INVESTING
WITHOUT A
SILVER
SPOON

How
Anyone
Can Build
Wealth
Through
Direct
Investing

JEFF FISCHER
Foreword by David Gardner

Published by The Motley Fool, Inc., 123 North Pitt Street,
Alexandria, Virginia, 22314, USA

First Printing, June 1999
10 9 8 7 6 5 4 3 2 1

This publication contains the opinions and ideas of its author and is designed to provide useful information in regard to the subject matter covered. It is sold with the understanding that the author and publisher are not engaged in rendering legal, financial, tax preparation, or other professional services. Laws vary from state to state, and if the reader requires expert assistance or legal advice, a competent professional should be consulted. Readers should not rely on this (or any other) publication for financial guidance, but should do their own homework and make their own decisions. The author and publisher reserve the right to be stupid, wrong, or even foolish (with a small "f"). Remember, past results are not necessarily an indication of future performance.

The author and publisher specifically disclaim any responsibility for any liability, loss, or risk, personal or otherwise, which is incurred as a consequence, directly or indirectly, of the use and application of any of the contents of this book.

ISBN 1-892547-04-X

Printed in the United States of America
Set in ITC Century Book

Distributed by Publishers Group West

Cover art by Johnson Design
Design and Layout by HBP, Inc.

Acknowledgments:

I first thank my outstanding parents, who had nothing to do with this book aside from cultivating its author from day one to day 6,570.

At The Motley Fool, many thanks go to Bob Bobala and Brian Bauer for their skillful and deliberate editing. Robyn Gearey deserves a hearty thank you for putting all of the pieces together in the final weeks and for editing with very Foolish skill as well. Selena Maranjian is also thanked for her insightful input and spry sense of humor and Mona Sharma is thanked and admired for her adept research skills during this age of information glut.

Demonstrating more patience than the Dalai Lama, in addition to a great sense of humor, Craig Fowler is given a Foolish tip of the jester cap for overseeing this book from start to finish. Well done, Craig.

Finally, David and Tom Gardner and Erik Rydholm are thanked for beginning The Motley Fool, a company with a heart and soul.

CONTENTS

FOREWORD
by David Gardner

First of all, it's always a pleasure to be asked to write a foreword. Generally, one is either asked to do so by a good friend, or because it is hoped that the presence of one's name on the cover will enhance sales of the book. As much as I like Jeff, I'm keeping my fingers crossed for what's behind door number two.

You say it didn't work? Drat!

I don't think *anyone* wants to – or will – read anything but a short and snappy foreword. So let me begin by asking a question, and then end by making an emphatic statement.

The question: *Why don't we all, ALL of us, consider ourselves investors?*

At what point in history, or by whom, was this word "investor" made to sound formidable, wonkish, mysterious, or rich? Why was saving and investing categorized as abnormal behavior? Why did getting started sound difficult? Who dreamed up this idea that the only way to make a lot was to have a lot?

Fool that I am, I am tempted to accuse the Wise. So indeed, *j'accuse!* Because *of course* they want to make it hard for you so that you'll turn your money over to them and they can charge you fees. *Of course* they are there to take away the "burden" of it all, the pressures, the cares, the sheer *time* it takes to think about (and actually begin) your future. The best brokers have traditionally been avuncular chaps, unctuous and exceptionally good at making you feel comfortable about – and a willing participant in – having your account "turned over" and "churned." Go to The Motley Fool on any given day and read our message boards for numerous such offhand comments, remarks, and direct retellings of such experiences from people like you and me across the U.S. of A.

But I'm still left here perched over my keyboard, regretfully staring into my computer monitor unable to name the Wise man first responsible for that very real question, *"Why don't we all, ALL of us, consider ourselves investors?"* I don't know which one of them it was, or when exactly. I hope he is in Purgatory, for his sake, because I know it could be no better.

Whoever, whenever, wherever, that time and place are long past now. And with your hands wrapped around this excellent get-started-cheap-and-*now* investment guide, you are presumably receptive to my application of the word "investor" to *you*, in whatever straits – dire or otherwise – that you presently find yourself. You are presumably already aware that we all *are* investors, have always been. What was your last purchase? A stick of gum? A bicycle? This book? You made an *investment*, you *invested* your cash in an experience, an object, or an entitlement to ownership that you considered worthwhile enough at the time. It is the last of those – the entitlement to ownership – that Jeff is focused on in *The Motley Fool's Investing Without a Silver Spoon*.

Which prepares me to make my emphatic statement, that peremptory declaration with which so few forewords ever dare to end.

Everyone living today in the United States of America should own at least one share of stock.

(How to start? Read on.)

Part I

AN INTRODUCTION TO DIRECT INVESTING

It is never too late to be what you might have been.

– GEORGE ELIOT

"Invest without a broker!"

"Stop paying commissions!"

"Buy stock in amounts as little as $10 per month!"

People are often attracted to direct investment plans by promotional hype of the kind that you see above. We aren't large fans of promotional hype, but we *do* want to grab your attention at the outset of this book, so permit us to tack on a few more exciting (and true) teasers:

"Turn $100 per month into $150,000 in 20 years!"

"Steadily win your life's financial race!"

"Build the nest egg that you need without sacrificing your quality of life!"

"Sleep soundly at night knowing that your financial needs are being met!"

Keep in mind as you read this guide that to us, "Foolish" is a positive adjective. The Motley Fool takes its name from Shakespeare. In Elizabethan drama, the Fool is usually the only one who can tell the king the truth without losing his head – literally. We Fools aim to tell you truth, too – that you can beat Wall Street at its own game. To learn more about The Motley Fool, drop by our website at www.fool.com or visit us on America Online at keyword: Fool.

"Appear on *Oprah* as a financial whiz guest!"

While all of these statements *can* come true (come on, Oprah!), each represents only a fraction of what direct investing offers to an investor smart enough to take advantage of it. If you weren't born with a titanium spoon in your mouth, it might seem inconceivable that you could – with relative ease and even enjoyment – amass a nest egg sizable enough to provide for your children's college tuition, buy a home in a peaceful wood alongside a shimmering lake, or provide yourself a criminally comfortable retirement. But it's true. You can. And you don't need hot stock tips from a suit-and-tie, you don't need $50,000 sitting at the ready in your bank account, and you certainly don't need a business school degree.

All you need is an open mind and an eagerness to learn. Okay, you also need at least $25 per month that you can sock away into leading public companies. And you need this book.

You're holding (or your pet monkey is holding for you) a comprehensive guide that explains everything you need to know to get started in and successfully use direct investment plans. They're called direct investment plans because they allow you to buy stock directly from companies without the need for a broker and his middleman fees. Direct investing is growing in popularity as the Internet makes it even easier; yet, if you're not online and all you have in the world is this book, a mailbox, a checkbook, and a pen, you can use these plans to build wealth as readily as anyone.

So, let's get rolling.

Here's what lies ahead: After we introduce the two types of direct investing available, we'll explain why you should begin to invest *sooner* rather than later. We'll show you how investing even very small dollar amounts can steadily build wealth, and we'll explain why direct investment plans are a great way for almost anyone to invest in the stock market. Then we'll describe how to begin direct investing plans.

Next, we'll discuss investment goals and the types of industries in which you should consider investing. We'll spotlight some favorite companies and show you how to recognize winning stocks. We'll also explain how to track your investing performance and how to deal with taxes (legally, that is). Finally, we'll show you how to whip up a great avocado dip (other investing books explicitly deny you that knowledge). The second part of this book supplies the necessary phone numbers and facts regarding direct investment plans offered by over 1,000 companies.

In sum, this book provides information that can be used for generations to create wealth without great sacrifice. And no, we're not trying to *sell* this book to you with that comment – after all, you've probably already bought it. (Thank you!)

The Two Types of Direct Investment Plans
There are two types of direct investment plans:

Dividend Reinvestment Plans (DRPs)

and...

Direct Stock Plans (DSPs)

The benefits offered by all of the direct investment plans that we're interested in include the ability to:

- Invest small amounts of money on a regular basis
- Easily buy more shares when prices are lower, and less when they're higher (as a result, you don't fret over the stock market's volatility)
- Reinvest dividends directly into more stock
- Avoid commissions and other costs
- Vary your investment amounts monthly, or not invest at all when you wish
- Diversify your stock portfolio even with very little money
- Sell shares readily

... and much more.

Dividend reinvestment plans are older than direct stock plans (which are also called direct initial purchase plans, or DIPs). Nearly 1,100 companies offer dividend reinvestment plans, while over 500 companies (and growing) provide direct stock plans. Partially due to the Internet, direct stock plans will likely outnumber dividend reinvestment plans in a few years.

Both plans allow an investor to purchase shares of stock directly from a company in amounts that can range from $10 per month to $50,000 per month without cost (or with very little cost), and almost all plans allow dividend payments to be reinvested in more stock. The only cost with a majority of these plans is a one-time start-up fee that averages around $12 to $15, and a similar fee when you sell stock. Usually these plans are administered through a transfer agent. A transfer agent is a financial firm, such as a bank, that handles the plan's transactions and record-keeping. You only need to be aware of transfer agents because they are the entities that you'll usually transact with when using direct investment plans, even though it'll often seem as if you're dealing directly with the companies in which you're investing.

Typically it is the large, long-established, dividend-paying company that offers a direct investment plan.

So, what're the *differences* between the two plans? They're slight and are mainly encountered at the outset.

To enroll in a company's dividend reinvestment plan, or DRP, you usually must be a registered owner of at least one share of the company's stock. In contrast, to enroll in a direct stock purchase plan, or DSP, you can begin to purchase shares directly from the company immediately. It's that simple: you usually must own at least one share of a company's stock to enroll in its DRP, but you needn't be a shareholder to begin a DSP. Once you begin, both plans are very similar in function and in purpose.

Each type of plan has slight advantages and disadvantages. The largest difference involves the money needed to start. Dividend reinvestment plans usually require you to own one share to enroll, meaning you typically must spend $60 to $100 to begin. By contrast, direct stock plans allow you to enroll immediately. However, you usually must start these plans with a minimum investment that can range from $250 to $500. So, DRPs typically require a smaller investment to start.

While it's important to understand the differences, it isn't necessary to contemplate them any more than we already have. A company may offer a dividend reinvestment plan or a direct stock plan, but you'll decide where to invest based on a company's merits, not on the plan that it offers. The plans are equally beneficial, no matter what start-up quirks they may have. What's more important is that you start to invest *sooner* rather than later.

Oh, and here's that recipe we promised you.

Linne's Ultimate Guacamole

The secret to really great guacamole is perfectly ripe avocados. Use the kind that are bumpy and turn black when they're ripe. (Don't use those big smooth–skinned green ones – they're too watery.) Don't buy the avocados black. They'll probably be overripe or have bad spots. Buy the avocados green, or just turning black, and put them in a paper bag on the counter (not in the fridge). If they're really green, they'll take five to seven days to ripen. If they're halfway there, it may take only two days. Check them every day by pressing *gently* near the stem. They should feel like a ripe peach – some give, but not mushy.

When they're ripe, cut with a sharp knife down to the seed all the way around. You can feel with the knife if they're ripe; if the knife doesn't glide easily to the seed, it's not ripe. (At this point, you can put it back in the paper bag to ripen further even though you've already cut into it.) Twist the halves to separate from the seed. Cut each half once more lengthwise (cut around the seed on the side that has the seed) and remove the seed. Peel the skin back – it should come off easily. Put the peeled avocado in a bowl. Mash with a fork. Do not use a blender – it will be too smooth. Cut one very thin slice of a large onion (or two slices of a small onion) per avocado and finely dice. Cut one slice of tomato per avocado and finely dice. Add the onion and tomato to the mashed avocado. Add salt and pepper to taste. (But remember that it will probably be eaten with salty chips, so go easy on the salt.) That's it!

You will see recipes telling you to add lemon juice to keep the guacamole from turning brown or to put the avocado seed in the bowl. Lemon juice will change the flavor of the guacamole, and it's not necessary. I never understood the seed bit. To keep the guacamole from turning brown, smooth the top so there are no air pockets. Place a piece of plastic wrap directly on the surface, and smooth out so there are no air bubbles. If you serve it the same day, there will be no discoloration. If you serve it the next day, there may be a faint brown on the very top layer. Just stir it in and no one will notice. If you wait two or more days, the top layer will turn brown (lemon juice or no); scrape off the top layer and discard it and the rest will be just fine. (Put it in a clean bowl, though.)

Sorry for the length of this *very* simple recipe! But I promise it will make *excellent* guacamole!

Thanks to Linne for posting this great guacamole recipe on The Motley Fool's message boards.

Chapter 1

WHY YOU SHOULD INVEST SOONER RATHER THAN LATER

The person who makes a success of living is the one

who sees his goal steadily and aims for it unswervingly.

— CECIL B. DeMILLE

Conventional wisdom holds that you need a pile of cash larger than Jabba the Hutt before you can begin to successfully invest in stocks. Investing via direct investment plans turns that notion on its head and proves that the opposite can be true. Whether you have $100 or $100,000, what's most meaningful is *when* you start to invest and *how* you invest. A common Fool beginning with only $100 can be in a much better position to succeed than a Wise man with $100,000.

How can this be?

We're glad you asked. It's because discipline, time, and compounding are the three main contributors to successful investing – not the amount of money with which you begin.

Discipline

Much more important to successful investing than starting with a large wad of money is beginning with the right *discipline*. (In fact, wealth can be a *detriment* if a person doesn't invest it with discipline – he can *lose* his wealth.) A new investor possessing a little money to start, the right discipline (which so many investors lack), and more than a few years to be invested in the stock market (ideally a decade or longer) can use compounding to build a nest egg that blows away many other investors' results. So, the first necessary factor is discipline.

Enter direct investment plans. These plans provide a framework that makes the discipline required for successful investing easier to maintain.

Time

As measured by the S&P 500 index – which represents 500 of the premier public companies in the United States – the stock market has risen 11% annually, on average and including reinvested dividends, since 1926. (This compares to the 2.5% that a savings account typically yields today.) The stock market has been the best-yielding investment available over its history, yet thousands of people have lost money on it. That's in part because it is *time* that awards you the highest return. Many years the stock market declines. The market cannot be predicted, however, and trying to do so is costly. Studies show that a majority of the stock market's gains take place during a condensed period – over a number of combined weeks each year. If an investor misses those weeks, her results suffer.

The longer that you can be invested in the stock market, and *stay* invested, the more likely it is that you'll be amply rewarded. If you invest just $3,000 in a handful of successful companies that return 12% annually, and you hold for 20 years, you'll have nearly $29,000. If you hold for another 10 years, you'll have nearly $90,000. When you couple the power of a successful investment style with a substantial amount of time, you get a one-two punch. Discipline combined with time results in the desired outcome: compounding.

Compounding

A dictionary definition of compound is "to intensify or make more serious." That definition *does* describe how we're using the word, but it isn't a perfect description.

To compound your money is to build wealth on top of newly built wealth, *as well as* on top of your original investment. If you start with $1,000 and earn 10% in year one, you'll earn $100 and have $1,100. If you earn 10% again in year two, you'll earn $110 this time, not just $100, because your investment base has grown. Now you'll have $1,210. The following year, another 10% gain will represent an even larger dollar amount earned – $121. Compounding is simple math that we learned in fifth grade, but it was all too promptly forgotten. (Who can blame us?) The math of compounding holds one of the other keys to building wealth.

Discipline + Time = Compounding

When you combine the three elements necessary to build wealth, you get the equation: Discipline + Time = Compounding. In the end, compounding is the goal. A Foolish investor will compound her money without compounding any problems, worry, or heartache. Just joy.

From here forward, we'll call the above equation The Foolish Equation. (We don't claim to be creative in our naming conventions.) Write down the equation and tape it to your computer screen if you actively watch stocks online, or affix it to your vanity mirror if you sometimes fret while staring in the glass reflecting on your finances.

The following tables illustrate the power of our Foolish Equation. Using discipline (saving money and then investing it regularly in strong companies) and committing to a meaningful period of time results in compounding, which creates wealth.

Our first table assumes that an investor named Cletus began with $500 in various direct investment plans and added $100 per month to his investments. The table demonstrates how his money grew over 5, 10, 15, 20, 30, and 40 years at annual appreciation rates of 7%, 11%, and 15%. The second table shows an investor, Fiona, who began with $1,000 and added $200 a month to her investments. We'll consider the same percentage returns for her.

Fool #1: Cletus – who sells fruit by the side of the road for a living – began with $500 in direct investment plans and added $100 per month for 20 years, investing a total of $24,500. When he achieved the stock market's average 11% annualized return, his portfolio grew to a total value of $91,031 after year 20. But remember that a full quarter of his money was invested only during the last five years, giving it less time to appreciate in value. If Cletus can let his money appreciate for another 10

Table I

Fool #1: Cletus began with $500 and added $100 monthly.
Total amount invested at the end of 20 years: $24,500. After 40 years: $48,500.

	Value when growing at 7%	Value when growing at 11%	Value when growing at 15%
Year 1	$1,745	$1,820	$1,866
Year 5	7,868	8,816	9,911
Year 10	18,313	23,194	29,741
Year 15	33,120	48,052	71,528
Year 20	54,112	91,031	159,581
Year 30	126,055	293,806	736,098
Year 40	270,637	899,929	3,295,955

Table II

Fool # 2: Fiona began with $1,000 and added $200 monthly.
Total amount invested at the end of 20 years: $49,000. After 40 years: $97,000.

	Value when growing at 7%	Value when growing at 11%	Value when growing at 15%
Year 1	$3,550	$3,640	$3,732
Year 5	15,736	17,632	19,822
Year 10	36,626	46,388	59,483
Year 15	66,241	96,105	143,057
Year 20	108,224	182,062	319,163
Year 30	252,110	587,612	1,472,196
Year 40	541,274	1,799,589	6,591,911

years, without adding an additional cent, he'll end with $259,241. That's after beginning with $500 and adding only $100 a month for 20 years, or $24,000. If Cletus continued to invest after year 20, by year 30 his portfolio would be worth nearly $300,000 if it grows at the stock market's average historic rate. After 40 years, he'd have nearly $900,000. If he earned a higher 15% annual return, he'd have $3.2 million.

Fool #2. Fiona is an accountant with a husband who is a world-renowned, award-winning poet. Last year, Fiona's husband earned $260, so she completely supports him and their family of four. Fiona began by investing $1,000 in a handful of direct investment plans, and then she added $200 a month for 20 years, resulting in a total investment of $49,000. After 20 years of achieving the stock market's average 11% annual return, her investments grew to $182,062. If she had earned a slightly better return of 15% annually (as she could have with Coke and Johnson & Johnson), she'd have $319,163 after 20 years. That's more than enough to put the two children through Yale University (where both will major in poetry).

What would Fiona's $319,000 become in 10 *more* years growing at just 11%, even if she didn't add another nickel? Her basket of stocks would exceed $905,775 in value. And remember, she only invested a total of $49,000 over the first 20 years, or about $2,400 per year. Look at the results when she continued to add more money each year. Year 30 finds her a millionaire (with $1.4 million) if she earns 15% annually. That's after investing only $72,000 over 30 years ($200 a month), plus her $1,000 seed money. By year 40, she'd have more than *$6.5 million*! Now imagine if her husband had a profession for which he actually got paid.

There are two important lessons to take away from these tables. Hopefully, they're obvious: 1) time matters greatly, and 2) your annual return matters greatly.

In the examples above, *most* of the value is created in years 20, 30, and 40 – and each decade represents much larger absolute dollar growth than the prior decade. If we carry the examples out further, a great deal more value (again, most of the value) would be created in still later years. That's how compounding works. Most value is created at the *tail end* of an investment's life. Always keep that in mind as you embark upon, and continue, your investment career.

You can also see from both tables that the annual return an investor achieves means a great deal. Every percentage point is significant, especially over long periods of compounding. That's part of the reason why it is so important that you learn to manage your money Foolishly and avoid mediocre companies. In Fiona's example, an annual return of 15% creates value of over $319,000 in 20 years, and $1.4 million in 30 years. If she earned just 11% per year, only four percentage points less, she'd have merely $182,000 after 20 years ($137,000 less), and $587,000 after 30 years ($800,000 *less*!). Even a 4% difference in annual returns over 20 years can mean hundreds of thousands of dollars.

"How Do I Become a Millionaire?"

Determining what you need to invest, for how long, and how much your money needs to compound to reach your financial goals is as easy as 1-2-3. Or almost, anyway.

Figuring the future value of a stream of regular payments that are growing at a consistent rate, as was done for Cletus and Fiona, requires a formula that is easily computed with a financial calculator – the kind that you threw away after high school – or on the Internet using free financial calculators offered by financial sites. The future value of an annuity, or FVA (a regular payment), refers to the amount that a person will accumulate by making regular payments (or investments) at certain rates of return over a period of time. This looks painful, but keep in mind that we'll use a calculator to compute it. The formula is (hold on to your hats):

$$FVA_n = PMT(1+r)1 + PMT(1+r)2 + \dots + PMT(1+r)n = PMT[(1+r)1 + (1+r)2 + \dots + (1+r)n]$$

The sum in the bracket is called the future value interest factor of an annuity. The "r" represents your rate of return, PMT is your payment or investment, and "n" is the year or ordered number of your payment.

As you can see, computing 20 years of monthly payments on paper, rather than with a calculator, will take you some time, so dig up a financial calculator or go online for The Motley Fool's "Compoundulator," at www.fool.com, specifically at http://www.fool.com/calculators/compoundulator.htm. The Compoundulator is a simple tool you can use to determine how much you need to save and earn on your investments to reach your goals.

When it comes to goals, the big question that many investors want answered is "How do I become a millionaire?" Whether you believe it or not, this goal is achievable even if you begin with very little. Here are several ways to become a millionaire:

1. Begin with $500, save $1,200 annually, or $100 a month, and earn 15% per year. In 33 years, you'll have over $1 million.
2. Begin broke, save $2,400 a year, or $200 monthly, earn the stock market's historic 11% annual return, and in 36 years you'll have more than one million clams.
3. Begin with nothing and save $3,600 per year, or $300 monthly, and earn 11% annually. In 32 years, you're a millionaire. Congratulations.
4. Begin with $5,000, save $250 monthly, earn 13% annually, and in 28 years: Boom! Hello, millionaire. Kiss your boss good-bye.
5. Begin with $10,000, save $250 a month, earn 10% annually, and in 33 years: Good-bye daily commute, hello French Riviera.

Each of these examples requires discipline and time, and compounding is the result. You needn't start with much more than discipline. In fact, notice that the starting dollar amount in each example is *not* very important. Each example requires about the same amount of time before reaching millionaire status.

Using the formula above, you can calculate what you need to save and what return you need to get on your savings in order to reach any goal in any amount of time. If you're looking to become a millionaire in one year, we hope you're beginning with a very royal sum. However, if you're near the age of the average American (34), you have 30 years until you reach traditional retirement age, so you can begin with a pauper's nickel.

By now it should be obvious that you should begin investing sooner rather than later. Now, why do you want to use direct investment plans?

Chapter 2

ADVANTAGES OF DIRECT INVESTMENT PLANS

Resolve and thou are free.

– HENRY WADSWORTH LONGFELLOW

Using direct investment plans, you'll likely avoid 95% of the mistakes that many other investors make repeatedly. According to studies, the most common mistake that would-be investors commit is to trade stock too frequently. Many people lack the patience that's needed to stick with an investment approach long enough to see it actually *succeed.* Another common mistake is to buy small, unknown companies with the dream of hitting a jackpot. Unfortunately, most small, obscure companies never amount to much and their investors can land in the poorhouse.

Direct investment plans steer you away from both mistakes. First, they help you adhere to an investment approach that's proven to work over the long term. Second, they guide you toward successful, powerhouse companies that will make almost any caliber investor money if he's patient. Beyond these good graces, the plans offer a multitude of other benefits that make them attractive to investors.

The Motley Fool website is host to a community of tens of thousands of investors who invest in direct investment plans. In addition, the Fool offers a real-money stock portfolio (called the Drip Portfolio) that employs direct investing. The portfolio managers provide a nightly column, but the real action takes place each day on the direct investment message boards. These are among the most popular message areas on the Fool website. It was here on the message boards that we asked investors why they enjoy direct investing. The following are a few of the responses.

An investor who calls himself LemmerShark on the message boards wrote: "I mainly like direct investing because it's a good way to pay yourself first. It's like a monthly bill that you pay toward your future. It

A screen shot of the Fool's message board main page.

Two posts from our Drip Investing message board.

The Motley **FOOL**

| Features | Messages | Quotes/Data | My Portfolio | Register | Login | 🛒 Shop FoolMart |
| Home | Folders | Search | Top 25 | Favorites | Register | Help |

Investors' Roundtable / Drip Investing – Companies

Post New • Post Reply   💙 good / bad POST?   Prev • Next

Subject: Industries ??   **Date:** 3/26/99 11:18 AM

Author: TLAjester ☺ ☹   **Number:** 10105 of 11314 GO

Long time reader (2 weeks), first time writer. I am vigorously collecting drip info from many sources and have determined that initial investment, minimum OCP and fees are big drivers for my portfolio. I believe I can properly track and contribute to 3-4 drips to start with. My question...are there any particular industries that are good starter industries?

I have read / heard about utilities as one good starting point. Is this true? Are there others?

Post New • Post Reply   Prev • Next

Save on business and investing titles at Amazon

❋ Drip Port Main Page

Stock Folders: A B C D E F G H I J K L M N O P Q R S T U V W X Y Z

Ticker [   ]   Board [   ]   Author [   ]   Find

| Home | • | Folders | • | Search | • | Top 25 | • | Favorites | • | Register | • | Help |

Hey! Look at our Disclaimer.

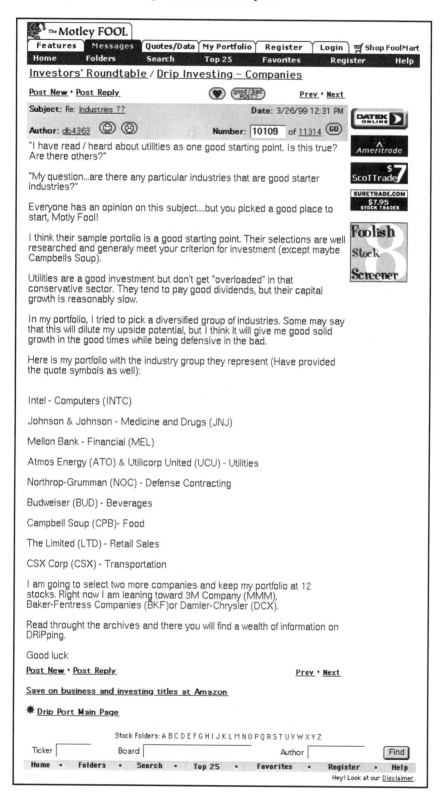

The Motley **FOOL**

| Features | Messages | Quotes/Data | My Portfolio | Register | Login | 🛒 Shop FoolMart |

| Home | Folders | Search | Top 25 | Favorites | Register | Help |

Investors' Roundtable / Drip Investing – Companies

Post New • **Post Reply**   ♥ (good/bad POST?)   **Prev** • **Next**

Subject: Re: Industries ??   **Date:** 3/26/99 12:31 PM

Author: db4363 ☺ ☹   **Number:** 10109 of 11314 **GO**

"I have read / heard about utilities as one good starting point. Is this true? Are there others?"

"My question...are there any particular industries that are good starter industries?"

Everyone has an opinion on this subject....but you picked a good place to start, Motly Fool!

I think their sample portolio is a good starting point. Their selections are well researched and generaly meet your criterion for investment (except maybe Campbells Soup).

Utilities are a good investment but don't get "overloaded" in that conservative sector. They tend to pay good dividends, but their capital growth is reasonably slow.

In my portfolio, I tried to pick a diversified group of industries. Some may say that this will dilute my upside potential, but I think it will give me good solid growth in the good times while being defensive in the bad.

Here is my portfolio with the industry group they represent (Have provided the quote symbols as well):

Intel - Computers (INTC)

Johnson & Johnson - Medicine and Drugs (JNJ)

Mellon Bank - Financial (MEL)

Atmos Energy (ATO) & Utilicorp United (UCU) - Utilities

Northrop-Grumman (NOC) - Defense Contracting

Budweiser (BUD) - Beverages

Campbell Soup (CPB)- Food

The Limited (LTD) - Retail Sales

CSX Corp (CSX) - Transportation

I am going to select two more companies and keep my portfolio at 12 stocks. Right now I am leaning toward 3M Company (MMM), Baker-Fentress Companies (BKF)or Damler-Chrysler (DCX).

Read throught the archives and there you will find a wealth of information on DRiPping.

Good luck

Post New • **Post Reply**   **Prev** • **Next**

Save on business and investing titles at Amazon

✳ **Drip Port Main Page**

Stock Folders: A B C D E F G H I J K L M N O P Q R S T U V W X Y Z

| Ticker | | Board | | Author | | Find |

| Home • | Folders • | Search • | Top 25 • | Favorites • | Register • | Help |

Hey! Look at our Disclaimer.

enables me to invest my money gradually as I get it, rather than trying to save a large block of cash and having it available to spend. I also like the fact that I'm not as worried about timing the market. I know that if the stock price goes down, when the next month rolls around I'll be buying more shares with the same amount of money that I always send."

Another investor in The Motley Fool community, named Racerboy because he races bikes, wrote: "I distinctly remember how I felt when I started my first DRPs with Intel and Exxon. It was as if I had been standing on a little suspension bridge that was blowing in the wind and had finally set foot on solid ground! It felt great. I am totally committed to the whole 'science' of this way of investing! First, it allows the small investor (but gee, I'm not that small!) an opportunity to have control over his financial future. It allows you to increase your contributions as your salary grows…. Investors are in total control of what they invest. Have a big insurance bill this month? You can simply back off on your contributions to your investments that month. On the flip side, when some extra money falls into your hands (and you're certain that you don't need another set of slicks for your race bike), then you can send more money to your companies! I just love it!"

Racerboy loved it so much that he eventually became a Fool employee. You can now find him on the message boards helping others under the name TMF Racer ("TMF" stands for The Motley Fool).

Finally, a woman named MotherofFools wrote: "I like direct investing because I'm a cheapskate. I never pay for anything I don't have to [pay for] because I can always find a better use for the money. So why should I pay a broker if I can buy direct?"

It's difficult to say it better ourselves, but we're going to try.

Advantages of Direct Investment Plans
You Need Little Money to Start
You can begin to invest in most direct investment plans for less than $100. Once begun, additional investments are voluntary (they're called optional cash payments, or OCPs) and there are low minimum investment requirements.

A majority of plans accept optional investments with a minimum of no more than $50 a shot, and many plans have minimum optional investments of only $10 to $25. This means that you can invest in a large company such as Coca-Cola even when you can't afford entire shares. You can buy *partial shares* each month. (You certainly can't order partial shares through a traditional broker!) Ten dollars will currently buy you 0.125 shares of Coca-Cola. Yes, you can buy that little through a direct investment plan – and you *should*. The important thing is that you *are* saving and investing whatever you can.

How frequently should you invest?

You should aim to send money to your companies every month or every quarter (three months). Building wealth requires that you have the discipline to consistently save and invest. Ideally, you should invest at least 10% of your pre-tax income, perhaps spread among your 401(k) or other retirement plan, and various direct investment plans. If you save consistently, you should invest just as frequently, which *should be every month*.

Can you afford to invest every month? If you're investing $50 to $100 per month, you probably won't even miss the money once you develop the habit; yet, it'll be out there growing for your future.

Commission-Free Investing

This advantage can't be emphasized enough. Once you've begun a commission-free direct investment plan, you're potentially done paying commissions on your investments for a lifetime. Forever. For an eternity. Until the end of time as we know it.

In a majority of cases, these plans are very inexpensive to begin, typically free to maintain – with free additional investments, free stock certificate safekeeping, and free dividend reinvestments – and it's very inexpensive to sell shares. Of course, some plans do charge fees for purchases (we avoid those plans), and almost all plans charge a small fee when you sell. That's not a big deal. It's typically $12 to $15, same as a discount broker.

The most important commission that you avoid with these plans is the commission that you'd normally pay to buy stock every month. Imagine you want to buy $100 worth of Coca-Cola each month. Using a discount broker with an $8 transaction fee, you'd pay $96 per year in fees. Using Coca-Cola's DRP, you pay $0.

Now consider the implications of that $96 cost. Aside from $96 being 8% of your total yearly investment (a giant bite!), that money would be compounding in value if you'd invested it. When $96 grows 15% annually in the stock market for 30 years, it becomes $6,356. Now you know why avoiding brokerage commissions is so meaningful.

Dollar-Cost Average and Avoid Worrying About the Stock Market's Volatility

Dollar-cost averaging is the process of regularly buying stock in equal dollar amounts, which means that you buy shares at various prices over time. This, in turn, means that you buy *more* of the stock when the price is lower, and *less* of the stock when the price is higher, resulting in a cost basis (or average cost) for your shares that favors the *low end* of the stock's price range over the years.

That's poetic.

Consider the real-life example offered by a Johnson & Johnson dividend reinvestment plan statement for 1998.

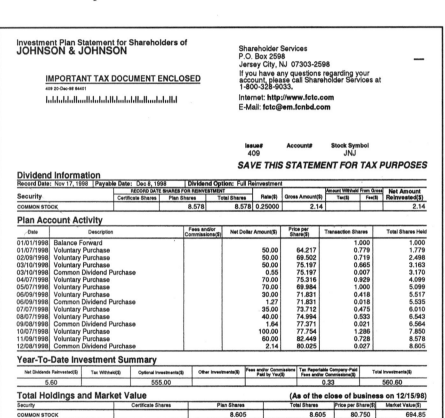

Investment Plan Statement for Shareholders of
JOHNSON & JOHNSON

Shareholder Services
P.O. Box 2598
Jersey City, NJ 07303-2598

IMPORTANT TAX DOCUMENT ENCLOSED
409 20-Dec-98 64401

|..|..|..|..|..|....|..|..|..|..|..|....|..|..|..|..|..|..|..|..|

If you have any questions regarding your account, please call Shareholder Services at 1-800-328-9033.
Internet: http://www.fctc.com
E-Mail: fctc@em.fcnbd.com

Issue#	Account#	Stock Symbol
409		JNJ

SAVE THIS STATEMENT FOR TAX PURPOSES

Dividend Information

Record Date: Nov 17, 1998 | Payable Date: Dec 8, 1998 | Dividend Option: Full Reinvestment

Security	RECORD DATE SHARES FOR REINVESTMENT			Rate($)	Gross Amount($)	Amount Withheld From Gross		Net Amount Reinvested($)
	Certificate Shares	Plan Shares	Total Shares			Tax($)	Fee($)	
COMMON STOCK		8.578	8.578	0.25000	2.14			2.14

Plan Account Activity

Date	Description	Fees and/or Commissions($)	Net Dollar Amount($)	Price per Share($)	Transaction Shares	Total Shares Held
01/01/1998	Balance Forward				1.000	1.000
01/07/1998	Voluntary Purchase		50.00	64.217	0.779	1.779
02/09/1998	Voluntary Purchase		50.00	69.502	0.719	2.498
03/10/1998	Voluntary Purchase		50.00	75.197	0.665	3.163
03/10/1998	Common Dividend Purchase		0.55	75.197	0.007	3.170
04/07/1998	Voluntary Purchase		70.00	75.316	0.929	4.099
05/07/1998	Voluntary Purchase		70.00	69.984	1.000	5.099
06/09/1998	Voluntary Purchase		30.00	71.831	0.418	5.517
06/09/1998	Common Dividend Purchase		1.27	71.831	0.018	5.535
07/07/1998	Voluntary Purchase		35.00	73.712	0.475	6.010
08/07/1998	Voluntary Purchase		40.00	74.994	0.533	6.543
09/08/1998	Common Dividend Purchase		1.64	77.371	0.021	6.564
10/07/1998	Voluntary Purchase		100.00	77.754	1.286	7.850
11/09/1998	Voluntary Purchase		60.00	82.449	0.728	8.578
12/08/1998	Common Dividend Purchase		2.14	80.025	0.027	8.605

Year-To-Date Investment Summary

Net Dividends Reinvested($)	Tax Withheld($)	Optional Investments($)	Other Investments($)	Fees and/or Commissions Paid by You($)	Tax Reportable Company-Paid Fees and/or Commissions($)	Total Investments($)
5.60		555.00			0.33	560.60

Total Holdings and Market Value

(As of the close of business on 12/15/98)

Security	Certificate Shares	Plan Shares	Total Shares	Price per Share($)	Market Value($)
COMMON STOCK		8.605	8.605	80.750	694.85

That is an account statement from The Motley Fool's real-money Drip Portfolio. The portfolio invests $100 per month and usually spreads it among a few companies. (You can read about it online as it happens.) This portfolio didn't invest the same dollar amount in Johnson & Johnson every month because it couldn't, but let's consider what would have happened if it had. If the portfolio had sent the same amount of money every month that it invested, it would have paid an average price of only $73.49 per share, even though it would have bought some stock at prices as high as $82.44 during 1998.

You can see why people using direct investment plans don't sweat falling stock prices; rather, they *encourage* them! People using these plans are often eager to buy more stock the next month at *lower* prices. They want prices to decline even when they already own shares because they want a *lower average cost per share* in the near term. That's smart.

This unconventional thought – the idea of cheering stocks *down* – is perfect for long-term investors. The most successful investor of our time, Warren Buffett (not Jimmy Buffett, though he's done well, too), reminds us that we always want lower prices on cars, houses, and appliances so we get more value for our dollar. Investors need to think this way, too. Long-term stock buyers should hope for lower prices on stocks if they're going to buy more shares over the coming years than they're going to sell, meaning that they're *net buyers*. This is precisely the case with new direct investment plan users who are beginning to dollar-cost average. They should have an investment time horizon that stretches into an era where bell bottoms are in style again, and then *out of style*, and then back in style – meaning a long way out. Dollar-cost averaging is the perfect means to take advantage of stock fluctuations while building wealth.

However, dollar-cost averaging isn't nearly so possible if you aren't using direct investment plans. These plans make averaging into your investments easy due to the low minimum investments required and the lack of commissions. If you were forced to invest $500 whenever you invested in Coca-Cola (instead of $10, the actual minimum with its plan), you probably couldn't invest every month and you'd lose the benefit of regular dollar-cost averaging. And we've already seen how brokerage commissions bite you.

Do you want to use direct investment plans yet? There are still more smart reasons why you should.

Time Diversification
When investing, diversification typically describes the act of mitigating risk by investing in several different companies in several different industries. But when it comes to diversification, there's a concept that we like better than spreading your money into several companies. It's called *time diversification.*

If you're investing in very strong companies, you needn't risk diluting your returns by owning 20 stocks. No matter what market pundits tell you, you can be adequately diversified owning just five stocks. So, once you locate and begin to invest in a small handful of truly great companies, the largest uncertainty is the stock market's direction and the amount of time that it'll take (as a result of the market's whims) to earn a sizable return. This uncertainty is especially present when you buy a large chunk of stock at once and stop at that. Imagine that you buy at the near-term high, and you don't see a higher price on your shares for five years – or longer. That certainly happens to thousands of investors. However, it can't happen if you're an investor who employs time diversification.

For example, if the stock market experienced a large decline during an investor's third, fourth, and fifth years of investing, it would represent a wonderful opportunity (a fire sale) for direct investors. Why? Because they'd buy more stock throughout the decline, they'd buy more at the bottom, and they'd purchase more again all the way back up. The ability to diversify *when* you invest (by investing month after month) actually makes it possible to *enjoy* and benefit from stock market volatility. Not many investment methods offer that.

Time diversification is clearly married to dollar-cost averaging, and together they make a great couple. Let's show what they can do.

An investor who uses time diversification by dollar-cost averaging can often achieve a better return than an investor who buys a block of the same stock in one fell swoop. Consider this example with Coca-Cola. The following table contrasts a direct investor who buys $100 in stock every month for one year with a traditional investor who buys $1,200 in stock the first day and nothing more.

	Table III	
	Direct Investor of $100 Monthly Using Dollar-Cost Averaging	Traditional Investor Investing $1,200 Lump Sum
Coke Price/Share		
Jan. 1	$68.50	$68.50
Feb. 1	$69.25	
Mar. 1	$71.50	
Apr. 1	$74.60	
May 1	$77.00	
June 1	$68.20	
July 1	$63.45	
Aug. 1	$57.13	
Sept. 1	$59.45	
Oct. 1	$57.25	
Nov. 1	$71.33	
Dec. 1	$64.60	
Average Price/Share	$66.85	$68.50

Each person invested the same total dollar amount in Coca-Cola after one year, but the investor using time diversification and dollar-cost averaging was able to buy the stock at a lower average price per share than the investor who spent all $1,200 on January 1. Subsequently, the investor using dollar-cost averaging also was able to buy *more* shares, and will achieve a better return and earn a higher dividend yield than the lump-sum investor. The direct investor's $66.85 average cost per share (obtained by adding all the prices she paid together and dividing by 12) beats his $68.50 per share cost, even though the direct investor paid as much as $77 per share one month and more than $70 per share four months out of 12.

It won't always work in the direct investor's favor (if a stock rises sharply early on and stays high, the lump-sum investor would have a lower price per share), but it often does, especially over several years. Therefore, averaging into your investment over time is a very attractive option (while being the most realistic option) for many investors. Direct investing makes time diversification possible.

By the way, if the above scenario seems unrealistic to you ("Coca-Cola could never trade from $57 to $71 and then back to $64 in three months!"), rest assured that that's *exactly* what Coca-Cola did at the end of 1998.

Easily Diversify Your Holdings

We criticized (albeit subtly) those who suggest that you must own a large basket of stocks in order to be properly diversified. We feel that owning more stocks than you can realistically follow and understand – typically about 8 to 15 – is not a good idea. Besides, there's only a small handful of extraordinary companies. Your goal is to find those (we'll help) and invest your money with them.

Of course, all investors *should* be adequately diversified in order to protect their portfolios from risk. If you put all of your money into Cup O' Bagel, Inc., the new company challenging Starbucks with its idea of selling coffee with a bagel already soaking in it (to the point of saturation), you're going to learn how bankruptcy court works. Or, suppose that you like the oil industry and therefore you buy just three different oil companies. When oil prices tumble, you're in a world of pain. You probably should have bought just one oil company and balanced your portfolio with other companies in other industries – perhaps a pharmaceutical company and a food and beverage company.

Diversification is certainly an investor's friend when appropriately employed. We suggest that you own different companies in a handful of industries that you understand. Five to eight well-chosen leaders should be sufficient for a long-term investor. Eight to 15 is more than enough.

Here's where our friend, the direct investment plan, proudly enters the picture again. Using direct investment plans, you can immediately begin your investing career as a diversified shareholder even if you have little money to start. With only about $500, you can start direct investment plans in five different industry leaders such as Coca-Cola, Intel, Johnson & Johnson, Pfizer, and Exxon. These five companies make for a well-diversified portfolio from day one.

Exactly how many companies *should* you own as you begin your investment career? First, that depends on how many leading companies you can understand well enough to merit investment. Second, before you begin to invest in direct investment plans, estimate the amount of money that you can save and send to your companies on a monthly basis. This guides you in deciding how many initial purchases to commit to, because you *do* want to be able to invest in all of your holdings regularly. If you own stock in too many different companies, some might be neglected and the benefit of dollar-cost averaging would be compromised.

No matter how much money you have, be extra careful not to *overdiversify*. Too many investors see how inexpensive and easy direct investment plans are and they load up, before long having 28 accounts with 28 companies and a pile of monthly recordkeeping that could choke a whale. Worse than that, though, they can't possibly keep pace with the news at all of their companies, even if they *can* send money to each on a regular basis (which is doubtful as well). Plus, owning too many companies makes it very difficult to outperform the stock market's average return. The more companies you own (and the more haphazardly you buy them), the more likely you are to have laggards in the group.

So, what are you to do?

A confident direct investor should consider "concentration investing" (also called "focus investing"), which means investing most of one's regular savings in a small handful of companies that one truly understands. Warren Buffett invests in this way. His largest positions have usually represented a majority of his investment holdings – companies such as Coca-Cola, American Express, Gillette, and Disney. At one point, Coca-Cola represented more than 40% of his holdings. Keep that in mind, and don't let the concentration of your wealth in your best investments frighten you. You want your investments to grow, and your most successful few stocks will likely grow to represent a great amount of your net worth. There's a reason they're growing. You should consider the reasons before taking any money out of them for the sake of "diversification."

Understanding what you're investing in is the best defense against risk and is the best way to create long-term wealth. It is much better than scattering your money across several companies and hoping for the best. Use direct investing to diversify easily and inexpensively, but don't overdiversify.

The Reinvestment of Dividends

Dividends are payments made from public companies to shareholders, usually every three months. They're one way profitable companies share corporate earnings with shareholders. When you're paid a dividend, you can do three things with it: blow it, save it, or invest it. Until you own hundreds or even thousands of shares, dividends are usually small (several dollars a year at the start), but that doesn't mean they aren't meaningful. Remember our Foolish Equation: Discipline + Time = Compounding. If you're disciplined about reinvesting dividends and you add time to them (like watering a plant), they'll compound to become meaningful in size.

Typically, the *very best thing* you can do with dividends is reinvest them for free in more shares of stock through your direct investment plan. Once cashed, a dividend check can't compound in value, but a reinvested dividend can begin to compound immediately. And not only does *it* grow in value, in the next quarter a reinvestor of dividends receives an even higher dividend payment than before, due in part to the dividend that was just received in the *last quarter* and used to buy more shares. That's growth on top of growth. That's compounding. Your dividends do it, too.

The practice of reinvesting dividends – even meager dividends – to buy more stock often separates the outstanding investor from the very good investor. As of 1999, the stock market, as measured by the S&P 500 index, has returned approximately 11% annually since 1926. That is the market's historic return with dividends reinvested. (Enter Ed McMahon voice here: "YES!") When dividends are *not* reinvested, the average yearly return of the S&P 500 withers to merely 7.4%. (Enter Ed McMahon again: "That is correct, sir. Only 7.4%." Lower and shake head. Walk off stage.)

Several brokerage firms do provide automatic reinvestment of dividends, but many of them charge a fee for the service and none of them, yet, allow for commission-free investing of additional cash in more shares – so, you still need a direct investment plan to dollar-cost average for free. However, if you're using a discount broker, it's worth asking for details on dividend reinvestment.

The table below shows how these two different annual returns play out over the lifetime of two investors. Imagine that the investors, named Speedy and Opie, each invested in leading S&P 500 companies with $3,000. Smart move. But imagine that Speedy didn't reinvest her dividends (bad move), so she earned 7.4% annually. Opie, on the other hand, reinvested all of his dividends, earning 11% annually.

	Table IV	
	The Power of Reinvested Dividends	
	(Each Invested $3,000)	
Years	Speedy: achieves a 7.4% return w/o dividends reinvested	Opie: achieves an 11% return with dividends reinvested
5	$4,286	$5,055
10	6,125	8,518
15	8,753	14,353
20	12,508	24,186
25	17,874	40,756
30	25,541	68,676
35	36,498	115,724

You can see that the performance difference is *enormous*. Monstrous, even. Opie reinvested the small dividend each year and ended up with more than three times as much money as Speedy. Speedy spent her dividends on Bon Bons and ended up with twice Opie's body weight. Hard to imagine!

An even more dramatic example of the power of dividends can be seen in the Coca-Cola Company. The carbonated soda leader was listed on the stock market in 1919. On day one, the shares cost $40 a pop. The stock has compounded over 16% annually on average since 1919, but that's *only* if all dividends were immediately reinvested in more shares. If an investor had reinvested dividends, a single $40 share from 1919 is now worth (get the calculator: *tap tap tap, tap tap* – you need a powerful calculator for this): $5.7 million! That's not a typo. Repeat: that's not a typo. Forty measly bucks in Coca-Cola turned into $5.7 million. (Compound $40 by 16% for 80 years and you get $5.7 million. Wealth is that easy. You just need time.) However, if dividends were *not* reinvested in Coca-Cola stock, an original $40 share is now worth only $250,000 – a difference of *$5.5 million.*

Over the 80-year period, one $40 share of Coca-Cola stock has paid more than $23,000 in dividends, which, reinvested when received every three months, accounts for the $5.5 million difference. $23,000 worth of reinvested dividends grew to $5.5 million. If dividends were not reinvested, the shareholder simply received small checks from Coca-Cola (worth $287 a year on average) that were likely frittered away – blown on hula-hoops and drive-in movies, beehive haircuts and bell-bottom pants, tickets to see Elvis and tickets to see Elvis's grave.

Perhaps no other example shows so plainly the power of reinvesting your dividends.

Table V

Coca-Cola (NYSE: KO)
1999 value of one $40 share purchased in 1919

Without Dividends Reinvested: $258,760

With Dividends Reinvested: $5,737,188

Source: The Coca-Cola Company

As smart as reinvesting dividends is, if dividends are needed for one's living expenses, most direct investment plans offer the option of receiving dividend payments in cash. Also, many plans allow partial reinvestment of dividends while paying the rest in cash. Finally, some plans charge small fees for the service of dividend reinvestment. An investor should weigh the fee against the benefits of investing in the particular company.

Putting It All Together

There are several reasons why so many investors use direct investment plans:

- You need little money to start and you may invest more voluntarily
- Commission-free investing
- Dollar-cost average and avoid worrying about the stock market's volatility
- Time diversification
- Easily diversify your holdings
- Dividend reinvestment

Given these advantages, direct investment plans are ideal when:

- You have varying (small to large) amounts of money to invest
- You have a long time horizon
- You will invest regularly

Like touring Willy Wonka's chocolate factory, we now move beyond the picturesque flowing chocolate rivers to the place behind the scenes – the mechanical stuff inside. It's time to learn how to open a direct investment plan. Come along!

Chapter 3

HOW TO ENROLL IN DIRECT INVESTMENT PLANS

I've never felt so accepted in all my life! These people looked deep within

my soul and assigned me a number based on the order in which I joined.

— HOMER SIMPSON, *THE SIMPSONS*

There are a number of ways to enroll in direct investment plans. One simple way is to marry someone who is already enrolled in one or more plans (the more the better). The more conventional ways vary depending on the plan you're joining. If you're enrolling in a dividend reinvestment plan that requires ownership of at least one share of stock to start (as most do), you can begin the enrollment process a few ways: through a discount broker, a DRP enrollment service, or with the help of a share-owning friend.

If you're enrolling in a direct stock plan, it's as simple as finding the minimum investment requirement and the plan's address (both of which are provided for each company in Part II of this book) and sending in your money. Direct stock plans are that easy to start, and dividend reinvestment plans aren't much more difficult.

Enrolling in Dividend Reinvestment Plans (DRPs)

When you know which company you want to invest in, find out how many shares are required to join its DRP. In most cases, it's one. When you're ready to invest, look at the direct investment plan information and phone numbers in this book. Call the companies you're interested in and request plan enrollment forms. (Note, however, that some companies won't send you the enrollment materials until you are already a registered shareholder.)

Aside from needing to own at least one share of stock to enroll in a DRP, the stock must be registered in your name, not in a brokerage house's name, not in your dog's name, and not even in your Uncle Bob's name. The stock certificate must be registered in your name to prove that you're a shareholder.

If you have a discount brokerage account, you can use it to buy the shares of stock necessary to enroll. If you already own shares in the company, you're set. Just have a broker register the shares in your name. Usually stocks are bought in a brokerage house's name (this is called "street name") and kept collectively in the house's account. You'll need to contact your brokerage house to request that the stock be registered in your name. When the stock is registered in your name, the certificate is often mailed to you and you're usually charged a small fee, but the certificate enables you to enroll in a dividend reinvestment plan.

The fee for placing a stock certificate in your name and having it mailed to you varies from broker to broker, but it generally costs from as low as $7 to as high as $50. Investors on The Motley Fool's message boards tend to favor the discount broker E*Trade (at www.etrade.com), because it charges a low $5 fee for stock certificates, and SureTrade (at www.suretrade.com), because it requires no minimum balance and it has *no charge* for stock certificates. Other brokers also charge no fee for this service, such as Waterhouse and Discover, but they have a minimum $2,000 deposit requirement to open an account. If you have a broker, ask what it costs to have shares put into your name.

Most brokers require minimum balances to open and maintain an account – and if you're only going to be investing in DRPs, you don't want that. A broker is just your way to buy the first necessary shares to enroll in a DRP. Grab the Yellow Pages or financial magazine or newspaper, or visit The Motley Fool's Discount Brokerage Center at www.fool.com (specifically at http://www.fool.com/media/Discount-BrokerageCenter/DiscountBrokerageCenter.htm) to see which broker suits you.

After you've found a discount broker, buy the necessary stock. Buy it online, if possible, because the commission is usually lower. (Smile. This will be one of the few commissions you'll ever pay on your investment.) If you can buy more than one share and want to, don't be shy about doing so. You can begin most DRPs with a minimum of one share and there's no maximum – you could buy 1,000 shares and enroll them all into a DRP. After your online purchase, call and inform the broker that you need the stock you just bought registered in your name. Or, if you're buying the share on the phone rather than online, tell them (as you're buying it) that:

1. You appreciate doing business with them;
2. You better get a smokin' good price on this stock; and...
3. You need the stock certificate registered in your name. Please.

The stock will be registered to you and the certificate will be mailed to your home within two to six weeks. Most direct investment plans will hold stock certificates for you (this is called "safekeeping"), so you'll probably want to mail your initial stock certificate to the DRP agent when you join. However, if you'd rather frame it and hang it above the bed, go ahead. Once you've become a registered shareholder in your company, you can enroll in its DRP even if you burn the stock certificate. Burning it isn't advised, however. Having the initial stock certificate kept with the direct investment plan's agent is the preferred route, because losing or burning your certificate results in paperwork to receive a replacement.

(Note that some companies, including Coca-Cola, accept your first share of stock directly from the stockbroker, so it needn't be mailed to your home first. When this option exists, ask the stockbroker to put the certificate in your name and transfer it to the company in which you wish to enroll. This simplifies the process.)

The DRP enrollment form is usually one page long. You provide your name, address, social security number, date of birth, favorite foods, etc. You'll also enter your dividend reinvestment preference (full reinvestment of dividends is ideal).

After you fill out the enrollment form, mail it in (typically with the stock certificate you received from the broker enclosed). After your enrollment has been mailed, congratulate yourself. You've done what you need to do to begin a DRP. Sit down and have a tall glass of lemonade. And then begin to wait.

And wait. And wait. And wait a little bit longer.

Wait a few weeks, usually no more than four, and you'll be enrolled in the company's DRP. If you haven't received mail from the company in six to eight weeks, call the company and give them your social security number to get your DRP account number, otherwise you'll probably have to wait until the next quarterly dividend payment to receive a DRP statement. Once you're enrolled and know your account number, you can begin to send additional investments (optional cash payments) immediately, and your dividends can buy more shares for you, too. In other words – you're on your way!

Here's an example of a DRP enrollment form, this one from Procter & Gamble.

THE PROCTER & GAMBLE SHAREHOLDER INVESTMENT PROGRAM
NEW ACCOUNT APPLICATION FORM   2.1

(Please use **BLACK INK**. Only one account per application is accepted. This form may be duplicated.)

CHECK HERE IF YOU ARE AN EMPLOYEE OR RETIREE OF PROCTER & GAMBLE (This form is not used for employee payroll deductions - check with your Personnel Contact)	CHECK HERE IF A DIRECT DEBIT FORM IS ENCLOSED	INITIAL PURCHASE ENCLOSED $
		($250.00 minimum -- see Prospectus)

This application form is for new accounts only. Once an account is established on the records of The Procter & Gamble Company, all future investments should accompany the OPTIONAL CASH PAYMENT FORM from your Shareholder Investment Program statement. Please return this form along with your remittance. A personal check or money order must be payable in U.S. dollars and drawn against a U.S. bank, made payable to: *THE PROCTER & GAMBLE SHAREHOLDER INVESTMENT PROGRAM* (Note: Third-party checks will not be accepted). Send completed application to the address shown on the bottom of this form.

ACCOUNT REGISTRATION

Check the appropriate box listed below for the desired account registration.

- [ ] INDIVIDUAL [ ] JOINT [ ] TRUST [ ] TOD (Transfer on Death)
- [ ] CUSTODIAL [ ] CORPORATE [ ] PARTNERSHIP [ ] OTHER _____

NOTE: The Procter & Gamble Company will not act as a custodian for an IRA registration. Please check with your financial institution to establish an IRA account.

ACCOUNT HOLDER'S SOCIAL SECURITY/TAXPAYER IDENTIFICATION NUMBER:

ACCOUNT TO BE REGISTERED AS: *(PLEASE PRINT CLEARLY IN ALL CAPS AND WITH BLACK INK)*

MAILING ADDRESS: *(PLEASE PRINT CLEARLY AND IN ALL CAPS)*

(Street Address)   (Apt.#, Unit #, etc.)

(City)   (State)   (Zip Code)

_____   _____   _____

Signature *(required from the person(s) requesting new account)*   ***Date***   *Daytime Phone*

TAXPAYER IDENTIFICATION - SUBSTITUTE W-9 FORM
IMPORTANT: MUST BE SIGNED BY THE REGISTERED ACCOUNT HOLDER ONLY

Under penalties of perjury, I certify that the Social Security/Taxpayer Identification Number indicated above is true and correct. Please note that if a Social Security Number/Taxpayer Identification Number is not provided, back-up withholding tax will be imposed on dividend and sale payments.

Signature: _____   **Date:** _____

[ ] Check here if you have been notified by the Internal Revenue Service that you are subject to back-up withholding.   7/01/98

The Procter & Gamble Company (Shareholders Services) · P.O. Box 5572 · Cincinnati, OH 45201-5572 · 1-800-742-6253

Enrolling in a DRP only takes a few steps:

1. Research company plan requirements and call for DRP enrollment forms.
2. Buy the initial share or shares of stock that you need to enroll in your chosen company's DRP.
3. Have the share(s) registered in your name.
4. Once your shares are registered, fill out the DRP enrollment form and mail it to your company or its transfer agent, as directed.

Not hard. Still, you've got to admit that marrying someone who's already enrolled is attractive. That *would* be easier.

Enrolling in Direct Stock Plans (DSPs)

Starting a direct investment plan that allows you to join before owning any shares is very simple. Many companies are moving away from the DRP format in favor of the DSP format.

To enroll in a DSP, get the plan information from this book, call the company for enrollment forms, and mail your check.

Presto. What could be simpler?

In contrast to DRPs, DSPs are incredibly simple to start. As we discussed earlier, however, DSPs usually require more significant initial investments (at least a few hundred dollars) and they have start-up fees averaging around $15. Also, unfortunately, more of these plans have ongoing fees compared to DRPs, so investigate any fees for optional cash payments and dividend reinvestments before enrolling, and aim to keep fees below 2% of any transaction's total value. Ideally, invest in plans without fees.

Direct Investment Plan Enrollment Services

DSPs are easy to begin, but if starting the other type of plan, a DRP, sounded at all complicated to you, you're not alone. How to begin a DRP is a frequently asked question. Fortunately, there are easier ways to start DRPs beyond the method that we just described using a discount broker.

A handful of independent services will enroll investors in direct investment plans at reasonable costs. There are good arguments for going this route. You can save time, hassle, and sometimes money. The enrollment services described here usually offer DRPs *and* DSPs. Realize that you usually don't need any help to enroll in a DSP, and you certainly shouldn't pay anything extra to an outside party. With DRPs, however, the help is often welcome. That's where these services come in handy.

First Share (www.firstshare.com). The First Share service links members who are willing to sell single shares in companies to one another in order to enroll in new DRPs. Members pay market value for the stock plus a $7.50 fee to the selling member. Membership in First Share is $24 for one year or $40 for two plus $10 for each transaction, or $5.00 for featured stocks (so each DRP usually costs $17.50 to begin, plus the annual membership fee and the price of the stock). More than a few thousand members hold shares in 400 companies, meaning that 400 DRPs are accessible. The program is meant for investors who want to enroll in at least three DRPs.

National Association of Investors Corporation (www.better investing. org). NAIC began the "Own Your Share of America" program to make it easier for new investors to begin DRPs. Similar to First Share, this not-for-profit organization pools members' resources. NAIC membership is $39 annually and you can start a DRP in 150 companies. A $7 start-up fee applies to each DRP. With membership comes many other benefits, including the monthly *Better Investing* magazine.

Netstock Direct Corporation (www.netstockdirect.com). An innovative young company, Netstock Direct provides information on DRPs and DSPs while allowing registered users to enroll in over 300 DSPs directly through its Internet site. The site is free and it offers information and enrollment forms on over 1,000 plans, and more and more companies are beginning to offer direct enrollment through Netstock. For Internet users, this is one of the easiest ways to enroll in DSPs – and at no additional cost beyond normal plan fees. However, Netstock can't yet help you enroll in DRPs; it provides DRP information and enrollment forms, but you need to buy your first share and enroll yourself. Netstock is ideal for DSPs, especially the 300 offered directly through the site.

Temper of the Times (www.moneypaper.com). If you use Netstock for DSPs, you might want to use Temper of the Times, a NASD member firm, for DRPs. Temper handles the enrollment process for most direct investment plans (over 900 plans). Its parent company, *The Moneypaper*, publishes three newsletters: *The Moneypaper* (monthly), *Direct Investing* (bimonthly), and *DRP Authority* (quarterly). An annual subscription to *The Moneypaper* is $90. For subscribers to *The Moneypaper*, most DRPs that you start through Temper have a one-time $15 fee. *The Moneypaper* also offers a complete list of DRPs and DSPs at its website.

Here's where the service becomes more affordable. If you *don't* subscribe to *The Moneypaper*, you can still use Temper to enroll in DRPs. The fee is merely increased to $20 per company, rather than $15 plus the subscription fee. At this $20 price, Temper is an option worth considering. For $20 apiece, Temper will buy your first shares and enroll you in as many DRPs as you wish, making it very convenient and easy for investors. For enrollment information, visit www.moneypaper.com or call 1-800-295-2550.

Alternative Ways to Invest

BUYandHOLD.com (www.buyandhold.com). Another innovative young company, BUYandHOLD.com opens for business in the fall of 1999. For a low transaction fee it will allow investors to buy shares of certain companies in any amount (including fractional shares) and it will reinvest dividends for free. The company will first offer only DRP-sporting companies, but it may later also provide the service for non-DRP companies such as Microsoft. This is where it really offers potential – as the cheapest brokerage-type service around, one that allows fractional shares, too. Keep an eye out for this service as a means to round out your investment options.

Direct investing is simply about having the ability to invest small amounts of money with minimal to zero costs, while being able to buy fractional shares of stock and reinvest dividends. If services such as BUYandHOLD.com proliferate, and if discount brokerage commissions continue to decline, these types of investment options could actually become more attractive than some direct investment plans. Some direct investment plans have $5 purchase fees. Discount brokerage commissions promise to be lower than $5, and the ability to buy fractional shares from brokers and easily reinvest dividends is probably around the corner if BUYandHOLD.com is an indicator.

As the online investment industry emerges, watch for this. The direct investment plans of some companies will likely become less attractive than other options available, such as BUYandHOLD.com. Of course, our hope is that declining brokerage commissions will cause companies to lower direct investment plan fees, too, or offer discounted share prices in order to attract investors to the plans. Either way, the low-cost investor wins.

Discount Brokers. Some traditional discount brokers offer free dividend reinvestments, although none offer fractional shares or commission-free investing. Depending on how infrequently you care to invest, however, discount brokers could work for you if you keep your commission below 2% of your investment each time and have dividends reinvested. This isn't a DRP, obviously, but a different way to invest. This option could allow you to have your dividends reinvested, and you could invest somewhat regularly if commissions are low enough.

Family or Friends. If anyone you know owns shares in companies you're interested in beginning DRPs with, ask if you can buy a share from them. They'll need to place the stock certificate in their name (if it isn't already), have it delivered, and then transfer it to you. You can enroll once you have company enrollment forms.

Seek Foolishness Online!

This chapter and the direct investment plan list in Part II of this book should provide all you need to know to enroll in plans. But, if you find that you have questions as you start to enroll in DRPs and DSPs, come online to get answers! The Motley Fool community graduates hundreds of new investors every month, lifting them from novice to Foolish in a matter of days, if not hours. Post your questions on our Direct Investing Basics message board at http://boards.fool.com/ (under the Investor's Roundtable listing). While there, you can ask everyone for their latest thoughts on which broker is best to buy first shares from or which DRP enrollment services excel.

Once you have the enrollment basics nailed down, you can move to the Direct Investing Companies message board to discuss interesting topics with other investors: companies and where to invest.

Which industries and companies should you consider for investment? Which should you avoid? What can you do to maximize your returns?

Our next chapter gets you started in the right direction.

Chapter 4

INDUSTRIES AND COMPANIES TO EMBRACE

For luck you carried a horse chestnut and a rabbit's foot in your right pocket.

— ERNEST HEMINGWAY, *A MOVEABLE FEAST*

You invest in order to build wealth, and with that, security. So when preparing to invest for the next decade or longer, seek companies that you have every reason to believe will build wealth for you without threatening your security. If you do, you shouldn't need luck. (A little won't hurt, however.)

Using direct investment plans, you're beginning a very long-term relationship with your companies. You're beginning to invest slowly and steadily, and it will probably be several years before you have substantial amounts of money invested. If you begin to invest in the wrong companies using direct investment plans, you'll lose valuable time and the opportunity to dollar-cost average into great companies over that time.

So what should you do?

Whatever you do, *don't* listen to *Barron's*, financial television shows, or any other stock market gurus who try to guess the market's direction or the fair value (and therefore the future price) of stocks. Nobody knows and nobody *can* know. And *you* don't care. You *hope* for lower prices from time to time. So rather than waste time trying to guess the unknowable, focus on finding the best companies in the world to buy – ideally, companies so great that you'll still own them when you retire.

To find strong companies you must first focus on strong industries. As you begin to build your portfolio, focus on industries that should prosper for decades no matter what befalls the world economy. Barring a Martian invasion, the impact of a major asteroid, the resurgence of disco, or nuclear destruction, there are industries that will survive (and thrive) in most any situation. These are known as "defensive industries," and there are more of them than you might think.

Defensive Long-Term Industries

One of our favorite industries is pharmaceuticals. Whatever the economy does, people need to fill prescriptions. Many other factors are working in the favor of pharmaceutical companies, including new Food and Drug Administration (FDA) regulations that hasten the drug approval process, advances in science bringing about new drugs, an aging world population, and long-term patent protection for new drugs. Leading pharmaceutical companies have benefited tremendously and should continue to do so for years. Industry leaders include Abbott Laboratories, American Home Products, Bristol-Myers Squibb, Glaxo Wellcome, Eli Lilly, Johnson & Johnson, Merck, Pfizer, Schering-Plough, and Warner-Lambert, among others. Not all of these companies have commission-free direct investment plans, but many do, including Johnson & Johnson and Pfizer (two of our favorites, incidentally).

Another defensive industry is food and beverages. Whatever the economy does, people need to eat and drink. Working in this industry's favor is a growing world population, the opening of new markets in Eastern Europe and former Soviet Block countries (the spread of democracy is slow but steady), and a lifestyle that increasingly favors prepared foods. Leading food and beverage giants with direct investment plans include Campbell Soup, Coca-Cola Co., General Mills, Heinz, Hershey, Kellogg, Philip Morris (one of the largest food companies in the world), PepsiCo, Sara Lee, Tricon, and dozens of others. All of them are listed in the back of this book. Again, not all of these companies have free direct investment plans, but many do, including Coca-Cola, one of the most respected companies on the planet.

Our next defensive industry might surprise you: technology. It's volatile and difficult to predict, but technology is the tuxedoed chauffeur driving this world to its destination. Invest in the consistent leaders and you'll be rewarded. Companies with direct investment plans include Ameritech, AT&T, General Electric, IBM, Intel, and Lucent Technologies. Investing in technology requires increased knowledge of a company and its competitors because the landscape can change so quickly, but you shouldn't bypass the industry unless you're uncomfortable investing in it. Be prepared for volatile stocks here, but with dollar-cost averaging, volatility can work in your favor.

A fourth defensive industry is consumer products. These are the little things that we all need to survive (or so we grow to believe), including razor blades, shampoo, toothpaste, shoes, shirts. You know. *Things.* We buy them whether or not the economy is thriving. We'll also include here the actual retail leaders that sell us necessary items for our home and hygiene, such as Home Depot and Wal-Mart. Leading consumer product companies include Gillette, many of our pharmaceutical companies, Colgate-Palmolive, and Clorox.

Two industries that straddle between defensive and cyclical (meaning that they rise and fall with economic cycles) are financial services and energy, including oil, gas, and utilities. Both industries are necessary for obvious reasons, but both can be at the mercy of external factors more than the other industries we just mentioned. Financial services and banks have good and bad years depending on interest rates, investments abroad, the value of the dollar, debtors' ability to repay loans, and so forth. Energy and oil prices are controlled largely by the government or international cartels. Still, both industries play vital roles in our lives and are worth consideration. Leaders in areas of finance include American Express, Fannie Mae, General Electric (it has an enormous financial wing), Mellon Bank, U.S. Bancorp, and dozens of others. In energy, Exxon and its pending partner, Mobil, and BP Amoco – alongside other giants – are typically the best investments. Energy is a challenging industry and sheer size is becoming increasingly important as consolidation occurs.

So, our top defensive industries are:

- Pharmaceuticals
- Food and Beverages
- Technology (even though others argue that tech is anything but defensive)
- Consumer Products
- Finance (though it's more cyclical)
- Energy (it's more cyclical, too)

Of course, as you go through the list of companies with DRPs and DSPs, don't ignore the industries we didn't cite. Other interesting possibilities include entertainment (Disney and General Electric again), construction and manufacturing (Caterpillar, Deere, and GE again), transportation (General Motors, Boeing, GE yet again – buy GE alone and you're diversified), telecommunications (which we lump with technology), and many more.

For beginners, we suggest that you focus on the more defensive list above (just about in that order, too) and try to find companies that you understand and respect, especially from the first three or four categories. The Motley Fool's real-money Drip Portfolio first invested in Intel, Johnson & Johnson, Campbell Soup, and Mellon Bank – representing diversity across strong industries. We might have bought Gillette for the portfolio, too, but its investment plan became fee-laden, as did Campbell Soup's after we began to buy it. We'll likely begin investing in Pfizer next, because we believe that owning two pharmaceutical companies makes great sense given the strengths and dynamics of the industry.

Any industry that you invest in should possess the following long-term characteristics:

- Viability and long-term opportunity
- Strong potential for growth
- Earnings predictability
- Reasonably clear competitive landscape
- Understandable (to you) business dynamics

We realize that some of these qualities are subjective or only modestly estimable. That's why you need to understand the industries in which you invest as well as possible. You should be knowledgeable enough to make comfortable judgments regarding any quality or a lack thereof. Most of us have industries that we understand better than others – industries we work in, industries we frequently patronize, and industries that interest us or support our hobbies. In these industries, we usually have favorite companies.

Focusing on attractive industries is the first step. Next you want to find the best companies by focusing on certain qualities.

Company Qualities to Embrace

As you study companies for potential investment, use the following list of desirable qualities as a lighthouse to help you steer your ship in the right direction. Assessing some of these qualities requires more research than others. All of the research can be done for free at www.fool.com. If you don't have online access, it can still be completed for free – at a library. A library should have computers with access to www.fool.com. If not, well, they have numerous publications on the shelves.

Ideally, you want your companies to possess the following attributes.

A "Most Respected" Company and Industry-Leading Management

If Johnson & Johnson didn't have strong management, the company wouldn't have increased annual sales, as it has, for 65 consecutive years. Due partially to this track record, Johnson & Johnson is one of the most respected companies on the stock market. Outside of historical performance, however, quality of management and how much respect a company deserves are subjective issues, making them more difficult to measure.

For insight, read financial magazines' "Most Respected Companies" issues. *Fortune*, for one, publishes lists of the most respected companies and management teams every year. Use that for reference as you strike out on your own, making a list of the companies that *you* respect most from industries fitting our criteria. The following is an example list of some of our favorite companies with direct investment plans, roughly in order.

Table VI	
Some of Our Most Respected Companies	**Why We Respect Them**
Johnson & Johnson	Consistent growth and it gives back to society
Pfizer	Steadily becoming the leading pharmaceutical company
Coca-Cola	Leading brand name in the world and in our refrigerator
Intel	Most trustworthy computer chips
General Electric	Unstoppable powerhouse across many industries
Lucent Technologies	Branded visionary in telecommunications equipment
IBM	Great laptop computers and software
Campbell Soup	Products are the leading brands, like Pepperidge Farm cookies, and are being sold in more and more places
Exxon	Leading oil conglomerate – and we like the Exxon tiger, too

Like our list, your list might only have companies on it that any five-year-old whipper snapper could name – Disney, Coca-Cola, Pepsi, Campbell Soup. That's perfectly fine. You don't need to invest in companies with names like Q-Logix 2001, or TriVisionCyclopes, Inc., to make money. Instead, you'll likely find that many of your most respected companies are known by everyone and are on the lists compiled by financial magazines, too. In fact, the recent list from *Fortune* included many of our companies: Johnson & Johnson, Pfizer, Coca-Cola, Intel, General Electric, and Lucent Technologies were named alongside Merck, Cisco Systems, Microsoft, and others. There's a reason for this. Companies possessing the brightest management teams for decades running are well known and are easily spotted – they're leading the pack. These companies are visionary and dominate their industries. They regularly make the evening news, and their stocks are usually among the most actively traded (and widely owned) on the market.

After you create your list, see if the companies have direct investment plans. If they do, investigate the fees involved. In the list above, GE, Lucent Technologies, IBM, and Campbell Soup charge fees for optional cash payments and dividend reinvestment. We'd weigh the fees in our decision as we considered each. If a company merits investment, we might forgive the fees and invest anyway.

After seeing if your companies have direct investment plans, call those that do and request investor information – namely an annual report, recent press releases, and direct investment plan forms. You'll need this information to see if the companies meet our next desired qualities.

A Profitable Business

Being respected and having visionary management only goes so far if a company isn't profitable. A shareholder invests in companies in hopes of sharing in the profits. If a company grows its earnings, the value of its stock should grow, too, benefiting shareholders. Unlike the first quality, this one is easy to quantify. You can find company profitability ratios at www.fool.com, in annual reports, or at the library. We'll discuss these ratios much more in the next chapter about valuing stocks. You simply want to invest in companies that are highly profitable and are becoming even more profitable, which leads to our next point.

Enduring Sales and Earnings Growth

You should focus on profitable companies that have historically grown annual sales and earnings at double-digit rates – at least 10% annually – and you want this growth to be sustainable. Look at the estimated long-term growth rates for your companies and see how well they've done in the past, too.

Johnson & Johnson has 65 consecutive years of sales growth and Pfizer has 49 years of the same. Both companies are poised to grow at market-beating rates for at least the next five years: Pfizer is expected to grow earnings per share 19% annually, and Johnson & Johnson could see 13% annual earnings growth. Consistent growth rates of above 11% (the S&P 500's historical return) typically earn a stock a premium valuation and lead to market-beating investments. Past growth rates and future growth estimates are available for free at www.fool.com in our quotes and portfolio area at http://quote.fool.com. They can also be obtained from research products (such as *ValueLine*) at the library.

The table below displays estimated five-year annual earnings per share (EPS) growth rates for some of our favorite companies. A growth rate above 11% is exceptional for established giants. It also proves that a company needn't be new to grow aggressively. Pfizer is 150 years old, and yet, over the past five years (1993 to 1998) a $10,000 investment in the company grew to $79,000.

Table VII	
Company	**Estimated Five-Year Earnings Per Share Growth Rate (Annual)***
Campbell Soup	11.8%
Coca-Cola	13.8%
General Electric	13.3%
Exxon	7.7%
IBM	12.3%
Intel	20.5%
Johnson & Johnson	12.8%
Lucent Technologies	20.4%
Pfizer	18.8%
Average Annual Growth	14.5%

Source: The Motley Fool (http://quote.fool.com), March 1999.

*Growth estimates often fluctuate – though if things go well, not dramatically.

Consistent earnings growth often leads to the fulfillment of our next quality.

Money in the Bank

Unfortunately, many public companies have more debt than the once-bankrupt Burt Reynolds. You want to avoid these companies. Leading companies usually have a growing pile of money in the bank. A company's financial health is revealed on its balance sheet. You don't need a degree in accounting to read a balance sheet correctly. The balance sheet tells you straight out the amount of cash and debt that the company holds. Think twice about companies with a great deal of the latter and little of the former. Avoid companies that are struggling under a heavy debt load and pique investors' interest merely with the promise of a big future. Companies need funds to fuel growth. Not coincidentally, a healthy cash balance also makes our next qualities possible.

Rising Dividend Payments

In chapter two, we demonstrated the role that dividends can play in a successful investment. We must also point out that when a company increases its dividend regularly, your investment can eventually earn a very large return from dividends alone. Johnson & Johnson has increased its dividend payment for 35 consecutive years, and in the last 10 years its dividend has increased by nearly 16% annually.

Imagine that you'd bought shares of Johnson & Johnson 10 years ago at $9 apiece (the split-adjusted price) when the stock paid a 2.5% dividend yield, or 22.5 cents per share. In the next 10 years, the dividend grew 16% annually to become $1 per share, which is where it stands as of March 1999. The stock is now $90 a share, so your original investment has grown 10 times in value. To boot, the dividend payment is now $1 per share, so your original $9 shares are each earning $1 in dividends alone, resulting in an 11% annual yield.

That yield is simply awesome. Ten years of patience – 3,653 days – has resulted in tremendous success.

An 11% yield all but guaranteed for the rest of one's investment life is wonderful, but with direct investment plans, a rising dividend is important in another way, too. Because investors who use direct investment plans typically reinvest dividends into more stock, a rising dividend will buy more and more stock over time. Remember our Coca-Cola example: $250,000 in value was created without dividends reinvested; $5.7 million was created *with* dividends reinvested. Reinvesting a growing dividend is definitely a smart move. Coca-Cola and many other leaders have increased dividends as reliably as Johnson & Johnson.

Now, before we move on, in a nefarious turnaround, we want to warn you about dividends that are *too high* and encourage you to buy some companies that pay barely any dividend at all.

First, be leery if companies pay 6%, 7%, 8% – or even higher – dividend yields. These yields are typically paid on stocks that don't have much chance to appreciate in value. An 8% yield is high, but alone it underperforms the stock market's long-term average return. If the stock can't rise, too, to boost the total return above 11%, forget it. Don't invest in laggards merely for the high (but often static) dividend payment. Next, sometimes you *want* to buy companies that pay a very small dividend.

Some of the stocks with the lowest dividends are the best performers. Intel and Lucent Technologies pay very slight dividends, but the stocks have appreciated so much that you don't need a dividend to prosper. Many leading companies (many of them technology leaders: Intel, Microsoft, Cisco, Lucent) choose to reinvest cash back into the business rather than pay it out to investors in dividends. That's profitable for shareholders if it results in a higher stock price.

In summary, rising dividend payments are an important quality to seek. Not only will they reward you, but they indicate that a company is strong. However, keep the two caveats from the previous paragraph in mind. Dividends *do* matter and often make a great difference in the long term, but they aren't the be-all and end-all to investing success.

Reliable Share Repurchase Programs
Profitable companies with cash in the bank often repurchase shares of the company stock. The practice of a company repurchasing its own shares is important, and what this practice *represents* is equally meaningful. It usually means that the company is generating a good sum of cash and that it sees enough value in its own stock to repurchase it. When a company is able to repurchase shares reliably, it's showing confidence in its future and in its cash balance. Campbell Soup currently buys back 2% of its shares each year, and Pfizer announced a $5 billion share repurchase program in 1998.

Share repurchases benefit you – the shareholder – in two ways. First, share buybacks increase a stock's price (if only temporarily) because the buyback represents increased demand for the stock. Campbell Soup buys its shares when the stock falls to certain levels. When Campbell's management steps to the plate with a large buy order, the stock often rises. Second, when companies repurchase shares, it reduces the total number of shares available to the public, which, in effect, means that each existing share is worth more. Let's explain.

Consider Ms. Selena's Governess Supply Company. Ms. Selena's has 100 million shares outstanding and the company is expected to earn $50 million in net income next year. That means Ms. Selena's is expected to earn $0.50 per share. ($50 million in income divided by 100 million shares equals $0.50 per share.) Imagine that Ms. Selena buys back 5% of her shares – 5 million, that is – with extra cash in the company coffers. The purchased shares are essentially retired (taken off the market), meaning that the company now has only 95 million shares outstanding. Ms. Selena's is still expected to earn the same amount of money next year. So now, when we divide $50 million by 95 million shares, we get $0.53. The earnings per share have risen from $0.50 to $0.53. Essentially, since there are fewer shares, each share is now worth more.

Similar to rising dividend payments, consistent share repurchase programs are a positive quality to look for. You can find a company's repurchase policy (or a lack of it) in company literature.

A Strong Stock

Too many investors seek weak, beaten down stocks on the argument that they're cheap and will rise again. Sometimes that happens, but usually it doesn't. One of the qualities that we seek represents contrarian thinking: We cotton to strong stocks that are valued more highly than others. Why? Because you typically get what you pay for. Therefore, we aren't afraid to buy stocks that are always making new 52-week highs. In fact, we interpret new highs as a sign that a company is strong and *should* be getting our attention, if not our investment dollars.

On the following pages, consider the long-term (10 years or longer) stock chart for each of our respected companies. Taking the long-term perspective as presented by these charts, ask yourself when these stocks *haven't* been making new highs. You'll notice they've consistently done so. Consistent new highs are the greatest indicator of long-term success. Plus, strong *past* performance, as shown by these charts, is usually an indicator of a strong *future* performance to come. We don't buy into the popular notion on Wall Street that "past performance is not an indicator of future results." History shows the opposite is frequently true. Past performance is often an indicator! Leaders with momentum usually continue to lead, while laggards lacking momentum usually continue to slog.

All charts below show company performance over the past decade as compared to the S&P 500 index.

Campbell Soup

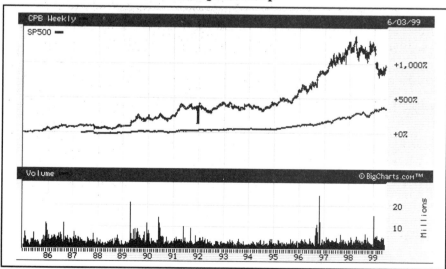

Coca-Cola

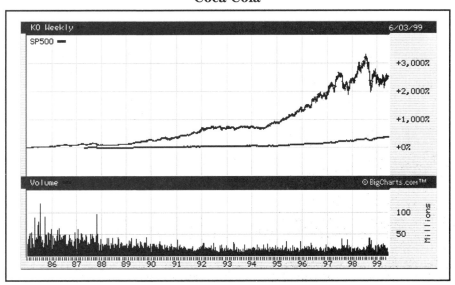

General Electric

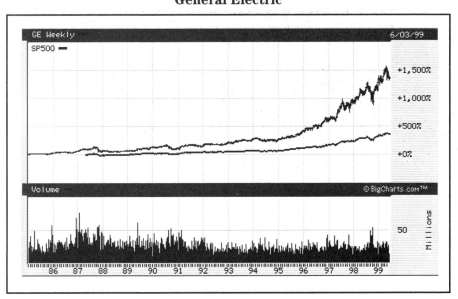

Exxon

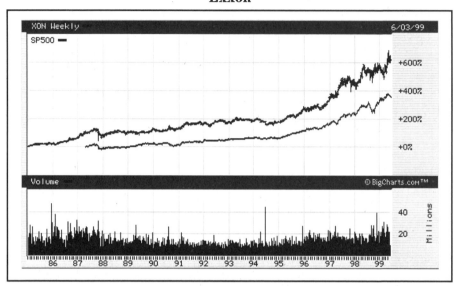

Reprinted with the permission of Big Charts Inc. www.BigCharts.com
Copyright 1999, Big Charts Inc.

IBM

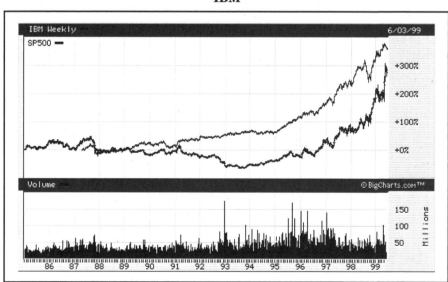

Reprinted with the permission of Big Charts Inc. www.BigCharts.com
Copyright 1999, Big Charts Inc.

Intel

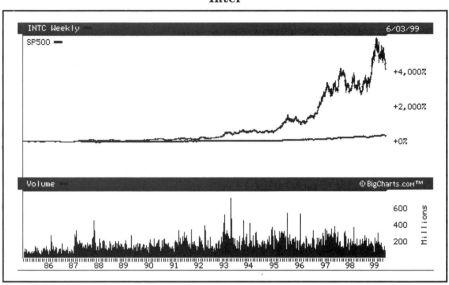

Reprinted with the permission of Big Charts Inc. www.BigCharts.com
Copyright 1999, Big Charts Inc.

Johnson & Johnson

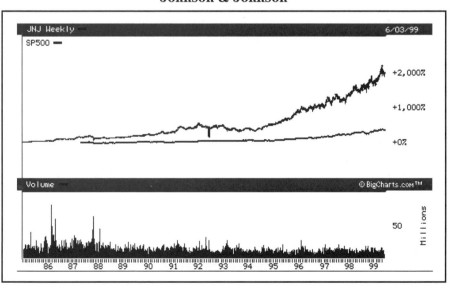

Reprinted with the permission of Big Charts Inc. www.BigCharts.com
Copyright 1999, Big Charts Inc.

Lucent Technologies

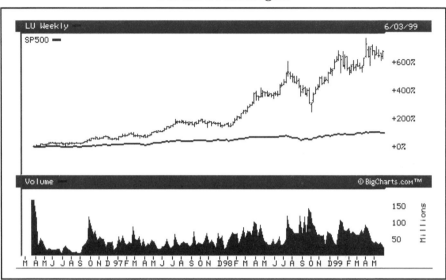

Lucent Technologies was spun off from AT&T in March 1996.
Reprinted with the permission of Big Charts Inc. www.BigCharts.com
Copyright 1999, Big Charts Inc.

Pfizer

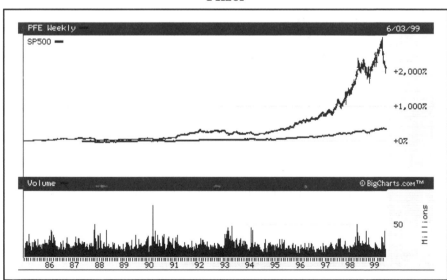

Reprinted with the permission of Big Charts Inc. www.BigCharts.com
Copyright 1999, Big Charts Inc.

Each of these charts teaches one lesson right off the bat: invest for the long term. The longer you own a leading stock, the more it should appreciate. Plus, if you invest in strong companies, you'll outperform the stock market's average return. Aside from IBM, all of our companies topped the S&P 500 over the measured time period. And all of these stocks, when measured from a considerably earlier year, have appreciated even more than shown here. Now consider the last chart. Pfizer's stock has been nothing short of phenomenal. There's plenty of volatility present when you tighten your scope, however. Consider a one-year chart of Pfizer and a one-year chart of Johnson & Johnson.

Pfizer

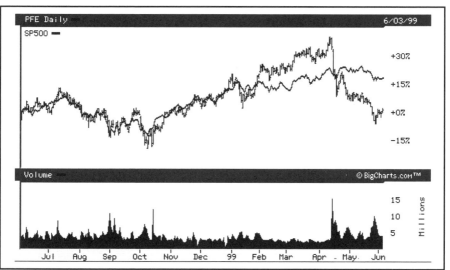

Reprinted with the permission of Big Charts Inc. www.BigCharts.com   Copyright 1999, Big Charts Inc.

Johnson & Johnson

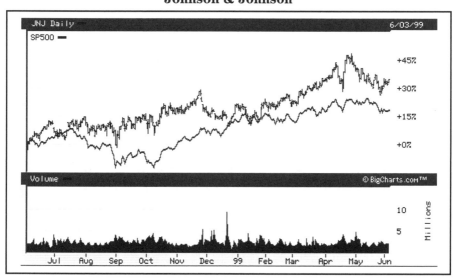

Reprinted with the permission of Big Charts Inc. www.BigCharts.com   Copyright 1999, Big Charts Inc.

Over a one-year period, these stocks swing high *and* low, sweet chariot. As you're investing, don't allow inevitable volatility to shake your resolve. You should always direct your attention to the looooooooong-term *trend* (sorry, the "o" stuck on the keyboooooard), rather than the short-term *swings*. If your companies fulfill most of the criteria in this chapter, your stocks should, over time, trend toward new highs. So, like that song says (kind of), don't fear new highs. Embrace them. And don't fear the reaper. Embrace...

Okay. Fear the reaper if you want.

But don't fear strong stocks that are at new highs. They're leading the market higher. They'd be leading your portfolio higher, too, if you owned them.

Domination of a Viable Industry

When fulfilled, the principles in this chapter should point you to strong companies. That's good. But even better is buying the *industry domi-nator*. This is the final quality to seek, and it's a biggie.

When seeking industry domination from companies, how does one measure for it?

Consider the market share possessed by your companies. Intel chips are inside 80% of personal computers. Campbell Soup controls 78% of North America's canned-soup market. Coca-Cola holds 50% of the domestic soft-drink market. All have leading brand names. You want your dollars riding on leaders of this magnitude.

Just as important as current market leadership is *future* leadership – and viability – both of the company in question and its industry. To the best of your ability, invest in companies that are most likely to lead profitable industries 10, 20, and 30 years from today. This is a subjective quality to measure (okay, it's a prediction), but if you consider past performance, current company strengths, market share, industry trends, and company initiatives, you should be able to draw confident conclusions regarding the staying power of a Coca-Cola, an Intel, a GE, and an IBM. Is it probable that each company will lead a significant portion of its market 10 years from now? Will its industry still be *important* 10 years from now? Once you know a company and its industry well enough, you should be able to answer these questions with enough confidence to make an investment decision.

Summary
Putting it all together, invest in industries that possess the following qualities:

- Viability and long-term opportunity
- Strong potential for growth
- Earnings predictability
- Reasonably clear competitive landscape
- Understandable (to you) business dynamics

Within such industries, seek companies that possess most or all of these qualities:

- A "most respected" company and industry-leading management
- A profitable business
- Enduring sales and earnings growth
- Money in the bank
- Rising dividend payments
- Reliable share repurchase programs
- A strong stock
- Domination of a viable industry

Note that the first and last items on the second list are the most subjective. This is because these subjective qualities, for better or worse, hold together – like a taco shell – all of the criteria in the middle. Look at the first and last criteria again. If a company *is* most respected, *does* have leading management, and *does* dominate a viable industry, all of the qualities in the middle will likely fall into place. Therefore, it's very important to know a company and its industry well enough that you can make subjective opinions about it. The middle criteria are easily measured. It's the end two, however – the subjective two – that hold everything together and have the most potential to make an investment great.

Seek the qualities on these lists and then add to them our Foolish Equation: Discipline + Time = Compounding. If you find all of the above qualities in a stock, use discipline to invest in the shares regularly over long periods of time. Eventually, you should achieve your goal: the compounding of your money.

While you will likely do very well by investing only in companies that possess these qualities, there are also arguments to be made for investing in beaten-down, mangy dog-like stocks now and again. Sometimes you can find great value in currently loathed stocks, but you need to know what to seek when digging through what other investors consider to be trash.

Investing in the "Fixer-Upper"

Many people dream of miraculously finding something a little less than perfect selling for pennies on the dollar (a home, a car, a boat), buying it for a pittance, fixing it up, and making an absolute killing. Many investors search for this on the stock market, too.

Indeed, there *are* some gems nestled in the sludge of downtrodden companies that are just waiting to be unearthed. Down in the muck, some investors are groping about for viable "turnaround" investments to make them rich. First, a company of considerable repute must suffer hardship for any number of reasons (lawsuits, bad management, competition), and next, its stock price must fall to levels never thought possible by the existing shareholders (poor fellows). When the shares are cheaper than a Las Vegas lounge act, so-called "value investors" will begin to buy the stock if they foresee a turnaround for the lagging company.

These types of situations can reward a patient investor extremely well. However, analyzing a company when it's under severe pressure and facing great uncertainty is very difficult, and this makes a challenging prospect (finding the right damaged company to invest in) even more daunting and risky. There's no magic formula – let alone *any* formula – for judging each of these disparate and *desperate* situations, so it's a risky proposition with more guesswork than your first dance steps in middle school.

So, what's an investor to do?

Avoid making guesses on investments outside of your realm of knowledge. Often something is cheap for a lasting reason and its low valuation won't change for years – if ever. We suggest that when investing in potential turnaround companies you *especially* only invest in what you know *very well*. If you work for an industry and you understand it better than you understand your spouse, you'll likely realize when there's value to be captured in the beaten-down industry stocks and when there isn't. Or, if you have a great deal of seasoned knowledge about certain industries, that could be enough to make good decisions on laggard companies. To help you make decisions regarding beaten-down, sleepy, and often forgotten stocks, use the following pointers:

- Consider a crushed company when its problems are external and temporary (lawsuits, a temporary decline in demand, or when a good stock falls because weak peers brought it down through guilt by association, etc.).

- Consider a fallen company when its problems are *internal* and are being properly addressed. (Intel's Pentium chip flaw is an excellent example – the stock fell over 40% on news of the chip's flaw, only to later recover to new highs. Another example is Microsoft: it usually falls when it delays the release of new software.)

- Buy only beaten-down companies with enough cash to ride out the bad times so that they won't risk bankruptcy.

- Be as certain as possible that a laggard has an excellent *reason* to turnaround – don't buy on faith alone, or just because "it's priced at a new low!"

- Make certain that there are no better places to invest your money – meaning, you don't know any healthy company that would likely serve you better in the long run (this implies that you'll very rarely buy a badly faltering stock – that's how it should be).

- Finally, the more uncertain a turnaround story is, the lower the percentage of your funds it should receive.

Recent turnaround stories that fit many of the above conditions and have worked out (or promise to work out) are plentiful. After five years of going nowhere but down, AT&T began to rise in 1997 after its management problems were addressed. In 1998, Gillette's stock was hammered down to new yearly lows because international currencies were weak. Also in 1998, Disney, owner of several film companies, fell on news of lower earnings due partially to slow box-office sales. In 1999, Campbell Soup was sucked dry (to new lows) because the warm winter decreased soup consumption and, at the same time, Campbell began to improve inventory methods at the cost of lower near-term earnings.

All of these are examples of temporary stumbles at respectable companies. There are many more drastic laggards and turnaround possibilities to be found (at much greater risk), but if the above situations represent the extent of your foray into beaten-down investing, that's quite acceptable and possibly even desirable. Severe turnaround investing is not for the typical investor. Investing in stumbling leaders can be.

However you choose to invest, keep in mind that even though lagging stocks are often the cheapest to buy statistically, you're committing to purchasing a company's shares on a regular basis over a long period of time. Therefore, a company's ability to grow over that time is much more important than the *current* valuation you pay. A cheap stock doesn't guarantee future price appreciation. The *quality* of a business is always the most enduring attribute to seek.

We listed some "do's." Now, it's time for some investing "don'ts."

Investing Situations to Avoid

When your aim is to build wealth by investing in businesses with clear, long-term futures, you should avoid three specific investment scenarios that will almost always work against you.

Avoid purchasing shares of a company that is operating in a declining industry; steer clear of an industry about to undergo serious competitive realignment; and run away screaming from an industry that is really, in the end, just a fad.

Declining Industries

Using a direct investment plan to regularly purchase shares of, say, a buggy whip manufacturer or an ice delivery service at the turn of the century would not have been a bright move. Both industries underwent long, painful declines during which shares of the related companies looked perpetually cheap on a statistical basis. However, they weren't cheap enough. They withered to zero. As a way to tell true decline from a few years' worth of softness, look for technological innovation or shifts in cultural norms that impact the industry in question. The Internet will pressure many industries into change, if not decline: retailing, full-service stockbrokers, and the media – including music, news, and information distribution. Changes aren't always so large and noticeable, however. Home-delivered milk used to be a thriving business. Cultural norms slowly shifted away from it. Keep your eyes and ears peeled.

Serious Competitive Realignment

Even when it's clear that demand in an industry will steadily increase, it's not always a good idea to commit funds to it over multi-decade periods, especially when the industry players are actively realigning.

When you invest for years, you want to end up betting on one of the top horses in an industry. But if intense competitive realignment is taking place, it may not be clear which horse leads, which horse could lead the next lap, and which horse will lead in the distant future. Your bet could turn up lame if the field is so jumbled that you can't even see your horse's stride. Local telephone companies and electric utilities have been in this situation for much of the 1990s. Although reform in both arenas has increased the potential for growth, it has also brought into question what the most successful business strategy will be over the next 5 years, let alone the next 20. Competition is inevitable in any business, but you want to know who will be competing, what they bring to the table, and who is likely to emerge victorious. If you can't reasonably form an answer to these questions, wait until the dust settles on the track before placing your investments.

Fad Companies

Although normally a fad company isn't viable long enough to offer a direct investment plan, this isn't always true, so this topic is worth mentioning quickly and then just as quickly forgetting. Sometimes a company will benefit from a fad in the near term even when it's clear there's no long-term business model to continue the growth. It's always worth questioning if a company's performance is the result of fad activity or anything that isn't sustainable. Some people have even called the Internet (the entire thing) a fad. [Insert raucous laughter here.]

A real example of a fad would be the once-booming hula-hoop industry, as documented in the film *The Hudsucker Proxy.* Another fad was the gyrating disco industry, as depicted in the film *Saturday Night Fever.*

Your Portfolio

Many financial publications tell you what your first portfolio should consist of, spitting out the four *precise companies* that you should buy. They even recommend an exact retirement portfolio for you. The publications probably mean well, but the Fool believes that this borders on preposterous. If you don't make your own investment decisions, it's very unlikely that you will *understand* what you're buying. That's plain wrong.

Build your portfolio based on your knowledge and interests. Fools online sometimes share their portfolios on the message boards. They vary greatly, with some holding Coca-Cola, Exxon, Intel, Pfizer, and an obscure utility stock, and others owning General Electric, PepsiCo, Philip Morris, Schering-Plough, and General Motors. Another portfolio holds Johnson & Johnson, Disney, Campbell Soup, IBM, and Hershey. There is no *right* portfolio for everyone – there is only one that is right for you.

You know our favorite industries and some of our favorite companies, but rather than limit you, our suggestions should lead you to more ideas. You might not buy any of our favorite companies, but perhaps you'll buy two pharmaceuticals because you agree it *is* a strong industry. Perhaps you won't. The important thing is that you make your own decisions for your own reasons.

As you build your portfolio, diversify modestly. Remember that being diversified across every industry known to man is *not* necessary. Being diversified doesn't automatically mean that you're well protected – it could actually mean that you're vulnerable to many things you don't understand, and to underperformance. Focus on the *best* companies that you *understand.* You'll feel comfortable about your portfolio only if you decide what goes into it, and only if you understand your reasoning behind each purchase. Most of all, we hope that you'll enjoy the process of building your portfolio over many years.

Find Foolishness Online!

In the same way that we ended the last chapter, we'll end this one reminding you that you're anything but alone. As you seek companies to buy, you should talk to friends, family, co-workers – anyone who has an interest (or should have an interest!) in building wealth by investing in great companies. Beyond your circle of friends, you can gather online with thousands of other Fools. Any direct investment plan stock that you might be curious about has its own message board at www.fool.com. If it doesn't yet, tell us, and we'll open it for you. Plus, The Motley Fool has six real-money stock portfolios that share daily investment lessons as real-life examples of how we invest *our* money. Come online to research, learn, and discuss companies for free.

Chapter 5

COMPANY VALUATION AND PERFORMANCE MEASURES

*What is a cynic? A man who knows the price of everything
and the value of nothing.*

– OSCAR WILDE

This popular quote from Oscar Wilde is a perfect characterization of the typical stock market guru. You frequently hear on financial television and read in Wall Street publications that stocks are "overpriced." You rarely hear it hypothesized that stocks might be bargains (as they were, it turns out, for most of the 1990s) or even reasonably priced. Instead, prices are quoted as "high," scoffs and warnings are registered, the interview or article ends, and the investor is left alone to worry...

"Hmm... should I sell and hope for a 15% decline in the market before buying again?"

Doing so would be foolhardy, if not idiotic.

First, nobody can guess the market's direction. Second, if you sold and waited for a 15% decline, you'd need to pay taxes of more than 15% on your gains, and this might leave you with less money than necessary to buy back what you just sold, especially if the market *rises*.

Too many people know "the price of everything and the value of nothing." How true this is on Wall Street. Think about it in the following way.

Market gurus (the Wise) will warn the public that stock *prices* are high at the moment, but they never say: "If you had bought 100 shares of this company 15 years ago, it'd be *valued* at over $1 million today. And, dear investor, whatever stocks are priced at currently, if you sold now, taxes would take a large chunk of your gain. Instead, if you hold this investment another 15 years it could grow to a total *value* of $3 million."

They *never* say things like that, even though one of the most important points to be made about the stock market is hidden in that paragraph: Value is created over many years. Current price, or valuation, is "of the moment." The two are *much less related* than you'd think.

Value is amassed by investing steadily for years. Valuation, or price, addresses the immediate. If you're investing in strong companies regularly, you will build value over 15 to 30 years whether you buy some shares at very "high" prices and other shares at so-called reasonable prices. However, many investors confuse the process of building value with the analysis of a stock's current price and it paralyzes them.

Make sure you don't get caught up in this confusion. Always act in the interest of creating long-term value. Seek great companies to use as direct investment "savings accounts" every month. That means you don't react to a stock price as if you know where it's headed in the near term. That's a game for market-lagging mutual fund managers: buy, sell, buy, sell! The bigger picture is that a stock's *price* might decline for a few years, but its *value* is going to be greater in 15 years if you've invested well.

You should aim to reverse Wilde's quote. You should aim to know the value of everything and the price of nothing. A leading company is *valuable* to own and invest in for 15 years or longer. The *price* you pay for a stock as you steadily invest is almost coincidental.

Using dollar-cost averaging, you'll buy the same stock at many different prices over several years. So within reason, the current valuation isn't very important as long as you find successful long-term investments. If you invest the same dollar amount each time, you'll always buy more stock when the price is lower, and less when it's higher. Over the years, your average price will favor the *low* end of the stock's range. You'll have created value regardless of the prices you paid. That's a concept the cynical gurus never seem to grasp.

Basic Valuation Measures

Although "mindless" dollar-cost averaging usually works out for the best with direct investing, valuation methods are important to know for investing in general. We'll now review some basics of valuation and offer thoughts on this far from perfect science.

First, what is the "fair value" of a stock?

Unfortunately, there's no correct answer, only many theories. The fair value of any stock is contingent upon hundreds of related factors, not the largest of which is the position of the U.S. economy at every moment. Given that the hundreds of variables affecting the stock market change constantly (interest rates, earnings growth, demand for stocks), the fair value of all stocks is always fluctuating. That's perfect for you, a regular user of direct investment plans. As your stocks fluctuate, the following are ways to measure their prices.

The Price-to-Earnings Ratio (P/E)

More common than an espresso bar in Italy, the Price-to-Earnings ratio is the most frequently used stock valuation measure. This is the number posted in the stock pages of just about any newspaper, from *The Washington Post* to the *Bimini Bazaar Daily* (assuming there were such a publication). So what is this P/E thing? Well, what it *isn't* is rocket science.

The Price-to-Earnings ratio compares a company's stock price to its trailing 12 months of earnings per share. It shows you what you're going to pay for a share of stock in relation to every dollar in net income earned for that share. Imagine that George's Jungle Gyms, Inc., trades at $60 per share and that the company has $2.00 in earnings per share for the past year. Dividing $60 by $2.00 gives you a P/E of 30. For every share of stock, you're paying 30 times what the company earned for that share. Is that expensive? It depends on several factors, such as how fast the company is growing. Many believe that a stock is fairly valued when its P/E ratio is equal to its earnings growth rate. So if George's earnings were growing at 30% per year, the P/E of 30 would be reasonable and the stock might be considered fairly valued – that is, until earnings grow again, which could take just a matter of months. (See why fair valuation is a fleeting subject, always changing?)

When investing in industry-leading companies, you'll often buy stock at a premium P/E ratio. Johnson & Johnson, for example, is expected to grow earnings 13% annually, but the stock recently has been trading at a P/E of 29. The company deserves a higher price because its growth is reliable and its market position is unquestioned. Coca-Cola is expected to grow earnings 14% annually and its stock has averaged a P/E of 45, or 45 times earnings, in recent years. The favorable economics of Coke's business have meant that many investors have been willing to pay a significant premium to the growth rate.

The strong stock market in the 1990s certainly padded that premium. Coca-Cola's P/E ranged from 18 to 53 from 1990 to 1999, so it's closer to the high end of the range as of this writing. Direct investors should be secure in buying a stock like Coca-Cola even at the higher end of the range, because they'll be dollar-cost averaging into the stock and they'll have a chance to buy additional shares at lower prices if the stock rises and falls as it has in the past. Plus, it's difficult to say what the fair valuation for Coca-Cola should be – other than admitting it deserves a premium price – but it's relatively easy to estimate that *value* will be created if you buy the stock and hold it for several years.

Small high-growth companies often have very high P/E ratios because they're expected to grow earnings rapidly. America Online's P/E has ranged from non-existent (no earnings) to over 1,200 in its young life. All over the map. With direct investment plans, however, you usually buy older, more stable companies, and the P/E ratio will almost always be in a smaller, tighter range.

As of March 1999, the average S&P 500 company (which is the type of company that a direct investor typically buys) traded at 29 times earnings (or a P/E of 29) and 26 times 1999 earnings estimates. The S&P 500 has traded at a P/E ranging from about 10 to 38 in its history, with 12 to 18 being the enduring average. You can surmise at this price that – contrary to the warnings of the Wise gurus – the S&P can go anywhere from here, higher or lower. And certainly it will do both. The longer your investment horizon and the stronger your commitment to dollar-cost averaging, the less vital the current valuation is. Focus instead on *businesses* and invest in the strongest companies you can find.

A warning is in order before we leave this valuation measure and saunter Foolishly to the next. Don't be suckered into a low P/E stock for the P/E alone. For one thing, P/E ratios vary widely by industry. Car manufacturers traditionally sport low P/Es, for example, while software and pharmaceutical companies often sport high ones. Examine a company's P/E in the context of its industry. If the Tennessee Gerbil Electric Co. trades at a P/E of 7, it's not necessarily attractive. Even if its P/E is low for its industry, it might just be a very low-growth company, perhaps unattractive at almost any price. An investment in Coca-Cola at a P/E of 45 might very well crush an investment in Tennessee Gerbil Electric at a P/E of 7.

The accompanying table shows P/E ratios on various stocks as of March 1999. You can obtain the P/E for a stock in most newspaper stock listings or online, and you can find company growth rate estimates (to compare to the company's P/E ratio if you wish) online at www.fool.com, specifically at http:quote.fool.com. Without exception, the companies in the table with higher P/E ratios are generally growing earnings more aggressively over the long term (and often with more certainty) than the companies with lower P/E ratios.

Table VIII

Company	P/E Ratio (March 1999)
Campbell Soup	32
Coca-Cola	45
Exxon	28
General Electric	37
IBM	27
Intel	34
Johnson & Johnson	29
Lucent Technologies	90
Pfizer	55
Caterpillar	11
Energy South Inc.	11
Ford	11
General Motors	19
Goodyear Tire	11
Home Depot	61
Mellon Bank	21
Microsoft	68
Sears	17
Starbucks	61
Wal-Mart	47

The Price-to-Sales Ratio (PSR)

Like the P/E ratio, the Price-to-Sales ratio measures the value of a company compared to a single performance measure. Where the P/E measures the stock price against net earnings, the PSR measures a company's overall market value in relation to its total sales (or total revenues). It's especially handy to use when a company isn't generating a profit. Not every company has earnings to report, but every company that you'll invest in sells *something* and has annual revenues. It better anyway, or you can pitch this book into a fire! (If you already planned to do that, we hope you at least enjoy a blast of warmth.)

The Price-to-Sales ratio is simply a company's market capitalization divided by its total sales for the past 12 months. Every company listed on the stock market has a *market capitalization,* or total market value.

To obtain the market value of a company, you multiply the current share price by the number of shares existing. (The number of shares existing – called diluted shares outstanding – can be found online or in recent quarterly and annual reports.) Imagine that Rip-em-Off, Inc., trades at $10 per share and has 1,000,000 shares on the market (making it a very small public company). The total market value of the company is $10,000,000. Next, imagine that the company has taken in $2,000,000 in sales over the past 12 months. Dividing the total market value of $10 million by $2 million in sales gives us a Price-to-Sales ratio of 5.

As of early 1999, the typical Dow Jones Industrial Average stock trades at a PSR of about 2, but the Dow companies are all mammoth, slower-growing firms. Faster growers often trade at much higher PSRs, like America Online with its recent PSR of 29, or Microsoft with its PSR of 26. American Express, by comparison, trades at 2.8 times sales (a PSR of 2.8), and Boeing trades at 0.59 times sales. In Boeing's case, the company's total market value is less than its annual sales. This is possible because sales are not the same as *net earnings*, which are the more important indicator of value creation. Boeing could have $100 billion in sales and zip for earnings, perhaps justifying a low PSR. A company's PSR, like its P/E, is dependent on numerous factors, ranging from the company's profit margins (our next topic) to its reliability and industry. Coca-Cola, though it's a giant Dow Jones Industrial stock, trades at a PSR of above 8, or over four times the average Dow Jones stock. Johnson & Johnson trades at over five times sales, more than double the average Dow stock.

If a company has a higher PSR than average, it's usually a leader with favorable economics and bright prospects. It is also most likely a company holding a defensible industry position, and often one of dominance. If a company has a *lower* PSR, like American Express, DuPont, Boeing, or General Motors, it doesn't necessarily mean that it's a weak business. Instead, it might have lower profit margins, operate in a cyclical industry, or have strong competition. The point to take away is that, as with the P/E ratio, a higher Price-to-Sales ratio often means a company is favored by the stock market because it has a strong business (and high profit margins) and it is growing aggressively or reliably – or usually both.

Table IX	
Company	**PSR Ratio (March 1999)**
Campbell Soup	2.9
Coca-Cola	8.4
Exxon	1.5
General Electric	3.5
IBM	2.1
Intel	7.8
Johnson & Johnson	5.1
Lucent Technologies	4.6
Pfizer	13.6
Caterpillar	0.8
Energy South Inc.	0.9
Ford	0.4
General Motors	0.3

Gross, Operating, and Net Profit Margins (GONG!)
One of the qualities to seek in a company is a profitable business. The more profitable, the better. This means the stronger a company's gross, operating, and net profit margins, the better. (And usually, the higher these margins the higher the company's P/E and PSR ratios.)

Gross margin indicates how much money is left from sales after the material cost of the product sold is subtracted. The operating margin shows earnings achieved from a company's sales after all of the expenses of running the business are subtracted, including salaries, advertising, research and development, *and* the product cost itself. At the time of this writing, Coca-Cola and Johnson & Johnson have operating margins of 27% and 21%, respectively. These are excellent results. With Coca-Cola, this means that for every dollar of sales, the company has 27 cents remaining after paying all product and business operation costs.

But wait... the company still has a few other costs to deduct from its operating earnings.

The net profit margin represents what a company actually keeps after paying *everything*, including interest expenses and the big, bad government – those guys who build highways, parks, national monuments, and generally protect your freedom. *That* big bad government. Every profitable company must pay income taxes. Many companies also pay interest expenses on borrowed money. These deductions are made from operating earnings. They're the final deduction and they leave you with a company's net profit margin. With Johnson & Johnson, this margin is above 14%. Coca-Cola's is above 18%. Any double-digit net profit margin is extraordinary. It means that a lot of money is staying with the company for every dollar of sales. (Profit margins at automobile companies hit 2% during *good* years, so you can surmise why their PSR and P/E ratios are low.)

To calculate gross margin, you divide gross income, or gross earnings, by total sales (or total revenue). From the Intel financial statement that follows, this means dividing 1998 gross income of $14.13 billion by total sales of $26.27 billion. Doing so, we arrive at gross margins of 53.77%. That means every dollar in product that Intel sold had a product cost to the company of 46.23 cents, and it cleared 53.77 cents per dollar of sales. Overall, this is very favorable. Companies like Microsoft (the cost to create software mainly involves people and rent) and Coca-Cola (it sells a basic syrup rather than silicon computer chips) have higher gross margins than Intel, but Intel's is still higher than most.

Next, to calculate operating margin you divide operating earnings by total sales. A company with $5 million in operating earnings and $25 million in sales has an operating margin of 20% ($5 million divided by $25 million equals 0.20, or 20%). Finally, if that company earns $3 million after taxes, it has a net profit margin of 12% ($3 million divided by $25 million equals 0.12, or 12%). The net profit margin is obtained by dividing net earnings by total sales.

So, the equations are:

Gross Earnings / Total Sales = Gross Margin
Operating Earnings / Total Sales = Operating Margin
Net Earnings / Total Sales = Net Margin

Remember their order by the word GONG, for Gross, Operating, Net, and GONG! – as in, you've got it! Using online resources or your companies' annual reports, you can calculate these numbers and compare companies to one another. The higher these margins, the better. Just like in your household. If you bring home $40,000 annually, you hope to have as much left over as possible after paying each of *your* gross, operating, and net expenses (which might be, in order, suits, car, commuting to work; followed by rent, utilities, food; followed by interest on bills and taxes).

To make certain that you can figure margins with your companies, grab a calculator or pen and paper and calculate the three margin equations for Intel with the 1998 numbers provided in the table. To help, the figures that you need to use are in bold.

Table X		
INTEL CORPORATION 1998 CONSOLIDATED SUMMARY FINANCIAL STATEMENTS		
(In millions, except per share amounts)		
		Twelve Months Ended
	Dec. 26, 1998	Dec. 27, 1997
TOTAL SALES (Revenue)	**$26,273**	$25,070
Cost of sales	12,144	9,945
GROSS EARNINGS	**14,129**	15,125
Research and development	2,509	2,347
Marketing, general, and administrative	3,076	2,891
Purchased in-process research and development	165	-
Operating costs and expenses	17,894	15,183
OPERATING EARNINGS	**8,379**	9,887
Interest and other	758	772
INCOME BEFORE TAXES	9,137	10,659
Income taxes	3,069	3,714
NET EARNINGS	**6,068**	6,945
BASIC EARNINGS PER SHARE	3.64	4.25

Tick, tock, tick, tock, tickity tick tick tock... GONG! Did you get it? You should find Intel's margins to be:

Gross = 53.7% (0.537 on the calculator)
Operating = 31.8% (0.318)
Net = 23.0% (0.230)

If your answers don't match, look at the equations and do the math again. Even Einstein made mistakes the first time around. For gross margin, divide $14,129 by $26,273. For operating margin divide $8,379 by $26,273. Finally, for net margin divide $6,068 by $26,273. (Let's pause to marvel. Intel had net income of $6.068 billion in 1998. That alone indicates it's an extraordinary company. But notice, while you're looking, that Intel made *less* money in 1998 than it did in 1997. Even extraordinary companies have slower years and experience difficult periods. The important concern is: Will the company grow over the long term?)

It's great to know these equations, and you should seek companies with lasting high margins, but – once you've found strong companies – none of these equations will be quite as important to you over the years as the Foolish Equation: Discipline + Time = Compounding.

Closing Thoughts on Valuation

One of the beautiful things about direct investing is that you needn't be a valuation genius to succeed. Time and dollar-cost averaging will smooth out the valuation aspect of your investments. Use discipline in your buy decisions, but don't forsake leading companies due to near-term valuation concerns ("the P/E is so high!") when you're a long-term investor.

If your interest has been piqued, there is much more to learn. These measures just scratch the surface. You know where to go for much more on the wide world of valuation: www.fool.com.

Chapter 6

PORTFOLIO TRACKING, RECORDKEEPING, AND TAXES

For every benefit you receive a tax is levied.

– RALPH WALDO EMERSON

Once you begin direct investment plans it's important to keep good records for your own knowledge and for tax purposes. Keep all of your investment plan statements organized. Don't throw them away. Your statements provide the price of each share or fractional share you buy and they're enough to get you through tax season. To make taxes easier, consider tracking your share costs and dividends in a computer spreadsheet, too. The Fool offers one online called Port Tracker. Recording your investments in a spreadsheet also makes it easier for you to track your performance. Some investors track their stocks on paper record sheets.

Tracking Your Performance with Share Price Accounting

One goal of Foolishness is to beat the performance of the major market indices, especially the S&P 500 – an index that 90% of mutual funds have lost to over the past 10 years. You should aim to outperform the S&P 500. (After all, if you can't beat it, you can always join it by putting your money in a low-cost S&P 500 index fund, which simply mirrors the S&P.)

You're at a disadvantage at the start, so don't be discouraged by your performance for at least a few years. Beginning with a small base and adding money regularly makes results slower to kick in because you're buying new stock every month at prevailing prices. It'll be a few years before you can realistically measure your performance against the stock market. You need to know how, though.

When you add money to your portfolio every month, measuring your results isn't simple, but it won't make your head explode, either. The process involves an accounting method that mutual funds use and that you would use if you were investing monthly in a mutual fund, or if you were investing in an S&P 500 fund through your 401(k).

Starting now, think of your portfolio as your own personal mutual fund. Just as mutual funds have "shares" (and companies do, too), you need to decide how many shares to begin your direct portfolio with as you begin to buy stocks. Then, in the future, every time you add money, you're simply buying new shares in your portfolio at that day's cost basis (which is determined by your portfolio's total performance up to that point). This is called "share price accounting."

When you're investing money on a regular basis, it's inaccurate to assess performance by counting the new money as if it had been invested for the entire life of your portfolio. If you start with $500 and invest $100 more per month for 12 months, you'll have $1,700 invested. But a lot of that money will have been invested for less than six months, meaning that it would've been difficult to earn much of a return on it. On the other hand, your initial $500 will have been invested for a year and it might have appreciated or depreciated a more significant amount.

If you judge your performance based only on your portfolio's total value, ignoring the fact that much of the money was invested only recently, you'll weigh the money you invested recently more than you will the older money. This means that if you have done poorly, your performance will look better, but if you have done well, your performance will look less impressive than it actually was. The share price accounting method smoothes this out by weighting each dollar *equally* as you convert them into shares.

Consider an example.

You begin your portfolio with $500. On that day, you decide that your direct investing portfolio has 20 shares. This means that, before you spent a single dollar, your 20 shares were each worth $25.

$$\text{Per Share Value} = \frac{\text{Total Port Value}}{\text{\# of Shares}} = \frac{\$500}{20} = \$25$$

Now imagine that you buy your first shares of stock (congratulations!), incurring some expenses in the process. At the end of one month, due to expenses, your portfolio is now worth $459.50 rather than $500. Beginning a new month, you want to add $100 in savings to the portfolio and buy more stock. Let's first calculate the current price per share. The current price per share of your portfolio is what you're going to "pay" for more shares of your portfolio when you add money.

Before you add money to the portfolio, you find the value per share to be $22.975.

$$\text{Per Share Value} = \frac{\text{Total Value}}{\text{\# of Shares}} = \frac{\$459.50}{20} = \$22.975$$

So, with the $100 you're adding, you'll buy 4.35 shares and add them to your portfolio's total share count.

$$\text{New Shares} = \frac{\text{Money Added}}{\text{Price Per Share}} = \frac{\$100}{\$22.975} = 4.35$$

You now have 24.35 shares of your portfolio worth $22.975 apiece, for a total portfolio value of $559.50. The portfolio's performance – rightly so – has not changed at all in the course of adding money. However, you've added $100 and the appropriate amount of new shares, and this permits you to continue to accurately measure your performance. To see the portfolio's performance to date, compare the current value per share against the previous value. As you can see, the portfolio is down 8.1% to date, with the price per share now being $22.975 vs. $25 when you began – that's ($25 - $22.975) divided by 25 = 0.081, or 8.1%. It could be this way in the beginning due to expenses alone.

To find the value of your portfolio's shares at any point, you need to know how many shares you have and the total cash and stock value of your portfolio. Divide the share count by the total portfolio value to arrive at the current value per share. Compare that to your $25 per share starting point. Each time that you add cash you need to know what your portfolio is worth so you can add the new shares at the correct price per share. And you only add shares to your portfolio's share count when you add cash or buy more shares with reinvested dividends.

Remember – the shares we're talking about here are not shares of company stock, but shares of your portfolio. For the purposes of calculating your performance, you're treating your portfolio like a mutual fund and are creating theoretical "shares" of it.

Even if you understand this completely, the paperwork can be a hassle. At the Fool we use an Excel spreadsheet called Portfolio Tracker to do all of the dirty work for our real-money Drip Portfolio online. That spreadsheet is available for a reasonable price from FoolMart at www.foolmart.com. There are also other computer programs that do the job, such as Quicken from Intuit (at www.intuit.com). If you're using a spreadsheet you must have a computer. To get more information on your spreadsheet and recordkeeping options, visit The Motley Fool's Direct Investing message boards (under the Investor's Roundtable board area) at http://boards.fool.com; ask there and you'll receive numerous suggestions.

If you'd rather track your investments by hand, that's perfectly acceptable and – allow us to say – even quite fanciful (maybe turn off the power and light candles while working, too). Many people track their direct investments in a ledger, much like an accountant would in the good old days. One downside is that it'll be difficult to track your actual performance because share price accounting isn't automatic when using paper and pencil. The choice is yours, however.

You may not want to use share price accounting at all. Instead, you might merely "eyeball" your performance over the years – sensing whether or not you're doing well based on the total value of your holdings. Although a Foolish investor should want to beat the S&P 500 and should know if she's doing so, the world won't end if your objective is less quantifiable. You might simply want to reach a certain dollar amount before retirement, for instance, and so you won't fret about your performance against the S&P as long as you meet your goal. Whatever you do, keep good records and keep all of your investment statements in a file. You need to know the cost basis for every full and fractional share you've ever bought when it comes to taxes.

Taxes and Direct Investing

For each direct investment plan you begin, get a folder and keep all of your statements in it. Most important are the cumulative year-end statements you'll receive (keep these on file *forever!*) and the 1099-DIV forms that are sent to you once each year.

Direct investment-related tax reporting can get a little complicated, but in most cases your experience will be straightforward. Assuming that you're not going to sell your shares for a number of years, the first taxable income that you'll have are the dividends that you receive, even if they're all reinvested in stock. Mutual fund investors deal with this same issue.

Dividends

The annual 1099-DIV form that your company will send you (see page 68) shows how much you received in dividend payments, even if it all **went** to buy more stock. Unless you typically dodge the IRS and plan to flee to Brazil when they catch on to you, you should report all dividends as income on your annual taxes. Pretty simple. It's much like reporting interest from a savings account – a one-line entry. As of 1998, you report the dividends you receive on Schedule B (see below), which is an interest and dividend income form, but only if you receive more than $400 worth in one year. Otherwise, you simply report dividend income on your main 1040 tax form.

Schedules A&B (Form 1040) 1998		OMB No. 1545-0074 Page **2**
Name(s) shown on Form 1040. Do not enter name and social security number if shown on other side.		**Your social security number**

Schedule B—Interest and Ordinary Dividends
Attachment Sequence No. **08**

Note: *If you had over $400 in taxable interest income, you must also complete Part III.*

			Amount
Part I **Interest** (See pages 20 and B-1.) **Note:** If you received a Form 1099-INT, Form 1099-OID, or substitute statement from a brokerage firm, list the firm's name as the payer and enter the total interest shown on that form.	**1**	List name of payer. If any interest is from a seller-financed mortgage and the buyer used the property as a personal residence, see page B-1 and list this interest first. Also, show that buyer's social security number and address ▶	**1**
	2	Add the amounts on line 1	**2**
	3	Excludable interest on series EE U.S. savings bonds issued after 1989 from Form 8815, line 14. You MUST attach Form 8815 to Form 1040	**3**
	4	Subtract line 3 from line 2. Enter the result here and on Form 1040, line 8a ▶	**4**

Note: *If you had over $400 in ordinary dividends, you must also complete Part III.*

			Amount
Part II **Ordinary** **Dividends** (See pages 21 and B-1.) **Note:** If you received a Form 1099-DIV or substitute statement from a brokerage firm, list the firm's name as the payer and enter the ordinary dividends shown on that form.	**5**	List name of payer. Include only ordinary dividends. Report any capital gain distributions on Schedule D, line 13 ▶	**5**
	6	Add the amounts on line 5. Enter the total here and on Form 1040, line 9 . ▶	**6**

		Yes	No
Part III **Foreign** **Accounts** **and Trusts** (See page B-2.)	You must complete this part if you **(a)** had over $400 of interest or ordinary dividends; **(b)** had a foreign account; or **(c)** received a distribution from, or were a grantor of, or a transferor to, a foreign trust.		
	7a At any time during 1998, did you have an interest in or a signature or other authority over a financial account in a foreign country, such as a bank account, securities account, or other financial account? See page B-2 for exceptions and filing requirements for Form TD F 90-22.1		
	b If "Yes," enter the name of the foreign country ▶		
	8 During 1998, did you receive a distribution from, or were you the grantor of, or transferor to, a foreign trust? If "Yes," you may have to file Form 3520. See page B-2		

For Paperwork Reduction Act Notice, see Form 1040 instructions.   ✪   Schedule B (Form 1040) 1998

Investment Plan Statement for Shareholders of
THE COCA-COLA COMPANY

Issue# 282 Account#

**** IMPORTANT ****
THIS IS YOUR IRS FORM 1099-DIV FOR 1998
KEEP FOR YOUR RECORDS

THIS IS IMPORTANT TAX INFORMATION AND IS BEING FURNISHED TO THE INTERNAL REVENUE SERVICE. IF YOU ARE REQUIRED TO FILE A RETURN, A NEGLIGENCE PENALTY OR OTHER SANCTION MAY BE IMPOSED ON YOU IF THIS INCOME IS TAXABLE AND THE IRS DETERMINES THAT IT HAS NOT BEEN REPORTED.

DIVIDENDS AND DISTRIBUTIONS

YEAR: 1998   OMB No. 1545-0110 FORM -1099-DIV

1 ORDINARY DIVIDENDS	2a TOTAL CAPITAL GAIN DISTR.	2b 28% RATE GAIN	2c UNRECAP. SEC. 1250 GAIN	2d SECTION 1202 GAIN
11.99				

3 NONTAXABLE DISTRIBUTIONS	4 FEDERAL INCOME TAX WITHHELD	5 INVESTMENT EXPENSES	6 FOREIGN TAX PAID	7 FOREIGN COUNTRY OR U.S. POSSESSION

8 CASH (LIQUIDATION DISTRIBUTIONS)	9 NONCASH (FAIR MARKET VALUE)	10 OTHER DIVIDEND INCOME INCLUDED IN BOX 1	11 BROKER'S COMMISSION INCLUDED IN BOX 1
			0.33

TO WHOM PAID ▶ JEFF M FISCHER

ACCOUNT NUMBER (OPTIONAL)   RECIPIENT'S IDENTIFICATION NUMBER

PAYER NAME, FEDERAL IDENTIFICATION NUMBER
THE COCA-COLA COMPANY COMMON

EIN: 58-0628465   Company Number: 282
REPORTED BY 13-3340857
FIRST CHICAGO TRUST COMPANY OF NY
P.O. BOX 2500
JERSEY CITY, NEW JERSEY 07303-2500

For inquiry: 888-265-3747

INSTRUCTIONS FOR RECIPIENT

Caution: If an amount appears in box 2a, you must report it on Schedule D (Form 1040). You may not file Form 1040A.

Box 1.--Ordinary dividends, which include any net short-term capital gains from a mutual fund, are fully taxable. Include this amount on the "Dividends" line of Form 1040 or 1040A. Also report it on Schedule B (Form 1040) or Schedule 1 (Form 1040A), as appropriate. This amount includes any amount shown in box 5. The amount shown may be a distribution from an employee stock ownership plan (ESOP). Report it as a dividend on your income tax return, but treat it as a plan distribution, not as investment income, for any other purpose.

Box 2a.--Total capital gain distributions (long-term) from a regulated investment company or real estate investment trust. Box 2a includes amount shown in boxes 2b, 2c, and 2d. Report the amount in box 2a in Part II, Schedule D (Form 1040). If an amount appears in boxes 2b-2d, you must report them on the proper lines of Schedule D (Form 1040).

Box 2b.--28% rate gain from sales or exchanges of assets (including installment payments received) held over 1 year but not over 18 months and all collectibles gains and losses. Report this amount on Schedule D (Form 1040), Part II.

Box 2c.--Unrecaptured section 1250 gain from certain depreciable real property. Report this amount on Schedule D (Form 1040), Part IV.

Box 2d.--Section 1202 gain from certain small business stock is subject to a 50% exclusion. See Schedule D (Form 1040) instructions.

Box 3.--This part of the distribution is nontaxable because it is a return of your cost (or other basis). You must reduce your cost (or other basis) by this amount for figuring gain or loss when you sell your stock. But if you get back all your cost (or other basis), you must report future nontaxable distributions as capital gains, even though this form shows them as nontaxable. For more information, see

Box 4.--Shows backup withholding. For example, persons not furnishing their taxpayer identification number to the payer become subject to backup withholding at a 31% rate on certain payments. See Form W-9, Request for Taxpayer Identification Number and Certification, for information on backup withholding. Include this amount on your income tax return as tax withheld.

Box 5.--Any amount shown is your share of expenses of a nonpublicly offered regulated investment company, generally a nonpublicly offered mutual fund. If you file Form 1040, you may deduct these expenses on the "Other expenses" line on Schedule A (Form 1040) subject to the 2% limit. This amount is included in box 1.

Box 6.--You may be able to claim this foreign tax as a deduction or a credit on Form 1040. See your Form 1040 instructions.

Boxes 10 and 11.--Amounts shown are applicable to Dividend Reinvestment Plan participants only and are included in box 1. The amount shown in box 10 represents the portion of dividend income resulting from the price discount offered by certain plans. The amount shown in box 11 is the portion of dividend income represented by brokerage commissions paid for by the Corporation. Consult your tax advisor as to the proper tax treatment of these amounts.

Nominees.--If your Federal identification number is shown on this form and the form includes amounts belonging to another person, you are considered a nominee recipient. You must file Form 1099-DIV for each of the other owners to show their share of the income, and you must furnish a Form 1099-DIV to each. A husband or wife is not required to file a nominee return to show amounts owned by the other. See the 1998 Instructions for Forms 1099, 1098, 5498, and W-2G.

282   5651-96720

Be aware that some companies don't send you the form 1099-DIV when the dividend payments that you received for the year amounted to less than $10. The dividends are still taxable, however. Your year-end account statement will show the total amount of dividends that you received. You should report that number as income, just as if you'd received a 1099-DIV.

Shares Purchased With Dividends

Shares purchased with dividends (dividend reinvestments) are accounted for exactly as if you had bought them with money sitting in your bank account. So, you must keep the statements showing your cost basis on dividend reinvestment-acquired shares just as you do when you make optional cash payments to buy shares. When it comes time to sell, you need to know the cost basis for all of your shares – those bought with reinvested dividends and those bought separately with your hard-earned money.

Commissions Paid *for* You

Although most direct investment plans are commission free, somebody *is* paying a brokerage commission for you, and that somebody is usually the company. Coca-Cola, Intel, Johnson & Johnson – these big guys are eating the cost for you. In return, they hope you'll be a loyal shareholder. But something even bigger than these companies (the government) requires that the companies report any commissions paid for you to the IRS and, in turn, you're required to report the commissions as well. You must report them as income. The argument is that you'd normally have to pay a commission, but since somebody paid it for you, it's similar to *income* for you.

The commission paid for you is included on the same annual 1099-DIV form that holds your dividend information and that you'll receive in the mail come January or February. The commission is usually minor. If you had bought shares of Coca-Cola almost every month in 1997, the total commission on your year-end 1099-DIV was $0.45. Yup, 45 cents total. It's incredibly cheap because your company buys every shareholder's shares at once and then divides the commission among the thousands (or hundreds of thousands in Coca-Cola's case) of direct investment participants. That 45 cents of "income" will hardly change your taxes, but if you don't report it you might find yourself on a midnight plane to Brazil (no cheap plane ticket, that one).

So, to stay in your home country, be aware that when companies pay commissions for you, you *usually* report it as income. Check your individual year-end direct investment plan statement for specifics, because in many cases, this minor commission "income" is lumped with your total dividend income and it's all reported together. That makes it much simpler for you – it's just one number to report. Look at your year-end statement to see how it's being reported and then proceed accordingly.

Commissions Paid *by* You

If there are commission fees that you pay when you buy or sell stock in your direct investment plan, these should, respectively, be added to the cost of shares bought and deducted from the proceeds when you sell shares. In other words, they decrease your taxes because they lower your overall amount of income by increasing your cost basis whenever you purchase, and by decreasing your income when selling – both times by the amount of the commission. Almost every direct investment plan has slight fees for selling stock, so remember to deduct the fee from your proceeds.

Also worth noting: when you begin your portfolio you might have additional fees to start. If it costs $20 through Temper of the Times to buy your first share of Coca-Cola, you can't add this to the share price that you paid for the first share for tax cost-basis purposes. This is because as the IRS sees it, it's a one-time expense for the production of income, not a direct commission paid to buy the stock. It doesn't become part of your cost basis. You can only deduct this fee if it is itemized on Schedule A, subject to the 2% of Adjusted Gross Income (AGI) limitation. Unless you already itemize deductions, it's probably not worth the trouble to record these small start-up costs.

Selling Shares

The most significant tax event occurs when you sell shares. At this point, you need to know all of the prices that you paid for any shares that you sell, as well as the length of time you've held the shares. This is why good recordkeeping is vitally important.

In the end, the taxation method is basically the same as with a regular stock sale. You pay a capital gains tax on any profit from shares held for over a year, and you pay a higher tax rate on profits that were achieved over a period of a year or less (typically 28% vs. 20% for investments held for more than a year). If you sustained losses, you can use them to offset any capital gains as well as other income up to $3,000 annually.

What's different with direct investment plans is that you'll have several different purchase dates and prices paid per stock – you'll even have fractional shares bought at varying prices. It sounds daunting, but it isn't too horrible. In fact, you'd probably rather do this than hear "Stairway to Heaven" played on the radio again.

So how do you do it?

Although you'd probably like to lump all of your shares together, figure the total amount that you invested, and then divide that by the total shares you sold to determine your average price paid per share, you can't do that. Mutual fund investors can, but direct investors must use one of two IRS-approved methods of accounting to figure their cost basis when selling shares. The following are the two methods.

First-In-First-Out (FIFO). This is a relatively self-explanatory system. With this method, the first shares that you sell are deemed to be the first shares that you purchased. First in, first out.

Assume you're selling 100 shares of a 230-share position in Exxon. You've been investing in Exxon's DRP regularly for five years. The 100 shares you sell could theoretically be the first 100 shares you bought, the last 100, or 100 randomly chosen shares. With this reporting system, however, in order to figure the price you paid per share, the 100 shares that you sell must be the *first* 100 shares you bought through both cash investments and dividend reinvestments. (This can work in your favor, because often you'd rather sell the oldest shares first and pay the lower long-term capital gains tax rate.) Notice how important recordkeeping is. If you don't sell for 20 years after your first purchase, you'll need your very first direct investment plan statement (or the first year-end statement) to show the prices you paid for your earliest shares. (Reminder: You'll need to know how many times the stock has split, too, if it has. You can track this from the start, or later call the company and ask or find the information online.)

If you sell only some of your shares at some point, as with this Exxon example, make a note of which early shares you sold in your records. Note the specific shares as "sold" and mark your complete records "sold up to this date." This way, the next time you sell shares you'll know the date to begin counting from and you won't incorrectly record the same shares as being sold twice.

If you sell all of your shares at once, you still need to determine your income on a "when bought" basis. If you sell shares that you bought within the last 12 months, you pay a higher, short-term tax rate on those shares (if you made money). Your oldest shares should qualify for the (lower) long-term tax rate assuming you owned them for more than one year. You simply must know all of your dates of purchase and the prices you paid. If all of your purchases occurred more than one year before selling, or all of them occurred within the last year, that makes things easier – all the shares will qualify for the same tax rate. If you're considering cashing out of an investment plan within the next year, you might want to stop investing in it in order to prevent a short-term tax headache. If all of your gains are long-term gains, the math is easier and the taxes are lower.

Specific Identification of Shares. The FIFO method determines which shares you're selling according to a set formula, but the second option of tax reporting, the "specific identification" method, allows you to specify the shares any way you wish. You could, for example, specify that the 100 shares you're selling include the first 27 shares you bought, the 44th share you bought, shares 109, 150, 201, and 212, and the last 68 shares you bought. Sound too good to be true? Well, it is.

Just as your family had strict rules against walking into the house with mud on your shoes and a frog in your hand, the IRS has strict rules when using the specific identification method of accounting. So strict, in fact, that the method usually doesn't work with direct investment plans. Why? One simple reason. Fractional shares and reinvested dividends tend to become commingled in direct investment plans, because the purchase price and the investment date for optional cash investments and dividend reinvestments is usually the same every three months. As you pay cash to buy new shares in your plan, the dividend that you're paid is buying you more shares, too, that same day and at the same cost. This fact alone usually works to disqualify this process of tax accounting. Don't ask us why. Ask the government.

So what can you do?

One laborious way to avoid this "commingling" problem is to have your stock certificates mailed to you by your transfer agent or plan administrator. If you have the actual certificates for each of your stock purchases, you can use the specific share method of accounting when you sell. One downside to this, however, is that the direct investment program will almost always send you stock certificates representing the highest amount of shares possible, not one certificate for every individual purchase made. Plus, if you request individual certificates, the fees get expensive.

So, unless you don't mind fees and hundreds of stock certificates, you must use the FIFO method or else not sell anything until you can afford to dump all of the work on an accountant. (Keep good records to keep the accountant's cost lower.) Using FIFO, the tax issue is easy enough, however. FIFO is straightforward if you keep clear records.

Reporting On Schedule D

When selling and using FIFO or *any* tax accounting method, having different cost bases for all of your shares would make reporting each share, and fractional share, individually on your Schedule D tax form (Capital Gains and Losses) a nightmare. You might need 20 pages to list your various purchase dates and prices over the years. Fortunately, the government cuts us some slack here. (They probably did it to save *themselves* the headache.)

SCHEDULE D (Form 1040) Department of the Treasury Internal Revenue Service (99) Name(s) shown on Form 1040	Capital Gains and Losses ► Attach to Form 1040. ► See Instructions for Schedule D (Form 1040). ► Use Schedule D-1 for more space to list transactions for lines 1 and 8.	OMB No. 1545-0074 1998 Attachment Sequence No. 12 Your social security number

Part I Short-Term Capital Gains and Losses—Assets Held One Year or Less

(a) Description of property (Example: 100 sh. XYZ Co.)	(b) Date acquired (Mo., day, yr.)	(c) Date sold (Mo., day, yr.)	(d) Sales price (see page D-6)	(e) Cost or other basis (see page D-6)	(f) GAIN or (LOSS) Subtract (e) from (d)	
1						
2 Enter your short-term totals, if any, from Schedule D-1, line 2		**2**				
3 Total short-term sales price amounts. Add column (d) of lines 1 and 2 . . .		**3**				
4 Short-term gain from Form 6252 and short-term gain or (loss) from Forms 4684, 6781, and 8824				**4**		
5 Net short-term gain or (loss) from partnerships, S corporations, estates, and trusts from Schedule(s) K-1				**5**		
6 Short-term capital loss carryover. Enter the amount, if any, from line 8 of your 1997 Capital Loss Carryover Worksheet				**6** (	)	
7 **Net short-term capital gain or (loss).** Combine lines 1 through 6 in column (f) . . . . ►				**7**		

Part II Long-Term Capital Gains and Losses—Assets Held More Than One Year

(a) Description of property (Example: 100 sh. XYZ Co.)	(b) Date acquired (Mo., day, yr.)	(c) Date sold (Mo., day, yr.)	(d) Sales price (see page D-6)	(e) Cost or other basis (see page D-6)	(f) GAIN or (LOSS) Subtract (e) from (d)	(g) 28% RATE GAIN * or (LOSS) (see instr. below)
8						
9 Enter your long-term totals, if any, from Schedule D-1, line 9		**9**				
10 Total long-term sales price amounts. Add column (d) of lines 8 and 9 . . .		**10**				
11 Gain from Form 4797, Part I; long-term gain from Forms 2439 and 6252; and long-term gain or (loss) from Forms 4684, 6781, and 8824				**11**		
12 Net long-term gain or (loss) from partnerships, S corporations, estates, and trusts from Schedule(s) K-1				**12**		
13 Capital gain distributions. See page D-2				**13**		
14 Long-term capital loss carryover. Enter in both columns (f) and (g) the amount, if any, from line 13 of your 1997 Capital Loss Carryover Worksheet . . .				**14** (	) (	)
15 Combine lines 8 through 14 in column (g)				**15**		
16 **Net long-term capital gain or (loss).** Combine lines 8 through 14 in column (f). ►				**16**		

Next: Go to Part III on the back.

** **28% Rate Gain or Loss** includes **all** "collectibles gains and losses" (as defined on page D-6) and up to 50% of the eligible gain on qualified small business stock (see page D-5).*

For Paperwork Reduction Act Notice, see Form 1040 instructions.   Cat. No. 11338H   Schedule D (Form 1040) 1998

Schedule D is where you report gains and losses on the sale of stock. If you read the instructions to Schedule D, you'll find that you don't need to disclose each and every share of stock. What you must do instead is separate the "blocks" of shares sold by holding period, with short-term currently being 0-12 months and long-term more than a year – so there are only two different kinds of holding periods. With direct investing, in the "date purchased" section of Schedule D you can simply state "various." Merely be ready to support this one-line entry by producing purchase records (run and get your folders!) if the IRS ever wants details. (Or, if you don't recognize the suited men or women holding briefcases at your front door, sneak out the back window.)

If you're selling all of your shares, break them into their respective holding periods (if they're all long-term, great). Write "various dates," enter the total costs for each time period, and finally state the money made or lost on the entire "time block" of shares. If you're selling only some of your shares, do the same, but remember – if you're using the FIFO system – the first shares that you bought need to be the first shares you sell. Use the earliest prices paid to determine the gains or losses to report.

As you can see, keeping good records is very important for direct investors. In order to track portfolio returns and the cost basis of your individual company shares, we highly recommend that you use a regular recordkeeping system – such as a computer accounting program or spreadsheet, or by keeping records on paper.

You can get more tax details in various IRS publications at the IRS website (or in the White Pages or library), where you can download all the necessary tax forms as well. The website is at http://www.irs.gov. The Fool has an entire area devoted to taxes, too, in its Money area. It's at http://www.fool.com/school/taxes/taxes.htm. And that's not all, because when it comes to taxes (*ahem*) that wouldn't be enough. The Fool has published a thorough tax guide for investors, aptly named *The Motley Fool Investment Tax Guide*, available at www.foolmart.com.

Chapter 7

WHEN NOT TO INVEST AND PLAN DISADVANTAGES

Between two evils, choose neither; between two goods, choose both.

– TYRON EDWARDS

We spent the first six chapters discussing why you should invest in the direct investment plans of strong companies. As rewarding as investing *is* over the long term, however, there are times when you shouldn't invest. Those times have nothing to do with warnings from market pundits, cliff-climbing stock charts, or the economic forecast. They have to do with *you*. The following are times you shouldn't invest.

You Carry High-Interest Debt
Eliminate all of your credit card debt before you start to invest in stocks. It doesn't make sense to invest money in companies in hopes of an 11% or 13% annual return if you're paying 16% to 18% annually on credit card debt. Even if it requires a handful of years of diligent payment, eliminate your credit card balances (and then make sure you can pay the entire balance every month to avoid finance charges) before you begin to invest.

Aside from credit card debt, you might have a mortgage or car payment (hopefully at agreeable interest rates) that you can't and perhaps shouldn't eliminate before investing. That's okay. Credit card debt is the main financial enemy to destroy before investing. For advice on how to pay down your credit card debt, visit the Fool's Money area at www.fool.com/money.

You Have a Short Time Horizon

If your time horizon is shorter than David Caruso's film career, you shouldn't invest in stocks. Typically, you should only use the stock market when your money can be invested – and not touched – for at least five years. If your money can only be invested for three or four years, consider a risk-free bank certificate of deposit (CD).

Why be so conservative even over a three- or four-year period?

Because there's too much uncertainty in the stock market over these shorter periods. If you need to withdraw your money from the stock market in three years to pay for tuition, for example, you might – during a weak market – find that you have less money than you started with after three years have passed. Time is required to lower your risk, mitigate stock market volatility, and build wealth. This is especially true with direct investment plans, because you typically begin these with little money and invest monthly. If you have only a four-year time horizon, after two years of investing the remainder of your monthly investments would only be invested for two years or less. That's far from ideal. Plus, the final year of your investments would be taxed, when sold, at a high short-term tax rate.

With direct investment plans, ideally your time horizon will be a minimum of seven to ten years; as compounding demonstrates, the longer the better.

You're Not Yet Comfortable Investing

If you don't know how to ride a horse, you don't leap into the saddle and yell, "Hi ho Silver... away!"

Investing shouldn't be any different. Don't leap into it.

Only you will know when you're ready to invest and which companies you're comfortable buying. If you rush, it's unlikely that you'll enjoy the experience or succeed. So take your time. Part of Foolish investing is enjoying the journey and having the confidence and patience to reach your destination. The journey shouldn't be frightening, intimidating, or worrisome. It should be calming, understandable, and reassuring. When you're confident that you'll be *securing* your future rather than risking it, your mind should be at ease. That's when you should begin to invest.

Direct Investment Plan Disadvantages and Solutions

When was the last time that anything in your life was absolutely, beyond any question, to the very last detail, *perfect*? Was your 10th birthday party perfect? Did you receive every gift you asked for? What about your high school graduation? Did people clap especially loud for you? Was your wedding perfect (if you're married)? Maybe your divorce?

Direct investment plans aren't perfect either, but their imperfections are minor and solutions exist.

Preset Purchase and Sell Dates

Most plans have preset purchase and sell dates, so investors can buy or sell stock only on specified days. This means that you can't always act immediately on your instinct to buy or sell, nor will you always get the exact stock price you wish (not that you can when investing with a broker, either). Each plan has its own investment schedule. Most purchases are made monthly, while sales are usually executed weekly or sometimes daily.

Solution: You want to build long-term wealth with these plans, not be a knee-jerk speculator acting on price swings, so buy and sell limitations are often *a good thing.*

As for stock prices: knowing a plan's investment dates, you'll always know the approximate price you pay, and your plan statement shows your exact price. A Fool named SmokingPopsicle wrote on our message board: "It gives me a real sense of accomplishment to fire off checks to my companies every month, and then I look forward to the statements that show me how many shares I bought and my new total account value. It's a sense of creating something, of building something for tomorrow. I don't watch prices. I buy every month and if I don't, I feel like I'm missing an opportunity."

Most plans are becoming more flexible and allowing frequent (weekly to daily) buying and selling, but be aware of limitations that each plan might have.

Increased Recordkeeping

Recording small monthly investments and reinvested dividend payments every three months requires organized recordkeeping for tax purposes. If you invest for decades, the problem can compound as quickly as your dollars.

Solution: Each time you open a direct investment account with a company, start a file for it and keep all of the plan's papers for as long as you own shares. Be certain to keep the year-end statements. If you keep good records, the process is not difficult (only time consuming) and is little different from what mutual fund owners or even index fund owners must do. When you sell, it will take time to sort out all of your buy prices. That is a disadvantage, but it's a result of dollar-cost averaging, which is an advantage too good to pass up.

Not All Companies Offer Plans

As of March 1999, approximately 1,100 companies offered DRPs and 500 offered DSPs, meaning thousands of public companies didn't offer a direct investment plan of any kind.

Solution: The companies that *do* offer direct plans are usually secure and established, if not leaders, and they tend to be large. Most small companies and those that don't pay dividends do not offer plans. For those companies, you'll probably want to use a discount broker to buy shares. If you have the funds and the desire, there's no reason that you can't open some direct investment accounts with giant and sturdy world leaders, and keep a traditional brokerage account for investing in smaller companies. Diversification of this kind can make great sense.

Some Plans Have Fees

Fees. They somewhat defeat the purpose of direct investing, don't they? With discount brokerage trading costs declining every year, it doesn't make sense to invest in an investment plan that charges substantial fees for every investment you make, or for dividend reinvestment.

Solution: Fees aren't necessarily unacceptable unless they're too steep. Aim to keep fees below 2% of each investment made. If you're investing $100 in a DRP and the fee for each optional investment is $5, it represents a 5% fee – far too much (5 divided by 100 equals 0.05, or 5%). On the other hand, a $1.50 fee on a $75 investment is 2% (1.5 divided by 75 equals 0.02, or 2%). You probably can't beat the $1.50 fee with any other investment method, even "Dirt Cheap Discount Brokers, Inc." Meanwhile, one way to lower the impact of plan fees is to save and invest more money each time. If you invest $150 rather than $75, the $1.50 fee in our example will only be 1% of your investment.

Luckily, most plans continue to be free, but investigate costs before beginning any plan. If you *do* find a superior company and its plan has fees, weigh them against the advantages you'll gain by investing in the company over the years. Don't preclude a plan due to fees alone, but do think twice about it. The Motley Fool's real-money Drip Portfolio avoids companies that charge fees for anything but selling.

Limited Investment Amounts

Most plans offer the opportunity to buy more stock every month, but the amount that you can buy is limited. There is a minimum that you must invest and a maximum that you can invest. To invest each month in Intel, for example, you must buy at *least* $25 and at *most* $15,000 worth of stock per month. With Coca-Cola and other plans, you can buy as little as $10 worth of stock per month, always buying fractional shares.

Solution: For most people, the lower limits don't present a problem (they're usually $25 to $100 each month you invest), while the upper limits on most plans are enormous – $350,000 to $500,000 per year, or higher. (If you're investing that much commission free, you can hardly afford to complain that you can't invest more.)

As long as you can save and invest as regularly as possible, the limitations are not important. What's important is that you *do* save and invest. If you own various direct investment plans, you should always be able to invest regularly. An example: if you own Mellon Bank, which has a minimum investment of $100, and you don't want to send all $100 that you save each month (assuming that's your limit) to Mellon, send $50 to Coke and $50 to Intel for two months (your other plans), and then send $100 to Mellon every third month. Set up a schedule that allows you to take advantage of, and adhere to, the investment limits of your various plans. The most important thing is to invest regularly in a handful of leading companies.

In summary, as great as investing in stocks is, and as wonderful as direct investment plans are, there are times to forego investing and there are some quirks involved with these plans. Don't invest in the stock market when:

- You carry high-interest debt
- You have a short time horizon
- You're not yet comfortable investing

And realize that disadvantages of direct investment plans include:

- Preset purchase and sell dates
- Increased recordkeeping
- Not all companies offer plans
- Some plans have fees
- Limited investment amounts

Assuming that we didn't talk you out of investing, you'll probably be enrolled in direct investment plans soon (as soon as you're ready!). Once you own stock, you'll need to consider selling at some point. We hope you won't need to sell until so long from now that, as you prepare to sell by retrieving this book from your attic, the pages will be yellow, faded, and crumble in your hands. If that proves true, you better read the next chapter on selling now.

Chapter 8

SELLING STOCK

An error doesn't become a mistake until you refuse to correct it.

– ORLANDO BATTISTA

The topic of selling was saved until last for a reason. When you begin to invest in the stock market, selling should be the *last thing* on your mind. A desire to quickly sell your stock should rank right up there with your desire to climb Mt. Everest with an unlicensed Sherpa guide, a thin windbreaker jacket, garden gloves, and flip-flop beach shoes. However, eventually there will, of course, come a time to sell.

When is it time? There are a few scenarios.

If you unexpectedly need money, you might need to sell. Try to exhaust other avenues first if you're selling only due to a short-term cash crunch; you'll lose the dollar-cost averaging benefits you achieved as soon as you sell, and you'll need to pay taxes that year on any gain. If you do need to sell, the only recommendation we have is this: consider keeping a minimal amount of shares in the plan (in most cases, one share will suffice) so the account isn't closed. This way you can always begin to invest in the plan again without fees or the enrollment hassle – even years later.

Selling a portion of your shares is easy. You merely specify the number of shares you wish to sell (keeping in mind the tax considerations discussed earlier) on a plan statement (or, with some plans, over the phone), and typically within a week or two your shares will be sold and you'll be sent a check. Another option is to have the plan administrator mail a stock certificate to you that you can then sell through a regular broker. This might make sense if your plan charges high fees for selling. Most don't, however. Most charge small fees – smaller fees than are charged to have a certificate mailed to you.

Completely closing a plan and selling all of the shares is equally easy. On a plan statement, you can ask to close the plan and request the sale of all shares and a cash payment, or request a stock certificate for the shares. With some plans you can at least begin this process over the phone, although closing the plan and requesting a check or a certificate requires your signature. This will often be completed within a few days of requesting it.

CAMPBELL SOUP COMPANY
Transaction Form

Issue#: 6795 Account#:   101

Optional Investment
Make check payable to:
Investment Plan Services
Amount enclosed in U.S.Dollars:
Your Optional Investment can be a minimum of $50.00 per
Investment and a maximum of $350,000.00 per year

Partial Withdrawal Continue Plan participation
Issue a certificate for
this number of shares

Sell this number of shares

Full Withdrawal Terminate Plan participation
Issue a certificate for all full shares and
a check for fractional shares

Sell all Plan shares

Deposit of Certificates
Deposit the enclosed
number of shares ➡

**Signature(s) for issuance or sale and/or
change of address.**
All joint owners must sign. Names must be signed exactly
as shown on this statement. (Partner/Officer/Trustee
must sign as Partner/Officer/Trustee.)

Address change or share transfer
Mark box and complete the appropriate
portion on the reverse side ■■■➡

06795

There are more subjective reasons to sell stock or close a direct investment plan. Beyond needing cash, if a company is failing you, you should consider selling – particularly if the failure appears to be long-term or permanent in nature. Don't be a hero when your ship is sinking. Even the best investors make mistakes. When you realize that you have made a mistake (and that could take months of thinking – don't rush to sell, just as you shouldn't rush to buy), admit the mistake and seek higher ground. Consider selling if your company:

• Is beginning to consistently lose money rather than make it.
• Is consistently accumulating debt rather than cash without apparent growth benefits (smart acquisitions *can* be made with debt, after all).
• Is falling behind industry changes and management seems to be foundering.
• Has changed its focus or business to something that you don't understand or admire.
• Institutes unreasonable fees in its direct investment plan.
• Cancels its dividend payment without apparent benefit to the growth of the company, meaning that the dividend money saved isn't reinvested in the business for growth, but goes to finance debt or losses (this indicates that something is amiss).

Do *not* sell just because:

• You think the stock market or your stock's price is temporarily too high (decrease your monthly investment if you must do anything about this temporary condition).
• Your company announced bad news that it will get past (selling on a downturn is a poor move for obvious reasons).

- Someone (a broker, a co-worker, a friend) thinks you should sell.
- You want favorable tax consequences. Selling a losing stock to offset gains in another stock is a poor investment decision, and, in general, you shouldn't let taxes affect your investment decisions except when considering short-term and long-term tax consequences under a neutral investment scenario.

You might also consider selling if your direct investing career eventually finds you eager to try different types of investing. If you wanted to invest in the Foolish Four (a popular approach to Dow Dividend investing addressed in the Frequently Asked Questions section) but you didn't have enough money to do so, you might have begun direct investment plans instead. After four or five years, perhaps you'd roll your direct investment plan money into a discount brokerage account and buy the Foolish Four. These plans make good stepping stones, although many investors find direct investing ideal whatever their initial intention, and they never leave them once they begin.

Keep in mind that selling a winning company almost never pays in the long run. The GEs and Coca-Colas of the world eventually climb to a higher plain. The goal is to find companies that you can hold into – and through – retirement. As you retire, perhaps you'll simply cancel your plans' dividend reinvestment options and live very well on cash dividend payments alone, never needing to sell much or any of your stock. That's a possibility for many investors.

Chapter 9

GOOD LUCK ON YOUR FOOLISH JOURNEY

You heavens, give me patience, patience I need.

– WILLIAM SHAKESPEARE

Money won't bring you ultimate happiness or provide you with a sense of freedom if you don't already feel that your spirit is free. The power of money is limited; it isn't the panacea that so many people believe it to be. However important money may seem to *you*, what money really boils down to is *opportunity*.

When you're fresh out of school, money provides you the opportunity to rent your own place, pay your bills, buy beer that doesn't taste like water (or so we've heard), and purchase new clothes. Later in life, money might grant you the opportunity to buy property, to pay your bills (yet again), to send children to school, or to start your own business. Also later in life, hopefully you'll have the opportunity to give money away, thereby granting new opportunity to those with little. Giving money away to good causes – giving *opportunity* to others – is the ultimate outcome of the Foolish Equation. Discipline + Time = Compounding, which equals Opportunity. As your opportunity compounds, you'll be in a position to share your good fortune with others.

Right now, giving on a large scale may be years away. As you begin to invest, keep your eye on the goal – the eventual outcome that can only result after many years. Remember that most wealth is created on the tail-end of an investment's lifetime (that's how compounding works) and that you can't reach that lucrative time in your investment career if you don't have a beginning and middle to your career, too. Start when you're comfortable and ready to be patient. Steadily invest in the greatest companies you know. There will be slow periods, stocks will decline periodically, and you may have bouts of sagging confidence contrasted with feelings of invincibility during the exceptionally good periods. Keep an even disposition throughout (your friends will appreciate it!) and enjoy yourself as you let time work for you.

Our final chart shows the historic movement of the United States stock market (as represented by the Dow Jones Industrial Average) over more than 100 years. See the chart. Read the chart. Be the chart. The direction of the stock market follows the progress of society. Unless disco revives, society will always progress upward when measured over many years. You want to invest in companies leading the progression. When you do, this steadily rising chart will belong to you. Your dollars will grow in kind with the line in the chart.

See the chart. Read the chart. Kiss the chart. (Now quickly dry off the page.)

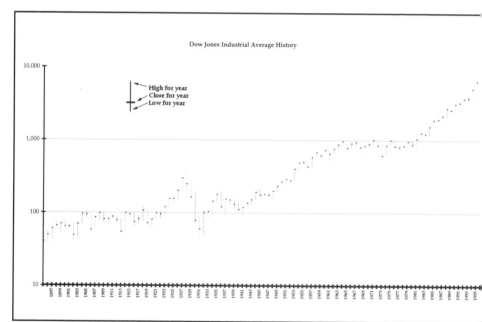

Use discipline, time, and compounding to build every possible opportunity into your future. It takes a Fool to tell you the following truth: with the right approach, you, better than *anyone* else, can invest your money most successfully.

We wish you the best of luck in your investment journey. You know where to find us as we enjoy ours and, collectively, help others along. (Pssst, that's at www.fool.com. Hope to see you there.)

Fool on!

FREQUENTLY ASKED QUESTIONS ABOUT DIRECT INVESTING

This section addresses many of the frequently asked questions related to direct investing – questions ranging from IRAs to the impact of stock splits to opening accounts for children. If you find that you have more questions about these topics, or if you have questions on topics we didn't cover, please visit our message boards at www.fool.com, call your companies, or visit the library.

What are Optional Cash Payments (OCPs) and how do they work?
Most direct investment plans allow for optional cash payments, and most don't charge fees for the service. OCPs make dollar-cost averaging possible and, by their nature, allow for fractional share purchases. An OCP usually entails mailing a check to your company's plan every month that you wish, while adhering to the set minimum and maximum investments. Most plans allow for OCPs to be made monthly and have set investment dates (the first of every month is common). You should send your payment before the investment date to have it arrive a few days before the cutoff. Many plans are now increasing the number of investment dates to weekly or biweekly, and some direct stock plans now buy shares for you within a week of your payment (or sooner), no matter when you send it.

Every time you send money, you'll receive a plan statement for the month. The statement usually contains an envelope for future payments. You tear off a portion of the statement and mail it with your next optional payment, much like a credit card statement (except – one large difference – you're paying yourself). If you don't send a payment, you typically receive a statement every three months with each dividend payment and at year-end for tax purposes, along with a 1099 form.

Can I make automatic electronic investments through my bank account?

Many direct investment plans offer automatic electronic investing. Your checking or savings account can be debited automatically and the funds used to buy more stock. Request enrollment from your company and then specify on the form how much money should be withdrawn from your account, usually on a monthly basis. Many companies charge a fee for this service, but it's typically only $1 every time that you invest (usually every month). Electronic investing saves you time, effort, checks, and stamps. Coca-Cola, Johnson & Johnson, and Intel are some of the companies that offer this option. Intel is free and the other two charge $1 per investment. Once you own a handful of companies and you're writing and mailing several checks a month to buy more stock, you might appreciate the simplicity of automatic investing. Consult plan literature to see if this option is available.

Eventually, most plans will allow for automatic investments directly over the Internet, we imagine, especially as more and more people bank and invest online. Some companies, such as Home Depot, have already begun to allow direct Internet investments.

I need my dividend payments to buy new shoes every three months. How do I reinvest just some (or none) of my dividends?

Most plans allow for partial dividend reinvestment, meaning only a percentage of your dividends are reinvested in stock. The rest is paid to you by check. Most plans offer the option of no dividend reinvestment at all and instead send the *entire* dividend amount to you. You can turn this option on and off like a faucet. Contact your plan administrator or look at your most recent plan statement for your options.

I like a bargain. Do some plans offer stock at a discount to market prices?

Fewer than 10% of all plans offer shares to plan holders at a discount to market prices. The discount is usually a few percent to five percent. A more common practice is to offer a discount on stock that is bought only with reinvested dividends. Still, not many companies offer this either. Appealing at first glance, the reality is that companies offering discounted shares often underperform the stock market. Companies offering this option are usually utilities, banks, and real estate investment trusts (REITs) that might not be growing much, so they entice shareholders with discounts. Be diligent in making certain that you find a strong company; don't invest in plans for a discount alone. We suggest finding investments based on a company's merits first and foremost. After you've chosen a company to buy, ask if they offer discounted shares. If they do: bonus!

Can I open an IRA in a direct investment plan?
Direct investment plans are logical vehicles for retirement investing as well as for tax-beneficial Individual Retirement Accounts (IRA). This is a great idea (congratulations for thinking of it!), however, using direct investing in an IRA takes a bit of doing.

Self-directed IRAs that hold individual stocks require a custodian for the account, and the custodian needs to be a brokerage house or a bank. Brokerage houses are not keen on providing you this service because providing the service does little for their business. If you *do* find a brokerage house willing to be a custodian, there will be an annual fee. Weigh the fee against the tax savings. (It could still be very worthwhile.)

A bank or credit union is much more likely to accommodate you. When you find a willing partner, deposit your funds with the bank or credit union in an IRA account. The bank or credit union should be named as your custodian. Then, from that account, establish a direct investment plan (or several) with the funds and you're all set – you can deposit as much from that IRA account into the plan as is allowed. One potential custodian for IRAs is First Trust (http://www.firsttrust.com). Consider the Roth IRA if you qualify (check IRA literature) and remember that you can't withdraw money from an IRA early without penalty.

Some direct investment plans do include an IRA option. This is the ideal option, and makes the process very easy, even though it's usually accompanied by an administrative fee. The annual fee typically ranges from $25 to $50. Some of the few dozen plans that offer IRAs include Campbell Soup, Barnett Banks, Bell Atlantic, Exxon, GTE, Lucent Technologies, McDonald's, Mobil, and Sears. Ask your company if it has an IRA option. Most won't, so you might suggest that you'd like to see one in the future.

For much more information, visit The Motley Fool's area, All About IRAs. It's at – what else – http://www.fool.com/money/allaboutiras/allaboutiras.htm.

Will a plan hold stock certificates for me?
Most direct investment plans offer stock certificate safekeeping free of charge. For convenience, you should try to keep all of your shares in one safe place. Having them held by the plan is usually a good idea. We said earlier that you could burn your shares without much consequence. That's true. You'd still be their registered owner and you could request a fresh certificate. But it's a hassle, it sometimes has a fee, and generally, the safer your shares are, the less chance you have of losing or forgetting about them. So placing them in safekeeping is the easiest and most Foolish choice.

If your plan doesn't offer safekeeping for certificates (very rare), keep them in a safety deposit box or in a lock box in your home. Either that or put them with your record album collection that's been gathering dust since the 1970s. They won't go anywhere from there. (Just don't forget where you put them!)

Nearly all plans will hold onto the shares that you buy through the plan. Some simply won't accept shares that you buy elsewhere, outside the plan, such as your initial share (that's rare, too).

What happens when a stock splits and I own partial shares?
When a stock splits 2-for-1 or 3-for-1, or whatever amount, your plan shares will do the same. If you owned 10 shares of Intel and it split 2-for-1, your next statement will show that you own 20 shares at half the price per share. (The total value doesn't change at all.) Partial shares will split as well, and all of your shares (partial and whole) always receive dividend payments (in fractions when necessary). Keep good records of splits and your adjusted cost bases for figuring your taxes.

I live in Bolivia. Can I make direct investments?
Many U.S. companies' direct investment plans are available to investors outside the United States. The plans typically operate as usual, although you must pay in U.S. dollars. The main difference when investing overseas is the tax consequence. If you're a citizen of another country (Texas doesn't count, though natives might argue otherwise) or are living in another country and are a U.S. citizen, investigate how dividend payments are taxed in your country of residence and pay accordingly (or face the slammer). The dividend payment (and capital gains) will also be taxed in the United States. The best way to learn if a company accepts international investors is simply to ask. Most do.

I live in the U.S., but U.S. companies bore me. Can I invest in international companies, like ones in Bolivia?
A handful of international companies trade on the New York Stock Exchange as American Depositary Receipts (ADRs) and offer direct investment plans. You can invest in these as you would any U.S. company on the exchange. These foreign companies include British Airways, British Petroleum, Glaxo Wellcome, Hanson PLC, Nestle S.A., Smith Kline Beecham, and Volvo. (As many of these companies are British, before investing you might want to visit The Motley Fool U.K. website at http://www.fool.co.uk)

When investing in international companies listed on the New York Stock Exchange, you send money to an American transfer agent, and all transactions will be in dollars. However, realize that currency fluctuations will impact your investments, and it will be more difficult to receive and understand information about these companies. British firms, for example, only report results every six months, rather than every three like U.S. companies. And a giant like Nestle reports results in Swiss Francs, making it difficult to read the operating results and relate them to U.S. food companies.

I have children. Can I begin direct investment plans for the little Fools?

Giving stock to children is a excellent idea, and giving it in direct investment plans is even better. Young people have the most to gain from the power of compounding, and since direct investment plans accept small deposits, they're perfect for getting young investors interested in and hooked on saving and investing.

You might open an account for your child and encourage her to contribute to it regularly from her allowance. Perhaps you can match her investments dollar for dollar: if she saves up $15, you'll throw in an additional $15 and mail off a check for $30 to the plan. There are many ways that you and your children (or grandchildren or nieces and nephews) can benefit by investing via this method.

To give a gift of stock to minors, you have two basic choices: a guardian account or a custodian account.

In a guardian account, the guardian (generally a parent, but it can be any legal adult) continues to be the owner of the assets. The guardian can withdraw funds for any purpose and remains liable for taxes on earnings. In a custodian account, the child is treated as the owner of the account. In other words, any gains, income, or dividends on the account are taxed at the child's level. In most cases, the use of a custodian account is more beneficial for tax purposes.

There are two major types of custodian accounts: One was formed under the Uniform Gift to Minors Act (UGMA) and the other under the Uniform Transfers to Minors Act (UTMA).

The second type of account, under UTMA, works in the same way as UGMA accounts, except that UTMA accounts allow the guardian to maintain control over the money for a longer period of time (until age 18, 21, or 25, depending upon the state). UGMA money is available to the child at the age of maturity (18).

As of 1999, there are a few tax differences with general custodian accounts to be aware of. From age 1 to age 13, the first $650 of investment income (typically dividends unless stock is sold for a gain) in any one year is taxed at zero. The next $650 is taxed at the child's rate (generally 15%). Anything over $1,300 will be taxed at the parents' rate. Once the child reaches age 14, the first $650 is not taxable, and any amount above $650 will be taxed at the child's rate.

Most direct investment plan enrollment forms ask if an account will be a custodian account, and the forms are self-explanatory. Be certain to keep good records for your child and hand them down (like a golden crown) when he or she is old enough to understand and maintain them.

I'm a generous sort. Can I give direct investing plans as gifts?

Once you're in a direct investment plan, you may transfer one share from your account into a new account that you open for a gift recipient. To do this you need a medallion or notarized signature on a share of stock (as is true for any stock transfer). Contact your plan for information on the procedure and to receive the forms.

You can also give stock by simply buying the shares through a discount broker, having them delivered, and then transfer them to your gift recipient's name. You could take it a step further, too, and have the share(s) enrolled in a direct plan for them. One option is to use an enrollment service, like Temper of the Times or Netstock Direct, which makes it easy to begin plans for others. You can use such a service for minors, too.

I'm very happily married. Can I establish joint direct investment accounts?

Easily done. When you enroll in a plan, you can designate it as either a joint or single account. This option can be changed with some paperwork from the plan administrator even after the plan is initiated.

Some DSPs require minimum investments of $1,000 or more to start! I can't afford that! Are there alternative minimum enrollment requirements with these direct stock plans?

Unlike DRPs where you normally need to own one share of stock to start, DSPs often require initial investments of $500 or more. However, many plans waive this requirement if you agree to make a regular monthly investment for a set time period (typically $50 a month or $100 a month for one year – or any amount that leads to the usual starting requirement or somewhat higher). If you have questions about this option, call the company you're interested in and ask.

I like the methodical Foolish Four investing approach. Can I direct invest in them?

The methodical Foolish Four investment approach is a popular derivative of the well-known Dow Dividend Approach, or Dogs of the Dow. At first glance, it might make sense to put this high voltage but sturdy approach to work with direct investing plans. At the time of this writing, almost all of the Dow Jones Industrial stocks have plans that have low fees or no fees. However, one concern is that the Foolish Four method, having a 12-month holding period for each cycle, is relatively short-term, and these direct plans require a few months to even get started. Plus, rolling the money over into new plans (representing the latest Foolish Four stocks) after a year wouldn't be easy given the time lag. Finally, the idea behind the Foolish Four is to buy the four stocks that qualify as the Foolish Four *on the day that you select the companies*, and then hold for a year. Direct investment plans would have you buying more stock frequently, and often you'd be buying shares that don't even qualify as Foolish Four holdings anymore.

However, one way Fools have used these plans with this method is to first buy the Foolish Four with a meaningful lump sum and then set up plans after being a shareholder. Next, they only send additional money to the direct plans when the companies qualify as Foolish Four stocks. Also, after a year they typically don't sell the stocks (too much tax and administrative work). Instead, they hold. These are, after all, leading companies paying some of the best dividend yields on the market – which can be perfect for a dividend reinvestment plan. So, these investors keep the shares and buy into the new Foolish Four as well, dollar-cost averaging into their older holdings when they qualify as Foolish Four stocks. After several years they might own a dozen Dow stocks – any that had qualified for the Foolish Four at certain times.

So, there *are* ways to utilize the Foolish Four method of investing when using these plans. It requires flexibility and an acceptance of limitations. For more on the Foolish Four, visit the Fool's real-money portfolios (http://www.fool.com/portfolios/portfolios) or consider the Fool's book on the topic, *The Foolish Four: How to Crush Your Mutual Funds in 15 Minutes a Year*.

I love Rule Maker stocks. Can I direct invest in Rule Makers?

In early 1998, Motley Fool co-founder Tom Gardner launched the Rule Maker Portfolio. Many Fools have asked if they should consider direct investing in Rule Maker stocks. The answer is a resounding "yes!" Being large industry leaders of the highest financial quality, Rule Maker stocks can be excellent candidates for direct investors. For more on these stocks and the Rule Maker method of investing, please visit the Rule Maker portfolio at www.fool.com, and consider David and Tom Gardner's 1999 book, *Rule Breakers, Rule Makers*.

Every so often I receive voting forms in the mail from my companies. What should I do with them?

As a shareholder, you have the right to vote on company issues. Periodically (at least annually) your companies will send you a voting form where you vote for or against a number of issues that are outlined for you. Generally, with good companies, you vote in favor of what the board of directors recommends – but it's up to you. Read the proposals and cast your vote! As a registered shareholder, you'll also receive a free annual report in the mail each year. Enjoy reading it and keep it in order to better understand your companies.

Whoa! I suddenly need some cash but I don't want to sell any stock. What can I do?

A fair number of direct investment plans allow you to borrow money against your stock holdings. Call the plan administrator or review the plan details that you received when you enrolled. You'll often be able to borrow against much of your account's value, though you'll pay interest on your borrowings. However, sometimes paying interest can be more favorable than selling shares, given the tax consequences of selling (and losing the dollar-cost averaging advantage that you may have achieved).

I'm retired. Do direct investment plans have anything to offer me?

Retirement. Whatever does it mean anymore? I mean, who truly "retires" these days, when an active life is the best life? Even so, no matter how active we remain throughout our lives, there typically comes a time when our salary ends or diminishes as we take more time (or *all* of our time) to enjoy ourselves while not pursuing money.

If you are retired or about to retire and you own direct investment plans, there is typically no reason to sell them unless you need the money held in the plans. Most plans allow for the safekeeping of shares, the inexpensive sale of shares, and the free reinvestment of dividends, so holding on to your existing direct investment plans is logical. Plus, if you need your dividend payments for anything from living expenses to luxuries, most plans allow you to choose partial or complete payment of dividends in cash rather than reinvesting them in stock.

Finally, if you're retired and you have more income than you need (nice going!), you might want to invest income that you don't foresee needing for at least three to five years. If you're in this situation, opening new direct plans can make sense. However, if you're in a retirement situation that doesn't provide you with additional investable income, opening new direct investment plans is typically not practical.

DIRECT INVESTMENT PLAN INFORMATION

All Data Provided by The Moneypaper / Temper Enrollment Service

www.moneypaper.com

1-800-295-2550

Definition of Terms

Other than USA: Indicates whether the company opens plans for foreign investors.

Safekeeping: Indicates whether the company will accept share certificates and deposit them into the plan account.

Invests: Indicates when investments in the plan are allowed.

Minimum: Minimum cash investment allowed.

Maximum: Maximum cash investment allowed.

Min. to qualify: Indicates the number of shares required to open a plan for that company.

Fee on cash inv.: Indicates whether the company charges a fee for cash investments.

Fee on div. inv.: Indicates whether the company charges a fee for dividends that are reinvested.

Discount (cash): Indicates whether the company offers a discount from the market price of the stock when optional cash investments are made.

Discount (div.): Indicates whether the company offers a discount from the market price of the stock when dividends are reinvested.

Auto invest: Indicates whether the company has a plan to automatically withdraw a fixed amount of money from your checking or savings account to make optional cash investments.

Auto invest fee: Indicates whether there is a fee associated with the auto invest service.

Selling info: Indicates when shares are sold, how sell orders can be placed, the price at which shares are sold, and the fee the company charges to sell shares through the plan.

!: An exclamation point on the FEES line indicates the fee is paid by the company.

Company:	**AAR Corp.**	Safekeeping:	No
Symbol:	AIR	Invests:	Every 90 days beginning 3/4
Exchange:	NYSE	Minimum:	$10
Industry:	Aviation parts & services	Maximum:	$3,000/quarter
Company Address:	1 AAR Pl.,1100 North Wood Dale Rd.	Min to qualify:	1
		Fee on cash inv.:	0
	Wood Dale, IL 60191	Fee on div. inv.:	0
Company Phone:	630-227-2043	Discount (cash):	0
Transfer Agent:	FCT (EquiServe)	Discount (div.):	0
Agent's Address:	P.O. Box 2500	Auto invest:	No
	Jersey City, NJ 07303-2500	Auto invest fee:	$0
Agent's Phone:	800-446-2617	Selling info:	Sells daily, by fax, mail, or phone,
Other than USA:	Yes		at market, for $10 +12¢/sh.

Company:	**Abbott Labs.**	Safekeeping:	Yes
Symbol:	ABT	Invests:	Every 45 days beginning 2/15
Exchange:	NYSE	Minimum:	$10
Industry:	Drugs, health care	Maximum:	$5,000/quarter
Company Address:	100 Abbott Park Rd.	Min to qualify:	1
	Abbott Park, IL 60064-3500	Fee on cash inv.:	0!
Company Phone:	847-937-6100	Fee on div. inv.:	0!
Transfer Agent:	Boston Eq. (EquiServe)	Discount (cash):	0
Agent's Address:	P.O. Box 8038	Discount (div.):	0
	Boston, MA 02266-8038	Auto invest:	No
Agent's Phone:	888-332-2268	Auto invest fee:	$0
Other than USA:	Yes	Selling info:	Sells within 10 bus. days, by mail,
			at market, for 15¢/sh.

Company:	**Abington Bancorp, Inc.**	Safekeeping:	Yes
Symbol:	ABBK	Invests:	Every 90 days beginning 1/23
Exchange:	OTC	Minimum:	$250
Industry:	Bank holding co.	Maximum:	$unlimited
Company Address:	536 Washington St.	Min to qualify:	1
	Abington, MA 02351	Fee on cash inv.:	$1
Company Phone:	781-982-3252	Fee on div. inv.:	0!
Transfer Agent:	Registrar & Transfer Co.	Discount (cash):	0
Agent's Address:	10 Commerce Drive	Discount (div.):	0
	Cranford, NJ 07016	Auto invest:	Yes
Agent's Phone:	800-368-5948	Auto invest fee:	$1
Other than USA:	No	Selling info:	Sells weekly, by mail, at market,
			for $5 + comm.

Company:	**ABN AMRO Holdings N.V.**	Safekeeping:	Yes
Symbol:	AAN	Invests:	Every 7 days beginning varies
Exchange:	NYSE	Minimum:	$50
Industry:	Banking operations in Netherlands	Maximum:	$100,000/year
Company Address:	c/o Morgan Guaranty Trust,	Min to qualify:	1
	Box 9073	Fee on cash inv.:	$5 + 12¢/sh.
	Boston, MA 02205-9948	Fee on div. inv.:	5% to $2.50
Company Phone:	800-428-4237	Discount (cash):	0
Transfer Agent:	Morgan Guaranty Trust Co.	Discount (div.):	0
Agent's Address:	P.O. Box 9073	Auto invest:	Yes
	Boston, MA 02205-9948	Auto invest fee:	$5 + 12¢/sh.
Agent's Phone:	800-428-4237	Selling info:	Sells daily, by mail or phone, at
Other than USA:	No		avg. price, for $5 +12¢/sh.

Company:	**Adams Express Co.**	Safekeeping:	Yes
Symbol:	ADX	Invests:	Every 7 days beginning varies
Exchange:	NYSE	Minimum:	$50
Industry:	Closed-end investment co.	Maximum:	$25,000/investment
Company Address:	7 St. Paul St., Ste.1140	Min to qualify:	1
	Baltimore, MD 21202	Fee on cash inv.:	$2.50 + 5¢/sh.
Company Phone:	410-752-5900	Fee on div. inv.:	10% to $2.50 + 5¢/sh.
Transfer Agent:	Bank of New York	Discount (cash):	0
Agent's Address:	P.O. Box 11258, Church St. Station	Discount (div.):	0
	New York, NY 10286	Auto invest:	Yes
Agent's Phone:	800-432-8224	Auto invest fee:	$0
Other than USA:	Yes	Selling info:	Sells weekly, by mail, at avg. price, for $10 + 5¢/sh.

Company:	**ADC Telecommunications, Inc.**	Safekeeping:	Yes
		Invests:	Every 5 days beginning varies
Symbol:	ADCT	Minimum:	$50
Exchange:	OTC	Maximum:	$250,000/year
Industry:	Communications equipment	Min to qualify:	1
Company Address:	12501 Whitewater Dr.	Fee on cash inv.:	$5 + 5¢/sh.
	Minnetonka, MN 55343	Fee on div. inv.:	0
Company Phone:	612-938-8080	Discount (cash):	0
Transfer Agent:	Norwest Bank Minnesota	Discount (div.):	0
Agent's Address:	P.O. Box 64854	Auto invest:	Yes
	St. Paul, MN 55164-0854	Auto invest fee:	$2 + 5¢/sh.
Agent's Phone:	800-468-9716	Selling info:	Sells daily, by mail or phone, at
Other than USA:	Yes		avg. price, for $10 +15¢/sh.

Company:	**Adecco ADR**	Safekeeping:	Yes
Symbol:	ADECY	Invests:	Every 7 days beginning varies
Exchange:	OTC	Minimum:	$50
Industry:	Business services	Maximum:	$100,000/year
Company Address:	c/o Morgan Guaranty Trust,	Min to qualify:	1
	Box 9073	Fee on cash inv.:	$5 + 12¢/sh.
	Boston, MA 02205-9948	Fee on div. inv.:	5% to $2.50
Company Phone:	800-428-4237	Discount (cash):	0
Transfer Agent:	Morgan Guaranty Trust Co.	Discount (div.):	0
Agent's Address:	P.O. Box 9073	Auto invest:	Yes
	Boston, MA 02205-9948	Auto invest fee:	$5
Agent's Phone:	800-428-4237	Selling info:	Sells daily, by phone or mail, at
Other than USA:	No		avg. price, for $5 +12¢/sh.

Company:	**Advanta Corp. B**	Safekeeping:	Yes
Symbol:	ADVNB	Invests:	Every 30 days beginning 1/18
Exchange:	OTC	Minimum:	$50
Industry:	Mkts. consumer fin'l prods.	Maximum:	$3,000/month
Company Address:	Welsh and McKean Rds., Box 844	Min to qualify:	25
	Spring House, PA 19477	Fee on cash inv.:	0!
Company Phone:	215-444-5315	Fee on div. inv.:	0!
Transfer Agent:	ChaseMellon Shareholder Services	Discount (cash):	0
Agent's Address:	P.O. Box 750	Discount (div.):	0
	Pittsburgh, PA 15230	Auto invest:	No
Agent's Phone:	800-851-9673	Auto invest fee:	$0
Other than USA:	Yes	Selling info:	Sells weekly, by mail, at market, for $15 +12¢/sh.

Company:	**Advest Group, Inc. (The)**
Symbol:	ADV
Exchange:	NYSE
Industry:	Financial services
Company Address:	90 State House Sq.
	Hartford, CT 06103
Company Phone:	860-509-1000
Transfer Agent:	American Stock Transfer
Agent's Address:	40 Wall St., 46th Floor
	New York, NY 10005
Agent's Phone:	800-937-5449 or 212-936-5100
Other than USA:	Yes

Safekeeping:	Yes
Invests:	Every 90 days beginning 1/15
Minimum:	$20
Maximum:	$2,500/quarter
Min to qualify:	1
Fee on cash inv.:	0
Fee on div. inv.:	0
Discount (cash):	0
Discount (div.):	0
Auto invest:	No
Auto invest fee:	$0
Selling info:	Sells weekly, by mail, at market, for $3 + 4¢/sh.

Company:	**AEGON N.V. NY Registry Shares**
Symbol:	AEG
Exchange:	NYSE
Industry:	Life, health ins., invest. prods.
Company Address:	c/o Citibank, NA. Box 7070
	Paramus, NJ 07653
Company Phone:	800-808-8010 or 212-657-1698
Transfer Agent:	FCT (Citibank)
Agent's Address:	111 Wall St., 20th Floor, Zone 9
	New York, NY 10043
Agent's Phone:	800-422-2066
Other than USA:	No

Safekeeping:	Yes
Invests:	Every 5 days beginning varies
Minimum:	$50
Maximum:	$100,000/year
Min to qualify:	1
Fee on cash inv.:	$5 + 10¢/sh.
Fee on div. inv.:	10¢/sh.
Discount (cash):	0
Discount (div.):	0
Auto invest:	Yes
Auto invest fee:	$5 + 10¢/sh.
Selling info:	Sells weekly, by mail, at avg. price, for $10 +10¢/sh.

Company:	**Aetna Inc.**
Symbol:	AET
Exchange:	NYSE
Industry:	Health, retirement svcs.
Company Address:	151 Farmington Ave.
	Hartford, CT 06156
Company Phone:	860-273-0123 or 860-273-3945
Transfer Agent:	FCT (EquiServe)
Agent's Address:	P.O. Box 2500
	Jersey City, NJ 07303-2500
Agent's Phone:	800-446-2617
Other than USA:	No

Safekeeping:	Yes
Invests:	Every 7 days beginning varies
Minimum:	$50
Maximum:	$3,000/quarter
Min to qualify:	1
Fee on cash inv.:	$5 + 10¢/sh.
Fee on div. inv.:	5% to $3 + 10¢/sh.
Discount (cash):	0
Discount (div.):	0
Auto invest:	Yes
Auto invest fee:	$1 + 10¢/sh.
Selling info:	Sells daily, by phone or mail, at market, for $15 +12¢/sh.

Company:	**AFLAC Inc.**
Symbol:	AFL
Exchange:	NYSE
Industry:	Insurance
Company Address:	1932 Wynnton Rd.
	Columbus, GA 31999
Company Phone:	800-227-4756 or 706-596-3589
Transfer Agent:	AFLAC Inc.
Agent's Address:	Worldwide Headquarters Share-
	holder Services Dept.
	Columbus, GA 31999
Agent's Phone:	800-227-4756
Other than USA:	Yes

Safekeeping:	Yes
Invests:	Every 15 days beginning 1/15
Minimum:	$50
Maximum:	$120,000/year
Min to qualify:	1
Fee on cash inv.:	0
Fee on div. inv.:	0
Discount (cash):	0
Discount (div.):	0
Auto invest:	Yes
Auto invest fee:	$0
Selling info:	Sells biweekly, by mail or fax, at market, for 5¢/sh.

Company:	**AFP Provida**		**Safekeeping:**	Yes
Symbol:	PVD		**Invests:**	Every 7 days beginning varies
Exchange:	NYSE		**Minimum:**	$50
Industry:	Pension fund administrators		**Maximum:**	$250,000/year
Company Address:	c/o BNY,101 Barclay St.,22 West		**Min to qualify:**	1
	New York, NY 10286		**Fee on cash inv.:**	$5 + 10¢/sh.
Company Phone:	800-943-9715		**Fee on div. inv.:**	5% to $5 + 10¢/sh.
Transfer Agent:	Bank of New York		**Discount (cash):**	0
Agent's Address:	P.O. Box 11258		**Discount (div.):**	0
	New York, NY 10286		**Auto invest:**	Yes
Agent's Phone:	888-269-2377		**Auto invest fee:**	$5 + 10¢/sh.
Other than USA:	Yes		**Selling info:**	Sells weekly, by mail, at market, for $5 +10¢/sh.

Company:	**AGL Resources Inc.**		**Safekeeping:**	Yes
Symbol:	ATG		**Invests:**	Every 15 days beginning 1/1
Exchange:	NYSE		**Minimum:**	$25
Industry:	Natural gas holding co.		**Maximum:**	$5,000/month
Company Address:	303 Peachtree St. N.E., Box 4569		**Min to qualify:**	1
	Atlanta, GA 30308		**Fee on cash inv.:**	0!
Company Phone:	404-584-3794		**Fee on div. inv.:**	0!
Transfer Agent:	Wachovia (EquiServe)		**Discount (cash):**	0
Agent's Address:	P.O. Box 8217		**Discount (div.):**	0
	Boston, MA 02266-8217		**Auto invest:**	Yes
Agent's Phone:	800-866-1543		**Auto invest fee:**	$0
Other than USA:	Yes		**Selling info:**	Sells within 10 bus. days, by mail, at market, for comm.

Company:	**Air Products & Chemicals, Inc.**		**Safekeeping:**	Yes
			Invests:	Every 5 days beginning varies
Symbol:	APD		**Minimum:**	$100
Exchange:	NYSE		**Maximum:**	$200,000/year
Industry:	Industrial gases		**Min to qualify:**	1
Company Address:	7201 Hamilton Blvd.		**Fee on cash inv.:**	$5 + 10¢/sh.
	Allentown, PA 18195-1501		**Fee on div. inv.:**	5% to $3 + 10¢/sh.
Company Phone:	610-481-5775 or 610-481-4911		**Discount (cash):**	0
Transfer Agent:	FCT (EquiServe)		**Discount (div.):**	0
Agent's Address:	P.O. Box 2598		**Auto invest:**	Yes
	Jersey City, NJ 07303-2598		**Auto invest fee:**	$2 +10¢/sh.
Agent's Phone:	800-519-3111		**Selling info:**	Sells daily, by phone or mail, at avg. price, for $10 +12¢/sh.
Other than USA:	Yes			

Company:	**AirTouch Communications, Inc.**		**Safekeeping:**	Yes
			Invests:	Every 7 days beginning varies
Symbol:	ATI		**Minimum:**	$100
Exchange:	NYSE		**Maximum:**	$10,000/transaction
Industry:	Wireless telecommunications servs.		**Min to qualify:**	1
Company Address:	One California St.		**Fee on cash inv.:**	$7.50 + 10¢/sh.
	San Francisco, CA 94111		**Fee on div. inv.:**	0
Company Phone:	415-658-2200		**Discount (cash):**	0
Transfer Agent:	Bank of New York		**Discount (div.):**	0
Agent's Address:	P.O. Box 11288, Church St. Station		**Auto invest:**	No
	New York, NY 10286-1288		**Auto invest fee:**	$0
Agent's Phone:	800-233-5601		**Selling info:**	Sells weekly, by phone or mail, at market, for $7.50 +10¢/sh.
Other than USA:	Yes			

Company:	**AK Steel Holding Corp.**
Symbol:	AKS
Exchange:	NYSE
Industry:	Integrated steel producer
Company Address:	703 Curtis St.
	Middeltown, OH 45053-0001
Company Phone:	513-425-5000 or 513-425-2821
Transfer Agent:	Fifth Third Bancorp
Agent's Address:	38 Fountain Sq. Plaza, MD
	1090F5-4129
	Cincinnati, OH 45263
Agent's Phone:	800-837-2755
Other than USA:	Yes

Safekeeping:	Yes
Invests:	Every 30 days beginning 1/15
Minimum:	$25
Maximum:	$4,000/month
Min to qualify:	1
Fee on cash inv.:	0!
Fee on div. inv.:	0!
Discount (cash):	0
Discount (div.):	0
Auto invest:	No
Auto invest fee:	$0
Selling info:	Sells weekly, by mail or fax, at market, for $5 + comm.

Company:	**Aktiebolaget Electrolux**
Symbol:	ELUXY
Exchange:	OTC
Industry:	Household appliances
Company Address:	c/o Morgan Guaranty Trust, Box 9073
	Boston, MA 02205-9948
Company Phone:	800-428-4237
Transfer Agent:	Morgan Guaranty Trust Co.
Agent's Address:	P.O. Box 9073
	Boston, MA 02205-9948
Agent's Phone:	800-428-4237
Other than USA:	No

Safekeeping:	Yes
Invests:	Every 7 days beginning varies
Minimum:	$50
Maximum:	$100,000/year
Min to qualify:	1
Fee on cash inv.:	$5 + 12¢/sh.
Fee on div. inv.:	5% to $2.50
Discount (cash):	0
Discount (div.):	0
Auto invest:	Yes
Auto invest fee:	$5
Selling info:	Sells daily, by phone or mail, at avg. price, for $5 +12¢/sh.

Company:	**Akzo Nobel NV**
Symbol:	AKZOY
Exchange:	OTC
Industry:	Produces chemicals, coatings, fibers & drugs
Company Address:	300 South Riverside Plz.
	Chicago, IL 60606
Company Phone:	312-906-7500
Transfer Agent:	Morgan Guaranty Trust Co.
Agent's Address:	P.O. Box 9073
	Boston, MA 02205-9948
Agent's Phone:	800-428-4237
Other than USA:	Yes

Safekeeping:	Yes
Invests:	Every 7 days beginning varies
Minimum:	$50
Maximum:	$100,000/year
Min to qualify:	1
Fee on cash inv.:	$5 + 12¢/sh.
Fee on div. inv.:	5% to $2.50
Discount (cash):	0
Discount (div.):	0
Auto invest:	Yes
Auto invest fee:	$5 +12¢/sh.
Selling info:	Sells daily, by phone or mail, at avg. price, for $5 +12¢/sh.

Company:	**Albany International**
Symbol:	AIN
Exchange:	NYSE
Industry:	Mfr. of paper, machine, clothing
Company Address:	Box 1907
	Albany, NY 12201-1907
Company Phone:	518-445-2284 or 518-445-2200
Transfer Agent:	Harris Trust & Savings Bank
Agent's Address:	P.O. Box A-3309
	Chicago, IL 60690-9939
Agent's Phone:	312-461-6001
Other than USA:	No

Safekeeping:	Yes
Invests:	Every 30 days beginning 1/1
Minimum:	$10
Maximum:	$5,000/month
Min to qualify:	1
Fee on cash inv.:	0!
Fee on div. inv.:	0!
Discount (cash):	0
Discount (div.):	0
Auto invest:	No
Auto invest fee:	$0
Selling info:	Sells weekly, by mail or fax, at market, for $10 + 8¢/sh.

Company:	**Albemarle Corp.**	**Safekeeping:**	No
Symbol:	ALB	**Invests:**	Every 30 days beginning 1/1
Exchange:	NYSE	**Minimum:**	$25
Industry:	Mfr. special and fine chemicals	**Maximum:**	$1,000/month
Company Address:	451 Florida St.	**Min to qualify:**	1
	Baton Rouge, LA 70801	**Fee on cash inv.:**	0
Company Phone:	225-388-7320 or 804-788-6000	**Fee on div. inv.:**	0
Transfer Agent:	Harris Trust & Savings Bank	**Discount (cash):**	0
Agent's Address:	P. O. Box A3504	**Discount (div.):**	0
	Chicago, IL 60690-3504	**Auto invest:**	No
Agent's Phone:	312-360-5146	**Auto invest fee:**	$0
Other than USA:	Yes	**Selling info:**	Sells irregularly, by mail, at market, for 7¢/sh.

Company:	**Alberta Energy Co. Ltd.**	**Safekeeping:**	No
Symbol:	AOG	**Invests:**	Every 90 days beginning 1/1
Exchange:	nyse	**Minimum:**	$50
Industry:	Oil & gas	**Maximum:**	$5,000/quarter
Company Address:	3900, 421-7 Ave. S.W.	**Min to qualify:**	1
	Calgary, Alberta T2P 4K9 Canada	**Fee on cash inv.:**	0
Company Phone:	403-266-8145	**Fee on div. inv.:**	0
Transfer Agent:	CIBC Mellon Trust	**Discount (cash):**	0
Agent's Address:	P.O.Box 2517	**Discount (div.):**	0
	Calgary, Alberta T2P 4P4 Canada	**Auto invest:**	No
Agent's Phone:	800-387-0825	**Auto invest fee:**	$0
Other than USA:	Yes-Cdn.	**Selling info:**	Not available

Company:	**Albertson's, Inc.**	**Safekeeping:**	Yes
Symbol:	ABS	**Invests:**	Every 90 days beginning 2/25
Exchange:	NYSE	**Minimum:**	$30
Industry:	Retail food & drug chain	**Maximum:**	$30,000/quarter
Company Address:	250 Parkcenter Blvd., Box 20	**Min to qualify:**	15
	Boise, ID 83726	**Fee on cash inv.:**	$5 + 12¢/sh.
Company Phone:	208-395-6200	**Fee on div. inv.:**	0
Transfer Agent:	ChaseMellon Shareholder Services	**Discount (cash):**	0
Agent's Address:	P.O. Box 3315	**Discount (div.):**	0
	South Hackensack, NJ 07606	**Auto invest:**	No
Agent's Phone:	800-982-7649	**Auto invest fee:**	$0
Other than USA:	No	**Selling info:**	Sells weekly, by mail , at avg. price, for $15 +15¢/sh.

Company:	**Alcan Aluminium Ltd.**	**Safekeeping:**	No
Symbol:	AL	**Invests:**	Every 30 days beginning 1/15
Exchange:	NYSE	**Minimum:**	$100
Industry:	Mining	**Maximum:**	$9,000/quarter
Company Address:	1188 Sherbrooke St. West,	**Min to qualify:**	1
	Box 6090	**Fee on cash inv.:**	0
	Montreal, Que. H3A 3G2 Canada	**Fee on div. inv.:**	0
Company Phone:	888-252-5226 or 514-848-8050	**Discount (cash):**	0
Transfer Agent:	Alcan Aluminium Ltd.	**Discount (div.):**	0
Agent's Address:	Box 6077	**Auto invest:**	No
	Montreal, Que. H3C 3A7 Canada	**Auto invest fee:**	$0
Agent's Phone:	888-252-5226	**Selling info:**	Not available
Other than USA:	Yes		

Company:	**Alcatel Alsthom S.A.**
Symbol:	ALA
Exchange:	NYSE
Industry:	Produces and distributes telecomm. equip. and manufactures equip. for electrical power generation.
Company Address:	c/o BNY,101 Barclay St.,22 West New York, NY 10286
Company Phone:	800-943-9715
Transfer Agent:	Bank of New York
Agent's Address:	P.O. Box 11258 New York, NY 10286
Agent's Phone:	888-269-2377
Other than USA:	Yes

Safekeeping:	Yes
Invests:	Every 7 days beginning varies
Minimum:	$50
Maximum:	$250,000/week
Min to qualify:	1
Fee on cash inv.:	$5 + 10¢/sh.
Fee on div. inv.:	5% to $5 + 10¢/sh.
Discount (cash):	0
Discount (div.):	0
Auto invest:	Yes
Auto invest fee:	$0
Selling info:	Sells Friday, by phone or mail, at avg. price, for $5 +10¢/sh.

Company:	**Alcoa**
Symbol:	AA
Exchange:	NYSE
Industry:	Metals
Company Address:	201 Isabella St. Pittsburgh, PA 15212-5858
Company Phone:	412-553-4545 or 412-553-2451
Transfer Agent:	FCT (EquiServe)
Agent's Address:	P.O. Box 2500 Jersey City, NJ 07303-2500
Agent's Phone:	800-317-4445
Other than USA:	Yes

Safekeeping:	Yes
Invests:	Every 30 days beginning 1/25
Minimum:	$25
Maximum:	$5,000/month
Min to qualify:	1
Fee on cash inv.:	0!
Fee on div. inv.:	0!
Discount (cash):	0
Discount (div.):	0
Auto invest:	No
Auto invest fee:	$0
Selling info:	Sells daily, by mail, at avg. price, for $10 +12¢/sh.

Company:	**Alfa Corp.**
Symbol:	ALFA
Exchange:	OTC
Industry:	Insurance holding co.
Company Address:	2108 East South Blvd., Box 11000 Montgomery, AL 36191
Company Phone:	334-288-3900
Transfer Agent:	Bank of New York
Agent's Address:	P.O. Box 11258, Church St. Station New York, NY 10286-1258
Agent's Phone:	800-524-4458
Other than USA:	Yes

Safekeeping:	Yes
Invests:	Every 90 days beginning 3/1
Minimum:	$25
Maximum:	$5,000/quarter
Min to qualify:	1
Fee on cash inv.:	0
Fee on div. inv.:	0
Discount (cash):	0
Discount (div.):	0
Auto invest:	No
Auto invest fee:	$0
Selling info:	Sells irregularly, by mail, at market, for comm.

Company:	**Aliant Communications Inc.**
Symbol:	ALNT
Exchange:	OTC
Industry:	Communication services
Company Address:	Box 81309 Lincoln, NE 68501-1309
Company Phone:	800-829-5832 or 402-436-5277
Transfer Agent:	ChaseMellon Shareholder Services
Agent's Address:	P.O. Box 3339 South Hackensack, NJ 07606-1939
Agent's Phone:	800-642-7236
Other than USA:	Yes

Safekeeping:	Yes
Invests:	Every 30 days beginning 1/10
Minimum:	$100
Maximum:	$3,000/quarter
Min to qualify:	1
Fee on cash inv.:	0!
Fee on div. inv.:	0!
Discount (cash):	0
Discount (div.):	0
Auto invest:	Yes
Auto invest fee:	$0
Selling info:	Sells daily, by mail or phone, at avg. price, for fee + comm.

Company:	**Allegheny Energy**	Safekeeping:	Yes
Symbol:	AYE	Invests:	Every 90 days beginning 3/31
Exchange:	NYSE	Minimum:	$50
Industry:	Utility-electric	Maximum:	$10,000/quarter
Company Address:	10435 Downsville Pike	Min to qualify:	1
	Hagerstown, MD 21740-1766	Fee on cash inv.:	$3
Company Phone:	301-790-3400	Fee on div. inv.:	3% to $3
Transfer Agent:	ChaseMellon Shareholder Services	Discount (cash):	0
Agent's Address:	P.O. Box 3340	Discount (div.):	0
	South Hackensack, NJ 07606-1940	Auto invest:	No
Agent's Phone:	800-648-8389	Auto invest fee:	$0
Other than USA:	No	Selling info:	Sells weekly, by mail , at market, for $15 + comm.

Company:	**Allegheny Teledyne Inc.**	Safekeeping:	Yes
Symbol:	ALT	Invests:	Every 7 days beginning varies
Exchange:	NYSE	Minimum:	$100
Industry:	Specialty metal, industrial, cons.	Maximum:	$10,000/month
	products, aerospace & electronics	Min to qualify:	1
Company Address:	1000 Six PPG Pl.	Fee on cash inv.:	12¢/sh.
	Pittsburgh, PA 15222	Fee on div. inv.:	0
Company Phone:	412-394-2800 or 412-394-2819	Discount (cash):	0
Transfer Agent:	ChaseMellon Shareholder Services	Discount (div.):	0
Agent's Address:	85 Challenger Road,	Auto invest:	Yes
	Overpeck Centre	Auto invest fee:	$0
	Ridgefield Park, NJ 07660	Selling info:	Sells weekly, by mail or phone, at market, for $15 +12¢/sh.
Agent's Phone:	800-406-4850		
Other than USA:	Yes		

Company:	**Allegiant Bancorp, Inc.**	Safekeeping:	No
Symbol:	ALLE	Invests:	Every 90 days beginning 1/30
Exchange:	OTC	Minimum:	$100
Industry:	Bank holding company	Maximum:	$15,000/quarter
Company Address:	2122 Kratky Rd.	Min to qualify:	1
	St. Louis, MO 63114	Fee on cash inv.:	$1 + comm.
Company Phone:	314-692-8200	Fee on div. inv.:	0
Transfer Agent:	UMB Bank, N.A.	Discount (cash):	0
Agent's Address:	P.O. Box 410064	Discount (div.):	0
	Kansas City, MO 64141	Auto invest:	No
Agent's Phone:	816-860-7888	Auto invest fee:	$0
Other than USA:	Yes	Selling info:	Sells daily, by mail, at market, for $2 + comm.

Company:	**Allergan, Inc.**	Safekeeping:	Yes
Symbol:	AGN	Invests:	Every 30 days beginning 1/10
Exchange:	NYSE	Minimum:	$10
Industry:	Drugs, eye & skin care prods.	Maximum:	$50,000/year
Company Address:	2525 Dupont Dr., Box 19534	Min to qualify:	1
	Irvine, CA 92623-9534	Fee on cash inv.:	0!
Company Phone:	800-790-4577 or 714-246-5541	Fee on div. inv.:	0!
Transfer Agent:	FCT (EquiServe)	Discount (cash):	0
Agent's Address:	P.O.Box 2598	Discount (div.):	0
	Jersey City, N.J. 07303-2598	Auto invest:	Yes
Agent's Phone:	201-324-1644	Auto invest fee:	$1
Other than USA:	Yes	Selling info:	Sells daily, by mail, at market, for $10 +12¢/sh.

Company:	**Alliant Energy Corp.**
Symbol:	LNT
Exchange:	NYSE
Industry:	Utility-electric, gas
Company Address:	222 West Washington Ave., Box 2568 Madison, WI 53701-2568
Company Phone:	800-356-5343 or 608-252-3110
Transfer Agent:	Alliant Energy (Interstate Energy Corp.)
Agent's Address:	P.O. Box 2568 Madison, WI 53701-2568
Agent's Phone:	800-356-5343
Other than USA:	No

Safekeeping:	Yes
Invests:	Every 30 days beginning 1/15
Minimum:	$25
Maximum:	$120,000/year
Min to qualify:	1
Fee on cash inv.:	0!
Fee on div. inv.:	0!
Discount (cash):	0
Discount (div.):	0
Auto invest:	Yes
Auto invest fee:	$0
Selling info:	Sells weekly, by mail, at market, for 2.5¢/sh.

Company:	**Allied Irish Banks, plc**
Symbol:	AIB
Exchange:	NYSE
Industry:	Regional banks
Company Address:	c/o BNY,101 Barclay St.,22 West New York, NY 10286
Company Phone:	800-943-9715
Transfer Agent:	Bank of New York
Agent's Address:	P.O. Box 11258 New York, NY 10286
Agent's Phone:	888-269-2377
Other than USA:	Yes

Safekeeping:	Yes
Invests:	Every 7 days beginning varies
Minimum:	$50
Maximum:	$250,000/year
Min to qualify:	1
Fee on cash inv.:	$5 + 10¢/sh.
Fee on div. inv.:	5% to $5 + 10¢/sh.
Discount (cash):	0
Discount (div.):	0
Auto invest:	Yes
Auto invest fee:	$5 + 10¢/sh.
Selling info:	Sells weekly, by mail, at market, for $5 +10¢/sh.

Company:	**AlliedSignal Inc.**
Symbol:	ALD
Exchange:	NYSE
Industry:	Automotive, chemicals, aerospace
Company Address:	101 Columbia Rd., Box 2245 Morristown, NJ 07962-2245
Company Phone:	800-255-4332 or 973-455-5402
Transfer Agent:	Bank of New York
Agent's Address:	P.O. Box 11258 New York, NY 10286
Agent's Phone:	800-432-0140
Other than USA:	No

Safekeeping:	Yes
Invests:	Every 30 days beginning 1/1
Minimum:	$25
Maximum:	$120,000/year
Min to qualify:	1
Fee on cash inv.:	0!
Fee on div. inv.:	0!
Discount (cash):	0
Discount (div.):	0
Auto invest:	No
Auto invest fee:	$0
Selling info:	Sells biweekly, by mail, at market, for 5¢/sh.

Company:	**Allmerica Securities Trust**
Symbol:	ALM
Exchange:	NYSE
Industry:	Corporate bond fund
Company Address:	440 Lincoln St. Worcester, MA 01653
Company Phone:	508-855-4330
Transfer Agent:	Bank of New York
Agent's Address:	Box 11258, Church St. Station New York, NY 10286
Agent's Phone:	800-432-8224
Other than USA:	Yes

Safekeeping:	Yes
Invests:	Every 30 days beginning 1/1
Minimum:	$25
Maximum:	$1,000/month
Min to qualify:	1
Fee on cash inv.:	$1 + 5¢/sh.
Fee on div. inv.:	0!
Discount (cash):	0
Discount (div.):	0
Auto invest:	No
Auto invest fee:	$0
Selling info:	Not available

Company:	**Allstate Corp.**	Safekeeping:	Yes
Symbol:	ALL	Invests:	Every 7 days beginning 1/7
Exchange:	NYSE	Minimum:	$100
Industry:	Insurance	Maximum:	$150,000/year
Company Address:	3075 Sanders Rd.,Ste. G2H	Min to qualify:	1
	Northbrook, IL 60062-6127	Fee on cash inv.:	5% to $5 + 3¢/sh.
Company Phone:	800-416-8803 or 847-402-2594	Fee on div. inv.:	5% to $3 + 3¢/sh.
Transfer Agent:	FCT (EquiServe)	Discount (cash):	0
Agent's Address:	P.O. Box 2500	Discount (div.):	0
	Jersey City, NJ 07303-2500	Auto invest:	Yes
Agent's Phone:	800-355-5191	Auto invest fee:	3¢/sh.
Other than USA:	Yes	Selling info:	Sells daily, by mail or phone, at avg. price, for $15 +12¢/sh.

Company:	**ALLTEL Corp.**	Safekeeping:	Yes
Symbol:	AT	Invests:	Every 30 days beginning 1/3
Exchange:	NYSE	Minimum:	$50
Industry:	Telecommunications	Maximum:	$25,000/quarter
Company Address:	One Allied Dr.	Min to qualify:	1
	Little Rock, AR 72202	Fee on cash inv.:	0
Company Phone:	888-838-4188 or 330-650-7250	Fee on div. inv.:	0
Transfer Agent:	First Union National Bank	Discount (cash):	0
Agent's Address:	1525 West W.T. Harris Blvd. 3C3	Discount (div.):	0
	Charlotte, NC 28288-1153	Auto invest:	No
Agent's Phone:	888-243-5445	Auto invest fee:	$0
Other than USA:	No	Selling info:	Sells weekly, by mail, at market, for $0

Company:	**Amcast Industrial Corp.**	Safekeeping:	Yes
Symbol:	AIZ	Invests:	Every 90 days beginning 3/1
Exchange:	NYSE	Minimum:	$25
Industry:	Manufacturing	Maximum:	$1,000/month
Company Address:	7887 Washington Village Dr.,	Min to qualify:	1
	Box 98	Fee on cash inv.:	0
	Dayton, OH 45401-0098	Fee on div. inv.:	0
Company Phone:	937-291-7000	Discount (cash):	0
Transfer Agent:	FCT (EquiServe)	Discount (div.):	0
Agent's Address:	P.O. Box 2500	Auto invest:	No
	Jersey City, NJ 07303-2500	Auto invest fee:	$0
Agent's Phone:	800-317-4445	Selling info:	Sells daily, by mail, at market, for $10 +12¢/sh.
Other than USA:	No		

Company:	**AMCOL International**	Safekeeping:	Yes
Symbol:	ACO	Invests:	Every 30 days beginning 1/4
Exchange:	NYSE	Minimum:	$25
Industry:	Produces minerals, specialty chemicals and environ. prods.	Maximum:	$2,000/month
		Min to qualify:	1
Company Address:	1500 West Shure Dr.	Fee on cash inv.:	0!
	Arlington Heights, IL 60004-7803	Fee on div. inv.:	0!
Company Phone:	800-426-5564 or 847-394-8730	Discount (cash):	0
Transfer Agent:	Harris Trust & Savings Bank	Discount (div.):	0
Agent's Address:	P.O. Box A-3309	Auto invest:	No
	Chicago, IL 60690	Auto invest fee:	$0
Agent's Phone:	312-360-5204	Selling info:	Sells weekly, by mail, at market, for 2¢/sh.
Other than USA:	Yes		

Company:	**AMCOR Ltd.**
Symbol:	AMCRY
Exchange:	OTC
Industry:	Mfr. paper prods.
Company Address:	c/o Morgan Guaranty Trust, Box 9073 Boston, MA 02205-9948
Company Phone:	800-428-4237
Transfer Agent:	Morgan Guaranty Trust Co.
Agent's Address:	P.O. Box 9073 Boston, MA 02205-9948
Agent's Phone:	800-428-4237
Other than USA:	No

Safekeeping:	Yes
Invests:	Every 7 days beginning varies
Minimum:	$50
Maximum:	$100,000/year
Min to qualify:	1
Fee on cash inv.:	$5 + 12¢/sh.
Fee on div. inv.:	5% to $2.50
Discount (cash):	0
Discount (div.):	0
Auto invest:	Yes
Auto invest fee:	$5
Selling info:	Sells daily, by phone or mail, at avg. price, for $5 +12¢/sh.

Company:	**Amcore Financial, Inc.**
Symbol:	AMFI
Exchange:	OTC
Industry:	Banking, mortgage, finance, insurance
Company Address:	501 Seventh St., Box 1537 Rockford, IL 61104
Company Phone:	815-968-2241 or 815-961-7003
Transfer Agent:	Firstar Bank Milwaukee, NA
Agent's Address:	P.O. Box 2077 Milwaukee, WI 53201-2077
Agent's Phone:	800-637-7549
Other than USA:	Yes

Safekeeping:	Yes
Invests:	Every 30 days beginning 1/1
Minimum:	$10
Maximum:	$7,500/quarter
Min to qualify:	1
Fee on cash inv.:	0
Fee on div. inv.:	0
Discount (cash):	0
Discount (div.):	0
Auto invest:	No
Auto invest fee:	$0
Selling info:	Not available

Company:	**Amerada Hess**
Symbol:	AHC
Exchange:	NYSE
Industry:	Oil & gas
Company Address:	1185 Ave. of the Americas New York, NY 10036
Company Phone:	212-997-8500 or 212-536-8597
Transfer Agent:	Bank of New York
Agent's Address:	P.O. Box 1958-DRP Dept. Newark, NJ 07101
Agent's Phone:	800-524-4458
Other than USA:	No

Safekeeping:	Yes
Invests:	Every 30 days beginning 1/30
Minimum:	$50
Maximum:	$5,000/quarter
Min to qualify:	1
Fee on cash inv.:	0!
Fee on div. inv.:	0
Discount (cash):	0
Discount (div.):	0
Auto invest:	No
Auto invest fee:	$0
Selling info:	Sells daily, by mail, at market, for $1

Company:	**Ameren Corp.**
Symbol:	AEE
Exchange:	NYSE
Industry:	Utility-electric, gas
Company Address:	Box 66887 St. Louis, MO 63166-6887
Company Phone:	800-255-2237 or 314-554-3502
Transfer Agent:	Ameren Services Co.
Agent's Address:	P.O. Box 66887 St. Louis, MO 63166-6887
Agent's Phone:	800-255-2237
Other than USA:	Yes

Safekeeping:	Yes
Invests:	Every 30 days beginning 1/30
Minimum:	$25
Maximum:	$10,000/month
Min to qualify:	1
Fee on cash inv.:	5¢/sh.
Fee on div. inv.:	5¢/sh.
Discount (cash):	0
Discount (div.):	0
Auto invest:	Yes
Auto invest fee:	$0
Selling info:	Sells weekly, by mail or phone, at market, for comm.

Company:	**American Business Products**	**Safekeeping:**	Yes
Symbol:	ABP	**Invests:**	Every 30 days beginning 1/15
Exchange:	NYSE	**Minimum:**	$10
Industry:	Specialty pkg. & printed office supplies	**Maximum:**	$1,000/month
		Min to qualify:	1
		Fee on cash inv.:	0!
Company Address:	2100 Riveredge Pkwy., Ste.1200 Atlanta, GA 30328	**Fee on div. inv.:**	0!
		Discount (cash):	0
Company Phone:	800-227-3390 or 770-953-8300	**Discount (div.):**	0
Transfer Agent:	Wachovia (EquiServe)	**Auto invest:**	No
Agent's Address:	P.O. Box 8217 Boston, MA 02266-8217	**Auto invest fee:**	$0
		Selling info:	Sells weekly, by phone, at avg.
Agent's Phone:	800-633-4236		price, for comm.
Other than USA:	Yes		

Company:	**American Electric Power**	**Safekeeping:**	Yes
Symbol:	AEP	**Invests:**	Every 7 days beginning varies
Exchange:	NYSE	**Minimum:**	$25
Industry:	Utility-electric	**Maximum:**	$150,000/year
Company Address:	1 Riverside Plaza, Box 6631 Columbus, OH 43215	**Min to qualify:**	1
		Fee on cash inv.:	0
Company Phone:	800-237-2667 or 614-223-1000	**Fee on div. inv.:**	0
Transfer Agent:	FCT (EquiServe)	**Discount (cash):**	0
Agent's Address:	P.O. Box 2500 Jersey City, NJ 07303-2500	**Discount (div.):**	0
		Auto invest:	Yes
Agent's Phone:	800-328-6955	**Auto invest fee:**	$0
Other than USA:	Yes	**Selling info:**	Sells daily, by phone or mail, at market, for $5 +12¢/sh.

Company:	**American Express Co.**	**Safekeeping:**	Yes
Symbol:	AXP	**Invests:**	Every 30 days beginning 1/10
Exchange:	NYSE	**Minimum:**	$50
Industry:	Financial services	**Maximum:**	$10,000/month
Company Address:	200 Vesey St. New York, NY 10285	**Min to qualify:**	10
		Fee on cash inv.:	$5 + 6¢/sh.
Company Phone:	212-640-5692 or 212-640-2000	**Fee on div. inv.:**	10% to 75¢ + 6¢/sh.
Transfer Agent:	ChaseMellon Shareholder Services	**Discount (cash):**	0
Agent's Address:	P.O. Box 3336 South Hackensack, NJ 07606	**Discount (div.):**	0
		Auto invest:	Yes
Agent's Phone:	800-463-5911	**Auto invest fee:**	$3 + 6¢/sh.
Other than USA:	Yes	**Selling info:**	Sells weekly, by mail or phone, at market, for $10 +12¢/sh.

Company:	**American General Corp.**	**Safekeeping:**	Yes
Symbol:	AGC	**Invests:**	Every 30 days beginning 1/1
Exchange:	NYSE	**Minimum:**	$25
Industry:	Financial services	**Maximum:**	$6,000/quarter
Company Address:	Box 3247 Houston, TX 77253	**Min to qualify:**	1
		Fee on cash inv.:	0!
Company Phone:	800-242-1111 or 713-522-1111	**Fee on div. inv.:**	0!
Transfer Agent:	FCT (EquiServe)	**Discount (cash):**	0
Agent's Address:	P.O. Box 2500 Jersey City, NJ 07303-2500	**Discount (div.):**	0
		Auto invest:	Yes
Agent's Phone:	800-519-3111	**Auto invest fee:**	$1
Other than USA:	Yes	**Selling info:**	Sells daily, by mail, at market, for comm.

Company:	**American Greetings Corp.**	Safekeeping:	Yes
Symbol:	AM	Invests:	Every 30 days beginning 3/10
Exchange:	NYSE	Minimum:	$100
Industry:	Consumer products, cards & gift	Maximum:	$10,000/quarter
	wrappings	Min to qualify:	10
Company Address:	One American Rd.	Fee on cash inv.:	0!
	Cleveland, OH 44144-2398	Fee on div. inv.:	0!
Company Phone:	216-252 7300	Discount (cash):	0
Transfer Agent:	National City Bank	Discount (div.):	0
Agent's Address:	P.O. Box 94946	Auto invest:	No
	Cleveland, OH 44101-4946	Auto invest fee:	$0
Agent's Phone:	800-622-6757	Selling info:	Sells weekly, by mail, at market,
Other than USA:	No		for $5 + comm.

Company:	**American Health Properties, Inc.**	Safekeeping:	No
		Invests:	Every 30 days beginning 1/31
Symbol:	AHE	Minimum:	$50
Exchange:	NYSE	Maximum:	$3,000/quarter
Industry:	REIT	Min to qualify:	1
Company Address:	6400 S. Fiddlers Green Cir., Ste.1800	Fee on cash inv.:	0!
	Englewood, CO 80111	Fee on div. inv.:	0!
Company Phone:	303-796-9793	Discount (cash):	0
Transfer Agent:	ChaseMellon Shareholder Services	Discount (div.):	0
Agent's Address:	400 South Hope St., 4th Floor	Auto invest:	No
	Los Angeles, CA 90071	Auto invest fee:	$0
Agent's Phone:	800-356-2017	Selling info:	Sells daily, by mail or phone, at
Other than USA:	Yes		market, for 0

Company:	**American Home Products**	Safekeeping:	Yes
Symbol:	AHP	Invests:	Every 30 days beginning 1/1
Exchange:	NYSE	Minimum:	$50
Industry:	Pharmaceuticals & consumer	Maximum:	$10,000/month
	products	Min to qualify:	1
Company Address:	5 Giralda Farms	Fee on cash inv.:	$5 + comm.
	Madison, NJ 07940	Fee on div. inv.:	$1.50 + comm.
Company Phone:	973-660-5000 or 973-660-6811	Discount (cash):	0
Transfer Agent:	ChaseMellon Shareholder Services	Discount (div.):	0
Agent's Address:	P.O. Box 3338	Auto invest:	No
	South Hackensack, NJ 07606-1938	Auto invest fee:	$0
Agent's Phone:	800-565-2067	Selling info:	Sells 2 to 3 times per wk., by mail
Other than USA:	Yes		or phone, at market, for $15 +
			comm.

Company:	**American Software, Inc.**	Safekeeping:	Yes
Symbol:	AMSWA	Invests:	Every 90 days beginning 3/20
Exchange:	otc	Minimum:	$25
Industry:	Software	Maximum:	$2,500/quarter
Company Address:	470 East Paces Rd.	Min to qualify:	1
	Atlanta, GA 30305	Fee on cash inv.:	0
Company Phone:	404-261-4381	Fee on div. inv.:	0
Transfer Agent:	Wachovia (EquiServe)	Discount (cash):	0
Agent's Address:	P.O. Box 8217	Discount (div.):	0
	Boston, MA 02266-8217	Auto invest:	No
Agent's Phone:	800-633-4236 or 910-770-4994	Auto invest fee:	$0
Other than USA:	No	Selling info:	Sells irregularly, by mail,
			at market, for comm.

Company:	**American States Water**	**Safekeeping:**	Yes
Symbol:	AWR	**Invests:**	Every 90 days beginning 3/1
Exchange:	NYSE	**Minimum:**	$50
Industry:	Utility-water	**Maximum:**	$12,000/year
Company Address:	630 East Foothill Blvd.	**Min to qualify:**	1
	San Dimas, CA 91773-1212	**Fee on cash inv.:**	0
Company Phone:	909-394-3600	**Fee on div. inv.:**	0
Transfer Agent:	ChaseMellon Shareholder Services	**Discount (cash):**	0
Agent's Address:	85 Challenger Road	**Discount (div.):**	0
	Ridgefield Park, NJ 07660	**Auto invest:**	No
Agent's Phone:	888-816-6998	**Auto invest fee:**	$0
Other than USA:	Yes	**Selling info:**	Not available

Company:	**American Water Works**	**Safekeeping:**	Yes
Symbol:	AWK	**Invests:**	Every 30 days beginning 1/15
Exchange:	NYSE	**Minimum:**	$100
Industry:	Utility-water	**Maximum:**	$5,000/month
Company Address:	1025 Laurel Oak Rd., Box 1770	**Min to qualify:**	1
	Voorhees, NJ 08043	**Fee on cash inv.:**	0!
Company Phone:	609-346-8200	**Fee on div. inv.:**	0!
Transfer Agent:	BankBoston (EquiServe)	**Discount (cash):**	2%
Agent's Address:	P.O. Box 8040, MS 45-02-64	**Discount (div.):**	2%
	Boston, MA 02266-8040	**Auto invest:**	No
Agent's Phone:	800-736-3001	**Auto invest fee:**	$0
Other than USA:	Yes	**Selling info:**	Sells daily, by mail, at market, for $1 to $10 + comm.

Company:	**Ameritech**	**Safekeeping:**	Yes
Symbol:	AIT	**Invests:**	Every 7 days beginning varies
Exchange:	NYSE	**Minimum:**	$100
Industry:	Telecommunications	**Maximum:**	$150,000/year
Company Address:	30 South Wacker Dr.	**Min to qualify:**	2
	Chicago, IL 60606	**Fee on cash inv.:**	$5 + 10¢/sh.
Company Phone:	800-257-0902 or 312-750-5353	**Fee on div. inv.:**	5% to $3
Transfer Agent:	FCT (EquiServe)	**Discount (cash):**	0
Agent's Address:	P.O. Box 2558	**Discount (div.):**	0
	Jersey City, NJ 07303-2558	**Auto invest:**	Yes
Agent's Phone:	800-233-1342	**Auto invest fee:**	$1 + 10¢/sh.
Other than USA:	Yes	**Selling info:**	Sells daily, by phone, mail, or fax, at market, for $10 +12¢/sh.

Company:	**AmSouth Bancorp.**	**Safekeeping:**	Yes
Symbol:	ASO	**Invests:**	Every 90 days beginning 1/1
Exchange:	NYSE	**Minimum:**	$10
Industry:	Banking	**Maximum:**	$5,000/quarter
Company Address:	Box 11007	**Min to qualify:**	1
	Birmingham, AL 35288	**Fee on cash inv.:**	0!
Company Phone:	205-320-7151	**Fee on div. inv.:**	0!
Transfer Agent:	Bank of New York	**Discount (cash):**	0
Agent's Address:	P.O. Box 11002, Church St. Station	**Discount (div.):**	0
	New York, NY 10286-1002	**Auto invest:**	No
Agent's Phone:	800-524-4458	**Auto invest fee:**	$0
Other than USA:	Yes	**Selling info:**	Sells irregularly, by mail, at market, for $0

Company:	**AMVESCAP plc**
Symbol:	AVZ
Exchange:	NYSE
Industry:	Investment management services
Company Address:	c/o BNY,101 Barclay St., 22 West New York, NY 10286
Company Phone:	212-815-2175
Transfer Agent:	Bank of New York
Agent's Address:	P.O. Box 11258 New York, NY 10286
Agent's Phone:	800-943-9715
Other than USA:	No

Safekeeping:	Yes
Invests:	Every 7 days beginning varies
Minimum:	$50
Maximum:	$100,000/year
Min to qualify:	1
Fee on cash inv.:	$5 + 12¢/sh.
Fee on div. inv.:	5% to $2.50
Discount (cash):	0
Discount (div.):	0
Auto invest:	Yes
Auto invest fee:	$5 + 12¢/sh.
Selling info:	Sells daily, by mail or phone, at avg. price, for $5 +12¢/sh.

Company:	**Amway Asia Pacific, Ltd.**
Symbol:	AAP
Exchange:	NYSE
Industry:	Distribution vehicle for Amway Products
Company Address:	c/o Bank of NY, Box 1958 Newark, NJ 07101-9774
Company Phone:	800-524-4458
Transfer Agent:	Bank of New York
Agent's Address:	P.O. Box 1958 Newark, NJ 07101-9774
Agent's Phone:	800-524-4458
Other than USA:	Yes

Safekeeping:	Yes
Invests:	Every 7 days beginning varies
Minimum:	$50
Maximum:	$10,000/investment
Min to qualify:	1
Fee on cash inv.:	$5 + 10¢/sh.
Fee on div. inv.:	10¢/sh.
Discount (cash):	0
Discount (div.):	0
Auto invest:	Yes
Auto invest fee:	$0
Selling info:	Sells weekly, by phone or mail, at market, for $5 +10¢/sh.

Company:	**Amway Japan Ltd.**
Symbol:	AJL
Exchange:	NYSE
Industry:	Dist. Amway prods. in Japan
Company Address:	c/o Morgan Guaranty Trust, Box 9073 Boston, MA 02205-9948
Company Phone:	800-428-4237
Transfer Agent:	Morgan Guaranty Trust Co.
Agent's Address:	P.O. Box 9073 Boston, MA 02205-9948
Agent's Phone:	800-428-4237
Other than USA:	Yes

Safekeeping:	Yes
Invests:	Every 7 days beginning varies
Minimum:	$50
Maximum:	$100,000 /year
Min to qualify:	1
Fee on cash inv.:	$5 + 12¢/sh.
Fee on div. inv.:	5% to $2.50
Discount (cash):	0
Discount (div.):	0
Auto invest:	Yes
Auto invest fee:	$5 + 12¢
Selling info:	Sells daily, by phone or mail, at avg. price, for $5 +12¢/sh.

Company:	**Anadarko Petroleum Corp.**
Symbol:	APC
Exchange:	NYSE
Industry:	Oil & gas
Company Address:	17001 Northchase Dr., Box 1330 Houston, TX 77251-1330
Company Phone:	281-875-1101
Transfer Agent:	ChaseMellon Shareholder Services
Agent's Address:	P.O. Box 3338 South Hackensack, NJ 07606-1938
Agent's Phone:	888-470-5786
Other than USA:	Yes

Safekeeping:	Yes
Invests:	Every 30 days beginning varies
Minimum:	$50
Maximum:	$10,000
Min to qualify:	1
Fee on cash inv.:	0
Fee on div. inv.:	0
Discount (cash):	0
Discount (div.):	5%
Auto invest:	Yes
Auto invest fee:	$0
Selling info:	Sells weekly, by mail, at market, for $15 +12¢/sh.

Company:	ANB Corp.	Safekeeping:	No
Symbol:	ANBC	Invests:	Every 90 days beginning 1/15
Exchange:	OTC	Minimum:	$100
Industry:	Bank holding co.	Maximum:	$5,000/quarter
Company Address:	110 East Main St.	Min to qualify:	100
	Muncie, IN 47305-2818	Fee on cash inv.:	0
Company Phone:	765-747-7600 ex. 513	Fee on div. inv.:	0
Transfer Agent:	Registrar & Transfer Co.	Discount (cash):	0
Agent's Address:	10 Commerce Drive	Discount (div.):	0
	Cranford, NJ 07016	Auto invest:	No
Agent's Phone:	800-368-5948	Auto invest fee:	$0
Other than USA:	No	Selling info:	Not available

Company:	Andover Bancorp, Inc.	Safekeeping:	Yes
Symbol:	ANDB	Invests:	Every 30 days beginning 1/1
Exchange:	NASD	Minimum:	$25
Industry:	Savings banks	Maximum:	$1,800/month
Company Address:	61 Main St., Box 2005	Min to qualify:	1
	Andover, MA 01810	Fee on cash inv.:	0!
Company Phone:	978-749-2000	Fee on div. inv.:	0!
Transfer Agent:	Boston Eq. (EquiServe)	Discount (cash):	0
Agent's Address:	P.O. Box 8040	Discount (div.):	0
	Boston, MA 02266	Auto invest:	No
Agent's Phone:	800-730-4001	Auto invest fee:	$0
Other than USA:	Yes	Selling info:	Sells within 10 bus. days, by mail, at avg. price, for 5% to $5 + comm.

Company:	Angelica Corp.	Safekeeping:	Yes
Symbol:	AGL	Invests:	Every 90 days beginning 2/1
Exchange:	NYSE	Minimum:	$10
Industry:	Uniforms	Maximum:	$3,000/quarter
Company Address:	424 South Woods Mill Rd.	Min to qualify:	1
	Chesterfield, MO 63017-3406	Fee on cash inv.:	0!
Company Phone:	314-854-3800	Fee on div. inv.:	0!
Transfer Agent:	UMB Bank, N.A.	Discount (cash):	0
Agent's Address:	P.O. Box 410064	Discount (div.):	0
	Kansas City, MO 64141-0064	Auto invest:	No
Agent's Phone:	800-884-4225 x7888	Auto invest fee:	$0
Other than USA:	Yes	Selling info:	Sells weekly, by mail, at market, for $2 + comm.

Company:	Anglogold Ltd.	Safekeeping:	Yes
Symbol:	AU	Invests:	Every 7 days beginning varies
Exchange:	NYSE	Minimum:	$50
Industry:	Gold & silver mining	Maximum:	$250,000/year
Company Address:	c/o BNY,101 Barclay St.,22 West	Min to qualify:	1
	New York, NY 10286	Fee on cash inv.:	$5 + 10¢/sh.
Company Phone:	800-943-9715	Fee on div. inv.:	5% to $5 + 10¢/sh.
Transfer Agent:	Bank of New York	Discount (cash):	0
Agent's Address:	P.O. Box 11258	Discount (div.):	0
	New York, NY 10286	Auto invest:	Yes
Agent's Phone:	888-269-2377	Auto invest fee:	$5 + 10¢/sh.
Other than USA:	Yes	Selling info:	Sells weekly, by mail, at market, for $5 +10¢/sh.

Company:	**Anheuser-Busch Cos.**	Safekeeping:	Yes
Symbol:	BUD	Invests:	Every 30 days beginning 1/9
Exchange:	NYSE	Minimum:	$25
Industry:	Food & beverages, distilling	Maximum:	$5,000/month
	brewers	Min to qualify:	1
Company Address:	One Busch Pl.	Fee on cash inv.:	0!
	St. Louis, MO 63118	Fee on div. inv.:	0!
Company Phone:	314-577-2000	Discount (cash):	0
Transfer Agent:	ChaseMellon Shareholder Services	Discount (div.):	0
Agent's Address:	P.O. Box 3336	Auto invest:	No
	South Hackensack, NJ 07606	Auto invest fee:	$0
Agent's Phone:	888-213-0964	Selling info:	Sells daily, by mail or phone, at
Other than USA:	Yes		avg. price, for 3¢/sh.

Company:	**Anthracite Capital**	Safekeeping:	Yes
Symbol:	AHR	Invests:	Every 30 days beginning varies
Exchange:	NYSE	Minimum:	$100
Industry:	REIT	Maximum:	$5,000/month
Company Address:	345 Park Ave.	Min to qualify:	1
	New York, NY 10154	Fee on cash inv.:	0!
Company Phone:	212-409-3333	Fee on div. inv.:	0!
Transfer Agent:	Bank of New York	Discount (cash):	0%-5%
Agent's Address:	P.O. Box 1958	Discount (div.):	0%-5%
	Newark, NJ 07101-9774	Auto invest:	Yes
Agent's Phone:	800-524-4458	Auto invest fee:	$0
Other than USA:	Yes	Selling info:	Sells weekly, by mail, at avg. price,
			for $10 +10¢/sh.

Company:	**Aon Corp.**	Safekeeping:	Yes
Symbol:	AOC	Invests:	Every 30 days beginning 1/15
Exchange:	NYSE	Minimum:	$20
Industry:	Insurance	Maximum:	$1,000/month
Company Address:	123 North Wacker Dr.	Min to qualify:	1
	Chicago, IL 60606	Fee on cash inv.:	0!
Company Phone:	312-701-3000	Fee on div. inv.:	0!
Transfer Agent:	FCT (Equiserve)	Discount (cash):	0
Agent's Address:	P.O. Box 2500	Discount (div.):	0
	Jersey City, NJ 07303-2500	Auto invest:	No
Agent's Phone:	800-446-2617	Auto invest fee:	$0
Other than USA:	Yes	Selling info:	Sells daily, by mail, at market, for
			$10 +12¢/sh.

Company:	**Apache Corp.**	Safekeeping:	Yes
Symbol:	APA	Invests:	Every 30 days beginning 1/31
Exchange:	NYSE	Minimum:	$50
Industry:	Oil exploration	Maximum:	$5,000/quarter
Company Address:	2000 Post Oak Blvd., Ste.100	Min to qualify:	1
	Houston, TX 77056-4400	Fee on cash inv.:	0!
Company Phone:	800-272-2434 x6504 or 713-296-6662	Fee on div. inv.:	0!
Transfer Agent:	Norwest Bank Minnesota	Discount (cash):	0
Agent's Address:	P.O. Box 64854	Discount (div.):	0
	St. Paul, MN 55164-0854	Auto invest:	No
Agent's Phone:	800-468-9716	Auto invest fee:	$0
Other than USA:	Yes	Selling info:	Sells within 5 bus. days, by mail or
			fax, at market, for $3 +15¢/sh.

Company:	**Applied Industrial Technologies, Inc.**	**Safekeeping:**	Yes
		Invests:	Every 30 days beginning 1/1
Symbol:	APZ	**Minimum:**	$10
Exchange:	NYSE	**Maximum:**	$1,000/month
Industry:	Dist. bearings & power	**Min to qualify:**	1
	transmissions	**Fee on cash inv.:**	0!
Company Address:	One Applied Plaza	**Fee on div. inv.:**	0!
	Cleveland, OH 44115-5000	**Discount (cash):**	0
Company Phone:	216-426-4212 or 216-426-4000	**Discount (div.):**	0
Transfer Agent:	Harris Trust & Savings Bank	**Auto invest:**	No
Agent's Address:	P.O. Box A3309	**Auto invest fee:**	$0
	Chicago, IL 60690	**Selling info:**	Sells weekly, by mail, at market,
Agent's Phone:	800-988-5291		for $5
Other than USA:	Yes		

Company:	**APT Satellite**	**Safekeeping:**	Yes
Symbol:	ATS	**Invests:**	Every 7 days beginning varies
Exchange:	NYSE	**Minimum:**	$50
Industry:	Communications equipment	**Maximum:**	$250,000/year
Company Address:	c/o BNY,101 Barclay St.,22 West	**Min to qualify:**	1
	New York, NY 10286	**Fee on cash inv.:**	$5 + 10¢/sh.
Company Phone:	800-943-9715	**Fee on div. inv.:**	0
Transfer Agent:	Bank of New York	**Discount (cash):**	0
Agent's Address:	P.O. Box 11258	**Discount (div.):**	0
	New York, NY 10286	**Auto invest:**	Yes
Agent's Phone:	888-269-2377	**Auto invest fee:**	$5 + 10¢/sh.
Other than USA:	Yes	**Selling info:**	Sells weekly, by mail, at market,
			for $5 +10¢/sh.

Company:	**Aquarion Co.**	**Safekeeping:**	No
Symbol:	WTR	**Invests:**	Every 30 days beginning 1/30
Exchange:	NYSE	**Minimum:**	$10
Industry:	Utility-water	**Maximum:**	$5,000/quarter
Company Address:	835 Main St	**Min to qualify:**	1
	Bridgeport, CT 06604-4995	**Fee on cash inv.:**	0
Company Phone:	203-336-7658 or 203-335-2333	**Fee on div. inv.:**	0
Transfer Agent:	ChaseMellon Shareholder Services	**Discount (cash):**	5%
Agent's Address:	P.O. Box 3338	**Discount (div.):**	5%
	South Hackensack, Nj 07606-1938	**Auto invest:**	No
Agent's Phone:	800-288-9541	**Auto invest fee:**	$0
Other than USA:	Yes	**Selling info:**	Sells daily, by mail , at market, for
			$5 + comm.

Company:	**Aracruz Celulose SA**	**Safekeeping:**	Yes
Symbol:	ARA	**Invests:**	Every 7 days beginning varies
Exchange:	NYSE	**Minimum:**	$50
Industry:	Produce eucalyptus kraft pulp	**Maximum:**	$100,000/year
Company Address:	c/o Morgan Guaranty Trust, Box	**Min to qualify:**	1
	9073	**Fee on cash inv.:**	$5 + 12¢/sh.
	Boston, MA 02205-9948	**Fee on div. inv.:**	5% to $2.50
Company Phone:	800-428-4237	**Discount (cash):**	0
Transfer Agent:	Morgan Guaranty Trust Co.	**Discount (div.):**	0
Agent's Address:	P.O. Box 9073	**Auto invest:**	Yes
	Boston, MA 02205-9948	**Auto invest fee:**	$5 + 12¢/sh.
Agent's Phone:	800-428-4237	**Selling info:**	Sells daily, by mail or phone, at
Other than USA:	No		avg. price, for $5 +12¢/sh.

Company:	**ARCADIS NV**
Symbol:	ARCAF
Exchange:	OTC
Industry:	Engineering company
Company Address:	c/o BNY,101 Barclay St.,22 West
	New York, NY 10286
Company Phone:	800-943-9715
Transfer Agent:	Bank of New York
Agent's Address:	P.O. Box 11258
	New York, NY 10286
Agent's Phone:	888-269-2377
Other than USA:	Yes

Safekeeping:	Yes
Invests:	Every 7 days beginning varies
Minimum:	$50
Maximum:	$250,000/year
Min to qualify:	1
Fee on cash inv.:	$5 + 10¢/sh.
Fee on div. inv.:	5% to $5 + 10¢/sh.
Discount (cash):	0
Discount (div.):	0
Auto invest:	Yes
Auto invest fee:	$5 + 10¢/sh.
Selling info:	Sells weekly, by mail, at market, for $5 +10¢/sh.

Company:	**Arch Coal, Inc.**
Symbol:	ACI
Exchange:	NYSE
Industry:	Metal, coal mining
Company Address:	CityPlace One, Ste. 300
	St. Louis, MO 63141
Company Phone:	314-994-2700
Transfer Agent:	FCT (EquiServe)
Agent's Address:	P.O. Box 2598
	Jersey City, NJ 07303-2598
Agent's Phone:	800-317-4445
Other than USA:	Yes

Safekeeping:	Yes
Invests:	Every 30 days beginning 1/15
Minimum:	$25
Maximum:	$100,000/year
Min to qualify:	1
Fee on cash inv.:	0!
Fee on div. inv.:	0!
Discount (cash):	0
Discount (div.):	0
Auto invest:	Yes
Auto invest fee:	$1
Selling info:	Sells daily, by mail or phone, at market, for $10 +12¢/sh.

Company:	**Archstone Communities Trust**
Symbol:	ASN
Exchange:	NYSE
Industry:	Real estate operations
Company Address:	7670 S. Chester St., Ste.100
	Englewood, CO 80112
Company Phone:	800-982-9293 or 303-708-5959
Transfer Agent:	ChaseMellon Shareholder Services
Agent's Address:	P.O. Box 3338
	S. Hackensack, NJ 07606-1938
Agent's Phone:	800-461-9257
Other than USA:	Yes

Safekeeping:	Yes
Invests:	Every 30 days beginning varies
Minimum:	$200
Maximum:	$5,000/month
Min to qualify:	1
Fee on cash inv.:	0
Fee on div. inv.:	0
Discount (cash):	2%
Discount (div.):	0
Auto invest:	Yes
Auto invest fee:	$0
Selling info:	Sells weekly, by mail, at market, for $15 +12¢/sh.

Company:	**Argentaria Caja Postal y Banco Hipotecario, SA**
Symbol:	AGR
Exchange:	NYSE
Industry:	Banking, Spain
Company Address:	c/o Morgan Guaranty Trust,
	Box 9073
	Boston, MA 02205-9948
Company Phone:	800-428-4237
Transfer Agent:	Morgan Guaranty Trust Co.
Agent's Address:	P.O. Box 9073
	Boston, MA 02205-9948
Agent's Phone:	800-428-4237
Other than USA:	No

Safekeeping:	Yes
Invests:	Every 7 days beginning varies
Minimum:	$50
Maximum:	$100,000/year
Min to qualify:	1
Fee on cash inv.:	$5 + 12¢/sh.
Fee on div. inv.:	5% to $2.50
Discount (cash):	0
Discount (div.):	0
Auto invest:	Yes
Auto invest fee:	$5
Selling info:	Sells daily, by phone or mail, at avg. price, for $5 +12¢/sh.

Company:	**Argentina Fund Inc. (The)**	**Safekeeping:**	No
Symbol:	AF	**Invests:**	Every 180 days beginning 2/15
Exchange:	NYSE	**Minimum:**	$100
Industry:	Closed-end fund	**Maximum:**	$3,000/investment
Company Address:	345 Park Ave	**Min to qualify:**	1
	New York, NY 10154	**Fee on cash inv.:**	75¢ + comm.
Company Phone:	800-349-4281	**Fee on div. inv.:**	0
Transfer Agent:	State Street Bank (EquiServe)	**Discount (cash):**	0
Agent's Address:	P.O. Box 8209	**Discount (div.):**	0-5%
	Boston, MA 02266-8209	**Auto invest:**	No
Agent's Phone:	800-426-5523	**Auto invest fee:**	$0
Other than USA:	Yes	**Selling info:**	Sells irregularly, by mail or phone, at market, for $2.50 + comm.

Company:	**Armstrong World Ind. Inc.**	**Safekeeping:**	Yes
Symbol:	ACK	**Invests:**	Every 30 days beginning 1/1
Exchange:	NYSE	**Minimum:**	$50
Industry:	Building materials	**Maximum:**	$3,000/month
Company Address:	Box 3001	**Min to qualify:**	1
	Lancaster, PA 17604-3001	**Fee on cash inv.:**	0
Company Phone:	717-396-3155 or 717-397-0611	**Fee on div. inv.:**	0
Transfer Agent:	ChaseMellon Shareholder Services	**Discount (cash):**	0
Agent's Address:	85 Challenger Road,	**Discount (div.):**	0
	Overpeck Centre	**Auto invest:**	No
	Ridgefield Park, NJ 07660-2108	**Auto invest fee:**	$0
Agent's Phone:	800-685-4541	**Selling info:**	Sells weekly, by mail , at market, for $10 + comm.
Other than USA:	Yes		

Company:	**Arnold Industries, Inc.**	**Safekeeping:**	Yes
Symbol:	AIND	**Invests:**	Every 90 days beginning 3/2
Exchange:	OTC	**Minimum:**	$25
Industry:	Trucking	**Maximum:**	$3,000/quarter
Company Address:	Box 210	**Min to qualify:**	1
	Lebanon, PA 17042	**Fee on cash inv.:**	0!
Company Phone:	717-273-9058	**Fee on div. inv.:**	0!
Transfer Agent:	Registrar & Transfer Co.	**Discount (cash):**	0
Agent's Address:	10 Commerce Drive	**Discount (div.):**	0
	Cranford, NJ 07016	**Auto invest:**	No
Agent's Phone:	800-368-5948	**Auto invest fee:**	$0
Other than USA:	No	**Selling info:**	Not available

Company:	**Arrow Financial Corp.**	**Safekeeping:**	Yes
Symbol:	AROW	**Invests:**	Every 30 days beginning 1/1
Exchange:	OTC	**Minimum:**	$50
Industry:	Banking	**Maximum:**	$10,000/quarter
Company Address:	250 Glen St., Box 307	**Min to qualify:**	1
	Glens Falls, NY 12801	**Fee on cash inv.:**	0!
Company Phone:	518-793-4121 or 518-745-1000	**Fee on div. inv.:**	0!
Transfer Agent:	American Stock Transfer	**Discount (cash):**	0
Agent's Address:	40 Wall St.	**Discount (div.):**	0
	New York, NY 10005	**Auto invest:**	No
Agent's Phone:	800-278-4353 or 718-921-8200	**Auto invest fee:**	$0
Other than USA:	No	**Selling info:**	Sells daily, by mail, at market, for 0!

Company:	**Arvin Ind.**	**Safekeeping:**	No
Symbol:	ARV	**Invests:**	Every 90 days beginning 2/15
Exchange:	NYSE	**Minimum:**	$25
Industry:	Automotive	**Maximum:**	$3,000/quarter
Company Address:	Box 3000	**Min to qualify:**	1
	Columbus, IN 47202-3000	**Fee on cash inv.:**	5% to $2.50
Company Phone:	800-652-7846 or 812-379-3206	**Fee on div. inv.:**	5% to $2.50
Transfer Agent:	Harris Trust & Savings Bank	**Discount (cash):**	0
Agent's Address:	P.O. Box A3504	**Discount (div.):**	0
	Chicago, IL 60690-3504	**Auto invest:**	No
Agent's Phone:	800-720-0418	**Auto invest fee:**	$0
Other than USA:	No	**Selling info:**	Sells irregularly, by mail, at market, for 0

Company:	**ASA Limited**	**Safekeeping:**	Yes
Symbol:	ASA	**Invests:**	Every 90 days beginning 2/24
Exchange:	NYSE	**Minimum:**	$50
Industry:	Closed-end fund	**Maximum:**	$3,000/quarter
Company Address:	Box 269	**Min to qualify:**	1
	Florham Park, NJ 07932	**Fee on cash inv.:**	5% to $2.50
Company Phone:	973-377-3535	**Fee on div. inv.:**	5% to $2.50
Transfer Agent:	FCT (EquiServe)	**Discount (cash):**	0
Agent's Address:	P.O. Box 2598	**Discount (div.):**	0
	Jersey City, NJ 07303-2598	**Auto invest:**	No
Agent's Phone:	201-324-0498	**Auto invest fee:**	$0
Other than USA:	Yes	**Selling info:**	Sells daily, by mail, at market, for $10 +12¢/sh.

Company:	**ASARCO Inc.**	**Safekeeping:**	Yes
Symbol:	AR	**Invests:**	Every 30 days beginning 1/1
Exchange:	NYSE	**Minimum:**	$25
Industry:	Metals-mining	**Maximum:**	$1,000/month
Company Address:	180 Maiden Lane	**Min to qualify:**	1
	New York, NY 10038	**Fee on cash inv.:**	0!
Company Phone:	212-510-2000	**Fee on div. inv.:**	0!
Transfer Agent:	Bank of New York	**Discount (cash):**	0
Agent's Address:	101 Barclay St.	**Discount (div.):**	0
	New York, NY 10286	**Auto invest:**	No
Agent's Phone:	800-524-4458	**Auto invest fee:**	$0
Other than USA:	Yes	**Selling info:**	Sells daily, by mail or phone, at avg. price, for $10 +12¢/sh.

Company:	**Ascent Entertainment Group, Inc.**	**Safekeeping:**	Yes
		Invests:	Every 7 days beginning varies
Symbol:	GOAL	**Minimum:**	$20
Exchange:	OTC	**Maximum:**	$5,000/quarter
Industry:	Diverse entertainment and media	**Min to qualify:**	1
Company Address:	1225 17th St., Ste. 1800	**Fee on cash inv.:**	$2 + 7¢/sh.
	Denver, CO 80202	**Fee on div. inv.:**	0
Company Phone:	303-308-7000	**Discount (cash):**	0
Transfer Agent:	Bank of New York	**Discount (div.):**	0
Agent's Address:	Box 11258, Church St. Station	**Auto invest:**	Yes
	New York, NY 10286	**Auto invest fee:**	$0
Agent's Phone:	800-433-7471	**Selling info:**	Sells weekly, by mail, fax ,or phone, at market, for $5 +10¢/sh.
Other than USA:	Yes		

Company:	**Ashland Inc.**	Safekeeping:	Yes
Symbol:	ASH	Invests:	Every 90 days beginning 3/15
Exchange:	NYSE	Minimum:	$10
Industry:	Oil refining, marketing	Maximum:	$5,000/quarter
Company Address:	Box 391	Min to qualify:	1
	Covington, KY 41114	Fee on cash inv.:	0
Company Phone:	606-815-3333 or 606-329-5757	Fee on div. inv.:	0
Transfer Agent:	Harris Trust & Savings Bank	Discount (cash):	0
Agent's Address:	P.O. Box A-3309	Discount (div.):	0
	Chicago, IL 60690	Auto invest:	No
Agent's Phone:	800-510-8199	Auto invest fee:	$0
Other than USA:	Yes	Selling info:	Sells irregularly, by mail, at market, for comm.

Company:	**Asia Pulp & Paper Co. Ltd.**	Safekeeping:	Yes
Symbol:	PAP	Invests:	Every 7 days beginning varies
Exchange:	NYSE	Minimum:	$50
Industry:	Pulp & paper producers	Maximum:	$250,000/week
Company Address:	c/o BNY,101 Barclay St.,22 West	Min to qualify:	1
	New York, NY 10286	Fee on cash inv.:	$5 + 10¢/sh.
Company Phone:	800-943-9715	Fee on div. inv.:	5% to $5 + 10¢/sh.
Transfer Agent:	Bank of New York	Discount (cash):	0
Agent's Address:	P.O. Box 11258	Discount (div.):	0
	New York, NY 10286	Auto invest:	Yes
Agent's Phone:	888-269-2377	Auto invest fee:	$0
Other than USA:	Yes	Selling info:	Sells weekly, by phone or mail, at market, for $5 +10¢/ADS

Company:	**Asia Satellite Tele. Holdings Ltd.**	Safekeeping:	Yes
		Invests:	Every 7 days beginning varies
Symbol:	SAT	Minimum:	$50
Exchange:	NYSE	Maximum:	$100,000/year
Industry:	Telecommunications	Min to qualify:	1
Company Address:	c/o Morgan Guaranty Trust,	Fee on cash inv.:	$5 + 12¢/sh.
	Box 9073	Fee on div. inv.:	5% to $2.50
	Boston, MA 02205-9948	Discount (cash):	0
Company Phone:	800-428-4237	Discount (div.):	0
Transfer Agent:	Morgan Guaranty Trust Co.	Auto invest:	Yes
Agent's Address:	P.O. Box 9073	Auto invest fee:	$5
	Boston, MA 02205-9948	Selling info:	Sells daily, by phone or mail, at avg. price, for $5 +12¢/sh.
Agent's Phone:	800-428-4237		
Other than USA:	No		

Company:	**ASM Lithography Holding N.V.**	Safekeeping:	Yes
		Invests:	Every 7 days beginning varies
Symbol:	ASMLF	Minimum:	$50
Exchange:	NYSE	Maximum:	$100,000/year
Industry:	Manufacturing photolithography systems	Min to qualify:	1
		Fee on cash inv.:	$5 + 12¢/sh.
Company Address:	c/o Morgan Guaranty Trust,	Fee on div. inv.:	5% to $2.50
	Box 9073	Discount (cash):	0
	Boston, MA 02205-9948	Discount (div.):	0
Company Phone:	800-428-4237	Auto invest:	Yes
Transfer Agent:	Morgan Guaranty Trust Co.	Auto invest fee:	$5
Agent's Address:	P.O. Box 9073	Selling info:	Sells daily, by phone or mail, at market, for $5 +12¢/sh.
	Boston, MA 02205-9948		
Agent's Phone:	800-428-4237		
Other than USA:	No		

Company:	**Associated Banc-Corp**	**Safekeeping:**	Yes
Symbol:	ASBC	**Invests:**	Every 90 days beginning 2/15
Exchange:	OTC	**Minimum:**	$100
Industry:	Bank holding company	**Maximum:**	$5,000/quarter
Company Address:	Box 13307	**Min to qualify:**	1
	Green Bay, WI 54307-3307	**Fee on cash inv.:**	0!
Company Phone:	800-236-2722 or 920-491-7006	**Fee on div. inv.:**	0!
Transfer Agent:	FCT (EquiServe)	**Discount (cash):**	0
Agent's Address:	P.O. Box 2500	**Discount (div.):**	0
	Jersey City, NJ 07303-2500	**Auto invest:**	No
Agent's Phone:	800-446-2617	**Auto invest fee:**	$0
Other than USA:	Yes	**Selling info:**	Sells daily, by mail or phone, at market, for 0!

Company:	**Associated Estates Realty Corp.**	**Safekeeping:**	Yes
		Invests:	Every 30 days beginning 1/1
Symbol:	AEC	**Minimum:**	$100
Exchange:	NYSE	**Maximum:**	$5,000/month
Industry:	REIT	**Min to qualify:**	1
Company Address:	5025 Swetland Ct.	**Fee on cash inv.:**	0
	Richmond Heights, OH 44143-1467	**Fee on div. inv.:**	0
Company Phone:	800-440-2372	**Discount (cash):**	0
Transfer Agent:	National City Bank	**Discount (div.):**	0
Agent's Address:	P.O. Box 92301	**Auto invest:**	No
	Cleveland, OH 44193-0900	**Auto invest fee:**	$0
Agent's Phone:	800-622-6757	**Selling info:**	Sells monthly, by mail, at market, for 8¢ to 20¢/sh.
Other than USA:	Yes		

Company:	**Associates First Capital Corp.**	**Safekeeping:**	Yes
		Invests:	Every 5 days beginning
Symbol:	AFS	**Minimum:**	$50
Exchange:	NYSE	**Maximum:**	$250,000/year
Industry:	Financial services	**Min to qualify:**	1
Company Address:	250 East Carpenter Freeway,	**Fee on cash inv.:**	$5 + 3¢/sh.
	Box 660237	**Fee on div. inv.:**	5% to $5 + 3¢/sh.
	Dallas, TX 75266-0237	**Discount (cash):**	0
Company Phone:	972-652-7294	**Discount (div.):**	0
Transfer Agent:	FCT (EquiServe)	**Auto invest:**	Yes
Agent's Address:	P.O. Box 2598	**Auto invest fee:**	$1 +3¢/sh.
	Jersey City, NJ 07303-2598	**Selling info:**	Sells weekly, by mail or phone, at market, for $15 +12¢/sh.
Agent's Phone:	800-975-2112		
Other than USA:	Yes		

Company:	**Astoria Financial Corp.**	**Safekeeping:**	Yes
Symbol:	ASFC	**Invests:**	Every 90 days beginning 3/12
Exchange:	OTC	**Minimum:**	$50
Industry:	Savings and loan	**Maximum:**	$5,000/quarter
Company Address:	One Astoria Federal Plaza	**Min to qualify:**	1
	Lake Success, NY 11042-1085	**Fee on cash inv.:**	0!
Company Phone:	516-327-3000	**Fee on div. inv.:**	0!
Transfer Agent:	ChaseMellon Shareholder Services	**Discount (cash):**	0
Agent's Address:	P.O. Box 3316	**Discount (div.):**	0
	South Hackensack, NJ 07606-1916	**Auto invest:**	No
Agent's Phone:	800-526-0801	**Auto invest fee:**	$0
Other than USA:	Yes	**Selling info:**	Sells weekly, by mail or phone, at market, for $15

Company:	**AT&T Corp.**
Symbol:	T
Exchange:	NYSE
Industry:	Telecommunications
Company Address:	32 Ave. of the Americas
	New York, NY 10013-2412
Company Phone:	908-221-5767 or 212-387-5400
Transfer Agent:	Boston Eq. (EquiServe)
Agent's Address:	P.O. Box 8035
	Boston, MA 02266-8035
Agent's Phone:	800-348-8288
Other than USA:	Yes

Safekeeping:	Yes
Invests:	Every 7 days beginning varies
Minimum:	$100
Maximum:	$250,000/year
Min to qualify:	1
Fee on cash inv.:	$5
Fee on div. inv.:	10%to$1
Discount (cash):	0
Discount (div.):	0
Auto invest:	Yes
Auto invest fee:	$5
Selling info:	Sells weekly, by phone, mail, or fax, at avg. price, for $20 + comm.

Company:	**Atlantic Richfield**
Symbol:	ARC
Exchange:	NYSE
Industry:	Petroleum refining, marketing
Company Address:	333 South Hope St.
	Los Angeles, CA 90071-1406
Company Phone:	213-486-3708
Transfer Agent:	FCT (EquiServe)
Agent's Address:	P.O. Box 2532
	Jersey City, NJ 07303-2532
Agent's Phone:	800-756-8200
Other than USA:	Yes

Safekeeping:	Yes
Invests:	Every 30 days beginning 1/20
Minimum:	$10
Maximum:	$60,000/year
Min to qualify:	1
Fee on cash inv.:	5% to $3 + comm.
Fee on div. inv.:	0
Discount (cash):	0
Discount (div.):	0
Auto invest:	Yes
Auto invest fee:	$1 + 5% to $3
Selling info:	Sells daily, by mail, at market, for $10 +12¢/sh.

Company:	**Atmos Energy Corp.**
Symbol:	ATO
Exchange:	NYSE
Industry:	Utility-gas and propane
Company Address:	Box 650205
	Dallas, TX 75265-0205
Company Phone:	800-382-8667 or 972-855-3729
Transfer Agent:	Boston Eq. (EquiServe)
Agent's Address:	P.O. Box 8040
	Boston, MA 02266-8040
Agent's Phone:	800-543-3038
Other than USA:	Yes

Safekeeping:	Yes
Invests:	Every 7 days beginning varies
Minimum:	$25
Maximum:	$100,000/year
Min to qualify:	1
Fee on cash inv.:	0!
Fee on div. inv.:	0!
Discount (cash):	0
Discount (div.):	3%
Auto invest:	Yes
Auto invest fee:	$0
Selling info:	Sells within 10 bus. days, by mail, at market, for $5 + 5¢/sh.

Company:	**Austria Fund (The)**
Symbol:	OST
Exchange:	NYSE
Industry:	Closed-end fund
Company Address:	1345 Ave. of the Americas
	New York, NY 10105-0302
Company Phone:	800-426-5523
Transfer Agent:	State Street Bank (EquiServe)
Agent's Address:	225 Franklin St.
	Boston, MA 02110
Agent's Phone:	800-219-4218
Other than USA:	No

Safekeeping:	No
Invests:	Every 180 days beginning 1/15
Minimum:	$100
Maximum:	$unlimited
Min to qualify:	1
Fee on cash inv.:	75¢
Fee on div. inv.:	0
Discount (cash):	0
Discount (div.):	5%
Auto invest:	No
Auto invest fee:	$0
Selling info:	Sells irregularly, by mail, at market, for $2.50 +15¢/sh.

Company:	AvalonBay Communities, Inc.	Safekeeping:	Yes
		Invests:	Every 90 days beginning 1/15
Symbol:	AVB	Minimum:	$100
Exchange:	NYSE	Maximum:	$25,000/quarter
Industry:	Real estate operations	Min to qualify:	1
Company Address:	2900 Eisenhower Ave., Ste. 300	Fee on cash inv.:	0
	Alexandria, VA 22314	Fee on div. inv.:	0
Company Phone:	703-329-6300	Discount (cash):	3%
Transfer Agent:	First Union National Bank	Discount (div.):	3%
Agent's Address:	1525 West W.T. Harris Blvd., 3C3	Auto invest:	No
	Charlotte, NC 28288-1153	Auto invest fee:	$0
Agent's Phone:	800-829-8432	Selling info:	Sells within 10 bus. days, by mail, at market, for 5¢/sh.
Other than USA:	No		

Company:	Avery Dennison Corp.	Safekeeping:	Yes
Symbol:	AVY	Invests:	Every 7 days beginning varies
Exchange:	NYSE	Minimum:	$100
Industry:	Adhesives, specialty chemicals	Maximum:	$12,500/month
Company Address:	Box 7090	Min to qualify:	1
	Pasadena, CA 91109-7090	Fee on cash inv.:	$5 + 3¢/sh.
Company Phone:	626-304-2032	Fee on div. inv.:	0!
Transfer Agent:	FCT (EquiServe)	Discount (cash):	0
Agent's Address:	P.O. Box 2598	Discount (div.):	0
	Jersey City, NJ 07303-2598	Auto invest:	Yes
Agent's Phone:	800-756-8200	Auto invest fee:	$2 +3¢/sh.
Other than USA:	Yes	Selling info:	Sells daily, by mail, at market, for $15 +12¢/sh.

Company:	Aviall, Inc.	Safekeeping:	Yes
Symbol:	AVL	Invests:	Every 30 days beginning 1/1
Exchange:	NYSE	Minimum:	$25
Industry:	Aviation services	Maximum:	$15,000/quarter
Company Address:	2075 Diplomat Dr.	Min to qualify:	10
	Dallas, TX 75234-8999	Fee on cash inv.:	0!
Company Phone:	972-406-6671	Fee on div. inv.:	0!
Transfer Agent:	Boston Eq. (EquiServe)	Discount (cash):	0
Agent's Address:	P.O.Box 8040	Discount (div.):	0
	Boston, MA 02266-8040	Auto invest:	No
Agent's Phone:	800-730-4001	Auto invest fee:	$0
Other than USA:	Yes	Selling info:	Sells 5 bus. days after receipt, by mail, at market, for 5% to $10 + comm.

Company:	Avista Corp.	Safekeeping:	Yes
Symbol:	AVA	Invests:	Every 30 days beginning 1/15
Exchange:	NYSE	Minimum:	$0
Industry:	Hydroelectric, gas utility	Maximum:	$100,000/year
Company Address:	Box 3647	Min to qualify:	1
	Spokane, WA 99220-3647	Fee on cash inv.:	4¢/sh.
Company Phone:	800-222-4931 or 509-495-4203	Fee on div. inv.:	4¢/sh.
Transfer Agent:	Bank of New York	Discount (cash):	0
Agent's Address:	Church St. Station, P.O. Box 11258	Discount (div.):	0
	New York, NY 10286-1258	Auto invest:	No
		Auto invest fee:	$0
Agent's Phone:	800-642-7365	Selling info:	Sells weekly, by mail, at market, for 4¢/sh.
Other than USA:	Yes		

Company:	**Avnet, Inc.**
Symbol:	AVT
Exchange:	NYSE
Industry:	Electronics
Company Address:	2211 South 47th St.
	Phoenix, AZ 85034
Company Phone:	602-643-2000
Transfer Agent:	Bank of New York
Agent's Address:	P.O. Box 11258, Church St. Station
	New York, NY 10286
Agent's Phone:	800-524-4458
Other than USA:	Yes

Safekeeping:	Yes
Invests:	Every 45 days beginning 1/1
Minimum:	$10
Maximum:	$unlimited
Min to qualify:	1
Fee on cash inv.:	0
Fee on div. inv.:	0
Discount (cash):	0
Discount (div.):	0
Auto invest:	No
Auto invest fee:	$0
Selling info:	Sells weekly, by mail, fax, or telephone, at market, for comm.

Company:	**Avon Products, Inc.**
Symbol:	AVP
Exchange:	NYSE
Industry:	Cosmetics, fragrances, jewelry, gift prod.
Company Address:	1345 Ave. of the Americas
	New York, NY 10105-0196
Company Phone:	212-282-5619 or 212-282-5000
Transfer Agent:	FCT (EquiServe)
Agent's Address:	P.O. Box 2500
	Jersey City, NJ 07303
Agent's Phone:	201-324-0498
Other than USA:	Yes

Safekeeping:	Yes
Invests:	Every 30 days beginning 1/1
Minimum:	$10
Maximum:	$5,000/month
Min to qualify:	1
Fee on cash inv.:	0!
Fee on div. inv.:	0!
Discount (cash):	0
Discount (div.):	0
Auto invest:	No
Auto invest fee:	$0
Selling info:	Sells daily, by mail, at market, for $5 +12¢/sh.

Company:	**AVX Corp.**
Symbol:	AVX
Exchange:	NYSE
Industry:	Electronic instr. & controls
Company Address:	801 17th Ave. South
	Myrtle Beach, SC 29577
Company Phone:	800-633-4236 or 843-448-9411
Transfer Agent:	Wachovia (EquiServe)
Agent's Address:	P.O. Box 8217
	Boston, MA 02266-8217
Agent's Phone:	800-633-4236
Other than USA:	Yes

Safekeeping:	Yes
Invests:	Every 30 days beginning 1/1
Minimum:	$20
Maximum:	$2,000/month
Min to qualify:	1
Fee on cash inv.:	0
Fee on div. inv.:	0
Discount (cash):	0
Discount (div.):	0
Auto invest:	No
Auto invest fee:	$0
Selling info:	Sells irregularly, by mail, at market, for comm.

Company:	**AXA-uap**
Symbol:	AXA
Exchange:	NYSE
Industry:	Life insurance
Company Address:	c/o BNY,101 Barclay St.,22 West
	New York, NY 10286
Company Phone:	800-943-9715
Transfer Agent:	Bank of New York
Agent's Address:	P.O. Box 11258
	New York, NY 10286
Agent's Phone:	888-269-2377
Other than USA:	Yes

Safekeeping:	Yes
Invests:	Every 7 days beginning varies
Minimum:	$50
Maximum:	$250,000/year
Min to qualify:	1
Fee on cash inv.:	$5 + 10¢/sh.
Fee on div. inv.:	5% to $5 + 10¢/sh.
Discount (cash):	0
Discount (div.):	0
Auto invest:	Yes
Auto invest fee:	$5 + 10¢/sh.
Selling info:	Sells weekly, by mail, at market, for $5 +10¢/sh.

Company:	**Baan Co. N.V.**	Safekeeping:	Yes
Symbol:	BAANF	Invests:	Every 7 days beginning varies
Exchange:	OTC	Minimum:	$50
Industry:	Network & management software	Maximum:	$100,000/year
Company Address:	c/o Morgan Guaranty Trust, Box 9073	Min to qualify:	1
		Fee on cash inv.:	$5 + 12¢/sh.
	Boston, MA 02205-9948	Fee on div. inv.:	5% to $2.50
Company Phone:	800-428-4237	Discount (cash):	0
Transfer Agent:	Morgan Guaranty Trust Co.	Discount (div.):	0
Agent's Address:	P.O. Box 9073	Auto invest:	Yes
	Boston, MA 02205-9948	Auto invest fee:	$5 + 12¢/sh.
Agent's Phone:	800-428-4237	Selling info:	Sells daily, by mail or phone, at
Other than USA:	No		avg. price, for $5 +12¢/sh.

Company:	**Baker Hughes Inc.**	Safekeeping:	Yes
Symbol:	BHI	Invests:	Every 30 days beginning 1/20
Exchange:	NYSE	Minimum:	$10
Industry:	Oil, gas, & mining, equip. svcs.	Maximum:	$350/month
Company Address:	Box 4740	Min to qualify:	1
	Houston, TX 77210-4740	Fee on cash inv.:	0!
Company Phone:	713-439-8739	Fee on div. inv.:	0!
Transfer Agent:	ChaseMellon Shareholder Services	Discount (cash):	0
		Discount (div.):	0
Agent's Address:	P.O. Box 3338	Auto invest:	No
	S. Hackensack, NJ 07606-1938	Auto invest fee:	$0
Agent's Phone:	888-216-8057	Selling info:	Sells weekly, by mail or phone, at
Other than USA:	Yes		market, for $15 +10¢/sh.

Company:	**Baker, Fentress & Co.**	Safekeeping:	No
Symbol:	BKF	Invests:	Every 30 days beginning 1/5
Exchange:	NYSE	Minimum:	$100
Industry:	Closed-end fund	Maximum:	$10,000/month
Company Address:	200 West Madison St., Ste. 3510	Min to qualify:	1
	Chicago, IL 60606	Fee on cash inv.:	comm.
Company Phone:	800-253-1891 or 312-236-9190	Fee on div. inv.:	comm.
Transfer Agent:	Harris Trust & Savings Bank	Discount (cash):	0
Agent's Address:	P.O. Box A3504	Discount (div.):	0
	Chicago, IL 60690-3504	Auto invest:	No
		Auto invest fee:	$0
Agent's Phone:	800-394-5187	Selling info:	Sells irregularly, by mail,
Other than USA:	Yes		at market price, for 5¢/sh.

Company:	**Baldor Electric Co.**	Safekeeping:	No
Symbol:	BEZ	Invests:	Every 30 days beginning 1/4
Exchange:	NYSE	Minimum:	$50
Industry:	Designs, mfrs. & mkts. electric	Maximum:	$10,000/month
	motors	Min to qualify:	1
Company Address:	Box 2400	Fee on cash inv.:	0!
	Fort Smith, AR 72902-2400	Fee on div. inv.:	0!
Company Phone:	501-646-4711	Discount (cash):	0
Transfer Agent:	Wachovia (EquiServe)	Discount (div.):	0
Agent's Address:	P.O. Box 8217	Auto invest:	No
	Boston, MA 02266-8217	Auto invest fee:	$0
Agent's Phone:	800-633-4236	Selling info:	Sells daily, by mail, at market, for
Other than USA:	Yes		5¢/sh.

Company:	**Ball Corp.**	Safekeeping:	No
Symbol:	BLL	Invests:	Every 30 days beginning 1/15
Exchange:	NYSE	Minimum:	$25
Industry:	Aerospace, metal and packaging	Maximum:	$3,000/quarter
Company Address:	10 Longs Peak Dr.	Min to qualify:	1
	Broomfield, CO 80021	Fee on cash inv.:	0!
Company Phone:	303-939-4000 or 303-460-3537	Fee on div. inv.:	0!
Transfer Agent:	FCT (EquiServe)	Discount (cash):	0
Agent's Address:	P.O. Box 2500	Discount (div.):	5%
	Jersey City, NJ 07303-2500	Auto invest:	No
Agent's Phone:	800-446-2617	Auto invest fee:	$0
Other than USA:	Yes	Selling info:	Sells daily, by phone, mail, or fax, at avg. price, for $10 +12¢/sh.

Company:	**Banco BHIF, S.A.**	Safekeeping:	Yes
Symbol:	BB	Invests:	Every 7 days beginning varies
Exchange:	NYSE	Minimum:	$50
Industry:	Money center banks	Maximum:	$250,000/year
Company Address:	c/o BNY,101 Barclay St.,22 West	Min to qualify:	1
	New York, NY 10286	Fee on cash inv.:	$5 + 10¢/sh.
Company Phone:	800-943-9715	Fee on div. inv.:	5% to $5 + 10¢/sh.
Transfer Agent:	Bank of New York	Discount (cash):	0
Agent's Address:	P.O. Box 11258	Discount (div.):	0
	New York, NY 10286	Auto invest:	Yes
Agent's Phone:	888-269-2377	Auto invest fee:	$5 + 10¢/sh.
Other than USA:	Yes	Selling info:	Sells weekly, by mail, at market, for $5 +10¢/sh.

Company:	**Banco Bilbao Vizcaya**	Safekeeping:	Yes
Symbol:	BBV	Invests:	Every 7 days beginning varies
Exchange:	NYSE	Minimum:	$50
Industry:	Regional banks	Maximum:	$250,000/year
Company Address:	c/o BNY,101 Barclay St.,22 West	Min to qualify:	1
	New York, NY 10286	Fee on cash inv.:	$5 + 10¢/sh.
Company Phone:	800-943-9715	Fee on div. inv.:	5% to $5 + 10¢/sh.
Transfer Agent:	Bank of New York	Discount (cash):	0
Agent's Address:	P.O. Box 11258	Discount (div.):	0
	New York, NY 10286	Auto invest:	Yes
Agent's Phone:	888-269-2377	Auto invest fee:	$5 + 10¢/sh.
Other than USA:	Yes	Selling info:	Sells weekly, by mail, at market, for $5 +10¢/sh.

Company:	**Banco Comercial Portugues SA ADS**	Safekeeping:	Yes
Symbol:	BPC	Invests:	Every 7 days beginning varies
Exchange:	NYSE	Minimum:	$50
Industry:	Commercial banking, Portugal	Maximum:	$100,000/year
Company Address:	c/o Morgan Guaranty Trust,	Min to qualify:	1
	Box 9073	Fee on cash inv.:	$$5 + 12¢/sh.
	Boston, MA 02205-9948	Fee on div. inv.:	5% to $2.50
Company Phone:	800-428-4237	Discount (cash):	0
Transfer Agent:	Morgan Guaranty Trust Co.	Discount (div.):	0
Agent's Address:	P.O. Box 9073	Auto invest:	Yes
	Boston, MA 02205-9948	Auto invest fee:	$5
Agent's Phone:	800-428-4237	Selling info:	Sells daily, by phone or mail, at avg. price, for $5 +12¢/sh.
Other than USA:	No		

Company:	**Banco de Galicia y Buenos Aires, S.A.**	**Safekeeping:**	Yes
		Invests:	Every 7 days beginning varies
Symbol:	BGALY	**Minimum:**	$50
Exchange:	OTC	**Maximum:**	$250,000/week
Industry:	Private banking, Argentina	**Min to qualify:**	1
Company Address:	c/o BNY,101 Barclay St.,22 West New York, NY 10286	**Fee on cash inv.:**	$5 + 10¢/sh.
		Fee on div. inv.:	5% to $5 + 10¢/sh.
Company Phone:	800-943-9715	**Discount (cash):**	0
Transfer Agent:	Bank of New York	**Discount (div.):**	0
Agent's Address:	P.O. Box 11258 New York, NY 10286	**Auto invest:**	Yes
		Auto invest fee:	$0
Agent's Phone:	888-269-2377	**Selling info:**	Sells weekly, by phone or mail, at market, for $5 +10¢/ADS
Other than USA:	Yes		

Company:	**Banco Ganadero (common)**	**Safekeeping:**	Yes
		Invests:	Every 7 days beginning varies
Symbol:	BGA	**Minimum:**	$50
Exchange:	NYSE	**Maximum:**	$250,000/year
Industry:	Regional banks	**Min to qualify:**	1
Company Address:	c/o BNY,101 Barclay St.,22 West New York, NY 10286	**Fee on cash inv.:**	$5 + 10¢/sh.
		Fee on div. inv.:	5% to $5 + 10¢/sh.
Company Phone:	800-943-9715	**Discount (cash):**	0
Transfer Agent:	Bank of New York	**Discount (div.):**	0
Agent's Address:	P.O. Box 11258 New York, NY 10286	**Auto invest:**	Yes
		Auto invest fee:	$5 + 10¢/sh.
Agent's Phone:	888-269-2377	**Selling info:**	Sells weekly, by mail, at market, for $5 +10¢/sh.
Other than USA:	Yes		

Company:	**Banco Ganadero (preferred)**	**Safekeeping:**	Yes
		Invests:	Every 7 days beginning varies
Symbol:	BGA.P	**Minimum:**	$50
Exchange:	NYSE	**Maximum:**	$250,000/year
Industry:	Regional banks	**Min to qualify:**	1
Company Address:	c/o BNY,101 Barclay St.,22 West New York, NY 10286	**Fee on cash inv.:**	$5 + 10¢/sh.
		Fee on div. inv.:	5% to $5 + 10¢/sh.
Company Phone:	800-943-9715	**Discount (cash):**	0
Transfer Agent:	Bank of New York	**Discount (div.):**	0
Agent's Address:	P.O. Box 11258 New York, NY 10286	**Auto invest:**	Yes
		Auto invest fee:	$5 + 10¢/sh.
Agent's Phone:	888-269-2377	**Selling info:**	Sells weekly, by mail, at market, for $5 +10¢/sh.
Other than USA:	Yes		

Company:	**Banco Ind. Colombiano, S.A.**	**Safekeeping:**	Yes
		Invests:	Every 7 days beginning varies
Symbol:	CIB	**Minimum:**	$50
Exchange:	NYSE	**Maximum:**	$250,000/year
Industry:	Banking	**Min to qualify:**	1
Company Address:	c/o BNY,101 Barclay St.,22 West New York, NY 10286	**Fee on cash inv.:**	$5 + 10¢/sh.
		Fee on div. inv.:	5% to $5 + 10¢/sh.
Company Phone:	800-943-9715	**Discount (cash):**	0
Transfer Agent:	Bank of New York	**Discount (div.):**	0
Agent's Address:	P.O. Box 11258 New York, NY 10286	**Auto invest:**	Yes
		Auto invest fee:	$5 + 10¢/sh.
Agent's Phone:	888-269-2377	**Selling info:**	Sells weekly, by mail, at market, for $5 +10¢/sh.
Other than USA:	Yes		

Company:	**Banco Rio de la Plata, S.A.**	**Safekeeping:**	Yes
		Invests:	Every 7 days beginning varies
Symbol:	BRS	**Minimum:**	$50
Exchange:	NYSE	**Maximum:**	$250,000/year
Industry:	Banking	**Min to qualify:**	1
Company Address:	c/o BNY,101 Barclay St.,22 West	**Fee on cash inv.:**	$5 + 10¢/sh.
	New York, NY 10286	**Fee on div. inv.:**	5% to $5 + 10¢/sh.
Company Phone:	800-943-9715	**Discount (cash):**	0
Transfer Agent:	Bank of New York	**Discount (div.):**	0
Agent's Address:	P.O. Box 11258	**Auto invest:**	Yes
	New York, NY 10286	**Auto invest fee:**	$5 + 10¢/sh.
Agent's Phone:	888-269-2377	**Selling info:**	Sells weekly, by mail, at market,
Other than USA:	Yes		for $5 +10¢/sh.

Company:	**Banco Santander Central Hispano SA**	**Safekeeping:**	Yes
		Invests:	Every 7 days beginning varies
Symbol:	STD	**Minimum:**	$50
Exchange:	NYSE	**Maximum:**	$100,000/year
Industry:	Financial services	**Min to qualify:**	1
Company Address:	c/o Morgan Guaranty Trust,	**Fee on cash inv.:**	$5 + 12¢/sh.
	Box 9073	**Fee on div. inv.:**	5% to $2.50
	Boston, MA 02205-9948	**Discount (cash):**	0
Company Phone:	800-428-4237	**Discount (div.):**	0
Transfer Agent:	Morgan Guaranty Trust Co.	**Auto invest:**	Yes
Agent's Address:	P.O. Box 9073	**Auto invest fee:**	$5
	Boston, MA 02205-9948	**Selling info:**	Sells daily, by phone or mail, at
Agent's Phone:	800-428-4237		market, for $5 +12¢/sh.
Other than USA:	No		

Company:	**Banco Santiago**	**Safekeeping:**	Yes
Symbol:	SAN	**Invests:**	Every 7 days beginning varies
Exchange:	NYSE	**Minimum:**	$50
Industry:	Commercial banking, Chile	**Maximum:**	$100,000/year
Company Address:	c/o Morgan Guaranty Trust,	**Min to qualify:**	1
	Box 9073	**Fee on cash inv.:**	$5 + 12¢/sh.
	Boston, MA 02205-9948	**Fee on div. inv.:**	5% to $2.50
Company Phone:	800-428-4237	**Discount (cash):**	0
Transfer Agent:	Morgan Guaranty Trust Co.	**Discount (div.):**	0
Agent's Address:	P.O. Box 9073	**Auto invest:**	Yes
	Boston, MA 02205-9948	**Auto invest fee:**	$5
Agent's Phone:	800-428-4237	**Selling info:**	Sells daily, by phone or mail, at
Other than USA:	No		avg. price, for $5 +12¢/sh.

Company:	**Banco Wiese Limitado**	**Safekeeping:**	Yes
Symbol:	BWP	**Invests:**	Every 7 days beginning varies
Exchange:	NYSE	**Minimum:**	$50
Industry:	Commercial banking, Peru	**Maximum:**	$100,000/year
Company Address:	c/o Morgan Guaranty Trust,	**Min to qualify:**	1
	Box 9073	**Fee on cash inv.:**	$5 + 12¢/sh.
	Boston, MA 02205-9948	**Fee on div. inv.:**	5% to $2.50
Company Phone:	800-428-4237	**Discount (cash):**	0
Transfer Agent:	Morgan Guaranty Trust Co.	**Discount (div.):**	0
Agent's Address:	P.O. Box 9073	**Auto invest:**	Yes
	Boston, MA 02205-9948	**Auto invest fee:**	$5
Agent's Phone:	800-428-4237	**Selling info:**	Sells daily, by phone or mail, at
Other than USA:	No		avg. price, for $5 +12¢/sh.

Company:	**BancorpSouth, Inc.**	**Safekeeping:**	No
Symbol:	BXS	**Invests:**	Every 90 days beginning 4/1
Exchange:	NYSE	**Minimum:**	$25
Industry:	Banking	**Maximum:**	$5,000/quarter
Company Address:	One Mississippi Plaza, Box 789	**Min to qualify:**	1
	Tupelo, MS 38802	**Fee on cash inv.:**	0!
Company Phone:	601-680-2000 or 601-680-2370	**Fee on div. inv.:**	0!
Transfer Agent:	SunTrust Bank, Atlanta	**Discount (cash):**	0
Agent's Address:	P.O. Box 4625	**Discount (div.):**	0
	Atlanta, GA 30302	**Auto invest:**	Yes
Agent's Phone:	800-568-3476	**Auto invest fee:**	$0
Other than USA:	Yes	**Selling info:**	Sells weekly, by mail, at market, for 0!

Company:	**Bancroft Convertible Fund, Inc.**	**Safekeeping:**	No
		Invests:	Every 30 days beginning 1/30
Symbol:	BCV	**Minimum:**	$25
Exchange:	ASE	**Maximum:**	$5,000/month
Industry:	Closed end fund	**Min to qualify:**	1
Company Address:	c/o Davis-Dinsmore, 65 Madison	**Fee on cash inv.:**	5% to $3 + comm.
	Ave., Ste. 550	**Fee on div. inv.:**	0
	Morristown, NJ 07960-7308	**Discount (cash):**	0
Company Phone:	973-631-1177	**Discount (div.):**	0
Transfer Agent:	ChaseMellon Shareholder Services	**Auto invest:**	No
Agent's Address:	P.O. Box 3322	**Auto invest fee:**	
	South Hackensack, NJ 07606-9980	**Selling info:**	Sells monthly, by mail, at market, for fee + comm.
Agent's Phone:	800-526-0801		
Other than USA:	Yes		

Company:	**BancWest Corp.**	**Safekeeping:**	Yes
Symbol:	BWE	**Invests:**	Every 30 days beginning 1/5
Exchange:	OTC	**Minimum:**	$50
Industry:	Banking	**Maximum:**	$10,0000/quarter
Company Address:	999 Bishop St., 29th fl.	**Min to qualify:**	25
	Honolulu, HI 96813	**Fee on cash inv.:**	0!
Company Phone:	808-525-7000	**Fee on div. inv.:**	0!
Transfer Agent:	American Stock Transfer	**Discount (cash):**	0
Agent's Address:	40 Wall Street	**Discount (div.):**	0
	New York, NY 10005	**Auto invest:**	No
Agent's Phone:	800-278-4353	**Auto invest fee:**	0
Other than USA:	No	**Selling info:**	Sells within 10 bus. days, by mail, at market, for comm.

Company:	**Bandag Inc.**	**Safekeeping:**	Yes
Symbol:	BDG	**Invests:**	Every 30 days beginning 1/20
Exchange:	NYSE	**Minimum:**	$50
Industry:	Manufacturing	**Maximum:**	$10,000/quarter
Company Address:	2905 N. Hwy. 61	**Min to qualify:**	1
	Muscatine, IA 52761-5886	**Fee on cash inv.:**	0
Company Phone:	319-262-1344 or 319-262-1260	**Fee on div. inv.:**	0
Transfer Agent:	BankBoston (EquiServe)	**Discount (cash):**	0
Agent's Address:	P.O. Box 8040	**Discount (div.):**	0
	Boston, MA 02266-8040	**Auto invest:**	No
Agent's Phone:	800-730-4001	**Auto invest fee:**	$0
Other than USA:	Yes	**Selling info:**	Sells daily, by mail, at avg. price, for $1 to $10 + comm.

Company:	**Bandag Inc. A**	**Safekeeping:**	Yes
Symbol:	BDGA	**Invests:**	Every 30 days beginning 1/20
Exchange:	NYSE	**Minimum:**	$50
Industry:	Manufacturing	**Maximum:**	$10,000/quarter
Company Address:	2905 N. Hwy. 61	**Min to qualify:**	1
	Muscatine, IA 52761-5886	**Fee on cash inv.:**	0
Company Phone:	319-262-1344 or 319-262-1260	**Fee on div. inv.:**	0
Transfer Agent:	BankBoston (EquiServe)	**Discount (cash):**	0
Agent's Address:	P.O. Box 8040	**Discount (div.):**	0
	Boston, MA 02266-8040	**Auto invest:**	No
Agent's Phone:	800-730-4001	**Auto invest fee:**	$0
Other than USA:	Yes	**Selling info:**	Sells daily, by mail, at avg. price, for $1 to $10 + comm.

Company:	**Bando McGlocklin Capital Corp.**	**Safekeeping:**	Yes
		Invests:	Every 90 days beginning 2/1
Symbol:	BMCC	**Minimum:**	$25
Exchange:	OTC	**Maximum:**	$3,000/quarter
Industry:	Financial	**Min to qualify:**	1
Company Address:	Box 190	**Fee on cash inv.:**	0!
	Pewaukee, WI 53072-0190	**Fee on div. inv.:**	0!
Company Phone:	414-523-4300	**Discount (cash):**	0
Transfer Agent:	Firstar Bank Milwaukee, NA	**Discount (div.):**	0
Agent's Address:	P.O. Box 2077	**Auto invest:**	No
	Milwaukee, WI 53201-2077	**Auto invest fee:**	$0
Agent's Phone:	800-637-7549	**Selling info:**	Sells biweekly, by mail or fax, at
Other than USA:	Yes		market, for comm.

Company:	**Bangor Hydro Electric**	**Safekeeping:**	Yes
Symbol:	BGR	**Invests:**	Every 30 days beginning 1/20
Exchange:	NYSE	**Minimum:**	$25
Industry:	Utility-electric	**Maximum:**	$25,000/year
Company Address:	Box 1599	**Min to qualify:**	1
	Bangor, ME 04402-1599	**Fee on cash inv.:**	0!
Company Phone:	207-990-6936 or 207-945-5621	**Fee on div. inv.:**	0!
Transfer Agent:	Boston Eq. (EquiServe)	**Discount (cash):**	0
Agent's Address:	Mail Stop 45-02-64, P.O. Box 644	**Discount (div.):**	0
	Boston, MA 02102-0644	**Auto invest:**	Yes
Agent's Phone:	800-736-3001	**Auto invest fee:**	$0
Other than USA:	No	**Selling info:**	Sells every 10 bus. days, by mail, at market, for $10 + comm.

Company:	**Bank of America Corp.**	**Safekeeping:**	Yes
Symbol:	BAC	**Invests:**	Every 7 days beginning varies
Exchange:	NYSE	**Minimum:**	$50
Industry:	Banking	**Maximum:**	$120,000/year
Company Address:	100 North Tryon St., 18th Fl.	**Min to qualify:**	1
	Charlotte, NC 28255	**Fee on cash inv.:**	0
Company Phone:	800-521-3984 or 704-386-5667	**Fee on div. inv.:**	0
Transfer Agent:	ChaseMellon Shareholder Services	**Discount (cash):**	0
Agent's Address:	P.O. Box 3336	**Discount (div.):**	0
	South Hackensack, NJ 07606-1936	**Auto invest:**	Yes
Agent's Phone:	800-642-9855	**Auto invest fee:**	$0
Other than USA:	Yes	**Selling info:**	Sells weekly, by mail or phone, at avg. price, for $15 + 8¢/sh.

Company:	**Bank of Granite Corp.**	Safekeeping:	Yes
Symbol:	GRAN	Invests:	Every 90 days beginning 1/30
Exchange:	OTC	Minimum:	$100
Industry:	Bank holding company	Maximum:	$2,000/quarter
Company Address:	Box 128	Min to qualify:	100
	Granite Falls, NC 28630	Fee on cash inv.:	0!
Company Phone:	828-496-2000	Fee on div. inv.:	0!
Transfer Agent:	Registrar & Transfer Company	Discount (cash):	0
Agent's Address:	10 Commerce Drive	Discount (div.):	0
	Cranford, NJ 07016	Auto invest:	Yes
Agent's Phone:	800-368-5948	Auto invest fee:	$0
Other than USA:	Yes	Selling info:	Not available

Company:	**Bank of Ireland**	Safekeeping:	Yes
Symbol:	IRE	Invests:	Every 7 days beginning varies
Exchange:	NYSE	Minimum:	$50
Industry:	Money center banks	Maximum:	$250,000/year
Company Address:	c/o BNY,101 Barclay St.,22 West	Min to qualify:	1
	New York, NY 10286	Fee on cash inv.:	$5 + 10¢/sh.
Company Phone:	800-943-9715	Fee on div. inv.:	5% to $5 + 10¢/sh.
Transfer Agent:	Bank of New York	Discount (cash):	0
Agent's Address:	P.O. Box 11258	Discount (div.):	0
	New York, NY 10286	Auto invest:	Yes
Agent's Phone:	888-269-2377	Auto invest fee:	$5 + 10¢/sh.
Other than USA:	Yes	Selling info:	Sells weekly, by mail, at market, for $5 +10¢/sh.

Company:	**Bank of Montreal**	Safekeeping:	No
Symbol:	BMO	Invests:	Every 30 days beginning 1/29
Exchange:	NYSE	Minimum:	$0
Industry:	Banking	Maximum:	$40,000/year
Company Address:	129 Saint Jacques St.	Min to qualify:	1
	Montreal, Que. H2Y 1L6 Canada	Fee on cash inv.:	0!
Company Phone:	514-867-6786	Fee on div. inv.:	0!
Transfer Agent:	Trust Co.-Bank Montreal	Discount (cash):	0
Agent's Address:	"A" Level North, 129 Saint Jacques	Discount (div.):	0
	St.	Auto invest:	No
	Montreal, Quebec H2Y 1L6	Auto invest fee:	$0
Agent's Phone:	514-877-2500	Selling info:	Sells irregularly, by mail or fax, at market, for comm.
Other than USA:	Yes		

Company:	**Bank of New York**	Safekeeping:	Yes
Symbol:	BK	Invests:	Every 7 days beginning varies
Exchange:	NYSE	Minimum:	$50
Industry:	Banking	Maximum:	$150,000/year
Company Address:	One Wall St., 13th Fl.	Min to qualify:	1
	New York, NY 10286	Fee on cash inv.:	0!
Company Phone:	212-495-1784 or 212-815-2128	Fee on div. inv.:	0!
Transfer Agent:	Bank of New York	Discount (cash):	0
Agent's Address:	P.O.Box 11258, Church St. Station	Discount (div.):	0
	New York, NY 10286-1258	Auto invest:	Yes
Agent's Phone:	800-432-0140	Auto invest fee:	$0
Other than USA:	Yes	Selling info:	Sells weekly, by mail or phone, at market, for $10 + 5¢/sh.

Company:	**Bank of Tokyo-Mitsubishi**	Safekeeping:	Yes
Symbol:	MBK	Invests:	Every 7 days beginning varies
Exchange:	NYSE	Minimum:	$50
Industry:	Banking	Maximum:	$250,000/week
Company Address:	c/o BNY,101 Barclay St., 22 West	Min to qualify:	1
	New York, NY 10286	Fee on cash inv.:	$5 + 10¢/sh.
Company Phone:	212-815-2175	Fee on div. inv.:	5% to $5 + 10¢/sh.
Transfer Agent:	Bank of New York	Discount (cash):	0
Agent's Address:	P.O. Box 11258	Discount (div.):	0
	New York, NY 10286	Auto invest:	Yes
Agent's Phone:	888-269-2377	Auto invest fee:	$0
Other than USA:	Yes	Selling info:	Sells weekly, by phone or mail, at avg. price, for $5 +10¢/ADS

Company:	**Bank One Corp.**	Safekeeping:	Yes
Symbol:	ONE	Invests:	Every 30 days beginning varies
Exchange:	NYSE	Minimum:	$25
Industry:	Banking	Maximum:	$5,000/month
Company Address:	100 East Broad St.	Min to qualify:	1
	Columbus, OH 43271	Fee on cash inv.:	0!
Company Phone:	614-248-5944	Fee on div. inv.:	0!
Transfer Agent:	FCT (EquiServe)	Discount (cash):	0
Agent's Address:	P.O. Box 2598	Discount (div.):	0
	Jersey City, NJ 07303-2598	Auto invest:	Yes
Agent's Phone:	888-764-5592	Auto invest fee:	$0
Other than USA:	Yes	Selling info:	Sells daily, by mail or phone, at market, for $10 +12¢/sh.

Company:	**BankBoston Corp.**	Safekeeping:	Yes
Symbol:	BKB	Invests:	Every 15 days beginning 1/15
Exchange:	NYSE	Minimum:	$50
Industry:	Bank holding company	Maximum:	$100,000/year
Company Address:	100 Federal St.	Min to qualify:	1
	Boston, MA 02110	Fee on cash inv.:	0
Company Phone:	800-730-4001	Fee on div. inv.:	0
Transfer Agent:	BankBoston (EquiServe)	Discount (cash):	0
Agent's Address:	P.O. Box 644	Discount (div.):	0
	Boston, MA 02102-0644	Auto invest:	Yes
Agent's Phone:	800-730-4001	Auto invest fee:	$0
Other than USA:	Yes	Selling info:	Sells within 5 bus. days, by mail, at avg. price, for comm.

Company:	**Banknorth Group, Inc.**	Safekeeping:	Yes
Symbol:	BKNG	Invests:	Every 90 days beginning 3/1
Exchange:	OTC	Minimum:	$25
Industry:	Banking	Maximum:	$5,000/quarter
Company Address:	300 Financial Plaza, Box 5420	Min to qualify:	1
	Burlington, VT 05402	Fee on cash inv.:	0!
Company Phone:	802-658-9959 or 802-658-2492	Fee on div. inv.:	0!
Transfer Agent:	Registrar & Transfer Co.	Discount (cash):	0
Agent's Address:	10 Commerce Drive	Discount (div.):	0
	Cranford, NJ 07016	Auto invest:	No
Agent's Phone:	800-368-5948	Auto invest fee:	$0
Other than USA:	Yes	Selling info:	Sells within 10 bus. days, by mail, at market, for $3 + comm.

Company:	**Banta Corp.**	Safekeeping:	Yes
Symbol:	BN	Invests:	Every 30 days beginning 1/1
Exchange:	NYSE	Minimum:	$25
Industry:	Printing	Maximum:	$7,500/quarter
Company Address:	225 Main St., Box 8003	Min to qualify:	1
	Menasha, WI 54952-8003	Fee on cash inv.:	0
Company Phone:	920-751-7770 or 920-751-7777	Fee on div. inv.:	0
Transfer Agent:	Firstar Bank Milwaukee, NA	Discount (cash):	0
Agent's Address:	P.O. Box 2077	Discount (div.):	0
	Milwaukee, WI 53201-2077	Auto invest:	Yes
Agent's Phone:	800-637-7549	Auto invest fee:	$0
Other than USA:	Yes	Selling info:	Sells irregularly, by mail, at market, for comm.

Company:	**Banyan Strategic Realty Trust**	Safekeeping:	Yes
		Invests:	Every 30 days beginning 1/20
Symbol:	BSRTS	Minimum:	$5
Exchange:	OTC	Maximum:	$120,000/year
Industry:	Real estate operations	Min to qualify:	1
Company Address:	150 South Wacker Dr., Ste. 2900	Fee on cash inv.:	0!
	Chicago, IL 60606	Fee on div. inv.:	0!
Company Phone:	312-553-9800	Discount (cash):	0%
Transfer Agent:	FCT (EquiServe)	Discount (div.):	3%
Agent's Address:	P.O. Box 2500	Auto invest:	Yes
	Jersey City, NJ 07303-0498	Auto invest fee:	$0
Agent's Phone:	201-324-0498	Selling info:	Sells daily, by mail or phone, at market, for $10 +12¢/sh.
Other than USA:	No		

Company:	**Barclays Bank plc**	Safekeeping:	Yes
Symbol:	BCS	Invests:	Every 7 days beginning varies
Exchange:	NYSE	Minimum:	$50
Industry:	Commercial banking	Maximum:	$5,000/month
Company Address:	75 Wall St.	Min to qualify:	1
	New York, NY 10265	Fee on cash inv.:	$5 + 12¢/sh.
Company Phone:	800-428-4237	Fee on div. inv.:	5% to $2.50
Transfer Agent:	Morgan Guaranty Trust Co.	Discount (cash):	0
Agent's Address:	P.O. Box 9073	Discount (div.):	0
	Boston, MA 02205-9948	Auto invest:	Yes
Agent's Phone:	800-428-4237	Auto invest fee:	$5
Other than USA:	No U.S.	Selling info:	Sells daily, by phone or mail, at avg. price, for $5 +12¢/sh.

Company:	**Bard, Inc. (C.R.)**	Safekeeping:	Yes
Symbol:	BCR	Invests:	Every 7 days beginning varies
Exchange:	NYSE	Minimum:	$25
Industry:	Health care	Maximum:	$unlimited
Company Address:	730 Central Ave.	Min to qualify:	1
	Murray Hill, NJ 07974	Fee on cash inv.:	$5 + 10¢/sh.
Company Phone:	908-277-8000 or 908-277-8059	Fee on div. inv.:	0!
Transfer Agent:	FCT (EquiServe)	Discount (cash):	0
Agent's Address:	P.O. Box 2598	Discount (div.):	0
	Jersey City, NJ 07303-2598	Auto invest:	Yes
Agent's Phone:	800-446-2617	Auto invest fee:	$1 +3¢/sh.
Other than USA:	Yes	Selling info:	Sells daily, by phone or mail, at market, for $15 +12¢/sh.

Company:	**Barnes Group Inc.**	Safekeeping:	No
Symbol:	B	Invests:	Every 90 days beginning 3/10
Exchange:	NYSE	Minimum:	$10
Industry:	Precision metal parts mfg. and dist.	Maximum:	$10,000/quarter
Company Address:	123 Main St., Box 489	Min to qualify:	1
	Bristol, CT 06011-0489	Fee on cash inv.:	0!
Company Phone:	860-583-7070	Fee on div. inv.:	0!
Transfer Agent:	ChaseMellon Shareholder Services	Discount (cash):	0
Agent's Address:	85 Challenger Road,	Discount (div.):	0
	Overpeck Centre	Auto invest:	No
	Ridgefield Park, NJ 07660	Auto invest fee:	$0
Agent's Phone:	800-288-9541	Selling info:	Sells weekly, by mail , at avg.
Other than USA:	No		price, for comm.

Company:	**Bausch & Lomb**	Safekeeping:	Yes
Symbol:	BOL	Invests:	Every 30 days beginning 1/1
Exchange:	NYSE	Minimum:	$25
Industry:	Health care and optics	Maximum:	$5,000/month
Company Address:	One Bausch & Lomb Pl.	Min to qualify:	1
	Rochester, NY 14604-2701	Fee on cash inv.:	0!
Company Phone:	800-344-8815 or 716-338-6025	Fee on div. inv.:	0!
Transfer Agent:	ChaseMellon Shareholder Services	Discount (cash):	0
		Discount (div.):	0
Agent's Address:	P.O. Box 3338	Auto invest:	No
	South Hackensack, NJ 07606-1938	Auto invest fee:	$0
Agent's Phone:	800-288-9541	Selling info:	Sells weekly, by mail, at market,
Other than USA:	No		for 5% to $5

Company:	**Baxter International Inc.**	Safekeeping:	Yes
Symbol:	BAX	Invests:	Every 30 days beginning 1/4
Exchange:	NYSE	Minimum:	$25
Industry:	Health care	Maximum:	$25,000/year
Company Address:	One Baxter Pkwy.	Min to qualify:	1
	Deerfield, IL 60015-4633	Fee on cash inv.:	0!
Company Phone:	847-948-4551 or 847-948-2000	Fee on div. inv.:	0!
Transfer Agent:	FCT (EquiServe)	Discount (cash):	0
Agent's Address:	P.O. Box 2598	Discount (div.):	0
	Jersey City, NJ 07303-2598	Auto invest:	No
Agent's Phone:	800-446-2617 or 201-324-0498	Auto invest fee:	$0
Other than USA:	No	Selling info:	Sells daily, by mail or fax,
			at market, for 12¢/sh.

Company:	**BB&T Corp.**	Safekeeping:	Yes
Symbol:	BBT	Invests:	Every 15 days beginning 1/1
Exchange:	NYSE	Minimum:	$25
Industry:	Banking	Maximum:	$10,000/month
Company Address:	Box 1489	Min to qualify:	1
	Lumberton, NC 28359-1489	Fee on cash inv.:	0
Company Phone:	910-671-2273 or 910-671-2283	Fee on div. inv.:	0
Transfer Agent:	Branch Bkg. & Trust Co., Corporate Trust Dept.	Discount (cash):	0
		Discount (div.):	0
Agent's Address:	Div. Reinvestment Plan, Box 2887	Auto invest:	Yes
	Wilson, NC 27894-2887	Auto invest fee:	$0
Agent's Phone:	910-671-2273	Selling info:	Sells bimonthly, by mail or fax, at
Other than USA:	No		avg. price, for 7¢/sh.

Company:	**BC Gas, Inc.**	Safekeeping:	No
Symbol:	BCG	Invests:	Every 90 days beginning 2/28
Exchange:	TSE	Minimum:	$0
Industry:	Energy & utility services	Maximum:	$20,000/year Cdn.
Company Address:	1111 West Georgia St.	Min to qualify:	1
	Vancouver, B.C. V6E 4M4 Canada	Fee on cash inv.:	0
Company Phone:	800-667-9177or 604-443-6559	Fee on div. inv.:	0
Transfer Agent:	CIBC Mellon Trust	Discount (cash):	0
Agent's Address:	Mall Level 1177 West Hastings St.	Discount (div.):	0
	Vancouver, B. C. V6E 2K3 Canada	Auto invest:	No
Agent's Phone:	800-387-0825	Auto invest fee:	$0
Other than USA:	No U S res	Selling info:	Not available

Company:	**BCE Inc.**	Safekeeping:	No
Symbol:	BCE	Invests:	Every 30 days beginning 1/16
Exchange:	NYSE	Minimum:	$0
Industry:	Telecommunications	Maximum:	$20,000/year
Company Address:	1000 rue de La Gauchetiere O.,	Min to qualify:	1
	Bureau 3700	Fee on cash inv.:	0
	Montreal, Que. H3B 4Y7 Canada	Fee on div. inv.:	0
Company Phone:	800-339-6353 or 514-397-7314	Discount (cash):	0
Transfer Agent:	Montreal Trust Company	Discount (div.):	0
Agent's Address:	P.O. Box 1100 Station B	Auto invest:	No
	Montreal, Que. H3B 3K9 Canada	Auto invest fee:	$0
Agent's Phone:	800-561-0934 or 514-982-7555 (out US)	Selling info:	Sells daily, by mail or fax, at avg. price, for 3¢/sh.
Other than USA:	Yes		

Company:	**BEC Energy**	Safekeeping:	Yes
Symbol:	BSE	Invests:	Every 30 days beginning 1/1
Exchange:	NYSE	Minimum:	$50
Industry:	Utility-electric	Maximum:	$40,000/year
Company Address:	800 Boylston St.	Min to qualify:	1
	Boston, MA 02199-8003	Fee on cash inv.:	0!
Company Phone:	617-424-2658 or 617-424-3562	Fee on div. inv.:	0!
Transfer Agent:	BankBoston (EquiServe)	Discount (cash):	0
Agent's Address:	P.O.Box 8040	Discount (div.):	0
	Boston, MA 02266-8040	Auto invest:	Yes
Agent's Phone:	800-338-8446	Auto invest fee:	$0
Other than USA:	Yes	Selling info:	Sells daily, by mail, at market, for 5% to $15

Company:	**Beckman Coulter Inc.**	Safekeeping:	Yes
Symbol:	BEC	Invests:	Every 30 days beginning 1/8
Exchange:	NYSE	Minimum:	$10
Industry:	Mfr. lab instr.	Maximum:	$60,000/year
Company Address:	4300 N. Harbor Blvd., Box 3100	Min to qualify:	1
	Fullerton, CA 92834-3100	Fee on cash inv.:	0!
Company Phone:	714-871-4848 or 714-773-7620	Fee on div. inv.:	0!
Transfer Agent:	FCT (EquiServe)	Discount (cash):	0
Agent's Address:	P.O. Box 2500	Discount (div.):	0
	Jersey City, NJ 07303-2500	Auto invest:	Yes
Agent's Phone:	201-324-1644	Auto invest fee:	$0
Other than USA:	Yes	Selling info:	Sells daily, by mail, phone, or fax, at market, for 0

Company:	**Becton Dickinson and Co.**	**Safekeeping:**	Yes
Symbol:	BDX	**Invests:**	Every 7 days beginning varies
Exchange:	NYSE	**Minimum:**	$50
Industry:	Health care	**Maximum:**	$unlimited
Company Address:	1 Becton Dr.	**Min to qualify:**	1
	Franklin Lakes, NJ 07417-1880	**Fee on cash inv.:**	3¢/sh.
Company Phone:	800-284-6845 or 201-847-6800 or	**Fee on div. inv.:**	3¢/sh.
	201-847-5873	**Discount (cash):**	0
Transfer Agent:	FCT (EquiServe)	**Discount (div.):**	0
Agent's Address:	P.O. Box 2598	**Auto invest:**	Yes
	Jersey City, NJ 07303-2598	**Auto invest fee:**	3¢/sh.
Agent's Phone:	800-955-4743	**Selling info:**	Sells daily, by mail or phone, at
Other than USA:	Yes		market, for $15 +15¢/sh.

Company:	**Bedford Property**	**Safekeeping:**	Yes
	Investors	**Invests:**	Every 30 days beginning 1/15
Symbol:	BED	**Minimum:**	$100
Exchange:	NYSE	**Maximum:**	$5,000/month
Industry:	Real estate, commercial	**Min to qualify:**	1
Company Address:	270 Lafayette Circle	**Fee on cash inv.:**	0
	Lafayette, CA 94549	**Fee on div. inv.:**	0
Company Phone:	925-283-8910	**Discount (cash):**	0
Transfer Agent:	ChaseMellon Shareholder Services	**Discount (div.):**	0
Agent's Address:	P.O. Box 3315	**Auto invest:**	No
	South Hackensack, NJ 07606	**Auto invest fee:**	$0
Agent's Phone:	800-774-5476	**Selling info:**	Sells weekly, by mail or phone, at
Other than USA:	No		market, for $15 +12¢/sh.

Company:	**Beijing Yanhua Pet. Co.**	**Safekeeping:**	Yes
	Ltd.	**Invests:**	Every 7 days beginning varies
Symbol:	BYH	**Minimum:**	$50
Exchange:	NYSE	**Maximum:**	$250,000/year
Industry:	Chemicals, plastics & rubber	**Min to qualify:**	1
Company Address:	c/o BNY,101 Barclay St.,22 West	**Fee on cash inv.:**	$5 + 10¢/sh.
	New York, NY 10286	**Fee on div. inv.:**	5% to $5 + 10¢/sh.
Company Phone:	800-943-9715	**Discount (cash):**	0
Transfer Agent:	Bank of New York	**Discount (div.):**	0
Agent's Address:	P.O. Box 11258	**Auto invest:**	Yes
	New York, NY 10286	**Auto invest fee:**	$5 + 10¢/sh.
Agent's Phone:	888-269-2377	**Selling info:**	Sells weekly, by mail, at market,
Other than USA:	Yes		for $5 +10¢/sh.

Company:	**Bell Atlantic**	**Safekeeping:**	Yes
Symbol:	BEL	**Invests:**	Every 7 days beginning Monday
Exchange:	NYSE	**Minimum:**	$50
Industry:	Telecommunications	**Maximum:**	$200,000/year
Company Address:	1095 Ave.of the Americas, Rm.	**Min to qualify:**	2
	3619	**Fee on cash inv.:**	$2.50 + 3¢/sh.
	New York, NY 10036	**Fee on div. inv.:**	$1 to $2 + 3¢/sh.
Company Phone:	212-395-2121 or 212-395-1525	**Discount (cash):**	0
Transfer Agent:	BankBoston (EquiServe)	**Discount (div.):**	0
Agent's Address:	P.O. Box 8038	**Auto invest:**	Yes
	Boston, MA 02266-8038	**Auto invest fee:**	$1
Agent's Phone:	800-631-2355	**Selling info:**	Sells weekly, by phone or mail, at
Other than USA:	Yes		avg. price, for $10 + 7¢/sh.

Company:	**BellSouth Corp.**	Safekeeping:	Yes
Symbol:	BLS	Invests:	Every 7 days beginning varies
Exchange:	NYSE	Minimum:	$50
Industry:	Telecommunications	Maximum:	$100,000/year
Company Address:	1155 Peachtree St. N.E., Rm.14B06	Min to qualify:	1
	Atlanta, GA 30309-3610	Fee on cash inv.:	3¢/sh.
Company Phone:	800-631-6001 or 404-249-2410	Fee on div. inv.:	3¢/sh.
Transfer Agent:	ChaseMellon Shareholder Services	Discount (cash):	0
Agent's Address:	P.O. Box 3341	Discount (div.):	0
	South Hackensack, NJ 07606	Auto invest:	Yes
Agent's Phone:	800-631-6001	Auto invest fee:	$0
Other than USA:	Yes	Selling info:	Sells daily, by mail or phone, at avg. price, for $10 + 8¢/sh.

Company:	**Bemis Co., Inc.**	Safekeeping:	Yes
Symbol:	BMS	Invests:	Every 30 days beginning 1/1
Exchange:	NYSE	Minimum:	$25
Industry:	Packaging	Maximum:	$10,000/quarter
Company Address:	222 South Ninth St., Ste. 2300	Min to qualify:	1
	Minneapolis, MN 55402-4099	Fee on cash inv.:	0
Company Phone:	612-376-3007 or 612-376-3030	Fee on div. inv.:	0
Transfer Agent:	Norwest Bank Minnesota	Discount (cash):	0
Agent's Address:	P.O. Box 738	Discount (div.):	0
	South St. Paul, MN 55075-0738	Auto invest:	No
Agent's Phone:	800-551-6161	Auto invest fee:	$0
Other than USA:	No	Selling info:	Sells daily, by phone, mail, or fax, at avg. price, for $3 +15¢/sh.

Company:	**Benckiser N.V.**	Safekeeping:	Yes
Symbol:	BNV	Invests:	Every 7 days beginning varies
Exchange:	NYSE	Minimum:	$50
Industry:	Manufacturing home cleaning	Maximum:	$100,000/year
	products	Min to qualify:	1
Company Address:	c/o Morgan Guaranty Trust,	Fee on cash inv.:	$5 + 12¢/sh.
	Box 9073	Fee on div. inv.:	5% to $2.50
	Boston, MA 02205-9948	Discount (cash):	0
Company Phone:	800-428-4237	Discount (div.):	0
Transfer Agent:	Morgan Guaranty Trust Co.	Auto invest:	Yes
Agent's Address:	P.O. Box 9073	Auto invest fee:	$5
	Boston, MA 02205-9948	Selling info:	Sells daily, by phone or mail, at market, for $5 +12¢/sh.
Agent's Phone:	800-428-4237		
Other than USA:	No		

Company:	**Benetton Grp. SpA**	Safekeeping:	Yes
Symbol:	BNG	Invests:	Every 7 days beginning varies
Exchange:	NYSE	Minimum:	$50
Industry:	Clothing manufacturer	Maximum:	$100,000/year
Company Address:	c/o Morgan Guaranty Trust, Box	Min to qualify:	1
	9073	Fee on cash inv.:	$5 + 12¢/sh.
	Boston, MA 02205-9948	Fee on div. inv.:	5% to $2.50
Company Phone:	800-428-4237	Discount (cash):	0
Transfer Agent:	Morgan Guaranty Trust Co.	Discount (div.):	0
Agent's Address:	P.O. Box 9073	Auto invest:	Yes
	Boston, MA 02205-9948	Auto invest fee:	$5
Agent's Phone:	800-428-4237	Selling info:	Sells daily, by phone or mail, at avg. price, for $5 +12¢/sh.
Other than USA:	No		

Company:	**Berkshire Energy Resources**	**Safekeeping:**	No
Symbol:	BERK	**Invests:**	Every 30 days beginning 1/15
Exchange:	OTC	**Minimum:**	$15
Industry:	Utility-gas	**Maximum:**	$5,000/quarter
Company Address:	115 Cheshire Rd.	**Min to qualify:**	10
	Pittsfield, MA 01201-1803	**Fee on cash inv.:**	0!
Company Phone:	800-292-5019 or 413-442-1511	**Fee on div. inv.:**	0!
Transfer Agent:	State Street Bank (EquiServe)	**Discount (cash):**	3%
Agent's Address:	P.O. Box 8209	**Discount (div.):**	3%
	Boston, MA 02101-8209	**Auto invest:**	No
Agent's Phone:	800-426-5523	**Auto invest fee:**	$0
Other than USA:	Yes	**Selling info:**	Sells daily, by mail, at market, for 5% to $5 +15¢/sh.

Company:	**Berkshire Realty Co.,Inc.**	**Safekeeping:**	Yes
Symbol:	BRI	**Invests:**	Every 15 days beginning 1/1
Exchange:	NYSE	**Minimum:**	$10
Industry:	REIT	**Maximum:**	$unlimited
Company Address:	One Beacon St., Ste. 1550	**Min to qualify:**	1
	Boston, MA 02108	**Fee on cash inv.:**	0
Company Phone:	888-867-0100 or 800-343-0989	**Fee on div. inv.:**	0
Transfer Agent:	American Stock Transfer	**Discount (cash):**	0
Agent's Address:	40 Wall St., 46th Fl.	**Discount (div.):**	0
	New York, NY 10005	**Auto invest:**	No
Agent's Phone:	800-937-5449	**Auto invest fee:**	$0
Other than USA:	Yes	**Selling info:**	Sells irregularly, by mail, at market, for $5 + 4¢/sh.

Company:	**Bestfoods**	**Safekeeping:**	Yes
Symbol:	BFO	**Invests:**	Every 30 days beginning 1/25
Exchange:	NYSE	**Minimum:**	$25
Industry:	Grocery	**Maximum:**	$25,000/year
Company Address:	International Plz., 700 Sylvan Ave.	**Min to qualify:**	1
	Englewood Cliffs, NJ 07632-9976	**Fee on cash inv.:**	0
Company Phone:	201-894-2837	**Fee on div. inv.:**	0
Transfer Agent:	FCT (EquiServe)	**Discount (cash):**	0
Agent's Address:	P.O. Box 2500	**Discount (div.):**	0
	Jersey City, NJ 07303	**Auto invest:**	Yes
Agent's Phone:	888-756-2632 or 800-519-3111	**Auto invest fee:**	$1
Other than USA:	Yes	**Selling info:**	Sells daily, by phone or mail, at market, for $10 +12¢/sh.

Company:	**Bethlehem Steel**	**Safekeeping:**	Yes
Symbol:	BS	**Invests:**	Every 30 days beginning 1/1
Exchange:	NYSE	**Minimum:**	$10
Industry:	Steel	**Maximum:**	$3,000/month
Company Address:	1170 Eighth Ave.	**Min to qualify:**	1
	Bethlehem, PA 18016-7699	**Fee on cash inv.:**	0!
Company Phone:	610-694-2261	**Fee on div. inv.:**	0!
Transfer Agent:	FCT (EquiServe)	**Discount (cash):**	0
Agent's Address:	P.O. Box 2500	**Discount (div.):**	0
	Jersey City, NJ 07303-2500	**Auto invest:**	No
Agent's Phone:	201-324-1225	**Auto invest fee:**	$0
Other than USA:	No	**Selling info:**	Sells daily, by mail, at market, for $10 +12¢/sh.

Company:	**Bindley Western Industries, Inc.**	Safekeeping:	Yes
		Invests:	Every 90 days beginning 3/29
Symbol:	BDY	Minimum:	$10
Exchange:	NYSE	Maximum:	$5,000/quarter
Industry:	Drug distribution	Min to qualify:	1
Company Address:	8909 Purdue Rd.	Fee on cash inv.:	0
	Indianapolis, IN 46268	Fee on div. inv.:	0
Company Phone:	317-704-4000 or 317-704-4305	Discount (cash):	0
Transfer Agent:	Harris Trust & Savings Bank	Discount (div.):	0
Agent's Address:	311 W. Monroe St. 11th Fl.,	Auto invest:	No
	Box A3504	Auto invest fee:	$0
	Chicago, IL 60690-3504	Selling info:	Sells weekly, by mail, at avg. price,
Agent's Phone:	800-942-5909		for $0
Other than USA:	Yes		

Company:	**Biora AB**	Safekeeping:	Yes
Symbol:	BIORY	Invests:	Every 7 days beginning varies
Exchange:	OTC	Minimum:	$50
Industry:	Develops, manufactures and sells	Maximum:	$250,000/week
	pharmaceutical products	Min to qualify:	1
Company Address:	c/o BNY,101 Barclay St.,22 West	Fee on cash inv.:	$5 + 10¢/sh.
	New York, NY 10286	Fee on div. inv.:	0
Company Phone:	800-943-9715	Discount (cash):	0
Transfer Agent:	Bank of New York	Discount (div.):	0
Agent's Address:	P.O. Box 11258	Auto invest:	Yes
	New York, NY 10286	Auto invest fee:	$0
Agent's Phone:	888-269-2377	Selling info:	Sells daily, by phone or mail, at
Other than USA:	Yes		market, for $5 +10¢/ADS

Company:	**Biper, SA de C.V.**	Safekeeping:	Yes
Symbol:	BIPRY	Invests:	Every 7 days beginning varies
Exchange:	OTC	Minimum:	$50
Industry:	Paging services	Maximum:	$250,000/year
Company Address:	c/o BNY,101 Barclay St.,22 West	Min to qualify:	1
	New York, NY 10286	Fee on cash inv.:	$5 + 10¢/sh.
Company Phone:	800-943-9715	Fee on div. inv.:	5% to $5 + 10¢/sh.
Transfer Agent:	Bank of New York	Discount (cash):	0
Agent's Address:	P.O. Box 11258	Discount (div.):	0
	New York, NY 10286	Auto invest:	Yes
Agent's Phone:	888-269-2377	Auto invest fee:	$5 + 10¢/sh.
Other than USA:	Yes	Selling info:	Sells weekly, by mail, at market,
			for $5 +10¢/sh.

Company:	**Birmingham Steel Corp.**	Safekeeping:	Yes
Symbol:	BIR	Invests:	Every 30 days beginning
Exchange:	NYSE	Minimum:	$20
Industry:	Produces steel & steel products	Maximum:	$2,000/month
Company Address:	1000 Urban Ctr. Pkwy., Ste. 300	Min to qualify:	1
	Birmingham, AL 35242-2516	Fee on cash inv.:	0!
Company Phone:	205-970-1200	Fee on div. inv.:	0!
Transfer Agent:	First Union National Bank	Discount (cash):	0
Agent's Address:	2 First Union Center, CMG-5	Discount (div.):	0
	Charlotte, NC 28288-1154	Auto invest:	No
Agent's Phone:	800-829-8432	Auto invest fee:	$0
Other than USA:	Yes	Selling info:	Sells bimonthly, by mail,
			at market, for fee + 5¢/sh.

Company:	**Black & Decker**		Safekeeping:	Yes
Symbol:	BDK		Invests:	Every 30 days beginning 4th Friday
Exchange:	NYSE		Minimum:	$50
Industry:	Home appl. & power tools		Maximum:	$60,000/year
Company Address:	701 East Joppa Rd., TW 266		Min to qualify:	1
	Towson, MD 21286		Fee on cash inv.:	0
Company Phone:	410-716-3979 or 410-716-3900		Fee on div. inv.:	0
Transfer Agent:	FCT (EquiServe)		Discount (cash):	0
Agent's Address:	P.O. Box 2500		Discount (div.):	0
	Jersey City, NJ 07303-2500		Auto invest:	Yes
Agent's Phone:	800-519-3111		Auto invest fee:	$1
Other than USA:	Yes		Selling info:	Sells daily, by phone or mail, at market, for $10 + comm.

Company:	**Black Hills Corp.**		Safekeeping:	Yes
Symbol:	BKH		Invests:	Every 30 days beginning 1/1
Exchange:	NYSE		Minimum:	$200
Industry:	Utility-electric		Maximum:	$50,000/quarter
Company Address:	Box 1400		Min to qualify:	1
	Rapid City, SD 57709		Fee on cash inv.:	0
Company Phone:	605-348-1700		Fee on div. inv.:	0
Transfer Agent:	Norwest Bank Minnesota		Discount (cash):	0
Agent's Address:	P.O. Box 64854		Discount (div.):	0
	St. Paul, MN 55164-0854		Auto invest:	No
Agent's Phone:	800-468-9716		Auto invest fee:	$0
Other than USA:	Yes		Selling info:	Sells weekly, by mail, at avg. price, for $15 + comm.

Company:	**Block (H&R)**		Safekeeping:	Yes
Symbol:	HRB		Invests:	Every 30 days beginning 1/31
Exchange:	NYSE		Minimum:	$25
Industry:	Tax & financial services		Maximum:	$2,000/month
Company Address:	4400 Main St.		Min to qualify:	1
	Kansas City, MO 64111		Fee on cash inv.:	3¢/sh.
Company Phone:	816-753-6900		Fee on div. inv.:	7¢/sh.
Transfer Agent:	ChaseMellon Shareholder Services		Discount (cash):	0
Agent's Address:	P.O. Box 3338		Discount (div.):	0
	South Hackensack, Nj 07606-1938		Auto invest:	No
Agent's Phone:	888-213-0968		Auto invest fee:	$0
Other than USA:	Yes		Selling info:	Sells 10 to 12 bus.days, by mail or phone, at market, for 7¢/sh.

Company:	**Blount Int'l,Inc. A**		Safekeeping:	No
Symbol:	BLTA		Invests:	Every 30 days beginning 1/1
Exchange:	NYSE		Minimum:	$10
Industry:	Diversified manufacturer		Maximum:	$25,000/year
Company Address:	4520 Executive Park Dr.		Min to qualify:	1
	Montgomery, AL 36116-1602		Fee on cash inv.:	0!
Company Phone:	334-244-4338 or 334-244-4229		Fee on div. inv.:	0!
Transfer Agent:	Boston Eq. (EquiServe)		Discount (cash):	0
Agent's Address:	Box 8040		Discount (div.):	5%
	Boston, MA 02266-8040		Auto invest:	No
Agent's Phone:	800-730-4001		Auto invest fee:	$0
Other than USA:	Yes		Selling info:	Sells daily, by mail, at market, for $0

Company:	**Blount Int'l,Inc. B**	**Safekeeping:**	No
Symbol:	BLTB	**Invests:**	Every 30 days beginning 1/1
Exchange:	NYSE	**Minimum:**	$10
Industry:	Diversified manufacturer	**Maximum:**	$25,000/year
Company Address:	4520 Executive Park Dr.	**Min to qualify:**	1
	Montgomery, AL 36116-1602	**Fee on cash inv.:**	0
Company Phone:	334-244-4000 or 334-244-4229	**Fee on div. inv.:**	0
Transfer Agent:	Boston Eq. (EquiServe)	**Discount (cash):**	0
Agent's Address:	Mail Stop: 45-02-09 P.O. Box 644	**Discount (div.):**	5%
	Boston, MA 02105-0644	**Auto invest:**	No
Agent's Phone:	800-730-4001	**Auto invest fee:**	$0
Other than USA:	Yes	**Selling info:**	Sells daily, by mail, at market, for $0

Company:	**Blue Square-Israel Ltd.**	**Safekeeping:**	Yes
Symbol:	BSI	**Invests:**	Every 7 days beginning varies
Exchange:	NYSE	**Minimum:**	$50
Industry:	Operator of Israeli retail stores	**Maximum:**	$250,000/week
Company Address:	c/o BNY,101 Barclay St.,22 West	**Min to qualify:**	1
	New York, NY 10286	**Fee on cash inv.:**	$5 + 10¢/sh.
Company Phone:	800-943-9715	**Fee on div. inv.:**	5% to $5 + 10¢/sh.
Transfer Agent:	Bank of New York	**Discount (cash):**	0
Agent's Address:	P.O. Box 11258	**Discount (div.):**	0
	New York, NY 10286	**Auto invest:**	Yes
Agent's Phone:	888-269-2377	**Auto invest fee:**	$0
Other than USA:	Yes	**Selling info:**	Sells weekly, by phone or mail, at market, for $5 +10¢/ADS

Company:	**Blyth Industries, Inc.**	**Safekeeping:**	Yes
Symbol:	BTH	**Invests:**	Every 30 days beginning varies
Exchange:	NYSE	**Minimum:**	$50
Industry:	Manufactures and dist. candles &	**Maximum:**	$10,000/month
	home fragrance products	**Min to qualify:**	1
Company Address:	100 Field Point Rd.	**Fee on cash inv.:**	$5 + 10¢/sh.
	Greenwich, CT 06830	**Fee on div. inv.:**	0
Company Phone:	203-661-1926	**Discount (cash):**	0
Transfer Agent:	Harris Bank & Trust	**Discount (div.):**	0
Agent's Address:	P.O. Box A3309	**Auto invest:**	Yes
	Chicago, IL 60690-3309	**Auto invest fee:**	$1.50 + 10¢/sh.
Agent's Phone:	877-424-1968	**Selling info:**	Sells within 5 bus. days, by mail, at avg. price, for $10 +10¢/sh.
Other than USA:	Yes		

Company:	**Bob Evans Farms**	**Safekeeping:**	Yes
Symbol:	BOBE	**Invests:**	Every 15 days beginning 1/1
Exchange:	OTC	**Minimum:**	$10
Industry:	Restaurant & sausage mfg.	**Maximum:**	$10,000/month
Company Address:	3776 South High St.	**Min to qualify:**	1
	Columbus, OH 43207-0863	**Fee on cash inv.:**	0!
Company Phone:	614-491-2225	**Fee on div. inv.:**	0!
Transfer Agent:	Bob Evans Farms Inc. Attn: Stock	**Discount (cash):**	0
	Transfer Dept.	**Discount (div.):**	0
Agent's Address:	3776 S. High St.	**Auto invest:**	Yes
	Columbus, OH 43207	**Auto invest fee:**	$0
Agent's Phone:	800-272-7675 or 614-492-4951	**Selling info:**	Sells weekly, by mail or fax, at market, for comm.
Other than USA:	Yes		

Company:	**BOC Group plc (The)**	**Safekeeping:**	Yes
Symbol:	BOX	**Invests:**	Every 7 days beginning varies
Exchange:	NYSE	**Minimum:**	$50
Industry:	Chemicals	**Maximum:**	$100,000/year
Company Address:	c/o Morgan Guaranty Trust,	**Min to qualify:**	1
	Box 9073	**Fee on cash inv.:**	$5 + 12¢/sh.
	Boston, MA 02205-9948	**Fee on div. inv.:**	5% to $2.50
Company Phone:	800-428-4237	**Discount (cash):**	0
Transfer Agent:	Morgan Guaranty Trust Co.	**Discount (div.):**	0
Agent's Address:	P.O. Box 9073	**Auto invest:**	Yes
	Boston, MA 02205-9948	**Auto invest fee:**	$5
Agent's Phone:	800-428-4237	**Selling info:**	Sells daily, by phone or mail, at
Other than USA:	No		avg. price, for $5 +12¢/sh.

Company:	**Boddie-Noell Properties**	**Safekeeping:**	Yes
Symbol:	BNP	**Invests:**	Every 90 days beginning 2/15
Exchange:	ASE	**Minimum:**	$25
Industry:	REIT	**Maximum:**	$10,000/quarter
Company Address:	3850 One First Union Ctr.	**Min to qualify:**	1
	Charlotte, NC 28202-6032	**Fee on cash inv.:**	0
Company Phone:	704-944-0100	**Fee on div. inv.:**	0
Transfer Agent:	First Union National Bank of NC	**Discount (cash):**	0
Agent's Address:	1525 West W.T. Harris Blvd, 3C3	**Discount (div.):**	0
	Charlotte, NC 28288-1153	**Auto invest:**	No
Agent's Phone:	800-829-8432	**Auto invest fee:**	$0
Other than USA:	Yes	**Selling info:**	Sells within 10 bus. days, by mail
			or fax, at market, for comm.

Company:	**Boeing Co. (The)**	**Safekeeping:**	Yes
Symbol:	BA	**Invests:**	Every 7 days beginning Friday
Exchange:	NYSE	**Minimum:**	$50
Industry:	Aerospace	**Maximum:**	$100,000/year
Company Address:	Box 3707, MC 13-08	**Min to qualify:**	1
	Seattle, WA 98124-2207	**Fee on cash inv.:**	$1 + comm.
Company Phone:	206-655-1990 or 206-655-2121	**Fee on div. inv.:**	$1 + comm.
Transfer Agent:	BankBoston (EquiServe)	**Discount (cash):**	0
Agent's Address:	P.O. Box 8040, Mail Stop 45-02-64	**Discount (div.):**	0
	Boston, MA 02266-8040	**Auto invest:**	Yes
Agent's Phone:	888-777-0923	**Auto invest fee:**	$0
Other than USA:	Yes	**Selling info:**	Sells daily, by mail, at avg. price,
			for $10 + 5¢/sh.

Company:	**Boise Cascade Corp.**	**Safekeeping:**	Yes
Symbol:	BCC	**Invests:**	Every 30 days beginning 1/15
Exchange:	NYSE	**Minimum:**	$10
Industry:	Paper & lumber products	**Maximum:**	$unlimited
Company Address:	1111 West Jefferson St., Box 50	**Min to qualify:**	1
	Boise, ID 83728-0001	**Fee on cash inv.:**	comm.
Company Phone:	800-544-6473 or 208-384-6161	**Fee on div. inv.:**	comm.
Transfer Agent:	Boise Cascade Corp.	**Discount (cash):**	0
Agent's Address:	P.O. Box 50	**Discount (div.):**	0
	Boise, ID 83728-0001	**Auto invest:**	No
Agent's Phone:	800-544-6473 or 208-384-7590	**Auto invest fee:**	$0
Other than USA:	Yes	**Selling info:**	Sells monthly, by mail or fax, at
			market, for comm.

Company:	**Boral Limited**	Safekeeping:	Yes
Symbol:	BORAY	Invests:	Every 7 days beginning varies
Exchange:	OTC	Minimum:	$50
Industry:	Building & construction	Maximum:	$250,000/week
	materials, energy	Min to qualify:	1
Company Address:	c/o BNY,101 Barclay St.,22 West	Fee on cash inv.:	$5 + 10¢/sh.
	New York, NY 10286	Fee on div. inv.:	5% to $5 + 10¢/sh.
Company Phone:	800-943-9715	Discount (cash):	0
Transfer Agent:	Bank of New York	Discount (div.):	0
Agent's Address:	P.O. Box 11258	Auto invest:	Yes
	New York, NY 10286	Auto invest fee:	$0
Agent's Phone:	888-269-2377	Selling info:	Sells weekly, by phone or mail, at
Other than USA:	Yes		market, for $5 +10¢/ADS

Company:	**Borg-Warner Automotive**	Safekeeping:	Yes
Symbol:	BWA	Invests:	Every 7 days beginning varies
Exchange:	NYSE	Minimum:	$50
Industry:	Auto powertrain components	Maximum:	$120,000/year
Company Address:	200 South Michigan Ave.	Min to qualify:	1
	Chicago, IL 60604	Fee on cash inv.:	0
Company Phone:	312-322-8536	Fee on div. inv.:	0
Transfer Agent:	ChaseMellon Shareholder Services	Discount (cash):	0
Agent's Address:	P.O. Box 382009	Discount (div.):	0
	Pittsburgh, PA 15250	Auto invest:	Yes
Agent's Phone:	800-851-4229	Auto invest fee:	$0
Other than USA:	Yes	Selling info:	Sells daily, by mail or phone, at
			market, for $15 +12¢/sh.

Company:	**Boston Beer Co. (The)**	Safekeeping:	Yes
Symbol:	SAM	Invests:	Every 7 days beginning varies
Exchange:	NYSE	Minimum:	$50
Industry:	Largest draft brewer in U.S.	Maximum:	$10,000/month
Company Address:	75 Arlington St.	Min to qualify:	1
	Boston, MA 02116	Fee on cash inv.:	$3 + 12¢/sh.
Company Phone:	617-368-5188 or 617-368-5000	Fee on div. inv.:	0
Transfer Agent:	ChaseMellon Shareholder Services	Discount (cash):	0
Agent's Address:	85 Challenger Road,	Discount (div.):	0
	Overpeck Centre	Auto invest:	Yes
	Ridgefield Park, NJ 07660	Auto invest fee:	$3 + 12¢/sh.
Agent's Phone:	888-877-2890	Selling info:	Sells weekly, by mail or phone, at
Other than USA:	Yes		market, for $25 +12¢/sh.

Company:	**Bowater Inc.**	Safekeeping:	No
Symbol:	BOW	Invests:	Every 30 days beginning 1/1
Exchange:	NYSE	Minimum:	$100
Industry:	Paper	Maximum:	$5,000/month
Company Address:	55 E. Camperdown Way, Box 1028	Min to qualify:	1
	Greenville, SC 29602-1028	Fee on cash inv.:	0
Company Phone:	864-271-7733x374	Fee on div. inv.:	0
Transfer Agent:	Bank of New York	Discount (cash):	0
Agent's Address:	P.O. Box 11258, Church St. Sta-	Discount (div.):	0
	tion,11E	Auto invest:	No
	New York, NY 10286	Auto invest fee:	$0
Agent's Phone:	800-524-4458	Selling info:	Sells weekly, by mail, at market,
Other than USA:	Yes		for $0

Company:	**Bowne & Co., Inc.**
Symbol:	BNE
Exchange:	ASE
Industry:	Printing services
Company Address:	345 Hudson St.
	New York, NY 10014
Company Phone:	212-924-5500 or 212-886-0614
Transfer Agent:	Bank of New York
Agent's Address:	P.O.Box 11258-Dept. 11E
	New York, NY 10286-1258
Agent's Phone:	800-524-4458
Other than USA:	Yes

Safekeeping:	Yes
Invests:	Every 7 days beginning varies
Minimum:	$50
Maximum:	$100,000/year
Min to qualify:	1
Fee on cash inv.:	0!
Fee on div. inv.:	0!
Discount (cash):	0
Discount (div.):	0
Auto invest:	Yes
Auto invest fee:	$0
Selling info:	Sells weekly, by mail, at market, for $15 +12¢/sh.

Company:	**BP Amoco plc**
Symbol:	BPA
Exchange:	NYSE
Industry:	World oil, petro chemicals
Company Address:	Box 87703, MC 0404
	Chicago, IL 60680-0703
Company Phone:	800-638-5672 or 312-856-6111
Transfer Agent:	Morgan Guaranty Trust Co.
Agent's Address:	P.O. Box 8205
	Boston, MA 02266-8205
Agent's Phone:	877-638-5672
Other than USA:	No

Safekeeping:	Yes
Invests:	Every 3 days beginning varies
Minimum:	$50
Maximum:	$150,000/year
Min to qualify:	1
Fee on cash inv.:	0
Fee on div. inv.:	0
Discount (cash):	0
Discount (div.):	0
Auto invest:	Yes
Auto invest fee:	$0
Selling info:	Sells daily, by mail or phone, at avg. price, for $10 +12¢/sh.

Company:	**Bradley Real Estate, Inc.**
Symbol:	BTR
Exchange:	NYSE
Industry:	Reit
Company Address:	40 Skokie Blvd., Ste.600
	Northbrook, IL 60062-1626
Company Phone:	847-272-9800 or 847-562-4115
Transfer Agent:	BankBoston (EquiServe)
Agent's Address:	P.O. Box 8040
	Boston, MA 02266-8040
Agent's Phone:	888-697-7873
Other than USA:	Yes

Safekeeping:	Yes
Invests:	Every 30 days beginning 1/30
Minimum:	$100
Maximum:	$10,000/quarter
Min to qualify:	100
Fee on cash inv.:	0!
Fee on div. inv.:	0!
Discount (cash):	0
Discount (div.):	0
Auto invest:	Yes
Auto invest fee:	$0
Selling info:	Sells weekly, by mail, at market, for $15 +1¢/sh.

Company:	**Brazil Fund, Inc.**
Symbol:	BZF
Exchange:	NYSE
Industry:	Closed end fund
Company Address:	c/o Scudder Inv.,345 Park Ave.
	New York, NY 10154
Company Phone:	800-349-4281
Transfer Agent:	Boston Eq. (EquiServe)
Agent's Address:	P.O. Box 8209
	Boston, MA 02266-8209
Agent's Phone:	800-426-5523
Other than USA:	No

Safekeeping:	No
Invests:	Every 180 days beginning 2/15
Minimum:	$100
Maximum:	$3,000/semiannually
Min to qualify:	1
Fee on cash inv.:	$1 + comm.
Fee on div. inv.:	0!
Discount (cash):	0
Discount (div.):	5%
Auto invest:	No
Auto invest fee:	$0
Selling info:	Sells within 10 bus. days, by mail, at market, for 5% to $3.50 + comm.

Company:	**BRE Properties, Inc.**	**Safekeeping:**	Yes
Symbol:	BRE	**Invests:**	Every 7 days beginning varies
Exchange:	NYSE	**Minimum:**	$100
Industry:	REIT	**Maximum:**	$10,000/month
Company Address:	44 Montgomery St., 36th Fl.	**Min to qualify:**	1
	San Francisco, CA 94104-4809	**Fee on cash inv.:**	0
Company Phone:	415-445-6500 or 415-445-6530	**Fee on div. inv.:**	0
Transfer Agent:	ChaseMellon Shareholder Services	**Discount (cash):**	0
Agent's Address:	85 Challenger Road	**Discount (div.):**	0
	Ridgefield Park, NJ 07660	**Auto invest:**	Yes
Agent's Phone:	800-368-8392	**Auto invest fee:**	$0
Other than USA:	Yes	**Selling info:**	Sells weekly, by mail or phone, at avg. price, for $15 +12¢/sh.

Company:	**Briggs & Stratton Corp.**	**Safekeeping:**	Yes
Symbol:	BGG	**Invests:**	Every 30 days beginning 1/2
Exchange:	NYSE	**Minimum:**	$25
Industry:	Mfr. small gas engines	**Maximum:**	$5,000/quarter
Company Address:	Box 702	**Min to qualify:**	1
	Milwaukee, WI 53201-0702	**Fee on cash inv.:**	0
Company Phone:	800-365-2759 or 414-259-5496	**Fee on div. inv.:**	0
Transfer Agent:	Firstar Bank Milwaukee, NA	**Discount (cash):**	0
Agent's Address:	P.O. Box 2077	**Discount (div.):**	0
	Milwaukee, WI 53201	**Auto invest:**	No
Agent's Phone:	800-637-7549	**Auto invest fee:**	$0
Other than USA:	Yes	**Selling info:**	Sells biweekly, by mail or fax, at market, for comm.

Company:	**Bristol-Myers Squibb**	**Safekeeping:**	Yes
Symbol:	BMY	**Invests:**	Every 7 days beginning Wed.
Exchange:	NYSE	**Minimum:**	$105
Industry:	Pharmaceutical & consumer products	**Maximum:**	$10,025/month
		Min to qualify:	50
Company Address:	345 Park Ave.	**Fee on cash inv.:**	$4.20 to $25
	New York, NY 10154-0037	**Fee on div. inv.:**	4% to $5
Company Phone:	212-546-4000	**Discount (cash):**	0
Transfer Agent:	ChaseMellon Shareholder Services	**Discount (div.):**	0
Agent's Address:	P.O. Box 3336	**Auto invest:**	No
	South Hackensack, NJ 07606	**Auto invest fee:**	$0
Agent's Phone:	800-356-2026	**Selling info:**	Sells daily, by mail, at market, for
Other than USA:	Yes		$15 + comm.

Company:	**British Airways plc**	**Safekeeping:**	Yes
Symbol:	BAB	**Invests:**	Every 7 days beginning Thurs.
Exchange:	NYSE	**Minimum:**	$50
Industry:	Major int'l U.K. airline	**Maximum:**	$100,000/year
Company Address:	c/o Morgan Guaranty Trust,	**Min to qualify:**	1
	Box 9073	**Fee on cash inv.:**	$5 + 12¢/sh.
	Boston, MA 02205-9948	**Fee on div. inv.:**	5% to $2.50
Company Phone:	800-428-4237	**Discount (cash):**	0
Transfer Agent:	Morgan Guaranty Trust Co.	**Discount (div.):**	0
Agent's Address:	P.O. Box 9073	**Auto invest:**	Yes
	Boston, MA 02205-9948	**Auto invest fee:**	$5
Agent's Phone:	800-428-4237	**Selling info:**	Sells daily, by phone or mail, at
Other than USA:	No		market, for $5 +12¢/sh.

Company:	**British American Tobacco plc**	Safekeeping:	No
		Invests:	Every 30 days beginning 1/10
Symbol:	BTI	Minimum:	$25
Exchange:	ASE	Maximum:	$5,000/month
Industry:	Tobacco prod., fin'l svcs., insurance	Min to qualify:	1
Company Address:	c/o BNY,101 Barclay St., 22 West	Fee on cash inv.:	$1.50 + 7¢/sh.
	New York, NY 10286	Fee on div. inv.:	0!
Company Phone:	800-943-9715	Discount (cash):	0
Transfer Agent:	Bank of New York	Discount (div.):	0
Agent's Address:	P.O. Box 11258	Auto invest:	No
	New York, NY 10286	Auto invest fee:	$0
Agent's Phone:	888-269-2377	Selling info:	Sells weekly, by mail or fax, at
Other than USA:	No		market, for $5 + 7¢/sh.

Company:	**British Telecommunications plc**	Safekeeping:	Yes
		Invests:	Every 7 days beginning Thurs.
Symbol:	BTY	Minimum:	$50
Exchange:	NYSE	Maximum:	$100,000/year
Industry:	Telecommunications	Min to qualify:	1
Company Address:	40 East 52nd St.	Fee on cash inv.:	$5 + 12¢/sh.
	New York, NY 10022	Fee on div. inv.:	5% to $2.50
Company Phone:	800-331-4568	Discount (cash):	0
Transfer Agent:	Morgan Guaranty Trust Co.	Discount (div.):	0
Agent's Address:	P.O. Box 9073	Auto invest:	Yes
	Boston, MA 02205-9948	Auto invest fee:	$5
Agent's Phone:	800-428-4237	Selling info:	Sells daily, by phone or mail, at
Other than USA:	Yes		avg. price, for $5 +12¢/sh.

Company:	**Brown Shoe Co., Inc.**	Safekeeping:	Yes
Symbol:	BWS	Invests:	Every 30 days beginning 1/1
Exchange:	NYSE	Minimum:	$25
Industry:	Shoes	Maximum:	$1,000/month
Company Address:	8300 Maryland Ave.	Min to qualify:	1
	St. Louis, MO 63105	Fee on cash inv.:	0
Company Phone:	314-854-4000	Fee on div. inv.:	0
Transfer Agent:	FCT (EquiServe)	Discount (cash):	0
Agent's Address:	P.O. Box 2500	Discount (div.):	0
	Jersey City, NJ 07303-2500	Auto invest:	No
Agent's Phone:	800-446-2617	Auto invest fee:	$0
Other than USA:	Yes	Selling info:	Sells weekly, by mail or fax, at
			market, for $10 +12¢/sh.

Company:	**Brown-Forman Corp. A**	Safekeeping:	No
Symbol:	BFA	Invests:	Every 30 days beginning 1/1
Exchange:	NYSE	Minimum:	$50
Industry:	Beverages, liquors, consumer durables	Maximum:	$3,000/quarter
		Min to qualify:	1
Company Address:	850 Dixie Hwy.	Fee on cash inv.:	0!
	Louisville, KY 40210	Fee on div. inv.:	0!
Company Phone:	502-585-1100	Discount (cash):	0
Transfer Agent:	FCT (EquiServe)	Discount (div.):	0
Agent's Address:	P.O. Box 2598	Auto invest:	No
	Jersey City, NJ 07303-2598	Auto invest fee:	$0
Agent's Phone:	201-324-0498	Selling info:	Sells daily, by phone, at market,
Other than USA:	Yes		for $15 +12¢/sh.

Company:	**Brown-Forman Corp. B**	**Safekeeping:**	No
Symbol:	BFB	**Invests:**	Every 30 days beginning 1/1
Exchange:	NYSE	**Minimum:**	$50
Industry:	Beverages, liquors, consumer durables	**Maximum:**	$3,000/quarter
		Min to qualify:	1
Company Address:	850 Dixie Hwy.	**Fee on cash inv.:**	0!
	Louisville, KY 40210	**Fee on div. inv.:**	0!
Company Phone:	502-585-1100	**Discount (cash):**	0
Transfer Agent:	FCT (EquiServe)	**Discount (div.):**	0
Agent's Address:	P.O. Box 2598	**Auto invest:**	No
	Jersey City, NJ 07303-2598	**Auto invest fee:**	$0
Agent's Phone:	201-324-0498	**Selling info:**	Sells daily, by phone, at market,
Other than USA:	Yes		for $15 +12¢/sh.

Company:	**Browning-Ferris Industries Inc.**	**Safekeeping:**	Yes
		Invests:	Every 30 days beginning 1/5
Symbol:	BFI	**Minimum:**	$25
Exchange:	NYSE	**Maximum:**	$60,000/year
Industry:	Waste removal	**Min to qualify:**	1
Company Address:	757 North Eldridge, Box 3151	**Fee on cash inv.:**	0
	Houston, TX 77253	**Fee on div. inv.:**	0
Company Phone:	281-870-8100	**Discount (cash):**	0
Transfer Agent:	FCT (EquiServe)	**Discount (div.):**	0
Agent's Address:	P.O. Box 2500	**Auto invest:**	No
	Jersey City, NJ 07303-2500	**Auto invest fee:**	$0
Agent's Phone:	800-519-3111	**Selling info:**	Sells irregularly, by mail,
Other than USA:	Yes		at market, for comm.

Company:	**Brunswick Corp.**	**Safekeeping:**	Yes
Symbol:	BC	**Invests:**	Every 30 days beginning 1/15
Exchange:	NYSE	**Minimum:**	$10
Industry:	Recreation prod.	**Maximum:**	$2,000/month
Company Address:	1 North Field Ct.	**Min to qualify:**	1
	Lake Forest, IL 60045-4811	**Fee on cash inv.:**	0!
Company Phone:	847-735-4294 or 847-735-4700	**Fee on div. inv.:**	0!
Transfer Agent:	Brunswick Corp.	**Discount (cash):**	0
Agent's Address:	1 North Field Ct.	**Discount (div.):**	0
	Lake Forest, IL 60045	**Auto invest:**	No
Agent's Phone:	800-546-9420	**Auto invest fee:**	$0
Other than USA:	Yes	**Selling info:**	Sells bimonthly, by mail or fax, at
			market, for 3¢/sh.

Company:	**Brush Wellman**	**Safekeeping:**	Yes
Symbol:	BW	**Invests:**	Every 30 days beginning 1/26
Exchange:	NYSE	**Minimum:**	$25
Industry:	Engineered materials	**Maximum:**	$5,000/quarter
Company Address:	17876 St. Clair Ave.	**Min to qualify:**	1
	Cleveland, OH 44110	**Fee on cash inv.:**	0!
Company Phone:	216-486-4200	**Fee on div. inv.:**	0!
Transfer Agent:	National City Bank	**Discount (cash):**	0
Agent's Address:	P.O. Box 92301	**Discount (div.):**	0
	Cleveland, OH 44193-0900	**Auto invest:**	No
Agent's Phone:	800-622-6757	**Auto invest fee:**	$0
Other than USA:	Yes	**Selling info:**	Sells weekly, by mail, at market,
			for $5 + comm.

Company:	**BSB Bancorp, Inc.**	**Safekeeping:**	Yes
Symbol:	BSBN	**Invests:**	Every 30 days beginning 1/10
Exchange:	OTC	**Minimum:**	$50
Industry:	Banking	**Maximum:**	$5,000/month
Company Address:	Box 1056	**Min to qualify:**	1
	Binghamton, NY 13902	**Fee on cash inv.:**	0
Company Phone:	607-779-2406	**Fee on div. inv.:**	0
Transfer Agent:	American Stock Transfer	**Discount (cash):**	0
Agent's Address:	40 Wall Street, 46th Fl.	**Discount (div.):**	0
	New York, NY 10005	**Auto invest:**	No
Agent's Phone:	800-937-5449 or 718-921-8200	**Auto invest fee:**	$0
Other than USA:	Yes	**Selling info:**	Sells weekly, by mail, at market, for 4¢/sh.

Company:	**BT Financial Corp.**	**Safekeeping:**	Yes
Symbol:	BTFC	**Invests:**	Every 90 days beginning 3/1
Exchange:	OTC	**Minimum:**	$20
Industry:	Bank holding co.	**Maximum:**	$2,500/quarter
Company Address:	551 Main St.	**Min to qualify:**	1
	Johnstown, PA 15907	**Fee on cash inv.:**	0
Company Phone:	814-536-2110	**Fee on div. inv.:**	0
Transfer Agent:	Laurel Trust Co.	**Discount (cash):**	0
Agent's Address:	Institutional Systs., 551 Main St.,	**Discount (div.):**	0
	Box 1110	**Auto invest:**	No
	Johnstown, PA 15907-1110	**Auto invest fee:**	$0
Agent's Phone:	814-536-2110	**Selling info:**	Sells daily, by mail, at market, for
Other than USA:	Yes		comm.

Company:	**Bufete Industrial, S.A.**	**Safekeeping:**	Yes
Symbol:	GBI	**Invests:**	Every 7 days beginning varies
Exchange:	NYSE	**Minimum:**	$50
Industry:	Integrated engineering, procurement and construction	**Maximum:**	$250,000/week
		Min to qualify:	1
Company Address:	c/o BNY,101 Barclay St.,22 West	**Fee on cash inv.:**	$5 + 10¢/sh.
	New York, NY 10286	**Fee on div. inv.:**	0
Company Phone:	800-943-9715	**Discount (cash):**	0
Transfer Agent:	Bank of New York	**Discount (div.):**	0
Agent's Address:	P.O. Box 11258	**Auto invest:**	Yes
	New York, NY 10286	**Auto invest fee:**	$0
Agent's Phone:	888-269-2377	**Selling info:**	Sells weekly, by phone or mail, at
Other than USA:	Yes		market, for $5 +10¢/ADS

Company:	**Burlington Northern Santa Fe Corp.**	**Safekeeping:**	Yes
		Invests:	Every 30 days beginning varies
Symbol:	BNI	**Minimum:**	$50
Exchange:	NYSE	**Maximum:**	$60,000/year
Industry:	Railroad	**Min to qualify:**	1
Company Address:	2650 Lou Menk Dr., 2nd Fl.	**Fee on cash inv.:**	5% to $2.50
	Fort Worth, TX 76131-2830	**Fee on div. inv.:**	5% to $2.50
Company Phone:	817-333-2000	**Discount (cash):**	0
Transfer Agent:	FCT (EquiServe)	**Discount (div.):**	0
Agent's Address:	P.O. Box 2500	**Auto invest:**	No
	Jersey City, NJ 07303	**Auto invest fee:**	$0
Agent's Phone:	800-526-5678	**Selling info:**	Sells daily, by phone or mail, at
Other than USA:	Yes		market, for $10 +12¢/sh.

Company:	**Burnham Pacific Properties Inc.**	Safekeeping:	Yes
		Invests:	Every 90 days beginning 3/30
Symbol:	BPP	Minimum:	$10
Exchange:	NYSE	Maximum:	$20,000/year
Industry:	REIT	Min to qualify:	1
Company Address:	610 West Ash St., 16th Fl.	Fee on cash inv.:	5% to $2.50 + comm.
	San Diego, CA 92112	Fee on div. inv.:	5% to $2.50 + comm.
Company Phone:	800-568-2722 or 619-652-4700	Discount (cash):	0
Transfer Agent:	FCT (EquiServe)	Discount (div.):	0
Agent's Address:	P.O. Box 2598	Auto invest:	No
	Jersey City, NJ 07303-2598	Auto invest fee:	$0
Agent's Phone:	800-756-8200	Selling info:	Sells daily, by phone or mail, at
Other than USA:	Yes		market, for $10 +12¢/sh.

Company:	**Cabot Corp.**	Safekeeping:	Yes
Symbol:	CBT	Invests:	Every 45 days beginning 3/1
Exchange:	NYSE	Minimum:	$10
Industry:	Chemicals	Maximum:	$10,000/quarter
Company Address:	75 State St.	Min to qualify:	1
	Boston, MA 02109-1806	Fee on cash inv.:	0
Company Phone:	617-345-0100 or 617-342-6366	Fee on div. inv.:	0
Transfer Agent:	Boston Eq. (EquiServe)	Discount (cash):	0
Agent's Address:	P.O. Box 8040, MS 45-02-64	Discount (div.):	0
	Boston, MA 02105-1681	Auto invest:	No
Agent's Phone:	800-730-4001	Auto invest fee:	$0
Other than USA:	Yes	Selling info:	Sells within 10 bus. days, by mail
			or phone, at market, for $0

Company:	**Cadbury Schweppes plc**	Safekeeping:	Yes
Symbol:	CSG	Invests:	Every 7 days beginning Thurs.
Exchange:	NYSE	Minimum:	$50
Industry:	Food & beverage	Maximum:	$100,000/year
Company Address:	1633 Broadway, 26th Fl.	Min to qualify:	1
	New York, NY 10019	Fee on cash inv.:	$5 + 12¢/sh.
Company Phone:	212-373-0200	Fee on div. inv.:	5% to $2.50
Transfer Agent:	Morgan Guaranty Trust Co.	Discount (cash):	0
Agent's Address:	P.O. Box 9073	Discount (div.):	0
	Boston, MA 02205-9948	Auto invest:	Yes
Agent's Phone:	800-428-4237	Auto invest fee:	$5
Other than USA:	No	Selling info:	Sells daily, by phone or mail, at
			avg. price, for $5 +12¢/sh.

Company:	**Cadmus Communications Corp.**	Safekeeping:	Yes
		Invests:	Every 90 days beginning 3/1
Symbol:	CDMS	Minimum:	$25
Exchange:	OTC	Maximum:	$3,000/quarter
Industry:	Printing, mktg., publ. & graphic arts	Min to qualify:	1
		Fee on cash inv.:	0
Company Address:	6620 W. Broad St., Ste.240,	Fee on div. inv.:	0
	Box 27367	Discount (cash):	0
	Richmond, VA 23261-7367	Discount (div.):	0
Company Phone:	804-287-5680	Auto invest:	No
Transfer Agent:	First Union National Bank of NC	Auto invest fee:	$0
Agent's Address:	1525 West W.T. Harris Blvd. 3C3	Selling info:	Sells 1st & 15th, by mail or fax, at
	Charlotte, NC 28288-1153		market, for $5
Agent's Phone:	800-829-8432		
Other than USA:	No		

Company:	**California Water Service Group**	Safekeeping:	Yes
		Invests:	Every 7 days beginning Wed.
Symbol:	CWT	Minimum:	$100
Exchange:	NYSE	Maximum:	$20,000/month
Industry:	Utility-water	Min to qualify:	1
Company Address:	1720 North First St.	Fee on cash inv.:	0
	San Jose, CA 95112	Fee on div. inv.:	0
Company Phone:	800-750-8200 or 408-367-8200	Discount (cash):	0
Transfer Agent:	Boston Eq. (EquiServe)	Discount (div.):	0
Agent's Address:	P.O. Box 8040	Auto invest:	Yes
	Boston, MA 02266-8040	Auto invest fee:	$0
Agent's Phone:	800-736-3001	Selling info:	Sells varies, by mail, at market,
Other than USA:	Yes		for $10 to $15 + comm.

Company:	**Callaway Golf Co.**	Safekeeping:	Yes
Symbol:	ELY	Invests:	Every 30 days beginning 1/15
Exchange:	NYSE	Minimum:	$50
Industry:	Mfr. golf clubs	Maximum:	$5,000/quarter
Company Address:	2285 Rutherford Rd.	Min to qualify:	1
	Carlsbad, CA 92008-8815	Fee on cash inv.:	0
Company Phone:	760-931-1771	Fee on div. inv.:	0
Transfer Agent:	ChaseMellon Shareholder Services	Discount (cash):	0
		Discount (div.):	0
Agent's Address:	85 Challenger Road	Auto invest:	No
	Ridgefirld, NJ 07660	Auto invest fee:	$0
Agent's Phone:	800-368-7068	Selling info:	Sells weekly, by mail or phone, at
Other than USA:	Yes		market, for $15 + comm.

Company:	**Camden Property Trust**	Safekeeping:	No
Symbol:	CPT	Invests:	Every 90 days beginning 1/19
Exchange:	NYSE	Minimum:	$100
Industry:	REIT	Maximum:	$10,000/quarter
Company Address:	3 Greenway Plz., Ste.1300	Min to qualify:	1
	Houston, TX 77046	Fee on cash inv.:	0
Company Phone:	713-354-2500	Fee on div. inv.:	0
Transfer Agent:	American Stock Transfer	Discount (cash):	0
Agent's Address:	40 Wall Street - 46th floor	Discount (div.):	0
	New York, N.Y. 10005	Auto invest:	No
Agent's Phone:	800-278-4353	Auto invest fee:	$0
Other than USA:	Yes	Selling info:	Sells irregularly, by mail,
			at market, for comm.

Company:	**Campbell Soup Co.**	Safekeeping:	Yes
Symbol:	CPB	Invests:	Every 5 days beginning 1/5
Exchange:	NYSE	Minimum:	$50
Industry:	Food proc.	Maximum:	$350,000/year
Company Address:	Campbell Pl.	Min to qualify:	1
	Camden, NJ 08103-1799	Fee on cash inv.:	$5 + 3¢/sh.
Company Phone:	609-342-6428	Fee on div. inv.:	5% to $3 + 10¢/sh.
Transfer Agent:	FCT (EquiServe)	Discount (cash):	0
Agent's Address:	P.O. Box 2500	Discount (div.):	0
	Jersey City, NJ 07303	Auto invest:	Yes
Agent's Phone:	800-446-2617	Auto invest fee:	$2 + 3¢/sh.
Other than USA:	Yes	Selling info:	Sells daily, by mail or phone, at
			market, for $15 +12¢/sh.

Company:	**Canadian General Investments, Ltd.**	Safekeeping:	No
		Invests:	Every 90 days beginning 3/15
Symbol:	CGI	Minimum:	$100
Exchange:	TSE	Maximum:	$5,000/quarter
Industry:	Closed-end fund	Min to qualify:	1
Company Address:	110 Yonge St., Ste.1601	Fee on cash inv.:	0
	Toronto, Ontario M5C 1T4 Canada	Fee on div. inv.:	0
Company Phone:	800-207-0067 or 416-366-2931x227	Discount (cash):	0
Transfer Agent:	Montreal Trust Company of Canada	Discount (div.):	0
Agent's Address:	151 Front St., W., 8th Fl.	Auto invest:	No
	Toronto, Ont. M5J 2N1 Canada	Auto invest fee:	$0
Agent's Phone:	416-981-9633	Selling info:	Sells irregularly, by mail or
Other than USA:	Yes		courier, at market, for comm.

Company:	**Canadian Imperial Bank of Commerce**	Safekeeping:	No
		Invests:	Every 30 days beginning 1/1
Symbol:	CM	Minimum:	$100
Exchange:	TSE	Maximum:	$50,000/year Cdn.
Industry:	Banking	Min to qualify:	1
Company Address:	Commerce Ct. West	Fee on cash inv.:	0
	Toronto, Ont. M5L 1A2 Canada	Fee on div. inv.:	0
Company Phone:	416-980-8306	Discount (cash):	0
Transfer Agent:	CIBC Mellon Trust	Discount (div.):	0
Agent's Address:	P.O. Box 7010, Adelaide Street	Auto invest:	No
	Postal Station	Auto invest fee:	$0
	Toronto, ON Canada M5C 2W9	Selling info:	Sells irregularly, by mail, at mar-
Agent's Phone:	800-387-0825		ket, for comm.
Other than USA:	Yes		

Company:	**Canadian Pacific Limited**	Safekeeping:	No
Symbol:	CP	Invests:	Every 30 days beginning 1/28
Exchange:	NYSE	Minimum:	$0
Industry:	Transportation, energy, & hotels	Maximum:	$30,000/year Cdn.
Company Address:	1800 Bankers Hall East, 855-2nd	Min to qualify:	1
	St. S.W.	Fee on cash inv.:	0
	Calgary, Alta.T2P 4Z5 Canada	Fee on div. inv.:	0
Company Phone:	403-218-8000 or 403-218-8176	Discount (cash):	0
Transfer Agent:	Trust Co. of Bank of Montreal	Discount (div.):	0
Agent's Address:	129 Saint -Jacques St., A Level	Auto invest:	No
	North	Auto invest fee:	$0
	Montreal, Que. H2Y 1L6 Canada	Selling info:	Not available
Agent's Phone:	800-332-0095 or 514-877-2584		
Other than USA:	Yes		

Company:	**Canon Inc.**	Safekeeping:	Yes
Symbol:	CANNY	Invests:	Every 7 days beginning varies
Exchange:	OTC	Minimum:	$50
Industry:	Business machines, cameras, and	Maximum:	$100,000/year
	optical products	Min to qualify:	1
Company Address:	c/o Morgan Guaranty Trust,	Fee on cash inv.:	$5 + 12¢/sh.
	Box 9073	Fee on div. inv.:	5% to $2.50
	Boston, MA 02205-9948	Discount (cash):	0
Company Phone:	800-428-4237	Discount (div.):	0
Transfer Agent:	Morgan Guaranty Trust Co.	Auto invest:	Yes
Agent's Address:	P.O. Box 9073	Auto invest fee:	$5 + 12¢/sh.
	Boston, MA 02205-9948	Selling info:	Sells daily, by mail or phone, at avg.
Agent's Phone:	800-428-4237		price, for $5 +12¢/sh.
Other than USA:	No		

Company:	**Cantab Pharmaceuticals plc**	**Safekeeping:**	Yes
		Invests:	Every 7 days beginning varies
Symbol:	CNTBY	**Minimum:**	$50
Exchange:	OTC	**Maximum:**	$250,000/week
Industry:	Develops drugs for human	**Min to qualify:**	1
	immune systems	**Fee on cash inv.:**	$5 + 10¢/sh.
Company Address:	c/o BNY,101 Barclay St.,22 West	**Fee on div. inv.:**	5% to $5 + 10¢/sh.
	New York, NY 10286	**Discount (cash):**	0
Company Phone:	800-943-9715	**Discount (div.):**	0
Transfer Agent:	Bank of New York	**Auto invest:**	Yes
Agent's Address:	P.O. Box 11258	**Auto invest fee:**	$0
	New York, NY 10286	**Selling info:**	Sells weekly, by phone or mail, at
Agent's Phone:	888-269-2377		market, for $5 +10¢/ADS
Other than USA:	Yes		

Company:	**Capital One Financial Corp.**	**Safekeeping:**	Yes
		Invests:	Every 30 days beginning 1/20
Symbol:	COF	**Minimum:**	$50
Exchange:	NYSE	**Maximum:**	$5,000/month
Industry:	Bank card issuer svcs.	**Min to qualify:**	1
Company Address:	2980 Fairview Park Dr., Ste.1300	**Fee on cash inv.:**	0!
	Falls Church, VA 22042-4525	**Fee on div. inv.:**	0!
Company Phone:	703-205-1000 or 703-205-1039	**Discount (cash):**	0% to 3%
Transfer Agent:	FCT (EquiServe)	**Discount (div.):**	0
Agent's Address:	P.O. Box 2598	**Auto invest:**	Yes
	Jersey City, NJ 07303-2598	**Auto invest fee:**	$1
Agent's Phone:	800-446-2617	**Selling info:**	Sells weekly, by mail or phone, at
Other than USA:	Yes		market, for fee + comm.

Company:	**Capitol Bancorp Ltd.**	**Safekeeping:**	Yes
Symbol:	CBCL	**Invests:**	Every 30 days beginning 1/19
Exchange:	OTC	**Minimum:**	$50
Industry:	Banking	**Maximum:**	$5,000/quarter
Company Address:	200 Washington Sq. North	**Min to qualify:**	1
	Lansing, MI 48933	**Fee on cash inv.:**	0!
Company Phone:	517-487-6555	**Fee on div. inv.:**	0!
Transfer Agent:	UMB Bank, N.A.	**Discount (cash):**	0
Agent's Address:	P.O. Box 410064	**Discount (div.):**	0
	Kansas City, MO 64141-0064	**Auto invest:**	No
Agent's Phone:	800-884-4225	**Auto invest fee:**	$0
Other than USA:	Yes	**Selling info:**	Sells monthly, by mail, at market,
			for $5 + comm.

Company:	**Caraustar Industries, Inc.**	**Safekeeping:**	Yes
Symbol:	CSAR	**Invests:**	Every 30 days beginning 1/31
Exchange:	OTC	**Minimum:**	$50
Industry:	Recycled packaging	**Maximum:**	$300,000/year
Company Address:	3100 Washington St., Box 115	**Min to qualify:**	1
	Austell, GA 30106	**Fee on cash inv.:**	10¢/sh.
Company Phone:	770-948-3101	**Fee on div. inv.:**	0
Transfer Agent:	Bank of New York	**Discount (cash):**	0
Agent's Address:	P.O. Box 11258	**Discount (div.):**	0
	New York, NY 10286-1258	**Auto invest:**	Yes
Agent's Phone:	800-524-4458	**Auto invest fee:**	10¢/sh.
Other than USA:	Yes	**Selling info:**	Sells weekly, by mail, at market,
			for $5 +10¢/sh.

Company:	**Carey Diversified LLC**	**Safekeeping:**	Yes
Symbol:	CDC	**Invests:**	Every 30 days beginning 1/21
Exchange:	NYSE	**Minimum:**	$500
Industry:	Real estate	**Maximum:**	$25,000/month
Company Address:	50 Rockefeller Plaza	**Min to qualify:**	1
	New York, NY 10020	**Fee on cash inv.:**	0!
Company Phone:	212-492-1100	**Fee on div. inv.:**	0!
Transfer Agent:	ChaseMellon Shareholder Services	**Discount (cash):**	0
Agent's Address:	P.O. Box 3338	**Discount (div.):**	0
	South Hackensack, NJ 07606-1938	**Auto invest:**	Yes
Agent's Phone:	800-200-8690	**Auto invest fee:**	$0
Other than USA:	Yes	**Selling info:**	Sells daily, by mail, at market, for $15 +12¢/sh.

Company:	**Carlisle Cos., Inc.**	**Safekeeping:**	Yes
Symbol:	CSL	**Invests:**	Every 30 days beginning 1/1
Exchange:	NYSE	**Minimum:**	$10
Industry:	Diversified manufacturing	**Maximum:**	$3,000/quarter
Company Address:	250 South Clinton St., Ste.201	**Min to qualify:**	1
	Syracuse, NY 13202-1258	**Fee on cash inv.:**	0!
Company Phone:	800-897-9071 or 315-474-2500	**Fee on div. inv.:**	0!
Transfer Agent:	Harris Trust & Savings Bank	**Discount (cash):**	0
Agent's Address:	P.O. Box A-3309	**Discount (div.):**	0
	Chicago, IL 60690	**Auto invest:**	No
Agent's Phone:	312-461-2302	**Auto invest fee:**	$0
Other than USA:	Yes	**Selling info:**	Sells daily, by mail, at avg. price, for 10¢/sh.

Company:	**Carlton Communications plc**	**Safekeeping:**	Yes
		Invests:	Every 7 days beginning varies
Symbol:	CCTVY	**Minimum:**	$50
Exchange:	OTC	**Maximum:**	$100,000/year
Industry:	TV production, programming	**Min to qualify:**	1
	& services	**Fee on cash inv.:**	$5 + 12¢/sh.
Company Address:	c/o Morgan Guaranty Trust,	**Fee on div. inv.:**	5% to $2.50
	Box 9073	**Discount (cash):**	0
	Boston, MA 02205-9948	**Discount (div.):**	0
Company Phone:	800-428-4237	**Auto invest:**	Yes
Transfer Agent:	Morgan Guaranty Trust Co.	**Auto invest fee:**	$5 + 12¢/sh.
Agent's Address:	P.O. Box 9073	**Selling info:**	Sells daily, by mail or phone, at
	Boston, MA 02205-9948		avg. price, for $5 +12¢/sh.
Agent's Phone:	800-428-4237		
Other than USA:	No		

Company:	**Carolina First Corp.**	**Safekeeping:**	Yes
Symbol:	CAFC	**Invests:**	Every 30 days beginning 1/1
Exchange:	OTC	**Minimum:**	$25
Industry:	Bank holding co.	**Maximum:**	$10,000/month
Company Address:	102 South Main St., Box 1029	**Min to qualify:**	1
	Greenville, SC 29602	**Fee on cash inv.:**	0
Company Phone:	800-951-2699 or 864-255-4919	**Fee on div. inv.:**	0
Transfer Agent:	Reliance Trust Co.	**Discount (cash):**	0
Agent's Address:	P.O. Box 48449	**Discount (div.):**	5%
	Atlanta, GA 30340-4099	**Auto invest:**	Yes
Agent's Phone:	800-241-5568	**Auto invest fee:**	$0
Other than USA:	No	**Selling info:**	Sells irregularly, by mail, at market, for comm.

Company:	**Carolina Power & Light**	Safekeeping:	No
Symbol:	CPL	Invests:	Every 30 days beginning 1/1
Exchange:	NYSE	Minimum:	$20
Industry:	Utility-electric	Maximum:	$2,000/month
Company Address:	Box 1551, Shareholder Relations	Min to qualify:	1
	Section	Fee on cash inv.:	0!
	Raleigh, NC 27602	Fee on div. inv.:	0!
Company Phone:	800-662-7232 or 919-546-7474	Discount (cash):	0
Transfer Agent:	Wachovia (EquiServe)	Discount (div.):	0
Agent's Address:	P.O. Box 8217	Auto invest:	Yes
	Boston, MA 02266-8217	Auto invest fee:	$0
Agent's Phone:	800-633-4236	Selling info:	Sells daily, by mail or fax, at avg.
Other than USA:	Yes		price, for 3.5¢/sh.

Company:	**Carpenter Technologies Corp.**	Safekeeping:	Yes
		Invests:	Every 7 days beginning Tuesday
Symbol:	CRS	Minimum:	$25
Exchange:	NYSE	Maximum:	$120,000/year
Industry:	Metals	Min to qualify:	1
Company Address:	101 West Bern St., Box 14662	Fee on cash inv.:	0
	Reading, PA 19642-4662	Fee on div. inv.:	0
Company Phone:	610-208-2301 or 610-208-2000	Discount (cash):	0
Transfer Agent:	FCT (EquiServe)	Discount (div.):	0
Agent's Address:	P.O. Box 2500	Auto invest:	Yes
	Jersey City, NJ 07303-2500	Auto invest fee:	$0
Agent's Phone:	800-519-3111	Selling info:	Sells weekly, by phone, mail, or
Other than USA:	No		fax, at avg. price, for $10 +12¢/sh.

Company:	**CarrAmerica**	Safekeeping:	Yes
Symbol:	CRE	Invests:	Every 30 days beginning 1/30
Exchange:	NYSE	Minimum:	$25
Industry:	Real estate operations	Maximum:	$25,000/year
Company Address:	1850 K St., N.W.	Min to qualify:	1
	Washington, DC 20006	Fee on cash inv.:	0!
Company Phone:	800-417-2277 or 202-729-7500	Fee on div. inv.:	0!
Transfer Agent:	Boston Eq. (EquiServe)	Discount (cash):	0
Agent's Address:	P.O. Box 8040	Discount (div.):	0
	Boston, MA 02266-8040	Auto invest:	No
Agent's Phone:	781-575-3100	Auto invest fee:	$0
Other than USA:	No	Selling info:	Sells weekly, by mail or phone, at
			market, for $1 to $10 +comm.

Company:	**Cascade Natural Gas**	Safekeeping:	Yes
Symbol:	CGC	Invests:	Every 30 days beginning 1/15
Exchange:	NYSE	Minimum:	$50
Industry:	Utility-gas	Maximum:	$20,000/year
Company Address:	222 Fairway Ave. North	Min to qualify:	1
	Seattle, WA 98109	Fee on cash inv.:	0!
Company Phone:	206-624-3900	Fee on div. inv.:	0!
Transfer Agent:	Bank of New York	Discount (cash):	0
Agent's Address:	P.O. Box 11258, Church St. Station	Discount (div.):	0
	New York, NY 10286	Auto invest:	No
Agent's Phone:	888-269-8845	Auto invest fee:	$0
Other than USA:	Yes	Selling info:	Sells weekly, by mail, at avg. price,
			for $5 +10¢/sh.

Company:	**Casey's General Store**	Safekeeping:	Yes
Symbol:	CASY	Invests:	Every 30 days beginning 1/15
Exchange:	OTC	Minimum:	$50
Industry:	Convenience stores	Maximum:	$10,000/quarter
Company Address:	One Convenience Blvd.	Min to qualify:	1
	Ankeny, IA 50021	Fee on cash inv.:	0!
Company Phone:	515-965-6100	Fee on div. inv.:	0!
Transfer Agent:	UMB Bank, N.A.	Discount (cash):	0
Agent's Address:	P.O. Box 410064	Discount (div.):	0
	Kansas City, MO 64141-0064	Auto invest:	Yes
Agent's Phone:	816-860-7891	Auto invest fee:	$0
Other than USA:	Yes	Selling info:	Sells daily, by mail, at avg. price, for $5 + comm.

Company:	**Castle (A.M.) & Co.**	Safekeeping:	No
Symbol:	CAS	Invests:	Every 90 days beginning varies
Exchange:	ASE	Minimum:	$100
Industry:	Metals service distribution	Maximum:	$10,000/quarter
	centers	Min to qualify:	1
Company Address:	3400 North Wolf Rd.	Fee on cash inv.:	0!
	Franklin Park, IL 60131	Fee on div. inv.:	0!
Company Phone:	847-455-7111	Discount (cash):	0
Transfer Agent:	American Stock Transfer	Discount (div.):	0
Agent's Address:	40 Wall St., 46th Fl.	Auto invest:	No
	New York, NY 10269-0436	Auto invest fee:	$0
Agent's Phone:	800-937-5449	Selling info:	Not available
Other than USA:	Yes		

Company:	**Caterpillar, Inc.**	Safekeeping:	Yes
Symbol:	CAT	Invests:	Every 7 days beginning varies
Exchange:	NYSE	Minimum:	$50
Industry:	Heavy machinery	Maximum:	$350,000/year
Company Address:	100 N.E. Adams St.	Min to qualify:	1
	Peoria, IL 61629-5310	Fee on cash inv.:	$5 + 3¢/sh.
Company Phone:	309-675-4619 or 309-675-1000	Fee on div. inv.:	5% to $3 + 10¢/sh.
Transfer Agent:	FCT (EquiServe)	Discount (cash):	0
Agent's Address:	P.O. Box 2500	Discount (div.):	0
	Jersey City, NJ 07303-2500	Auto invest:	Yes
Agent's Phone:	800-446-2617 or 201-324-0498	Auto invest fee:	$2 + 3¢/sh.
Other than USA:	Yes	Selling info:	Sells daily, by phone or mail, at market, for $15 +12¢/sh.

Company:	**Cathay Bancorp, Inc.**	Safekeeping:	Yes
Symbol:	CATY	Invests:	Every 30 days beginning 1/20
Exchange:	OTC		(varies)
Industry:	Bank holding co.	Minimum:	$600
Company Address:	777 North Broadway	Maximum:	$15,000/quarter
	Los Angeles, CA 90012	Min to qualify:	1
Company Phone:	213-625-4700 or 213-625-4749	Fee on cash inv.:	0!
Transfer Agent:	American Stock Transfer	Fee on div. inv.:	0!
Agent's Address:	40 Wall Street	Discount (cash):	0
	New York, NY 10005	Discount (div.):	5%
Agent's Phone:	800-937-5449	Auto invest:	No
Other than USA:	Yes	Auto invest fee:	$0
		Selling info:	Not available

Company:	**CBL & Associates Properties**
Symbol:	CBL
Exchange:	NYSE
Industry:	REIT
Company Address:	1Park Pl., 6148 Lee Hwy., Ste.300
	Chattanooga, TN 37421-6511
Company Phone:	423-855-0001
Transfer Agent:	Boston Eq. (EquiServe)
Agent's Address:	P.O. Box 8040
	Boston, MA 02266-8040
Agent's Phone:	781-575-3400
Other than USA:	Yes

Safekeeping:	Yes
Invests:	Every 30 days beginning 1/15
Minimum:	$100
Maximum:	$5,000/quarter
Min to qualify:	1
Fee on cash inv.:	0
Fee on div. inv.:	0
Discount (cash):	0
Discount (div.):	5%
Auto invest:	No
Auto invest fee:	$0
Selling info:	Sells within 10 bus. days, by mail, at market, for 5% to $10 + comm.

Company:	**CBRL Group, Inc.**
Symbol:	CBRL
Exchange:	OTC
Industry:	Restaurant, gift shop
Company Address:	305 Hartmann Dr., Box 787
	Lebanon, TN 37088-0787
Company Phone:	615-444-5533
Transfer Agent:	SunTrust Bank, Atlanta
Agent's Address:	P.O. Box 4625
	Atlanta, GA 30302
Agent's Phone:	800-568-3476
Other than USA:	Yes

Safekeeping:	Yes
Invests:	Every 30 days beginning 1/30
Minimum:	$100
Maximum:	$5,000/quarter
Min to qualify:	1
Fee on cash inv.:	0
Fee on div. inv.:	0
Discount (cash):	0
Discount (div.):	0
Auto invest:	No
Auto invest fee:	$0
Selling info:	Sells within 10 bus.days , by mail, at avg. price, for $0

Company:	**CBS Corp.**
Symbol:	CBS
Exchange:	NYSE
Industry:	Comm., financial, & manufacturing
Company Address:	51 West 52nd St.
	New York, NY 10019
Company Phone:	212-975-4321 or 412-642-4835
Transfer Agent:	Bank of New York
Agent's Address:	P.O. Box 11258-Church St. Station
	New York, NY 10286
Agent's Phone:	800-507-7799
Other than USA:	No

Safekeeping:	Yes
Invests:	Every 30 days beginning 1/1
Minimum:	$100
Maximum:	$5,000/month
Min to qualify:	1
Fee on cash inv.:	0
Fee on div. inv.:	0
Discount (cash):	0
Discount (div.):	0
Auto invest:	No
Auto invest fee:	$0
Selling info:	Sells daily, by phone, mail, or fax, at market, for 5¢/sh.

Company:	**CBT Group plc**
Symbol:	CBTSY
Exchange:	OTC
Industry:	Software & programming
Company Address:	1005 Hamilton Courtare
	Menlo Park, CA 94025
Company Phone:	650-614-5900
Transfer Agent:	Bank of New York
Agent's Address:	P.O. Box 11258
	New York, NY 10286
Agent's Phone:	888-269-2377
Other than USA:	Yes

Safekeeping:	Yes
Invests:	Every 7 days beginning varies
Minimum:	$50
Maximum:	$250,000/year
Min to qualify:	1
Fee on cash inv.:	$5 + 10¢/sh.
Fee on div. inv.:	0
Discount (cash):	0
Discount (div.):	0
Auto invest:	Yes
Auto invest fee:	$5 + 10¢/sh.
Selling info:	Sells weekly, by mail, at market, for $5 +10¢/sh.

Company:	**CCB Financial Corp.**	Safekeeping:	Yes
Symbol:	CCB	Invests:	Every 30 days beginning 1/8
Exchange:	NYSE	Minimum:	$25
Industry:	Banking	Maximum:	$10,000/month
Company Address:	Box 931	Min to qualify:	1
	Durham, NC 27702	Fee on cash inv.:	0!
Company Phone:	919-683-7646	Fee on div. inv.:	0!
Transfer Agent:	Registrar & Transfer Co.	Discount (cash):	0
Agent's Address:	10 Commerce Drive	Discount (div.):	0
	Cranford, NJ 07016-9982	Auto invest:	Yes
Agent's Phone:	800-368-5948	Auto invest fee:	$0
Other than USA:	Yes	Selling info:	Sells bimonthly, by mail, at market, for 2¢ to 5¢/sh.

Company:	**CCFNB Bancorp, Inc.**	Safekeeping:	No
Symbol:	CCFN	Invests:	Every 90 days beginning 1/15
Exchange:	OTC	Minimum:	$25
Industry:	Banking	Maximum:	$1,500/quarter
Company Address:	232 East St.	Min to qualify:	1
	Bloomsburg, PA 17815	Fee on cash inv.:	0
Company Phone:	717-387-4016	Fee on div. inv.:	0
Transfer Agent:	American Stock Transfer	Discount (cash):	0
Agent's Address:	40 Wall Street 46th Floor	Discount (div.):	0
	New York, NY 10005	Auto invest:	No
Agent's Phone:	800-937-5449	Auto invest fee:	$0
Other than USA:	Yes	Selling info:	Sells irregularly, by mail, at market, for comm.

Company:	**Cedar Fair L.P.**	Safekeeping:	Yes
Symbol:	FUN	Invests:	Every 30 days beginning 1/15
Exchange:	NYSE	Minimum:	$50
Industry:	Retail, amusement parks	Maximum:	$5,000/quarter
Company Address:	Cedar Point Dr.	Min to qualify:	50
	Sandusky, OH 44871-5006	Fee on cash inv.:	0!
Company Phone:	419-627-2173	Fee on div. inv.:	0!
Transfer Agent:	ChaseMellon Shareholder Services	Discount (cash):	0
Agent's Address:	P.O. Box 750	Discount (div.):	0
	Pittsburgh, PA 15230-9625	Auto invest:	No
Agent's Phone:	800-756-3353	Auto invest fee:	$0
Other than USA:	Yes	Selling info:	Sells daily, by mail, at market, for $0

Company:	**Center Bancorp, Inc.**	Safekeeping:	Yes
Symbol:	CNBC	Invests:	Every 30 days beginning 1/1
Exchange:	OTC	Minimum:	$100
Industry:	Regional banks	Maximum:	$30,000/year
Company Address:	2455 Morris Ave.	Min to qualify:	1
	Union, NJ 07083	Fee on cash inv.:	0!
Company Phone:	908-688-9500	Fee on div. inv.:	0!
Transfer Agent:	American Stock Transfer	Discount (cash):	0
Agent's Address:	6201 15th Ave.	Discount (div.):	0
	Brooklyn, NY 11219	Auto invest:	No
Agent's Phone:	800-937-5449	Auto invest fee:	$0
Other than USA:	Yes	Selling info:	Sells daily, by mail, at market, for comm.

Company:	**CenterPoint Properties Trust**	**Safekeeping:**	Yes
		Invests:	Every 90 days beginning 3/30
Symbol:	CNT	**Minimum:**	$25
Exchange:	NYSE	**Maximum:**	$100,000/year
Industry:	REIT	**Min to qualify:**	1
Company Address:	1808 Swift Dr.	**Fee on cash inv.:**	0!
	Oak Brook, IL 60523-1501	**Fee on div. inv.:**	0!
Company Phone:	630-586-8000	**Discount (cash):**	0
Transfer Agent:	FCT (EquiServe)	**Discount (div.):**	0
Agent's Address:	P.O. Box 2598	**Auto invest:**	No
	Jersey City, NJ 07303-2598	**Auto invest fee:**	$0
Agent's Phone:	800-446-2617	**Selling info:**	Sells daily, by mail, at market, for
Other than USA:	Yes		$10 +12¢/sh.

Company:	**Central & South West Corp.**	**Safekeeping:**	Yes
		Invests:	Every 7 days beginning Mon.
Symbol:	CSR	**Minimum:**	$25
Exchange:	NYSE	**Maximum:**	$100,000/year
Industry:	Utility-electric	**Min to qualify:**	1
Company Address:	Box 660164	**Fee on cash inv.:**	0
	Dallas, TX 75266-0164	**Fee on div. inv.:**	0
Company Phone:	800-527-5797 or 214-777-1277	**Discount (cash):**	0
Transfer Agent:	Central & South West Corporation	**Discount (div.):**	0
Agent's Address:	P.O. Box 660164	**Auto invest:**	Yes
	Dallas, TX 75266-0614	**Auto invest fee:**	$0
Agent's Phone:	800-527-5797	**Selling info:**	Sells weekly, by mail or fax, at
Other than USA:	Yes		market, for $0

Company:	**Central European Equity Fund**	**Safekeeping:**	Yes
		Invests:	Every 30 days beginning 1/15
Symbol:	CEE	**Minimum:**	$100
Exchange:	NYSE	**Maximum:**	$36,000/year
Industry:	Closed-end fund	**Min to qualify:**	1
Company Address:	c/o Deutsche Bk.,31 West 52nd St.	**Fee on cash inv.:**	comm.
	New York, NY 10019	**Fee on div. inv.:**	0!
Company Phone:	800-334-1898 or 212-469-7052	**Discount (cash):**	0
Transfer Agent:	Investors Bank & Trust Company-	**Discount (div.):**	0
	Shareholder Svcs.	**Auto invest:**	No
Agent's Address:	P.O. Box 1537	**Auto invest fee:**	$0
	Boston, MA 02205-1537	**Selling info:**	Not available
Agent's Phone:	800-356-2754 or 617-443-6867		
Other than USA:	Yes		

Company:	**Central European Value Fund**	**Safekeeping:**	No
		Invests:	Every 365 days beginning 9/15
Symbol:	CRF	**Minimum:**	$100
Exchange:	NYSE	**Maximum:**	$3,000/year
Industry:	Closed-end fund	**Min to qualify:**	1
Company Address:	Box 8209	**Fee on cash inv.:**	comm.
	Boston, MA 02266-8209	**Fee on div. inv.:**	comm.
Company Phone:	800-421-4777	**Discount (cash):**	0
Transfer Agent:	Boston Eq. (EquiServe)	**Discount (div.):**	0
Agent's Address:	P.O. Box 8200	**Auto invest:**	No
	Boston, MA 02266-8200	**Auto invest fee:**	$0
Agent's Phone:	800-426-5523	**Selling info:**	Sells 7-10 bus. days upon request,
Other than USA:	Yes		by mail or phone, at market, for
			$2.50 +15¢/sh.

Company:	**Central Hudson G&E Corp.**		Safekeeping:	Yes
			Invests:	Every 30 days beginning 1/1
Symbol:	CNH		Minimum:	$50
Exchange:	NYSE		Maximum:	$150,000/year
Industry:	Utility-electric, gas		Min to qualify:	1
Company Address:	284 South Ave.		Fee on cash inv.:	0!
	Poughkeepsie, NY 12601-4879		Fee on div. inv.:	0!
Company Phone:	914-486-5204		Discount (cash):	0
Transfer Agent:	FCT (EquiServe)		Discount (div.):	0
Agent's Address:	P.O. Box 2500		Auto invest:	Yes
	Jersey City, NJ 07303-2500		Auto invest fee:	$0
Agent's Phone:	800-428-9578		Selling info:	Sells irregularly, by mail, at market, for $10 +12¢/sh.
Other than USA:	Yes			

Company:	**Central Vermont Public Service**		Safekeeping:	Yes
			Invests:	Every 30 days beginning 1/15
Symbol:	CV		Minimum:	$100
Exchange:	NYSE		Maximum:	$6,000/quarter
Industry:	Utility-electric		Min to qualify:	1
Company Address:	77 Grove St.		Fee on cash inv.:	5¢/sh.
	Rutland, VT 05701		Fee on div. inv.:	5¢/sh.
Company Phone:	800-354-2877 or 802-747-5205		Discount (cash):	0
Transfer Agent:	BankBoston (EquiServe)		Discount (div.):	0
Agent's Address:	P.O. Box 8040		Auto invest:	Yes
	Boston, MA 02266-8040		Auto invest fee:	$0
Agent's Phone:	800-736-3001		Selling info:	Sells within 10 bus. days, by mail, at avg. price, for 10¢/sh.
Other than USA:	Yes			

Company:	**Centura Banks, Inc.**		Safekeeping:	Yes
Symbol:	CBC		Invests:	Every 30 days beginning 1/15
Exchange:	NYSE		Minimum:	$25
Industry:	Banking		Maximum:	$10,000/month
Company Address:	134 North Church St., Box 1220		Min to qualify:	100
	Rocky Mount, NC 27802		Fee on cash inv.:	comm.
Company Phone:	800-436-5898 or 919-977-4400		Fee on div. inv.:	comm.
Transfer Agent:	Registrar & Transfer Co.		Discount (cash):	0
Agent's Address:	10 Commerce Drive		Discount (div.):	0
	Cranford, NJ 07016		Auto invest:	Yes
Agent's Phone:	800-368-5948		Auto invest fee:	$0
Other than USA:	Yes		Selling info:	Sells within 10 bus. days, by mail, at avg. price, for comm.

Company:	**CenturyTel, Inc.**		Safekeeping:	Yes
Symbol:	CTL		Invests:	Every 30 days beginning 1/15
Exchange:	NYSE		Minimum:	$25
Industry:	Telecommunications		Maximum:	$5,000/quarter
Company Address:	Box 4065		Min to qualify:	1
	Monroe, LA 71211-4065		Fee on cash inv.:	0!
Company Phone:	800-833-1188 or 318-388-9648		Fee on div. inv.:	0!
Transfer Agent:	Harris Trust & Savings Bank		Discount (cash):	0
Agent's Address:	P.O. Box A3504		Discount (div.):	0
	Chicago, IL 60690-3504		Auto invest:	Yes
			Auto invest fee:	$0
Agent's Phone:	800-969-6718		Selling info:	Sells monthly, by mail or fax, at market, for comm.
Other than USA:	Yes			

Company:	**CFW Communications Co.**	Safekeeping:	Yes
Symbol:	CFWC	Invests:	Every 30 days beginning 1/29
Exchange:	OTC	Minimum:	$50
Industry:	Communications	Maximum:	$10,000/quarter
Company Address:	401 Spring Ln., Ste. 300, Box 1990	Min to qualify:	1
	Waynesboro, VA 22980	Fee on cash inv.:	0!
Company Phone:	888-221-4239 or 540-946-3500	Fee on div. inv.:	comm.
Transfer Agent:	CFW Communications Co.,	Discount (cash):	0
	Shareholder Services	Discount (div.):	0
Agent's Address:	P.O. Box 1990	Auto invest:	No
	Waynesboro, VA 22980	Auto invest fee:	$0
Agent's Phone:	888-221-4239	Selling info:	Sells monthly, by mail, at market,
Other than USA:	Yes		for comm.

Company:	**Champion International**	Safekeeping:	No
Symbol:	CHA	Invests:	Every 30 days beginning 1/10
Exchange:	NYSE	Minimum:	$10
Industry:	Forest prod.	Maximum:	$5,000/month
Company Address:	One Champion Plz.	Min to qualify:	1
	Stamford, CT 06921	Fee on cash inv.:	0
Company Phone:	203-358-7000	Fee on div. inv.:	0
Transfer Agent:	ChaseMellon Shareholder Services	Discount (cash):	0
Agent's Address:	P.O. Box 3338	Discount (div.):	0
	South Hackensack, NJ 07606	Auto invest:	No
Agent's Phone:	800-663-8236	Auto invest fee:	$0
Other than USA:	No	Selling info:	Sells biweekly, by mail or phone,
			at avg. price, for $0!

Company:	**Charles E. Smith Res. Rlty. Inc.**	Safekeeping:	Yes
		Invests:	Every 30 days beginning 1/15
Symbol:	SRW	Minimum:	$200
Exchange:	NYSE	Maximum:	$25,000/year
Industry:	REIT	Min to qualify:	1
Company Address:	2345 Crystal Dr.	Fee on cash inv.:	0
	Arlington, VA 22202	Fee on div. inv.:	0
Company Phone:	703-769-1000 or 703-769-1334	Discount (cash):	0
Transfer Agent:	First Union National Bank of NC	Discount (div.):	0
Agent's Address:	1525 West W.T. Harris Blvd.	Auto invest:	No
	NC-1153	Auto invest fee:	$0
	Charlotte, NC 28288-1153	Selling info:	Sells daily, by mail, at market, for
Agent's Phone:	800-829-8432		5¢/sh.
Other than USA:	Yes		

Company:	**Chart Industries**	Safekeeping:	Yes
Symbol:	CTI	Invests:	Every 30 days beginning 1/15
Exchange:	NYSE	Minimum:	$10
Industry:	Mfr. custom built industrial equipment	Maximum:	$5,000/month
		Min to qualify:	1
Company Address:	5885 Landerbrook Dr., Ste.150	Fee on cash inv.:	0
	Cleveland, OH 44124	Fee on div. inv.:	0
Company Phone:	440-753-1490	Discount (cash):	0
Transfer Agent:	National City Bank	Discount (div.):	0
Agent's Address:	P.O. Box 92301	Auto invest:	No
	Cleveland, OH 44193-0900	Auto invest fee:	$0
Agent's Phone:	800-622-6757	Selling info:	Sells weekly, by mail, at market,
Other than USA:	Yes		for 20¢/sh.

Company:	**Charter One Financial Inc.**
Symbol:	COFI
Exchange:	OTC
Industry:	Banking
Company Address:	1215 Superior Ave.
	Cleveland, OH 44114
Company Phone:	800-262-6301 or 216-566-5300
Transfer Agent:	BankBoston (EquiServe)
Agent's Address:	P.O. Box 8040
	Boston, MA 02266-8040
Agent's Phone:	800-733-5001
Other than USA:	No

Safekeeping:	Yes
Invests:	Every 30 days beginning 1/20
Minimum:	$50
Maximum:	$5,000/month
Min to qualify:	10
Fee on cash inv.:	$5
Fee on div. inv.:	0
Discount (cash):	0
Discount (div.):	0
Auto invest:	No
Auto invest fee:	$0
Selling info:	Sells daily, by mail, at market, for $15 + comm.

Company:	**Chemed Corp.**
Symbol:	CHE
Exchange:	NYSE
Industry:	Diversified services
Company Address:	2600 Chemed Ctr., 255 East Fifth St.
	Cincinnati, OH 45202-4726
Company Phone:	800-2CHEMED or 513-762-6900
Transfer Agent:	Norwest Bank Minnesota, N.A.
Agent's Address:	P.O. Box 64854
	St. Paul, MN 55164-0854
Agent's Phone:	800-468-9716
Other than USA:	Yes

Safekeeping:	Yes
Invests:	Every 30 days beginning 1/10
Minimum:	$50
Maximum:	$5,000/month
Min to qualify:	25
Fee on cash inv.:	0!
Fee on div. inv.:	0!
Discount (cash):	0
Discount (div.):	0
Auto invest:	Yes
Auto invest fee:	$0
Selling info:	Sells irregularly, by mail or phone, at market, for $5 + comm.

Company:	**Chemical Financial Corp.**
Symbol:	CHFC
Exchange:	OTC
Industry:	Banking
Company Address:	333 East Main St., Box 569
	Midland, MI 48640-0569
Company Phone:	517-631-3310 or 517-839-5358
Transfer Agent:	Harris Trust & Savings Bank
Agent's Address:	311 W. Monroe St., 11th Floor
	Chicago, IL 60690-3504
Agent's Phone:	800-942-5909
Other than USA:	Yes

Safekeeping:	Yes
Invests:	Every 15 days beginning 1/15
Minimum:	$10
Maximum:	$3,000/quarter
Min to qualify:	1
Fee on cash inv.:	0
Fee on div. inv.:	0
Discount (cash):	0
Discount (div.):	0
Auto invest:	No
Auto invest fee:	$0
Selling info:	Sells weekly, by mail or fax, at market, for 0

Company:	**Chesapeake Corp.**
Symbol:	CSK
Exchange:	NYSE
Industry:	Packaging & tissue
Company Address:	1021 East Cary St., Box 2350
	Richmond, VA 23218-2350
Company Phone:	804-697-1160
Transfer Agent:	Harris Trust & Savings Bank
Agent's Address:	P.O. Box A-3309
	Chicago, IL 60690
Agent's Phone:	312-360-5163
Other than USA:	Yes

Safekeeping:	No
Invests:	Every 30 days beginning 1/15
Minimum:	$10
Maximum:	$5,000/quarter
Min to qualify:	1
Fee on cash inv.:	0
Fee on div. inv.:	0
Discount (cash):	0
Discount (div.):	0
Auto invest:	No
Auto invest fee:	$0
Selling info:	Sells irregularly, by mail, at market, for 7¢ to 10¢/sh.

Company:	**Chesapeake Utilities Corp.**	Safekeeping:	Yes
		Invests:	Every 30 days beginning 1/5
Symbol:	CPK	Minimum:	$50
Exchange:	NYSE	Maximum:	$15,000/quarter
Industry:	Natural gas	Min to qualify:	1
Company Address:	909 Silver Lake Blvd.	Fee on cash inv.:	0
	Dover, DE 19904	Fee on div. inv.:	0
Company Phone:	888-742-5275	Discount (cash):	0
Transfer Agent:	Boston Eq. (EquiServe)	Discount (div.):	0
Agent's Address:	P.O. Box 8040	Auto invest:	No
	Boston, MA 02266-8040	Auto invest fee:	$0
Agent's Phone:	800-736-3001	Selling info:	Sells daily, by mail, at market, for
Other than USA:	Yes		comm.

Company:	**Chester Valley Bancorp**	Safekeeping:	Yes
Symbol:	CVAL	Invests:	Every 90 days beginning 3/1
Exchange:	OTC	Minimum:	$50
Industry:	Savings and loan	Maximum:	$10,000/year
Company Address:	100 East Lancaster Ave.	Min to qualify:	1
	Downington, PA 19335	Fee on cash inv.:	0
Company Phone:	610-269-9700	Fee on div. inv.:	0
Transfer Agent:	American Stock Transfer	Discount (cash):	5%
Agent's Address:	40 Wall Street-46th floor	Discount (div.):	5%
	New York, NY 10005	Auto invest:	No
Agent's Phone:	800-937-5449 or 718-921-8200	Auto invest fee:	$0
Other than USA:	No	Selling info:	Sells n/o, by N/o, at n/o, for n/o

Company:	**Chevron Corp.**	Safekeeping:	Yes
Symbol:	CHV	Invests:	Every 5 days beginning 1/1
Exchange:	NYSE	Minimum:	$50
Industry:	Oil refining, marketing	Maximum:	$100,000/year
Company Address:	575 Market St., Rm. 3444	Min to qualify:	1
	San Francisco, CA 94105-2856	Fee on cash inv.:	$3 + 8¢/sh.
Company Phone:	800-926-7372 or 415-894-5690	Fee on div. inv.:	5% to $2.50 + 8¢/sh.
Transfer Agent:	ChaseMellon Shareholder Services	Discount (cash):	0
		Discount (div.):	0
Agent's Address:	P.O. Box 3337	Auto invest:	Yes
	South Hackensack, NJ 07606	Auto invest fee:	$1.50 + 8¢/sh.
Agent's Phone:	800-368-8357	Selling info:	Sells weekly, by mail or phone, at
Other than USA:	Yes		market, for $10 + 8¢/sh.

Company:	**Chicago Bridge & Iron Co. N.V.**	Safekeeping:	Yes
		Invests:	Every 7 days beginning varies
Symbol:	CBI	Minimum:	$50
Exchange:	NYSE	Maximum:	$250,000/year
Industry:	Construction services	Min to qualify:	1
Company Address:	c/o BNY,101 Barclay St.,22 West	Fee on cash inv.:	$5 + 10¢/sh.
	New York, NY 10286	Fee on div. inv.:	5% to $5 + 10¢/sh.
Company Phone:	800-943-9715	Discount (cash):	0
Transfer Agent:	Bank of New York	Discount (div.):	0
Agent's Address:	P.O. Box 11258	Auto invest:	Yes
	New York, NY 10286	Auto invest fee:	$5 + 10¢/sh.
Agent's Phone:	888-269-2377	Selling info:	Sells weekly, by mail, at market,
Other than USA:	Yes		for $5 +10¢/sh.

Company:	**Chicago Title Corp.**	**Safekeeping:**	Yes
Symbol:	CTZ	**Invests:**	Every 30 days beginning varies
Exchange:	NYSE	**Minimum:**	$100
Industry:	Insurance, property & casualty	**Maximum:**	$30,000/quarter
Company Address:	171 North Clark St.	**Min to qualify:**	1
	Chicago, IL 60601-3294	**Fee on cash inv.:**	$5 + 10¢/sh.
Company Phone:	888-431-4288 or 312-223-2959	**Fee on div. inv.:**	0!
Transfer Agent:	Harris Trust & Savings Bank	**Discount (cash):**	0
Agent's Address:	P.O. Box A3309	**Discount (div.):**	0
	Chicago, IL 06090-3309	**Auto invest:**	Yes
Agent's Phone:	877-424-1981	**Auto invest fee:**	$1.50 + 10¢/sh.
Other than USA:	Yes	**Selling info:**	Sells within 10 bus. days, by mail, at market, for $10 +10¢/sh.

Company:	**Chile Fund**	**Safekeeping:**	Yes
Symbol:	CH	**Invests:**	Every 5 days beginning Wed.
Exchange:	NYSE	**Minimum:**	$100
Industry:	Closed-end fund	**Maximum:**	$100,000/year
Company Address:	c/o Credit Suisse, 153 East 53rd	**Min to qualify:**	1
	St.	**Fee on cash inv.:**	$5 + 8¢/sh.
	New York, NY 10022	**Fee on div. inv.:**	0!
Company Phone:	800-293-1232 or 212-238-5674	**Discount (cash):**	0
Transfer Agent:	BankBoston (EquiServe)	**Discount (div.):**	0
Agent's Address:	P.O. Box 8040	**Auto invest:**	Yes
	Boston, MA 02266-8040	**Auto invest fee:**	$5 + 8¢/sh.
Agent's Phone:	800-730-6001	**Selling info:**	Sells weekly, by mail, at market, for $10 +15¢/sh.
Other than USA:	Yes		

Company:	**China Eastern Airlines Corp.**	**Safekeeping:**	Yes
		Invests:	Every 7 days beginning varies
Symbol:	CEA	**Minimum:**	$50
Exchange:	NYSE	**Maximum:**	$250,000/year
Industry:	Airline	**Min to qualify:**	1
Company Address:	c/o BNY,101 Barclay St.,22 West	**Fee on cash inv.:**	$5 + 10¢/sh.
	New York, NY 10286	**Fee on div. inv.:**	0
Company Phone:	800-943-9715	**Discount (cash):**	0
Transfer Agent:	Bank of New York	**Discount (div.):**	0
Agent's Address:	P.O. Box 11258	**Auto invest:**	Yes
	New York, NY 10286	**Auto invest fee:**	$5 + 10¢/sh.
Agent's Phone:	888-269-2377	**Selling info:**	Sells weekly, by mail, at market, for $5 +10¢/sh.
Other than USA:	Yes		

Company:	**China Southern Airlines Co. Ltd.**	**Safekeeping:**	Yes
		Invests:	Every 7 days beginning varies
Symbol:	ZNH	**Minimum:**	$50
Exchange:	NYSE	**Maximum:**	$250,000/year
Industry:	Airline	**Min to qualify:**	1
Company Address:	c/o BNY,101 Barclay St.,22 West	**Fee on cash inv.:**	$5 + 10¢/sh.
	New York, NY 10286	**Fee on div. inv.:**	0
Company Phone:	800-943-9715	**Discount (cash):**	0
Transfer Agent:	Bank of New York	**Discount (div.):**	0
Agent's Address:	P.O. Box 11258	**Auto invest:**	Yes
	New York, NY 10286	**Auto invest fee:**	$5 + 10¢/sh.
Agent's Phone:	888-269-2377	**Selling info:**	Sells weekly, by mail, at market, for $5 +10¢/sh.
Other than USA:	Yes		

Company:	**China Telecom Ltd.**	Safekeeping:	Yes
Symbol:	CHL	Invests:	Every 7 days beginning varies
Exchange:	NYSE	Minimum:	$50
Industry:	Communications services	Maximum:	$250,000/year
Company Address:	c/o BNY,101 Barclay St.,22 West	Min to qualify:	1
	New York, NY 10286	Fee on cash inv.:	$5 + 10¢/sh.
Company Phone:	800-943-9715	Fee on div. inv.:	0
Transfer Agent:	Bank of New York	Discount (cash):	0
Agent's Address:	P.O. Box 11258	Discount (div.):	0
	New York, NY 10286	Auto invest:	Yes
Agent's Phone:	888-269-2377	Auto invest fee:	$5 + 10¢/sh.
Other than USA:	Yes	Selling info:	Sells weekly, by mail, at market, for $5 +10¢/sh.

Company:	**Chittenden Corp.**	Safekeeping:	Yes
Symbol:	CHZ	Invests:	Every 90 days beginning 2/21
Exchange:	NYSE	Minimum:	$25
Industry:	Banking	Maximum:	$10,000/quarter
Company Address:	Box 820	Min to qualify:	1
	Burlington, VT 05402-0820	Fee on cash inv.:	0!
Company Phone:	802-660-1412	Fee on div. inv.:	0!
Transfer Agent:	BankBoston (EquiServe)	Discount (cash):	0
Agent's Address:	P.O. Box 8040	Discount (div.):	0
	Boston, MA 02266	Auto invest:	No
Agent's Phone:	800-730-4001	Auto invest fee:	$0
Other than USA:	Yes	Selling info:	Sells daily, by mail, at market, for 5% to $10

Company:	**Chock Full O' Nuts**	Safekeeping:	Yes
Symbol:	CHF	Invests:	Every 7 days beginning varies
Exchange:	NYSE	Minimum:	$50
Industry:	Roasts, packs, & markets coffee	Maximum:	$10,000/transaction
Company Address:	370 Lexington Ave.	Min to qualify:	1
	New York, NY 10017	Fee on cash inv.:	$7.50 + 10¢/sh.
Company Phone:	212-532-0300	Fee on div. inv.:	0
Transfer Agent:	American Stock Transfer	Discount (cash):	0
Agent's Address:	40 Wall St.	Discount (div.):	0
	New York, NY 10005	Auto invest:	Yes
Agent's Phone:	718-921-8200	Auto invest fee:	$0
Other than USA:	Yes	Selling info:	Sells weekly, by mail, at market, for $7.50 +10¢/sh.

Company:	**Chubb Corp.**	Safekeeping:	Yes
Symbol:	CB	Invests:	Every 30 days beginning 1/10
Exchange:	NYSE	Minimum:	$10
Industry:	Insurance	Maximum:	$60,000/year
Company Address:	15 Mountain View Rd., Box 1615	Min to qualify:	1
	Warren, NJ 07061-1615	Fee on cash inv.:	5% to $3
Company Phone:	908-903-2000	Fee on div. inv.:	5% to $3
Transfer Agent:	FCT (EquiServe)	Discount (cash):	0
Agent's Address:	P.O. Box 2500	Discount (div.):	0
	Jersey City, NJ 07303-2500	Auto invest:	Yes
Agent's Phone:	800-317-4445	Auto invest fee:	$1
Other than USA:	Yes	Selling info:	Sells daily, by mail or phone, at market, for $10 +12¢/sh.

Company:	**Church & Dwight Co., Inc.**	Safekeeping:	Yes
Symbol:	CHD	Invests:	Every 90 days beginning 5/30
Exchange:	NYSE	Minimum:	$250
Industry:	Consumer products	Maximum:	$5,000/quarter
Company Address:	469 North Harrison St.	Min to qualify:	1
	Princeton, NJ 08543-5297	Fee on cash inv.:	0!
Company Phone:	609-683-7078 or 609-683-5900	Fee on div. inv.:	0!
Transfer Agent:	ChaseMellon Shareholder Services	Discount (cash):	0
Agent's Address:	P.O. Box 3338	Discount (div.):	0
	South Hackensack, NJ 07606	Auto invest:	No
Agent's Phone:	800-851-9677	Auto invest fee:	$0
Other than USA:	Yes	Selling info:	Sells daily, by mail, at market, for $15 + comm.

Company:	**CIGNA Corp.**	Safekeeping:	Yes
Symbol:	CI	Invests:	Every 30 days beginning 1/10
Exchange:	NYSE	Minimum:	$10
Industry:	Insurance	Maximum:	$5,000/month
Company Address:	2 Liberty Pl., Box 7716	Min to qualify:	1
	Philadelphia, PA 19192-2378	Fee on cash inv.:	0!
Company Phone:	215-761-3516	Fee on div. inv.:	0!
Transfer Agent:	FCT (EquiServe)	Discount (cash):	0
Agent's Address:	P.O. Box 2598	Discount (div.):	0
	Jersey City, NJ 07303-2598	Auto invest:	No
Agent's Phone:	800-317-4445	Auto invest fee:	$0
Other than USA:	Yes	Selling info:	Sells daily, by phone or mail, at market, for $15 +12¢/sh.

Company:	**CILCORP Inc.**	Safekeeping:	Yes
Symbol:	CER	Invests:	Every 30 days beginning 1/1
Exchange:	NYSE	Minimum:	$25
Industry:	Utility-electic, gas	Maximum:	$25,000/quarter
Company Address:	300 Hamilton Blvd., Ste.300	Min to qualify:	1
	Peoria, IL 61602-8892	Fee on cash inv.:	0!
Company Phone:	800-622-5514	Fee on div. inv.:	0!
Transfer Agent:	CILCORP Inc.	Discount (cash):	0
Agent's Address:	300 Hamilton Blvd., Suite 300	Discount (div.):	0
	Peoria, IL 61602-1238	Auto invest:	No
Agent's Phone:	800-622-5514	Auto invest fee:	$0
Other than USA:	Yes	Selling info:	Sells within 10 bus. days, by mail or fax, at avg. price, for 5¢/sh.

Company:	**Cincinnati Bell Inc.**	Safekeeping:	No
Symbol:	CSN	Invests:	Every 30 days beginning 1/1
Exchange:	NYSE	Minimum:	$25
Industry:	Telecommunications	Maximum:	$5,000/month
Company Address:	Box 2301	Min to qualify:	1
	Cincinnati, OH 45201	Fee on cash inv.:	0!
Company Phone:	800-345-6301 or 513-397-6462	Fee on div. inv.:	0!
Transfer Agent:	Fifth Third Bancorp	Discount (cash):	0
Agent's Address:	38 Fountain Sq. Plz., MD 1090F5	Discount (div.):	0
	Cincinnati, OH 45263	Auto invest:	No
Agent's Phone:	800-837-2755	Auto invest fee:	$0
Other than USA:	Yes	Selling info:	Sells weekly, by mail, at market, for comm.

Company:	**Cincinnati Financial Corp.**	Safekeeping:	Yes
Symbol:	CINF	Invests:	Every 30 days beginning 1/8
Exchange:	OTC	Minimum:	$25
Industry:	Insurance	Maximum:	$5,000/month
Company Address:	Box 145496	Min to qualify:	1
	Fairfield, OH 45250-5496	Fee on cash inv.:	$3
		Fee on div. inv.:	5% to $3
Company Phone:	513-870-2639 or 513-870-2000	Discount (cash):	0
Transfer Agent:	Fifth Third Bank	Discount (div.):	0
Agent's Address:	P.O. Box 478	Auto invest:	No
	Cincinnati, OH 45273-9611	Auto invest fee:	$0
Agent's Phone:	513-744-7343	Selling info:	Sells weekly, by mail, at market,
Other than USA:	No		for 0!

Company:	**Cinergy Corp.**	Safekeeping:	Yes
Symbol:	CIN	Invests:	Every 30 days beginning 1/15
Exchange:	NYSE	Minimum:	$25
Industry:	Utility-electric, gas	Maximum:	$100,000/year
Company Address:	139 East Fourth St., Box 900	Min to qualify:	1
	Cincinnati, OH 45201-0900	Fee on cash inv.:	0!
Company Phone:	800-325-2945 or 513-287-1940	Fee on div. inv.:	0!
Transfer Agent:	Cinergy Corp.	Discount (cash):	0
Agent's Address:	P.O. Box 900	Discount (div.):	0
	Cincinnati, OH 45201-0900	Auto invest:	No
Agent's Phone:	800-325-2945	Auto invest fee:	$0
Other than USA:	Yes	Selling info:	Sells weekly, by mail or fax, at
			market, for 4¢/sh.

Company:	**Citizens Banking Corp.**	Safekeeping:	Yes
Symbol:	CBCF	Invests:	Every 30 days beginning 1/15
Exchange:	OTC	Minimum:	$25
Industry:	Banking	Maximum:	$2,000/month
Company Address:	328 South Saginaw St.	Min to qualify:	1
	Flint, MI 48502-2401	Fee on cash inv.:	0!
Company Phone:	810-766-7500 or 810-257-2593	Fee on div. inv.:	0!
Transfer Agent:	Harris Trust & Savings Bank	Discount (cash):	0
Agent's Address:	P.O.Box A3504	Discount (div.):	0
	Chicago, IL 60690-3504	Auto invest:	No
Agent's Phone:	877-795-0772	Auto invest fee:	$0
Other than USA:	No	Selling info:	Sells daily, by mail or phone, at
			market, for 10¢/sh.

Company:	**Citizens Utilities B**	Safekeeping:	Yes
Symbol:	CZN	Invests:	Every 30 days beginning 1/15
Exchange:	NYSE	Minimum:	$100
Industry:	Telecomm., gas, electric, water,	Maximum:	$25,000/quarter
	wastewater	Min to qualify:	1
Company Address:	3 High Ridge Park	Fee on cash inv.:	$6 + 2¢/sh.
	Stamford, CT 06905-1390	Fee on div. inv.:	0
Company Phone:	800-248-8845 or 203-614-5003	Discount (cash):	0
Transfer Agent:	Illinois Stock Transfer Co.-Direct	Discount (div.):	0
	Stock Purchase Plan	Auto invest:	Yes
Agent's Address:	209 W. Jackson Blvd., Ste. 1210	Auto invest fee:	$0
	Chicago, IL 60606-6905	Selling info:	Sells weekly, by mail or fax, at avg.
Agent's Phone:	800-757-5755		price, for $15 +2¢/sh.
Other than USA:	No		

Company:	**City Holding Co.**	**Safekeeping:**	Yes
Symbol:	CHCO	**Invests:**	Every 90 days beginning 3/15
Exchange:	OTC	**Minimum:**	$50
Industry:	Banking	**Maximum:**	$5,000/quarter
Company Address:	25 Gatewater Rd.	**Min to qualify:**	1
	Cross Lanes, WV 25313	**Fee on cash inv.:**	0!
Company Phone:	304-925-6611	**Fee on div. inv.:**	0!
Transfer Agent:	SunTrust Bank, Atlanta	**Discount (cash):**	0
Agent's Address:	P.O. Box 4625	**Discount (div.):**	0
	Atlanta, GA 30302	**Auto invest:**	No
Agent's Phone:	800-568-3476	**Auto invest fee:**	$0
Other than USA:	Yes	**Selling info:**	Sells daily, by n/o, at market, for n/o

Company:	**CLARCOR Inc.**	**Safekeeping:**	No
Symbol:	CLC	**Invests:**	Every 30 days beginning 1/31
Exchange:	NYSE	**Minimum:**	$25
Industry:	Manufacturing, filters, packaging	**Maximum:**	$3,000/month
Company Address:	2323 6th St., Box 7007	**Min to qualify:**	1
	Rockford, IL 61125	**Fee on cash inv.:**	0!
Company Phone:	815-962-8867	**Fee on div. inv.:**	0!
Transfer Agent:	FCT (EquiServe)	**Discount (cash):**	0
Agent's Address:	P.O. Box 2506	**Discount (div.):**	0
	Jersey City, NJ 07303-2506	**Auto invest:**	No
Agent's Phone:	800-446-2617	**Auto invest fee:**	$0
Other than USA:	No	**Selling info:**	Sells within 10 bus. days, by mail, at market, for $0

Company:	**Clayton Homes, Inc.**	**Safekeeping:**	No
Symbol:	CMH	**Invests:**	Every 15 days beginning 1/5
Exchange:	NYSE	**Minimum:**	$100
Industry:	Mobile home manufacturer	**Maximum:**	$5,000/quarter
Company Address:	Box 15169	**Min to qualify:**	1
	Knoxville, TN 37901	**Fee on cash inv.:**	0
Company Phone:	423-380-3000	**Fee on div. inv.:**	0
Transfer Agent:	American Stock Transfer	**Discount (cash):**	0
Agent's Address:	40 Wall Street	**Discount (div.):**	0
	New York, NY 10005	**Auto invest:**	No
Agent's Phone:	800-937-5449 or 800-278-4353	**Auto invest fee:**	$0
Other than USA:	Yes	**Selling info:**	Sells irregularly, by mail, at market, for comm.

Company:	**CLECO Corp.**	**Safekeeping:**	Yes
Symbol:	CNL	**Invests:**	Every 30 days beginning 1/1
Exchange:	NYSE	**Minimum:**	$25
Industry:	Utility-electric, gas	**Maximum:**	$5,000/month
Company Address:	Box 5000	**Min to qualify:**	1
	Pineville, LA 71361-5000	**Fee on cash inv.:**	0!
Company Phone:	800-253-2652 or 318-484-7400	**Fee on div. inv.:**	0!
Transfer Agent:	FCT (EquiServe)	**Discount (cash):**	0
Agent's Address:	P.O. Box 2500	**Discount (div.):**	0
	Jersey City, NJ 07303	**Auto invest:**	No
Agent's Phone:	201-324-0137	**Auto invest fee:**	$0
Other than USA:	No	**Selling info:**	Sells daily, by mail or fax, at market, for $10 + comm.

Company:	**Cleveland-Cliffs Inc.**	**Safekeeping:**	Yes
Symbol:	CLF	**Invests:**	Every 30 days beginning 1/1
Exchange:	NYSE	**Minimum:**	$20
Industry:	Metals	**Maximum:**	$30,000/year
Company Address:	1100 Superior Ave., 18th Fl.	**Min to qualify:**	1
	Cleveland, OH 44114-2589	**Fee on cash inv.:**	0!
Company Phone:	800-214-0739 or 216-694-5459	**Fee on div. inv.:**	0!
Transfer Agent:	FCT (EquiServe)	**Discount (cash):**	0
Agent's Address:	P.O. Box 2500	**Discount (div.):**	0
	Jersey City, NJ 07303-2500	**Auto invest:**	Yes
Agent's Phone:	800-446-2617	**Auto invest fee:**	$1
Other than USA:	No	**Selling info:**	Sells daily, by phone, mail, or fax, at market, for $5 +12¢/sh.

Company:	**Clorox**	**Safekeeping:**	Yes
Symbol:	CLX	**Invests:**	Every 30 days beginning 1/15
Exchange:	NYSE	**Minimum:**	$10
Industry:	Consumer products	**Maximum:**	$60,000/year
Company Address:	1221 Broadway	**Min to qualify:**	1
	Oakland, CA 94612	**Fee on cash inv.:**	0
Company Phone:	888-259-6973 or 510-271-7000	**Fee on div. inv.:**	0
Transfer Agent:	FCT (EquiServe)	**Discount (cash):**	0
Agent's Address:	P.O. Box 2500	**Discount (div.):**	0
	Jersey City, NJ 07303-2500	**Auto invest:**	Yes
Agent's Phone:	201-324-1644	**Auto invest fee:**	$1
Other than USA:	Yes	**Selling info:**	Sells daily, by phone or mail, at market, for $10 +12¢/sh.

Company:	**CMP Group Inc.**	**Safekeeping:**	No
Symbol:	CTP	**Invests:**	Every 30 days beginning 1/2
Exchange:	NYSE	**Minimum:**	$10
Industry:	Utility-electric	**Maximum:**	$40,000/year
Company Address:	83 Edison Dr.	**Min to qualify:**	1
	Augusta, ME 04336	**Fee on cash inv.:**	0
Company Phone:	207-623-3521 or 207-621-3985	**Fee on div. inv.:**	0
Transfer Agent:	BankBoston (EquiServe)	**Discount (cash):**	0
Agent's Address:	P.O. Box 8040	**Discount (div.):**	0
	Boston, MA 02266-8040	**Auto invest:**	Yes
Agent's Phone:	800-736-3001	**Auto invest fee:**	$0
Other than USA:	Yes	**Selling info:**	Sells biweekly, by mail, at market, for 5¢/sh.

Company:	**CMS Energy**	**Safekeeping:**	Yes
Symbol:	CMS	**Invests:**	Every 30 days beginning 1/1
Exchange:	NYSE	**Minimum:**	$25
Industry:	Utility-electric	**Maximum:**	$120,000/year
Company Address:	212 West Michigan Ave.	**Min to qualify:**	1
	Jackson, MI 49201-2277	**Fee on cash inv.:**	0!
Company Phone:	517-788-1868	**Fee on div. inv.:**	0!
Transfer Agent:	CMS Investor Services Dept.	**Discount (cash):**	0
Agent's Address:	212 West Michigan Avenue	**Discount (div.):**	0
	Jackson, MI 49201-2236	**Auto invest:**	Yes
Agent's Phone:	517-788-1868	**Auto invest fee:**	$0
Other than USA:	Yes	**Selling info:**	Sells weekly, by mail or fax, at market, for 5¢/sh.

Company:	**CMS Energy G**
Symbol:	CPG
Exchange:	NYSE
Industry:	Utility-gas
Company Address:	212 West Michigan Ave.
	Jackson, MI 49201-2236
Company Phone:	517-788-1868
Transfer Agent:	CMS Investor Services Dept.
Agent's Address:	212 West Michigan Avenue
	Jackson, MI 49201-2236
Agent's Phone:	517-788-1868
Other than USA:	Yes

Safekeeping:	Yes
Invests:	Every 30 days beginning 1/1
Minimum:	$25
Maximum:	$120,000/year
Min to qualify:	1
Fee on cash inv.:	0
Fee on div. inv.:	0
Discount (cash):	0
Discount (div.):	0
Auto invest:	Yes
Auto invest fee:	$0
Selling info:	Sells weekly, by mail or fax, at market, for 5¢/sh.

Company:	**CNA Income Shares**
Symbol:	CNN
Exchange:	NYSE
Industry:	Closed-end bond fund
Company Address:	CNA Plaza 23-S
	Chicago, IL 60685
Company Phone:	312-822-4181
Transfer Agent:	Bank of New York
Agent's Address:	P.O. Box 11258, Church St. Station
	New York, NY 10286
Agent's Phone:	800-432-8224
Other than USA:	Yes

Safekeeping:	No
Invests:	Every 30 days beginning 1/1
Minimum:	$25
Maximum:	$unlimited
Min to qualify:	1
Fee on cash inv.:	comm.
Fee on div. inv.:	0
Discount (cash):	0
Discount (div.):	0
Auto invest:	No
Auto invest fee:	$0
Selling info:	Not available

Company:	**CNB Bancshares, Inc.**
Symbol:	BNK
Exchange:	NYSE
Industry:	Banking
Company Address:	Box 778
	Evansville, IN 47705-0778
Company Phone:	812-456-3416 or 812-456-3400
Transfer Agent:	Citizens National Bank of
	Evansville
Agent's Address:	Kathryn P. Williams, Box 778
	Evansville, IN 47705-0778
Agent's Phone:	812-456-3416
Other than USA:	No

Safekeeping:	Yes
Invests:	Every 30 days beginning 1/1
Minimum:	$50
Maximum:	$5,000/month
Min to qualify:	1
Fee on cash inv.:	0
Fee on div. inv.:	0
Discount (cash):	0
Discount (div.):	3%
Auto invest:	Yes
Auto invest fee:	$0
Selling info:	Not available

Company:	**CNB Financial Corp.**
Symbol:	CNBF
Exchange:	OTC
Industry:	Community banks
Company Address:	24 Church St.
	Canajoharie, NY 13317
Company Phone:	518-673-3243
Transfer Agent:	CNB Financial Corp
Agent's Address:	24 Church Street
	Canajoharie, NY 13317
Agent's Phone:	518-673-3243
Other than USA:	Yes

Safekeeping:	No
Invests:	Every 90 days beginning 3/10
Minimum:	$10
Maximum:	$3,000/quarter
Min to qualify:	1
Fee on cash inv.:	0!
Fee on div. inv.:	0!
Discount (cash):	0
Discount (div.):	0
Auto invest:	No
Auto invest fee:	$0
Selling info:	Not available

Company:	Coastal Corp.	**Safekeeping:**	Yes
Symbol:	CGP	**Invests:**	Every 15 days beginning 1/1-1/15
Exchange:	NYSE	**Minimum:**	$50
Industry:	Diversified energy	**Maximum:**	$120,000/year
Company Address:	9 Greenway Plaza	**Min to qualify:**	1
	Houston, TX 77046-0995	**Fee on cash inv.:**	5¢/sh.
Company Phone:	713-877-6821	**Fee on div. inv.:**	5¢/sh.
Transfer Agent:	The Coastal Corp.	**Discount (cash):**	0
Agent's Address:	Nine Greenway Plaza	**Discount (div.):**	0
	Houston, TX 77046-0995	**Auto invest:**	No
Agent's Phone:	800-788-2500 or 713-877-6821	**Auto invest fee:**	$0
Other than USA:	Yes	**Selling info:**	Sells bimonthly-1st & 15th, by mail or fax, at market, for 5¢/sh.

Company:	Coca-Cola Bottling Co. Consolidated	**Safekeeping:**	Yes
		Invests:	Every 30 days beginning 1/5
Symbol:	COKE	**Minimum:**	$10
Exchange:	OTC	**Maximum:**	$1,000/month
Industry:	Soft drink distr.	**Min to qualify:**	1
Company Address:	Box 31487	**Fee on cash inv.:**	4% to $2.50
	Charlotte, NC 28231	**Fee on div. inv.:**	4% to $2.50
Company Phone:	704-551-4038 or 704-551-4400	**Discount (cash):**	0
Transfer Agent:	First Union National Bank of NC	**Discount (div.):**	0
Agent's Address:	230 South Tryon St.	**Auto invest:**	Yes
	Charlotte, NC 28288-1154	**Auto invest fee:**	$0
Agent's Phone:	800-829-8432	**Selling info:**	Sells bimonthly, by mail, at avg. price, for 4% to $2.50
Other than USA:	No		

Company:	Coca-Cola Co.	**Safekeeping:**	Yes
Symbol:	KO	**Invests:**	Every 30 days beginning 1/1 except 12/15
Exchange:	NYSE		
Industry:	Beverages	**Minimum:**	$10
Company Address:	One Coca-Cola Plz.	**Maximum:**	$125,000/year
	Atlanta, GA 30313	**Min to qualify:**	1
Company Phone:	404-676-2121	**Fee on cash inv.:**	0!
Transfer Agent:	FCT (EquiServe)	**Fee on div. inv.:**	0!
Agent's Address:	P.O. Box 2500	**Discount (cash):**	0
	Jersey City, NJ 07303	**Discount (div.):**	0
Agent's Phone:	888-265-3747	**Auto invest:**	Yes
Other than USA:	Yes	**Auto invest fee:**	$1
		Selling info:	Sells daily, by phone, mail, or fax, at market, for $10 +12¢/sh.

Company:	Coca-Cola Enterprises Inc.	**Safekeeping:**	Yes
		Invests:	Every 15 days beginning 1/1
Symbol:	CCE	**Minimum:**	$10
Exchange:	NYSE	**Maximum:**	$100,000/year
Industry:	Non-alcoholic bottling company	**Min to qualify:**	1
Company Address:	Box 723040	**Fee on cash inv.:**	0!
	Atlanta, GA 31139-0040	**Fee on div. inv.:**	0!
Company Phone:	800-233-7210 or 770-989-3796	**Discount (cash):**	0
Transfer Agent:	FCT (EquiServe)	**Discount (div.):**	0
Agent's Address:	P.O. Box 2598	**Auto invest:**	Yes
	Jersey City, NJ 07303-2598	**Auto invest fee:**	$1
Agent's Phone:	800-418-4223	**Selling info:**	Sells daily, by mail or phone, at market, for $10 +12¢/sh.
Other than USA:	Yes		

Company:	**Coca-Cola FEMSA**	Safekeeping:	Yes
Symbol:	KOF	Invests:	Every 7 days beginning varies
Exchange:	NYSE	Minimum:	$50
Industry:	Beverages (non-alchoholic)	Maximum:	$250,000/year
Company Address:	c/o BNY,101 Barclay St.,22 West	Min to qualify:	1
	New York, NY 10286	Fee on cash inv.:	$5 + 10¢/sh.
Company Phone:	800-943-9715	Fee on div. inv.:	5% to $5 + 10¢/sh.
Transfer Agent:	Bank of New York	Discount (cash):	0
Agent's Address:	P.O. Box 11258	Discount (div.):	0
	New York, NY 10286	Auto invest:	Yes
Agent's Phone:	888-269-2377	Auto invest fee:	$5 + 10¢/sh.
Other than USA:	Yes	Selling info:	Sells weekly, by mail, at market, for $5 +10¢/sh.

Company:	**Codorus Valley Bancorp, Inc.**	Safekeeping:	Yes
		Invests:	Every 90 days beginning 2/26
Symbol:	CVLY	Minimum:	$100
Exchange:	OTC	Maximum:	$3,000/quarter
Industry:	Bank holding company	Min to qualify:	1
Company Address:	105 Leader Heights Rd., Box 2887	Fee on cash inv.:	0!
	York, PA 17405-2887	Fee on div. inv.:	0!
Company Phone:	717-846-1970	Discount (cash):	0
Transfer Agent:	Norwest Bank Minnesota, N.A.	Discount (div.):	0
Agent's Address:	P.O. Box 64856	Auto invest:	Yes
	St. Paul, MN 55164-0856	Auto invest fee:	$0
Agent's Phone:	800-468-9716	Selling info:	Sells monthly, by mail, at market,
Other than USA:	Yes		for $5 + 8¢/sh.

Company:	**Colgate-Palmolive**	Safekeeping:	Yes
Symbol:	CL	Invests:	Every 30 days beginning 1/15
Exchange:	NYSE	Minimum:	$20
Industry:	Household products	Maximum:	$60,000/year
Company Address:	300 Park Ave.	Min to qualify:	1
	New York, NY 10022-7499	Fee on cash inv.:	0!
Company Phone:	212-310-3312 or 800-850-2654	Fee on div. inv.:	0!
Transfer Agent:	FCT (EquiServe)	Discount (cash):	0
Agent's Address:	P.O. Box 2500	Discount (div.):	0
	Jersey City, NJ 07303-2500	Auto invest:	Yes
Agent's Phone:	800-756-8700	Auto invest fee:	$1
Other than USA:	Yes	Selling info:	Sells irregularly, by mail, at market, for $10 +12¢/sh.

Company:	**Colonial BancGroup, Inc. (The)**	Safekeeping:	Yes
		Invests:	Every 90 days beginning 2/9
Symbol:	CNB	Minimum:	$10
Exchange:	NYSE	Maximum:	$3,000/quarter
Industry:	Banking	Min to qualify:	1
Company Address:	Box 1108	Fee on cash inv.:	0
	Montgomery, AL 36101	Fee on div. inv.:	0
Company Phone:	888-843-0622 or 334-240-5061	Discount (cash):	0
Transfer Agent:	SunTrust Bank, Atlanta	Discount (div.):	0
Agent's Address:	P.O. Box 4625	Auto invest:	No
	Atlanta, GA 30302	Auto invest fee:	$0
Agent's Phone:	800-568-3476	Selling info:	Sells weekly, by mail or fax, at
Other than USA:	No		market, for comm.

Company:	**Columbia Bancorp**	**Safekeeping:**	No
Symbol:	CBMD	**Invests:**	Every 90 days beginning 1/5
Exchange:	OTC	**Minimum:**	$250
Industry:	Banking	**Maximum:**	$2,500/quarter
Company Address:	10480 Little Patuxent Pkwy.	**Min to qualify:**	1
	Columbia, MD 21044	**Fee on cash inv.:**	0!
Company Phone:	410-465-4800	**Fee on div. inv.:**	0!
Transfer Agent:	Registrar & Transfer Co.	**Discount (cash):**	0
Agent's Address:	10 Commerce Drive	**Discount (div.):**	3%
	Cranford, NJ 07016	**Auto invest:**	No
Agent's Phone:	800-368-5948	**Auto invest fee:**	$0
Other than USA:	Yes	**Selling info:**	Sells monthly, by mail, at market, for $10 + comm.

Company:	**Columbia Energy Group**	**Safekeeping:**	Yes
Symbol:	CG	**Invests:**	Every 30 days beginning 1/15
Exchange:	NYSE	**Minimum:**	$100
Industry:	Utility-gas	**Maximum:**	$25,000/quarter
Company Address:	13880 Dulles Corner Lane	**Min to qualify:**	1
	Herndon, VA 20171-4600	**Fee on cash inv.:**	0!
Company Phone:	703-561-6002 or 703-561-6000	**Fee on div. inv.:**	0!
Transfer Agent:	Harris Trust & Savings Bank	**Discount (cash):**	0
Agent's Address:	311 W. Monroe St.-11th Floor	**Discount (div.):**	0
	Chicago, IL 60606-4607	**Auto invest:**	No
Agent's Phone:	800-296-3913	**Auto invest fee:**	$0
Other than USA:	Yes	**Selling info:**	Sells within 5 bus. days, by mail, at market, for $1 +10¢/sh.

Company:	**Comerica Inc.**	**Safekeeping:**	Yes
Symbol:	CMA	**Invests:**	Every 90 days beginning 1/1
Exchange:	NYSE	**Minimum:**	$10
Industry:	Banking	**Maximum:**	$3,000/quarter
Company Address:	500 Woodward Ave., MC 3391	**Min to qualify:**	1
	Detroit, MI 48226	**Fee on cash inv.:**	0!
Company Phone:	800-521-1190 or 313-222-6317	**Fee on div. inv.:**	0!
Transfer Agent:	Norwest Bank Minnesota	**Discount (cash):**	0
Agent's Address:	P.O. Box 64854	**Discount (div.):**	0
	St. Paul, MN 55164-0854	**Auto invest:**	No
Agent's Phone:	800-468-9716	**Auto invest fee:**	$0
Other than USA:	No	**Selling info:**	Sells daily, by mail, at market, for $3 +15¢/sh.

Company:	**Commerce Bancorp, Inc.**	**Safekeeping:**	Yes
Symbol:	CBH	**Invests:**	Every 30 days beginning 1/15
Exchange:	NYSE	**Minimum:**	$100
Industry:	Bank holding company	**Maximum:**	$5,000/month
Company Address:	1701 Route 70 E.	**Min to qualify:**	1
	Cherry Hill, NJ 08034-5400	**Fee on cash inv.:**	0!
Company Phone:	609-751-9000 or 888-751-9000 x7108	**Fee on div. inv.:**	0!
Transfer Agent:	ChaseMellon Shareholder Services	**Discount (cash):**	3%
Agent's Address:	P.O. Box 750	**Discount (div.):**	3%
	Pittsburgh, PA 15230	**Auto invest:**	No
Agent's Phone:	888-470-5884	**Auto invest fee:**	$0
Other than USA:	Yes	**Selling info:**	Sells weekly, by mail, at market, for $15 +12¢/sh.

Company:	**Commercial Intertech**	Safekeeping:	Yes
Symbol:	TEC	Invests:	Every 90 days beginning 3/1
Exchange:	NYSE	Minimum:	$30
Industry:	Manufacturer	Maximum:	$5,000/quarter
Company Address:	1775 Logan Ave., Box 239	Min to qualify:	1
	Youngstown, OH 44501-0239	Fee on cash inv.:	comm.
Company Phone:	330-746-8011	Fee on div. inv.:	comm.
Transfer Agent:	ChaseMellon Shareholder Services	Discount (cash):	0
Agent's Address:	P.O. Box 3338	Discount (div.):	0
	South Hackensack, NJ 07606-8009	Auto invest:	No
Agent's Phone:	800-526-0801	Auto invest fee:	$0
Other than USA:	Yes	Selling info:	Not available

Company:	**Commonwealth Bank**	Safekeeping:	Yes
Symbol:	CMSB	Invests:	Every 30 days beginning 1/15
Exchange:	OTC	Minimum:	$100
Industry:	Banking	Maximum:	$2,500/quarter
Company Address:	2 West Lafayette St.	Min to qualify:	1
	Morristown, PA 19401	Fee on cash inv.:	$5
Company Phone:	610-251-1600	Fee on div. inv.:	0
Transfer Agent:	Registrar & Transfer Co.	Discount (cash):	0
Agent's Address:	P.O. Box 1010	Discount (div.):	0
	Cranford, NJ 07016	Auto invest:	No
Agent's Phone:	800-368-5948	Auto invest fee:	$0
Other than USA:	Yes	Selling info:	Sells irregularly, by mail, at market, for $15

Company:	**Commonwealth Energy System**	Safekeeping:	No
		Invests:	Every 30 days beginning 1/1
Symbol:	CES	Minimum:	$10
Exchange:	NYSE	Maximum:	$5,000/month
Industry:	Utility-electric, gas	Min to qualify:	1
Company Address:	One Main St., Box 9150	Fee on cash inv.:	0!
	Cambridge, MA 02142	Fee on div. inv.:	0!
Company Phone:	800-447-1183 or 617-225-4000	Discount (cash):	0
Transfer Agent:	BankBoston (EquiServe)	Discount (div.):	0
Agent's Address:	P.O. Box 8040	Auto invest:	No
	Boston, MA 02266	Auto invest fee:	$0
Agent's Phone:	800-730-4001	Selling info:	Not available
Other than USA:	Yes		

Company:	**Community Bank System, Inc.**	Safekeeping:	Yes
		Invests:	Every 30 days beginning 1/10
Symbol:	CBU	Minimum:	$100
Exchange:	NYSE	Maximum:	$5,000/month
Industry:	Banking	Min to qualify:	10
Company Address:	5790 Widewaters Pkwy.	Fee on cash inv.:	12¢/sh.
	DeWitt, NY 13214-1883	Fee on div. inv.:	0
Company Phone:	800-724-2262 or 315-445-2282	Discount (cash):	0
Transfer Agent:	ChaseMellon Shareholder Services	Discount (div.):	0
Agent's Address:	P.O. Box 3338	Auto invest:	Yes
	S. Hackensack, NJ 07606-1938	Auto invest fee:	$0
Agent's Phone:	888-213-0883	Selling info:	Sells weekly, by mail or phone, at market, for $15 +12¢/sh.
Other than USA:	Yes		

Company:	**Community First Bank-shares**	Safekeeping:	Yes
		Invests:	Every 30 days beginning 1/15
Symbol:	CFBX	Minimum:	$25
Exchange:	OTC	Maximum:	$3,000/quarter
Industry:	Banking	Min to qualify:	1
Company Address:	520 Main Ave.	Fee on cash inv.:	0
	Fargo, ND 58124-0001	Fee on div. inv.:	0
Company Phone:	701-298-5601 or 701-298-5600	Discount (cash):	0
Transfer Agent:	Norwest Bank Minnesota	Discount (div.):	0
Agent's Address:	P.O. Box 64854	Auto invest:	No
	St. Paul, MN 55164-0854	Auto invest fee:	$0
Agent's Phone:	800-468-9716	Selling info:	Not available
Other than USA:	Yes		

Company:	**Community Savings Bank-shares, Inc.**	Safekeeping:	Yes
		Invests:	Every 30 days beginning 1/1
Symbol:	CMSV	Minimum:	$25
Exchange:	OTC	Maximum:	$5,000/month
Industry:	Financial	Min to qualify:	1
Company Address:	660 U.S. Hwy. One, Box 14547	Fee on cash inv.:	0!
	North Palm Beach, FL 33408-0547	Fee on div. inv.:	0!
Company Phone:	561-881-2212	Discount (cash):	0
Transfer Agent:	ChaseMellon Shareholder Services	Discount (div.):	0
Agent's Address:	P.O. Box 3338	Auto invest:	No
	South Hackensack, NJ 07606-1938	Auto invest fee:	$0
Agent's Phone:	800-526-0801	Selling info:	Sells within 2 bus. days, by mail or
Other than USA:	Yes		fax, at market, for $15 + 6¢/sh.

Company:	**Companhia Brasileira de Distribuicao**	Safekeeping:	Yes
		Invests:	Every 7 days beginning varies
Symbol:	CBD	Minimum:	$50
Exchange:	NYSE	Maximum:	$250,000/year
Industry:	Retail supermarkets	Min to qualify:	1
Company Address:	c/o BNY,101 Barclay St., 22 West	Fee on cash inv.:	$5 + 10¢/sh.
	New York, NY 10286	Fee on div. inv.:	5% to $5 + 10¢/sh.
Company Phone:	800-943-9715	Discount (cash):	0
Transfer Agent:	Bank of New York	Discount (div.):	0
Agent's Address:	P.O. Box 11258	Auto invest:	Yes
	New York, NY 10286	Auto invest fee:	$5 + 10¢/sh.
Agent's Phone:	888-269-2377	Selling info:	Sells weekly, by mail, at market,
Other than USA:	Yes		for $5 +10¢/sh.

Company:	**Companhia Cervejaria Brahma**	Safekeeping:	Yes
		Invests:	Every 7 days beginning varies
Symbol:	BRHC	Minimum:	$50
Exchange:	NYSE	Maximum:	$250,000/year
Industry:	Beverages	Min to qualify:	1
Company Address:	c/o BNY,101 Barclay St.,22 West	Fee on cash inv.:	$5 + 10¢/sh.
	New York, NY 10286	Fee on div. inv.:	5% to $5 + 10¢/sh.
Company Phone:	800-943-9715	Discount (cash):	0
Transfer Agent:	Bank of New York	Discount (div.):	0
Agent's Address:	P.O. Box 11258	Auto invest:	Yes
	New York, NY 10286	Auto invest fee:	$5 + 10¢/sh.
Agent's Phone:	888-269-2377	Selling info:	Sells weekly, by mail, at market,
Other than USA:	Yes		for $5 +10¢/sh.

Company:	**Companhia Cervejaria Brahma, Preferred Preferred**	Safekeeping:	Yes
		Invests:	Every 7 days beginning varies
		Minimum:	$50
Symbol:	BRH	Maximum:	$250,000/year
Exchange:	NYSE	Min to qualify:	1
Industry:	Beverages	Fee on cash inv.:	$5 + 10¢/sh.
Company Address:	c/o BNY,101 Barclay St.,22 West	Fee on div. inv.:	5% to $5 + 10¢/sh.
	New York, NY 10286	Discount (cash):	0
Company Phone:	800-943-9715	Discount (div.):	0
Transfer Agent:	Bank of New York	Auto invest:	Yes
Agent's Address:	P.O. Box 11258	Auto invest fee:	$5 + 10¢/sh.
	New York, NY 10286	Selling info:	Sells weekly, by mail, at market,
Agent's Phone:	888-269-2377		for $5 +10¢/sh.
Other than USA:	Yes		

Company:	**Companhia Paranaense de Energia**	Safekeeping:	Yes
		Invests:	Every 7 days beginning varies
Symbol:	ELP	Minimum:	$50
Exchange:	NYSE	Maximum:	$250,000/year
Industry:	Electric utilities	Min to qualify:	1
Company Address:	c/o BNY,101 Barclay St.,22 West	Fee on cash inv.:	$5 + 10¢/sh.
	New York, NY 10286	Fee on div. inv.:	5% to $5 + 10¢/sh.
Company Phone:	800-943-9715	Discount (cash):	0
Transfer Agent:	Bank of New York	Discount (div.):	0
Agent's Address:	P.O. Box 11258	Auto invest:	Yes
	New York, NY 10286	Auto invest fee:	$5 + 10¢/sh.
Agent's Phone:	888-269-2377	Selling info:	Sells weekly, by mail, at market,
Other than USA:	Yes		for $5 +10¢/sh.

Company:	**Compania Cervecerias Unida SA**	Safekeeping:	Yes
		Invests:	Every 7 days beginning varies
Symbol:	CU	Minimum:	$50
Exchange:	OTC	Maximum:	$100,000/year
Industry:	Beverage mfr., bottler & distributor	Min to qualify:	1
Company Address:	c/o Morgan Guaranty Trust,	Fee on cash inv.:	$5 + 12¢/sh.
	Box 9073	Fee on div. inv.:	5% to $2.50
	Boston, MA 02205-9948	Discount (cash):	0
Company Phone:	800-428-4237	Discount (div.):	0
Transfer Agent:	Morgan Guaranty Trust Co.	Auto invest:	Yes
Agent's Address:	P.O. Box 9073	Auto invest fee:	$5
	Boston, MA 02205-9948	Selling info:	Sells daily, by phone or mail, at
Agent's Phone:	800-428-4237		avg. price, for $5 +12¢/sh.
Other than USA:	No		

Company:	**Compania de Minas Buenaventura**	Safekeeping:	Yes
		Invests:	Every 7 days beginning varies
Symbol:	BVN	Minimum:	$50
Exchange:	NYSE	Maximum:	$250,000/year
Industry:	Minerals	Min to qualify:	1
Company Address:	c/o BNY,101 Barclay St.,22 West	Fee on cash inv.:	$5 + 10¢/sh.
	New York, NY 10286	Fee on div. inv.:	5% to $5 + 10¢/sh.
Company Phone:	800-943-9715	Discount (cash):	0
Transfer Agent:	Bank of New York	Discount (div.):	0
Agent's Address:	P.O. Box 11258	Auto invest:	Yes
	New York, NY 10286	Auto invest fee:	$5 + 10¢/sh.
Agent's Phone:	888-269-2377	Selling info:	Sells weekly, by mail, at market,
Other than USA:	Yes		for $5 +10¢/sh.

Company:	**Compaq Computer**
Symbol:	CPQ
Exchange:	NYSE
Industry:	Manufacturer of personal computers
Company Address:	20555 State Hwy. 249 Houston, TX 77070
Company Phone:	281-370-0670
Transfer Agent:	Boston Eq. (EquiServe)
Agent's Address:	P.O. Box 8040 Boston, MA 02266-8040
Agent's Phone:	888-218-4373
Other than USA:	Yes

Safekeeping:	Yes
Invests:	Every 7 days beginning varies
Minimum:	$50
Maximum:	$10,000/month
Min to qualify:	1
Fee on cash inv.:	$5 + 4¢/sh.
Fee on div. inv.:	0
Discount (cash):	0
Discount (div.):	0
Auto invest:	Yes
Auto invest fee:	$2.50 + 4¢/ sh.
Selling info:	Sells daily, by mail or fax, at avg. price, for $10 +7¢/sh.

Company:	**Compass Bancshares, Inc.**
Symbol:	CBSS
Exchange:	OTC
Industry:	Banking
Company Address:	15 South 20th St. Birmingham, AL 35233
Company Phone:	205-933-3000 or 205-933-3331
Transfer Agent:	Continental Stock Transfer & Trust
Agent's Address:	2 Broadway, 19th Floor New York, NY 10004
Agent's Phone:	212-509-4000
Other than USA:	No

Safekeeping:	Yes
Invests:	Every 30 days beginning 1/1
Minimum:	$25
Maximum:	$500/month
Min to qualify:	1
Fee on cash inv.:	5% to $2.50
Fee on div. inv.:	5% to $2.50
Discount (cash):	0
Discount (div.):	0
Auto invest:	No
Auto invest fee:	$0
Selling info:	Sells within 10 bus. days , by mail, at market, for 5% to $2.50

Company:	**Computer Associates International**
Symbol:	CA
Exchange:	NYSE
Industry:	Computer software
Company Address:	One Computer Associates Plaza Islandia, NY 11788-7000
Company Phone:	516-342-5224
Transfer Agent:	ChaseMellon Shareholder Services
Agent's Address:	P.O. Box 3338 South Hackensack, Nj 07606-1938
Agent's Phone:	800-244-7155
Other than USA:	Yes

Safekeeping:	Yes
Invests:	Every 30 days beginning 1/5
Minimum:	$25
Maximum:	$3,000/month
Min to qualify:	1
Fee on cash inv.:	$1.50 + 6¢ to10¢/sh.
Fee on div. inv.:	$1.50 + 6¢ to 10¢/sh.
Discount (cash):	0
Discount (div.):	0
Auto invest:	No
Auto invest fee:	$0
Selling info:	Sells weekly, by mail or phone, at market, for $5 + 3¢ to 18¢/sh.

Company:	**COMSAT Corp.**
Symbol:	CQ
Exchange:	NYSE
Industry:	Global telecommunications
Company Address:	6560 Rock Spring Dr. Bethesda, MD 20817
Company Phone:	301-214-3244 or 301-214-3000
Transfer Agent:	Bank of New York
Agent's Address:	P.O. Box 11258, Church St. Station New York, NY 10286-1258
Agent's Phone:	800-432-0140
Other than USA:	Yes

Safekeeping:	Yes
Invests:	Every 30 days beginning 1/10
Minimum:	$50
Maximum:	$10,000/month
Min to qualify:	1
Fee on cash inv.:	0
Fee on div. inv.:	0
Discount (cash):	0
Discount (div.):	0
Auto invest:	No
Auto invest fee:	$0
Selling info:	Sells weekly, by mail, at market, for $5 + 6¢/sh.

Company:	**ConAgra, Inc.**	Safekeeping:	Yes
Symbol:	CAG	Invests:	Every 15 days beginning 1/1-1/15
Exchange:	NYSE	Minimum:	$50
Industry:	Food	Maximum:	$50,000/year
Company Address:	One ConAgra Dr.	Min to qualify:	1
	Omaha, NE 68102	Fee on cash inv.:	0!
Company Phone:	402-595-4005	Fee on div. inv.:	0!
Transfer Agent:	Norwest Bank Minnesota, NA	Discount (cash):	0
Agent's Address:	P.O. Box 64854	Discount (div.):	0
	St. Paul, MN 55164-0854	Auto invest:	Yes
Agent's Phone:	800-214-0349	Auto invest fee:	$0
Other than USA:	Yes	Selling info:	Sells weekly, by mail, at market, for $10 +15¢/sh.

Company:	**Conectiv**	Safekeeping:	Yes
Symbol:	CIV	Invests:	Every 7 days beginning varies
Exchange:	NYSE	Minimum:	$50
Industry:	Utility-electric	Maximum:	$200,000/year
Company Address:	800 King St., Box 231	Min to qualify:	1
	Wilmington, DE 19899	Fee on cash inv.:	3¢/sh.
Company Phone:	302-429-3114 or 888-424-8401	Fee on div. inv.:	3¢/sh.
Transfer Agent:	Bank of New York	Discount (cash):	0
Agent's Address:	Box 11258,Church Street Station	Discount (div.):	0
	New York, NY 10286	Auto invest:	Yes
Agent's Phone:	800-365-6495	Auto invest fee:	$0
Other than USA:	Yes	Selling info:	Sells weekly, by mail, at market, for $5 + 3¢/sh.

Company:	**Conestoga Enterprises, Inc.**	Safekeeping:	No
		Invests:	Every 90 days beginning 3/15
Symbol:	CENI	Minimum:	$100
Exchange:	OTC	Maximum:	$2,500/quarter
Industry:	Communications services	Min to qualify:	1
Company Address:	202 East First St.	Fee on cash inv.:	0
	Birdsboro, PA 19508	Fee on div. inv.:	0
Company Phone:	610-582-8711	Discount (cash):	0
Transfer Agent:	Conestoga Enterprises, Inc.	Discount (div.):	0
Agent's Address:	202 East First St.	Auto invest:	No
	Birdsboro, PA 19508	Auto invest fee:	$0
Agent's Phone:	610-582-8711	Selling info:	Not available
Other than USA:	No		

Company:	**Connecticut Energy Corp.**	Safekeeping:	Yes
Symbol:	CNE	Invests:	Every 30 days beginning 1/30
Exchange:	NYSE	Minimum:	$50
Industry:	Utility-gas	Maximum:	$50,000/year
Company Address:	855 Main St., Box 1540	Min to qualify:	1
	Bridgeport, CT 06601	Fee on cash inv.:	0!
Company Phone:	800-760-7776	Fee on div. inv.:	0!
Transfer Agent:	Boston Eq. (EquiServe)	Discount (cash):	0
Agent's Address:	P.O. Box 8040	Discount (div.):	0
	Boston, MA 02266-8040	Auto invest:	Yes
Agent's Phone:	800-736-3001	Auto invest fee:	$0
Other than USA:	Yes	Selling info:	Sells within 10 bus. days, by mail, at market, for 5% to $5 + comm.

Company:	**Connecticut Water Service Inc.**
Symbol:	CTWS
Exchange:	OTC
Industry:	Utility-water
Company Address:	93 West Main St.
	Clinton, CT 06413
Company Phone:	800-428-3985x305 or 860-669-8636
Transfer Agent:	State Street Bank (EquiServe)
Agent's Address:	P.O. Box 8200
	Boston, MA 02266-8200
Agent's Phone:	800-426-5523
Other than USA:	Yes

Safekeeping:	Yes
Invests:	Every 30 days beginning 1/4
Minimum:	$25
Maximum:	$1,000/month
Min to qualify:	1
Fee on cash inv.:	0
Fee on div. inv.:	0
Discount (cash):	0
Discount (div.):	0
Auto invest:	Yes
Auto invest fee:	$0
Selling info:	Sells within 10 bus. days, by phone or mail, at market, for $5 + comm.

Company:	**Consolidated Edison**
Symbol:	ED
Exchange:	NYSE
Industry:	Utility-electric, gas
Company Address:	4 Irving Pl., Rm. 249-S
	New York, NY 10003
Company Phone:	212-460-4600 or 212-460-3911
Transfer Agent:	Bank of New York
Agent's Address:	P.O. Box 11258, Church St. Station
	New York, NY 10286-1258
Agent's Phone:	800-522-5522
Other than USA:	Yes

Safekeeping:	Yes
Invests:	Every 7 days beginning varies
Minimum:	$100
Maximum:	$24,000/year
Min to qualify:	50
Fee on cash inv.:	$2
Fee on div. inv.:	0
Discount (cash):	0
Discount (div.):	0
Auto invest:	No
Auto invest fee:	$0
Selling info:	Sells weekly, by mail, at market, for $2 +10¢/sh.

Company:	**Consolidated Freightways Corp.**
Symbol:	CFWY
Exchange:	OTC
Industry:	Trucking & air freight
Company Address:	175 Linfield Dr.
	Menlo Park, CA 94025
Company Phone:	650-326-1700
Transfer Agent:	Bank of New York
Agent's Address:	Dividend Reinvestment Dept.,
	P.O. Box 1958
	Newark, NJ 07101-9774
Agent's Phone:	800-524-4458
Other than USA:	Yes

Safekeeping:	Yes
Invests:	Every 7 days beginning varies
Minimum:	$25
Maximum:	$50,000/year
Min to qualify:	1
Fee on cash inv.:	$2 + 5¢/sh.
Fee on div. inv.:	0
Discount (cash):	0
Discount (div.):	0
Auto invest:	Yes
Auto invest fee:	$2 + 5¢/sh.
Selling info:	Sells weekly, by mail, at avg. price, for $10 + 5¢/sh.

Company:	**Consolidated Natural Gas**
Symbol:	CNG
Exchange:	NYSE
Industry:	Gas distributor
Company Address:	CNG Tower, 625 Liberty Ave.
	Pittsburgh, PA 15222-3199
Company Phone:	412-690-1000 or 412-690-1482
Transfer Agent:	FCT (EquiServe)
Agent's Address:	P.O. Box 2500
	Jersey City, NJ 07303-2500
Agent's Phone:	800-414-6443
Other than USA:	Yes

Safekeeping:	Yes
Invests:	Every 90 days beginning 2/15
Minimum:	$25
Maximum:	$5,000/quarter
Min to qualify:	1
Fee on cash inv.:	0
Fee on div. inv.:	0
Discount (cash):	0
Discount (div.):	0
Auto invest:	No
Auto invest fee:	$0
Selling info:	Sells within 2 bus. days, by mail, at market, for $5 +12¢/sh.

Company:	**Consolidated Papers, Inc.**	Safekeeping:	No
Symbol:	CDP	Invests:	Every 30 days beginning 1/1
Exchange:	NYSE	Minimum:	$100
Industry:	Manufacturer paper	Maximum:	$3,000/quarter
Company Address:	Box 8050	Min to qualify:	1
	Wisconsin Rapids, WI 54495-8050	Fee on cash inv.:	0!
Company Phone:	715-422-3111	Fee on div. inv.:	0!
Transfer Agent:	Harris Trust & Savings Bank	Discount (cash):	0
Agent's Address:	P.O. Box A3309	Discount (div.):	0
	Chicago, IL 60690-3309	Auto invest:	No
Agent's Phone:	312-461-3157	Auto invest fee:	$0
Other than USA:	Yes	Selling info:	Sells within 10 bus. days, by mail, at market, for 7¢ to 10¢/sh.

Company:	**Consorcio G Grupo Dina SA de C.V.**	Safekeeping:	Yes
		Invests:	Every 7 days beginning varies
Symbol:	DIN	Minimum:	$50
Exchange:	NYSE	Maximum:	$100,000/year
Industry:	Truck & bus. mfr. in Mexico	Min to qualify:	1
Company Address:	c/o Morgan Guaranty Trust,	Fee on cash inv.:	$5 + 12¢/sh.
	Box 9073	Fee on div. inv.:	5% to $2.50
	Boston, MA 02205-9948	Discount (cash):	0
Company Phone:	800-428-4237	Discount (div.):	0
Transfer Agent:	Morgan Guaranty Trust Co.	Auto invest:	Yes
Agent's Address:	P.O. Box 9073	Auto invest fee:	$5
	Boston, MA 02205-9948	Selling info:	Sells daily, by phone or mail, at
Agent's Phone:	800-428-4237		avg. price, for $5 +12¢/sh.
Other than USA:	No		

Company:	**Constellation Energy Grp., Inc.**	Safekeeping:	Yes
		Invests:	Every 30 days beginning 1/1
Symbol:	CEG	Minimum:	$25
Exchange:	NYSE	Maximum:	$100,000/year
Industry:	Utility-electric	Min to qualify:	1
Company Address:	Box 1642, Rm. 820	Fee on cash inv.:	2.5¢ to 4¢/sh.
	Baltimore, MD 21203-1642	Fee on div. inv.:	2.5¢ to 4¢/sh.
Company Phone:	800-258-0499	Discount (cash):	0
Transfer Agent:	Baltimore G & E Co.	Discount (div.):	0
Agent's Address:	P.O. Box 1642	Auto invest:	No
	Baltimore, MD 21203-1642	Auto invest fee:	$0
Agent's Phone:	800-258-0499	Selling info:	Sells biweekly, by mail, at avg.
Other than USA:	Yes		price, for $5 + 2.5¢ to 4¢/sh.

Company:	**Cooper Industries**	Safekeeping:	No
Symbol:	CBE	Invests:	Every 30 days beginning 1/1
Exchange:	NYSE	Minimum:	$25
Industry:	Mfg.of electrical prods. & tools	Maximum:	$24,000/year
Company Address:	Box 4446	Min to qualify:	1
	Houston, TX 77210-4446	Fee on cash inv.:	0
Company Phone:	713-209-8610 or 713-209-8400	Fee on div. inv.:	0
Transfer Agent:	FCT (EquiServe)	Discount (cash):	0
Agent's Address:	P.O. Box 2500	Discount (div.):	0
	Jersey City, NJ 07303-2500	Auto invest:	No
Agent's Phone:	800-446-2617	Auto invest fee:	$0
Other than USA:	Yes (with restrictions)	Selling info:	Sells daily, by mail, at avg. price, for $10 +12¢/sh.

Company:	**Cornerstone Bancorp, Inc.**	Safekeeping:	Yes
		Invests:	Every 90 days beginning 1/15
Symbol:	CBN	Minimum:	$50
Exchange:	ASE	Maximum:	$5,000/quarter
Industry:	Bank holding co.	Min to qualify:	50
Company Address:	550 Summer St.	Fee on cash inv.:	0
	Stamford, CT 06901	Fee on div. inv.:	0
Company Phone:	203-356-0111	Discount (cash):	0
Transfer Agent:	American Stock Transfer & Trust	Discount (div.):	0
Agent's Address:	40 Wall St.	Auto invest:	No
	New York, NY 10005	Auto invest fee:	$0
Agent's Phone:	800-278-4353	Selling info:	Sells weekly, by mail, at market,
Other than USA:	Yes		for 4¢/sh.

Company:	**Cornerstone Realty Income Trust, Inc.**	Safekeeping:	Yes
		Invests:	Every 90 days beginning 1/1
Symbol:	TCR	Minimum:	$50
Exchange:	NYSE	Maximum:	$15,000/quarter
Industry:	REIT	Min to qualify:	1
Company Address:	306 E. Main St.	Fee on cash inv.:	0!
	Richmond, VA 23219	Fee on div. inv.:	0!
Company Phone:	804-643-1761	Discount (cash):	0
Transfer Agent:	First Union National Bank	Discount (div.):	0
Agent's Address:	1525 West W.T. Harris Blvd., 3c3	Auto invest:	Yes
	Charlotte, NC 23288-1153	Auto invest fee:	$0
Agent's Phone:	800-829-8432	Selling info:	Sells weekly, by mail, at avg. price,
Other than USA:	Yes		for comm.

Company:	**Corning Inc.**	Safekeeping:	Yes
Symbol:	GLW	Invests:	Every 30 days beginning 1/31
Exchange:	NYSE	Minimum:	$10
Industry:	Communication, cons. products,	Maximum:	$5,000/month
	mfg.	Min to qualify:	1
Company Address:	1 Riverfront Plz.	Fee on cash inv.:	0
	Corning, NY 14831-0001	Fee on div. inv.:	0
Company Phone:	607-974-8188607-947-9000	Discount (cash):	0
Transfer Agent:	Harris Trust & Savings Bank	Discount (div.):	0
Agent's Address:	P.O. Box 755, 311 W. Monroe St.	Auto invest:	Yes
	Chicago, IL 60690-0755	Auto invest fee:	$0
Agent's Phone:	800-255-0461	Selling info:	Sells within 10 bus. days, by mail,
Other than USA:	Yes		at market, for $10 + 5¢ to 10¢/sh.

Company:	**Cortland Bancorp**	Safekeeping:	Yes
Symbol:	CLDB	Invests:	Every 180 days beginning 6/1
Exchange:	OTC	Minimum:	$100
Industry:	Banking	Maximum:	$1,000/year
Company Address:	194 West Main St.	Min to qualify:	1
	Cortland, OH 44410	Fee on cash inv.:	0
Company Phone:	330-637-8040	Fee on div. inv.:	0
Transfer Agent:	Cortland Savings Bank	Discount (cash):	0
Agent's Address:	194 West Main St.	Discount (div.):	0
	Cortland, OH 44410	Auto invest:	Yes
Agent's Phone:	330-637-8040 x240	Auto invest fee:	$0
Other than USA:	No	Selling info:	Not available

Company:	**Countrywide Credit Industries, Inc.**	Safekeeping:	Yes
		Invests:	Every 30 days beginning varies
Symbol:	CCR	Minimum:	$100
Exchange:	NYSE	Maximum:	$3,000/month
Industry:	Mortgage banking	Min to qualify:	1
Company Address:	4500 Park Granada Blvd., MS CH-19	Fee on cash inv.:	0
	Calabasas, CA 91302	Fee on div. inv.:	0
Company Phone:	818-225-3601	Discount (cash):	0
Transfer Agent:	Bank of New York	Discount (div.):	0-5%
Agent's Address:	P.O. Box 1958	Auto invest:	No
	Newark, NJ 07101-9774	Auto invest fee:	$0
Agent's Phone:	800-524-4458	Selling info:	Sells daily, by mail, at market, for nominal fee
Other than USA:	No		

Company:	**CoVest Bancshares, Inc.**	Safekeeping:	Yes
Symbol:	COVB	Invests:	Every 90 days beginning 3/30
Exchange:	OTC	Minimum:	$25
Industry:	Banking	Maximum:	$5,000/quarter
Company Address:	749 Lee St.	Min to qualify:	1
	Des Plaines, IL 60016-6471	Fee on cash inv.:	0
Company Phone:	847-294-6500	Fee on div. inv.:	0
Transfer Agent:	Harris Trust & Savings Bank	Discount (cash):	0
Agent's Address:	P.O. Box A3309	Discount (div.):	0
	Chicago, IL 60690	Auto invest:	No
Agent's Phone:	312-360-5106	Auto invest fee:	$0
Other than USA:	Yes	Selling info:	Sells weekly, by mail or fax, at market, for 5% to $3 +7¢/sh.

Company:	**CPI Corp.**	Safekeeping:	Yes
Symbol:	CPY	Invests:	Every 30 days beginning 3/1
Exchange:	NYSE	Minimum:	$10
Industry:	Portrait studio and wall decor.	Maximum:	$10,000/quarter
Company Address:	1706 Washington Ave.	Min to qualify:	1
	St. Louis, MO 63103-1717	Fee on cash inv.:	0!
Company Phone:	314-231-1575 x.3469	Fee on div. inv.:	0!
Transfer Agent:	Harris Trust & Savings Bank	Discount (cash):	0
Agent's Address:	Box 755	Discount (div.):	0
	Chicago, IL 60690-0755	Auto invest:	No
Agent's Phone:	800-441-9673	Auto invest fee:	$0
Other than USA:	Yes	Selling info:	Sells weekly, by mail, at market, for $5 + 5¢ to 7¢/sh.

Company:	**Crane Co.**	Safekeeping:	Yes
Symbol:	CR	Invests:	Every 30 days beginning 1/14
Exchange:	NYSE	Minimum:	$10
Industry:	Manufacturing	Maximum:	$5,000/month
Company Address:	100 First Stamford Pl.	Min to qualify:	1
	Stamford, CT 06902	Fee on cash inv.:	0!
Company Phone:	203-363-7300	Fee on div. inv.:	0!
Transfer Agent:	FCT (EquiServe)	Discount (cash):	0
Agent's Address:	P.O. Box 2598	Discount (div.):	0
	Jersey City, NJ 07303-2598	Auto invest:	No
Agent's Phone:	800-446-2617	Auto invest fee:	$0
Other than USA:	No	Selling info:	Sells daily, by phone, mail, or fax, at market, for $10 +12¢/sh.

Company:	**Cresud S.A.C.I.F. y A.**	Safekeeping:	Yes
Symbol:	CRESY	Invests:	Every 7 days beginning varies
Exchange:	NYSE	Minimum:	$50
Industry:	Agricultural	Maximum:	$250,000/year
Company Address:	c/o BNY,101 Barclay St.,22 West	Min to qualify:	1
	New York, NY 10286	Fee on cash inv.:	$5 + 10¢/sh.
Company Phone:	800-943-9715	Fee on div. inv.:	5% to $5 + 10¢/sh.
Transfer Agent:	Bank of New York	Discount (cash):	0
Agent's Address:	P.O. Box 11258	Discount (div.):	0
	New York, NY 10286	Auto invest:	Yes
Agent's Phone:	888-269-2377	Auto invest fee:	$5 + 10¢/sh.
Other than USA:	Yes	Selling info:	Sells weekly, by mail, at market, for $5 +10¢/sh.

Company:	**Crompton-Knowles Corp.**	Safekeeping:	Yes
Symbol:	CNK	Invests:	Every 90 days beginning 2/1
Exchange:	NYSE	Minimum:	$30
Industry:	Specialty chemicals	Maximum:	$3,000/quarter
Company Address:	One Station Pl., Metro Ctr.	Min to qualify:	50
	Stamford, CT 06902	Fee on cash inv.:	0
Company Phone:	203-573-2000 or 203-573-3441	Fee on div. inv.:	0
Transfer Agent:	ChaseMellon Shareholder Services	Discount (cash):	0
Agent's Address:	85 Challenger Road	Discount (div.):	0
	Ridgefield Park, NJ 07660	Auto invest:	No
Agent's Phone:	800-851-9677	Auto invest fee:	$0
Other than USA:	No	Selling info:	Sells weekly, by mail or phone, at market, for $5 + comm.

Company:	**Cross Timbers Oil Co.**	Safekeeping:	Yes
Symbol:	XTO	Invests:	Every 7 days beginning varies
Exchange:	NYSE	Minimum:	$50
Industry:	Oil & gas development, production	Maximum:	$10,000/month
Company Address:	810 Houston St., Ste. 2000	Min to qualify:	1
	Fort Worth, TX 76102-6298	Fee on cash inv.:	0
Company Phone:	817-870-2800 or 817-882-7260	Fee on div. inv.:	0
Transfer Agent:	ChaseMellon Shareholder Services	Discount (cash):	0
Agent's Address:	P.O. Box 3338	Discount (div.):	0
	South Hackensack, NJ 07606-1938	Auto invest:	Yes
Agent's Phone:	888-877-2892	Auto invest fee:	$0
Other than USA:	Yes	Selling info:	Sells weekly, by mail or phone, at market, for $15 +12¢/sh.

Company:	**Crown American Realty Trust**	Safekeeping:	Yes
		Invests:	Every 30 days beginning 1/31
Symbol:	CWN	Minimum:	$100
Exchange:	NYSE	Maximum:	$5,000/quarter
Industry:	REIT	Min to qualify:	1
Company Address:	Pasquerilla Plaza	Fee on cash inv.:	0!
	Johnstown, PA 15907	Fee on div. inv.:	0!
Company Phone:	800-860-2011 or 814-535-9364	Discount (cash):	0
Transfer Agent:	American Stock Transfer	Discount (div.):	0
Agent's Address:	40 Wall St.	Auto invest:	No
	New York, NY 10005	Auto invest fee:	$0
Agent's Phone:	800-937-5449	Selling info:	Sells weekly, by mail, at market, for comm.
Other than USA:	Yes		

Company:	**Crown Cork & Seal Co., Inc.**	**Safekeeping:**	Yes
		Invests:	Every 30 days beginning 1/20
Symbol:	CCK	**Minimum:**	$25
Exchange:	NYSE	**Maximum:**	$25,000/year
Industry:	Mfr. metal & plastic packaging prods.	**Min to qualify:**	1
		Fee on cash inv.:	0
Company Address:	One Crown Way	**Fee on div. inv.:**	0
	Philadelphia, PA 19154-4599	**Discount (cash):**	0
Company Phone:	215-698-5100 or 215-698-5156	**Discount (div.):**	0
Transfer Agent:	FCT (EquiServe)	**Auto invest:**	Yes
Agent's Address:	P.O. Box 2500	**Auto invest fee:**	$1
	Jersey City, NJ 07303-2500	**Selling info:**	Sells daily, by phone or mail, at avg. price, for $10 +12¢/sh.
Agent's Phone:	800-317-4445		
Other than USA:	Yes		

Company:	**CSR Ltd.**	**Safekeeping:**	Yes
Symbol:	CSRLY	**Invests:**	Every 7 days beginning varies
Exchange:	OTC	**Minimum:**	$50
Industry:	Diversified mfr. in Australia	**Maximum:**	$100,000/year
Company Address:		**Min to qualify:**	1
	Boston, MA 02205-9948	**Fee on cash inv.:**	$5 + 12¢/sh.
Company Phone:	800-428-4237	**Fee on div. inv.:**	5% to $2.50
Transfer Agent:	Morgan Guaranty Trust Co.	**Discount (cash):**	0
Agent's Address:	P.O. Box 9073	**Discount (div.):**	0
	Boston, MA 02205-9948	**Auto invest:**	Yes
Agent's Phone:	800-428-4237	**Auto invest fee:**	$5
Other than USA:	No	**Selling info:**	Sells daily, by phone or mail, at avg. price, for $5 +12¢/sh.

Company:	**CSX Corp.**	**Safekeeping:**	Yes
Symbol:	CSX	**Invests:**	Every 7 days beginning varies
Exchange:	NYSE	**Minimum:**	$50
Industry:	Transportation, railroad	**Maximum:**	$10,000/month
Company Address:	Box 85629	**Min to qualify:**	1
	Richmond, VA 23285-5629	**Fee on cash inv.:**	0!
Company Phone:	804-782-1400 or 804-782-1465	**Fee on div. inv.:**	0!
Transfer Agent:	Harris Trust & Savings Bank	**Discount (cash):**	0
Agent's Address:	P.O. Box A3309	**Discount (div.):**	0
	Chicago, IL 60690-3309	**Auto invest:**	Yes
Agent's Phone:	800-521-5571	**Auto invest fee:**	$0
Other than USA:	Yes	**Selling info:**	Sells weekly, by mail or fax, at avg. price, for $10 +15¢/sh.

Company:	**CTG Resources**	**Safekeeping:**	Yes
Symbol:	CTG	**Invests:**	Every 90 days beginning 3/21
Exchange:	NYSE	**Minimum:**	$25
Industry:	Utility-gas	**Maximum:**	$5,000/quarter
Company Address:	100 Columbus Blvd., Box 1500	**Min to qualify:**	1
	Hartford, CT 06144-1500	**Fee on cash inv.:**	0!
Company Phone:	860-727-3155 or 860-727-3203	**Fee on div. inv.:**	0!
Transfer Agent:	ChaseMellon Shareholder Services	**Discount (cash):**	0
Agent's Address:	P.O. Box 3338	**Discount (div.):**	0
	South Hackensack, Nj 07606-1938	**Auto invest:**	No
Agent's Phone:	800-279-1262	**Auto invest fee:**	$0
Other than USA:	Yes	**Selling info:**	Sells weekly, by mail or phone, at avg. price, for comm.

Company:	**Cummins Engine**	Safekeeping:	Yes
Symbol:	CUM	Invests:	Every 30 days beginning 1/15
Exchange:	NYSE	Minimum:	$10
Industry:	Machinery	Maximum:	$6,000/quarter
Company Address:	Box 3005, MC 60118	Min to qualify:	1
	Columbus, IN 47202-3005	Fee on cash inv.:	0!
Company Phone:	812-377-3121	Fee on div. inv.:	0!
Transfer Agent:	FCT (EquiServe)	Discount (cash):	0
Agent's Address:	P.O. Box 2598	Discount (div.):	0
	Jersey City, NJ 07303-2598	Auto invest:	Yes
Agent's Phone:	800-446-2617	Auto invest fee:	$0
Other than USA:	Yes	Selling info:	Sells daily, by phone or mail, at market, for $10 +12¢/sh.

Company:	**Curtiss-Wright Corp.**	Safekeeping:	Yes
Symbol:	CW	Invests:	Every 7 days beginning varies
Exchange:	NYSE	Minimum:	$100
Industry:	Equipment for aerospace and	Maximum:	$10,000/month
	defense	Min to qualify:	1
Company Address:	1200 Wall St. West	Fee on cash inv.:	$5 + 12¢/sh.
	Lyndhurst, NJ 07071	Fee on div. inv.:	5% to $2.50 + 12¢/sh.
Company Phone:	201-896-8400 or 201-896-1751	Discount (cash):	0
Transfer Agent:	ChaseMellon Shareholder Services	Discount (div.):	0
Agent's Address:	P.O. Box 3315	Auto invest:	Yes
	South Hackensack, NJ 07606	Auto invest fee:	$0
Agent's Phone:	800-416-3743	Selling info:	Sells weekly, by mail or phone, at
Other than USA:	No		market, for $15 +12¢/sh.

Company:	**CVS Corp.**	Safekeeping:	Yes
Symbol:	CVS	Invests:	Every 7 days beginning varies
Exchange:	NYSE	Minimum:	$100
Industry:	Retail drugstore chain	Maximum:	$50,000/inv.
Company Address:	670 White Plains Rd., Ste. 210	Min to qualify:	1
	Scarsdale, NY 10583	Fee on cash inv.:	$2.50 + 10¢/sh.
Company Phone:	800-201-0938 or 401-765-1500	Fee on div. inv.:	0
Transfer Agent:	Bank of New York	Discount (cash):	0
Agent's Address:	P.O. Box 1958	Discount (div.):	0
	Newark, NJ 07101-9774	Auto invest:	Yes
Agent's Phone:	877-287-7526	Auto invest fee:	$1 + 10¢/sh.
Other than USA:	Yes	Selling info:	Sells weekly, by mail or phone, at market, for $10 +10¢/sh.

Company:	**Cyprus Amax Minerals Co.**	Safekeeping:	Yes
		Invests:	Every 30 days beginning 1/1
Symbol:	CYM	Minimum:	$50
Exchange:	NYSE	Maximum:	$3,000/month
Industry:	Minerals, mining & exploration	Min to qualify:	1
Company Address:	9100 East Mineral Circle	Fee on cash inv.:	$1.10 + 5¢/sh.
	Englewood, CO 80155	Fee on div. inv.:	$1.10 to $2.10
Company Phone:	303-643-5625 or 303-643-5000	Discount (cash):	0
Transfer Agent:	Bank of New York	Discount (div.):	0
Agent's Address:	P.O. Box 11258, Church St. Station	Auto invest:	No
	New York, NY 10286-1258	Auto invest fee:	$0
Agent's Phone:	800-643-4296	Selling info:	Sells weekly, by mail, at market,
Other than USA:	Yes		for $5 + 5¢/sh.

Company:	**D&E Communications, Inc.**	Safekeeping:	No
		Invests:	Every 90 days beginning 1/15
Symbol:	DECC	Minimum:	$100
Exchange:	OTC	Maximum:	$5,000/quarter
Industry:	Communications	Min to qualify:	1
Company Address:	124 East Main St., Box 458	Fee on cash inv.:	0!
	Ephrata, PA 17522-0458	Fee on div. inv.:	0!
Company Phone:	717-738-8304	Discount (cash):	0
Transfer Agent:	D&E Communications Inc.	Discount (div.):	0
Agent's Address:	Brossman Business Complex-124	Auto invest:	No
	East Main St.	Auto invest fee:	$0
	Ephrata, Penn. 17522-0458	Selling info:	Not available
Agent's Phone:	717-738-8304		
Other than USA:	Yes		

Company:	**DaimlerChrysler AG**	Safekeeping:	Yes
Symbol:	DCX	Invests:	Every daily days beginning varies
Exchange:	NYSE	Minimum:	$50
Industry:	Automobiles	Maximum:	$350,000/year
Company Address:	1000 Chrysler Dr.	Min to qualify:	1
	Auburn Hills, MI 48326	Fee on cash inv.:	$5 + 3¢/sh.
Company Phone:	248-576-5741	Fee on div. inv.:	5% to $3 + 3¢/sh.
Transfer Agent:	Bank of New York	Discount (cash):	0
Agent's Address:	P.O. Box 11258	Discount (div.):	0
	New York, NY 10286	Auto invest:	Yes
Agent's Phone:	800-470-7418	Auto invest fee:	$2 + 3¢/sh.
Other than USA:	Yes	Selling info:	Sells daily, by mail or phone, at market, for $15 +12¢/sh.

Company:	**Dana Corp.**	Safekeeping:	Yes
Symbol:	DCN	Invests:	Every 30 days beginning 1/12
Exchange:	NYSE	Minimum:	$25
Industry:	Mfr. auto parts	Maximum:	$2,000/month
Company Address:	Box 1000	Min to qualify:	1
	Toledo, OH 43637	Fee on cash inv.:	0
Company Phone:	800-537-8823 or 419-535-4725	Fee on div. inv.:	0
Transfer Agent:	ChaseMellon Shareholder Services	Discount (cash):	0
Agent's Address:	85 Challenger Road,	Discount (div.):	0
	Overpeck Centre	Auto invest:	No
	Ridgefield Park, NJ 07660	Auto invest fee:	$0
Agent's Phone:	800-298-6810	Selling info:	Sells biweekly, by mail or phone, at market, for $15
Other than USA:	Yes		

Company:	**Darden Restaurants**	Safekeeping:	Yes
Symbol:	DRI	Invests:	Every 7 days beginning varies
Exchange:	NYSE	Minimum:	$50
Industry:	Restaurants	Maximum:	$25,000/quarter
Company Address:	5900 Lake Ellenor Dr.	Min to qualify:	50
	Orlando, FL 32809	Fee on cash inv.:	$5 + 10¢/sh.
Company Phone:	407-245-4000	Fee on div. inv.:	5% to $5 + 10¢/sh.
Transfer Agent:	First Union National Bank	Discount (cash):	0
Agent's Address:	1525 W. W.T. Harris Blvd., 3C3, NC 1153	Discount (div.):	0
	Charlotte, NC	Auto invest:	No
		Auto invest fee:	$0
Agent's Phone:	800-829-8432	Selling info:	Sells weekly, by mail, at market, for $15 +10¢/sh.
Other than USA:	No		

Company:	**Dassault Systemes SA**	Safekeeping:	Yes
Symbol:	DASTY	Invests:	Every 7 days beginning varies
Exchange:	OTC	Minimum:	$50
Industry:	Computer aided design mfg. software	Maximum:	$100,000/year
		Min to qualify:	1
Company Address:	c/o Morgan Guaranty Trust, Box 9073	Fee on cash inv.:	$5 + 12¢/sh.
		Fee on div. inv.:	5% to $2.50
	Boston, MA 02205-9948	Discount (cash):	0
Company Phone:	800-428-4237	Discount (div.):	0
Transfer Agent:	Morgan Guaranty Trust Co.	Auto invest:	Yes
Agent's Address:	P.O. Box 9073	Auto invest fee:	$5
	Boston, MA 02205-9948	Selling info:	Sells daily, by phone or mail, at
Agent's Phone:	800-428-4237		avg. price, for $5 +12¢/sh.
Other than USA:	No		

Company:	**Dayton Hudson**	Safekeeping:	Yes
Symbol:	DH	Invests:	Every 7 days beginning varies
Exchange:	NYSE	Minimum:	$50
Industry:	Retail stores	Maximum:	$100,000/year
Company Address:	777 Nicollet Mall	Min to qualify:	1
	Minneapolis, MN 55402	Fee on cash inv.:	$5 + 10¢/sh.
Company Phone:	612-370-6948 or 612-370-6736	Fee on div. inv.:	5% to $3 + 10¢/sh.
Transfer Agent:	FCT (EquiServe)	Discount (cash):	0
Agent's Address:	P.O. Box 2598	Discount (div.):	0
	Jersey City, NJ 07303-2598	Auto invest:	Yes
Agent's Phone:	888-268-0203	Auto invest fee:	$2 +10¢/sh.
Other than USA:	Yes	Selling info:	Sells daily, by mail or phone, at
			market, for $10 +12¢/sh.

Company:	**DCB Financial Corp.**	Safekeeping:	Yes
Symbol:	DCBF	Invests:	Every 90 days beginning 2/15
Exchange:	OTC	Minimum:	$100
Industry:	Bank holding company	Maximum:	$2,000/quarter
Company Address:	41 N. Sandusky St.	Min to qualify:	1
	Delaware, OH 43015	Fee on cash inv.:	0
Company Phone:	740-363-1133	Fee on div. inv.:	0
Transfer Agent:	Delaware County Bank & Trust	Discount (cash):	0
Agent's Address:	41 North Sandusky St.	Discount (div.):	0
	Delaware, OH 43015	Auto invest:	No
Agent's Phone:	740-363-1133	Auto invest fee:	$0
Other than USA:	Yes	Selling info:	Sells within 10 bus. days, by mail,
			at market, for comm.

Company:	**De Rigo S.p.A.**	Safekeeping:	Yes
Symbol:	DER	Invests:	Every 7 days beginning varies
Exchange:	NYSE	Minimum:	$50
Industry:	Manufacturer of sun & prescription eyeglasses	Maximum:	$250,000/week
		Min to qualify:	1
Company Address:	c/o BNY,101 Barclay St.,22 West	Fee on cash inv.:	$5 + 10¢/sh.
	New York, NY 10286	Fee on div. inv.:	5% to $5 + 10¢/sh.
Company Phone:	800-943-9715	Discount (cash):	0
Transfer Agent:	Bank of New York	Discount (div.):	0
Agent's Address:	P.O. Box 11258	Auto invest:	Yes
	New York, NY 10286	Auto invest fee:	$0
Agent's Phone:	888-269-2377	Selling info:	Sells weekly, by phone or mail, at
Other than USA:	Yes		market, for $5 +10¢/ADS

Company:	**Dean Foods Co.**	**Safekeeping:**	Yes
Symbol:	DF	**Invests:**	Every 90 days beginning 3/15
Exchange:	NYSE	**Minimum:**	$25
Industry:	Food	**Maximum:**	$3,000/quarter
Company Address:	3600 North River Rd.	**Min to qualify:**	25
	Franklin Park, IL 60131	**Fee on cash inv.:**	0!
Company Phone:	847-678-1680	**Fee on div. inv.:**	0!
Transfer Agent:	Harris Trust & Savings Bank	**Discount (cash):**	0
Agent's Address:	P.O. Box A-3309	**Discount (div.):**	0
	Chicago, IL 60690	**Auto invest:**	No
Agent's Phone:	800-721-5167	**Auto invest fee:**	$0
Other than USA:	No	**Selling info:**	Not available

Company:	**Deere & Co.**	**Safekeeping:**	Yes
Symbol:	DE	**Invests:**	Every 7 days beginning varies
Exchange:	NYSE	**Minimum:**	$100
Industry:	Machinery	**Maximum:**	$10,000/month
Company Address:	One John Deere Pl.	**Min to qualify:**	1
	Moline, IL 61265-8098	**Fee on cash inv.:**	$3 + 5¢/sh.
Company Phone:	309-765-8000 or 309-765-4491	**Fee on div. inv.:**	5% to $3 + 5¢/sh.
Transfer Agent:	Bank of New York	**Discount (cash):**	0
Agent's Address:	PO Box 1958	**Discount (div.):**	0
	Newark, NJ 07101-9774	**Auto invest:**	Yes
Agent's Phone:	800-268-7369	**Auto invest fee:**	$1
Other than USA:	Yes	**Selling info:**	Sells weekly, by mail, at market, for $10 + 5¢/sh

Company:	**Delta Air Lines, Inc.**	**Safekeeping:**	Yes
Symbol:	DAL	**Invests:**	Every 30 days beginning 1/1
Exchange:	NYSE	**Minimum:**	$25
Industry:	Airline services	**Maximum:**	$10,000/year
Company Address:	Box 20706, Dept. 829	**Min to qualify:**	1
	Atlanta, GA 30320-6001	**Fee on cash inv.:**	0
Company Phone:	404-715-2391	**Fee on div. inv.:**	0
Transfer Agent:	FCT (EquiServe)	**Discount (cash):**	0
Agent's Address:	P.O. Box 2598	**Discount (div.):**	0
	Jersey City, NJ 07303-2598	**Auto invest:**	No
Agent's Phone:	201-324-1225	**Auto invest fee:**	$0
Other than USA:	No	**Selling info:**	Sells irregularly, by mail or phone, at market, for $10 +12¢/sh.

Company:	**Delta Natural Gas Co., Inc.**	**Safekeeping:**	Yes
		Invests:	Every 30 days beginning 1/15
Symbol:	DGAS	**Minimum:**	$25
Exchange:	OTC	**Maximum:**	$50,000/year
Industry:	Utility-gas	**Min to qualify:**	1
Company Address:	3617 Lexington Rd.	**Fee on cash inv.:**	0
	Winchester, KY 40391-9706	**Fee on div. inv.:**	0
Company Phone:	606-744-6171	**Discount (cash):**	0
Transfer Agent:	Fifth Third Bancorp	**Discount (div.):**	0
Agent's Address:	38 Fountain Sq. Plz., Mail Drop 10-90-F5	**Auto invest:**	No
		Auto invest fee:	$0
	Cincinnati, OH 45202	**Selling info:**	Not available
Agent's Phone:	800-837-2755		
Other than USA:	Yes		

Company:	**Developers Diversified Realty**	Safekeeping:	Yes
		Invests:	Every 90 days beginning 3/31
Symbol:	DDR	Minimum:	$100
Exchange:	NYSE	Maximum:	$5,000/quarter
Industry:	REIT	Min to qualify:	1
Company Address:	300 Enterprise Pkwy.	Fee on cash inv.:	0!
	Beechwood, OH 44122	Fee on div. inv.:	0!
Company Phone:	216-755-5500	Discount (cash):	0
Transfer Agent:	National City Bank	Discount (div.):	0
Agent's Address:	P.O. Box 92301	Auto invest:	No
	Cleveland, OH 44193-0900	Auto invest fee:	$0
Agent's Phone:	800-622-6757	Selling info:	Sells weekly, by mail, at market,
Other than USA:	No		for comm.

Company:	**Dexter Corp.**	Safekeeping:	Yes
Symbol:	DEX	Invests:	Every 30 days beginning 1/10
Exchange:	NYSE	Minimum:	$25
Industry:	Specialty materials company	Maximum:	$3,000/quarter
Company Address:	One Elm St.	Min to qualify:	1
	Windsor Locks, CT 06096-2334	Fee on cash inv.:	0
Company Phone:	860-292-7675	Fee on div. inv.:	0
Transfer Agent:	ChaseMellon Shareholder Services	Discount (cash):	0
Agent's Address:	85 Challenger Road, Overpeck Centre	Discount (div.):	0
		Auto invest:	No
	Ridgefield Park, NJ 07660	Auto invest fee:	$0
Agent's Phone:	800-288-9541	Selling info:	Sells weekly, by mail or phone, at
Other than USA:	Yes		market, for comm.

Company:	**Diageo plc ADS**	Safekeeping:	Yes
Symbol:	DEO	Invests:	Every 30 days beginning
Exchange:	NYSE	Minimum:	$50
Industry:	Food & beverage (alcoholic)	Maximum:	$250,000/investment
Company Address:	c/o BNY,101 Barclay St.,22 West	Min to qualify:	1
	New York, NY 10286	Fee on cash inv.:	$5 + 10¢/sh.
Company Phone:	800-943-9715	Fee on div. inv.:	5% to $5 + 10¢/sh.
Transfer Agent:	Bank of New York	Discount (cash):	
Agent's Address:	P.O. Box 11258	Discount (div.):	
	New York, NY 10286	Auto invest:	Yes
Agent's Phone:	888-269-2377	Auto invest fee:	$5 + 10¢/sh.
Other than USA:	No	Selling info:	Sells daily, by mail, at market, for
			$5 +10¢/sh.

Company:	**Diebold, Inc.**	Safekeeping:	No
Symbol:	DBD	Invests:	Every 30 days beginning 1/9
Exchange:	NYSE	Minimum:	$10
Industry:	Self-service prods., security equip.	Maximum:	$5,000/quarter
Company Address:	5995 Mayfair Rd., Box 3077	Min to qualify:	1
	North Canton, OH 44720-8077	Fee on cash inv.:	0!
Company Phone:	800-766-5859 or 330-490-3767	Fee on div. inv.:	0!
Transfer Agent:	Bank of New York	Discount (cash):	0
Agent's Address:	P.O. Box 11258, Church St. Station	Discount (div.):	0
	New York, NY 10286-1258	Auto invest:	No
Agent's Phone:	800-432-0140	Auto invest fee:	$0
Other than USA:	Yes	Selling info:	Sells weekly, by mail, at market,
			for $5 + 3¢/sh.

Company:	**Digitale Telekabel AG**	Safekeeping:	Yes
Symbol:	DTAGY	Invests:	Every 7 days beginning varies
Exchange:	OTC	Minimum:	$50
Industry:	Cable television and radio programming	Maximum:	$250,000/week
		Min to qualify:	1
Company Address:	c/o BNY,101 Barclay St.,22 West New York, NY 10286	Fee on cash inv.:	$5 + 10¢/sh.
		Fee on div. inv.:	5% to $5 + 10¢/sh.
Company Phone:	800-943-9715	Discount (cash):	0
Transfer Agent:	Bank of New York	Discount (div.):	0
Agent's Address:	P.O. Box 11258 New York, NY 10286	Auto invest:	Yes
		Auto invest fee:	$0
Agent's Phone:	888-269-2377	Selling info:	Sells weekly, by phone or mail, at market, for $5 +10¢/ADS
Other than USA:	Yes		

Company:	**Dominion Resources**	Safekeeping:	Yes
Symbol:	D	Invests:	Every 15 days beginning 1/5
Exchange:	NYSE	Minimum:	$40
Industry:	Utility-electric	Maximum:	$100,000/quarter
Company Address:	Box 26532 Richmond, VA 23261-6532	Min to qualify:	5
		Fee on cash inv.:	0
Company Phone:	800-552-4034 or 804-775-2500	Fee on div. inv.:	0
Transfer Agent:	Dominion Resources	Discount (cash):	0
Agent's Address:	P.O. Box 26532 Richmond, VA 23261-6532	Discount (div.):	0
		Auto invest:	Yes
Agent's Phone:	800-552-4034	Auto invest fee:	$0
Other than USA:	Yes	Selling info:	Sells weekly, by mail or fax, at market, for 2.5¢/sh.

Company:	**Donaldson Co., Inc.**	Safekeeping:	Yes
Symbol:	DCI	Invests:	Every 30 days beginning 1/13
Exchange:	NYSE	Minimum:	$10
Industry:	Diesel engine & filtration products	Maximum:	$1,000/month
		Min to qualify:	1
Company Address:	Box 1299, MS101 Minneapolis, MN 55440	Fee on cash inv.:	0
		Fee on div. inv.:	0
Company Phone:	651-450-4064	Discount (cash):	0
Transfer Agent:	Norwest Bank Minnesota	Discount (div.):	0
Agent's Address:	P.O. Box 64854 St. Paul, MN 55164-0854	Auto invest:	No
		Auto invest fee:	$0
Agent's Phone:	800-468-9716	Selling info:	Sells daily, by mail, at market, for $3 +15¢/sh.
Other than USA:	Yes		

Company:	**Donnelley (RR) & Sons Co.**	Safekeeping:	Yes
		Invests:	Every 30 days beginning 1/1
Symbol:	DNY	Minimum:	$10
Exchange:	NYSE	Maximum:	$60,000/year
Industry:	Printing	Min to qualify:	1
Company Address:	77 West Wacker Dr. Chicago, IL 60601-1696	Fee on cash inv.:	0!
		Fee on div. inv.:	0!
Company Phone:	312-326-8000 or 312-326-7754	Discount (cash):	0
Transfer Agent:	FCT (EquiServe)	Discount (div.):	0
Agent's Address:	P.O. Box 2500 Jersey City, NJ 07303-2500	Auto invest:	No
		Auto invest fee:	$0
Agent's Phone:	800-446-2617	Selling info:	Sells daily, by phone or mail, at market, for $10 +12¢/sh.
Other than USA:	Yes		

Company:	**Dow Chemical**	Safekeeping:	Yes
Symbol:	DOW	Invests:	Every 15 days beginning 1/15
Exchange:	NYSE	Minimum:	$25
Industry:	Chemicals	Maximum:	$25,000/quarter
Company Address:	2030 Dow Ctr.	Min to qualify:	1
	Midland, MI 48674	Fee on cash inv.:	0!
Company Phone:	800-422-8193 or 517-636-1463	Fee on div. inv.:	0!
Transfer Agent:	Boston Eq. (EquiServe)	Discount (cash):	0
Agent's Address:	P.O. Box 8038	Discount (div.):	0
	Boston, MA 02266-8038	Auto invest:	No
Agent's Phone:	800-369-5606 or 617-575-3899	Auto invest fee:	$0
Other than USA:	Yes	Selling info:	Sells weekly, by mail, at market, for $5 + comm.

Company:	**Dow Jones & Co.**	Safekeeping:	Yes
Symbol:	DJ	Invests:	Every 30 days beginning 1/1
Exchange:	NYSE	Minimum:	$100
Industry:	Publishing	Maximum:	$10,000/month
Company Address:	200 Liberty St.	Min to qualify:	10
	New York, NY 10281	Fee on cash inv.:	0!
Company Phone:	212-416-2679 or 212-416-2951	Fee on div. inv.:	0!
Transfer Agent:	ChaseMellon Shareholder Services	Discount (cash):	0
		Discount (div.):	0
Agent's Address:	85 Challenger Road	Auto invest:	Yes
	Ridgefield Park, NJ 07660	Auto invest fee:	$0
Agent's Phone:	800-851-4228	Selling info:	Sells weekly, by mail or phone, at market, for $15 +12¢/sh.
Other than USA:	Yes		

Company:	**DPL Inc.**	Safekeeping:	Yes
Symbol:	DPL	Invests:	Every 90 days beginning 3/1
Exchange:	NYSE	Minimum:	$25
Industry:	Utility-electric, gas	Maximum:	$1,000/quarter
Company Address:	Box 8825	Min to qualify:	1
	Dayton, OH 45401	Fee on cash inv.:	0
Company Phone:	800-322-9244 or 937-259-7150	Fee on div. inv.:	0
Transfer Agent:	Boston Eq. (EquiServe)	Discount (cash):	0
Agent's Address:	P.O. Box 8040	Discount (div.):	0
	Boston, MA 02266-8040	Auto invest:	No
Agent's Phone:	800-736-3001	Auto invest fee:	$0
Other than USA:	Yes	Selling info:	Sells daily, by mail , at avg. price, for 15¢/sh.

Company:	**DQE**	Safekeeping:	Yes
Symbol:	DQE	Invests:	Every 30 days beginning 1/1
Exchange:	NYSE	Minimum:	$10
Industry:	Utility-electric	Maximum:	$60,000/year
Company Address:	Box 68	Min to qualify:	1
	Pittsburgh, PA 15230-0068	Fee on cash inv.:	5¢/sh.
Company Phone:	800-247-0400 or 412-393-6193	Fee on div. inv.:	5¢/sh.
Transfer Agent:	DQE Shareholder Services	Discount (cash):	0
Agent's Address:	Shareholder Relations 2-050, 411 Seventh Ave	Discount (div.):	0
		Auto invest:	Yes
	Pittsburgh, PA 15219	Auto invest fee:	$0
Agent's Phone:	800-247-0400	Selling info:	Sells weekly, by mail or fax, at market, for 7¢/sh.
Other than USA:	Yes		

Company:	**Drovers Bancshares Corp.**	Safekeeping:	Yes
Symbol:	DROV	Invests:	Every 90 days beginning 3/31
Exchange:	OTC	Minimum:	$10
Industry:	Bank holding company	Maximum:	$2,000/quarter
Company Address:	30 South George St.	Min to qualify:	1
	York, PA 17401	Fee on cash inv.:	0!
Company Phone:	717-843-1586	Fee on div. inv.:	0!
Transfer Agent:	Registrar & Transfer Company	Discount (cash):	0
Agent's Address:	10 Commerce Drive	Discount (div.):	0
	Cranford, NJ 07016	Auto invest:	No
Agent's Phone:	800-368-5948	Auto invest fee:	$0
Other than USA:	No	Selling info:	Not available

Company:	**DTE Energy Co.**	Safekeeping:	Yes
Symbol:	DTE	Invests:	Every 30 days beginning 1/10
Exchange:	NYSE	Minimum:	$25
Industry:	Utility-electric	Maximum:	$100,000/year
Company Address:	2000 2nd Ave., 434 W.C.B.	Min to qualify:	1
	Detroit, MI 48226-1279	Fee on cash inv.:	$1 + 4¢/sh.
Company Phone:	800-551-5009 or 313-235-7881	Fee on div. inv.:	$1 + 4¢/sh.
Transfer Agent:	DTE Energy Company	Discount (cash):	0
Agent's Address:	P.O. Box 33380	Discount (div.):	0
	Detroit, MI 48232-5380	Auto invest:	No
Agent's Phone:	800-551-5009	Auto invest fee:	$0
Other than USA:	No	Selling info:	Sells weekly, by mail, at market, for 12.5¢/sh.

Company:	**Duff & Phelps Utilities Income Inc.**	Safekeeping:	Yes
		Invests:	Every 30 days beginning 1/10
Symbol:	DNP	Minimum:	$100
Exchange:	NYSE	Maximum:	$5,000/month
Industry:	Closed-end invest co.	Min to qualify:	1
Company Address:	55 East Monroe St.	Fee on cash inv.:	$2.50 + 7¢/sh.
	Chicago, IL 60603-5802	Fee on div. inv.:	0
Company Phone:	800-680-4367 or 312-368-5510	Discount (cash):	0
Transfer Agent:	Bank of New York	Discount (div.):	0-5%
Agent's Address:	PO Box 11258,Church Street Station	Auto invest:	No
		Auto invest fee:	$0
	New York, NY 10286-1258	Selling info:	Sells weekly, by mail, at market, for $2.50 + 7¢/sh.
Agent's Phone:	800-432-8224		
Other than USA:	No		

Company:	**Duke Energy**	Safekeeping:	Yes
Symbol:	DUK	Invests:	Every 15 days beginning 1/3
Exchange:	NYSE	Minimum:	$50
Industry:	Utility-electric, gas	Maximum:	$100,000/year
Company Address:	Box 1005	Min to qualify:	1
	Charlotte, NC 28201-1005	Fee on cash inv.:	0!
Company Phone:	800-488-3853 or 704-382-3853	Fee on div. inv.:	0!
Transfer Agent:	Duke Energy Corp.	Discount (cash):	0
Agent's Address:	P.O. Box 1005	Discount (div.):	0
	Charlotte, NC 28201-1005	Auto invest:	Yes
		Auto invest fee:	$0
Agent's Phone:	800-488-3853	Selling info:	Sells weekly, by mail or fax, at market, for 5¢/sh.
Other than USA:	Yes		

Company:	**Duke Realty Investments, Inc.**	Safekeeping:	Yes
		Invests:	Every 30 days beginning 1/31
Symbol:	DRE	Minimum:	$50
Exchange:	NYSE	Maximum:	$10,000/month
Industry:	REIT	Min to qualify:	1
Company Address:	8888 Keystone Crossing, Ste.1200	Fee on cash inv.:	0!
	Indianapolis, IN 46240-2182	Fee on div. inv.:	0!
Company Phone:	317-846-4700 or 317-574-3531	Discount (cash):	0
Transfer Agent:	American Stock Transfer	Discount (div.):	3%
Agent's Address:	40 Wall Street	Auto invest:	Yes
	New York, NY 10005	Auto invest fee:	$0
Agent's Phone:	800-937-5449 or 212-936-5100	Selling info:	Sells weekly, by mail, at avg. price,
Other than USA:	Yes		for 5¢ to 10¢/sh.

Company:	**DuPont (E.I.)**	Safekeeping:	Yes
Symbol:	DD	Invests:	Every 30 days beginning varies
Exchange:	NYSE	Minimum:	$20
Industry:	Chemicals, oil, gas	Maximum:	$5,000/month
Company Address:	1007 Market St., Rm.10006	Min to qualify:	1
	Wilmington, DE 19898	Fee on cash inv.:	5% to $3 + 3¢/sh.
Company Phone:	302-774-0195 or 302-774-4994	Fee on div. inv.:	5% to $3 + 10¢/sh.
Transfer Agent:	FCT (EquiServe)	Discount (cash):	0
Agent's Address:	P O Box 2500	Discount (div.):	0
	Jersey City, NJ 07303-2500	Auto invest:	No
Agent's Phone:	888-983-8766	Auto invest fee:	$0
Other than USA:	Yes	Selling info:	Sells daily, by mail or phone, at market, for $10 + 12¢/sh.

Company:	**Durbam Roodeport Deep Ltd.**	Safekeeping:	Yes
		Invests:	Every 7 days beginning varies
Symbol:	DROOY	Minimum:	$50
Exchange:	OTC	Maximum:	$250,000/year
Industry:	Gold mining	Min to qualify:	1
Company Address:	c/o BNY,101 Barclay St.,22 West	Fee on cash inv.:	$5 + 10¢/sh.
	New York, NY 10286	Fee on div. inv.:	5% to $5 + 10¢/sh.
Company Phone:	800-943-9715	Discount (cash):	0
Transfer Agent:	Bank of New York	Discount (div.):	0
Agent's Address:	P.O. Box 11258	Auto invest:	Yes
	New York, NY 10286	Auto invest fee:	$5 + 10¢/sh.
Agent's Phone:	888-269-2377	Selling info:	Sells weekly, by mail, at market,
Other than USA:	Yes		for $5 +10¢/sh.

Company:	**E'Town Corp.**	Safekeeping:	No
Symbol:	ETW	Invests:	Every 30 days beginning 1/30
Exchange:	NYSE	Minimum:	$100
Industry:	Utility-water	Maximum:	$2,000/month
Company Address:	600 South Ave., Box 788	Min to qualify:	20
	Westfield, NJ 07091-0788	Fee on cash inv.:	0!
Company Phone:	908-654-1234x283	Fee on div. inv.:	0!
Transfer Agent:	Bank of New York	Discount (cash):	5%
Agent's Address:	P.O. Box 11258, Church St. Station	Discount (div.):	5%
	New York, NY 10286	Auto invest:	No
Agent's Phone:	888-269-8845	Auto invest fee:	$0
Other than USA:	Yes	Selling info:	Sells within 10 bus. days, by mail, at market, for comm.

Company:	**Eagle Bancshares, Inc.**	Safekeeping:	Yes
Symbol:	EBSI	Invests:	Every 90 days beginning 1/21
Exchange:	OTC	Minimum:	$25
Industry:	Savings and loan	Maximum:	$5,000/quarter
Company Address:	4305 Lynburn Dr.	Min to qualify:	1
	Tucker, GA 30884-4441	Fee on cash inv.:	0!
Company Phone:	770-908-6690	Fee on div. inv.:	0!
Transfer Agent:	SunTrust Bank, Atlanta	Discount (cash):	0
Agent's Address:	P.O. Box 4625	Discount (div.):	0
	Atlanta, GA 30302	Auto invest:	No
Agent's Phone:	800-568-3476	Auto invest fee:	$0
Other than USA:	Yes	Selling info:	Sells weekly, by mail, at market, for comm.

Company:	**Eastern Co. (The)**	Safekeeping:	Yes
Symbol:	EML	Invests:	Every 30 days beginning 2ndThurs.
Exchange:	ASE	Minimum:	$50
Industry:	Mfr. locks & metal products	Maximum:	$150,000/year
Company Address:	112 Bridge St., Box 460	Min to qualify:	1
	Naugatuck, CT 06770-0460	Fee on cash inv.:	0!
Company Phone:	203-729-2255 x 241	Fee on div. inv.:	0!
Transfer Agent:	Boston Eq. (EquiServe)	Discount (cash):	0
Agent's Address:	P.O. Box 8040	Discount (div.):	0
	Boston, MA 02266	Auto invest:	Yes
Agent's Phone:	800-633-3455	Auto invest fee:	$0
Other than USA:	Yes	Selling info:	Sells weekly, by mail, at avg. price, for $10 +15¢/sh.

Company:	**Eastern Enterprises**	Safekeeping:	Yes
Symbol:	EFU	Invests:	Every 90 days beginning 3/30
Exchange:	NYSE	Minimum:	$10
Industry:	Natural gas distrib. & marine transportation	Maximum:	$3,000/quarter
		Min to qualify:	1
Company Address:	9 Riverside Rd.	Fee on cash inv.:	0!
	Weston, MA 02493	Fee on div. inv.:	0!
Company Phone:	781-647-2316 or 781-647-2300	Discount (cash):	0
Transfer Agent:	BankBoston (EquiServe)	Discount (div.):	0
Agent's Address:	P.O. Box 8040	Auto invest:	No
	Boston, MA 02266-8040	Auto invest fee:	$0
Agent's Phone:	800-736-3001	Selling info:	Sells weekly, by mail, at avg. price, for 5% to $10 + comm.
Other than USA:	Yes		

Company:	**Eastern Utilities Associates**	Safekeeping:	Yes
		Invests:	Every 30 days beginning 1/15
Symbol:	EUA	Minimum:	$0
Exchange:	NYSE	Maximum:	$5,000/quarter
Industry:	Utility-electric	Min to qualify:	1
Company Address:	Box 2333	Fee on cash inv.:	0!
	Boston, MA 02107	Fee on div. inv.:	0!
Company Phone:	617-357-9590	Discount (cash):	0
Transfer Agent:	Boston Eq. (EquiServe)	Discount (div.):	0
Agent's Address:	P.O. Box 8040	Auto invest:	No
	Boston, MA 02266-8040	Auto invest fee:	$0
Agent's Phone:	800-736-3001	Selling info:	Sells daily, by mail, at market, for 15¢/sh.
Other than USA:	Yes		

	Eastman Chemical Co.		
Company:		Safekeeping:	Yes
Symbol:	EMN	Invests:	Every 7 days beginning Wed.
Exchange:	NYSE	Minimum:	$0
Industry:	Chemical manufacturer	Maximum:	$60,000/year
Company Address:	100 North Eastman Rd.. Box 511	Min to qualify:	1
	Kingsport, TN 37662-5075	Fee on cash inv.:	0!
Company Phone:	800-930-3278 or 423-229-2000	Fee on div. inv.:	0!
Transfer Agent:	FCT (EquiServe)	Discount (cash):	0
Agent's Address:	P.O. Box 2598	Discount (div.):	0
	Jersey City, NJ 07303-2598	Auto invest:	Yes
Agent's Phone:	800-323-1404	Auto invest fee:	$1
Other than USA:	No	Selling info:	Sells daily, by phone or mail, at market, for $10 +12¢/sh.

	Eastman Kodak		
Company:		Safekeeping:	Yes
Symbol:	EK	Invests:	Every 7 days beginning varies
Exchange:	NYSE	Minimum:	$50
Industry:	Photography	Maximum:	$120,000/year
Company Address:	343 State St.	Min to qualify:	1
	Rochester, NY 14650	Fee on cash inv.:	0!
Company Phone:	716-724-5492 or 716-724-4000	Fee on div. inv.:	0!
Transfer Agent:	BankBoston (EquiServe)	Discount (cash):	0
Agent's Address:	P.O. Box 8023	Discount (div.):	0
	Boston, MA 02266-8023	Auto invest:	Yes
Agent's Phone:	800-253-6057	Auto invest fee:	$0
Other than USA:	Yes	Selling info:	Sells daily, by mail or phone, at avg. price, for $10 +10¢/sh.

	Eaton Corp.		
Company:		Safekeeping:	Yes
Symbol:	ETN	Invests:	Every 30 days beginning 1/25
Exchange:	NYSE	Minimum:	$10
Industry:	Manufacturer electrical equipment	Maximum:	$60,000/year
Company Address:	Eaton Ctr.	Min to qualify:	1
	Cleveland, OH 44114-2584	Fee on cash inv.:	0!
Company Phone:	888-328-6647 or 216-523-4724	Fee on div. inv.:	0!
Transfer Agent:	FCT (EquiServe)	Discount (cash):	0
Agent's Address:	P.O. Box 2500	Discount (div.):	0
	Jersey City, NJ 07503-2500	Auto invest:	Yes
Agent's Phone:	800-317-4445	Auto invest fee:	$1
Other than USA:	Yes	Selling info:	Sells daily, by mail or phone, at market, for $10 + comm.

	Ecolab Inc.		
Company:		Safekeeping:	Yes
Symbol:	ECL	Invests:	Every 30 days beginning 1/15
Exchange:	NYSE	Minimum:	$10
Industry:	Cleaning & sanitizing products	Maximum:	$60,000/year
Company Address:	Ecolab Ctr.	Min to qualify:	1
	St. Paul, MN 55102-1390	Fee on cash inv.:	0
Company Phone:	612-293-2233 or 612-293-2809	Fee on div. inv.:	0
Transfer Agent:	FCT (EquiServe)	Discount (cash):	0
Agent's Address:	P.O. Box 2598	Discount (div.):	0
	Jersey City, NJ 07303-2598	Auto invest:	No
Agent's Phone:	201-324-0313	Auto invest fee:	$0
Other than USA:	Yes	Selling info:	Sells irregularly, by mail, at market, for $10 + comm.

Company:	**ECsoft Group plc.**	Safekeeping:	Yes
Symbol:	ECSGY	Invests:	Every 7 days beginning varies
Exchange:	OTC	Minimum:	$50
Industry:	Systems integration, info. tech. consulting, applications development	Maximum:	$250,000/week
		Min to qualify:	1
Company Address:	c/o BNY,101 Barclay St.,22 West New York, NY 10286	Fee on cash inv.:	$5 + 10¢/sh.
		Fee on div. inv.:	0
Company Phone:	800-943-9715	Discount (cash):	0
Transfer Agent:	Bank of New York	Discount (div.):	0
Agent's Address:	P.O. Box 11258 New York, NY 10286	Auto invest:	Yes
		Auto invest fee:	$0
Agent's Phone:	888-269-2377	Selling info:	Sells weekly, by phone or mail, at market, for $5 +10¢/ADS
Other than USA:	Yes		

Company:	**Edison International**	Safekeeping:	Yes
Symbol:	EIX	Invests:	Every 30 days beginning 1/1
Exchange:	NYSE	Minimum:	$25
Industry:	Utility-electric	Maximum:	$10,000/month
Company Address:	Box 400 Rosemead, CA 91770	Min to qualify:	1
		Fee on cash inv.:	0!
Company Phone:	800-347-8625 or 626-302-7206	Fee on div. inv.:	0!
Transfer Agent:	Southern CA Edison Co.	Discount (cash):	0
Agent's Address:	P.O. Box 400 Rosemead, CA 91770-9975	Discount (div.):	0
		Auto invest:	No
Agent's Phone:	800-347-8625	Auto invest fee:	$0
Other than USA:	Yes	Selling info:	Sells weekly, by mail or fax, at market, for 3¢/sh.

Company:	**EG&G Inc.**	Safekeeping:	Yes
Symbol:	EGG	Invests:	Every 30 days beginning 1/1
Exchange:	NYSE	Minimum:	$25
Industry:	Mfr. scientific instruments & equipment	Maximum:	$5,000/month
		Min to qualify:	1
Company Address:	45 William St. Wellesley, MA 02181-4078	Fee on cash inv.:	0!
		Fee on div. inv.:	0!
Company Phone:	781-237-5100 or 781-431-4306	Discount (cash):	0
Transfer Agent:	BankBoston (EquiServe)	Discount (div.):	0
Agent's Address:	P.O. Box 8040 Boston, MA 02266	Auto invest:	No
		Auto invest fee:	$0
Agent's Phone:	800-730-4001	Selling info:	Sells weekly, by mail or phone, at market, for $1 to $5 + comm.
Other than USA:	Yes		

Company:	**Eidos plc**	Safekeeping:	Yes
Symbol:	EIDSY	Invests:	Every 7 days beginning varies
Exchange:	OTC	Minimum:	$50
Industry:	Software development	Maximum:	$100,000/year
Company Address:	c/o Morgan Guaranty Trust, Box 9073 Boston, MA 02205-9948	Min to qualify:	1
		Fee on cash inv.:	$5 + 12¢/sh.
		Fee on div. inv.:	5% to $2.50
Company Phone:	800-428-4237	Discount (cash):	0
Transfer Agent:	Morgan Guaranty Trust Co.	Discount (div.):	0
Agent's Address:	P.O. Box 9073 Boston, MA 02205-9948	Auto invest:	Yes
		Auto invest fee:	$5
Agent's Phone:	800-428-4237	Selling info:	Sells daily, by phone or mail, at market, for $5 +12¢/sh.
Other than USA:	No		

Company:	**EKCO Group, Inc.**	Safekeeping:	No
Symbol:	EKO	Invests:	Every 30 days beginning 1/10
Exchange:	NYSE	Minimum:	$10
Industry:	Mfr. kitchen, household products	Maximum:	$10,000/quarter
Company Address:	98 Spit Brook Rd., Ste.102	Min to qualify:	1
	Nashua, NH 03062-5738	Fee on cash inv.:	0
Company Phone:	603-888-1212	Fee on div. inv.:	0
Transfer Agent:	American Stock Transfer	Discount (cash):	0
Agent's Address:	40 Wall St., 46th Fl.	Discount (div.):	0
	New York, NY 10005	Auto invest:	No
Agent's Phone:	800-278-4353	Auto invest fee:	$0
Other than USA:	Yes	Selling info:	Not available

Company:	**El Paso Energy Corp.**	Safekeeping:	Yes
Symbol:	EPG	Invests:	Every 30 days beginning varies
Exchange:	NYSE	Minimum:	$10
Industry:	Natural gas	Maximum:	$10,000/month
Company Address:	1001 Louisiana St., Box 2511	Min to qualify:	1
	Houston, TX 77252-2511	Fee on cash inv.:	0!
Company Phone:	888-202-9971 or 713-420-5597	Fee on div. inv.:	0!
Transfer Agent:	Boston Eq. (EquiServe)	Discount (cash):	0
Agent's Address:	P.O. Box 644	Discount (div.):	0
	Boston, MA 02102	Auto invest:	No
Agent's Phone:	800-736-3001	Auto invest fee:	$0
Other than USA:	Yes	Selling info:	Sells within 10 days, by mail, at market, for $1 to $10 + comm.

Company:	**ELAN Corp., plc**	Safekeeping:	Yes
Symbol:	ELN	Invests:	Every 7 days beginning varies
Exchange:	NYSE	Minimum:	$50
Industry:	Biotechnology & drugs	Maximum:	$250,000/year
Company Address:	c/o BNY,101 Barclay St.,22 West	Min to qualify:	1
	New York, NY 10286	Fee on cash inv.:	$5 + 10¢/sh.
Company Phone:	800-943-9715	Fee on div. inv.:	0
Transfer Agent:	Bank of New York	Discount (cash):	0
Agent's Address:	P.O. Box 11258	Discount (div.):	0
	New York, NY 10286	Auto invest:	Yes
Agent's Phone:	888-269-2377	Auto invest fee:	$5 + 10¢/sh.
Other than USA:	Yes	Selling info:	Sells weekly, by mail, at market, for $5 +10¢/sh.

Company:	**Electronic Data Systems**	Safekeeping:	Yes
Symbol:	EDS	Invests:	Every 30 days beginning 1/15
Exchange:	NYSE	Minimum:	$100
Industry:	Computer system services	Maximum:	$15,000/quarter
Company Address:	5400 Legacy Dr., MS H1-2D-05	Min to qualify:	50
	Plano, TX 75024	Fee on cash inv.:	$2 + 10¢/sh.
Company Phone:	972-604-6661 or 972-604-6000	Fee on div. inv.:	50¢ + 5¢/sh.
Transfer Agent:	Bank of New York	Discount (cash):	0
Agent's Address:	P.O. Box 11258, Church St. Station	Discount (div.):	0
	New York, NY 10286	Auto invest:	No
Agent's Phone:	800-250-5016	Auto invest fee:	$0
Other than USA:	Yes	Selling info:	Sells daily, by phone or mail, at avg. price, for $5 +10¢/sh.

Company:	**Elf Aquitaine**	Safekeeping:	Yes
Symbol:	ELF	Invests:	Every 7 days beginning varies
Exchange:	NYSE	Minimum:	$50
Industry:	Oil & gas, integrated	Maximum:	$250,000/year
Company Address:	c/o BNY,101 Barclay St.,22 West	Min to qualify:	1
	New York, NY 10286	Fee on cash inv.:	$5 + 10¢/sh.
Company Phone:	800-943-9715	Fee on div. inv.:	5% to $5 + 10¢/sh.
Transfer Agent:	Bank of New York	Discount (cash):	0
Agent's Address:	P.O. Box 11258	Discount (div.):	0
	New York, NY 10286	Auto invest:	Yes
Agent's Phone:	888-269-2377	Auto invest fee:	$5 + 10¢/sh.
Other than USA:	Yes	Selling info:	Sells weekly, by mail, at market, for $5 +10¢/sh.

Company:	**Ellsworth Convertible Growth & Income Fund**	Safekeeping:	No
		Invests:	Every 30 days beginning 1/15
Symbol:	ECF	Minimum:	$100
Exchange:	ASE	Maximum:	$1,000/month
Industry:	Convertible bond fund	Min to qualify:	1
Company Address:	65 Madison Ave., 5th Fl.	Fee on cash inv.:	0!
	Morristown, NJ 07960	Fee on div. inv.:	0!
Company Phone:	973-631-1177	Discount (cash):	0
Transfer Agent:	Bank of New York	Discount (div.):	0
Agent's Address:	Dividend Reinvestment,	Auto invest:	No
	PO Box 11258	Auto invest fee:	$0
	New York, NY 10286-1258	Selling info:	Sells irregularly, by mail,
Agent's Phone:	800-432-8224		at market, for comm.
Other than USA:	Yes		

Company:	**Embratel Participacoes SA**	Safekeeping:	Yes
		Invests:	Every 7 days beginning varies
Symbol:	EMT	Minimum:	$50
Exchange:	NYSE	Maximum:	$250,000/year
Industry:	Telecommunications	Min to qualify:	1
Company Address:	c/o BNY,101 Barclay St.,22 West	Fee on cash inv.:	$5 + 10¢/sh.
	New York, NY 10286	Fee on div. inv.:	5% to $5 + 10¢/sh.
Company Phone:	800-943-9715	Discount (cash):	0
Transfer Agent:	Bank of New York	Discount (div.):	0
Agent's Address:	P.O. Box 11258	Auto invest:	Yes
	New York, NY 10286	Auto invest fee:	$5 + 10¢/sh.
Agent's Phone:	888-269-2377	Selling info:	Sells weekly, by mail, at market,
Other than USA:	Yes		for $5 +10¢/sh.

Company:	**EMC Insurance Group**	Safekeeping:	Yes
Symbol:	EMCI	Invests:	Every 90 days beginning 3/23
Exchange:	OTC	Minimum:	$50
Industry:	Insurance holding co.	Maximum:	$5,000/month
Company Address:	717 Mulberry St.	Min to qualify:	1
	Des Moines, IA 50309	Fee on cash inv.:	0!
Company Phone:	515-280-2515 or 515-280-2511	Fee on div. inv.:	0!
Transfer Agent:	UMB Bank, N.A.	Discount (cash):	0
Agent's Address:	P.O. Box 410064,13th Floor	Discount (div.):	0
	Kansas City, MO 64141-0064	Auto invest:	No
Agent's Phone:	800-884-4225	Auto invest fee:	$0
Other than USA:	Yes	Selling info:	Sells daily, by mail, at market, for $5 + comm.

Company:	**Emcee Broadcast Products, Inc.**	Safekeeping:	Yes
		Invests:	Every 7 days beginning 1/1
Symbol:	ECIN	Minimum:	$50
Exchange:	OTC	Maximum:	$10,000/invest
Industry:	Communications equipment	Min to qualify:	1
Company Address:	Susquehanna St. Ext., Box 68	Fee on cash inv.:	$7.50 + 10¢/sh.
	White Haven, PA 18661	Fee on div. inv.:	0
Company Phone:	717-443-9575	Discount (cash):	0
Transfer Agent:	American Stock Transfer	Discount (div.):	0
Agent's Address:	40 Wall Street	Auto invest:	Yes
	New York, NY 10005	Auto invest fee:	$0
Agent's Phone:	888-200-3167	Selling info:	Sells weekly, by mail or fax, at
Other than USA:	Yes		market, for $7.50 +10¢/sh.

Company:	**Emerald Financial Corp.**	Safekeeping:	Yes
Symbol:	EMLD	Invests:	Every 15 days beginning 1/15
Exchange:	OTC	Minimum:	$10
Industry:	Savings banks	Maximum:	$25,000/year
Company Address:	14092 Pearl Rd.	Min to qualify:	1
	Strongsville, OH 44136	Fee on cash inv.:	0!
Company Phone:	440-238-7311	Fee on div. inv.:	0!
Transfer Agent:	National City Bank	Discount (cash):	0
Agent's Address:	P.O. Box 94946	Discount (div.):	0
	Cleveland, OH 44101-4946	Auto invest:	No
Agent's Phone:	800-622-6757	Auto invest fee:	$0
Other than USA:	Yes	Selling info:	Sells weekly, by mail, at market,
			for 20¢/sh.

Company:	**Emerging Markets Infrastructure Fund, Inc. (The)**	Safekeeping:	Yes
		Invests:	Every 7 days beginning Wed.
		Minimum:	$100
Symbol:	EMG	Maximum:	$100,000/year
Exchange:	NYSE	Min to qualify:	1
Industry:	Closed end fund	Fee on cash inv.:	$5 + 8¢/sh.
Company Address:	c/o Credit Suisse, 153 E. 53rd St.,	Fee on div. inv.:	0
	58th Fl.	Discount (cash):	0
	New York, NY 10022	Discount (div.):	0
Company Phone:	800-293-1232 or 212-238-5674	Auto invest:	Yes
Transfer Agent:	BankBoston (EquiServe)	Auto invest fee:	$5 + 8¢/sh.
Agent's Address:	P.O. Box 8040	Selling info:	Sells within 4 bus. days, by mail,
	Boston, MA 02266		at avg. price, for $10 + 15¢/sh.
Agent's Phone:	800-730-6001		
Other than USA:	Yes		

Company:	**Emerging Markets Telecomm. Fund, Inc. (The)**	Safekeeping:	Yes
		Invests:	Every 7 days beginning Wed.
Symbol:	ETF	Minimum:	$100
Exchange:	NYSE	Maximum:	$100,000/year
Industry:	Closed end fund	Min to qualify:	1
Company Address:	c/o Credit Suisse, 153 E. 53rd St.,	Fee on cash inv.:	$5 + 8¢/sh.
	58th Fl.	Fee on div. inv.:	0
	New York, NY 10022	Discount (cash):	0
Company Phone:	800-293-1232 or 212-238-5674	Discount (div.):	0
Transfer Agent:	BankBoston (EquiServe)	Auto invest:	Yes
Agent's Address:	P.O. Box 8040	Auto invest fee:	$5 + 8¢/sh.
	Boston, MA 02266	Selling info:	Sells within 4 bus. days, by mail,
Agent's Phone:	800-730-6001		at avg. price, for $10 + 15¢/sh.
Other than USA:	Yes		

Company:	**Emerson Electric Co.**	Safekeeping:	Yes
Symbol:	EMR	Invests:	Every 15 days beginning 1/10
Exchange:	NYSE	Minimum:	$50
Industry:	Electric equipment	Maximum:	$120,000/year
Company Address:	8000 West Florissant, Box 4100	Min to qualify:	1
	St. Louis, MO 63136	Fee on cash inv.:	0!
Company Phone:	314-553-2197	Fee on div. inv.:	0!
Transfer Agent:	ChaseMellon Shareholder Services	Discount (cash):	0
Agent's Address:	P.O. Box 3338	Discount (div.):	0
	South Hackensack, NJ 07606-1938	Auto invest:	No
Agent's Phone:	888-213-0970	Auto invest fee:	$0
Other than USA:	Yes	Selling info:	Sells weekly, by mail or phone, at market, for $5 + comm.

Company:	**Empire District Electric Co.**	Safekeeping:	No
		Invests:	Every 90 days beginning 2/15
Symbol:	EDE	Minimum:	$50
Exchange:	NYSE	Maximum:	$3,000/quarter
Industry:	Utility-electric	Min to qualify:	1
Company Address:	Box 127, 602 Joplin St.	Fee on cash inv.:	0
	Joplin, MO 64802	Fee on div. inv.:	0
Company Phone:	417-625-5100 x 2223	Discount (cash):	0
Transfer Agent:	ChaseMellon Shareholder Services	Discount (div.):	5%
Agent's Address:	85 Challenger Road	Auto invest:	No
	Ridgefield Park, NJ 07660	Auto invest fee:	$0
Agent's Phone:	888-261-6784	Selling info:	Sells daily, by mail or phone, at market, for $15
Other than USA:	Yes		

Company:	**Empresas ICA, S.A. de C.V.**	Safekeeping:	Yes
		Invests:	Every 7 days beginning varies
Symbol:	ICA	Minimum:	$50
Exchange:	NYSE	Maximum:	$250,000/week
Industry:	Construction	Min to qualify:	1
Company Address:	c/o BNY,101 Barclay St.,22 West	Fee on cash inv.:	$5 + 10¢/sh.
	New York, NY 10286	Fee on div. inv.:	5% to $5 + 10¢/sh.
Company Phone:	800-943-9715	Discount (cash):	0
Transfer Agent:	Bank of New York	Discount (div.):	0
Agent's Address:	P.O. Box 11258	Auto invest:	Yes
	New York, NY 10286	Auto invest fee:	$0
Agent's Phone:	888-269-2377	Selling info:	Sells weekly, by phone or mail, at market, for $5 +10¢/ADS
Other than USA:	Yes		

Company:	**Empresas Telex-Chile**	Safekeeping:	Yes
Symbol:	TL	Invests:	Every 7 days beginning varies
Exchange:	NYSE	Minimum:	$50
Industry:	Telecommunications	Maximum:	$250,000/year
Company Address:	c/o BNY,101 Barclay St.,22 West	Min to qualify:	1
	New York, NY 10286	Fee on cash inv.:	$5 + 10¢/sh.
Company Phone:	800-943-9715	Fee on div. inv.:	5% to $5 + 10¢/sh.
Transfer Agent:	Bank of New York	Discount (cash):	0
Agent's Address:	P.O. Box 11258	Discount (div.):	0
	New York, NY 10286	Auto invest:	Yes
Agent's Phone:	888-269-2377	Auto invest fee:	$5 + 10¢/sh.
Other than USA:	Yes	Selling info:	Sells weekly, by mail, at market, for $5 +10¢/sh.

Company:	**Enbridge, Inc.**	Safekeeping:	No
Symbol:	ENBRF	Invests:	Every 90 days beginning 3/1
Exchange:	TSE	Minimum:	$0
Industry:	Pipeline operator	Maximum:	$5,000/quarter Cdn.
Company Address:	2900, 421-7 Ave. S.W.	Min to qualify:	1
	Calgary, Alta.,T2P 4K9 Canada	Fee on cash inv.:	0
Company Phone:	800-481-2804 or 403-231-3973	Fee on div. inv.:	0
Transfer Agent:	CIBC Mellon Trust Company	Discount (cash):	0
Agent's Address:	320 Bay St., 3rd Fl.	Discount (div.):	5%
	Toronto, Ontario M5H 4A6	Auto invest:	No
Agent's Phone:	800-387-0825	Auto invest fee:	$0
Other than USA:	Yes	Selling info:	Sells within 3 weeks, by mail, at avg. price, for comm.

Company:	**Endesa SA**	Safekeeping:	Yes
Symbol:	ELE	Invests:	Every 7 days beginning varies
Exchange:	NYSE	Minimum:	$50
Industry:	Electric utility	Maximum:	$100,000/year
Company Address:	c/o Morgan Guaranty Trust, Box 9073	Min to qualify:	1
		Fee on cash inv.:	$5 + 12¢/sh.
	Boston, MA 02205-9948	Fee on div. inv.:	5% to $2.50
Company Phone:	800-428-4237	Discount (cash):	0
Transfer Agent:	Morgan Guaranty Trust Co.	Discount (div.):	0
Agent's Address:	P.O. Box 9073	Auto invest:	Yes
	Boston, MA 02205-9948	Auto invest fee:	$5
Agent's Phone:	800-428-4237	Selling info:	Sells daily, by phone or mail, at market, for $5 +12¢/sh.
Other than USA:	No		

Company:	**Energen Corp.**	Safekeeping:	Yes
Symbol:	EGN	Invests:	Every 7 days beginning varies
Exchange:	NYSE	Minimum:	$25
Industry:	Utility-gas, oil & gas exploration & prod.	Maximum:	$250,000/year
		Min to qualify:	1
Company Address:	605 21st St. North	Fee on cash inv.:	0!
	Birmingham, AL 35203-2707	Fee on div. inv.:	0
Company Phone:	800-654-3206 or 205-326-2700	Discount (cash):	0
Transfer Agent:	FCT (EquiServe)	Discount (div.):	0
Agent's Address:	P.O. Box 2598	Auto invest:	Yes
	Jersey City, NJ 07303-2598	Auto invest fee:	$0
Agent's Phone:	888-764-5603	Selling info:	Sells daily, by mail, fax or phone, at avg. price, for $15 +12¢/sh.
Other than USA:	Yes		

Company:	**Energy East Corp.**	Safekeeping:	Yes
Symbol:	NEG	Invests:	Every 30 days beginning 1/1
Exchange:	NYSE	Minimum:	$25
Industry:	Utility-electric, gas	Maximum:	$100,000/year
Company Address:	Box 3200	Min to qualify:	1
	Ithaca, NY 14852-3200	Fee on cash inv.:	0!
Company Phone:	800-225-5643 or 607-347-2561	Fee on div. inv.:	0!
Transfer Agent:	Energy East Corp.	Discount (cash):	0
Agent's Address:	P. O. Box 3200	Discount (div.):	0
	Ithaca, NY 14852-3200	Auto invest:	No
Agent's Phone:	800-225-5643	Auto invest fee:	$0
Other than USA:	Yes	Selling info:	Sells weekly, by mail, at avg. price, for 7¢ to 8¢/sh.

Company:	**EnergyNorth, Inc.**	Safekeeping:	Yes
Symbol:	EI	Invests:	Every 30 days beginning 1/15
Exchange:	NYSE	Minimum:	$50
Industry:	Utility-gas	Maximum:	$2,500/quarter
Company Address:	1260 Elm St., Box 329	Min to qualify:	1
	Manchester, NH 03105	Fee on cash inv.:	0
Company Phone:	603-625-4000 x4267	Fee on div. inv.:	0
Transfer Agent:	Boston Eq. (EquiServe)	Discount (cash):	0
Agent's Address:	P.O. Box 8040	Discount (div.):	0
	Boston, MA 02266	Auto invest:	No
Agent's Phone:	800-736-3001	Auto invest fee:	$0
Other than USA:	Yes	Selling info:	Sells within 10 bus. days, by mail, at avg. price, for 5% to $10 + comm.

Company:	**EnergySouth, Inc.**	Safekeeping:	Yes
Symbol:	ENSI	Invests:	Every 30 days beginning 1/1
Exchange:	OTC	Minimum:	$25
Industry:	Utility-gas	Maximum:	$5,000/quarter
Company Address:	Box 2607	Min to qualify:	1
	Mobile, AL 36652	Fee on cash inv.:	0
Company Phone:	334-450-4638	Fee on div. inv.:	0
Transfer Agent:	Boston Eq. (EquiServe)	Discount (cash):	0
Agent's Address:	P.O. Box 8040	Discount (div.):	0
	Boston, MA 02266-8040	Auto invest:	No
Agent's Phone:	800-736-3001	Auto invest fee:	$0
Other than USA:	Yes	Selling info:	Sells irregularly, by mail, at market, for comm.

Company:	**Enesco Group, Inc.**	Safekeeping:	Yes
Symbol:	ENC	Invests:	Every 90 days beginning 1/1
Exchange:	NYSE	Minimum:	$10
Industry:	Giftware, collectibles, consumer prods. household items	Maximum:	$5,000/quarter
		Min to qualify:	1
Company Address:	225 Windsor Dr.	Fee on cash inv.:	0
	Itasca, IL 60143	Fee on div. inv.:	0
Company Phone:	630-875-5856 or 630-875-5300	Discount (cash):	0
Transfer Agent:	ChaseMellon Shareholder Services	Discount (div.):	0
Agent's Address:	P.O. Box 3338	Auto invest:	No
	South Hackensack, NJ 07606-1938	Auto invest fee:	$0
Agent's Phone:	800-288-9541	Selling info:	Sells weekly, by mail or phone, at market, for $3 + comm.
Other than USA:	Yes		

Company:	**Engelhard Corp.**	Safekeeping:	Yes
Symbol:	EC	Invests:	Every 30 days beginning 1/30
Exchange:	NYSE	Minimum:	$10
Industry:	Specialty chemicals	Maximum:	$3,000/month
Company Address:	101 Wood Ave., Box 770	Min to qualify:	1
	Iselin, NJ 08830	Fee on cash inv.:	0
Company Phone:	800-458-9823 or 732-205-5000 or 732-205-6065	Fee on div. inv.:	0
		Discount (cash):	0
Transfer Agent:	ChaseMellon Shareholder Services	Discount (div.):	0
Agent's Address:	85 Challenger Road	Auto invest:	No
	Ridgefield Park, NJ 07660	Auto invest fee:	$0
Agent's Phone:	800-851-9677	Selling info:	Sells weekly, by mail or phone, at market, for $5 + comm.
Other than USA:	No		

Company:	**ENI SpA**	Safekeeping:	Yes
Symbol:	E	Invests:	Every 7 days beginning varies
Exchange:	NYSE	Minimum:	$50
Industry:	Oil & gas company	Maximum:	$100,000/year
Company Address:	c/o Morgan Guaranty Trust, Box	Min to qualify:	1
	9073	Fee on cash inv.:	$5 + 12¢/sh.
	Boston, MA 02205-9948	Fee on div. inv.:	5% to $2.50
Company Phone:	800-428-4237	Discount (cash):	0
Transfer Agent:	Morgan Guaranty Trust Co.	Discount (div.):	0
Agent's Address:	P.O. Box 9073	Auto invest:	Yes
	Boston, MA 02205-9948	Auto invest fee:	$5
Agent's Phone:	800-428-4237	Selling info:	Sells daily, by phone or mail, at
Other than USA:	No		market, for $5 +12¢/sh.

Company:	**Enron Corp.**	Safekeeping:	Yes
Symbol:	ENE	Invests:	Every 7 days beginning Wed.
Exchange:	NYSE	Minimum:	$25
Industry:	Gas distr. & electricity	Maximum:	$120,000/year
Company Address:	1400 Smith St.	Min to qualify:	1
	Houston, TX 77002	Fee on cash inv.:	0!
Company Phone:	713-853-9864 or 713-853-6161	Fee on div. inv.:	0!
Transfer Agent:	FCT (EquiServe)	Discount (cash):	0
Agent's Address:	P.O. Box 2598	Discount (div.):	0
	Jersey City, NJ 07303-2598	Auto invest:	Yes
Agent's Phone:	800-519-3111	Auto invest fee:	$1
Other than USA:	Yes	Selling info:	Sells daily, by phone or mail, at
			avg. price, for $15 +12¢/sh.

Company:	**Entergy Corp.**	Safekeeping:	Yes
Symbol:	ETR	Invests:	Every 30 days beginning 1/4
Exchange:	NYSE	Minimum:	$100
Industry:	Utility-electric	Maximum:	$3,000/month
Company Address:	Box 61000	Min to qualify:	1
	New Orleans, LA 70161	Fee on cash inv.:	$5 + comm.
Company Phone:	504-569-4365	Fee on div. inv.:	0
Transfer Agent:	ChaseMellon Shareholder Ser-	Discount (cash):	0
	vices	Discount (div.):	0
Agent's Address:	85 Challenger Road	Auto invest:	No
	Ridgefield Park, NJ 07660	Auto invest fee:	$0
Agent's Phone:	800-333-4368	Selling info:	Sells biweekly, by mail or phone,
Other than USA:	No		at market, for $15 +12¢/sh.

Company:	**Entertainment Properties Trust**	Safekeeping:	Yes
		Invests:	Every 30 days beginning 1/15
Symbol:	EPR	Minimum:	$50
Exchange:	NYSE	Maximum:	$100,000/year
Industry:	REIT	Min to qualify:	1
Company Address:	1200 Main St., Ste. 3250	Fee on cash inv.:	0!
	Kansas City, MO 64105	Fee on div. inv.:	0!
Company Phone:	816-472-1700	Discount (cash):	0
Transfer Agent:	UMB Bank, NA	Discount (div.):	0
Agent's Address:	P.O. Box 410064	Auto invest:	Yes
	Kansas City, MO 64141	Auto invest fee:	$0
Agent's Phone:	800-884-4225	Selling info:	Sells monthly, by mail, at market,
Other than USA:	No		for $10

Company:	**Equant NV**	Safekeeping:	Yes
Symbol:	ENT	Invests:	Every 7 days beginning varies
Exchange:	NYSE	Minimum:	$50
Industry:	Provider of data network services	Maximum:	$100,000/year
Company Address:	c/o Morgan Guaranty Trust,	Min to qualify:	1
	Box 9073	Fee on cash inv.:	$5 + 12¢/sh.
	Boston, MA 02205-9948	Fee on div. inv.:	5% to $2.50
Company Phone:	800-428-4237	Discount (cash):	0
Transfer Agent:	Morgan Guaranty Trust Co.	Discount (div.):	0
Agent's Address:	P.O. Box 9073	Auto invest:	Yes
	Boston, MA 02205-9948	Auto invest fee:	$5
Agent's Phone:	800-428-4237	Selling info:	Sells daily, by phone or mail, at
Other than USA:	No		market, for $5 +12¢/sh.

Company:	**Equifax**	Safekeeping:	Yes
Symbol:	EFX	Invests:	Every 7 days beginning Wed.
Exchange:	NYSE	Minimum:	$50
Industry:	Business information services	Maximum:	$10,000/month
Company Address:	Box 4081	Min to qualify:	1
	Atlanta, GA 30302	Fee on cash inv.:	$5 + 7¢/sh.
Company Phone:	800-462-9853 or 404-885-8000	Fee on div. inv.:	0
Transfer Agent:	SunTrust Bank, Atlanta	Discount (cash):	0
Agent's Address:	P.O. Box 4625	Discount (div.):	0
	Atlanta, GA 30302	Auto invest:	Yes
Agent's Phone:	800-568-3476	Auto invest fee:	$0
Other than USA:	Yes	Selling info:	Sells biweekly, by mail or fax, at
			market, for $15 +7¢/sh.

Company:	**Equitable Companies Direct Invest**	Safekeeping:	Yes
		Invests:	Every 7 days beginning Wed.
Symbol:	EQ	Minimum:	$50
Exchange:	NYSE	Maximum:	$50,000/year
Industry:	Financial & insurance	Min to qualify:	1
Company Address:	787 Seventh Ave.	Fee on cash inv.:	0
	New York, NY 10019	Fee on div. inv.:	0
Company Phone:	212-554-1234	Discount (cash):	0
Transfer Agent:	FCT (EquiServe)	Discount (div.):	0
Agent's Address:	P.O. Box 2512	Auto invest:	Yes
	Jersey City, NJ 07303	Auto invest fee:	$0
Agent's Phone:	800-437-8736	Selling info:	Sells daily, by mail, at market, for
Other than USA:	No		$10 +12¢/sh.

Company:	**Equitable Companies, Inc. (The)**	Safekeeping:	Yes
		Invests:	Every 30 days beginning 1/15
Symbol:	EQ	Minimum:	$50
Exchange:	NYSE	Maximum:	$60,000/year
Industry:	Financial & insurance	Min to qualify:	1
Company Address:	1290 Ave. of the Americas	Fee on cash inv.:	0!
	New York, NY 10104	Fee on div. inv.:	0!
Company Phone:	212-314-3081	Discount (cash):	0
Transfer Agent:	FCT (EquiServe)	Discount (div.):	0
Agent's Address:	P.O. Box 2512, MS 4672	Auto invest:	Yes
	Jersey City, NJ 07303-2512	Auto invest fee:	$0
Agent's Phone:	800-437-8736	Selling info:	Sells daily, by mail or fax,
Other than USA:	No		at market, for $10 +12¢/sh.

Company:	Equitable Resources Inc.	**Safekeeping:**	Yes
Symbol:	EQT	**Invests:**	Every 30 days beginning 1/1
Exchange:	NYSE	**Minimum:**	$25
Industry:	Energy company	**Maximum:**	$5,000/month
Company Address:	One Oxford Center, Ste. 3300	**Min to qualify:**	1
	Pittsburgh, PA 15219	**Fee on cash inv.:**	0!
Company Phone:	412-553-5700 or 412-553-5768	**Fee on div. inv.:**	0!
Transfer Agent:	ChaseMellon Shareholder Services	**Discount (cash):**	0
Agent's Address:	P.O. Box 3315	**Discount (div.):**	0
	S. Hackensack, NJ 07606	**Auto invest:**	No
Agent's Phone:	800-589-9026	**Auto invest fee:**	$0
Other than USA:	Yes	**Selling info:**	Sells weekly, by mail , at market, for $5 +10¢/sh.

Company:	Equity Residential Prop. Trust	**Safekeeping:**	Yes
		Invests:	Every 30 days beginning 1/10
Symbol:	EQR	**Minimum:**	$250
Exchange:	NYSE	**Maximum:**	$5,000/month
Industry:	REIT	**Min to qualify:**	1
Company Address:	Two North Riverside Plaza-	**Fee on cash inv.:**	0
	Ste. 600	**Fee on div. inv.:**	0
	Chicago, IL 60606	**Discount (cash):**	0
Company Phone:	888-879-6356 or 312-474-1300	**Discount (div.):**	0-5%
Transfer Agent:	Boston Eq. (EquiServe)	**Auto invest:**	No
Agent's Address:	P.O. Box 8040	**Auto invest fee:**	$0
	Boston, MA 02266-8040	**Selling info:**	Sells within 10 days, by mail, at
Agent's Phone:	800-733-5001		market, for $10 +15¢/sh.
Other than USA:	Yes		

Company:	ESB Financial Corp.	**Safekeeping:**	No
Symbol:	ESBF	**Invests:**	Every 30 days beginning 1/25
Exchange:	OTC	**Minimum:**	$25
Industry:	Banking	**Maximum:**	$15,000/quarter
Company Address:	600 Lawrence Ave.	**Min to qualify:**	1
	Ellwood City, PA 16117-1930	**Fee on cash inv.:**	0!
Company Phone:	724-758-5584	**Fee on div. inv.:**	0!
Transfer Agent:	Registrar & Transfer Co.	**Discount (cash):**	0
Agent's Address:	10 Commerce Drive	**Discount (div.):**	0
	Cranford, NJ 07016	**Auto invest:**	No
Agent's Phone:	800-368-5948	**Auto invest fee:**	$0
Other than USA:	Yes	**Selling info:**	Not available

Company:	Espirito Santo Financial Grp., SA	**Safekeeping:**	Yes
		Invests:	Every 7 days beginning varies
Symbol:	ESF	**Minimum:**	$50
Exchange:	NYSE	**Maximum:**	$250,000/year
Industry:	Banking	**Min to qualify:**	1
Company Address:	c/o BNY,101 Barclay St.,22 West	**Fee on cash inv.:**	$5 + 10¢/sh.
	New York, NY 10286	**Fee on div. inv.:**	5% to $5 + 10¢/sh.
Company Phone:	800-943-9715	**Discount (cash):**	0
Transfer Agent:	Bank of New York	**Discount (div.):**	0
Agent's Address:	P.O. Box 11258	**Auto invest:**	Yes
	New York, NY 10286	**Auto invest fee:**	$5 + 10¢/sh.
Agent's Phone:	888-269-2377	**Selling info:**	Sells weekly, by mail, at market,
Other than USA:	Yes		for $5 +10¢/sh.

Company:	**Esprit Telecom Group plc**	**Safekeeping:**	Yes
Symbol:	ESPRY	**Invests:**	Every 7 days beginning varies
Exchange:	OTC	**Minimum:**	$50
Industry:	Telecommunications	**Maximum:**	$250,000/week
Company Address:	c/o BNY,101 Barclay St., 22 West	**Min to qualify:**	1
	New York, NY 10286	**Fee on cash inv.:**	$5 + 10¢/sh.
Company Phone:	212-815-2175	**Fee on div. inv.:**	5% to $5 + 10¢/sh.
Transfer Agent:	Bank of New York	**Discount (cash):**	0
Agent's Address:	P.O. Box 11258	**Discount (div.):**	0
	New York, NY 10286	**Auto invest:**	Yes
Agent's Phone:	888-269-2377	**Auto invest fee:**	$0
Other than USA:	Yes	**Selling info:**	Sells weekly, by phone or mail, at market, for $5 +10¢/sh.

Company:	**Essex Property Trust, Inc.**	**Safekeeping:**	Yes
Symbol:	ESS	**Invests:**	Every 7 days beginning Friday
Exchange:	NYSE	**Minimum:**	$100
Industry:	REIT	**Maximum:**	$20,000/month
Company Address:	925 E. Meadow Dr.	**Min to qualify:**	1
	Palo Alto, CA 94303	**Fee on cash inv.:**	$5
Company Phone:	650-494-3700	**Fee on div. inv.:**	0
Transfer Agent:	BankBoston (EquiServe)	**Discount (cash):**	0
Agent's Address:	P.O. Box 8040	**Discount (div.):**	0
	Boston, MA 02266-8040	**Auto invest:**	Yes
Agent's Phone:	800-730-6001	**Auto invest fee:**	$5
Other than USA:	Yes	**Selling info:**	Sells within 10 bus. days, by mail, at avg. price, for $10 +15¢/sh.

Company:	**Ethyl Corp.**	**Safekeeping:**	No
Symbol:	EY	**Invests:**	Every 30 days beginning 1/1
Exchange:	NYSE	**Minimum:**	$25
Industry:	Chemicals	**Maximum:**	$1,000/month
Company Address:	330 South Fourth St., Box 2189	**Min to qualify:**	1
	Richmond, VA 23218-2189	**Fee on cash inv.:**	0
Company Phone:	804-788-5000	**Fee on div. inv.:**	0
Transfer Agent:	Harris Trust & Savings Bank	**Discount (cash):**	0
Agent's Address:	P.O. Box A-3309	**Discount (div.):**	0
	Chicago, IL 60690-3309	**Auto invest:**	No
Agent's Phone:	800-625-5191	**Auto invest fee:**	$0
Other than USA:	No	**Selling info:**	Sells weekly, by mail or fax, at market, for comm.

Company:	**Exxon Corp.**	**Safekeeping:**	Yes
Symbol:	XON	**Invests:**	Every 7 days beginning Thursday
Exchange:	NYSE	**Minimum:**	$50
Industry:	Oil refining	**Maximum:**	$200,000/year
Company Address:	Box 140369	**Min to qualify:**	1
	Irving, TX 75014-0369	**Fee on cash inv.:**	0
Company Phone:	972-444-1000	**Fee on div. inv.:**	0
Transfer Agent:	BankBoston (EquiServe)	**Discount (cash):**	0
Agent's Address:	P.O. Box 8033	**Discount (div.):**	0
	Boston, MA 02266-8033	**Auto invest:**	Yes
Agent's Phone:	800-252-1800	**Auto invest fee:**	$0
Other than USA:	Yes	**Selling info:**	Sells weekly, by mail or fax, at avg. price, for $5 +10¢/sh.

Company:	**F & M Bancorp**	Safekeeping:	No
Symbol:	FMBN	Invests:	Every 90 days beginning 1/1
Exchange:	OTC	Minimum:	$25
Industry:	Bank holding co.	Maximum:	$3,000/quarter
Company Address:	110 Thomas Johnson Dr., Box 518	Min to qualify:	1
	Frederick, MD 21705	Fee on cash inv.:	0!
Company Phone:	888-694-4170 or 301-694-4000	Fee on div. inv.:	0!
Transfer Agent:	Norwest Shareowner Services	Discount (cash):	0
Agent's Address:	P.O. Box 64854	Discount (div.):	5%
	St. Paul, MN 55164-0854	Auto invest:	No
Agent's Phone:	800-468-9716	Auto invest fee:	$0
Other than USA:	Yes	Selling info:	Not available

Company:	**FAI Insurances Ltd.**	Safekeeping:	Yes
Symbol:	FAI	Invests:	Every 7 days beginning varies
Exchange:	NYSE	Minimum:	$50
Industry:	Insurance	Maximum:	$250,000/week
Company Address:	c/o BNY,101 Barclay St.,22 West	Min to qualify:	1
	New York, NY 10286	Fee on cash inv.:	$5 + 10¢/sh.
Company Phone:	800-943-9715	Fee on div. inv.:	5% to $5 + 10¢/sh.
Transfer Agent:	Bank of New York	Discount (cash):	0
Agent's Address:	P.O. Box 11258	Discount (div.):	0
	New York, NY 10286	Auto invest:	Yes
Agent's Phone:	888-269-2377	Auto invest fee:	$0
Other than USA:	Yes	Selling info:	Sells weekly, by phone or mail, at market, for $5 +10¢/ADS

Company:	**Fall River Gas Co.**	Safekeeping:	Yes
Symbol:	FAL	Invests:	Every 30 days beginning 1/15
Exchange:	ASE	Minimum:	$15
Industry:	Natural gas utility	Maximum:	$5,000/quarter
Company Address:	155 N. Main St., Box 911	Min to qualify:	10
	Fall River, MA 02722-0911	Fee on cash inv.:	0!
Company Phone:	506-675-7811	Fee on div. inv.:	0!
Transfer Agent:	State St. Bank & Trust	Discount (cash):	3%
Agent's Address:	P.O. Box 8209	Discount (div.):	0
	Boston, MA 02101-8209	Auto invest:	No
Agent's Phone:	800-426-5523	Auto invest fee:	$0
Other than USA:	Yes	Selling info:	Sells within 3 bus. days, by mail, at market, for 5% to $5 + 15¢/sh.

Company:	**Fannie Mae**	Safekeeping:	Yes
Symbol:	FNM	Invests:	Every 7 days beginning varies
Exchange:	NYSE	Minimum:	$25
Industry:	Mortgage and financing	Maximum:	$250,000/year
Company Address:	3900 Wisconsin Ave. NW	Min to qualify:	1
	Washington, DC 20016-2892	Fee on cash inv.:	$5
Company Phone:	888-289-3266 or 202-752-7115	Fee on div. inv.:	0
Transfer Agent:	FCT (EquiServe)	Discount (cash):	0
Agent's Address:	P.O. Box 2598	Discount (div.):	0
	Jersey City, NJ 07303-2598	Auto invest:	Yes
Agent's Phone:	800-910-8277	Auto invest fee:	$2
Other than USA:	Yes	Selling info:	Sells daily, by mail or phone, at market, for $15 +12¢/sh.

Company:	**FBL Financial Group, Inc. A**	**Safekeeping:**	No
Symbol:	FFG	**Invests:**	Every 30 days beginning 1/31
Exchange:	NYSE	**Minimum:**	$25
Industry:	Markets and distributes insurance	**Maximum:**	$5,000/month
Company Address:	5400 University Ave.	**Min to qualify:**	1
	West Des Moines, IA 50266	**Fee on cash inv.:**	0
Company Phone:	515-225-5400 or 515-225-5799	**Fee on div. inv.:**	0
Transfer Agent:	ChaseMellon Shareholder Services	**Discount (cash):**	0
		Discount (div.):	0
Agent's Address:	P.O. Box 3338	**Auto invest:**	Yes
	South Hackensack, NJ 07606-1938	**Auto invest fee:**	$0
Agent's Phone:	888-213-0965	**Selling info:**	Sells weekly, by mail or phone, at market, for $15 +12¢/sh.
Other than USA:	No		

Company:	**FCNB Corp.**	**Safekeeping:**	Yes
Symbol:	FCNB	**Invests:**	Every 90 days beginning 1/8
Exchange:	OTC	**Minimum:**	$20
Industry:	Bank holding company	**Maximum:**	$2,500/quarter
Company Address:	7200 FCNB Ct., Box 240	**Min to qualify:**	1
	Frederick, MD 21705-0240	**Fee on cash inv.:**	0
Company Phone:	800-622-2191 or 301-624-2306	**Fee on div. inv.:**	0
Transfer Agent:	American Stock Transfer	**Discount (cash):**	3%
Agent's Address:	40 Wall Street	**Discount (div.):**	3%
	New York, NY 10005	**Auto invest:**	No
Agent's Phone:	800-278-4353 or 718-921-8283	**Auto invest fee:**	$0
Other than USA:	Yes	**Selling info:**	Sells weekly, by mail or fax, at market, for 4¢/sh.

Company:	**Federal Realty Investment Trust**	**Safekeeping:**	Yes
Symbol:	FRT	**Invests:**	Every 30 days beginning 1/15
Exchange:	NYSE	**Minimum:**	$50
Industry:	REIT	**Maximum:**	$15,000/quarter
Company Address:	1626 East Jefferson St.	**Min to qualify:**	1
	Rockville, MD 20852-4041	**Fee on cash inv.:**	0
Company Phone:	800-658-8980 or 301-998-8320	**Fee on div. inv.:**	0
Transfer Agent:	American Stock Transfer	**Discount (cash):**	0
Agent's Address:	40 Wall Street	**Discount (div.):**	0
	New York, NY 10005	**Auto invest:**	Yes
Agent's Phone:	800-937-5449 or 212-936-5100	**Auto invest fee:**	$0
Other than USA:	Yes	**Selling info:**	Sells weekly, by mail, at market, for comm.

Company:	**Federal Signal Corp.**	**Safekeeping:**	Yes
Symbol:	FSS	**Invests:**	Every 45 days beginning 1/1
Exchange:	NYSE	**Minimum:**	$100
Industry:	Elec. equip., vehicles, tools & signs	**Maximum:**	$5,000/quarter
		Min to qualify:	50
Company Address:	1415 West 22nd St.	**Fee on cash inv.:**	0!
	Oak Brook, IL 60523-2004	**Fee on div. inv.:**	0!
Company Phone:	630-954-2000 or 630-954-2020	**Discount (cash):**	0
Transfer Agent:	Harris Trust & Savings Bank	**Discount (div.):**	0
Agent's Address:	P.O. Box A3309	**Auto invest:**	No
	Chicago, IL 60690	**Auto invest fee:**	$0
Agent's Phone:	312-461-3309	**Selling info:**	Sells irregularly, by mail, at market, for $0
Other than USA:	Yes		

Company:	**Federal-Mogul**
Symbol:	FMO
Exchange:	NYSE
Industry:	Auto parts
Company Address:	26555 Northwestern Hwy.
	Southfield, MI 48034
Company Phone:	248-354-8847 or 248-354-7700
Transfer Agent:	Bank of New York
Agent's Address:	P.O. Box 11258, Church St. Station
	New York, NY 10286-1258
Agent's Phone:	800-524-4458
Other than USA:	Yes

Safekeeping:	Yes
Invests:	Every 30 days beginning 1/11
Minimum:	$10
Maximum:	$25,000/year
Min to qualify:	1
Fee on cash inv.:	5% to $3
Fee on div. inv.:	5% to $3
Discount (cash):	0
Discount (div.):	0
Auto invest:	No
Auto invest fee:	$0
Selling info:	Sells weekly, by mail, at avg. price, for $5 + comm.

Company:	**Ferro Corp.**
Symbol:	FOE
Exchange:	NYSE
Industry:	Specialty chemicals
Company Address:	1000 Lakeside Ave., Box 147000
	Cleveland, OH 44114-7000
Company Phone:	216-641-8580
Transfer Agent:	National City Bank
Agent's Address:	P.O. Box 92301
	Cleveland, OH 44193-0900
Agent's Phone:	800-622-6757 x2532
Other than USA:	Yes

Safekeeping:	Yes
Invests:	Every 30 days beginning 1/1
Minimum:	$10
Maximum:	$3,000/month
Min to qualify:	1
Fee on cash inv.:	0
Fee on div. inv.:	0
Discount (cash):	0
Discount (div.):	0
Auto invest:	No
Auto invest fee:	$0
Selling info:	Sells irregularly, by mail, at market, for comm.

Company:	**Fiat SpA**
Symbol:	FIA
Exchange:	NYSE
Industry:	Mfr. automobiles, farm equip.
Company Address:	c/o Morgan Guaranty Trust, Box 9073
	Boston, MA 02205-9948
Company Phone:	800-428-4237
Transfer Agent:	Morgan Guaranty Trust Co.
Agent's Address:	P.O. Box 9073
	Boston, MA 02205-9948
Agent's Phone:	800-428-4237
Other than USA:	No

Safekeeping:	Yes
Invests:	Every 7 days beginning varies
Minimum:	$50
Maximum:	$100,000/year
Min to qualify:	1
Fee on cash inv.:	$5 + 12¢/sh.
Fee on div. inv.:	5% to $2.50
Discount (cash):	0
Discount (div.):	0
Auto invest:	Yes
Auto invest fee:	$0
Selling info:	Sells daily, by phone or mail, at avg. price, for $5 +12¢/sh.

Company:	**Fidelity Bancorp**
Symbol:	FSBI
Exchange:	OTC
Industry:	Bank holding co.
Company Address:	1009 Perry Hwy.
	Pittsburgh, PA 15237-2105
Company Phone:	412-367-3300 x3139
Transfer Agent:	Registrar & Transfer Co.
Agent's Address:	10 Commerce Drive
	Cranford, NJ 07016
Agent's Phone:	800-866-1340 or 800-346-6084
Other than USA:	Yes

Safekeeping:	Yes
Invests:	Every 90 days beginning 2/10
Minimum:	$10
Maximum:	$3,500/quarter
Min to qualify:	1
Fee on cash inv.:	0
Fee on div. inv.:	0
Discount (cash):	0
Discount (div.):	0
Auto invest:	No
Auto invest fee:	$0
Selling info:	Sells daily, by mail, at market, for comm.

Company:	**Fidelity National Corp.**	**Safekeeping:**	Yes
Symbol:	LION	**Invests:**	Every 30 days beginning 1/15
Exchange:	OTC	**Minimum:**	$100
Industry:	Bank holding company	**Maximum:**	$50,000/quarter
Company Address:	3490 Piedmont Rd., Ste. 1550	**Min to qualify:**	100
	Atlanta, GA 30305	**Fee on cash inv.:**	$2 + 6¢/sh.
Company Phone:	404-639-6500	**Fee on div. inv.:**	0!
Transfer Agent:	Bank of New York	**Discount (cash):**	0
Agent's Address:	P.O. Box 11258, Church St. Station	**Discount (div.):**	0
	New York, NY 10286-1258	**Auto invest:**	No
Agent's Phone:	800-524-4458	**Auto invest fee:**	$0
Other than USA:	Yes	**Selling info:**	Sells daily, by mail, at avg. price, for $5 + 6¢/sh.

Company:	**Fifth Third Bancorp**	**Safekeeping:**	Yes
Symbol:	FITB	**Invests:**	Every 30 days beginning 1/14
Exchange:	OTC	**Minimum:**	$25
Industry:	Banking	**Maximum:**	$2,500/month
Company Address:	38 Fountain Sq. Plz., MS 10AT	**Min to qualify:**	1
	Cincinnati, OH 45263	**Fee on cash inv.:**	0!
Company Phone:	513-579-5320	**Fee on div. inv.:**	0!
Transfer Agent:	Fifth Third Bancorp	**Discount (cash):**	0
Agent's Address:	38 Fountain Square Plaza Dept.	**Discount (div.):**	0
	00855	**Auto invest:**	No
	Cincinnati, OH 45263	**Auto invest fee:**	$0
Agent's Phone:	800-837-2755	**Selling info:**	Sells weekly, by mail, at market,
Other than USA:	Yes		for $0

Company:	**Fila Holding S.p.A.**	**Safekeeping:**	Yes
Symbol:	FLH	**Invests:**	Every 7 days beginning varies
Exchange:	NYSE	**Minimum:**	$50
Industry:	Footwear	**Maximum:**	$250,000/year
Company Address:	c/o BNY,101 Barclay St.,22 West	**Min to qualify:**	1
	New York, NY 10286	**Fee on cash inv.:**	$5 + 10¢/sh.
Company Phone:	800-943-9715	**Fee on div. inv.:**	5% to $5 + 10¢/sh.
Transfer Agent:	Bank of New York	**Discount (cash):**	0
Agent's Address:	P.O. Box 11258	**Discount (div.):**	0
	New York, NY 10286	**Auto invest:**	Yes
Agent's Phone:	888-269-2377	**Auto invest fee:**	$5 + 10¢/sh.
Other than USA:	Yes	**Selling info:**	Sells weekly, by mail, at market, for $5 +10¢/sh.

Company:	**FINOVA Group Inc. (The)**	**Safekeeping:**	Yes
Symbol:	FNV	**Invests:**	Every 7 days beginning varies
Exchange:	NYSE	**Minimum:**	$50
Industry:	Commercial finance	**Maximum:**	$25,000/quarter
Company Address:	1850 North Central Ave., Box 2209	**Min to qualify:**	1
	Phoenix, AZ 85002-2209	**Fee on cash inv.:**	0!
Company Phone:	800-734-6682 or 602-207-4900	**Fee on div. inv.:**	0!
Transfer Agent:	Harris Trust & Savings Bank	**Discount (cash):**	0
Agent's Address:	P.O. Box A3504	**Discount (div.):**	0
	Chicago, IL 60690-3504	**Auto invest:**	Yes
Agent's Phone:	888-445-6428	**Auto invest fee:**	$0
Other than USA:	Yes	**Selling info:**	Sells every 5 bus. days, by mail, at avg. price, for $10 +8¢/sh.

Company:	**First American Corp.**	**Safekeeping:**	Yes
Symbol:	FAM	**Invests:**	Every 30 days beginning 1/1
Exchange:	NYSE	**Minimum:**	$25
Industry:	Banking	**Maximum:**	$15,000/quarter
Company Address:	First American Ctr.	**Min to qualify:**	1
	Nashville, TN 37237	**Fee on cash inv.:**	0!
Company Phone:	615-748-1500 or 615-770-4025	**Fee on div. inv.:**	0!
Transfer Agent:	FCT (EquiServe)	**Discount (cash):**	0
Agent's Address:	P.O. Box 2500	**Discount (div.):**	5%
	Jersey City, NJ 07303-2500	**Auto invest:**	Yes
Agent's Phone:	888-322-6927	**Auto invest fee:**	$0
Other than USA:	No	**Selling info:**	Sells irregularly, by mail, at market, for $0

Company:	**First American Financial Corp. (The)**	**Safekeeping:**	Yes
		Invests:	Every 5 days beginning varies
Symbol:	FAF	**Minimum:**	$50
Exchange:	NYSE	**Maximum:**	$5,000/quarter
Industry:	Financial services	**Min to qualify:**	1
Company Address:	114 East Fifth St.	**Fee on cash inv.:**	0!
	Santa Ana, CA 92701	**Fee on div. inv.:**	0!
Company Phone:	800-854-3643x6414	**Discount (cash):**	0
Transfer Agent:	Norwest Bank	**Discount (div.):**	0
Agent's Address:	P.O. Box 64854	**Auto invest:**	Yes
	St. Paul, MN 55164-0854	**Auto invest fee:**	$0
Agent's Phone:	800-468-9716	**Selling info:**	Sells daily, by mail or phone, at market, for $10 +15¢/sh.
Other than USA:	Yes		

Company:	**First Australia Prime Income Fund, Inc.**	**Safekeeping:**	No
		Invests:	Every 30 days beginning 1/15
Symbol:	FAX	**Minimum:**	$100
Exchange:	ASE	**Maximum:**	$unlimited
Industry:	Closed-end fund	**Min to qualify:**	1
Company Address:	c/o State St. Bank, Box 8200	**Fee on cash inv.:**	75¢ + comm.
	Boston, MA 02266-8200	**Fee on div. inv.:**	0
Company Phone:	800-323-9995 or 800-451-6788	**Discount (cash):**	0
Transfer Agent:	State Street Bank (EquiServe)	**Discount (div.):**	5%
Agent's Address:	P.O. Box 8200	**Auto invest:**	No
	Boston, MA 02266-8200	**Auto invest fee:**	$0
Agent's Phone:	800-451-6788	**Selling info:**	Sells irregularly, by mail, at market, for $2.50 +15¢/sh.
Other than USA:	Yes		

Company:	**First Bancorp**	**Safekeeping:**	Yes
Symbol:	FBNC	**Invests:**	Every 30 days beginning 1/25
Exchange:	OTC	**Minimum:**	$25
Industry:	Bank holding company	**Maximum:**	$2,500/quarter
Company Address:	341 North Main St., Box 508	**Min to qualify:**	1
	Troy, NC 27371-0508	**Fee on cash inv.:**	0
Company Phone:	800-548-9377 or 910-576-2265 x216	**Fee on div. inv.:**	0
Transfer Agent:	Registrar & Transfer Co.	**Discount (cash):**	0
Agent's Address:	10 Commerce Drive	**Discount (div.):**	0
	Cranford, NJ 07016-3572	**Auto invest:**	No
Agent's Phone:	800-368-5948	**Auto invest fee:**	$0
Other than USA:	Yes	**Selling info:**	Sells monthly, by mail, at market, for 6¢ to 8¢/sh.

Company:	**First Charter Corp.**		Safekeeping:	Yes
Symbol:	FCTR		Invests:	Every 30 days beginning 1/15
Exchange:	OTC		Minimum:	$25
Industry:	Banking		Maximum:	$3,000/quarter
Company Address:	Box 228		Min to qualify:	1
	North Concord, NC 28026-0228		Fee on cash inv.:	0
Company Phone:	800-422-4650 or 704-786-3300		Fee on div. inv.:	0
			Discount (cash):	0
Transfer Agent:	Registrar & Transfer Co.		Discount (div.):	0
Agent's Address:	P.O. Box 1010		Auto invest:	Yes
	Cranford, NJ 07016		Auto invest fee:	$0
Agent's Phone:	800-368-5948		Selling info:	Sells irregularly, by mail,
Other than USA:	Yes			at market, for $0

Company:	**First Colonial Group**		Safekeeping:	Yes
Symbol:	FTCG		Invests:	Every 90 days beginning 2/22
Exchange:	OTC		Minimum:	$100
Industry:	Banking		Maximum:	$1,000/quarter
Company Address:	76 South Main St.		Min to qualify:	1
	Nazareth, PA 18064-2053		Fee on cash inv.:	0
Company Phone:	610-746-7317 or 610-746-7300		Fee on div. inv.:	0
Transfer Agent:	Nazareth National Bank and		Discount (cash):	5%
	Trust Co.		Discount (div.):	5%
Agent's Address:	76 South Main St.		Auto invest:	No
	Nazareth, PA 18064		Auto invest fee:	$0
Agent's Phone:	610-746-7317		Selling info:	Not available
Other than USA:	N/A			

Company:	**First Commerce Banc-shares**		Safekeeping:	No
			Invests:	Every 30 days beginning 1/5
Symbol:	FCBIB		Minimum:	$25
Exchange:	OTC		Maximum:	$500/month
Industry:	Regional banks		Min to qualify:	1
Company Address:	1248 'O' St., NBC Ctr., Box 82408		Fee on cash inv.:	0!
	Lincoln, NE 68508		Fee on div. inv.:	0!
Company Phone:	402-434-4110		Discount (cash):	0
Transfer Agent:	ChaseMellon Shareholder Services		Discount (div.):	0
Agent's Address:	P.O. Box 3338		Auto invest:	No
	South Hackensack, Nj 07606-1938		Auto invest fee:	$0
Agent's Phone:	800-765-3353		Selling info:	Sells daily, by mail or phone, at
Other than USA:	No			market, for $5 + comm.

Company:	**First Commonwealth Financial**		Safekeeping:	No
			Invests:	Every 30 days beginning 1/15
Symbol:	FCF		Minimum:	$25
Exchange:	NYSE		Maximum:	$10,000/quarter
Industry:	Banking		Min to qualify:	1
Company Address:	Old Courthouse Sq., 22 North 6th St.		Fee on cash inv.:	0
	Indiana, PA 15701		Fee on div. inv.:	0
Company Phone:	800-331-4107 or 724-349-7220		Discount (cash):	0
Transfer Agent:	Bank of New York		Discount (div.):	5%
Agent's Address:	P.O. Box 11258, Church St. Station		Auto invest:	No
	New York, NY 10286		Auto invest fee:	$0
Agent's Phone:	800-524-4458		Selling info:	Sells irregularly, by mail,
Other than USA:	Yes			at market, for comm.

Company:	**First Federal Capital Corp.**	**Safekeeping:**	Yes
		Invests:	Every 90 days beginning 3/1
Symbol:	FTFC	**Minimum:**	$50
Exchange:	OTC	**Maximum:**	$5,000/quarter
Industry:	Banking	**Min to qualify:**	1
Company Address:	605 State St., Box 1868	**Fee on cash inv.:**	0!
	La Crosse, WI 54602	**Fee on div. inv.:**	0!
Company Phone:	608-784-8000 X231	**Discount (cash):**	0
Transfer Agent:	Norwest Bank Minnesota	**Discount (div.):**	0
Agent's Address:	P.O. Box 64854	**Auto invest:**	No
	St. Paul, MN 55164-0854	**Auto invest fee:**	$0
Agent's Phone:	800-468-9716 or 651-450-4057	**Selling info:**	Sells daily, by mail or fax,
Other than USA:	Yes		at market, for comm.

Company:	**First Financial Holdings Inc.**	**Safekeeping:**	Yes
		Invests:	Every 7 days beginning varies
Symbol:	FFCH	**Minimum:**	$100
Exchange:	OTC	**Maximum:**	$5,000/month
Industry:	Savings and loan	**Min to qualify:**	1
Company Address:	Box 118068	**Fee on cash inv.:**	0!
	Charleston, SC 29423-8068	**Fee on div. inv.:**	0!
Company Phone:	843-529-5933 or 843-529-5800	**Discount (cash):**	0
Transfer Agent:	Registrar & Transfer Co.	**Discount (div.):**	0
Agent's Address:	10 Commerce Drive	**Auto invest:**	Yes
	Cranford, NJ 07106-9982	**Auto invest fee:**	$0
Agent's Phone:	800-368-5948	**Selling info:**	Sells irregularly, by mail,
Other than USA:	Yes		at market, for $3.50 + comm.

Company:	**First Indiana Corp.**	**Safekeeping:**	No
Symbol:	FISB	**Invests:**	Every 90 days beginning 3/15
Exchange:	OTC	**Minimum:**	$100
Industry:	Savings banks	**Maximum:**	$5,000/quarter
Company Address:	135 North Pennsylvania St.	**Min to qualify:**	1
	Indianapolis, IN 46204	**Fee on cash inv.:**	0!
Company Phone:	317-269-1200 or 317-269-1363	**Fee on div. inv.:**	0!
Transfer Agent:	Harris Trust & Savings Bank	**Discount (cash):**	0
Agent's Address:	P.O. Box A3309	**Discount (div.):**	0
	Chicago, IL 60690-9939	**Auto invest:**	No
Agent's Phone:	312-461-5545	**Auto invest fee:**	$0
Other than USA:	Yes	**Selling info:**	Sells weekly, by mail or fax, at
			market, for $5 + comm.

Company:	**First M & F Corp.**	**Safekeeping:**	Yes
Symbol:	FMFC	**Invests:**	Every 30 days beginning 1/30
Exchange:	OTC	**Minimum:**	$50
Industry:	Bank holding company	**Maximum:**	$5,000/quarter
Company Address:	221 E. Washington St., Box 520	**Min to qualify:**	100
	Kosciusko, MS 39090	**Fee on cash inv.:**	0!
Company Phone:	601-289-5121	**Fee on div. inv.:**	0!
Transfer Agent:	Registrar & Transfer Company	**Discount (cash):**	0
Agent's Address:	10 Commerce Drive	**Discount (div.):**	0
	Cranford, NJ 07016-3572	**Auto invest:**	Yes
Agent's Phone:	800-368-5948	**Auto invest fee:**	$0
Other than USA:	Yes	**Selling info:**	Sells within 10 bus. days, by mail,
			at avg. price, for $10 + comm.

Company:	**First Midwest Bancorp, Inc.**	**Safekeeping:**	Yes
		Invests:	Every 30 days beginning varies
Symbol:	FMBI	**Minimum:**	$100
Exchange:	OTC	**Maximum:**	$5,000/quarter
Industry:	Banking	**Min to qualify:**	1
Company Address:	300 Park Blvd., Ste.405, Box 459	**Fee on cash inv.:**	0
	Itasca, IL 60143-9768	**Fee on div. inv.:**	0
Company Phone:	630-875-7452	**Discount (cash):**	0
Transfer Agent:	American Securities Transfer	**Discount (div.):**	0
Agent's Address:	938 Quail St., Ste. 101	**Auto invest:**	No
	Lakewood, CO 80215	**Auto invest fee:**	$0
Agent's Phone:	800-962-4284	**Selling info:**	Not available
Other than USA:	No		

Company:	**First Northern Capital Corp.**	**Safekeeping:**	Yes
		Invests:	Every 90 days beginning 2/15
Symbol:	FNGB	**Minimum:**	$25
Exchange:	OTC	**Maximum:**	$3,000/quarter
Industry:	Banking	**Min to qualify:**	50
Company Address:	201 North Monroe, Box 23100	**Fee on cash inv.:**	0
	Green Bay, WI 54305-3100	**Fee on div. inv.:**	0
Company Phone:	800-999-3675	**Discount (cash):**	0
Transfer Agent:	Firstar Bank Milwaukee, NA	**Discount (div.):**	0
Agent's Address:	615 East Michigan St., P.O.	**Auto invest:**	Yes
	Box 2077	**Auto invest fee:**	$0
	Milwaukee, WI 53201-2077	**Selling info:**	Not available
Agent's Phone:	800-637-7549 or 414-276-3737		
Other than USA:	Yes		

Company:	**First Savings Bancorp, Inc.**	**Safekeeping:**	No
Symbol:	SOPN	**Invests:**	Every 90 days beginning 1/22
Exchange:	OTC	**Minimum:**	$25
Industry:	Banking	**Maximum:**	$3,000/quarter
Company Address:	205 S.E. Broad St., Box 1657	**Min to qualify:**	1
	Southern Pines, NC 28387	**Fee on cash inv.:**	8¢/sh.
Company Phone:	910-692-6222	**Fee on div. inv.:**	0
Transfer Agent:	Registrar & Transfer Company	**Discount (cash):**	0
Agent's Address:	10 Commerce Drive	**Discount (div.):**	0
	Cranford, NJ 07016-3572	**Auto invest:**	No
Agent's Phone:	800-368-5948	**Auto invest fee:**	$0
Other than USA:	Yes	**Selling info:**	Sells irregularly, by mail, at market, for comm.

Company:	**First Security Corp.**	**Safekeeping:**	Yes
Symbol:	FSCO	**Invests:**	Every 30 days beginning 1/1
Exchange:	OTC	**Minimum:**	$50
Industry:	Banking, financial, insurance	**Maximum:**	$5,000/month
Company Address:	15 East 100 South, 2nd Fl.	**Min to qualify:**	1
	Salt Lake City, UT 84111	**Fee on cash inv.:**	0!
Company Phone:	800-574-6695 or 801-246-5289	**Fee on div. inv.:**	0!
Transfer Agent:	FCT (EquiServe)	**Discount (cash):**	0
Agent's Address:	P.O. Box 2500	**Discount (div.):**	0
	Jersey City, NJ 07303-2500	**Auto invest:**	No
Agent's Phone:	800-756-8200	**Auto invest fee:**	$0
Other than USA:	Yes	**Selling info:**	Sells monthly, by mail, at avg. price, for comm.

Company:	First Tennessee National Corp.	**Safekeeping:**	Yes
		Invests:	Every 30 days beginning 1/1
Symbol:	FTEN	**Minimum:**	$25
Exchange:	OTC	**Maximum:**	$10,000/quarter
Industry:	Banking	**Min to qualify:**	1
Company Address:	Box 84	**Fee on cash inv.:**	0
	Memphis, TN 38101-0084	**Fee on div. inv.:**	0
Company Phone:	800-489-4040 or 901-523-5620	**Discount (cash):**	0
Transfer Agent:	Norwest Bank Minnesota	**Discount (div.):**	0
Agent's Address:	P.O. Box 64854	**Auto invest:**	No
	St. Paul, MN 55164-0854	**Auto invest fee:**	$0
Agent's Phone:	800-468-9716	**Selling info:**	Sells weekly, by mail, at market,
Other than USA:	Yes		for comm.

Company:	First Union Corp.	**Safekeeping:**	Yes
Symbol:	FTU	**Invests:**	Every 30 days beginning 1/15
Exchange:	NYSE	**Minimum:**	$25
Industry:	Banking	**Maximum:**	$2,000/month
Company Address:	301 S. College St., Ste. 4000	**Min to qualify:**	10
	Charlotte, NC 28288-0570	**Fee on cash inv.:**	0!
Company Phone:	888-257-9919 or 704-374-6782	**Fee on div. inv.:**	0!
Transfer Agent:	First Union National Bank	**Discount (cash):**	0
Agent's Address:	1525 West W.T. Harris Blvd.,3C3	**Discount (div.):**	1%
	Charlotte, NC 28288-1153	**Auto invest:**	Yes
Agent's Phone:	800-347-1246	**Auto invest fee:**	$0
Other than USA:	Yes	**Selling info:**	Sells monthly, by mail, at market,
			for 0!

Company:	First Union REIT	**Safekeeping:**	Yes
Symbol:	FUR	**Invests:**	Every 30 days beginning 1/1
Exchange:	NYSE	**Minimum:**	$20
Industry:	REIT	**Maximum:**	$5,000/month
Company Address:	55 Public Sq., Ste.1900	**Min to qualify:**	1
	Cleveland, OH 44113-1937	**Fee on cash inv.:**	5% to $3
Company Phone:	216-781-4030x1039	**Fee on div. inv.:**	0
Transfer Agent:	National City Bank	**Discount (cash):**	0
Agent's Address:	4100 W. 150th St., 3rd Fl., N.	**Discount (div.):**	0
	Annex, Loc 5352	**Auto invest:**	No
	Cleveland, OH 44135-1385	**Auto invest fee:**	$0
Agent's Phone:	800-622-6757	**Selling info:**	Sells weekly, by mail or fax, at
Other than USA:	Yes		market, for comm.

Company:	First United Corp.	**Safekeeping:**	Yes
Symbol:	FUNC	**Invests:**	Every 90 days beginning 2/1
Exchange:	OTC	**Minimum:**	$50
Industry:	Regional banks	**Maximum:**	$10,000/quarter
Company Address:	19 South Second St.	**Min to qualify:**	1
	Oakland, MD 21550	**Fee on cash inv.:**	0!
Company Phone:	301-334-9471	**Fee on div. inv.:**	0!
Transfer Agent:	ChaseMellon Shareholder Services	**Discount (cash):**	0
Agent's Address:	P.O. Box 3338	**Discount (div.):**	0
	South Hackensack, Nj 07606-1938	**Auto invest:**	No
Agent's Phone:	800-953-2593	**Auto invest fee:**	$0
Other than USA:	No	**Selling info:**	Sells weekly, by mail or phone, at
			market, for $3.50 + comm.

Company:	**First Virginia Banks, Inc.**	**Safekeeping:**	Yes
Symbol:	FVB	**Invests:**	Every 30 days beginning 1/1
Exchange:	NYSE	**Minimum:**	$25
Industry:	Banking	**Maximum:**	$5,000/quarter
Company Address:	6400 Arlington Blvd.	**Min to qualify:**	1
	Falls Church, VA 22042-2336	**Fee on cash inv.:**	0!
Company Phone:	800-995-9416 or 703-241-3657,	**Fee on div. inv.:**	0!
	4000	**Discount (cash):**	0
Transfer Agent:	Registrar & Transfer Co.	**Discount (div.):**	0
Agent's Address:	10 Commerce Drive	**Auto invest:**	Yes
	Cranford, NJ 07016-3572	**Auto invest fee:**	$0
Agent's Phone:	800-368-5948	**Selling info:**	Not available
Other than USA:	Yes		

Company:	**First Western Bancorp Inc.**	**Safekeeping:**	Yes
		Invests:	Every 30 days beginning 1/15
Symbol:	FWBI	**Minimum:**	$25
Exchange:	OTC	**Maximum:**	$10,000/quarter
Industry:	Banking	**Min to qualify:**	1
Company Address:	Box 1488	**Fee on cash inv.:**	0!
	New Castle, PA 16103-1488	**Fee on div. inv.:**	0!
Company Phone:	800-696-2572 or 724-652-8550	**Discount (cash):**	0
Transfer Agent:	BankBoston (EquiServe)	**Discount (div.):**	0
Agent's Address:	P.O. Box 8040	**Auto invest:**	No
	Boston, MA 02266-8040	**Auto invest fee:**	$0
Agent's Phone:	800-730-4001	**Selling info:**	Sells within 10 bus. days, by mail,
Other than USA:	Yes		at market, for 15¢/sh.

Company:	**Firstar Corp.**	**Safekeeping:**	Yes
Symbol:	FSR	**Invests:**	Every 30 days beginning 1/15
Exchange:	NYSE	**Minimum:**	$50
Industry:	Banking	**Maximum:**	$10,000/quarter
Company Address:	777 East Wisconsin Ave., Ste. 301	**Min to qualify:**	1
	Milwaukee, WI 53202	**Fee on cash inv.:**	0!
Company Phone:	414-765-4321	**Fee on div. inv.:**	0!
Transfer Agent:	Firstar Bank Milwaukee, NA	**Discount (cash):**	0
Agent's Address:	1555 North River Center Dr.,	**Discount (div.):**	0
	Suite 301	**Auto invest:**	Yes
	Milwaukee, WI 53212	**Auto invest fee:**	$0
Agent's Phone:	800-637-7549	**Selling info:**	Sells avg. price, by mail or fax, at
Other than USA:	No		market, for 3¢/sh.

Company:	**FirstEnergy**	**Safekeeping:**	Yes
Symbol:	FE	**Invests:**	Every 15 days beginning 1/1
Exchange:	NYSE	**Minimum:**	$25
Industry:	Utility-electric	**Maximum:**	$100,000/year
Company Address:	76 South Main St.	**Min to qualify:**	1
	Akron, OH 44308-1890	**Fee on cash inv.:**	9¢/sh.
Company Phone:	800-736-3402	**Fee on div. inv.:**	9¢/sh.
Transfer Agent:	FirstEnergy Corp. Investor Services	**Discount (cash):**	0
Agent's Address:	76 South Main Street	**Discount (div.):**	0
	Akron, OH 44308-1890	**Auto invest:**	Yes
Agent's Phone:	800-736-3402	**Auto invest fee:**	$0
Other than USA:	Yes	**Selling info:**	Sells biweekly, by phone, mail, or
			fax, at avg. price, for 9¢/sh.

Company:	**FIRSTFED Bancorp, Inc.**	Safekeeping:	Yes
Symbol:	FFDB	Invests:	Every 30 days beginning 1/10
Exchange:	OTC	Minimum:	$50
Industry:	Banking	Maximum:	$2,000/month
Company Address:	1630 Fourth Ave. North	Min to qualify:	1
	Bessemer, AL 35020	Fee on cash inv.:	0
Company Phone:	205-428-8472	Fee on div. inv.:	0
Transfer Agent:	Reliance Trust Company	Discount (cash):	0
Agent's Address:	P.O. Box 48449	Discount (div.):	5%
	Atlanta, GA 30362-1409	Auto invest:	Yes
Agent's Phone:	800-241-5568	Auto invest fee:	$0
Other than USA:	Yes	Selling info:	Sells monthly, by mail, at market, for comm.

Company:	**FirstMerit Corp.**	Safekeeping:	Yes
Symbol:	FMER	Invests:	Every 90 days beginning 3/12
Exchange:	OTC	Minimum:	$25
Industry:	Banking	Maximum:	$5,000/quarter
Company Address:	111 Cascade Plaza	Min to qualify:	1
	Akron, OH 44308-1103	Fee on cash inv.:	0
Company Phone:	888-384-6388 or 330-996-6300	Fee on div. inv.:	0
Transfer Agent:	FirstMerit Bank, N.A.-Div.	Discount (cash):	0
	Reinvestment	Discount (div.):	0
Agent's Address:	121 S. Main Street, Suite 200	Auto invest:	No
	Akron, OH 44308-1440	Auto invest fee:	$0
Agent's Phone:	800-261-0406	Selling info:	Sells daily, by phone, at market,
Other than USA:	Yes		for $2.50 + comm.

Company:	**Flamel Technologies**	Safekeeping:	Yes
Symbol:	FLMLY	Invests:	Every 7 days beginning varies
Exchange:	OTC	Minimum:	$50
Industry:	Health care	Maximum:	$250,000/week
Company Address:	c/o Bank of NY, 101 Barclay St.,	Min to qualify:	1
	22 West	Fee on cash inv.:	$5 + 10¢/sh.
	New York, NY 10286	Fee on div. inv.:	0
Company Phone:	800-943-9715	Discount (cash):	0
Transfer Agent:	Bank of New York	Discount (div.):	0
Agent's Address:	P.O. Box 11258	Auto invest:	Yes
	New York, NY 10286	Auto invest fee:	$0
Agent's Phone:	888-269-2377	Selling info:	Sells weekly, by phone or mail, at
Other than USA:	Yes		avg. price, for $5 +10¢/ADS

Company:	**Fleet Financial Group**	Safekeeping:	No
Symbol:	FLT	Invests:	Every 30 days beginning 1/1
Exchange:	NYSE	Minimum:	$10
Industry:	Banking	Maximum:	$10,000/quarter
Company Address:	One Federal St.	Min to qualify:	1
	Boston, MA 02110-2010	Fee on cash inv.:	0!
Company Phone:	800-944-0786 or 617-346-0142	Fee on div. inv.:	0!
Transfer Agent:	FCT (EquiServe)	Discount (cash):	0
Agent's Address:	P.O. Box 2500	Discount (div.):	0
	Jersey City, NJ 07303-2500	Auto invest:	No
Agent's Phone:	800-317-4445	Auto invest fee:	$0
Other than USA:	No	Selling info:	Not available

Company:	**Fleming Companies, Inc.**
Symbol:	FLM
Exchange:	NYSE
Industry:	Food marketing, distribution
Company Address:	Box 26647
	Oklahoma City, OK 73126-0647
Company Phone:	405-840-7200 or 405-841-8121
Transfer Agent:	Bank One Trust Co., N.A.
Agent's Address:	P.O. Box 25848
	Oklahoma City, OK 73125-0848
Agent's Phone:	800-395-2662
Other than USA:	Yes

Safekeeping:	Yes
Invests:	Every 30 days beginning 1/10
Minimum:	$25
Maximum:	$5,000/quarter
Min to qualify:	1
Fee on cash inv.:	0!
Fee on div. inv.:	0!
Discount (cash):	0
Discount (div.):	5%
Auto invest:	No
Auto invest fee:	$0
Selling info:	Sells within 10 bus. days, by mail or fax, at market, for 10¢/sh.

Company:	**Florida Progress Corp.**
Symbol:	FPC
Exchange:	NYSE
Industry:	Utility-electric
Company Address:	Box 33028
	St. Petersburg, FL 33733-9765
Company Phone:	800-937-2640 or 727-820-5738
Transfer Agent:	Boston Eq. (EquiServe)
Agent's Address:	P.O. Box 8040-Mail Stop 45-02-64
	Boston, MA 02266-8040
Agent's Phone:	800-352-1121
Other than USA:	Yes

Safekeeping:	Yes
Invests:	Every 30 days beginning 1/20
Minimum:	$10
Maximum:	$100,000/year
Min to qualify:	1
Fee on cash inv.:	0
Fee on div. inv.:	0
Discount (cash):	0
Discount (div.):	0
Auto invest:	No
Auto invest fee:	$0
Selling info:	Sells twice weekly, by mail or phone, at market, for 8¢/sh.

Company:	**Florida Public Utilities Co.**
Symbol:	FPU
Exchange:	ASE
Industry:	Utility-electric, gas
Company Address:	Box 3395
	West Palm Beach, FL 33402-3395
Company Phone:	561-832-2461 or 561-838-1729
Transfer Agent:	Bank of New York
Agent's Address:	Church St. Station, P.O. Box 11258
	New York, NY 10286-1258
Agent's Phone:	800-524-4458
Other than USA:	Yes

Safekeeping:	No
Invests:	Every 90 days beginning 1/1
Minimum:	$25
Maximum:	$2,000/quarter
Min to qualify:	1
Fee on cash inv.:	0!
Fee on div. inv.:	0!
Discount (cash):	0
Discount (div.):	0
Auto invest:	No
Auto invest fee:	$0
Selling info:	Sells irregularly, by mail, at market, for $2.50

Company:	**Flowers Industries, Inc.**
Symbol:	FLO
Exchange:	NYSE
Industry:	Baked goods
Company Address:	1919 Flowers Circle
	Thomasville, GA 31757
Company Phone:	912-226-9110
Transfer Agent:	First Union National Bank
Agent's Address:	1525 West W.T. Harris Blvd., 3C#
	Charlotte, NC 28288-1153
Agent's Phone:	800-829-8432
Other than USA:	No

Safekeeping:	Yes
Invests:	Every 30 days beginning 1/20
Minimum:	$25
Maximum:	$3,000/month
Min to qualify:	1
Fee on cash inv.:	0
Fee on div. inv.:	0
Discount (cash):	0
Discount (div.):	0
Auto invest:	No
Auto invest fee:	$0
Selling info:	Sells daily, by mail, at market, for 9¢/sh.

Company:	**Flowserve Corp.**	Safekeeping:	Yes
Symbol:	FLS	Invests:	Every 90 days beginning 3/1
Exchange:	OTC	Minimum:	$25
Industry:	Corrosion resist. equip	Maximum:	$1,000/quarter
Company Address:	222 West Las Colinas Blvd.,	Min to qualify:	1
	Ste.1500	Fee on cash inv.:	0
	Irving, TX 75039	Fee on div. inv.:	0
Company Phone:	972-443-6500	Discount (cash):	0
Transfer Agent:	National City Bank	Discount (div.):	0
Agent's Address:	P.O. Box 92301	Auto invest:	No
	Cleveland, Ohio 44101	Auto invest fee:	$0
Agent's Phone:	800-622-6757	Selling info:	Sells weekly, by mail or fax, at
Other than USA:	Yes		market, for $3.00

Company:	**Fluor Corp.**	Safekeeping:	Yes
Symbol:	FLR	Invests:	Every 30 days beginning 1/15
Exchange:	NYSE	Minimum:	$100
Industry:	Energy & construction	Maximum:	$10,000/quarter
Company Address:	3353 Michelson Dr.	Min to qualify:	50
	Irvine, CA 92698	Fee on cash inv.:	$1.50 + 7¢/sh.
Company Phone:	949-975-6961 or 949-975-2000	Fee on div. inv.:	0!
Transfer Agent:	ChaseMellon Shareholder Services	Discount (cash):	0
Agent's Address:	85 Challenger Road	Discount (div.):	0
	Ridgefield Park, NJ 07660	Auto invest:	No
Agent's Phone:	800-813-2847	Auto invest fee:	$0
Other than USA:	Yes	Selling info:	Sells weekly, by mail or phone, at
			market, for $15 +7¢/sh.

Company:	**FNB Corp.**	Safekeeping:	Yes
Symbol:	FBAN	Invests:	Every 30 days beginning 1/15
Exchange:	OTC	Minimum:	$100
Industry:	Banking	Maximum:	$10,000/quarter
Company Address:	One FNB Blvd.	Min to qualify:	1
	Hermitage, PA 16148	Fee on cash inv.:	0!
Company Phone:	800-490-3951 or 412-981-6000	Fee on div. inv.:	0!
Transfer Agent:	FNB Shareholder Services	Discount (cash):	0
Agent's Address:	P.O. Box 11929	Discount (div.):	0
	Naples, FL 34101	Auto invest:	No
Agent's Phone:	888-441-4362	Auto invest fee:	$0
Other than USA:	Yes	Selling info:	Sells bimonthly, by mail,
			at market, for comm.

Company:	**FNB Financial Services Corp.**	Safekeeping:	Yes
		Invests:	Every 90 days beginning 3/31
Symbol:	FNBF	Minimum:	$25
Exchange:	OTC	Maximum:	$1,000/quarter
Industry:	Banking	Min to qualify:	1
Company Address:	202 East Main St.	Fee on cash inv.:	0
	Reidsville, NC 27320	Fee on div. inv.:	0
Company Phone:	336-342-3346	Discount (cash):	0
Transfer Agent:	SunTrust Bank, Atlanta	Discount (div.):	0
Agent's Address:	P.O. Box 4625	Auto invest:	No
	Atlanta, GA 30302	Auto invest fee:	$0
Agent's Phone:	800-568-3476	Selling info:	Sells within 10 bus. days, by mail,
Other than USA:	Yes		at market, for 6¢ to 12¢/sh.

Company:	**Food Lion Inc. B**	**Safekeeping:**	Yes
Symbol:	FDLNB	**Invests:**	Every 7 days beginning varies
Exchange:	OTC	**Minimum:**	$50
Industry:	Grocery	**Maximum:**	$150,000/year
Company Address:	2110 Executive Dr., Box 1330	**Min to qualify:**	1
	Salisbury, NC 28145-1330	**Fee on cash inv.:**	$5 + 3¢/sh.
Company Phone:	704-633-8250 ex.2285	**Fee on div. inv.:**	0!
Transfer Agent:	FCT (EquiServe)	**Discount (cash):**	0
Agent's Address:	P.O. Box 2500	**Discount (div.):**	0
	Jersey City, NJ 07303-2500	**Auto invest:**	Yes
Agent's Phone:	888-236-5466	**Auto invest fee:**	$2 + 3¢/sh.
Other than USA:	Yes	**Selling info:**	Sells weekly, by mail or phone, at avg. price, for $15 +12¢/sh.

Company:	**Food Lion Inc. A**	**Safekeeping:**	Yes
Symbol:	FDLNA	**Invests:**	Every 7 days beginning varies
Exchange:	OTC	**Minimum:**	$50
Industry:	Grocery	**Maximum:**	$150,000/year
Company Address:	2110 Executive Dr.,Box 1330	**Min to qualify:**	1
	Salisbury, NC 28145-1330	**Fee on cash inv.:**	$5 + 3¢/sh.
Company Phone:	704-633-8250 ex.2285	**Fee on div. inv.:**	0!
Transfer Agent:	FCT (EquiServe)	**Discount (cash):**	0
Agent's Address:	P.O. Box 2500	**Discount (div.):**	0
	Jersey City, NJ 07303-2500	**Auto invest:**	Yes
Agent's Phone:	888-236-5466	**Auto invest fee:**	$2 + 3¢/sh.
Other than USA:	Yes	**Selling info:**	Sells weekly, by mail or phone, at avg. price, for $15 +12¢/sh.

Company:	**Foothill Independent Bancorp**	**Safekeeping:**	Yes
		Invests:	Every 30 days beginning 1/27
Symbol:	FOOT	**Minimum:**	$100
Exchange:	OTC	**Maximum:**	$10,000/quarter
Industry:	Banking	**Min to qualify:**	1
Company Address:	510 South Grand Ave.	**Fee on cash inv.:**	0
	Glendora, CA 91741	**Fee on div. inv.:**	0
Company Phone:	626-963-8551	**Discount (cash):**	0
Transfer Agent:	ChaseMellon Shareholder Services	**Discount (div.):**	0
Agent's Address:	400 S. Hope St., 4th Floor	**Auto invest:**	No
	Los Angeles, CA 90071	**Auto invest fee:**	$0
Agent's Phone:	800-356-2017	**Selling info:**	Sells weekly, by mail or phone, at market, for $15
Other than USA:	No		

Company:	**Ford Motor Co.**	**Safekeeping:**	Yes
Symbol:	F	**Invests:**	Every 7 days beginning varies
Exchange:	NYSE	**Minimum:**	$50
Industry:	Automotive	**Maximum:**	$250,000/year
Company Address:	The American Rd., Box 1899	**Min to qualify:**	1
	Dearborn, MI 48121-1899	**Fee on cash inv.:**	$5 + 3¢/sh.
Company Phone:	800-555-5259 or 313-322-3000	**Fee on div. inv.:**	5% to $5 + 3¢/sh.
Transfer Agent:	FCT (EquiServe)	**Discount (cash):**	0
Agent's Address:	P.O. Box 2566	**Discount (div.):**	0
	Jersey City, NJ 07303-2566	**Auto invest:**	Yes
Agent's Phone:	800-279-1237	**Auto invest fee:**	$1 + 3¢/sh.
Other than USA:	Yes	**Selling info:**	Sells daily, by mail, at avg. price, for $15 +12¢/sh.

Company:	**Formula Co.**	Safekeeping:	Yes
Symbol:	FORM	Invests:	Every 30 days beginning 1/1
Exchange:	NYSE	Minimum:	$100
Industry:	Beverages	Maximum:	$125,000/year
Company Address:	One Coca-Cola Plz.	Min to qualify:	1
	Atlanta, GA 30313	Fee on cash inv.:	0!
Company Phone:	404-676-2121	Fee on div. inv.:	0!
Transfer Agent:	Bank of New York	Discount (cash):	0
Agent's Address:	P.O. Box 11258	Discount (div.):	0
	New York, NY 10286	Auto invest:	Yes
Agent's Phone:	888-269-2377	Auto invest fee:	$1
Other than USA:	Yes	Selling info:	Sells daily, by phone, mail, or fax, at market, for $10 +12¢/sh.

Company:	**Formula Systems Ltd.**	Safekeeping:	Yes
Symbol:	FORTY	Invests:	Every 7 days beginning varies
Exchange:	NYSE	Minimum:	$50
Industry:	Software & programming	Maximum:	$250,000/year
Company Address:	c/o BNY,101 Barclay St.,22 West	Min to qualify:	1
	New York, NY 10286	Fee on cash inv.:	$5 + 10¢/sh.
Company Phone:	800-943-9715	Fee on div. inv.:	0
Transfer Agent:	Bank of New York	Discount (cash):	0
Agent's Address:	P.O. Box 11258	Discount (div.):	0
	New York, NY 10286	Auto invest:	Yes
Agent's Phone:	888-269-2377	Auto invest fee:	$5 + 10¢/sh.
Other than USA:	Yes	Selling info:	Sells weekly, by mail, at market, for $5 +10¢/sh.

Company:	**Fort James Corp.**	Safekeeping:	Yes
Symbol:	FJ	Invests:	Every 30 days beginning 1/31
Exchange:	NYSE	Minimum:	$100
Industry:	Consumer products, paper	Maximum:	$5,000/month
Company Address:	1650 Lake Cook Rd., Box 89	Min to qualify:	1
	Deerfield, IL, 60015	Fee on cash inv.:	0!
Company Phone:	847-317-5341 or 847-317-5000	Fee on div. inv.:	0!
Transfer Agent:	Norwest Bank Minnesota	Discount (cash):	0
Agent's Address:	P.O. Box 64854	Discount (div.):	0
	St. Paul, MN 55164-0854	Auto invest:	No
Agent's Phone:	800-468-9716	Auto invest fee:	$0
Other than USA:	Yes	Selling info:	Sells daily, by mail, at market, for comm.

Company:	**Fortune Brands**	Safekeeping:	Yes
Symbol:	FO	Invests:	Every 30 days beginning 1/1
Exchange:	NYSE	Minimum:	$50
Industry:	Consumer products, hardware,	Maximum:	$15,000/quarter
	and distilled beverages	Min to qualify:	1
Company Address:	1700 East Putnam Ave.	Fee on cash inv.:	0!
	Old Greenwich, CT 06870-3163	Fee on div. inv.:	0!
Company Phone:	800-225-2719 or 203-698-5462	Discount (cash):	0
Transfer Agent:	Fortune Brands	Discount (div.):	0
Agent's Address:	1700 East Putnam Ave., Box 815	Auto invest:	No
	Old Greenwich, CT 06870-0815	Auto invest fee:	$0
Agent's Phone:	800-225-2719	Selling info:	Sells Friday, by mail, at market, for 10¢/sh.
Other than USA:	Yes		

Company:	**Foster Wheeler**	Safekeeping:	No
Symbol:	FWC	Invests:	Every 30 days beginning 1/4
Exchange:	NYSE	Minimum:	$10
Industry:	Engineering, construction	Maximum:	$unlimited
Company Address:	Perryville Corp.Park, Inv. Relations	Min to qualify:	1
	Clinton, NJ 08809-4000	Fee on cash inv.:	0!
Company Phone:	908-730-4270 or 908-730-4000	Fee on div. inv.:	0!
Transfer Agent:	ChaseMellon Shareholder Services	Discount (cash):	0
Agent's Address:	P.O. Box 3339	Discount (div.):	0
	South Hackensack, NJ 07606-1939	Auto invest:	No
Agent's Phone:	800-851-9677	Auto invest fee:	$0
Other than USA:	Yes	Selling info:	Sells daily, by mail or phone, at market, for $3.50 + comm.

Company:	**FPL Group, Inc.**	Safekeeping:	Yes
Symbol:	FPL	Invests:	Every 90 days beginning 3/15
Exchange:	NYSE	Minimum:	$100
Industry:	Utility-electric	Maximum:	$100,000/year
Company Address:	700 Universe Blvd., Box 14000	Min to qualify:	1
	Juno Beach, FL 33408-0420	Fee on cash inv.:	0!
Company Phone:	800-222-4511 or 561-694-4693	Fee on div. inv.:	0!
Transfer Agent:	Boston Eq. (EquiServe)	Discount (cash):	0
Agent's Address:	P.O. Box 8040	Discount (div.):	0
	Boston, MA 02266-8040	Auto invest:	No
Agent's Phone:	888-218-4392	Auto invest fee:	$0
Other than USA:	Yes	Selling info:	Sells weekly, by mail or phone, at market, for 15¢/sh.

Company:	**Franklin Resources**	Safekeeping:	Yes
Symbol:	BEN	Invests:	Every 30 days beginning 1/15
Exchange:	NYSE	Minimum:	$100
Industry:	Financial	Maximum:	$50,000/month
Company Address:	777 Mariners Island Blvd.	Min to qualify:	1
	San Mateo, CA 94404	Fee on cash inv.:	0!
Company Phone:	650-525-7584	Fee on div. inv.:	0!
Transfer Agent:	Bank of New York	Discount (cash):	0
Agent's Address:	P.O. Box 11002, Church St. Station	Discount (div.):	0
	New York, NY 10277-0702	Auto invest:	No
Agent's Phone:	800-524-4458	Auto invest fee:	$0
Other than USA:	Yes	Selling info:	Sells weekly, by mail or fax, at market, for $3 + comm.

Company:	**Fresenius Medical AG**	Safekeeping:	Yes
Symbol:	FMS	Invests:	Every 7 days beginning varies
Exchange:	NYSE	Minimum:	$50
Industry:	Pharmaceutical mfr. & dist.	Maximum:	$100,000/year
Company Address:	c/o Morgan Guaranty Trust,	Min to qualify:	1
	Box 9073	Fee on cash inv.:	$5 + 12¢/sh.
	Boston, MA 02205-9948	Fee on div. inv.:	5% to $2.50
Company Phone:	800-428-4237	Discount (cash):	0
Transfer Agent:	Morgan Guaranty Trust Co.	Discount (div.):	0
Agent's Address:	P.O. Box 9073	Auto invest:	Yes
	Boston, MA 02205-9948	Auto invest fee:	$5
Agent's Phone:	800-428-4237	Selling info:	Sells daily, by phone or mail, at avg. price, for $5 +12¢/sh.
Other than USA:	No		

Company:	**Frontier Corp.**	**Safekeeping:**	Yes
Symbol:	FRO	**Invests:**	Every 30 days beginning 1/1
Exchange:	NYSE	**Minimum:**	$25
Industry:	Telecommunications	**Maximum:**	$50,000/month
Company Address:	180 South Clinton Ave.	**Min to qualify:**	1
	Rochester, NY 14646-0700	**Fee on cash inv.:**	0!
Company Phone:	800-836-0342 or 716-777-6179	**Fee on div. inv.:**	0!
Transfer Agent:	Boston Eq. (EquiServe)	**Discount (cash):**	0
Agent's Address:	P.O. Box 8040	**Discount (div.):**	0
	Boston, MA 02266-8040	**Auto invest:**	No
Agent's Phone:	800-836-7370	**Auto invest fee:**	$0
Other than USA:	Yes	**Selling info:**	Sells daily, by mail, at market, for $5 +15¢/sh.

Company:	**Frontier Insurance Group, Inc.**	**Safekeeping:**	Yes
		Invests:	Every 7 days beginning varies
Symbol:	FTR	**Minimum:**	$50
Exchange:	NYSE	**Maximum:**	$10,000/investment
Industry:	Property and casualty insurance	**Min to qualify:**	1
Company Address:	195 Lake Louise Marie Rd.	**Fee on cash inv.:**	$7.50 + 10¢/sh.
	Rock Hill, NY 12775	**Fee on div. inv.:**	0
Company Phone:	800-836-2100 or 914-796-2100	**Discount (cash):**	0
Transfer Agent:	American Stock Transfer	**Discount (div.):**	0
Agent's Address:	40 Wall Street	**Auto invest:**	Yes
	New York, NY 10005	**Auto invest fee:**	$7.50 + $10¢/sh.
Agent's Phone:	800-278-4353	**Selling info:**	Sells weekly, by mail, at market, for $7.50 +10¢/sh.
Other than USA:	Yes		

Company:	**Fuller (H.B.)**	**Safekeeping:**	Yes
Symbol:	FULL	**Invests:**	Every 30 days beginning 1/10
Exchange:	OTC	**Minimum:**	$25
Industry:	Chemicals	**Maximum:**	$6,000/month
Company Address:	Box 64683	**Min to qualify:**	1
	St. Paul, MN 55164-0683	**Fee on cash inv.:**	0!
Company Phone:	800-214-2523 or 651-236-5900	**Fee on div. inv.:**	0!
Transfer Agent:	Norwest Bank Minnesota	**Discount (cash):**	0
Agent's Address:	P.O. Box 64854	**Discount (div.):**	3%
	St. Paul, MN 55164-0854	**Auto invest:**	Yes
Agent's Phone:	800-468-9716	**Auto invest fee:**	$0
Other than USA:	Yes	**Selling info:**	Sells daily, by mail, at market, for $3 +15¢/sh.

Company:	**Fulton Bank**	**Safekeeping:**	Yes
Symbol:	FULT	**Invests:**	Every 30 days beginning 1/15
Exchange:	OTC	**Minimum:**	$25
Industry:	Banking	**Maximum:**	$5,000/month
Company Address:	One Penn Sq., Box 4887	**Min to qualify:**	1
	Lancaster, PA 17604-4887	**Fee on cash inv.:**	0!
Company Phone:	717-291-2411	**Fee on div. inv.:**	0!
Transfer Agent:	Fulton Bank	**Discount (cash):**	0
Agent's Address:	P.O. Box 3215	**Discount (div.):**	0
	Lancaster, PA 17604	**Auto invest:**	No
Agent's Phone:	800-626-0255	**Auto invest fee:**	$0
Other than USA:	Yes	**Selling info:**	Sells within 15 days, by mail, at market, for $35

Company:	**Gabelli Convertible Securities Fund**	Safekeeping:	Yes
		Invests:	Every 30 days beginning 1/15
Symbol:	GCV	Minimum:	$250
Exchange:	NYSE	Maximum:	$10,000/month
Industry:	Closed-end fund	Min to qualify:	1
Company Address:	One Corporate Ctr.	Fee on cash inv.:	75¢ + comm.
	Rye, NY 10580	Fee on div. inv.:	0
Company Phone:	914-921-5246	Discount (cash):	0
Transfer Agent:	State Street Bank (EquiServe)	Discount (div.):	5%
Agent's Address:	P.O. Box 8200	Auto invest:	No
	Boston, MA 02266-8200	Auto invest fee:	$0
Agent's Phone:	800-336-6983	Selling info:	Sells daily, by mail or phone, at
Other than USA:	Yes		avg. price, for $2.50 +10¢/sh.

Company:	**Gabelli Equity Trust**	Safekeeping:	Yes
Symbol:	GAB	Invests:	Every 30 days beginning 1/15
Exchange:	NYSE	Minimum:	$250
Industry:	Closed-end fund	Maximum:	$10,000/month
Company Address:	One Corporate Ctr.	Min to qualify:	1
	Rye, NY 10580-1434	Fee on cash inv.:	75¢ + comm.
		Fee on div. inv.:	0
Company Phone:	914-921-5070	Discount (cash):	0
Transfer Agent:	State Street Bank (EquiServe)	Discount (div.):	5%
Agent's Address:	P.O. Box 8200	Auto invest:	No
	Boston, MA 02266-8200	Auto invest fee:	$0
Agent's Phone:	800-336-6983	Selling info:	Sells daily, by phone or mail, at
Other than USA:	Yes		market, for 75¢ +10¢/sh.

Company:	**Gabelli Global Multimedia Trust**	Safekeeping:	Yes
		Invests:	Every 30 days beginning 1/15
Symbol:	GGT	Minimum:	$250
Exchange:	NYSE	Maximum:	$10,000/month
Industry:	Closed-end fund	Min to qualify:	1
Company Address:	One Corporate Ctr.	Fee on cash inv.:	75¢ + comm.
	Rye, NY 10580	Fee on div. inv.:	0
Company Phone:	914-921-5246	Discount (cash):	0
Transfer Agent:	State Street Bank (EquiServe)	Discount (div.):	5%
Agent's Address:	P.O. Box 8200	Auto invest:	No
	Boston, MA 02266-8200	Auto invest fee:	$0
Agent's Phone:	800-336-6983	Selling info:	Sells daily, by mail or phone, at
Other than USA:	Yes		avg. price, for $2.50 +10¢/sh.

Company:	**Gallaher Group Plc**	Safekeeping:	Yes
Symbol:	GLH	Invests:	Every 7 days beginning varies
Exchange:	NYSE	Minimum:	$50
Industry:	Largest manufacturer of tobacco products for UK	Maximum:	$250,000/year
		Min to qualify:	1
Company Address:	c/o BNY,101 Barclay St.,22 West	Fee on cash inv.:	$5 + 10¢/sh.
	New York, NY 10286	Fee on div. inv.:	5% to $5 + 10¢/sh.
Company Phone:	800-943-9715	Discount (cash):	0
Transfer Agent:	Bank of New York	Discount (div.):	0
Agent's Address:	P.O. Box 11258	Auto invest:	Yes
	New York, NY 10286	Auto invest fee:	$0
Agent's Phone:	888-269-2377	Selling info:	Sells weekly, by phone or mail, at
Other than USA:	No		avg. price, for $5 +10¢/sh.

Company:	**Gannett Co., Inc.**	Safekeeping:	Yes
Symbol:	GCI	Invests:	Every 30 days beginning 1/1
Exchange:	NYSE	Minimum:	$10
Industry:	Publishing, broadcasting	Maximum:	$5,000/month
Company Address:	1100 Wilson Blvd.	Min to qualify:	1
	Arlington, VA 22234	Fee on cash inv.:	0!
Company Phone:	800-778-3299 or 703-284-6922	Fee on div. inv.:	0!
Transfer Agent:	Norwest Bank Minnesota	Discount (cash):	0
Agent's Address:	P.O. Box 64854	Discount (div.):	0
	St. Paul, MN 55164-0854	Auto invest:	Yes
Agent's Phone:	800-778-3299	Auto invest fee:	$0
Other than USA:	Yes	Selling info:	Sells daily, by mail or fax, at market, for $5 +15¢/sh.

Company:	**Gardner Denver Inc.**	Safekeeping:	Yes
Symbol:	GDI	Invests:	Every 7 days beginning varies
Exchange:	NYSE	Minimum:	$25
Industry:	Capital goods	Maximum:	$150,000/year
Company Address:	1800 Gardner Exp.	Min to qualify:	1
	Quincy, IL 62301	Fee on cash inv.:	$5 + 12¢/sh.
Company Phone:	800-682-9868 or 217-222-5400	Fee on div. inv.:	0
Transfer Agent:	FCT (EquiServe)	Discount (cash):	0
Agent's Address:	P.O. Box 2598	Discount (div.):	0
	Jersey City, NJ 07303-2598	Auto invest:	Yes
Agent's Phone:	800-317-4445	Auto invest fee:	$5 to $20 +12¢/sh.
Other than USA:	Yes	Selling info:	Sells daily, by mail or phone, at avg. price, for $10 +12¢/sh.

Company:	**GATX Corp.**	Safekeeping:	Yes
Symbol:	GMT	Invests:	Every 30 days beginning 1/30
Exchange:	NYSE	Minimum:	$25
Industry:	Railcar leasing equip. financing	Maximum:	$36,000/year
Company Address:	500 West Monroe St.	Min to qualify:	1
	Chicago, IL 60661-3676	Fee on cash inv.:	0!
Company Phone:	312-621-6200 or	Fee on div. inv.:	0!
312-621-6603		Discount (cash):	0
Transfer Agent:	ChaseMellon Shareholder Services	Discount (div.):	0
Agent's Address:	P.O. Box 590	Auto invest:	No
	Ridgefield Park, NJ 07660-0590	Auto invest fee:	$0
Agent's Phone:	800-851-9677	Selling info:	Sells weekly, by mail or phone, at
Other than USA:	Yes		avg. price, for $0!

Company:	**GB&T Bancshares, Inc.**	Safekeeping:	Yes
Symbol:	GBTB	Invests:	Every 90 days beginning 1/30
Exchange:	OTC	Minimum:	$25
Industry:	Banking	Maximum:	$2,500/quarter
Company Address:	500 Jesse Jewell Pkwy., Box 2760	Min to qualify:	1
	Gainesville, GA 30503	Fee on cash inv.:	0
Company Phone:	770-532-1212	Fee on div. inv.:	0
Transfer Agent:	Reliance Trust Company, Attn:	Discount (cash):	0
	GB&T DRP Plan	Discount (div.):	0
Agent's Address:	P.O. Box 48449	Auto invest:	No
	Atlanta, GA 30340-4099	Auto invest fee:	$0
Agent's Phone:	404-266-0663	Selling info:	Not available
Other than USA:	Yes		

Company:	**GenCorp Inc.**
Symbol:	GY
Exchange:	NYSE
Industry:	Aerospace, auto, & polymer products
Company Address:	175 Ghent Rd.
	Fairlawn, OH 44333-3300
Company Phone:	800-689-0851 or 330-869-4411
Transfer Agent:	Bank of New York
Agent's Address:	P.O. Box 1958
	Newark, NJ 07101-9774
Agent's Phone:	800-524-4458
Other than USA:	Yes

Safekeeping:	Yes
Invests:	Every 7 days beginning varies
Minimum:	$50
Maximum:	$10,000/month
Min to qualify:	1
Fee on cash inv.:	0!
Fee on div. inv.:	0!
Discount (cash):	0
Discount (div.):	0
Auto invest:	Yes
Auto invest fee:	$0
Selling info:	Sells weekly, by mail, at market, for $5 +10¢/sh.

Company:	**General Cable**
Symbol:	GCABY
Exchange:	OTC
Industry:	Communications services
Company Address:	c/o BNY,101 Barclay St.,22 West
	New York, NY 10286
Company Phone:	800-943-9715
Transfer Agent:	Bank of New York
Agent's Address:	P.O. Box 11258
	New York, NY 10286
Agent's Phone:	888-269-2377
Other than USA:	Yes

Safekeeping:	Yes
Invests:	Every 7 days beginning varies
Minimum:	$50
Maximum:	$250,000/year
Min to qualify:	1
Fee on cash inv.:	$5 + 10¢/sh.
Fee on div. inv.:	0
Discount (cash):	0
Discount (div.):	0
Auto invest:	Yes
Auto invest fee:	$5 + 10¢/sh.
Selling info:	Sells weekly, by mail, at market, for $5 +10¢/sh.

Company:	**General Electric**
Symbol:	GE
Exchange:	NYSE
Industry:	Elec. equip., broadcasting, fin'l serv. & mfg.
Company Address:	3135 Easton Turnpike
	Fairfield, CT 06431
Company Phone:	203-373-2211 or 800-786-2543
Transfer Agent:	Bank of New York
Agent's Address:	P.O. Box 11402
	New York, NY 10286-1402
Agent's Phone:	800-786-2543
Other than USA:	Yes

Safekeeping:	Yes
Invests:	Every 7 days beginning Wed.
Minimum:	$10
Maximum:	$10,000/week
Min to qualify:	1
Fee on cash inv.:	$3
Fee on div. inv.:	0!
Discount (cash):	0
Discount (div.):	0
Auto invest:	Yes
Auto invest fee:	$1
Selling info:	Sells biweekly, by mail, at market price, for $10 +15¢/sh.

Company:	**General Growth Properties**
Symbol:	GGP
Exchange:	NYSE
Industry:	REIT
Company Address:	110 N. Wacker Dr.
	Chicago, IL 60606
Company Phone:	312-960-5000 or 312-960-5081
Transfer Agent:	Norwest Bank Minnesota
Agent's Address:	P.O. Box 64854
	St. Paul, MN 55164-0854
Agent's Phone:	888-291-3713
Other than USA:	Yes

Safekeeping:	Yes
Invests:	Every 7 days beginning varies
Minimum:	$50
Maximum:	$125,000/quarter
Min to qualify:	1
Fee on cash inv.:	$5 + 5¢/sh.
Fee on div. inv.:	4% to $2.50 + 5¢/sh.
Discount (cash):	0
Discount (div.):	0
Auto invest:	Yes
Auto invest fee:	$3 + 5¢/sh.
Selling info:	Sells daily, by mail or phone, at avg. price, for $10 +15¢/sh.

Company:	**General Housewares Corp.**	**Safekeeping:**	Yes
Symbol:	GHW	**Invests:**	Every 30 days beginning 1/30
Exchange:	NYSE	**Minimum:**	$10
Industry:	Consumer products	**Maximum:**	$1,000/month
Company Address:	1536 Beech St., Box 4066	**Min to qualify:**	1
	Terre Haute, IN 47804	**Fee on cash inv.:**	0!
Company Phone:	800-457-2665 or 812-232-1000	**Fee on div. inv.:**	0!
Transfer Agent:	FCT (EquiServe)	**Discount (cash):**	0
Agent's Address:	P.O. Box 3506, Church St. Station	**Discount (div.):**	0
	New York, NY 10008-3506	**Auto invest:**	No
Agent's Phone:	800-446-2617	**Auto invest fee:**	$0
Other than USA:	No	**Selling info:**	Sells daily, by mail or fax, at market, for $10 +12¢/sh.

Company:	**General Mills**	**Safekeeping:**	Yes
Symbol:	GIS	**Invests:**	Every 30 days beginning 1/1
Exchange:	NYSE	**Minimum:**	$10
Industry:	Foods	**Maximum:**	$3,000/quarter
Company Address:	1 General Mills Blvd., Box 1113	**Min to qualify:**	1
	Minneapolis, MN 55426	**Fee on cash inv.:**	0!
Company Phone:	800-245-5703 or 612-540-3888	**Fee on div. inv.:**	0!
Transfer Agent:	Norwest Bank Minnesota	**Discount (cash):**	0
Agent's Address:	P.O. Box 64854	**Discount (div.):**	0
	St. Paul, MN 55164-0854	**Auto invest:**	Yes
Agent's Phone:	800-670-4763	**Auto invest fee:**	$0
Other than USA:	Yes	**Selling info:**	Sells daily, by mail or fax, at market, for $5 + 5¢/sh.

Company:	**General Motors**	**Safekeeping:**	Yes
Symbol:	GM	**Invests:**	Every 30 days beginning 1/20 or nest business day
Exchange:	NYSE		
Industry:	Automotive	**Minimum:**	$25
Company Address:	767 5th Ave.,14th Fl.	**Maximum:**	$4,000/month
	New York, NY 10153-0013	**Min to qualify:**	1
Company Phone:	212-418-6270	**Fee on cash inv.:**	0!
Transfer Agent:	Boston Eq. (EquiServe)	**Fee on div. inv.:**	0!
Agent's Address:	P.O. Box 9255	**Discount (cash):**	0
	Boston, MA 02205-9255	**Discount (div.):**	0
Agent's Phone:	800-331-9922	**Auto invest:**	No
Other than USA:	Yes	**Auto invest fee:**	$0
		Selling info:	Sells daily, by mail, at market, for $5 +7¢/sh.

Company:	**Genuine Parts Co.**	**Safekeeping:**	Yes
Symbol:	GPC	**Invests:**	Every 30 days beginning 1/1
Exchange:	NYSE	**Minimum:**	$10
Industry:	Distr. & retails auto parts, electronics	**Maximum:**	$3,000/quarter
		Min to qualify:	1
Company Address:	2999 Circle 75 Pkwy.	**Fee on cash inv.:**	0
	Atlanta, GA 30339-3050	**Fee on div. inv.:**	0
Company Phone:	770-953-1700	**Discount (cash):**	0
Transfer Agent:	SunTrust Bank, Atlanta	**Discount (div.):**	0
Agent's Address:	P.O. Box 4625	**Auto invest:**	No
	Atlanta, GA 30302-4625	**Auto invest fee:**	$0
Agent's Phone:	800-568-3476	**Selling info:**	Sells biweekly, by mail, at avg. price, for 9¢/sh.
Other than USA:	No		

Company:	**Georgia-Pacific Grp.**	Safekeeping:	Yes
Symbol:	GP	Invests:	Every 30 days beginning 1/10
Exchange:	NYSE	Minimum:	$25
Industry:	Pulp, paper, and building products	Maximum:	$5,000/month
	manufacturing	Min to qualify:	1
Company Address:	133 Peachtree St. N.E., Box 105605	Fee on cash inv.:	5% to $3
	Atlanta, GA 30348	Fee on div. inv.:	5% to $3
Company Phone:	404-652-5555 or 404-652-4000	Discount (cash):	0
Transfer Agent:	FCT (EquiServe)	Discount (div.):	0
Agent's Address:	P.O. Box 2500	Auto invest:	Yes
	Jersey City, NJ 07303-2500	Auto invest fee:	5% to $3 + $2 comm.
Agent's Phone:	800-519-3111	Selling info:	Sells daily, by phone, mail, or fax,
Other than USA:	Yes		at avg. price, for $10 +12¢/sh.

Company:	**German American**	Safekeeping:	No
	Bancorp	Invests:	Every 90 days beginning 1/31
Symbol:	GABC	Minimum:	$100
Exchange:	OTC	Maximum:	$3,000/quarter
Industry:	Banking	Min to qualify:	1
Company Address:	Box 810	Fee on cash inv.:	0
	Jasper, IN 47547-0810	Fee on div. inv.:	0
Company Phone:	812-482-1314	Discount (cash):	0
Transfer Agent:	Fifth Third Bank	Discount (div.):	0
Agent's Address:	38 Fountain Sq. MD 1090 F5	Auto invest:	No
	Cincinnati, OH 45263	Auto invest fee:	$0
Agent's Phone:	513-579-4355	Selling info:	Sells weekly, by mail, at market,
Other than USA:	Yes		for comm.

Company:	**Germany Fund (The)**	Safekeeping:	Yes
Symbol:	GER	Invests:	Every 30 days beginning 1/15
Exchange:	NYSE	Minimum:	$100
Industry:	Closed-end fund	Maximum:	$36,000/year
Company Address:	c/o Deutsche Bk., 31 West 52nd St.	Min to qualify:	1
	New York, NY 10019	Fee on cash inv.:	comm.
Company Phone:	800-334-1898 or 212-469-7052	Fee on div. inv.:	0!
Transfer Agent:	Investors Bank & Trust Co.-	Discount (cash):	
	Shareholder Svcs.	Discount (div.):	
Agent's Address:	P.O. Box 1537	Auto invest:	No
	Boston, MA 02205-1537	Auto invest fee:	$0
Agent's Phone:	800-356-2754	Selling info:	Not available
Other than USA:	Yes		

Company:	**Gillette**	Safekeeping:	Yes
Symbol:	G	Invests:	Every 7 days beginning varies
Exchange:	NYSE	Minimum:	$100
Industry:	Consumer products	Maximum:	$120,000/year
Company Address:	Prudential Twr. Bldg.	Min to qualify:	10
	Boston, MA 02199	Fee on cash inv.:	$5 + 8¢/sh.
Company Phone:	617-421-8499 or 617-421-7761	Fee on div. inv.:	0 to $1.25 + 8¢/sh.
Transfer Agent:	BankBoston (EquiServe)	Discount (cash):	0
Agent's Address:	P.O. Box 8040	Discount (div.):	0
	Boston, MA 02266-8040	Auto invest:	Yes
Agent's Phone:	888-218-2841	Auto invest fee:	$2.50 + 8¢/sh.
Other than USA:	Yes	Selling info:	Sells daily, by phone, mail, or fax,
			at avg. price, for $10 +15¢/sh.

Company:	**Glacier Bancorp, Inc.**	**Safekeeping:**	Yes
Symbol:	GBCI	**Invests:**	Every 90 days beginning 1/22
Exchange:	OTC	**Minimum:**	$100
Industry:	Commercial bank holding co.	**Maximum:**	$2,000/quarter
Company Address:	49 Commons Loop	**Min to qualify:**	1
	Kalispell, MT 59901	**Fee on cash inv.:**	0!
Company Phone:	406-756-4200	**Fee on div. inv.:**	0!
Transfer Agent:	Davidson Trust	**Discount (cash):**	0
Agent's Address:	P.O Box 2309	**Discount (div.):**	0
	Great Falls, MT 59401	**Auto invest:**	No
Agent's Phone:	800-634-5526	**Auto invest fee:**	$0
Other than USA:	Yes	**Selling info:**	Sells irregularly, by mail, at market, for $3.50 + comm.

Company:	**Glaxo Wellcome plc ADR**	**Safekeeping:**	No
Symbol:	GLX	**Invests:**	Every 30 days beginning 1/1
Exchange:	NYSE	**Minimum:**	$25
Industry:	Ethical pharmaceuticals	**Maximum:**	$50,000/month
Company Address:	499 Park Ave.	**Min to qualify:**	1
	New York, NY 10022	**Fee on cash inv.:**	5% to $2.50
Company Phone:	888-308-5112	**Fee on div. inv.:**	0!
Transfer Agent:	Bank of New York	**Discount (cash):**	0
Agent's Address:	P.O. Box 11258	**Discount (div.):**	0
	New York, NY 10286	**Auto invest:**	No
Agent's Phone:	888-269-2377	**Auto invest fee:**	$0
Other than USA:	Yes	**Selling info:**	Sells irregularly, by mail, at market, for $5

Company:	**Gleason Corp.**	**Safekeeping:**	Yes
Symbol:	GLE	**Invests:**	Every 30 days beginning 1/25
Exchange:	NYSE	**Minimum:**	$50
Industry:	Machinery	**Maximum:**	$5,000/month
Company Address:	1000 University Ave., Box 22970	**Min to qualify:**	1
	Rochester, NY 14692-2970	**Fee on cash inv.:**	0
Company Phone:	716-473-1000	**Fee on div. inv.:**	0
Transfer Agent:	ChaseMellon Shareholder Services	**Discount (cash):**	0
Agent's Address:	P.O. Box 3338	**Discount (div.):**	0
	South Hackensack, NJ 07606-1938	**Auto invest:**	No
Agent's Phone:	888-816-7319	**Auto invest fee:**	$0
Other than USA:	Yes	**Selling info:**	Sells weekly, by mail, at market, for 10¢/sh.

Company:	**Glenborough Realty Trust**	**Safekeeping:**	Yes
Symbol:	GLB	**Invests:**	Every 7 days beginning varies
Exchange:	NYSE	**Minimum:**	$100
Industry:	Real estate operations	**Maximum:**	$10,000/transaction
Company Address:	400 South El Camino Real, Ste.1100	**Min to qualify:**	1
	San Mateo, CA 94402	**Fee on cash inv.:**	$5 + comm.
Company Phone:	650-343-9300	**Fee on div. inv.:**	comm.
Transfer Agent:	Registrar & Transfer Co.	**Discount (cash):**	0
Agent's Address:	10 Commerce Drive	**Discount (div.):**	0
	Cranford, NJ 07016	**Auto invest:**	Yes
Agent's Phone:	800-368-5968	**Auto invest fee:**	$0
Other than USA:	Yes	**Selling info:**	Sells daily, by mail, fax, or e-mail, at avg. price, for $7.50 + comm.

Company:	**Glimcher Realty Trust**	Safekeeping:	Yes
Symbol:	GRT	Invests:	Every 30 days beginning 1/15
Exchange:	NYSE	Minimum:	$100
Industry:	REIT	Maximum:	$3,000/quarter
Company Address:	20 South Third St.	Min to qualify:	1
	Columbus, OH 43215-3602	Fee on cash inv.:	0
Company Phone:	614-621-9000	Fee on div. inv.:	0
Transfer Agent:	Harris Trust & Savings	Discount (cash):	0%-3%
Agent's Address:	P.O. Box A3309	Discount (div.):	0
	Chicago, IL 60690	Auto invest:	No
Agent's Phone:	800-738-4931	Auto invest fee:	$0
Other than USA:	Yes	Selling info:	Sells weekly, by mail, at market, for $10 +10¢/sh.

Company:	**Golden Triangle Industries, Inc.**	Safekeeping:	Yes
		Invests:	Every 30 days beginning 1/29
Symbol:	GTII	Minimum:	$25
Exchange:	OTC	Maximum:	$5,000/month
Industry:	Energy services	Min to qualify:	1
Company Address:	Box 17029	Fee on cash inv.:	$2.50
	Sugar Land, TX 77496-7029	Fee on div. inv.:	0
Company Phone:	281-565-7300	Discount (cash):	2%
Transfer Agent:	Golden Triangle Industries, Inc.	Discount (div.):	0
Agent's Address:	104 Fossil Court	Auto invest:	No
	Springtown, TX 76082-6626	Auto invest fee:	$0
Agent's Phone:	800-940-4484	Selling info:	Not available
Other than USA:	Yes		

Company:	**Goodrich (B.F.) Co.**	Safekeeping:	Yes
Symbol:	GR	Invests:	Every 30 days beginning 1/30
Exchange:	NYSE	Minimum:	$25
Industry:	Chemicals & aerospace	Maximum:	$1,000/month
Company Address:	4020 Kinross Lakes Pkwy.	Min to qualify:	1
	Richfield, OH 44286-9368	Fee on cash inv.:	0!
Company Phone:	330-659-7600 or 330-659-7788	Fee on div. inv.:	0!
Transfer Agent:	Bank of New York	Discount (cash):	0
Agent's Address:	P.O. Box 11258, Church St.	Discount (div.):	0
	Station, 11E	Auto invest:	No
	New York, NY 10286-1258	Auto invest fee:	$0
Agent's Phone:	800-524-4458	Selling info:	Sells weekly, by mail, at market, for $2 + 3¢ to 5¢/sh.
Other than USA:	Yes		

Company:	**Goodyear Tire & Rubber**	Safekeeping:	Yes
Symbol:	GT	Invests:	Every 7 days beginning Friday
Exchange:	NYSE	Minimum:	$25
Industry:	Tire and rubber mfr.	Maximum:	$150,000/year
Company Address:	1144 East Market St.	Min to qualify:	1
	Akron, OH 44316-0001	Fee on cash inv.:	3¢/sh.
Company Phone:	330-796-2121	Fee on div. inv.:	$1 + 3¢/sh.
Transfer Agent:	FCT (EquiServe)	Discount (cash):	0
Agent's Address:	P.O. Box 2598	Discount (div.):	0
	Jersey City, NJ 07303-2598	Auto invest:	Yes
Agent's Phone:	800-317-4445	Auto invest fee:	$1 + comm.
Other than USA:	Yes	Selling info:	Sells daily, by mail, at avg. price, for $15 +15¢/sh.

Company:	**Gorman-Rupp Co.**	Safekeeping:	Yes
Symbol:	GRC	Invests:	Every 30 days beginning 1/10
Exchange:	ASE	Minimum:	$20
Industry:	Mfr. const. & ind'l pumps & parts	Maximum:	$1,000/month
Company Address:	305 Bowman St., Box 1217	Min to qualify:	1
	Mansfield, OH 44901-1217	Fee on cash inv.:	0
Company Phone:	419-755-1011 or 419-755-1294	Fee on div. inv.:	0
Transfer Agent:	National City Bank	Discount (cash):	0
Agent's Address:	P.O. Box 92301	Discount (div.):	0
	Cleveland, OH 44135-0900	Auto invest:	No
Agent's Phone:	800-622-6757	Auto invest fee:	$0
Other than USA:	Yes	Selling info:	Sells weekly, by mail or fax, at market, for comm.

Company:	**GPU, Inc.**	Safekeeping:	Yes
Symbol:	GPU	Invests:	Every 30 days beginning 1/29
Exchange:	NYSE	Minimum:	$50
Industry:	Utility-holding co.	Maximum:	$6,000/quarter
Company Address:	300 Madison Ave., Box 1911	Min to qualify:	1
	Morristown, NJ 07962-1911	Fee on cash inv.:	0
Company Phone:	973-455-8204 or 973-455-8200	Fee on div. inv.:	0
Transfer Agent:	ChaseMellon Shareholder Services	Discount (cash):	0
Agent's Address:	P.O. Box 3315	Discount (div.):	0
	South Hackensack, NJ 07606-1915	Auto invest:	No
Agent's Phone:	800-263-1310	Auto invest fee:	$0
Other than USA:	Yes	Selling info:	Sells weekly, by mail or phone, at market, for $15 + comm.

Company:	**Grace (W.R.)**	Safekeeping:	Yes
Symbol:	GRA	Invests:	Every 30 days beginning 1/10
Exchange:	NYSE	Minimum:	$100
Industry:	Chemicals	Maximum:	$100,000/year
Company Address:	1750 Clint Moore Rd.	Min to qualify:	50
	Boca Raton, FL 33487-2707	Fee on cash inv.:	0
Company Phone:	561-362-1331 or 561-362-2107	Fee on div. inv.:	0
Transfer Agent:	ChaseMellon Shareholder Services	Discount (cash):	0
Agent's Address:	P.O. Box 750	Discount (div.):	0
	Pittsburgh, PA 15230	Auto invest:	No
Agent's Phone:	800-648-8392	Auto invest fee:	$0
Other than USA:	Yes	Selling info:	Sells weekly, by mail, at market, for $5 +10¢/sh.

Company:	**Graco, Inc.**	Safekeeping:	Yes
Symbol:	GGG	Invests:	Every 30 days beginning 1/15
Exchange:	NYSE	Minimum:	$25
Industry:	Mfr. spray equipment	Maximum:	$1,000/quarter
Company Address:	Box 1441	Min to qualify:	1
	Minneapolis, MN 55440-1441	Fee on cash inv.:	0!
Company Phone:	612-623-6778 or 612-623-6000	Fee on div. inv.:	0!
Transfer Agent:	Norwest Bank Minnesota	Discount (cash):	0
Agent's Address:	P.O. Box 64854	Discount (div.):	0
	St. Paul, MN 55164-0854	Auto invest:	No
Agent's Phone:	800-468-9716	Auto invest fee:	$0
Other than USA:	Yes	Selling info:	Sells daily, by mail, at market, for $3 +15¢/sh.

Company:	**Great Central Mines**		**Safekeeping:**	Yes
Symbol:	GTCMY		**Invests:**	Every 7 days beginning varies
Exchange:	OTC		**Minimum:**	$50
Industry:	Precious Metals		**Maximum:**	$250,000/year
Company Address:	c/o BNY,101 Barclay St.,22 West		**Min to qualify:**	1
	New York, NY 10286		**Fee on cash inv.:**	$5 + 10¢/sh.
Company Phone:	800-943-9715		**Fee on div. inv.:**	5% to $5 + 10¢/sh.
Transfer Agent:	Bank of New York		**Discount (cash):**	0
Agent's Address:	P.O. Box 11258		**Discount (div.):**	0
	New York, NY 10286		**Auto invest:**	Yes
Agent's Phone:	888-269-2377		**Auto invest fee:**	$5 + 10¢/sh.
Other than USA:	Yes		**Selling info:**	Sells weekly, by mail, at market, for $5 +10¢/sh.

Company:	**Great Southern Bancorp, Inc.**		**Safekeeping:**	Yes
			Invests:	Every 90 days beginning 1/1
Symbol:	GSBC		**Minimum:**	$25
Exchange:	OTC		**Maximum:**	$2,500/quarter
Industry:	Savings and trust service		**Min to qualify:**	1
Company Address:	Box 9009		**Fee on cash inv.:**	5% to $2.50
	Springfield, MO 65808		**Fee on div. inv.:**	5% to $2.50
Company Phone:	800-725-6651		**Discount (cash):**	0
Transfer Agent:	Registrar & Transfer Co.		**Discount (div.):**	0
Agent's Address:	10 Commerce Drive		**Auto invest:**	No
	Cranford, NJ 07016		**Auto invest fee:**	$0
Agent's Phone:	800-368-5948		**Selling info:**	Not available
Other than USA:	Yes			

Company:	**Green Mountain Power**		**Safekeeping:**	Yes
Symbol:	GMP		**Invests:**	Every 30 days beginning 1/30
Exchange:	NYSE		**Minimum:**	$50
Industry:	Utility-electric		**Maximum:**	$40,000/year
Company Address:	Box 850		**Min to qualify:**	1
	South Burlington, VT 05402-0850		**Fee on cash inv.:**	0!
Company Phone:	888-434-4467 or 802-660-5787		**Fee on div. inv.:**	0!
Transfer Agent:	ChaseMellon Shareholder Services		**Discount (cash):**	0
Agent's Address:	85 Challenger Road, Overpeck Centre		**Discount (div.):**	5%
			Auto invest:	No
	Ridgefield Park, NJ 07660		**Auto invest fee:**	$0
Agent's Phone:	800-851-9677		**Selling info:**	Sells daily, by mail or phone, at market, for comm.
Other than USA:	Yes			

Company:	**Greenpoint Financial**		**Safekeeping:**	Yes
Symbol:	GPT		**Invests:**	Every 7 days beginning varies
Exchange:	NYSE		**Minimum:**	$100
Industry:	Savings bank		**Maximum:**	$10,000/month
Company Address:	90 Park Ave.		**Min to qualify:**	1
	New York, NY 10016		**Fee on cash inv.:**	$5 + 12¢/sh.
Company Phone:	212-834-1710		**Fee on div. inv.:**	0!
Transfer Agent:	ChaseMellon Shareholder Services		**Discount (cash):**	0
Agent's Address:	P.O. Box 750		**Discount (div.):**	0
	Pittsburgh, PA 15230		**Auto invest:**	Yes
			Auto invest fee:	$5 + 12¢/sh.
Agent's Phone:	888-224-2741		**Selling info:**	Sells weekly, by mail or phone, at market, for $15 +12¢/sh.
Other than USA:	Yes			

Company:	**Greif Brothers Corp. A**	**Safekeeping:**	Yes
Symbol:	GBCOA	**Invests:**	Every 30 days beginning 1/15
Exchange:	OTC	**Minimum:**	$100
Industry:	Shipping containers	**Maximum:**	$1,000/month
Company Address:	425 Winter Rd.	**Min to qualify:**	1
	Delaware, OH 43015	**Fee on cash inv.:**	0!
Company Phone:	740-549-6000 or 614-876-2000	**Fee on div. inv.:**	0!
Transfer Agent:	National City Bank	**Discount (cash):**	0
Agent's Address:	P.O. Box 94946	**Discount (div.):**	0
	Cleveland, OH 44101-4946	**Auto invest:**	No
Agent's Phone:	800-622-6757	**Auto invest fee:**	$0
Other than USA:	No	**Selling info:**	Sells weekly, by mail, at market, for comm.

Company:	**Groupe AB ADS**	**Safekeeping:**	Yes
Symbol:	ABG	**Invests:**	Every 7 days beginning varies
Exchange:	NYSE	**Minimum:**	$50
Industry:	Communications	**Maximum:**	$250,000/transaction
Company Address:	c/o Bank of NY,101 Barclay St.,	**Min to qualify:**	1
	22 West	**Fee on cash inv.:**	$5 + 10¢/sh.
	New York, NY 10286	**Fee on div. inv.:**	5% to $5 + 10¢/sh.
Company Phone:	800-943-9715	**Discount (cash):**	0
Transfer Agent:	Bank of New York	**Discount (div.):**	0
Agent's Address:	P.O. Box 11258	**Auto invest:**	Yes
	New York, NY 10286	**Auto invest fee:**	$0
Agent's Phone:	888-269-2377	**Selling info:**	Sells daily, by phone or mail, at
Other than USA:	Yes		avg. price, for $5 +10¢/ADS

Company:	**Grupo Casa Autrey SA de C.V.**	**Safekeeping:**	Yes
		Invests:	Every 7 days beginning varies
Symbol:	ATY	**Minimum:**	$50
Exchange:	NYSE	**Maximum:**	$100,000/year
Industry:	Dist. consumer prods. &	**Min to qualify:**	1
	pharmaceuticals	**Fee on cash inv.:**	$5 + 12¢/sh.
Company Address:	c/o Morgan Guaranty Trust,	**Fee on div. inv.:**	5% to $2.50
	Box 9073	**Discount (cash):**	0
	Boston, MA 02205-9948	**Discount (div.):**	0
Company Phone:	800-428-4237	**Auto invest:**	Yes
Transfer Agent:	Morgan Guaranty Trust Co.	**Auto invest fee:**	$5
Agent's Address:	P.O. Box 9073	**Selling info:**	Sells daily, by phone or mail, at
	Boston, MA 02205-9948		avg. price, for $5 +12¢/sh.
Agent's Phone:	800-428-4237		
Other than USA:	No		

Company:	**Grupo Elektra, SA de C.V.**	**Safekeeping:**	Yes
Symbol:	EKT	**Invests:**	Every 7 days beginning varies
Exchange:	NYSE	**Minimum:**	$50
Industry:	Retail	**Maximum:**	$250,000/year
Company Address:	c/o BNY,101 Barclay St.,22 West	**Min to qualify:**	1
	New York, NY 10286	**Fee on cash inv.:**	$5 + 10¢/sh.
Company Phone:	800-943-9715	**Fee on div. inv.:**	5% to $5 + 10¢/sh.
Transfer Agent:	Bank of New York	**Discount (cash):**	0
Agent's Address:	P.O. Box 11258	**Discount (div.):**	0
	New York, NY 10286	**Auto invest:**	Yes
Agent's Phone:	888-269-2377	**Auto invest fee:**	$5 + 10¢/sh.
Other than USA:	Yes	**Selling info:**	Sells weekly, by mail, at market, for $5 +10¢/sh.

Company:	**Grupo Imsa, S.A. de C.V.**	**Safekeeping:**	Yes
Symbol:	IMY	**Invests:**	Every 7 days beginning varies
Exchange:	NYSE	**Minimum:**	$50
Industry:	Iron & steel	**Maximum:**	$250,000/year
Company Address:	c/o BNY,101 Barclay St.,22 West	**Min to qualify:**	1
	New York, NY 10286	**Fee on cash inv.:**	$5 + 10¢/sh.
Company Phone:	800-943-9715	**Fee on div. inv.:**	5% to $5 + 10¢/sh.
Transfer Agent:	Bank of New York	**Discount (cash):**	0
Agent's Address:	P.O. Box 11258	**Discount (div.):**	0
	New York, NY 10286	**Auto invest:**	Yes
Agent's Phone:	888-269-2377	**Auto invest fee:**	$5 + 10¢/sh.
Other than USA:	Yes	**Selling info:**	Sells weekly, by mail, at market, for $5 +10¢/sh.

Company:	**Grupo Industrial Durango, S.A.**	**Safekeeping:**	Yes
		Invests:	Every 7 days beginning varies
Symbol:	GID	**Minimum:**	$50
Exchange:	NYSE	**Maximum:**	$250,000/week
Industry:	Integrated paper packaging and forest products	**Min to qualify:**	1
		Fee on cash inv.:	$5 + 10¢/sh.
Company Address:	c/o BNY,101 Barclay St.,22 West	**Fee on div. inv.:**	0
	New York, NY 10286	**Discount (cash):**	0
Company Phone:	800-943-9715	**Discount (div.):**	0
Transfer Agent:	Bank of New York	**Auto invest:**	Yes
Agent's Address:	P.O. Box 11258	**Auto invest fee:**	$0
	New York, NY 10286	**Selling info:**	Sells weekly, by phone or mail, at market, for $5 +10¢/ADS
Agent's Phone:	888-269-2377		
Other than USA:	Yes		

Company:	**Grupo Iusacell D**	**Safekeeping:**	Yes
Symbol:	CELD	**Invests:**	Every 7 days beginning varies
Exchange:	NYSE	**Minimum:**	$50
Industry:	Telecommunications	**Maximum:**	$250,000/year
Company Address:	c/o BNY,101 Barclay St.,22 West	**Min to qualify:**	1
	New York, NY 10286	**Fee on cash inv.:**	$5 + 10¢/sh.
Company Phone:	800-943-9715	**Fee on div. inv.:**	5% to $5 + 10¢/sh.
Transfer Agent:	Bank of New York	**Discount (cash):**	0
Agent's Address:	P.O. Box 11258	**Discount (div.):**	0
	New York, NY 10286	**Auto invest:**	Yes
Agent's Phone:	888-269-2377	**Auto invest fee:**	$5 + 10¢/sh.
Other than USA:	Yes	**Selling info:**	Sells weekly, by mail, at market, for $5 +10¢/sh.

Company:	**Grupo Iusacell, Series L**	**Safekeeping:**	Yes
Symbol:	CEL	**Invests:**	Every 7 days beginning varies
Exchange:	NYSE	**Minimum:**	$50
Industry:	Telecommunications	**Maximum:**	$250,000/year
Company Address:	c/o BNY,101 Barclay St.,22 West	**Min to qualify:**	1
	New York, NY 10286	**Fee on cash inv.:**	$5 + 10¢/sh.
Company Phone:	800-943-9715	**Fee on div. inv.:**	5% to $5 + 10¢/sh.
Transfer Agent:	Bank of New York	**Discount (cash):**	0
Agent's Address:	P.O. Box 11258	**Discount (div.):**	0
	New York, NY 10286	**Auto invest:**	Yes
Agent's Phone:	888-269-2377	**Auto invest fee:**	$5 + 10¢/sh.
Other than USA:	Yes	**Selling info:**	Sells weekly, by mail, at market, for $5 +10¢/sh.

Company:	**Grupo Tribasa**	**Safekeeping:**	Yes
Symbol:	GTR	**Invests:**	Every 7 days beginning varies
Exchange:	NYSE	**Minimum:**	$50
Industry:	Large scale infrastructure	**Maximum:**	$250,000/week
	construction projects	**Min to qualify:**	1
Company Address:	c/o BNY,101 Barclay St.,22 West	**Fee on cash inv.:**	$5 + 10¢/sh.
	New York, NY 10286	**Fee on div. inv.:**	0
Company Phone:	800-943-9715	**Discount (cash):**	0
Transfer Agent:	Bank of New York	**Discount (div.):**	0
Agent's Address:	P.O. Box 11258	**Auto invest:**	Yes
	New York, NY 10286	**Auto invest fee:**	$0
Agent's Phone:	888-269-2377	**Selling info:**	Sells weekly, by phone or mail, at
Other than USA:	Yes		market, for $5 +10¢/ADS

Company:	**GTE Corp.**	**Safekeeping:**	Yes
Symbol:	GTE	**Invests:**	Every 30 days beginning 1/1
Exchange:	NYSE	**Minimum:**	$25
Industry:	Telecommunications	**Maximum:**	$100,000/year
Company Address:	1225 Corporate Dr.	**Min to qualify:**	1
	Irving, TX 75038	**Fee on cash inv.:**	0
Company Phone:	972-507-2789	**Fee on div. inv.:**	5% to $1
Transfer Agent:	BankBoston (EquiServe)	**Discount (cash):**	0
Agent's Address:	P.O. Box 8031	**Discount (div.):**	0
	Boston, MA 02266-8031	**Auto invest:**	Yes
Agent's Phone:	800-225-5160	**Auto invest fee:**	$0
Other than USA:	Yes	**Selling info:**	Sells daily, by phone or mail, at
			market, for 15¢/sh.

Company:	**Guangshen Railway Co.**	**Safekeeping:**	Yes
	Ltd.	**Invests:**	Every 7 days beginning varies
Symbol:	GSH	**Minimum:**	$50
Exchange:	NYSE	**Maximum:**	$100,000/year
Industry:	Chinese railroad operations	**Min to qualify:**	1
Company Address:	c/o Morgan Guaranty Trust,	**Fee on cash inv.:**	$5 + 12¢/sh.
	Box 9073	**Fee on div. inv.:**	5% to $2.50
	Boston, MA 02205-9948	**Discount (cash):**	0
Company Phone:	800-428-4237	**Discount (div.):**	0
Transfer Agent:	Morgan Guaranty Trust Co.	**Auto invest:**	Yes
Agent's Address:	P.O. Box 9073	**Auto invest fee:**	$5
	Boston, MA 02205-9948	**Selling info:**	Sells daily, by phone or mail, at
Agent's Phone:	800-428-4237		avg. price, for $5 +12¢/sh.
Other than USA:	No		

Company:	**Guidant Corp.**	**Safekeeping:**	Yes
Symbol:	GDT	**Invests:**	Every 7 days beginning varies
Exchange:	NYSE	**Minimum:**	$50
Industry:	Design & mfr. medical devices	**Maximum:**	$unlimited
Company Address:	111 Monument Cir., 29th Fl.,	**Min to qualify:**	1
	Box 44906	**Fee on cash inv.:**	5% to $7.50 + comm.
	Indianapolis, IN 46204-5129	**Fee on div. inv.:**	0
Company Phone:	317-971-2000	**Discount (cash):**	0
Transfer Agent:	FCT (EquiServe)	**Discount (div.):**	0
Agent's Address:	P.O. Box 2500	**Auto invest:**	Yes
	Jersey City, NJ 07303-2500	**Auto invest fee:**	$1
Agent's Phone:	800-317-4445	**Selling info:**	Sells daily, by phone, mail, or fax,
Other than USA:	Yes		at avg. price, for $15 +12¢/sh.

Company:	**Hancock Holding Co.**	Safekeeping:	No
Symbol:	HBHC	Invests:	Every 90 days beginning 3/15
Exchange:	OTC	Minimum:	$50
Industry:	Banking	Maximum:	$5,000/quarter
Company Address:	One Hancock Plaza, Box 4019	Min to qualify:	1
	Gulfport, MS 39502	Fee on cash inv.:	0
Company Phone:	228-868-4414	Fee on div. inv.:	0
Transfer Agent:	Hancock Bank Trust Dept.	Discount (cash):	0
Agent's Address:	One Hancock Plaza, POB 4019	Discount (div.):	0
	Gulfport, MS 39502-4019	Auto invest:	Yes
Agent's Phone:	228-868-4414	Auto invest fee:	$0
Other than USA:	No	Selling info:	Sells weekly, by mail, at market, for comm.

Company:	**Hanna (M.A.) Co.**	Safekeeping:	Yes
Symbol:	MAH	Invests:	Every 30 days beginning 1/12
Exchange:	NYSE	Minimum:	$25
Industry:	Specialty chemicals	Maximum:	$3,000/month
Company Address:	200 Public Sq., Ste.36-5000	Min to qualify:	1
	Cleveland, OH 44114-2304	Fee on cash inv.:	0!
Company Phone:	800-688-4259 or 216-589-4200	Fee on div. inv.:	0!
Transfer Agent:	FCT (EquiServe)	Discount (cash):	0
Agent's Address:	P.O. Box 2500	Discount (div.):	0
	Jersey City, NJ 07303	Auto invest:	No
Agent's Phone:	800-446-2617	Auto invest fee:	$0
Other than USA:	Yes	Selling info:	Sells daily, by mail, at market, for $10 +12¢/sh.

Company:	**Hannaford Bros. Co.**	Safekeeping:	Yes
Symbol:	HRD	Invests:	Every 30 days beginning 1/31
Exchange:	NYSE	Minimum:	$25
Industry:	Retail stores	Maximum:	$2,000/month
Company Address:	Box 1000	Min to qualify:	1
	Portland, ME 04104	Fee on cash inv.:	0!
Company Phone:	207-883-2911	Fee on div. inv.:	0!
Transfer Agent:	Continental Stock Transfer &	Discount (cash):	0
	Trust	Discount (div.):	0
Agent's Address:	2 Broadway, 19th Floor	Auto invest:	No
	New York, NY 10004	Auto invest fee:	$0
Agent's Phone:	212-509-4000	Selling info:	Sells within 10 bus. days, by mail, at
Other than USA:	Yes		market, for 5% to $2.50 + comm.

Company:	**Hanover Bancorp, Inc.**	Safekeeping:	Yes
Symbol:	HOVB	Invests:	Every 90 days beginning 2/1
Exchange:	OTC	Minimum:	$50
Industry:	Banking	Maximum:	$2,500/quarter
Company Address:	25 Carlisle St.	Min to qualify:	1
	Hanover, PA 17331	Fee on cash inv.:	0!
Company Phone:	717-637-2201 x 233	Fee on div. inv.:	0!
Transfer Agent:	Bank of Hanover & Trust Co.	Discount (cash):	0
Agent's Address:	33 Carlisle Street	Discount (div.):	0
	Hanover, PA 17331	Auto invest:	No
Agent's Phone:	717-637-2201 x233	Auto invest fee:	$0
Other than USA:	No	Selling info:	Sells irregularly, by mail, at market, for $5

Company:	**Hanson plc**	Safekeeping:	Yes
Symbol:	HAN	Invests:	Every 30 days beginning 1/1
Exchange:	NYSE	Minimum:	$50
Industry:	Conglomerates	Maximum:	$60,000/year
Company Address:	1350 Campus Pkwy., Ste.302	Min to qualify:	1
	Neptune, NJ 07753	Fee on cash inv.:	$2.50 + 6¢/sh.
Company Phone:	732-919-2314 or 732-919-9777	Fee on div. inv.:	6¢/sh.
Transfer Agent:	FCT (Citibank)	Discount (cash):	0
Agent's Address:	111 Wall St., 5th Fl., ADR Dept.	Discount (div.):	0
	New York, NY 10043-0111	Auto invest:	No
Agent's Phone:	800-422-2066	Auto invest fee:	$0
Other than USA:	Yes	Selling info:	Sells monthly, by mail, at market, for $2.50 + 6¢/sh.

Company:	**Harcourt General**	Safekeeping:	Yes
Symbol:	H	Invests:	Every 45 days beginning 1/30
Exchange:	NYSE	Minimum:	$25
Industry:	Specialty retail, publishing	Maximum:	$2,500/quarter
Company Address:	27 Boylston St.	Min to qualify:	1
	Chestnut Hill, MA 02167	Fee on cash inv.:	0!
Company Phone:	617-232-8200	Fee on div. inv.:	0!
Transfer Agent:	Boston Eq. (EquiServe)	Discount (cash):	0
Agent's Address:	P.O. Box 8040	Discount (div.):	0
	Boston, MA 02266	Auto invest:	No
Agent's Phone:	800-736-3001	Auto invest fee:	$0
Other than USA:	No	Selling info:	Sells daily, by mail, at market, for $10 + comm.

Company:	**Harland (John H.) Co.**	Safekeeping:	Yes
Symbol:	JH	Invests:	Every 30 days beginning 1/15
Exchange:	NYSE	Minimum:	$50
Industry:	Printer, financial services provider	Maximum:	$250,000/year
		Min to qualify:	1
Company Address:	Box 105250	Fee on cash inv.:	$5 + 3¢/sh.
	Atlanta, GA 30348	Fee on div. inv.:	0!
Company Phone:	770-593-5128 or 770-981-9460	Discount (cash):	0
Transfer Agent:	FCT (EquiServe)	Discount (div.):	0
Agent's Address:	P.O. Box 2500	Auto invest:	Yes
	Jersey City, NJ 07303-2500	Auto invest fee:	$2 + comm.
Agent's Phone:	800-519-3111	Selling info:	Sells daily, by phone, mail, or fax, at avg. price, for $15 +12¢/sh.
Other than USA:	Yes		

Company:	**Harley-Davidson**	Safekeeping:	No
Symbol:	HDI	Invests:	Every 30 days beginning 1/1
Exchange:	NYSE	Minimum:	$30
Industry:	Mfr. motorcycles	Maximum:	$5,000/quarter
Company Address:	3700 W. Juneau Ave., Box 653	Min to qualify:	1
	Milwaukee, WI 53201	Fee on cash inv.:	0!
Company Phone:	414-343-4680	Fee on div. inv.:	0!
Transfer Agent:	Firstar Bank Milwaukee, NA	Discount (cash):	0
Agent's Address:	P.O. Box 2077	Discount (div.):	0
	Milwaukee, WI 53201	Auto invest:	No
Agent's Phone:	800-637-7549	Auto invest fee:	$0
Other than USA:	Yes	Selling info:	Sells daily, by mail or fax, at market, for 2¢ to 5¢/sh.

Company:	**Harleysville Group, Inc.**	**Safekeeping:**	No
Symbol:	HGIC	**Invests:**	Every 90 days beginning 3/30
Exchange:	OTC	**Minimum:**	$100
Industry:	Insurance, prop. & casualty	**Maximum:**	$25,000/year
Company Address:	355 Maple Ave.	**Min to qualify:**	1
	Harleysville, PA 19438-2297	**Fee on cash inv.:**	0!
Company Phone:	215-256-5000 or 215-256-5151	**Fee on div. inv.:**	0!
Transfer Agent:	ChaseMellon Shareholder Services	**Discount (cash):**	0
Agent's Address:	450 W. 33rd St.-15th Floor	**Discount (div.):**	0
	New York, NY 10001	**Auto invest:**	No
Agent's Phone:	800-851-9677	**Auto invest fee:**	$0
Other than USA:	No	**Selling info:**	Sells weekly, by mail or phone, at market, for comm.

Company:	**Harmony Gold Mining Co. Ltd.**	**Safekeeping:**	Yes
		Invests:	Every 7 days beginning varies
Symbol:	HGMCY	**Minimum:**	$50
Exchange:	OTC	**Maximum:**	$250,000/year
Industry:	Gold mining	**Min to qualify:**	1
Company Address:	c/o BNY,101 Barclay St.,22 West	**Fee on cash inv.:**	$5 + 10¢/sh.
	New York, NY 10286	**Fee on div. inv.:**	5% to $5 + 10¢/sh.
Company Phone:	800-943-9715	**Discount (cash):**	0
Transfer Agent:	Bank of New York	**Discount (div.):**	0
Agent's Address:	P.O. Box 11258	**Auto invest:**	Yes
	New York, NY 10286	**Auto invest fee:**	$5 + 10¢/sh.
Agent's Phone:	888-269-2377	**Selling info:**	Sells weekly, by mail, at market,
Other than USA:	Yes		for $5 +10¢/sh.

Company:	**Harris Corp.**	**Safekeeping:**	Yes
Symbol:	HRS	**Invests:**	Every 30 days beginning 1/15
Exchange:	NYSE	**Minimum:**	$10
Industry:	Electronic sys., comm. & office	**Maximum:**	$5,000/quarter
	equip.	**Min to qualify:**	1
Company Address:	1025 West NASA Blvd.	**Fee on cash inv.:**	0!
	Melbourne, FL 32919	**Fee on div. inv.:**	0!
Company Phone:	407-727-9100 or 407-727-9283	**Discount (cash):**	0
Transfer Agent:	ChaseMellon Shareholder Services	**Discount (div.):**	0
Agent's Address:	P.O. Box 3339	**Auto invest:**	Yes
	South Hackensack, NJ 07606-1939	**Auto invest fee:**	$0
Agent's Phone:	800-313-9450	**Selling info:**	Sells within 2 bus. days, by mail or
Other than USA:	Yes		phone, at market, for $0!

Company:	**Harsco Corp.**	**Safekeeping:**	Yes
Symbol:	HSC	**Invests:**	Every 30 days beginning 1/15
Exchange:	NYSE	**Minimum:**	$10
Industry:	Manufacturing & service	**Maximum:**	$unlimited
Company Address:	350 Poplar Church Rd., Box 8888	**Min to qualify:**	1
	Camp Hill, PA 17001-8888	**Fee on cash inv.:**	0!
Company Phone:	717-975-5677 or 717-763-7064	**Fee on div. inv.:**	0!
Transfer Agent:	ChaseMellon Shareholder Services	**Discount (cash):**	0
Agent's Address:	P.O. Box 3315	**Discount (div.):**	0
	South Hackensack, NJ 07606	**Auto invest:**	No
Agent's Phone:	800-526-0801	**Auto invest fee:**	$0
Other than USA:	Yes	**Selling info:**	Sells only for termination, by mail or phone, at market, for $5 + comm.

Company:	**Hartford Financial Services Group Inc**	Safekeeping:	Yes
Symbol:	HIG	Invests:	Every 7 days beginning Monday
Exchange:	NYSE	Minimum:	$50
Industry:	Multiline insurance	Maximum:	$5,000/month
Company Address:	Hartford Plaza, HO-1-01	Min to qualify:	1
	Hartford, CT 06115	Fee on cash inv.:	0!
Company Phone:	860-547-2537 or 860-547-5000	Fee on div. inv.:	0!
Transfer Agent:	Bank of New York	Discount (cash):	0
Agent's Address:	P.O. Box 1958	Discount (div.):	0
	Newark, NJ 07101-9774	Auto invest:	No
Agent's Phone:	800-254-2823	Auto invest fee:	$0
Other than USA:	Yes	Selling info:	Sells weekly, by mail, at market, for $3 + 7¢/sh.

Company:	**Hartford Life, Inc.**	Safekeeping:	Yes
Symbol:	HLI	Invests:	Every 7 days beginning varies
Exchange:	NYSE	Minimum:	$50
Industry:	Life insurance, financial services	Maximum:	$5,000/month
Company Address:	200 Hopmeadow St.	Min to qualify:	1
	Simsbury, CT 06089	Fee on cash inv.:	0!
Company Phone:	860-843-8418 or 860-843-8034	Fee on div. inv.:	0!
Transfer Agent:	Bank of New York	Discount (cash):	0
Agent's Address:	P.O. Box 11258, Church St. Station	Discount (div.):	0
	New York, NY 10286-1258	Auto invest:	No
Agent's Phone:	800-254-2823	Auto invest fee:	$0
Other than USA:	Yes	Selling info:	Sells weekly, by mail, at avg. price, for $5 + 10¢/sh.

Company:	**Hartmarx Corp.**	Safekeeping:	No
Symbol:	HMX	Invests:	Every 30 days beginning 1/15
Exchange:	NYSE	Minimum:	$25
Industry:	Apparel, retail clothing	Maximum:	$1,000/month
Company Address:	101 North Wacker Dr.	Min to qualify:	1
	Chicago, IL 60606	Fee on cash inv.:	0
Company Phone:	312-372-6300 or 312-357-5331	Fee on div. inv.:	0
Transfer Agent:	FCT (EquiServe)	Discount (cash):	0
Agent's Address:	P.O. Box 2500	Discount (div.):	0
	Jersey City, NJ 07303	Auto invest:	No
Agent's Phone:	201-324-0498	Auto invest fee:	$0
Other than USA:	Yes	Selling info:	Not available

Company:	**Hasbro Inc.**	Safekeeping:	Yes
Symbol:	HAS	Invests:	Every 30 days beginning 1/15
Exchange:	ASE	Minimum:	$25
Industry:	Manufactures toys and games	Maximum:	$2,000/month
Company Address:	1027 Newport Ave., Box 1059	Min to qualify:	1
	Pawtucket, RI 02862-1059	Fee on cash inv.:	0!
Company Phone:	401-431-8697 or 401-727-5701	Fee on div. inv.:	0!
Transfer Agent:	BankBoston (EquiServe)	Discount (cash):	0
Agent's Address:	P.O. Box 644, MS 45-02-64	Discount (div.):	0
	Boston, MA 02102-0644	Auto invest:	Yes
Agent's Phone:	800-733-5001	Auto invest fee:	$0
Other than USA:	No	Selling info:	Sells daily, by mail, at market, for $10 +15¢/sh.

Company:	**Hawaiian Elec. Ind.**	**Safekeeping:**	Yes
Symbol:	HE	**Invests:**	Every 15 days beginning 1/15 & 1/30
Exchange:	NYSE	**Minimum:**	$25
Industry:	Utility-electric, holding co.	**Maximum:**	$120,000/year
Company Address:	Box 730	**Min to qualify:**	1
	Honolulu, HI 96808-0730	**Fee on cash inv.:**	3¢/sh.
Company Phone:	808-543-5841 or 808-543-7385	**Fee on div. inv.:**	3¢/sh. + 50¢/qtr.
Transfer Agent:	Hawaiian Electric Industries Inc.	**Discount (cash):**	0
Agent's Address:	P.O. Box 730	**Discount (div.):**	0
	Honolulu, HI 96808-0730	**Auto invest:**	Yes
Agent's Phone:	808-532-5841	**Auto invest fee:**	$0
Other than USA:	Yes	**Selling info:**	Sells weekly, by mail or fax, at market, for $15 + 3.2¢/sh.

Company:	**Health Care REIT**	**Safekeeping:**	No
Symbol:	HCN	**Invests:**	Every 90 days beginning 2/20
Exchange:	NYSE	**Minimum:**	$50
Industry:	REIT	**Maximum:**	$5,000/quarter
Company Address:	1SeaGate, Ste.1500, Box 1475	**Min to qualify:**	1
	Toledo, OH 43603-1475	**Fee on cash inv.:**	0
Company Phone:	419-247-2800 or 419-247-2835	**Fee on div. inv.:**	0
Transfer Agent:	ChaseMellon Shareholder Services	**Discount (cash):**	4%
		Discount (div.):	4%
Agent's Address:	85 Challenger Road	**Auto invest:**	No
	Ridgefield Park, NJ 07660	**Auto invest fee:**	$0
Agent's Phone:	888-216-7206	**Selling info:**	Sells weekly, by mail or phone, at market, for $15 + comm.
Other than USA:	Yes		

Company:	**Healthcare Realty Trust**	**Safekeeping:**	Yes
Symbol:	HR	**Invests:**	Every 90 days beginning 2/15
Exchange:	NYSE	**Minimum:**	$25
Industry:	REIT	**Maximum:**	$5,000/quarter
Company Address:	3310 West End Ave., Ste.700	**Min to qualify:**	1
	Nashville, TN 37203	**Fee on cash inv.:**	0!
Company Phone:	615-269-8175	**Fee on div. inv.:**	0!
Transfer Agent:	BankBoston (EquiServe)	**Discount (cash):**	0
Agent's Address:	P.O. Box 8040	**Discount (div.):**	5%
	Boston, MA 02266-8040	**Auto invest:**	No
Agent's Phone:	781-575-3400	**Auto invest fee:**	$0
Other than USA:	Yes	**Selling info:**	Not available

Company:	**Heilig-Meyers Co.**	**Safekeeping:**	Yes
Symbol:	HMY	**Invests:**	Every 30 days beginning 1/1
Exchange:	NYSE	**Minimum:**	$10
Industry:	Retail	**Maximum:**	$2,500/month
Company Address:	12560 West Creek Pkwy.	**Min to qualify:**	1
	Richmond, VA 23230	**Fee on cash inv.:**	0!
Company Phone:	804-784-7300	**Fee on div. inv.:**	0!
Transfer Agent:	Wachovia (EquiServe)	**Discount (cash):**	0
Agent's Address:	P.O. Box 8217	**Discount (div.):**	0
	Boston, MA 02266-8217	**Auto invest:**	No
Agent's Phone:	800-633-4236	**Auto invest fee:**	$0
Other than USA:	Yes	**Selling info:**	Sells within 10 bus. days, by mail, at market, for 5¢/sh.

Company:	**Heinz (H.J.)**	**Safekeeping:**	Yes
Symbol:	HNZ	**Invests:**	Every 30 days beginning 1/10
Exchange:	NYSE	**Minimum:**	$25
Industry:	Food processor	**Maximum:**	$5,000/month
Company Address:	600 Grant St., Box 57	**Min to qualify:**	1
	Pittsburgh, PA 15230-0057	**Fee on cash inv.:**	0!
Company Phone:	412-456-5700	**Fee on div. inv.:**	0!
Transfer Agent:	ChaseMellon Shareholder Services	**Discount (cash):**	0
Agent's Address:	P.O. Box 3315	**Discount (div.):**	0
	South Hackensack, NJ 07606-1915	**Auto invest:**	No
Agent's Phone:	800-253-3399	**Auto invest fee:**	$0
Other than USA:	Yes	**Selling info:**	Sells daily, by mail or phone, at market, for $2.50 + comm.

Company:	**Hercules, Inc.**	**Safekeeping:**	Yes
Symbol:	HPC	**Invests:**	Every 30 days beginning 1/30
Exchange:	NYSE	**Minimum:**	$50
Industry:	Chemicals & plastics	**Maximum:**	$2,000/month
Company Address:	Hercules Plaza,1313 N. Market St.	**Min to qualify:**	1
	Wilmington, DE 19894-0001	**Fee on cash inv.:**	$5 + comm.
Company Phone:	800-441-9274 or 302-594-5000	**Fee on div. inv.:**	0!
Transfer Agent:	ChaseMellon Shareholder Services	**Discount (cash):**	0
Agent's Address:	P.O. Box 3338	**Discount (div.):**	0
	South Hackensack NJ 07606-1938	**Auto invest:**	No
Agent's Phone:	800-237-9980	**Auto invest fee:**	$0
Other than USA:	No	**Selling info:**	Sells monthly, by mail or phone, at market, for $15 + comm.

Company:	**Herman Miller, Inc.**	**Safekeeping:**	Yes
Symbol:	MLHR	**Invests:**	Every 30 days beginning 1/15
Exchange:	OTC	**Minimum:**	$25
Industry:	Office equipment and systems	**Maximum:**	$60,000/year
Company Address:	855 East Main Ave., Box 302	**Min to qualify:**	1
	Zeeland, MI 49464-0302	**Fee on cash inv.:**	5% to $3 + 5¢/sh.
Company Phone:	616-654-5044	**Fee on div. inv.:**	0!
Transfer Agent:	FCT (EquiServe)	**Discount (cash):**	0
Agent's Address:	P.O. Box 2598	**Discount (div.):**	0
	Jersey City, NJ 07303-2598	**Auto invest:**	Yes
Agent's Phone:	800-446-2617	**Auto invest fee:**	$1 + fee
Other than USA:	No	**Selling info:**	Sells daily, by mail or phone, at market, for $15 +12¢/sh.

Company:	**Hershey Foods**	**Safekeeping:**	Yes
Symbol:	HSY	**Invests:**	Every 7 days beginning varies
Exchange:	NYSE	**Minimum:**	$100
Industry:	Mfg. of chocolate & grocery prod.	**Maximum:**	$10,000/month
Company Address:	100 Crystal Dr., Box 810	**Min to qualify:**	10
	Hershey, PA 17033-0810	**Fee on cash inv.:**	$5 + 12¢/sh.
Company Phone:	717-534-7530 or 717-534-4000	**Fee on div. inv.:**	0
Transfer Agent:	ChaseMellon Shareholder Services	**Discount (cash):**	0
Agent's Address:	P.O. Box 3338	**Discount (div.):**	0
	South Hackensack, NJ 07606-1938	**Auto invest:**	Yes
Agent's Phone:	800-851-4216	**Auto invest fee:**	$3 + 12¢/sh.
Other than USA:	Yes	**Selling info:**	Sells weekly, by mail or phone, at market, for $15 +12¢/sh.

Company:	**Hewlett-Packard**
Symbol:	HWP
Exchange:	NYSE
Industry:	Manufacturer of computer products
Company Address:	3000 Hanover St. Palo Alto, CA 94304
Company Phone:	650-857-2067
Transfer Agent:	Harris Trust & Savings Bank
Agent's Address:	P.O. Box A3309 Chicago, IL 60690
Agent's Phone:	800-286-5977
Other than USA:	Yes

Safekeeping:	Yes
Invests:	Every 30 days beginning 1/15
Minimum:	$50
Maximum:	$10,000/month
Min to qualify:	10
Fee on cash inv.:	$2.50 + 8¢/sh.
Fee on div. inv.:	5% to $2.50 + 8¢/sh.
Discount (cash):	0
Discount (div.):	0
Auto invest:	Yes
Auto invest fee:	$1.25
Selling info:	Sells weekly, by mail or fax, at avg. price, for $10 + 8¢/sh.

Company:	**Hibernia Corp.**
Symbol:	HIB
Exchange:	NYSE
Industry:	Banking
Company Address:	Box 61540 New Orleans, LA 70161
Company Phone:	800-245-4388 or 504-533-2180
Transfer Agent:	ChaseMellon Shareholder Services
Agent's Address:	85 Challenger Road, Overpeck Centre Ridgefield Park, NJ 07660
Agent's Phone:	800-814-0305
Other than USA:	Yes

Safekeeping:	Yes
Invests:	Every 30 days beginning 1/20
Minimum:	$100
Maximum:	$3,000/month
Min to qualify:	1
Fee on cash inv.:	0
Fee on div. inv.:	0
Discount (cash):	0
Discount (div.):	5%
Auto invest:	No
Auto invest fee:	$0
Selling info:	Sells daily, by mail or phone, at avg. price, for comm.

Company:	**Highwoods Properties, Inc.**
Symbol:	HIW
Exchange:	NYSE
Industry:	REIT
Company Address:	3100 Smoketree Ct., Ste. 600 Raleigh, NC 27604-1051
Company Phone:	919-872-4924
Transfer Agent:	First Union National Bank of NC
Agent's Address:	1525 West W.T. Harris Blvd. 3C2 Charlotte, NC 28288-1153
Agent's Phone:	800-829-8432
Other than USA:	Yes

Safekeeping:	Yes
Invests:	Every 90 days beginning 2/16
Minimum:	$25
Maximum:	$20,000/quarter
Min to qualify:	1
Fee on cash inv.:	0!
Fee on div. inv.:	0!
Discount (cash):	0
Discount (div.):	5%
Auto invest:	No
Auto invest fee:	$0
Selling info:	Sells within 10 bus. days, by mail, at market, for comm.

Company:	**Hillenbrand Industries**
Symbol:	HB
Exchange:	NYSE
Industry:	Hospital equip., caskets, life insurance
Company Address:	700 State Route 46 East Batesville, IN 47006-8835
Company Phone:	812-934-8400 or 812-934-7000
Transfer Agent:	Harris Trust & Savings Bank
Agent's Address:	111 W. Monroe St., Box 755 Chicago, IL 60690-0755
Agent's Phone:	888-665-9611
Other than USA:	Yes

Safekeeping:	Yes
Invests:	Every 7 days beginning varies
Minimum:	$100
Maximum:	$50,000/year
Min to qualify:	1
Fee on cash inv.:	$5 + 10¢/sh.
Fee on div. inv.:	0
Discount (cash):	0
Discount (div.):	0
Auto invest:	Yes
Auto invest fee:	$2.50 + 10¢/sh.
Selling info:	Sells weekly, by mail, at avg. price, for $10 + 10¢/sh.

Company:	**Hoechst AG**	**Safekeeping:**	Yes
Symbol:	HOE	**Invests:**	Every 7 days beginning varies
Exchange:	NYSE	**Minimum:**	$50
Industry:	Pharmaceutical products, chemicals	**Maximum:**	$250,000/year
		Min to qualify:	1
Company Address:	c/o BNY,101 Barclay St.,22 West New York, NY 10286	**Fee on cash inv.:**	$5 + 10¢/sh.
		Fee on div. inv.:	5% to $5 + 10¢/sh.
Company Phone:	800-943-9715	**Discount (cash):**	0
Transfer Agent:	Bank of New York	**Discount (div.):**	0
Agent's Address:	P.O. Box 11258 New York, NY 10286	**Auto invest:**	Yes
		Auto invest fee:	$5 + 10¢/sh.
Agent's Phone:	888-269-2377	**Selling info:**	Sells weekly, by mail, at market, for $5 +10¢/sh.
Other than USA:	Yes		

Company:	**Home Depot**	**Safekeeping:**	Yes
Symbol:	HD	**Invests:**	Every 3 days beginning Tues. & Thurs.
Exchange:	NYSE		
Industry:	Retail building materials	**Minimum:**	$25
Company Address:	2455 Paces Ferry Rd., C17 Atlanta, GA 30339-4024	**Maximum:**	$100,000/year
		Min to qualify:	1
		Fee on cash inv.:	5% to $2.50 + comm.
Company Phone:	770-433-8211 or 770-384-4388	**Fee on div. inv.:**	5% to $2.50 + comm.
Transfer Agent:	BankBoston (EquiServe)	**Discount (cash):**	0
Agent's Address:	P.O. Box 8040 Boston, MA 02266-8040	**Discount (div.):**	0
		Auto invest:	Yes
Agent's Phone:	800-577-0177	**Auto invest fee:**	5% to $2.50 + comm.
Other than USA:	Yes	**Selling info:**	Sells biweekly, by mail, at market, for $10 + comm.

Company:	**Home Properties of NY**	**Safekeeping:**	Yes
Symbol:	HME	**Invests:**	Every 30 days beginning 1/10
Exchange:	NYSE	**Minimum:**	$50
Industry:	REIT	**Maximum:**	$5,000/month
Company Address:	850 Clinton Sq. Rochester, NY 14604	**Min to qualify:**	1
		Fee on cash inv.:	0
Company Phone:	716-546-4900 or 716-246-4192	**Fee on div. inv.:**	0
Transfer Agent:	ChaseMellon Shareholder Services	**Discount (cash):**	0-3%
Agent's Address:	P.O. Box 3338 South Hackensack, NJ 07606-1938	**Discount (div.):**	0-3%
		Auto invest:	Yes
Agent's Phone:	888-245-0458	**Auto invest fee:**	$0
Other than USA:	Yes	**Selling info:**	Sells weekly, by mail, at market, for $15 +12¢/sh.

Company:	**Homestake Mining Co.**	**Safekeeping:**	Yes
Symbol:	HM	**Invests:**	Every 30 days beginning 1/15
Exchange:	NYSE	**Minimum:**	$25
Industry:	Gold mining	**Maximum:**	$5,000/quarter
Company Address:	650 California St. San Francisco, CA 94108-2788	**Min to qualify:**	1
		Fee on cash inv.:	$3
Company Phone:	888-272-9123 or 415-981-8150	**Fee on div. inv.:**	0
Transfer Agent:	Boston Eq. (EquiServe)	**Discount (cash):**	0
Agent's Address:	P.O. Box 8040 Boston, MA 02266	**Discount (div.):**	0
		Auto invest:	No
Agent's Phone:	800-730-4001	**Auto invest fee:**	$0
Other than USA:	No	**Selling info:**	Sells weekly, by mail, at market, for $10 +15¢/sh.

Company:	**Honeywell Inc.**	
Symbol:	HON	
Exchange:	NYSE	
Industry:	Electronic controls	
Company Address:	Honeywell Plaza, Box 524	
	Minneapolis, MN 55440-0524	
Company Phone:	800-345-6770 or 612-951-1000	
Transfer Agent:	ChaseMellon Shareholder Services	
Agent's Address:	P.O. Box 3336	
	South Hackensack, NJ 07606-1936	
Agent's Phone:	800-647-7147	
Other than USA:	Yes	

Safekeeping:	No
Invests:	Every 30 days beginning 1/20
Minimum:	$25
Maximum:	$3,000/month
Min to qualify:	1
Fee on cash inv.:	0
Fee on div. inv.:	0
Discount (cash):	0
Discount (div.):	0
Auto invest:	No
Auto invest fee:	$0
Selling info:	Sells weekly, by mail, at market, for comm.

Company:	**Hormel Foods Corp.**
Symbol:	HRL
Exchange:	NYSE
Industry:	Food processor, marketer
Company Address:	1 Hormel Pl.
	Austin, MN 55912-3680
Company Phone:	507-437-5737 or 507-437-5669
Transfer Agent:	Norwest Bank Minnesota
Agent's Address:	P.O. Box 64854
	South St. Paul, MN 55164-0854
Agent's Phone:	800-468-9716
Other than USA:	No

Safekeeping:	Yes
Invests:	Every 30 days beginning 1/15
Minimum:	$25
Maximum:	$20,000/quarter
Min to qualify:	1
Fee on cash inv.:	0!
Fee on div. inv.:	0!
Discount (cash):	0
Discount (div.):	0
Auto invest:	Yes
Auto invest fee:	$0
Selling info:	Sells daily, by mail or fax, at market, for $3 +15¢/sh.

Company:	**Houghton Mifflin Co.**
Symbol:	HTN
Exchange:	NYSE
Industry:	Publishing
Company Address:	222 Berkeley St.
	Boston, MA 02116-3764
Company Phone:	617-351-5114 or 617-351-5000
Transfer Agent:	BankBoston (EquiServe)
Agent's Address:	P.O. Box 8040
	Boston, MA 02266
Agent's Phone:	800-730-4001
Other than USA:	Yes

Safekeeping:	Yes
Invests:	Every 45 days beginning varies
Minimum:	$25
Maximum:	$3,000/quarter
Min to qualify:	1
Fee on cash inv.:	0!
Fee on div. inv.:	0!
Discount (cash):	0
Discount (div.):	0
Auto invest:	No
Auto invest fee:	$0
Selling info:	Sells daily, by mail, at market, for 5% to $5

Company:	**Household International, Inc.**
Symbol:	HI
Exchange:	NYSE
Industry:	Financial services
Company Address:	2700 Sanders Rd.
	Prospect Heights, IL 60070-2799
Company Phone:	847-564-6990 or 847-564-5000
Transfer Agent:	Harris Trust & Savings Bank
Agent's Address:	P.O. Box A3309
	Chicago, IL 60690-3309
Agent's Phone:	800-926-2335
Other than USA:	Yes

Safekeeping:	Yes
Invests:	Every 30 days beginning 1/15
Minimum:	$50
Maximum:	$5,000/quarter
Min to qualify:	1
Fee on cash inv.:	0
Fee on div. inv.:	0
Discount (cash):	0
Discount (div.):	2.5%
Auto invest:	No
Auto invest fee:	$0
Selling info:	Sells weekly, by mail, at market, for 5¢/sh.

HRPT Properties Trust

Company:	HRPT Properties Trust	**Safekeeping:**	No
Symbol:	HRP	**Invests:**	Every 90 days beginning 2/20
Exchange:	NYSE	**Minimum:**	$0
Industry:	REIT	**Maximum:**	$10,000/quarter
Company Address:	400 Centre St.	**Min to qualify:**	1
	Newton, MA 02458	**Fee on cash inv.:**	0!
Company Phone:	617-332-3990	**Fee on div. inv.:**	0!
Transfer Agent:	State Street Bank (EquiServe)	**Discount (cash):**	0
Agent's Address:	P.O. Box 8200	**Discount (div.):**	0
	Boston, MA 02266-8200	**Auto invest:**	No
Agent's Phone:	800-426-5523	**Auto invest fee:**	$0
Other than USA:	Yes	**Selling info:**	Sells daily, by mail or phone, at market, for $2.50 +15¢/sh.

HSB Group, Inc.

Company:	HSB Group, Inc.	**Safekeeping:**	Yes
Symbol:	HSB	**Invests:**	Every 30 days beginning 1/31
Exchange:	NYSE	**Minimum:**	$10
Industry:	Insurance & engineering services	**Maximum:**	$1,000/month
Company Address:	One State St., Box 5024	**Min to qualify:**	1
	Hartford, CT 06102-5024	**Fee on cash inv.:**	0
Company Phone:	860-722-5724	**Fee on div. inv.:**	0
Transfer Agent:	Boston Eq. (EquiServe)	**Discount (cash):**	0
Agent's Address:	P.O. Box 8040	**Discount (div.):**	0
	Boston, MA 02266-8040	**Auto invest:**	No
Agent's Phone:	800-730-4001	**Auto invest fee:**	$0
Other than USA:	Yes	**Selling info:**	Sells daily, by mail, at market, for 5% to $5 + comm.

HSBC Holding plc ADR

Company:	HSBC Holding plc ADR	**Safekeeping:**	Yes
Symbol:	HSBHY	**Invests:**	Every 30 days beginning 1/7
Exchange:	OTC	**Minimum:**	$50
Industry:	Banking	**Maximum:**	$100,000/year
Company Address:	c/o Marine Midland Bank, Box 1022	**Min to qualify:**	1
	New York, NY 10269-0400	**Fee on cash inv.:**	$5 + 12¢/sh.
Company Phone:	800-638-6347	**Fee on div. inv.:**	5% to $2.50
Transfer Agent:	Marine Midland Bank-HSBC Issuer Services	**Discount (cash):**	0
		Discount (div.):	0
Agent's Address:	P.O.Box 1022	**Auto invest:**	Yes
	New York, NY 10269-0400	**Auto invest fee:**	$0
Agent's Phone:	800-638-6347	**Selling info:**	Sells daily, by mail, at market, for $5 +12¢/sh.
Other than USA:	Yes		

Huaneng Power Int'l, Inc.

Company:	Huaneng Power Int'l, Inc.	**Safekeeping:**	Yes
Symbol:	HNP	**Invests:**	Every 7 days beginning varies
Exchange:	NYSE	**Minimum:**	$50
Industry:	Power company	**Maximum:**	$100,000/year
Company Address:	c/o Morgan Guaranty Trust,	**Min to qualify:**	1
	Box 9073	**Fee on cash inv.:**	$5 + 12¢/sh.
	Boston, MA 02205-9948	**Fee on div. inv.:**	5% to $2.50
Company Phone:	800-428-4237	**Discount (cash):**	0
Transfer Agent:	Morgan Guaranty Trust Co.	**Discount (div.):**	0
Agent's Address:	P.O. Box 9073	**Auto invest:**	Yes
	Boston, MA 02205-9948	**Auto invest fee:**	$5
Agent's Phone:	800-428-4237	**Selling info:**	Sells daily, by phone or mail, at avg. price, for $5 +12¢/sh.
Other than USA:	No		

Company:	**Hubbell, Inc. A**	**Safekeeping:**	Yes
Symbol:	HUBA	**Invests:**	Every 30 days beginning 1/15
Exchange:	NYSE	**Minimum:**	$100
Industry:	Mfr. elec. equipment	**Maximum:**	$5,000/quarter
Company Address:	584 Derby Milford Rd., Box 549	**Min to qualify:**	1
	Orange, CT 06477-4024	**Fee on cash inv.:**	0!
Company Phone:	203-799-4100	**Fee on div. inv.:**	0!
Transfer Agent:	ChaseMellon Shareholder Services	**Discount (cash):**	0
Agent's Address:	P.O. Box 3338	**Discount (div.):**	0
	South Hackensack, NJ 07606-1938	**Auto invest:**	No
Agent's Phone:	800-851-9677	**Auto invest fee:**	$0
Other than USA:	Yes	**Selling info:**	Sells biweekly, by mail, at market, for $15 + comm.

Company:	**Hubbell, Inc. B**	**Safekeeping:**	Yes
Symbol:	HUBB	**Invests:**	Every 30 days beginning 1/15
Exchange:	NYSE	**Minimum:**	$100
Industry:	Mfr. elec. equipment	**Maximum:**	$5,000/quarter
Company Address:	584 Derby Milford Rd., Box 549	**Min to qualify:**	1
	Orange, CT 06477-4024	**Fee on cash inv.:**	0!
Company Phone:	203-799-4100	**Fee on div. inv.:**	0!
Transfer Agent:	ChaseMellon Shareholder Services	**Discount (cash):**	0
Agent's Address:	P.O. Box 3338	**Discount (div.):**	0
	S. Hackensack, NJ 07606-1938	**Auto invest:**	No
Agent's Phone:	800-851-9677	**Auto invest fee:**	$0
Other than USA:	Yes	**Selling info:**	Sells biweekly, by mail, at market, for $15 + comm.

Company:	**Hudson United Bancorp**	**Safekeeping:**	Yes
Symbol:	HU	**Invests:**	Every 30 days beginning 1/31
Exchange:	NYSE	**Minimum:**	$10
Industry:	Banking	**Maximum:**	$20,000/quarter
Company Address:	1000 MacArthur Blvd.	**Min to qualify:**	1
	Mahwah, NJ 07430	**Fee on cash inv.:**	0
Company Phone:	201-236-2641 or 201-236-2600	**Fee on div. inv.:**	0
Transfer Agent:	American Stock Transfer	**Discount (cash):**	0
Agent's Address:	40 Wall Street, 46th Fl.	**Discount (div.):**	0
	New York, NY 10005	**Auto invest:**	Yes
Agent's Phone:	800-278-4353 or 718-921-8283	**Auto invest fee:**	$0
Other than USA:	No	**Selling info:**	Sells weekly, by mail, at avg. price, for $0

Company:	**Huffy Corp.**	**Safekeeping:**	No
Symbol:	HUF	**Invests:**	Every 30 days beginning 1/1
Exchange:	NYSE	**Minimum:**	$10
Industry:	Recreation & leisure products	**Maximum:**	$1,000/month
Company Address:	225 Byers Rd.	**Min to qualify:**	25
	Miamisburg, OH 45342	**Fee on cash inv.:**	0!
Company Phone:	937-866-6251 or 937-865-2867	**Fee on div. inv.:**	0!
Transfer Agent:	Harris Trust & Savings Bank	**Discount (cash):**	0
Agent's Address:	P.O. BOX A3309	**Discount (div.):**	0
	Chicago, IL 60690-3309	**Auto invest:**	No
Agent's Phone:	800-942-5909	**Auto invest fee:**	$0
Other than USA:	No	**Selling info:**	Sells daily, by mail, at market, for $1 + comm.

Company:	Huntingdon Life Sciences Group plc	Safekeeping:	Yes
		Invests:	Every 7 days beginning varies
Symbol:	HTD	Minimum:	$50
Exchange:	OTC	Maximum:	$250,000/year
Industry:	Biotechnology & drugs	Min to qualify:	1
Company Address:	c/o BNY,101 Barclay St.,22 West New York, NY 10286	Fee on cash inv.:	$5 + 10¢/sh.
		Fee on div. inv.:	0
Company Phone:	800-943-9715	Discount (cash):	0
Transfer Agent:	Bank of New York	Discount (div.):	0
Agent's Address:	P.O. Box 11258 New York, NY 10286	Auto invest:	Yes
		Auto invest fee:	$5 + 10¢/sh.
Agent's Phone:	888-269-2377	Selling info:	Sells weekly, by mail, at market, for $5 +10¢/sh.
Other than USA:	Yes		

Company:	Huntington Bancshares	Safekeeping:	Yes
Symbol:	HBAN	Invests:	Every 90 days beginning 1/1
Exchange:	OTC	Minimum:	$200
Industry:	Banking	Maximum:	$10,000/quarter
Company Address:	Huntington Ctr., HCO635 Columbus, OH 43287	Min to qualify:	1
		Fee on cash inv.:	0
Company Phone:	614-480-3803 or 614-480-3878	Fee on div. inv.:	0
Transfer Agent:	Harris Trust & Savings Bank	Discount (cash):	0
Agent's Address:	311 West Monroe St.11th Flr., Box A-3504 Chicago, IL 60690-3504	Discount (div.):	0
		Auto invest:	Yes
		Auto invest fee:	$0
Agent's Phone:	800-725-0674	Selling info:	Sells weekly, by mail, at market, for $10 + comm.
Other than USA:	Yes		

Company:	IDACORP, Inc.	Safekeeping:	Yes
Symbol:	IDA	Invests:	Every 90 days beginning 2/20
Exchange:	NYSE	Minimum:	$10
Industry:	Utility-electric	Maximum:	$15,000/quarter
Company Address:	P.O. Box 70 Boise, ID 83707	Min to qualify:	1
		Fee on cash inv.:	4¢/sh.
Company Phone:	800-635-5406 or 208-388-6955	Fee on div. inv.:	4¢/sh.
Transfer Agent:	Idaho Power	Discount (cash):	0
Agent's Address:	Box 70 Boise, ID 83702	Discount (div.):	0
		Auto invest:	No
Agent's Phone:	800-635-5406	Auto invest fee:	$0
Other than USA:	Yes	Selling info:	Sells weekly, by mail or fax, at avg. price, for 4¢/sh.

Company:	IKON Office Solutions, Inc.	Safekeeping:	Yes
Symbol:	IKN	Invests:	Every 30 days beginning 1/10
Exchange:	NYSE	Minimum:	$25
Industry:	Paper, office products	Maximum:	$5,000/month
Company Address:	70 Valley Stream Pkwy. Valley Forge, PA 19355	Min to qualify:	1
		Fee on cash inv.:	comm.
Company Phone:	610-408-7280 or 610-408-7279	Fee on div. inv.:	comm.
Transfer Agent:	National City Bank	Discount (cash):	0
Agent's Address:	P.O. Box 92301-N Cleveland, OH 44193-0900	Discount (div.):	0
		Auto invest:	No
Agent's Phone:	800-622-6757 x2532	Auto invest fee:	$0
Other than USA:	Yes	Selling info:	Sells weekly, by mail, at market, for $2.50 + comm.

Company:	**Illinois Tool Works, Inc.**	Safekeeping:	No
Symbol:	ITW	Invests:	Every 90 days beginning 3/1
Exchange:	NYSE	Minimum:	$25
Industry:	Industrial systems	Maximum:	$5,000/quarter
Company Address:	3600 West Lake Ave.	Min to qualify:	1
	Glenview, IL 60025-5811	Fee on cash inv.:	0
Company Phone:	847-724-7500 or 847-657-4104	Fee on div. inv.:	0
Transfer Agent:	Harris Trust & Savings Bank	Discount (cash):	0
Agent's Address:	P.O. Box A3504	Discount (div.):	0
	Chicago, IL 60690-3504	Auto invest:	No
Agent's Phone:	888-829-7424	Auto invest fee:	$0
Other than USA:	Yes	Selling info:	Sells weekly, by mail or fax, at market, for 10¢/sh. + comm.

Company:	**Illinova Corp.**	Safekeeping:	Yes
Symbol:	ILN	Invests:	Every 15 days beginning 1/1
Exchange:	NYSE	Minimum:	$25
Industry:	Energy services holding co.	Maximum:	$60,000/year
Company Address:	500 South 27th St.	Min to qualify:	1
	Decatur, IL 62521-2200	Fee on cash inv.:	0
Company Phone:	800-800-8220 or 217-424-8715	Fee on div. inv.:	0
Transfer Agent:	Ilinois Power Company	Discount (cash):	0
Agent's Address:	500 S. 27th St.	Discount (div.):	0
	Decatur, IL 62521-2200	Auto invest:	Yes
Agent's Phone:	800-800-8220	Auto invest fee:	$0
Other than USA:	Yes	Selling info:	Sells weekly, by mail or fax, at market, for 5¢/sh.

Company:	**Imasco Limited**	Safekeeping:	No
Symbol:	IMS	Invests:	Every 90 days beginning 3/30
Exchange:	TSE	Minimum:	$75
Industry:	Tobacco, fin'l services, drugstore, land development	Maximum:	$4,000/quarter Cdn.
		Min to qualify:	1
Company Address:	600 de Maisonneuve Bl. W., 20th Fl.	Fee on cash inv.:	0!
	Montreal, Que. H3A 3K7 Canada	Fee on div. inv.:	0!
Company Phone:	514-982-9111 or 514-982-6415	Discount (cash):	0
Transfer Agent:	CIBC Mellon Trust Company	Discount (div.):	0
Agent's Address:	P.O. Box 700, Station B	Auto invest:	No
	Montreal, Quebec H3B 3K3	Auto invest fee:	$0
Agent's Phone:	800-387-0825	Selling info:	Not available
Other than USA:	Yes		

Company:	**IMPAC Mortgage Holdings**	Safekeeping:	No
		Invests:	Every 30 days beginning 1/29
Symbol:	IMH	Minimum:	$50
Exchange:	ASE	Maximum:	$10,000/month
Industry:	REIT	Min to qualify:	1
Company Address:	20371 Irvine Ave.	Fee on cash inv.:	$0 to 15¢/sh.
	Santa Ana Heights, CA 92707	Fee on div. inv.:	$0 to 15¢/sh.
Company Phone:	714-556-0122	Discount (cash):	1-2.25%
Transfer Agent:	Boston Eq. (EquiServe)	Discount (div.):	3%
Agent's Address:	P.O. Box 8040	Auto invest:	No
	Boston, MA 02266	Auto invest fee:	$0
Agent's Phone:	800-730-4001	Selling info:	Sells within 10 bus. days, by mail, at market, for comm.
Other than USA:	No		

Company:	**Imperial Chemical Ind. plc**	Safekeeping:	Yes
Symbol:	ICI	Invests:	Every 7 days beginning varies
Exchange:	NYSE	Minimum:	$50
Industry:	Int'l chemical co.	Maximum:	$100,000/year
Company Address:	645 Fifth Ave.	Min to qualify:	1
	New York, NY 10022	Fee on cash inv.:	$5 + 12¢/sh.
		Fee on div. inv.:	5% to $2.50
Company Phone:	212-644-9292	Discount (cash):	0
Transfer Agent:	Morgan Guaranty Trust Co.	Discount (div.):	0
Agent's Address:	P.O. Box 9073	Auto invest:	Yes
	Boston, MA 02205-9948	Auto invest fee:	$0
Agent's Phone:	800-428-4237	Selling info:	Sells daily, by phone or mail, at
Other than USA:	No		avg. price, for $5 +12¢/sh.

Company:	**Imperial Oil Limited**	Safekeeping:	No
Symbol:	IMO	Invests:	Every 90 days beginning 1/4
Exchange:	ASE	Minimum:	$50
Industry:	Energy	Maximum:	$5,000/quarter (Cdn.)
Company Address:	111 St. Clair Ave. West, Rm.1721	Min to qualify:	1
	Toronto, Ont. M5W 1K3 Canada	Fee on cash inv.:	comm.
Company Phone:	800-388-1518 or 468-968-5387	Fee on div. inv.:	comm.
Transfer Agent:	Trust Co.-Bk Montreal	Discount (cash):	0
Agent's Address:	129 Saint-Jacques St., Level B	Discount (div.):	0
	North	Auto invest:	No
	Montreal, Que. H2Y 1L6	Auto invest fee:	$0
Agent's Phone:	514-877-2584	Selling info:	Not available
Other than USA:	Yes		

Company:	**Imperial Sugar Co.**	Safekeeping:	Yes
Symbol:	IHK	Invests:	Every 30 days beginning 1/10
Exchange:	ASE	Minimum:	$100
Industry:	Food, sugar & sweeteners	Maximum:	$5,000/quarter
Company Address:	One Imperial Sq., Box 9	Min to qualify:	1
	Sugar Land, TX 77487-0009	Fee on cash inv.:	0!
Company Phone:	713-491-9181 or 281-491-9181	Fee on div. inv.:	0!
Transfer Agent:	Bank of New York	Discount (cash):	0
Agent's Address:	P.O. Box 11258 , Church Street	Discount (div.):	0
	Station	Auto invest:	No
	New York, NY 10286-1258	Auto invest fee:	$0
Agent's Phone:	800-524-4458	Selling info:	Sells upon term. of accnt., by
Other than USA:	Yes		mail, at market, for $5 + comm.

Company:	**Inco Ltd.**	Safekeeping:	No
Symbol:	N	Invests:	Every 90 days beginning 3/11
Exchange:	NYSE	Minimum:	$50
Industry:	Metals	Maximum:	$10,000/quarter
Company Address:	145 King St.West, Ste.1500	Min to qualify:	1
	Toronto, Ont. M5H 4B7 Canada	Fee on cash inv.:	0!
Company Phone:	416-361-7511 or 212-612-5500	Fee on div. inv.:	0!
Transfer Agent:	CIBC Mellon Trust Company	Discount (cash):	0
Agent's Address:	Box 7010, Adelaide St. Postal Sta-	Discount (div.):	0
	tion	Auto invest:	No
	Toronto, Ontario M5C 2W9	Auto invest fee:	$0
Agent's Phone:	800-387-0825	Selling info:	Sells within 10 days, by mail or
Other than USA:	Yes		fax, at market, for comm.

Company:	**Independent Bank Corp.**	
Symbol:	IBCP	
Exchange:	OTC	
Industry:	Banking	
Company Address:	230 West Main St., Box 491	
	Ionia, MI 48846	
Company Phone:	616-527-5820x1217 or 616-527-9450	
Transfer Agent:	State Street Bank (EquiServe)	
Agent's Address:	P.O. Box 8209	
	Boston, Mass 02266-8209	
Agent's Phone:	800-257-1770 or 800-426-5523	
Other than USA:	No	

Safekeeping:	Yes
Invests:	Every 90 days beginning 1/30
Minimum:	$50
Maximum:	$5,000/quarter
Min to qualify:	1
Fee on cash inv.:	0
Fee on div. inv.:	0
Discount (cash):	0
Discount (div.):	0
Auto invest:	Yes
Auto invest fee:	$0
Selling info:	Sells irregularly, by mail or phone, at market, for $5 + comm.

Company:	**India Fund**
Symbol:	IFN
Exchange:	NYSE
Industry:	Closed-end fund
Company Address:	Oppenheimer Tower,
	200 Liberty St.
	New York, NY 10281
Company Phone:	800-421-4777
Transfer Agent:	Bank of New York
Agent's Address:	101 Barclay St.
	New York, NY 10286
Agent's Phone:	800-432-8224
Other than USA:	Yes

Safekeeping:	No
Invests:	Every 365 days beginning 2/15
Minimum:	$100
Maximum:	$3,000/year
Min to qualify:	1
Fee on cash inv.:	comm.
Fee on div. inv.:	0
Discount (cash):	0
Discount (div.):	0
Auto invest:	No
Auto invest fee:	$0
Selling info:	Sells weekly, by mail, at avg. price, for $5 + 3¢ to 5¢/sh.

Company:	**Indiana Energy**
Symbol:	IEI
Exchange:	NYSE
Industry:	Utility-gas
Company Address:	1630 North Meridian St.
	Indianapolis, IN 46202-1496
Company Phone:	800-777-3389 or 317-321-0588
Transfer Agent:	FCT (EquiServe)
Agent's Address:	P.O. Box 2598
	Jersey City, NJ 07303-2598
Agent's Phone:	800-446-2617
Other than USA:	Yes

Safekeeping:	Yes
Invests:	Every 30 days beginning 1/1
Minimum:	$25
Maximum:	$50,000/year
Min to qualify:	1
Fee on cash inv.:	0!
Fee on div. inv.:	0!
Discount (cash):	0
Discount (div.):	0
Auto invest:	Yes
Auto invest fee:	$2
Selling info:	Sells irregularly, by phone or mail, at avg. price, for $10 +12¢/sh.

Company:	**Indonesia Fund, Inc. (The)**
Symbol:	IF
Exchange:	NYSE
Industry:	Closed end fund
Company Address:	c/o Credit Suisse, 153 E. 53rd St.,
	58th Fl.
	New York, NY 10022
Company Phone:	800-293-1232 or 212-238-5674
Transfer Agent:	BankBoston (EquiServe)
Agent's Address:	P.O. Box 8040
	Boston, MA 02266
Agent's Phone:	800-730-6001
Other than USA:	Yes

Safekeeping:	Yes
Invests:	Every 7 days beginning Wed.
Minimum:	$100
Maximum:	$100,000/year
Min to qualify:	1
Fee on cash inv.:	$5 + 8¢/sh.
Fee on div. inv.:	0
Discount (cash):	0
Discount (div.):	0
Auto invest:	Yes
Auto invest fee:	$5 + 8¢/sh.
Selling info:	Sells within 4 bus. days, by mail, at avg. price, for $10 + 15¢/sh.

Company:	**Industrias Bachoco**	Safekeeping:	Yes
Symbol:	IBA	Invests:	Every 7 days beginning varies
Exchange:	NYSE	Minimum:	$50
Industry:	Food products	Maximum:	$250,000/year
Company Address:	c/o BNY,101 Barclay St.,22 West	Min to qualify:	1
	New York, NY 10286	Fee on cash inv.:	$5 + 10¢/sh.
Company Phone:	800-943-9715	Fee on div. inv.:	0
Transfer Agent:	Bank of New York	Discount (cash):	0
Agent's Address:	P.O. Box 11258	Discount (div.):	0
	New York, NY 10286	Auto invest:	Yes
Agent's Phone:	888-269-2377	Auto invest fee:	$5 + 10¢/sh.
Other than USA:	Yes	Selling info:	Sells weekly, by mail, at market, for $5 +10¢/sh.

Company:	**Industrie Natuzzi SPA ADS**	Safekeeping:	Yes
		Invests:	Every 7 days beginning varies
Symbol:	NTZ	Minimum:	$50
Exchange:	NYSE	Maximum:	$250,000/week
Industry:	Consumer products	Min to qualify:	1
Company Address:	c/o BNY,101 Barclay St., 22 West	Fee on cash inv.:	$5 + 10¢/sh.
	New York, NY 10286	Fee on div. inv.:	5% to $5 + 10¢/sh.
Company Phone:	800-943-9715	Discount (cash):	0
Transfer Agent:	Bank of New York	Discount (div.):	0
Agent's Address:	P.O. Box 11258	Auto invest:	Yes
	New York, NY 10286	Auto invest fee:	$0
Agent's Phone:	888-269-2377	Selling info:	Sells weekly, by phone or mail, at
Other than USA:	Yes		avg. price, for $5 +10¢/ADS

Company:	**IndyMac Mortgage Holdings, Inc.**	Safekeeping:	No
		Invests:	Every 30 days beginning 1/22
Symbol:	NDE	Minimum:	$50
Exchange:	NYSE	Maximum:	$10,000/month
Industry:	REIT	Min to qualify:	1
Company Address:	155 North Lake Ave.	Fee on cash inv.:	0
	Pasadena, CA 91101-7211	Fee on div. inv.:	0
Company Phone:	800-669-2300x5019 or 626-535-5019	Discount (cash):	0
Transfer Agent:	Bank of New York	Discount (div.):	1%
Agent's Address:	P.O. Box 11258, Church Street	Auto invest:	No
	Station	Auto invest fee:	$0
	New York, NY 10286-1258	Selling info:	Not available
Agent's Phone:	800-524-4458		
Other than USA:	No		

Company:	**ING Groep N.V.**	Safekeeping:	Yes
Symbol:	ING	Invests:	Every 7 days beginning varies
Exchange:	NYSE	Minimum:	$50
Industry:	Life Insurance	Maximum:	$100,000/year
Company Address:	c/o Morgan Guaranty Trust,	Min to qualify:	1
	Box 9073	Fee on cash inv.:	$5 + 12¢/sh.
	Boston, MA 02205-9948	Fee on div. inv.:	5% to $2.50
Company Phone:	800-428-4237	Discount (cash):	0
Transfer Agent:	Morgan Guaranty Trust Co.	Discount (div.):	0
Agent's Address:	P.O. Box 9073	Auto invest:	Yes
	Boston, MA 02205-9948	Auto invest fee:	$5 + 12¢/sh.
Agent's Phone:	800-428-4237	Selling info:	Sells daily, by mail or phone, at
Other than USA:	No		avg. price, for $5 +12¢/sh.

Company:	**Ingersoll-Rand**	Safekeeping:	Yes
Symbol:	IR	Invests:	Every 30 days beginning 1/1
Exchange:	NYSE	Minimum:	$10
Industry:	Machinery	Maximum:	$3,000/quarter
Company Address:	200 Chestnut Ridge Rd.	Min to qualify:	1
	Woodcliff Lake, NJ 07675	Fee on cash inv.:	0!
Company Phone:	201-573-3113	Fee on div. inv.:	0!
Transfer Agent:	Bank of New York	Discount (cash):	0
Agent's Address:	P.O. Box 11258-Church St. Station	Discount (div.):	0
	New York, NY 10286-1258	Auto invest:	No
Agent's Phone:	800-524-4458	Auto invest fee:	$0
Other than USA:	No	Selling info:	Sells daily, by mail, at market, for comm.

Company:	**Innkeepers USA Trust**	Safekeeping:	Yes
Symbol:	KPA	Invests:	Every 30 days beginning 4/15
Exchange:	NYSE	Minimum:	$250
Industry:	Ownership of hotels	Maximum:	$3,000/investment
Company Address:	306 Royal Poinciana Plaza	Min to qualify:	1
	Palm Beach., FL 33480	Fee on cash inv.:	0!
Company Phone:	561-835-1800	Fee on div. inv.:	0!
Transfer Agent:	Harris Bank & Trust	Discount (cash):	0-3%
Agent's Address:	P.O. Box A3309	Discount (div.):	4%
	Chicago, IL 60690-3309	Auto invest:	No
Agent's Phone:	800-942-5909	Auto invest fee:	$0
Other than USA:	No	Selling info:	Sells monthly, by mail or e-mail, at avg. price, for $5 + comm.

Company:	**Insteel Ind., Inc.**	Safekeeping:	Yes
Symbol:	III	Invests:	Every 30 days beginning 1/5
Exchange:	NYSE	Minimum:	$10
Industry:	Mfr. wire & wire products	Maximum:	$unlimited
Company Address:	1373 Boggs Dr.	Min to qualify:	1
	Mount Airy, NC 27030	Fee on cash inv.:	0!
Company Phone:	336-786-2141	Fee on div. inv.:	0!
Transfer Agent:	First Union National Bank of NC	Discount (cash):	0
Agent's Address:	200 S. Tryon St., 10th floor	Discount (div.):	0
	Charlotte, NC 28288	Auto invest:	No
Agent's Phone:	800-829-8432	Auto invest fee:	$0
Other than USA:	Yes	Selling info:	Sells bimonthly, by mail, at market, for 5¢/sh.

Company:	**Intel Corp.**	Safekeeping:	Yes
Symbol:	INTC	Invests:	Every 30 days beginning 1/1
Exchange:	OTC	Minimum:	$25
Industry:	Computer chips	Maximum:	$15,000/month
Company Address:	2200 Mission College Blvd.,	Min to qualify:	1
	RN5-24	Fee on cash inv.:	0!
	Santa Clara, CA 95052-8119	Fee on div. inv.:	0!
Company Phone:	800-628-8686 or 408-765-1480	Discount (cash):	0
Transfer Agent:	Harris Trust & Savings Bank	Discount (div.):	0
Agent's Address:	P.O. Box A3309	Auto invest:	Yes
	Chicago, IL 60690	Auto invest fee:	$0
Agent's Phone:	800-298-0146	Selling info:	Sells within 10 bus. days, by mail or fax, at avg. price, for 0!
Other than USA:	Yes		

Company:	**Interchange Financial Services**	**Safekeeping:**	No
		Invests:	Every 30 days beginning 1/5
Symbol:	ISB	**Minimum:**	$25
Exchange:	ASE	**Maximum:**	$unlimited
Industry:	Commercial banking	**Min to qualify:**	1
Company Address:	Park 80 West, Plaza Two	**Fee on cash inv.:**	comm.
	Saddle Brook, NJ 07663	**Fee on div. inv.:**	comm.
Company Phone:	201-703-4508 or 201-703-2265	**Discount (cash):**	0
Transfer Agent:	Continental Stock Transfer &	**Discount (div.):**	0
	Trust	**Auto invest:**	Yes
Agent's Address:	2 Broadway, 19th Floor	**Auto invest fee:**	$0
	New York, NY 10004	**Selling info:**	Sells irregularly, by n/a,
Agent's Phone:	212-509-4000		at market, for comm.
Other than USA:	Yes		

Company:	**International Business Machines**	**Safekeeping:**	Yes
		Invests:	Every 7 days beginning varies
Symbol:	IBM	**Minimum:**	$50
Exchange:	NYSE	**Maximum:**	$250,000/year
Industry:	Mfr. of bus. machines and	**Min to qualify:**	1
	info.tech.	**Fee on cash inv.:**	$5
Company Address:	New Orchard Rd.	**Fee on div. inv.:**	2% to $3
	Armonk, NY 10504	**Discount (cash):**	0
Company Phone:	914-499-5305 or 914-499-1900	**Discount (div.):**	0
Transfer Agent:	FCT (EquiServe)	**Auto invest:**	Yes
Agent's Address:	P.O. Box 2530, Mail Ste. 4688	**Auto invest fee:**	$1
	Jersey City, NJ 07303-2530	**Selling info:**	Sells daily, by mail or phone, at
Agent's Phone:	888-421-8860 or 888-IBM-6700		market, for $15 +10¢/sh.
Other than USA:	Yes		

Company:	**International Flavors & Fragrances**	**Safekeeping:**	Yes
		Invests:	Every 30 days beginning 1/1
Symbol:	IFF	**Minimum:**	$25
Exchange:	NYSE	**Maximum:**	$5,000/month
Industry:	Specialty chemicals	**Min to qualify:**	1
Company Address:	521 West 57th St.	**Fee on cash inv.:**	0!
	New York, NY 10019-2960	**Fee on div. inv.:**	0!
Company Phone:	212-765-5500	**Discount (cash):**	0
Transfer Agent:	Bank of New York	**Discount (div.):**	0
Agent's Address:	Church St. Station-P.O. Box 11258	**Auto invest:**	No
	New York, NY 10286	**Auto invest fee:**	$0
Agent's Phone:	800-524-4458	**Selling info:**	Sells weekly, by phone or mail, at
Other than USA:	Yes		market, for $0

Company:	**International Multifoods Corp.**	**Safekeeping:**	Yes
		Invests:	Every 30 days beginning 1/15
Symbol:	IMC	**Minimum:**	$10
Exchange:	NYSE	**Maximum:**	$60,000/year
Industry:	Food processing	**Min to qualify:**	1
Company Address:	200 East Lake St.	**Fee on cash inv.:**	0!
	Wayzata, MN 55391-1662	**Fee on div. inv.:**	0!
Company Phone:	612-594-3300 or 612-594-3385	**Discount (cash):**	0
Transfer Agent:	Norwest Bank Minnesota	**Discount (div.):**	0
Agent's Address:	161 N. Concord Ex., Box 738	**Auto invest:**	No
	South St. Paul, MN 55075-0738	**Auto invest fee:**	$0
Agent's Phone:	800-468-9716	**Selling info:**	Sells daily, by mail, at market, for
Other than USA:	No		$3 +15¢/sh.

Company:	**International Paper**	Safekeeping:	Yes
Symbol:	IP	Invests:	Every 7 days beginning varies
Exchange:	NYSE	Minimum:	$50
Industry:	Forest products	Maximum:	$20,000/year
Company Address:	2 Manhattanville Rd.	Min to qualify:	1
	Purchase, NY 10577	Fee on cash inv.:	0!
Company Phone:	914-397-1625 or 914-397-1500	Fee on div. inv.:	0!
Transfer Agent:	ChaseMellon Shareholder Services	Discount (cash):	0
Agent's Address:	P.O. Box 3338	Discount (div.):	0
	South Hackensack, NJ 07606-1938	Auto invest:	Yes
Agent's Phone:	800-678-8715	Auto invest fee:	$0
Other than USA:	Yes	Selling info:	Sells within 4 bus. days, by mail or phone, at avg. price, for $15 +12¢/sh.

Company:	**Interpublic Group of Companies**	Safekeeping:	Yes
		Invests:	Every 90 days beginning 3/15
Symbol:	IPG	Minimum:	$10
Exchange:	NYSE	Maximum:	$3,000/quarter
Industry:	Advertising	Min to qualify:	1
Company Address:	1271 Ave. of the Americas	Fee on cash inv.:	5% to $2.50
	New York, NY 10020	Fee on div. inv.:	5% to $2.50
Company Phone:	212-399-8000	Discount (cash):	0
Transfer Agent:	FCT (EquiServe)	Discount (div.):	0
Agent's Address:	P.O. Box 2500	Auto invest:	No
	Jersey City, NJ 07303-2500	Auto invest fee:	$0
Agent's Phone:	201-324-0498	Selling info:	Sells daily, by mail or fax, at market, for $10 +12¢/sh.
Other than USA:	No		

Company:	**Interstate Bakeries Corp.**	Safekeeping:	Yes
Symbol:	IBC	Invests:	Every 30 days beginning 1/30
Exchange:	NYSE	Minimum:	$50
Industry:	Food & beverage	Maximum:	$3,000/quarter
Company Address:	12 East Armour Blvd., Box 419627	Min to qualify:	1
	Kansas City, MO 64111	Fee on cash inv.:	0!
Company Phone:	816-502-4000	Fee on div. inv.:	0!
Transfer Agent:	UMB Bank, N.A.	Discount (cash):	0
Agent's Address:	P.O. Box 410064	Discount (div.):	0
	Kansas City, MO 64141-0064	Auto invest:	No
Agent's Phone:	816-860-7761	Auto invest fee:	$0
Other than USA:	Yes	Selling info:	Sells daily, by mail, at market, for $2 +10¢ to 12¢/sh.

Company:	**Invacare**	Safekeeping:	Yes
Symbol:	IVCR	Invests:	Every 30 days beginning 1/15
Exchange:	OTC	Minimum:	$10
Industry:	Home health care medical equip.	Maximum:	$5,000/month
Company Address:	Box 4028	Min to qualify:	1
	Elyria, OH 44036-2125	Fee on cash inv.:	0!
Company Phone:	800-333-6900 or 440-329-6001	Fee on div. inv.:	0!
Transfer Agent:	National City Bank	Discount (cash):	0
Agent's Address:	P.O. Box 92301	Discount (div.):	0
	Cleveland, OH 44193-0900	Auto invest:	No
Agent's Phone:	800-622-6757	Auto invest fee:	$0
Other than USA:	Yes	Selling info:	Sells weekly, by mail or fax, at market, for comm.

Company:	**Investors Financial Services Corp.**
Symbol:	IFIN
Exchange:	OTC
Industry:	Financial
Company Address:	200 Clarendon St., Box 9130
	Boston, MA 02117
Company Phone:	617-330-6700
Transfer Agent:	FCT (EquiServe)
Agent's Address:	P.O. Box 2598
	Jersey City, NJ 07303-2598
Agent's Phone:	201-324-0313
Other than USA:	Yes

Safekeeping:	Yes
Invests:	Every 7 days beginning Tuesday
Minimum:	$100
Maximum:	$unlimited
Min to qualify:	1
Fee on cash inv.:	$5 + 10¢/sh.
Fee on div. inv.:	0
Discount (cash):	0
Discount (div.):	0
Auto invest:	Yes
Auto invest fee:	$2 + 10¢/sh.
Selling info:	Sells daily, by mail or phone, at market, for $15 +12¢/sh.

Company:	**IPALCO Enterprises Inc.**
Symbol:	IPL
Exchange:	NYSE
Industry:	Utility-electric
Company Address:	Box 798
	Indianapolis, IN 46206-0798
Company Phone:	800-877-0153 or 317-261-8394
Transfer Agent:	IPALCO Enterprises Inc. Shareholder services
Agent's Address:	Shareholder Services,Box 798
	Indianapolis, IN 46206
Agent's Phone:	800-877-0153 or 317-261-8394
Other than USA:	Yes

Safekeeping:	Yes
Invests:	Every 15 days beginning 1/1
Minimum:	$25
Maximum:	$100,000/year
Min to qualify:	1
Fee on cash inv.:	6¢/sh.
Fee on div. inv.:	6¢/sh.
Discount (cash):	0
Discount (div.):	0
Auto invest:	Yes
Auto invest fee:	$0
Selling info:	Sells weekly, by fax, at avg. price, for 6¢/sh.

Company:	**IPSCO, Inc.**
Symbol:	IPS
Exchange:	NYSE
Industry:	Manufacturing of steel products
Company Address:	Box 1670, Regina
	Saskatchewan, S4P 3C7 Canada
Company Phone:	306-924-7700
Transfer Agent:	Montreal Trust Company
Agent's Address:	DRP Services, 660,
	1783 Hamilton St.
	Regina, Saskatchewan, Canada
	S4P 2B6
Agent's Phone:	888-334-3305
Other than USA:	Yes

Safekeeping:	Yes
Invests:	Every 90 days beginning 3/30
Minimum:	$0
Maximum:	$5,000/quarter Cdn.
Min to qualify:	1
Fee on cash inv.:	0!
Fee on div. inv.:	0!
Discount (cash):	0
Discount (div.):	0
Auto invest:	No
Auto invest fee:	$0
Selling info:	Not available

Company:	**Irish Investment Fund**
Symbol:	IRL
Exchange:	NYSE
Industry:	Closed-end fund
Company Address:	c/o Amer.Stk., 40 Wall St., 46th fl.
	New York, NY 10005
Company Phone:	800-937-5449
Transfer Agent:	American Stock Transfer
Agent's Address:	40 Wall St.
	New York, NY 10005
Agent's Phone:	800-937-5449
Other than USA:	No

Safekeeping:	No
Invests:	Every 365 days beginning 1/15
Minimum:	$100
Maximum:	$3,000/year
Min to qualify:	1
Fee on cash inv.:	comm.
Fee on div. inv.:	comm.
Discount (cash):	0
Discount (div.):	0
Auto invest:	No
Auto invest fee:	$0
Selling info:	Not available

Company:	**Iroquois Bancorp**	**Safekeeping:**	Yes
Symbol:	IROQ	**Invests:**	Every 30 days beginning 1/1
Exchange:	OTC	**Minimum:**	$25
Industry:	Banking	**Maximum:**	$3,000/quarter
Company Address:	115 Genesee St.	**Min to qualify:**	1
	Auburn, NY 13021	**Fee on cash inv.:**	0!
Company Phone:	315-252-9521	**Fee on div. inv.:**	0!
Transfer Agent:	American Stock Transfer	**Discount (cash):**	0
Agent's Address:	40 Wall Street	**Discount (div.):**	0
	New York, NY 10005	**Auto invest:**	No
Agent's Phone:	800-937-5449 or 718-921-8200	**Auto invest fee:**	$0
Other than USA:	No	**Selling info:**	Sells weekly, by mail or fax, at market, for 4¢/sh.

Company:	**IRSA Inversiones y Representaciones S.A.**	**Safekeeping:**	Yes
		Invests:	Every 7 days beginning varies
Symbol:	IRS	**Minimum:**	$50
Exchange:	NYSE	**Maximum:**	$250,000/year
Industry:	Real estate operations	**Min to qualify:**	1
Company Address:	c/o BNY,101 Barclay St.,22 West	**Fee on cash inv.:**	$5 + 10¢/sh.
	New York, NY 10286	**Fee on div. inv.:**	5% to $5 + 10¢/sh.
Company Phone:	800-943-9715	**Discount (cash):**	0
Transfer Agent:	Bank of New York	**Discount (div.):**	0
Agent's Address:	P.O. Box 11258	**Auto invest:**	Yes
	New York, NY 10286	**Auto invest fee:**	$5 + 10¢/sh.
Agent's Phone:	888-269-2377	**Selling info:**	Sells weekly, by mail, at market, for $5 +10¢/sh.
Other than USA:	Yes		

Company:	**Irvine Apartment Communities, Inc.**	**Safekeeping:**	Yes
		Invests:	Every 90 days beginning 2/29
Symbol:	IAC	**Minimum:**	$100
Exchange:	NYSE	**Maximum:**	$30,000/quarter
Industry:	REIT	**Min to qualify:**	1
Company Address:	550 Newport Ctr. Dr., #300	**Fee on cash inv.:**	0
	Newport Beach, CA 92660-7011	**Fee on div. inv.:**	0
Company Phone:	949-720-5558 or 949-720-5500	**Discount (cash):**	0
Transfer Agent:	Boston Eq. (EquiServe)	**Discount (div.):**	2%
Agent's Address:	P.O. Box 8040	**Auto invest:**	No
	Boston, MA 02266-8040	**Auto invest fee:**	$0
Agent's Phone:	800-733-5001	**Selling info:**	Sells weekly, by mail, at avg. price, for $10 + comm.
Other than USA:	Yes		

Company:	**Island Telecom Inc.**	**Safekeeping:**	No
Symbol:	IT	**Invests:**	Every 90 days beginning 3/16
Exchange:	TSE	**Minimum:**	$0
Industry:	Telecommunications	**Maximum:**	$5,000/quarter Cdn.
Company Address:	69 Belvedere Ave., Box 820	**Min to qualify:**	1
	Charlottetown, PEI C1A 7M1	**Fee on cash inv.:**	0!
Company Phone:	800-565-7168	**Fee on div. inv.:**	0!
Transfer Agent:	CIBC Mellon Trust	**Discount (cash):**	0
Agent's Address:	1660 Hollis St., 4th Fl.	**Discount (div.):**	0
	Halifax, NS B3J 1V7 Canada	**Auto invest:**	No
Agent's Phone:	800-566-2188	**Auto invest fee:**	$0
Other than USA:	Yes	**Selling info:**	Not available

Company:	**Ispat International N.V.**	**Safekeeping:**	Yes
Symbol:	IST	**Invests:**	Every 7 days beginning varies
Exchange:	NYSE	**Minimum:**	$50
Industry:	Steel	**Maximum:**	$250,000/year
Company Address:	c/o BNY,101 Barclay St.,22 West	**Min to qualify:**	1
	New York, NY 10286	**Fee on cash inv.:**	$5 + 10¢/sh.
Company Phone:	800-943-9715	**Fee on div. inv.:**	0
Transfer Agent:	Bank of New York	**Discount (cash):**	0
Agent's Address:	P.O. Box 11258	**Discount (div.):**	0
	New York, NY 10286	**Auto invest:**	Yes
Agent's Phone:	888-269-2377	**Auto invest fee:**	$5 + 10¢/sh.
Other than USA:	Yes	**Selling info:**	Sells weekly, by mail, at market, for $5 +10¢/sh.

Company:	**Israel Land Dev. Corp. Ltd.**	**Safekeeping:**	Yes
Symbol:	ILDCY	**Invests:**	Every 7 days beginning varies
Exchange:	OTC	**Minimum:**	$50
Industry:	Real estate	**Maximum:**	$250,000/year
Company Address:	c/o BNY,101 Barclay St.,22 West	**Min to qualify:**	1
	New York, NY 10286	**Fee on cash inv.:**	$5 + 10¢/sh.
Company Phone:	800-943-9715	**Fee on div. inv.:**	5% to $5 + 10¢/sh.
Transfer Agent:	Bank of New York	**Discount (cash):**	0
Agent's Address:	P.O. Box 11258	**Discount (div.):**	0
	New York, NY 10286	**Auto invest:**	Yes
Agent's Phone:	888-269-2377	**Auto invest fee:**	$5 + 10¢/sh.
Other than USA:	Yes	**Selling info:**	Sells weekly, by mail, at market, for $5 +10¢/sh.

Company:	**Istituto Mobilare Italiano SpA**	**Safekeeping:**	Yes
		Invests:	Every 7 days beginning varies
Symbol:	IMI	**Minimum:**	$50
Exchange:	NYSE	**Maximum:**	$100,000/year
Industry:	Financial services	**Min to qualify:**	1
Company Address:	c/o Morgan Guaranty Trust,	**Fee on cash inv.:**	$5 + 12¢/sh.
	Box 9073	**Fee on div. inv.:**	5% to $2.50
	Boston, MA 02205-9948	**Discount (cash):**	0
Company Phone:	800-428-4237	**Discount (div.):**	0
Transfer Agent:	Morgan Guaranty Trust Co.	**Auto invest:**	Yes
Agent's Address:	P.O. Box 9073	**Auto invest fee:**	$5
	Boston, MA 02205-9948	**Selling info:**	Sells daily, by phone or mail, at avg. price, for $5 +12¢/sh.
Agent's Phone:	800-428-4237		
Other than USA:	No		

Company:	**Istituto Nationale Delle Assicurazioni, SpA**	**Safekeeping:**	Yes
		Invests:	Every 7 days beginning varies
Symbol:	INZ	**Minimum:**	$50
Exchange:	NYSE	**Maximum:**	$250,000/year
Industry:	Insurance	**Min to qualify:**	1
Company Address:	c/o BNY,101 Barclay St.,22 West	**Fee on cash inv.:**	$5 + 10¢/sh.
	New York, NY 10286	**Fee on div. inv.:**	5% to $5 + 10¢/sh.
Company Phone:	800-943-9715	**Discount (cash):**	0
Transfer Agent:	Bank of New York	**Discount (div.):**	0
Agent's Address:	P.O. Box 11258	**Auto invest:**	Yes
	New York, NY 10286	**Auto invest fee:**	$5 + 10¢/sh.
Agent's Phone:	888-269-2377	**Selling info:**	Sells weekly, by mail, at market, for $5 +10¢/sh.
Other than USA:	Yes		

Company:	**Italy Fund Inc. (The)**	**Safekeeping:**	No
Symbol:	ITA	**Invests:**	Every 180 days beginning 2/15
Exchange:	NYSE	**Minimum:**	$100
Industry:	Closed-end fund	**Maximum:**	$3,000/semiannually
Company Address:	c/o SSBC Fund Mgmnt.,388	**Min to qualify:**	1
	Greenwich St.	**Fee on cash inv.:**	0
	New York, NY 10013	**Fee on div. inv.:**	0
Company Phone:	212-816-6082	**Discount (cash):**	0
Transfer Agent:	First Data Investor Services Grp.,	**Discount (div.):**	5%
	Inc.	**Auto invest:**	No
Agent's Address:	150 Royal St.	**Auto invest fee:**	$0
	Canton, MA 02021	**Selling info:**	Sells daily, by mail, at market, for
Agent's Phone:	800-331-1710		$5
Other than USA:	Yes		

Company:	**ITT Industries**	**Safekeeping:**	Yes
Symbol:	IIN	**Invests:**	Every 7 days beginning varies
Exchange:	NYSE	**Minimum:**	$50
Industry:	Diversified	**Maximum:**	$10,000/investment
Company Address:	4 West Red Oak Lane	**Min to qualify:**	1
	White Plains, NY 10604	**Fee on cash inv.:**	0!
Company Phone:	914-641-2000 or 914-641-2033	**Fee on div. inv.:**	0!
Transfer Agent:	Bank of New York	**Discount (cash):**	0
Agent's Address:	P.O. Box 11258, Church St. Station	**Discount (div.):**	0
	New York, NY 10286-1258	**Auto invest:**	Yes
Agent's Phone:	800-254-2823	**Auto invest fee:**	$0
Other than USA:	Yes	**Selling info:**	Sells weekly, by mail, at market,
			for $5 +10¢/sh.

Company:	**Jacobson Stores Inc.**	**Safekeeping:**	Yes
Symbol:	JCBS	**Invests:**	Every 30 days beginning 1/10
Exchange:	OTC	**Minimum:**	$10
Industry:	Retail stores	**Maximum:**	$1,000/month
Company Address:	3333 Sargent Rd.	**Min to qualify:**	1
	Jackson, MI 49201-8847	**Fee on cash inv.:**	0!
Company Phone:	517-764-6400	**Fee on div. inv.:**	0
Transfer Agent:	Norwest Bank Minnesota	**Discount (cash):**	0
Agent's Address:	P.O. Box 738	**Discount (div.):**	0
	South St. Paul, MN 55075-0738	**Auto invest:**	No
Agent's Phone:	800-468-9716	**Auto invest fee:**	$0
Other than USA:	No	**Selling info:**	Sells daily, by phone, mail, or fax
			to bank, at market, for $5
			+15¢/sh.

Company:	**Jameson Inns, Inc.**	**Safekeeping:**	Yes
Symbol:	JAMS	**Invests:**	Every 30 days beginning 1/15
Exchange:	OTC	**Minimum:**	$100
Industry:	REIT	**Maximum:**	$5,000/quarter
Company Address:	8 Perimeter Center East, Ste.	**Min to qualify:**	1
	8050	**Fee on cash inv.:**	0!
	Atlanta, GA 30346	**Fee on div. inv.:**	0!
Company Phone:	770-901-9020	**Discount (cash):**	0
Transfer Agent:	First Union National Bank	**Discount (div.):**	5%
Agent's Address:	1525 West W.T. Harris Blvd.	**Auto invest:**	No
	Charlotte, NC 28288-1153	**Auto invest fee:**	$0
Agent's Phone:	800-829-8432	**Selling info:**	Sells bimonthly, by mail or fax, at
Other than USA:	Yes		market, for 5¢ to $5

Company:	**Jefferson-Pilot Corp.**	Safekeeping:	Yes
Symbol:	JP	Invests:	Every 30 days beginning 1/6
Exchange:	NYSE	Minimum:	$20
Industry:	Insurance holding co.	Maximum:	$2,000/month
Company Address:	100 North Greene St., Box 21008	Min to qualify:	1
	Greensboro, NC 27420	Fee on cash inv.:	0!
Company Phone:	336-691-3379 or 336-691-3283	Fee on div. inv.:	0!
Transfer Agent:	First Union National Bank	Discount (cash):	0
Agent's Address:	230 S. Tryon Street	Discount (div.):	0
	Charlotte, NC 28288-1154	Auto invest:	No
Agent's Phone:	800-829-8432	Auto invest fee:	$0
Other than USA:	Yes	Selling info:	Sells bimonthly, by mail, at market, for comm.

Company:	**Jilin Chemical Ind. Co. Ltd.**	Safekeeping:	Yes
		Invests:	Every 7 days beginning varies
Symbol:	JCC	Minimum:	$50
Exchange:	NYSE	Maximum:	$250,000/year
Industry:	Oil & gas operations	Min to qualify:	1
Company Address:	c/o BNY,101 Barclay St.,22 West	Fee on cash inv.:	$5 + 10¢/sh.
	New York, NY 10286	Fee on div. inv.:	5% to $5 + 10¢/sh.
Company Phone:	800-943-9715	Discount (cash):	0
Transfer Agent:	Bank of New York	Discount (div.):	0
Agent's Address:	P.O. Box 11258	Auto invest:	Yes
	New York, NY 10286	Auto invest fee:	$5 + 10¢/sh.
Agent's Phone:	888-269-2377	Selling info:	Sells weekly, by mail, at market, for $5 +10¢/sh.
Other than USA:	Yes		

Company:	**Johnson & Johnson**	Safekeeping:	Yes
Symbol:	JNJ	Invests:	Every 30 days beginning 1/7
Exchange:	NYSE	Minimum:	$25
Industry:	Health care & consumer products	Maximum:	$50,000/year
Company Address:	One Johnson & Johnson Plaza	Min to qualify:	1
	New Brunswick, NJ 08933	Fee on cash inv.:	0!
Company Phone:	800-950-5089 or 732-524-0400	Fee on div. inv.:	0!
Transfer Agent:	FCT (EquiServe)	Discount (cash):	0
Agent's Address:	P.O. Box 2598	Discount (div.):	0
	Jersey City, NJ 07303-2598	Auto invest:	Yes
Agent's Phone:	800-328-9033	Auto invest fee:	$1
Other than USA:	Yes	Selling info:	Sells daily, by phone, mail, or fax, at market, for $10 +12¢/sh.

Company:	**Johnson Controls**	Safekeeping:	Yes
Symbol:	JCI	Invests:	Every 30 days beginning last bus. day
Exchange:	NYSE	Minimum:	$50
Industry:	Elec.equip., batteries, auto seats, interiors	Maximum:	$15,000/quarter
		Min to qualify:	1
Company Address:	5757 N. Green Bay Ave., Box 591	Fee on cash inv.:	0
	Milwaukee, WI 53201	Fee on div. inv.:	0
Company Phone:	800-524-6220 or 414-228-1200	Discount (cash):	0
Transfer Agent:	Firstar Bank Milwaukee, NA	Discount (div.):	0
Agent's Address:	P.O. Box 3078	Auto invest:	Yes
	Milwaukee, WI 53201	Auto invest fee:	$0
Agent's Phone:	800-828-1489	Selling info:	Sells biweekly, by mail or fax, at market, for 5¢ to 8¢/sh.
Other than USA:	Yes		

Company:	**Jostens**	**Safekeeping:**	Yes
Symbol:	JOS	**Invests:**	Every 30 days beginning 1/1
Exchange:	NYSE	**Minimum:**	$25
Industry:	School rings, yearbooks, award products	**Maximum:**	$1,000/month
		Min to qualify:	1
Company Address:	5501 Norman Ctr. Dr.	**Fee on cash inv.:**	0!
	Minneapolis, MN 55437	**Fee on div. inv.:**	0!
Company Phone:	612-830-3300	**Discount (cash):**	0
Transfer Agent:	Norwest Bank Minnesota	**Discount (div.):**	0
Agent's Address:	P.O. Box 64854	**Auto invest:**	No
	St. Paul, MN 55164-0854	**Auto invest fee:**	$0
Agent's Phone:	800-468-9716	**Selling info:**	Sells daily, by mail, at market, for
Other than USA:	Yes		$3 +15¢/sh.

Company:	**Justin Ind., Inc.**	**Safekeeping:**	Yes
Symbol:	JSTN	**Invests:**	Every daily days beginning varies
Exchange:	OTC	**Minimum:**	$25
Industry:	Bricks, tile, & footwear	**Maximum:**	$100,000/year
Company Address:	2821 West 7th St., Box 425	**Min to qualify:**	1
	Fort Worth, TX 76101	**Fee on cash inv.:**	10¢/sh.
Company Phone:	817-336-5125 or 817-390-2446	**Fee on div. inv.:**	10¢/sh.
Transfer Agent:	Bank of New York	**Discount (cash):**	0
Agent's Address:	Box 11258, Church St. Station-11E	**Discount (div.):**	0
	New York, NY 10286	**Auto invest:**	Yes
Agent's Phone:	800-524-4458	**Auto invest fee:**	$0
Other than USA:	Yes	**Selling info:**	Sells irregularly, by mail,
			at market, for 10¢/sh.

Company:	**Kaman Corp. A**	**Safekeeping:**	Yes
Symbol:	KAMNA	**Invests:**	Every 30 days beginning 1/15
Exchange:	OTC	**Minimum:**	$50
Industry:	Diversified mfr.	**Maximum:**	$60,000/year
Company Address:	1332 Blue Hills Ave., Box 1	**Min to qualify:**	10
	Bloomfield, CT 06002	**Fee on cash inv.:**	$5 + 12¢/sh.
Company Phone:	203-243-6307	**Fee on div. inv.:**	0!
Transfer Agent:	ChaseMellon Shareholder Services	**Discount (cash):**	0
		Discount (div.):	0
Agent's Address:	P.O. Box 590	**Auto invest:**	Yes
	Ridgefield Park, NJ 07660	**Auto invest fee:**	$3 +12¢/sh.
Agent's Phone:	800-227-0291	**Selling info:**	Sells weekly, by mail or phone, at
Other than USA:	Yes		market, for $15 +12¢/sh.

Company:	**Kansas City Southern Ind., Inc.**	**Safekeeping:**	Yes
		Invests:	Every 30 days beginning 1/18
Symbol:	KSU	**Minimum:**	$50
Exchange:	NYSE	**Maximum:**	$5,000/quarter
Industry:	Railroad financial serv., mutual funds	**Min to qualify:**	1
		Fee on cash inv.:	0
Company Address:	114 West 11th St.	**Fee on div. inv.:**	0
	Kansas City, MO 64105-1804	**Discount (cash):**	0
Company Phone:	816-983-1303	**Discount (div.):**	0
Transfer Agent:	UMB Bank, N.A.	**Auto invest:**	No
Agent's Address:	P.O. Box 410064	**Auto invest fee:**	$0
	Kansas City, MO 64141	**Selling info:**	Sells weekly, by mail, at market,
Agent's Phone:	816-860-7787		for $5 +12¢ to 25¢/sh.
Other than USA:	Yes		

Company:	**Keithley Instruments**	Safekeeping:	Yes
Symbol:	KEI	Invests:	Every 30 days beginning 1/31
Exchange:	NYSE	Minimum:	$10
Industry:	Maker of electronic instrumenta-	Maximum:	$4,000/month
	tion test and measurement	Min to qualify:	1
Company Address:	28775 Aurora Rd.	Fee on cash inv.:	0
	Cleveland, OH 44139	Fee on div. inv.:	0
Company Phone:	440-248-0400	Discount (cash):	0
Transfer Agent:	FCT (EquiServe)	Discount (div.):	0
Agent's Address:	P.O. Box 2500	Auto invest:	Yes
	Jersey City, NJ 07303-2500	Auto invest fee:	$0
Agent's Phone:	800-446-2617	Selling info:	Sells daily, by phone or mail, at
Other than USA:	Yes		market, for comm.

Company:	**Kellogg**	Safekeeping:	Yes
Symbol:	K	Invests:	Every 30 days beginning 1/15
Exchange:	NYSE	Minimum:	$25
Industry:	Food	Maximum:	$25,000/year
Company Address:	One Kellogg Sq., Box 3599	Min to qualify:	1
	Battle Creek, MI 49016-3599	Fee on cash inv.:	0
Company Phone:	616-961-2380 or 616-961-2767	Fee on div. inv.:	0
Transfer Agent:	Harris Trust & Savings Bank	Discount (cash):	0
Agent's Address:	P.O. Box A3309	Discount (div.):	0
	Chicago, IL 60690-3504	Auto invest:	Yes
Agent's Phone:	800-323-6138	Auto invest fee:	$0
Other than USA:	Yes	Selling info:	Sells irregularly, by mail,
			at market, for 7¢/sh.

Company:	**Kellwood Co.**	Safekeeping:	Yes
Symbol:	KWD	Invests:	Every 30 days beginning 1/20
Exchange:	NYSE	Minimum:	$25
Industry:	Apparel	Maximum:	$3,000/month
Company Address:	Box 14374	Min to qualify:	1
	St. Louis, MO 63178	Fee on cash inv.:	0
Company Phone:	314-576-3350 or 314-576-3100	Fee on div. inv.:	0
Transfer Agent:	Harris Trust & Savings Bank	Discount (cash):	0
Agent's Address:	P.O. Box A3504	Discount (div.):	0
	Chicago, IL 60690-3504	Auto invest:	No
Agent's Phone:	312-360-5168	Auto invest fee:	$0
Other than USA:	No	Selling info:	Sells weekly, by mail, at market,
			for 10¢/sh.

Company:	**Kennametal, Inc.**	Safekeeping:	No
Symbol:	KMT	Invests:	Every 90 days beginning 2/25
Exchange:	NYSE	Minimum:	$25
Industry:	Metals fabricating	Maximum:	$4,000/quarter
Company Address:	Box 231, 1600 Technology Way	Min to qualify:	1
	Latrobe, PA 15650-0231	Fee on cash inv.:	0!
Company Phone:	724-539-5137 or 724-539-4617	Fee on div. inv.:	0!
Transfer Agent:	ChaseMellon Shareholder Ser-	Discount (cash):	0
	vices	Discount (div.):	5%
Agent's Address:	P.O. Box 3338	Auto invest:	No
	South Hackensack, NJ 07606-1938	Auto invest fee:	$0
Agent's Phone:	800-756-3353	Selling info:	Sells within 2 bus. days, by mail ,
Other than USA:	Yes		at market, for comm.

Company:	**Kerr-McGee**	Safekeeping:	Yes
Symbol:	KMG	Invests:	Every 30 days beginning 1/1
Exchange:	NYSE	Minimum:	$10
Industry:	Oil & gas exploring & production	Maximum:	$3,000/quarter
Company Address:	Kerr-McGee Ctr., Box 25861	Min to qualify:	1
	Oklahoma City, OK 73125	Fee on cash inv.:	0!
Company Phone:	800-786-2556 or 405-270-3561	Fee on div. inv.:	0!
Transfer Agent:	UMB Bank, N.A.-Securities	Discount (cash):	0
	Transfer Division	Discount (div.):	0
Agent's Address:	P.O. Box 410064	Auto invest:	No
	Kansas City, MO 64141-0064	Auto invest fee:	$0
Agent's Phone:	877-860-5820	Selling info:	Sells weekly, by mail, at market,
Other than USA:	Yes		for $0

Company:	**KeyCorp**	Safekeeping:	Yes
Symbol:	KEY	Invests:	Every 30 days beginning 1/15
Exchange:	NYSE	Minimum:	$10
Industry:	Banking, financial services	Maximum:	$10,000/month
Company Address:	127 Public Sq., OH 01-27-1113	Min to qualify:	1
	Cleveland, OH 44114-1306	Fee on cash inv.:	0
Company Phone:	216-689-4221 or 216-689-3196	Fee on div. inv.:	0
Transfer Agent:	Harris Trust & Savings Bank	Discount (cash):	0
Agent's Address:	311 W. Monroe St., P.O. Box A3504	Discount (div.):	0
	Chicago, IL 60690-3504	Auto invest:	No
Agent's Phone:	800-539-7216	Auto invest fee:	$0
Other than USA:	Yes	Selling info:	Sells irregularly, by mail,
			at market, for $10 + comm.

Company:	**Keyspan Energy**	Safekeeping:	Yes
Symbol:	KSE	Invests:	Every 7 days beginning Thurs.
Exchange:	NYSE	Minimum:	$25
Industry:	Utility-gas	Maximum:	$150,000/year
Company Address:	One MetroTech Ctr.	Min to qualify:	1
	Brooklyn, NY 11201-3850	Fee on cash inv.:	0!
Company Phone:	718-403-3196	Fee on div. inv.:	0!
Transfer Agent:	Bank of New York	Discount (cash):	0
Agent's Address:	P.O. Box 11258	Discount (div.):	0
	New York, NY 10286-1258	Auto invest:	Yes
Agent's Phone:	800-482-3638	Auto invest fee:	$0
Other than USA:	Yes	Selling info:	Sells daily, by phone or mail, at
			market, for $5 + 5¢/sh.

Company:	**Keystone Financial, Inc.**	Safekeeping:	Yes
Symbol:	KSTN	Invests:	Every 90 days beginning 1/20
Exchange:	OTC	Minimum:	$100
Industry:	Banking	Maximum:	$5,000/quarter
Company Address:	Box 708	Min to qualify:	1
	Altoona, PA 16603	Fee on cash inv.:	0
Company Phone:	814-946-6691 or 717-233-1555	Fee on div. inv.:	0
Transfer Agent:	American Stock Transfer	Discount (cash):	0
Agent's Address:	40 Wall Street	Discount (div.):	0
	New York, NY 10005	Auto invest:	No
Agent's Phone:	718-921-8200	Auto invest fee:	$0
Other than USA:	Yes	Selling info:	Sells weekly, by mail or fax, at
			market, for $1 + comm.

Company:	**Kimberly-Clark Corp.**	Safekeeping:	Yes
Symbol:	KMB	Invests:	Every 45 days beginning 1/1
Exchange:	NYSE	Minimum:	$25
Industry:	Paper, newsprint, & consumer products	Maximum:	$3,000/quarter
		Min to qualify:	1
Company Address:	Box 619100	Fee on cash inv.:	0!
	Dallas, TX 75261-9100	Fee on div. inv.:	0!
Company Phone:	800-639-1352 or 972-281-1478	Discount (cash):	0
Transfer Agent:	BankBoston (EquiServe)	Discount (div.):	0
Agent's Address:	P.O. Box 8040	Auto invest:	No
	Boston, MA 02266	Auto invest fee:	$0
Agent's Phone:	800-730-4001	Selling info:	Sells within 10 bus. days, by mail,
Other than USA:	Yes		at market, for 5% to $10 + comm.

Company:	**Kimco Realty Corp.**	Safekeeping:	No
Symbol:	KIM	Invests:	Every 30 days beginning 1/15
Exchange:	NYSE	Minimum:	$100
Industry:	REIT	Maximum:	$25,000/quarter
Company Address:	3333 New Hyde Park Rd., Ste.100	Min to qualify:	1
	New Hyde Park, NY 11042	Fee on cash inv.:	0
Company Phone:	516-869-9000	Fee on div. inv.:	0
Transfer Agent:	BankBoston (EquiServe)	Discount (cash):	0
Agent's Address:	P.O. Box 8040	Discount (div.):	0
	Boston, MA 02266-8040	Auto invest:	No
Agent's Phone:	781-575-3400	Auto invest fee:	$0
Other than USA:	Yes	Selling info:	Sells within 10 bus. days, by mail,
			at market, for $5 + comm.

Company:	**Kleinwort Benson Australian Income Fund**	Safekeeping:	No
		Invests:	Every 90 days beginning 2/15
Symbol:	KBA	Minimum:	$100
Exchange:	NYSE	Maximum:	$3,000/quarter
Industry:	Closed-end fund	Min to qualify:	1
Company Address:	Four Embarcadero Ctr., Ste.3000	Fee on cash inv.:	comm.
	San Francisco, CA 94111	Fee on div. inv.:	comm.
Company Phone:	800-237-4218	Discount (cash):	0
Transfer Agent:	Boston Eq. (EquiServe)	Discount (div.):	5%
Agent's Address:	P.O. Box 1684, Mail Stop 45-01-06	Auto invest:	No
	Boston, MA 02105-1681	Auto invest fee:	$0
Agent's Phone:	800-730-6001	Selling info:	Sells daily, by mail, at avg. price,
Other than USA:	Yes		for comm.

Company:	**Kmart Corp.**	Safekeeping:	Yes
Symbol:	KM	Invests:	Every 30 days beginning 1/10
Exchange:	NYSE	Minimum:	$25
Industry:	Retail stores	Maximum:	$100,000/year
Company Address:	3100 West Big Beaver Rd.	Min to qualify:	10
	Troy, MI 48084	Fee on cash inv.:	0!
Company Phone:	248-643-1040	Fee on div. inv.:	0!
Transfer Agent:	BankBoston (EquiServe)	Discount (cash):	0
Agent's Address:	P.O.Box 8038	Discount (div.):	0
	Boston, MA 02266-8038	Auto invest:	No
Agent's Phone:	800-336-6981	Auto invest fee:	$0
Other than USA:	No	Selling info:	Sells irregularly, by mail, at avg.
			price, for $10 + 5¢/sh.

Company:	**KN Energy, Inc.**	Safekeeping:	Yes
Symbol:	KNE	Invests:	Every 7 days beginning varies
Exchange:	NYSE	Minimum:	$25
Industry:	Oil & gas, & gas distrib.	Maximum:	$8,000/quarter
Company Address:	370 Van Gorden St., Box 281304	Min to qualify:	1
	Lakewood, CO 80228-8304	Fee on cash inv.:	0!
Company Phone:	303-763-3618	Fee on div. inv.:	0!
Transfer Agent:	FCT (EquiServe)	Discount (cash):	0
Agent's Address:	P.O. Box 2500	Discount (div.):	0
	Jersey City, NJ 07303-2500	Auto invest:	Yes
Agent's Phone:	800-847-4351	Auto invest fee:	$0
Other than USA:	Yes	Selling info:	Sells weekly, by mail, at market, for $0

Company:	**Knape & Vogt Manufacturing Co.**	Safekeeping:	No
		Invests:	Every 30 days beginning 1/1
Symbol:	KNAP	Minimum:	$25
Exchange:	OTC	Maximum:	$1,000/month
Industry:	Manufacturing	Min to qualify:	1
Company Address:	2700 Oak Industrial Dr., NE	Fee on cash inv.:	0!
	Grand Rapids, MI 49505	Fee on div. inv.:	0!
Company Phone:	800-253-1561 or 616-459-3311	Discount (cash):	0
Transfer Agent:	Harris Trust & Savings Bank	Discount (div.):	0
Agent's Address:	P.O. Box A-3309	Auto invest:	No
	Chicago, IL 60690	Auto invest fee:	$0
Agent's Phone:	312-360-5341	Selling info:	Sells within 10 bus. days, by mail, at market, for $0
Other than USA:	Yes		

Company:	**Knight Ridder Inc.**	Safekeeping:	Yes
Symbol:	KRI	Invests:	Every 7 days beginning Mondays
Exchange:	NYSE	Minimum:	$25
Industry:	Newspaper publisher	Maximum:	$10,000/month
Company Address:	One Herald Plaza	Min to qualify:	50
	Miami, FL 33132-1693	Fee on cash inv.:	0
Company Phone:	305-376-3800 or 305-376-3938	Fee on div. inv.:	0
Transfer Agent:	ChaseMellon Shareholder Services	Discount (cash):	0
Agent's Address:	P.O. Box 3338	Discount (div.):	0
	South Hackensack, NJ 07606	Auto invest:	No
Agent's Phone:	800-758-4672	Auto invest fee:	$0
Other than USA:	Yes	Selling info:	Sells biweekly, by mail or phone, at market, for $15 +10¢/sh.

Company:	**Kollmorgen Corp.**	Safekeeping:	Yes
Symbol:	KOL	Invests:	Every 30 days beginning 1/30
Exchange:	NYSE	Minimum:	$25
Industry:	Mfr. of motion control products	Maximum:	$1,000/month
Company Address:	1601 Trapelo Rd.	Min to qualify:	1
	Waltham, MA 02154	Fee on cash inv.:	0
Company Phone:	781-890-5655	Fee on div. inv.:	0
Transfer Agent:	Boston Eq. (EquiServe)	Discount (cash):	0
Agent's Address:	P.O. Box 8040, MS 45-02-64	Discount (div.):	0
	Boston, MA 02266-8040	Auto invest:	No
Agent's Phone:	800-730-4001	Auto invest fee:	$0
Other than USA:	No	Selling info:	Sells within 10 bus. days, by mail, at market, for 5% to $5 + comm.

Company:	**Koor Industries Ltd.**	Safekeeping:	Yes
Symbol:	KOR	Invests:	Every 7 days beginning 1/2
Exchange:	NYSE	Minimum:	$200
Industry:	Conglomerates	Maximum:	$250,000/year
Company Address:	c/o BNY,101 Barclay St.,22 West	Min to qualify:	1
	New York, NY 10286	Fee on cash inv.:	$5 + 10¢/sh.
Company Phone:	800-943-9715	Fee on div. inv.:	5% to $5 + 10¢/sh.
Transfer Agent:	Bank of New York	Discount (cash):	0
Agent's Address:	P.O. Box 11258	Discount (div.):	0
	New York, NY 10286	Auto invest:	Yes
Agent's Phone:	888-269-2377	Auto invest fee:	$5 + 10¢/sh.
Other than USA:		Selling info:	Sells weekly, by mail, at market, for $5 +10¢/sh.

Company:	**Korea Electric Power Corp.**	Safekeeping:	Yes
		Invests:	Every 7 days beginning varies
Symbol:	KEP	Minimum:	$50
Exchange:	NYSE	Maximum:	$250,000/year
Industry:	Electric utilities	Min to qualify:	1
Company Address:	c/o BNY,101 Barclay St.,22 West	Fee on cash inv.:	$5 + 10¢/sh.
	New York, NY 10286	Fee on div. inv.:	5% to $5 + 10¢/sh.
Company Phone:	800-943-9715	Discount (cash):	0
Transfer Agent:	Bank of New York	Discount (div.):	0
Agent's Address:	P.O. Box 11258	Auto invest:	Yes
	New York, NY 10286	Auto invest fee:	$5 + 10¢/sh.
Agent's Phone:	888-269-2377	Selling info:	Sells weekly, by mail, at market, for $5 +10¢/sh.
Other than USA:	Yes		

Company:	**Korea Fund, Inc. (The)**	Safekeeping:	No
Symbol:	KF	Invests:	Every 180 days beginning 2/15
Exchange:	NYSE	Minimum:	$100
Industry:	Closed-end fund	Maximum:	$3,000/semiannually
Company Address:	345 Park Ave.	Min to qualify:	1
	New York, NY 10154	Fee on cash inv.:	75¢ + comm.
Company Phone:	800-349-4281	Fee on div. inv.:	0
Transfer Agent:	Boston Eq. (EquiServe)	Discount (cash):	0
Agent's Address:	P.O. Box 8200	Discount (div.):	0·5%
	Boston, MA 02266-8200	Auto invest:	No
Agent's Phone:	800-426-5523	Auto invest fee:	$0
Other than USA:	Yes	Selling info:	Sells 7 to10 bus. days , by mail or phone, at avg. price, for $2.50 + comm.

Company:	**Kranzco Realty Trust**	Safekeeping:	Yes
Symbol:	KRT	Invests:	Every 30 days beginning 1/10
Exchange:	NYSE	Minimum:	$100
Industry:	REIT	Maximum:	$5,000/quarter
Company Address:	128 Fayette St.	Min to qualify:	1
	Conshohocken, PA 19428-0805	Fee on cash inv.:	0!
Company Phone:	610-941-9292	Fee on div. inv.:	0!
Transfer Agent:	First Union National Bank of NC	Discount (cash):	0
Agent's Address:	1525 West W.T. Harris Blvd., 3C3	Discount (div.):	0
	Charlotte, NC 28288-1153	Auto invest:	No
Agent's Phone:	800-829-8432	Auto invest fee:	$0
Other than USA:	No	Selling info:	Sells bimonthly, by mail, at market, for 0!

Company:	**La-Z-Boy, Inc.**	Safekeeping:	No
Symbol:	LZB	Invests:	Every 30 days beginning 1/1
Exchange:	NYSE	Minimum:	$25
Industry:	Furniture manufacturer	Maximum:	$1,000/month
Company Address:	1284 North Telegraph Rd.	Min to qualify:	1
	Monroe, MI 48162-3390	Fee on cash inv.:	0!
Company Phone:	734-241-4414	Fee on div. inv.:	0!
Transfer Agent:	American Stock Transfer	Discount (cash):	0
Agent's Address:	40 Wall Street, 46th Fl.	Discount (div.):	0
	New York, NY 10005	Auto invest:	No
Agent's Phone:	212-936-5100	Auto invest fee:	$0
Other than USA:	No	Selling info:	Sells weekly, by mail, at market, for $5 + 4¢/sh.

Company:	**Lab Holdings, Inc.**	Safekeeping:	No
Symbol:	LABH	Invests:	Every 90 days beginning 3/1
Exchange:	OTC	Minimum:	$25
Industry:	Insurance, health care services	Maximum:	$5,000/quarter
Company Address:	Box 7568	Min to qualify:	1
	Shawnee Mission, KS 66207	Fee on cash inv.:	0!
Company Phone:	913-648-3600	Fee on div. inv.:	0!
Transfer Agent:	American Stock Transfer	Discount (cash):	0
Agent's Address:	40 Wall Street	Discount (div.):	0
	New York, NY 10005	Auto invest:	No
Agent's Phone:	800-937-5449 or 718-921-8200	Auto invest fee:	$0
Other than USA:	No	Selling info:	Sells weekly, by mail, at market, for 4¢/sh.

Company:	**Laclede Gas Co.**	Safekeeping:	No
Symbol:	LG	Invests:	Every 90 days beginning 1/1
Exchange:	NYSE	Minimum:	$100
Industry:	Utility-gas	Maximum:	$30,000/year
Company Address:	720 Olive St.	Min to qualify:	1
	St. Louis, MO 63101	Fee on cash inv.:	0
Company Phone:	314-342-0503 or 314-342-0500	Fee on div. inv.:	0
Transfer Agent:	UMB Bank, NA	Discount (cash):	0
Agent's Address:	P.O. Box 410064	Discount (div.):	0
	Kansas City, MO 64141-0064	Auto invest:	No
Agent's Phone:	800-884-4225	Auto invest fee:	$0
Other than USA:	Yes	Selling info:	Sells monthly, by mail or phone, at market, for comm.

Company:	**Lancaster Colony Corp.**	Safekeeping:	Yes
Symbol:	LANC	Invests:	Every 30 days beginning 1/10
Exchange:	OTC	Minimum:	$50
Industry:	Household	Maximum:	$20,000/year
Company Address:	37 West Broad St.	Min to qualify:	1
	Columbus, OH 43215-4177	Fee on cash inv.:	0!
Company Phone:	614-224-7141	Fee on div. inv.:	0!
Transfer Agent:	American Stock Transfer	Discount (cash):	0
Agent's Address:	40 Wall Street-46th Floor	Discount (div.):	0
	New York, NY 10005	Auto invest:	No
Agent's Phone:	800-937-5449	Auto invest fee:	$0
Other than USA:	Yes	Selling info:	Sells daily, by mail, at market, for 4¢/sh.

Company:	**Lance, Inc.**	Safekeeping:	Yes
Symbol:	LNCE	Invests:	Every 30 days beginning 1/15
Exchange:	OTC	Minimum:	$10
Industry:	Snack foods, vending	Maximum:	$1,000/month
Company Address:	Box 32368	Min to qualify:	1
	Charlotte, NC 28232-2368	Fee on cash inv.:	4% to $2.50
Company Phone:	704-554-1421	Fee on div. inv.:	0
Transfer Agent:	Wachovia (EquiServe)	Discount (cash):	0
Agent's Address:	P.O. Box 8217	Discount (div.):	0
	Boston, MA 02266-8217	Auto invest:	No
Agent's Phone:	800-633-4236	Auto invest fee:	$0
Other than USA:	No	Selling info:	Sells daily, by mail, at market, for 0

Company:	**Lear Corp.**	Safekeeping:	Yes
Symbol:	LEA	Invests:	Every 30 days beginning 1/25
Exchange:	NYSE	Minimum:	$50
Industry:	Automotive supplier	Maximum:	$150,000/year
Company Address:	21557 Telegraph Rd., Box 5008	Min to qualify:	1
	Southfield, MI 48086-5008	Fee on cash inv.:	$2
Company Phone:	800-413-5327 or 248-746-1500	Fee on div. inv.:	0
Transfer Agent:	Bank of New York	Discount (cash):	0
Agent's Address:	P.O. Box 11258	Discount (div.):	0
	New York, NY 10286-1258	Auto invest:	No
Agent's Phone:	800-524-4458	Auto invest fee:	$0
Other than USA:	Yes	Selling info:	Sells weekly, by mail, at market, for $5 + 7¢/sh.

Company:	**Lehman Brothers Holdings Inc.**	Safekeeping:	Yes
		Invests:	Every 7 days beginning varies
Symbol:	LEH	Minimum:	$50
Exchange:	NYSE	Maximum:	$175,000/year
Industry:	Investment banking	Min to qualify:	1
Company Address:	c/o Bank of New York, Box 11019	Fee on cash inv.:	0!
	New York, NY 10286	Fee on div. inv.:	0!
Company Phone:	212-526-7000	Discount (cash):	0
Transfer Agent:	Bank of New York	Discount (div.):	0
Agent's Address:	P.O. Box 11258, Church St. Station	Auto invest:	Yes
	New York, NY 10286-1258	Auto invest fee:	$0
Agent's Phone:	800-824-5707	Selling info:	Sells daily, by mail, at market, for $10 +10¢/sh.
Other than USA:	No		

Company:	**LESCO, Inc.**	Safekeeping:	Yes
Symbol:	LSCO	Invests:	Every 30 days beginning 1/10
Exchange:	OTC	Minimum:	$25
Industry:	Mfr. & dist. of turf grass & lawn equip.	Maximum:	$5,000/month
		Min to qualify:	1
Company Address:	20005 Lake Rd.	Fee on cash inv.:	0
	Rocky River, OH 44116	Fee on div. inv.:	0
Company Phone:	800-321-5325 or 440-333-9250	Discount (cash):	0
Transfer Agent:	National City Bank	Discount (div.):	0
Agent's Address:	P.O. Box 92301- Locator #5352	Auto invest:	No
	Cleveland, OH 44193-0900	Auto invest fee:	$0
Agent's Phone:	800-622-6757	Selling info:	Sells weekly, by mail or fax, at avg. price, for 5% to $5
Other than USA:	Yes		

Company:	**LG&E Energy Corp.**	**Safekeeping:**	Yes
Symbol:	LGE	**Invests:**	Every 30 days beginning 1/15
Exchange:	NYSE	**Minimum:**	$25
Industry:	Utility-electric, gas	**Maximum:**	$40,000/year
Company Address:	Box 32030	**Min to qualify:**	1
	Louisville, KY 40232-2030	**Fee on cash inv.:**	0!
Company Phone:	800-235-9705 or 502-627-3867	**Fee on div. inv.:**	0!
Transfer Agent:	Harris Trust & Savings Bank	**Discount (cash):**	0
Agent's Address:	P.O. Box A3504	**Discount (div.):**	0
	Chicago, IL 60690-3504	**Auto invest:**	No
Agent's Phone:	800-245-7630	**Auto invest fee:**	$0
Other than USA:	No	**Selling info:**	Sells within 10 bus. days, by mail, at avg. price, for 5¢/sh.

Company:	**Libbey Inc.**	**Safekeeping:**	Yes
Symbol:	LBY	**Invests:**	Every 7 days beginning Thursday
Exchange:	NYSE	**Minimum:**	$20
Industry:	Produces glass tableware	**Maximum:**	$5,000/investment
Company Address:	300 Madison Ave., Box 10060	**Min to qualify:**	1
	Toledo, OH 43699-0060	**Fee on cash inv.:**	7¢/sh.
Company Phone:	419-325-2100 or 419-325-2490	**Fee on div. inv.:**	7¢/sh.
Transfer Agent:	Bank of New York	**Discount (cash):**	0
Agent's Address:	P.O. Box 11258, Church St. Station	**Discount (div.):**	0
	New York, NY 10286-1258	**Auto invest:**	Yes
Agent's Phone:	800-524-4458 or 212-815-2451	**Auto invest fee:**	$0
Other than USA:	Yes	**Selling info:**	Sells weekly, by mail, at avg. price, for $5 + 7¢/sh.

Company:	**Liberty ALL-STAR Equity Fund**	**Safekeeping:**	Yes
		Invests:	Every 30 days beginning 1/15
Symbol:	USA	**Minimum:**	$0
Exchange:	NYSE	**Maximum:**	$unlimited
Industry:	Closed-end fund	**Min to qualify:**	1
Company Address:	600 Atlantic Ave.	**Fee on cash inv.:**	$1.25 + comm.
	Boston, MA 02210-2214	**Fee on div. inv.:**	comm.
Company Phone:	800-542-3863	**Discount (cash):**	0
Transfer Agent:	Boston Eq. (EquiServe)	**Discount (div.):**	0
Agent's Address:	P.O. Box 8200	**Auto invest:**	No
	Boston, MA 02266-8200	**Auto invest fee:**	$0
Agent's Phone:	800-542-3863	**Selling info:**	Sells daily, by phone or mail, at market, for $2.50 + comm.
Other than USA:	Yes		

Company:	**Liberty ALL-STAR Growth Fund, Inc.**	**Safekeeping:**	Yes
		Invests:	Every 30 days beginning 1/15
Symbol:	ASG	**Minimum:**	$100
Exchange:	NYSE	**Maximum:**	$3,000/month
Industry:	Closed-end fund	**Min to qualify:**	1
Company Address:	600 Atlantic Ave.	**Fee on cash inv.:**	$1.25 + comm.
	Boston, MA 02210-2214	**Fee on div. inv.:**	comm.
Company Phone:	800-542-3863 or 617-722-6036	**Discount (cash):**	0
Transfer Agent:	Boston Eq. (EquiServe)	**Discount (div.):**	0
Agent's Address:	P.O. Box 8200	**Auto invest:**	No
	Boston, MA 02266-8200	**Auto invest fee:**	$0
Agent's Phone:	800-542-3863	**Selling info:**	Sells daily, by mail or phone, at market, for $2.50 + comm.
Other than USA:	Yes		

Company:	**Liberty Property Trust**	Safekeeping:	Yes
Symbol:	LRY	Invests:	Every 30 days beginning 1/15
Exchange:	NYSE	Minimum:	$250
Industry:	REIT	Maximum:	$7,500/month
Company Address:	65 Valley Stream Pkwy.	Min to qualify:	10
	Malvern, PA 19355	Fee on cash inv.:	0
Company Phone:	610-648-1704 or 610-648-1700	Fee on div. inv.:	0
Transfer Agent:	Boston Eq. (EquiServe)	Discount (cash):	0
Agent's Address:	P.O. Box 8040	Discount (div.):	3%
	Boston, MA 02266	Auto invest:	Yes
Agent's Phone:	800-944-2214	Auto invest fee:	$0
Other than USA:	No	Selling info:	Sells daily, by mail, at market, for $10 + comm.

Company:	**Lihir Gold Ltd. ADS**	Safekeeping:	Yes
Symbol:	LIHRY	Invests:	Every 7 days beginning varies
Exchange:	OTC	Minimum:	$50
Industry:	Minerals & mining	Maximum:	$250,000/week
Company Address:	c/o BNY,101 Barclay St., 22 West	Min to qualify:	1
	New York, NY 10286	Fee on cash inv.:	$5 + 10¢/sh.
Company Phone:	800-943-9715	Fee on div. inv.:	5% to $5 + 10¢/sh.
Transfer Agent:	Bank of New York	Discount (cash):	0
Agent's Address:	P.O. Box 11258	Discount (div.):	0
	New York, NY 10286	Auto invest:	Yes
Agent's Phone:	888-269-2377	Auto invest fee:	$0
Other than USA:	Yes	Selling info:	Sells weekly, by phone or mail, at avg. price, for $5 +10¢/ADS

Company:	**Lilly (Eli) & Co.**	Safekeeping:	Yes
Symbol:	LLY	Invests:	Every 7 days beginning varies
Exchange:	NYSE	Minimum:	$50
Industry:	Drugs	Maximum:	$150,000/year
Company Address:	Lilly Corporate Ctr.	Min to qualify:	1
	Indianapolis, IN 46285	Fee on cash inv.:	$5 + 3¢/sh.
Company Phone:	800-833-8699	Fee on div. inv.:	$1 to $3 + 3¢/sh.
Transfer Agent:	FCT (EquiServe)	Discount (cash):	0
Agent's Address:	Box 2500	Discount (div.):	0
	Jersey City, NJ 07303-2500	Auto invest:	Yes
Agent's Phone:	800-833-8699	Auto invest fee:	$2 + 3¢/sh.
Other than USA:	Yes	Selling info:	Sells daily, by mail or phone, at market, for $10 +12¢/sh.

Company:	**Lilly Industries, Inc. A**	Safekeeping:	Yes
Symbol:	LI	Invests:	Every 30 days beginning 1/1
Exchange:	NYSE	Minimum:	$100
Industry:	Specialty chemicals	Maximum:	$5,000/month
Company Address:	733 S. West St.	Min to qualify:	1
	Indianapolis, IN 46225	Fee on cash inv.:	0!
Company Phone:	317-687-6700	Fee on div. inv.:	0!
Transfer Agent:	Harris Trust & Savings Bank	Discount (cash):	0
Agent's Address:	311 W. Monroe St., 2nd flr, Box 3309	Discount (div.):	0
	Chicago, IL 60690	Auto invest:	No
Agent's Phone:	800-942-5909	Auto invest fee:	$0
Other than USA:	Yes	Selling info:	Sells within 10 bus. days, by mail, at market, for $1 + comm.

Company:	**Limited (The)**	**Safekeeping:**	No
Symbol:	LTD	**Invests:**	Every 45 days beginning 2/5
Exchange:	NYSE	**Minimum:**	$30
Industry:	Retail stores	**Maximum:**	$6,000/quarter
Company Address:	3 Limited Pkwy.	**Min to qualify:**	1
	Columbus, OH 43216	**Fee on cash inv.:**	0!
Company Phone:	614-415-7000	**Fee on div. inv.:**	0!
Transfer Agent:	FCT (EquiServe)	**Discount (cash):**	0
Agent's Address:	P.O. Box 2500	**Discount (div.):**	0
	Jersey City, NJ 07303-2500	**Auto invest:**	No
Agent's Phone:	800-317-4445	**Auto invest fee:**	$0
Other than USA:	No	**Selling info:**	Sells daily, by mail, at market, for $10 +12¢/sh.

Company:	**Lincoln Nat'l Convert. Sec. Fund**	**Safekeeping:**	Yes
		Invests:	Every 90 days beginning 3/7
Symbol:	LNV	**Minimum:**	$100
Exchange:	NYSE	**Maximum:**	$3,000/quarter
Industry:	Closed-end fund	**Min to qualify:**	1
Company Address:	200 East Berry St.	**Fee on cash inv.:**	0!
	Fort Wayne, IN 46802	**Fee on div. inv.:**	0!
Company Phone:	219-455-2210	**Discount (cash):**	0
Transfer Agent:	FCT (Equiserve)	**Discount (div.):**	0
Agent's Address:	P.O. Box 2500	**Auto invest:**	No
	Jersey City, NJ 07303-2500	**Auto invest fee:**	$0
Agent's Phone:	800-317-4445	**Selling info:**	Sells daily, by mail, at market, for $10 +12¢/sh.
Other than USA:	Yes		

Company:	**Lincoln Nat'l Income Fund**	**Safekeeping:**	Yes
		Invests:	Every 90 days beginning 3/7
Symbol:	LND	**Minimum:**	$100
Exchange:	NYSE	**Maximum:**	$3,000/quarter
Industry:	Closed-end fund	**Min to qualify:**	1
Company Address:	200 East Berry St.	**Fee on cash inv.:**	0!
	Fort Wayne, IN 46802	**Fee on div. inv.:**	0!
Company Phone:	219-455-3142	**Discount (cash):**	0
Transfer Agent:	FCT (EquiServe)	**Discount (div.):**	0
Agent's Address:	P.O. Box 2500	**Auto invest:**	No
	Jersey City, NJ 07303-2500	**Auto invest fee:**	$0
Agent's Phone:	800-317-4445	**Selling info:**	Sells daily, by mail, at market, for $10 +12¢/sh.
Other than USA:	Yes		

Company:	**Lincoln National Corp.**	**Safekeeping:**	Yes
Symbol:	LNC	**Invests:**	Every 30 days beginning 1/1
Exchange:	NYSE	**Minimum:**	$25
Industry:	Insurance	**Maximum:**	$5,000/month
Company Address:	200 East Berry St., Box 7845	**Min to qualify:**	1
	Fort Wayne, IN 46801-7845	**Fee on cash inv.:**	0!
Company Phone:	800-237-2920 or 219-455-2697	**Fee on div. inv.:**	0!
Transfer Agent:	FCT (EquiServe)	**Discount (cash):**	0
Agent's Address:	P.O. Box 2500	**Discount (div.):**	0
	Jersey City, NJ 07303-2500	**Auto invest:**	No
Agent's Phone:	800-317-4445	**Auto invest fee:**	$0
Other than USA:	Yes	**Selling info:**	Sells within 10 bus. days, by mail, at market, for $1 + comm.

Company:	**Liz Claiborne, Inc.**	Safekeeping:	Yes
Symbol:	LIZ	Invests:	Every 30 days beginning 1/30
Exchange:	NYSE	Minimum:	$25
Industry:	Apparel	Maximum:	$60,000/year
Company Address:	One Claiborne Ave.	Min to qualify:	1
	North Bergen, NJ 07047	Fee on cash inv.:	0!
Company Phone:	201-662-6000	Fee on div. inv.:	0!
Transfer Agent:	FCT (EquiServe)	Discount (cash):	0
Agent's Address:	P.O. Box 2500	Discount (div.):	0
	Jersey City, NJ 07303	Auto invest:	No
Agent's Phone:	201-324-0313	Auto invest fee:	$0
Other than USA:	No	Selling info:	Sells daily, by mail, at market, for $10 +12¢/sh.

Company:	**LNB Bancorp, Inc.**	Safekeeping:	Yes
Symbol:	LNBB	Invests:	Every 90 days beginning 12/1
Exchange:	OTC	Minimum:	$100
Industry:	Bank holding company	Maximum:	$5,000/quarter
Company Address:	457 Broadway	Min to qualify:	1
	Lorain, OH 44052-1769	Fee on cash inv.:	0
Company Phone:	440-244-6000	Fee on div. inv.:	0
Transfer Agent:	Registrar & Transfer Company	Discount (cash):	0
Agent's Address:	10 Commerce Drive	Discount (div.):	0
	Cranford, NJ 07016-3572	Auto invest:	No
Agent's Phone:	800-368-5948	Auto invest fee:	$0
Other than USA:	No	Selling info:	Not available

Company:	**Lockheed Martin**	Safekeeping:	No
Symbol:	LMT	Invests:	Every 30 days beginning 1/31
Exchange:	NYSE	Minimum:	$50
Industry:	Aeronautics, electronics, missiles	Maximum:	$100,000/year
Company Address:	6801 Rockledge Dr.	Min to qualify:	1
	Bethesda, MD 20817-1836	Fee on cash inv.:	0
Company Phone:	301-897-6310	Fee on div. inv.:	0
Transfer Agent:	FCT (EquiServe)	Discount (cash):	0
Agent's Address:	P.O. Box 2536, Suite 4694	Discount (div.):	0
	Jersey City, NJ 07303-2536	Auto invest:	No
Agent's Phone:	800-519-3111 or 201-324-0498	Auto invest fee:	$0
Other than USA:	Yes	Selling info:	Sells irregularly, by mail, at market, for $10 +12¢/sh.

Company:	**London Int'l**	Safekeeping:	Yes
Symbol:	LONDY	Invests:	Every 7 days beginning varies
Exchange:	OTC	Minimum:	$50
Industry:	Personal care products	Maximum:	$250,000/week
Company Address:	c/o BNY,101 Barclay St., 22 West	Min to qualify:	1
	New York, NY 10286	Fee on cash inv.:	$5 + 10¢/sh.
Company Phone:	800-943-9715	Fee on div. inv.:	5% to $5 + 10¢/sh.
Transfer Agent:	Bank of New York	Discount (cash):	0
Agent's Address:	P.O. Box 11258	Discount (div.):	0
	New York, NY 10286	Auto invest:	Yes
Agent's Phone:	888-269-2377	Auto invest fee:	$0
Other than USA:	Yes	Selling info:	Sells weekly, by phone or mail, at avg. price, for $5 +10¢/ADS

Company:	**Longs Drug Stores**	Safekeeping:	Yes
Symbol:	LDG	Invests:	Every 7 days beginning varies
Exchange:	NYSE	Minimum:	$25
Industry:	Self service drug store chain	Maximum:	$5,000/quarter
Company Address:	141 North Civic Dr.	Min to qualify:	1
	Walnut Creek, CA 94596	Fee on cash inv.:	$5 + 12¢/sh.
Company Phone:	925-937-1170	Fee on div. inv.:	5% to $10
Transfer Agent:	ChaseMellon Shareholder Services	Discount (cash):	0
Agent's Address:	P.O. Box 3338	Discount (div.):	0
	South Hackensack, NJ 07606-1938	Auto invest:	Yes
Agent's Phone:	888-213-0886	Auto invest fee:	$0
Other than USA:	Yes	Selling info:	Sells weekly, by mail, at market, for $15 +12¢/sh.

Company:	**Louisiana-Pacific Corp.**	Safekeeping:	Yes
Symbol:	LPX	Invests:	Every 30 days beginning 1/31
Exchange:	NYSE	Minimum:	$25
Industry:	Lumber	Maximum:	$12,000/year
Company Address:	111 S.W. 5th Ave.	Min to qualify:	1
	Portland, OR 97204-3601	Fee on cash inv.:	0
Company Phone:	800-547-6331 or 503-221-0800	Fee on div. inv.:	0
Transfer Agent:	FCT (EquiServe)	Discount (cash):	0
Agent's Address:	P.O. Box 2598	Discount (div.):	0
	Jersey City, NJ 07303	Auto invest:	No
Agent's Phone:	201-324-1644	Auto invest fee:	$0
Other than USA:	Yes	Selling info:	Sells daily, by phone or mail, at market, for $10 +12¢/sh.

Company:	**Lowe's Companies, Inc.**	Safekeeping:	Yes
Symbol:	LOW	Invests:	Every 45 days beginning 1/1
Exchange:	NYSE	Minimum:	$10
Industry:	Retail	Maximum:	$1,000/month
Company Address:	Box 1111	Min to qualify:	1
	North Wilkesboro, NC 28656	Fee on cash inv.:	0
Company Phone:	336-658-4000 or 336-658-4022	Fee on div. inv.:	0
Transfer Agent:	Wachovia (EquiServe)	Discount (cash):	0
Agent's Address:	P.O. Box 8217	Discount (div.):	0
	Boston, MA 02266-8217	Auto invest:	No
Agent's Phone:	800-633-4236	Auto invest fee:	$0
Other than USA:	No	Selling info:	Sells irregularly, by mail, at market, for 5¢/sh.

Company:	**LSB Bancshares, Inc.**	Safekeeping:	Yes
Symbol:	LXBK	Invests:	Every 90 days beginning 1/15
Exchange:	OTC	Minimum:	$25
Industry:	Bank holding company	Maximum:	$1,000/quarter
Company Address:	One LSB Plaza, Box 867	Min to qualify:	1
	Lexington, NC 27292	Fee on cash inv.:	0
Company Phone:	336-248-6500	Fee on div. inv.:	0
Transfer Agent:	Wachovia (EquiServe)	Discount (cash):	0
Agent's Address:	P.O. Box 8217	Discount (div.):	0
	Boston, MA 02266-8217	Auto invest:	No
Agent's Phone:	800-633-4236	Auto invest fee:	$0
Other than USA:	Yes	Selling info:	Sells weekly, by mail, at market, for 5¢/sh.

Company:	**LTC Properties, Inc.**	**Safekeeping:**	Yes
Symbol:	LTC	**Invests:**	Every 30 days beginning 1/15
Exchange:	NYSE	**Minimum:**	$25
Industry:	Health care REIT	**Maximum:**	$1,000/month
Company Address:	300 Esplanade Dr., Ste.1860	**Min to qualify:**	1
	Oxnard, CA 93030	**Fee on cash inv.:**	comm.
Company Phone:	805-981-8655	**Fee on div. inv.:**	0
Transfer Agent:	Harris Trust & Savings Bank	**Discount (cash):**	0
Agent's Address:	P.O. Box A3504	**Discount (div.):**	0
	Chicago, IL 60690	**Auto invest:**	No
Agent's Phone:	312-461-3309	**Auto invest fee:**	$0
Other than USA:	Yes	**Selling info:**	Sells weekly, by mail, at market, for 8¢/sh.

Company:	**Lubrizol Corp.**	**Safekeeping:**	Yes
Symbol:	LZ	**Invests:**	Every 90 days beginning 3/9
Exchange:	NYSE	**Minimum:**	$25
Industry:	Chemicals	**Maximum:**	$5,000/quarter
Company Address:	29400 Lakeland Blvd.	**Min to qualify:**	1
	Wickliffe, OH 44092-2298	**Fee on cash inv.:**	0
Company Phone:	440-943-4200	**Fee on div. inv.:**	0
Transfer Agent:	American Stock Transfer	**Discount (cash):**	0
Agent's Address:	40 Wall Street	**Discount (div.):**	0
	New York, NY 10005	**Auto invest:**	No
Agent's Phone:	800-937-5449	**Auto invest fee:**	$0
Other than USA:	No	**Selling info:**	Sells every 2 weeks, by mail, at market, for $5 + comm.

Company:	**Luby's Inc.**	**Safekeeping:**	Yes
Symbol:	LUB	**Invests:**	Every 30 days beginning 1/1
Exchange:	NYSE	**Minimum:**	$20
Industry:	Cafeteria style restaurants	**Maximum:**	$5,000/quarter
Company Address:	2211 Northeast Loop 410,	**Min to qualify:**	1
	Box 33069	**Fee on cash inv.:**	0
	San Antonio, TX 78265-3069	**Fee on div. inv.:**	0
Company Phone:	210-871-7509 or 210-654-9000	**Discount (cash):**	0
Transfer Agent:	American Stock Transfer	**Discount (div.):**	0
Agent's Address:	40 Wall St.	**Auto invest:**	No
	New York, NY 10005	**Auto invest fee:**	$0
Agent's Phone:	800-937-5449 or 212-936-5100	**Selling info:**	Sells weekly, by mail, at market, for 4¢/sh.
Other than USA:	Yes		

Company:	**Lucent Technologies Inc.**	**Safekeeping:**	Yes
Symbol:	LU	**Invests:**	Every daily days beginning 1/1
Exchange:	NYSE	**Minimum:**	$100
Industry:	Mfr. telecommunications systems	**Maximum:**	$50,000/investment
Company Address:	600 Mountain Ave., Rm. 3D 548	**Min to qualify:**	1
	Murray Hill, NJ 07974-0636	**Fee on cash inv.:**	10% to $2 + 10¢/sh.
Company Phone:	888-LUCENT6	**Fee on div. inv.:**	10% to $2 + 10¢/sh.
Transfer Agent:	Bank of New York	**Discount (cash):**	0
Agent's Address:	P.O. Box 1362	**Discount (div.):**	0
	Newark, NJ 07101-1632	**Auto invest:**	Yes
Agent's Phone:	888-582-3686	**Auto invest fee:**	$0
Other than USA:	Yes	**Selling info:**	Sells daily, by mail or phone, at market, for $10 + 10¢/sh.

Company:	**Luxottica Grp. ADS**
Symbol:	LUX
Exchange:	NYSE
Industry:	Eyeware
Company Address:	c/o BNY,101 Barclay St., 22 West New York, NY 10286
Company Phone:	800-943-9715
Transfer Agent:	Bank of New York
Agent's Address:	P.O. Box 11258 New York, NY 10286
Agent's Phone:	888-269-2377
Other than USA:	Yes

Safekeeping:	Yes
Invests:	Every 7 days beginning varies
Minimum:	$50
Maximum:	$250,000/week
Min to qualify:	1
Fee on cash inv.:	$5 + 10¢/sh.
Fee on div. inv.:	5% to $5 + 10¢/sh.
Discount (cash):	0
Discount (div.):	0
Auto invest:	Yes
Auto invest fee:	$0
Selling info:	Sells weekly, by phone or mail, at avg. price, for $5 +10¢/ADS

Company:	**Lyondell Chemical Co.**
Symbol:	LYO
Exchange:	NYSE
Industry:	Petrochemicals & refining
Company Address:	Box 3646 Houston, TX 77253-3646
Company Phone:	713-652-4590 or 713-652-7200
Transfer Agent:	Bank of New York
Agent's Address:	P.O. Box 11258, Church St. Station New York, NY 10286
Agent's Phone:	800-524-4458
Other than USA:	No

Safekeeping:	Yes
Invests:	Every 90 days beginning 3/15
Minimum:	$25
Maximum:	$10,000/quarter
Min to qualify:	1
Fee on cash inv.:	0
Fee on div. inv.:	0
Discount (cash):	0
Discount (div.):	0
Auto invest:	No
Auto invest fee:	$0
Selling info:	Sells irregularly, by mail, at market, for $5 + comm.

Company:	**M & T Bank Corp.**
Symbol:	MTB
Exchange:	NYSE
Industry:	Banking
Company Address:	One M & T Plaza, Box 223 Buffalo, NY 14240
Company Phone:	716-842-5445 or 716-842-4200
Transfer Agent:	Boston Eq. (EquiServe)
Agent's Address:	P.O. Box 8040, MS:45-02-64 Boston, MA 02266-8040
Agent's Phone:	800-730-4001
Other than USA:	No

Safekeeping:	Yes
Invests:	Every 30 days beginning 1/1
Minimum:	$10
Maximum:	$1,000/month
Min to qualify:	1
Fee on cash inv.:	5% to $2.50 + comm.
Fee on div. inv.:	5% to $2.50 + comm.
Discount (cash):	0
Discount (div.):	0
Auto invest:	Yes
Auto invest fee:	5% to $2.50 +comm.
Selling info:	Sells within10 bus. days, by mail, at market, for 5% to $10 + comm.

Company:	**MacDermid, Inc.**
Symbol:	MRD
Exchange:	NYSE
Industry:	Industrial metal finishing chemicals
Company Address:	245 Freight St. Waterbury, CT 06702
Company Phone:	203-575-5700 or 203-575-5813
Transfer Agent:	Harris Trust & Savings Bank
Agent's Address:	P.O. Box 2857, Church St. Station New York, NY 10008
Agent's Phone:	312-461-2302
Other than USA:	Yes

Safekeeping:	No
Invests:	Every 90 days beginning 1/1
Minimum:	$50
Maximum:	$unlimited
Min to qualify:	1
Fee on cash inv.:	0
Fee on div. inv.:	0
Discount (cash):	0
Discount (div.):	0
Auto invest:	No
Auto invest fee:	$0
Selling info:	Sells irregularly, by mail, at market, for $1 + comm.

Company:	**Macerich Co.**	Safekeeping:	Yes
Symbol:	MAC	Invests:	Every 7 days beginning varies
Exchange:	NYSE	Minimum:	$50
Industry:	Real estate operations	Maximum:	$250,000/year
Company Address:	Box 2172	Min to qualify:	1
	Santa Monica, CA 90407-2172	Fee on cash inv.:	0!
Company Phone:	800-421-7237 or 310-394-6911	Fee on div. inv.:	0!
Transfer Agent:	FCT (EquiServe)	Discount (cash):	0
Agent's Address:	P.O. Box 2598	Discount (div.):	0
	Jersey City, NJ 07303-2598	Auto invest:	Yes
Agent's Phone:	800-567-0169	Auto invest fee:	$0
Other than USA:	Yes	Selling info:	Sells daily, by mail or phone, at market, for $10 +12¢/sh.

Company:	**Mack-Cali Realty Corp.**	Safekeeping:	Yes
Symbol:	CLI	Invests:	Every 30 days beginning 3/31
Exchange:	NYSE	Minimum:	$100
Industry:	REIT	Maximum:	$5,000/month
Company Address:	11 Commerce Dr.	Min to qualify:	1
	Cranford, NJ 07016	Fee on cash inv.:	0
Company Phone:	908-272-8000	Fee on div. inv.:	0
Transfer Agent:	ChaseMellon Shareholder Services	Discount (cash):	0
Agent's Address:	P.O. Box 3338	Discount (div.):	0
	South Hackensack, NJ 07606-1938	Auto invest:	No
Agent's Phone:	888-816-7320	Auto invest fee:	$0
Other than USA:	Yes	Selling info:	Sells weekly, by mail, at market, for $15 + 12¢/sh.

Company:	**MacMillan Bloedel Ltd.**	Safekeeping:	Yes
Symbol:	MB	Invests:	Every 90 days beginning 3/14
Exchange:	TSE	Minimum:	$500
Industry:	Paper & lumber	Maximum:	$25,000/year Cdn.
Company Address:	925 West Georgia St.	Min to qualify:	1
	Vancouver, B.C. V6C 3L2 Canada	Fee on cash inv.:	0
Company Phone:	604-661-8312	Fee on div. inv.:	0
Transfer Agent:	Montreal Trust Company of	Discount (cash):	0
	Canada	Discount (div.):	0
Agent's Address:	Montreal Trust Centre, 2nd Fl.,	Auto invest:	No
	510 Burrard St.	Auto invest fee:	$0
	Vancouver, B.C. V6C 3B9 Canada	Selling info:	Not available
Agent's Phone:	604-661-0222		
Other than USA:	Yes		

Company:	**Macronix Int'l. Co. Ltd.**	Safekeeping:	Yes
Symbol:	MXICY	Invests:	Every 7 days beginning varies
Exchange:	OTC	Minimum:	$50
Industry:	Integrated circuits	Maximum:	$250,000/week
Company Address:	c/o BNY,101 Barclay St.,22 West	Min to qualify:	1
	New York, NY 10286	Fee on cash inv.:	$5 + 10¢/sh.
Company Phone:	800-943-9715	Fee on div. inv.:	5% to $5 + 10¢/sh.
Transfer Agent:	Bank of New York	Discount (cash):	0
Agent's Address:	P.O. Box 11258	Discount (div.):	0
	New York, NY 10286	Auto invest:	Yes
Agent's Phone:	888-269-2377	Auto invest fee:	$0
Other than USA:	Yes	Selling info:	Sells weekly, by phone or mail, at market, for $5 +10¢/ADS

Company:	**Maderas y Sinteticos Sociedad Anonima**	**Safekeeping:**	Yes
		Invests:	Every 7 days beginning varies
Symbol:	MYS	**Minimum:**	$50
Exchange:	NYSE	**Maximum:**	$250,000/year
Industry:	Construction, supplies & fixtures	**Min to qualify:**	1
Company Address:	c/o BNY,101 Barclay St.,22 West	**Fee on cash inv.:**	$5 + 10¢/sh.
	New York, NY 10286	**Fee on div. inv.:**	0
Company Phone:	800-943-9715	**Discount (cash):**	0
Transfer Agent:	Bank of New York	**Discount (div.):**	0
Agent's Address:	P.O. Box 11258	**Auto invest:**	Yes
	New York, NY 10286	**Auto invest fee:**	$5 + 10¢/sh.
Agent's Phone:	888-269-2377	**Selling info:**	Sells weekly, by mail, at market,
Other than USA:	Yes		for $5 +10¢/sh.

Company:	**Madison Gas & Electric Co.**	**Safekeeping:**	Yes
		Invests:	Every 30 days beginning 1/15
Symbol:	MDSN	**Minimum:**	$25
Exchange:	OTC	**Maximum:**	$25,000/quarter
Industry:	Utility-electric, gas	**Min to qualify:**	1
Company Address:	Box 1231	**Fee on cash inv.:**	comm.
	Madison, WI 53701-1231	**Fee on div. inv.:**	comm.
Company Phone:	800-356-6423 or 608-252-7000	**Discount (cash):**	0
Transfer Agent:	Madison G&E Co.	**Discount (div.):**	0
Agent's Address:	133 South Blair St.	**Auto invest:**	Yes
	Madison, WI 53703	**Auto invest fee:**	$0
Agent's Phone:	800-356-6423	**Selling info:**	Sells weekly, by phone or mail, at
Other than USA:	Yes		market, for comm.

Company:	**Magyar Tavkozlesi Rt. (MATAV)**	**Safekeeping:**	Yes
		Invests:	Every 7 days beginning varies
Symbol:	MTA	**Minimum:**	$50
Exchange:	NYSE	**Maximum:**	$100,000/year
Industry:	Telecommunications	**Min to qualify:**	1
Company Address:	c/o Morgan Guaranty Trust, Box 9073	**Fee on cash inv.:**	$5 + 12¢/sh.
		Fee on div. inv.:	5% to $2.50
	Boston, MA 02205-9948	**Discount (cash):**	0
Company Phone:	800-428-4237	**Discount (div.):**	0
Transfer Agent:	Morgan Guaranty Trust Co.	**Auto invest:**	Yes
Agent's Address:	P.O. Box 9073	**Auto invest fee:**	$5
	Boston, MA 02205-9948	**Selling info:**	Sells daily, by phone or mail, at
Agent's Phone:	800-428-4237		market, for $5 +12¢/sh.
Other than USA:	No		

Company:	**Mahaska Investment Co.**	**Safekeeping:**	Yes
Symbol:	OSKY	**Invests:**	Every 30 days beginning 1/1
Exchange:	OTC	**Minimum:**	$25
Industry:	Regional banks	**Maximum:**	$5,000/month
Company Address:	222 First Ave. East, Box 1104	**Min to qualify:**	1
	Oskaloosa, IA 52577-1104	**Fee on cash inv.:**	0!
Company Phone:	515-673-8448	**Fee on div. inv.:**	0!
Transfer Agent:	Illinois Stock Transfer Company	**Discount (cash):**	0
Agent's Address:	223 West Jackson Blvd., Suite 1210	**Discount (div.):**	0
		Auto invest:	No
	Chicago, IL 60606	**Auto invest fee:**	$0
Agent's Phone:	312-427-2953	**Selling info:**	Sells within 10 bus. days, by mail,
Other than USA:	No		at market, for $3

Company:	**Mahoning National Bancorp, Inc.**	Safekeeping:	Yes
		Invests:	Every 90 days beginning 3/15
Symbol:	MGNB	Minimum:	$30
Exchange:	OTC	Maximum:	$5,000/quarter
Industry:	Bank holding company	Min to qualify:	1
Company Address:	23 Federal Plaza, Box 479	Fee on cash inv.:	$1.50
	Youngstown, OH 44501	Fee on div. inv.:	$1.50
Company Phone:	330-742-7097 or 330-742-7000	Discount (cash):	0
Transfer Agent:	Mahoning Nat'l Bank of	Discount (div.):	0
	Youngstown	Auto invest:	No
Agent's Address:	P.O. Box 479	Auto invest fee:	$0
	Youngstown, OH 44501-0479	Selling info:	Not available
Agent's Phone:	330-742-7040		
Other than USA:	Yes		

Company:	**Makita**	Safekeeping:	Yes
Symbol:	MKTAY	Invests:	Every 7 days beginning varies
Exchange:	OTC	Minimum:	$50
Industry:	Elec. equip.	Maximum:	$250,000/week
Company Address:	c/o BNY,101 Barclay St., 22 West	Min to qualify:	1
	New York, NY 10286	Fee on cash inv.:	$5 + 10¢/sh.
Company Phone:	800-943-9715	Fee on div. inv.:	5% to $5 + 10¢/sh.
Transfer Agent:	Bank of New York	Discount (cash):	0
Agent's Address:	P.O. Box 11258	Discount (div.):	0
	New York, NY 10286	Auto invest:	Yes
Agent's Phone:	888-269-2377	Auto invest fee:	$0
Other than USA:	Yes	Selling info:	Sells weekly, by phone or mail, at avg. price, for $5 +10¢/ADS

Company:	**Mallinckrodt Inc.**	Safekeeping:	Yes
Symbol:	MKG	Invests:	Every 30 days beginning 1/31
Exchange:	NYSE	Minimum:	$100
Industry:	Medical	Maximum:	$100,000/year
Company Address:	675 McDonnell Blvd., Box 5840	Min to qualify:	1
	St. Louis, MO 63134	Fee on cash inv.:	$5 + 3¢/sh.
Company Phone:	800-323-5039 or 314-654-3190	Fee on div. inv.:	5% to $3 + 10¢/sh.
Transfer Agent:	FCT (EquiServe)	Discount (cash):	0
Agent's Address:	P.O. Box 2598	Discount (div.):	0
	Jersey City, NJ 07303-2598	Auto invest:	Yes
Agent's Phone:	800-446-2617	Auto invest fee:	$2 + 3¢/sh.
Other than USA:	Yes	Selling info:	Sells daily, by phone or mail, at market, for $10 +12¢/sh.

Company:	**Manitowoc Co.**	Safekeeping:	Yes
Symbol:	MTW	Invests:	Every 30 days beginning 1/10
Exchange:	NYSE	Minimum:	$10
Industry:	Machinery	Maximum:	$60,000/year
Company Address:	500 South 16th St., Box 66	Min to qualify:	1
	Manitowoc, WI 54221-0066	Fee on cash inv.:	0!
Company Phone:	920-684-4410 or 920-683-8150	Fee on div. inv.:	0!
Transfer Agent:	FCT (EquiServe)	Discount (cash):	0
Agent's Address:	P.O. Box 2571	Discount (div.):	0
	Jersey City, NJ 07303-2571	Auto invest:	No
Agent's Phone:	800-446-2617	Auto invest fee:	$0
Other than USA:	No	Selling info:	Sells daily, by mail, at market, for $10 +12¢/sh.

Company:	**Manpower**	Safekeeping:	Yes
Symbol:	MAN	Invests:	Every 30 days beginning 1/15
Exchange:	NYSE	Minimum:	$25
Industry:	Nongovernmental temp.	Maximum:	$10,000/year
	employment services	Min to qualify:	1
Company Address:	5301 N. Ironwood Rd., Box 2053	Fee on cash inv.:	0!
	Milwaukee, WI 53201	Fee on div. inv.:	0!
Company Phone:	414-961-1000 or 414-906-6350	Discount (cash):	0
Transfer Agent:	ChaseMellon Shareholder Services	Discount (div.):	0
Agent's Address:	P.O. Box 3338	Auto invest:	No
	South Hackensack, NJ 07606-1938	Auto invest fee:	$0
Agent's Phone:	800-851-9677	Selling info:	Sells biweekly, by mail,
Other than USA:	Yes		at market, for $5 + comm.

Company:	**Marcus Corp. (The)**	Safekeeping:	Yes
Symbol:	MCS	Invests:	Every 30 days beginning 1/15
Exchange:	NYSE	Minimum:	$100
Industry:	Hotels, restaurants & movie	Maximum:	$1,500/month
	theaters	Min to qualify:	1
Company Address:	250 East Wisconsin Ave., Ste.1700	Fee on cash inv.:	0
	Milwaukee, WI 53202-4220	Fee on div. inv.:	0
Company Phone:	414-905-1000	Discount (cash):	0
Transfer Agent:	Firstar Bank Milwaukee, NA	Discount (div.):	0
Agent's Address:	P.O. Box 2077	Auto invest:	No
	Milwaukee, WI 53201-2077	Auto invest fee:	$0
Agent's Phone:	800-637-7549	Selling info:	Sells biweekly, by mail or fax, at
Other than USA:	Yes		market, for $5 + comm.

Company:	**Maritime Telegraph & Telephone Co.**	Safekeeping:	No
		Invests:	Every 90 days beginning 1/16
Symbol:	MTT	Minimum:	$0
Exchange:	TSE	Maximum:	$5,000/quarter Cdn.
Industry:	Communications	Min to qualify:	1
Company Address:	Box 880 Stn. Central RPO	Fee on cash inv.:	0!
	Halifax, NS B3J 2W3	Fee on div. inv.:	0!
Company Phone:	800-565-7168 or 902-487-4311	Discount (cash):	0
Transfer Agent:	CIBC Mellon Trust	Discount (div.):	0
Agent's Address:	P.O. Box 2082, Station "C"	Auto invest:	No
	Halifax, NS B3J 3B7 Canada	Auto invest fee:	$0
Agent's Phone:	800-565-2188	Selling info:	Not available
Other than USA:	Yes		

Company:	**Mark IV Industries**	Safekeeping:	Yes
Symbol:	IV	Invests:	Every 30 days beginning 1/1
Exchange:	NYSE	Minimum:	$50
Industry:	Power transfer equipment	Maximum:	$5,000/month
Company Address:	501 John James Audubon	Min to qualify:	1
	Pkwy.,Box 810	Fee on cash inv.:	0!
	Amherst, NY 14226-0810	Fee on div. inv.:	0!
Company Phone:	716-689-4972	Discount (cash):	0
Transfer Agent:	American Stock Transfer	Discount (div.):	0
Agent's Address:	40 Wall St., 46th Floor	Auto invest:	No
	New York, NY 10005	Auto invest fee:	$0
Agent's Phone:	800-278-4353	Selling info:	Sells weekly, by mail, at market,
Other than USA:	Yes		for $10 + comm.

Company:	**Marriott International, Inc.**	Safekeeping:	Yes
		Invests:	Every 30 days beginning 1/15
Symbol:	MAR	Minimum:	$25
Exchange:	NYSE	Maximum:	$60,000/year
Industry:	Hotels, food service mgt.	Min to qualify:	1
Company Address:	Marriott Dr.	Fee on cash inv.:	5% to $3 + comm.
	Washington, DC 20058	Fee on div. inv.:	5% to $3 + comm.
Company Phone:	301-380-3000 or 301-380-6500	Discount (cash):	0
Transfer Agent:	FCT (EquiServe)	Discount (div.):	0
Agent's Address:	P.O. Box 2598	Auto invest:	No
	Jersey City, NJ 07303-2598	Auto invest fee:	$0
Agent's Phone:	800-311-4816	Selling info:	Sells daily, by mail, at market, for
Other than USA:	Yes		$15 +12¢/sh.

Company:	**Marsh & McLennan Co., Inc.**	Safekeeping:	Yes
		Invests:	Every 90 days beginning 2/15
Symbol:	MMC	Minimum:	$10
Exchange:	NYSE	Maximum:	$3,000/quarter
Industry:	Insurance	Min to qualify:	1
Company Address:	1166 Ave. of the Americas	Fee on cash inv.:	5% to $2.50
	New York, NY 10036	Fee on div. inv.:	5% to $2.50
Company Phone:	212-345-5161 or 212-345-5000	Discount (cash):	0
Transfer Agent:	Bank of New York	Discount (div.):	0
Agent's Address:	P.O. Box 11258, Church St. Station	Auto invest:	No
	New York, NY 10286	Auto invest fee:	$0
Agent's Phone:	212-815-2560	Selling info:	Sells daily, by mail, at market, for
Other than USA:	No		$0

Company:	**Marsh Supermarkets A**	Safekeeping:	Yes
Symbol:	MARSA	Invests:	Every 30 days beginning 1/1
Exchange:	OTC		monthly
Industry:	Supermarkets	Minimum:	$100
Company Address:	9800 Crosspoint Blvd.	Maximum:	$5,000/month
	Indianapolis, IN 46256-3350	Min to qualify:	1
Company Phone:	317-594-2345 or 317-594-2100	Fee on cash inv.:	0
Transfer Agent:	National City Bank	Fee on div. inv.:	0
Agent's Address:	P.O. Box 94915	Discount (cash):	0
	Cleveland, OH 44101-4915	Discount (div.):	0
Agent's Phone:	800-622-6757	Auto invest:	No
Other than USA:	Yes	Auto invest fee:	$0
		Selling info:	Sells weekly, by mail, at market, for $2.50 + 8¢ to 20¢/sh.

Company:	**Marsh Supermarkets B**	Safekeeping:	Yes
Symbol:	MARSB	Invests:	Every 30 days beginning 1/1
Exchange:	OTC	Minimum:	$100
Industry:	Supermarkets	Maximum:	$5,000/month
Company Address:	9800 Crosspoint Blvd.	Min to qualify:	1
	Indianapolis, IN 46256	Fee on cash inv.:	0
Company Phone:	317-594-2345 or 317-594-2100	Fee on div. inv.:	0
Transfer Agent:	National City Bank	Discount (cash):	0
Agent's Address:	P.O. Box 94915	Discount (div.):	0
	Cleveland, OH 44101-4915	Auto invest:	No
Agent's Phone:	800-622-6757	Auto invest fee:	$0
Other than USA:	Yes	Selling info:	Sells weekly, by mail, at market, for $2.50 + 8¢ to 20¢/sh.

Company:	**Marshall & Ilsley Corp.**	Safekeeping:	Yes
Symbol:	MRIS	Invests:	Every 30 days beginning 1/1
Exchange:	OTC	Minimum:	$25
Industry:	Banking	Maximum:	$3,000/quarter
Company Address:	770 N. Water St., Box 2035	Min to qualify:	1
	Milwaukee, WI 53202	Fee on cash inv.:	0
Company Phone:	414-765-7801	Fee on div. inv.:	0
Transfer Agent:	BankBoston (EquiServe)	Discount (cash):	0
Agent's Address:	P.O. Box 8040	Discount (div.):	0
	Boston Ma, 02266-8040	Auto invest:	No
Agent's Phone:	800-730-4001	Auto invest fee:	$0
Other than USA:	No	Selling info:	Sells within 10 bus. days, by mail, at market, for $5

Company:	**Martin Industries**	Safekeeping:	Yes
Symbol:	MTIN	Invests:	Every 90 days beginning 2/16
Exchange:	OTC	Minimum:	$25
Industry:	Supplies, heaters & fixtures	Maximum:	$6,000/quarter
Company Address:	301 E. Tennessee St., Box 128	Min to qualify:	1
	Florence, AL 35631	Fee on cash inv.:	0!
Company Phone:	205-767-0330	Fee on div. inv.:	0!
Transfer Agent:	SunTrust Bank, Atlanta	Discount (cash):	5%
Agent's Address:	P.O. Box 4625	Discount (div.):	5%
	Atlanta, GA 30302	Auto invest:	No
Agent's Phone:	800-568-3476	Auto invest fee:	$0
Other than USA:	Yes	Selling info:	Sells weekly, by mail, at market, for 20¢/sh.

Company:	**Masco Corp.**	Safekeeping:	Yes
Symbol:	MAS	Invests:	Every 30 days beginning 1/10
Exchange:	NYSE	Minimum:	$50
Industry:	Bldg. & home improvement products	Maximum:	$5,000/month
		Min to qualify:	1
Company Address:	21001 Van Born Rd.	Fee on cash inv.:	0!
	Taylor, MI 48180	Fee on div. inv.:	0!
Company Phone:	313-274-7400 or 313-792-6226	Discount (cash):	0
Transfer Agent:	Bank of New York	Discount (div.):	0
Agent's Address:	P.O. Box 1958	Auto invest:	No
	Newark, NJ 07101-9774	Auto invest fee:	$0
Agent's Phone:	800-524-4458	Selling info:	Sells weekly, by mail or fax, at market, for $5 + 5¢/sh.
Other than USA:	No		

Company:	**Mason-Dixon Bancshares**	Safekeeping:	Yes
Symbol:	MSDX	Invests:	Every 30 days beginning 1/20
Exchange:	OTC	Minimum:	$100
Industry:	Banking	Maximum:	$5,000/month
Company Address:	Box 1100, 45 West Main St.	Min to qualify:	1
	Westminster, MD 21158-0199	Fee on cash inv.:	0!
Company Phone:	410-857-3401	Fee on div. inv.:	0!
Transfer Agent:	American Stock Transfer & Trust	Discount (cash):	0
Agent's Address:	40 Wall St., 46th Fl.	Discount (div.):	0
	New York, NY 10005	Auto invest:	No
Agent's Phone:	800-278-4353	Auto invest fee:	$0
Other than USA:	Yes	Selling info:	Sells weekly, by mail, at market, for $15 + 4¢/sh.

Company:	**MASSBANK Corp.**	Safekeeping:	Yes
Symbol:	MASB	Invests:	Every 90 days beginning 2/15
Exchange:	OTC	Minimum:	$50
Industry:	Banking	Maximum:	$5,000/quarter
Company Address:	159 Haven St.	Min to qualify:	1
	Reading, MA 01867	Fee on cash inv.:	0
Company Phone:	781-662-0100 or 978-446-9200	Fee on div. inv.:	0
Transfer Agent:	Boston Eq. (EquiServe)	Discount (cash):	0
Agent's Address:	P.O. Box 644	Discount (div.):	0
	Canton, MA 02021	Auto invest:	No
Agent's Phone:	800-730-4001	Auto invest fee:	$0
Other than USA:	No	Selling info:	Sells within 10 bus. days, by mail, at market, for comm.

Company:	**Matav-Cable Systems Media**	Safekeeping:	Yes
		Invests:	Every 7 days beginning varies
Symbol:	MATVY	Minimum:	$50
Exchange:	OTC	Maximum:	$250,000/week
Industry:	Israeli cable television provider	Min to qualify:	1
Company Address:	c/o BNY,101 Barclay St.,22 West	Fee on cash inv.:	$5 + 10¢/sh.
	New York, NY 10286	Fee on div. inv.:	5% to $5 + 10¢/sh.
Company Phone:	800-943-9715	Discount (cash):	0
Transfer Agent:	Bank of New York	Discount (div.):	0
Agent's Address:	P.O. Box 11258	Auto invest:	Yes
	New York, NY 10286	Auto invest fee:	$0
Agent's Phone:	888-269-2377	Selling info:	Sells weekly, by phone or mail, at
Other than USA:	Yes		market, for $5 +10¢/sh.

Company:	**Matsushita Electric Ind. Co.,Ltd.**	Safekeeping:	Yes
		Invests:	Every 7 days beginning varies
Symbol:	MC	Minimum:	$50
Exchange:	NYSE	Maximum:	$100,000/year
Industry:	Electric	Min to qualify:	1
Company Address:	c/o Morgan Guaranty Trust,	Fee on cash inv.:	$5 + 12¢/sh.
	Box 9073	Fee on div. inv.:	5% to $2.50
	Boston, MA 02205-9948	Discount (cash):	0
Company Phone:	800-428-4237	Discount (div.):	0
Transfer Agent:	Morgan Guaranty Trust Co.	Auto invest:	Yes
Agent's Address:	P.O. Box 9073	Auto invest fee:	$5 + 12¢/sh.
	Boston, MA 02205-9948	Selling info:	Sells daily, by mail or phone, at
Agent's Phone:	800-428-4237		avg. price, for $5 +12¢/sh.
Other than USA:	No		

Company:	**Mattel Inc.**	Safekeeping:	Yes
Symbol:	MAT	Invests:	Every 7 days beginning Wed.
Exchange:	NYSE	Minimum:	$100
Industry:	Mfg., marketing toys	Maximum:	$100,000/year
Company Address:	333 Continental Blvd.	Min to qualify:	1
	El Segundo, CA 90245	Fee on cash inv.:	$5 + 8¢/sh.
Company Phone:	310-252-4600	Fee on div. inv.:	0
Transfer Agent:	BankBoston (EquiServe)	Discount (cash):	0
Agent's Address:	P.O. Box 644	Discount (div.):	0
	Boston, MA 02102	Auto invest:	Yes
Agent's Phone:	888-909-9922	Auto invest fee:	$0
Other than USA:	Yes	Selling info:	Sells within 10 bus. days, by mail, at market, for $10 +15¢/sh.

Company:	**Mavesa, S.A.**
Symbol:	MAV
Exchange:	NYSE
Industry:	Manufacturer of food & soap products
Company Address:	c/o BNY,101 Barclay St.,22 West New York, NY 10286
Company Phone:	800-943-9715
Transfer Agent:	Bank of New York
Agent's Address:	P.O. Box 11258 New York, NY 10286
Agent's Phone:	888-269-2377
Other than USA:	Yes

Safekeeping:	Yes
Invests:	Every 7 days beginning varies
Minimum:	$50
Maximum:	$250,000/week
Min to qualify:	1
Fee on cash inv.:	$5 + 10¢/sh.
Fee on div. inv.:	5% to $5 + 10¢/sh.
Discount (cash):	0
Discount (div.):	0
Auto invest:	Yes
Auto invest fee:	$0
Selling info:	Sells weekly, by phone or mail, at market, for $5 +10¢/ADS

Company:	**May Dept. Stores Co.**
Symbol:	MAY
Exchange:	NYSE
Industry:	Retail stores
Company Address:	611 Olive St. St. Louis, MO 63101-1799
Company Phone:	314-342-6413 or 314-342-6300
Transfer Agent:	Bank of New York
Agent's Address:	P.O. Box 11260, Church St. Station New York, NY 10286-1260
Agent's Phone:	800-524-4458
Other than USA:	Yes

Safekeeping:	Yes
Invests:	Every daily days beginning 1/1
Minimum:	$25
Maximum:	$unlimited
Min to qualify:	1
Fee on cash inv.:	$2
Fee on div. inv.:	5% to $2
Discount (cash):	0
Discount (div.):	0
Auto invest:	No
Auto invest fee:	$0
Selling info:	Sells irregularly, by mail, at avg. price, for $2.50

Company:	**Maytag Corp.**
Symbol:	MYG
Exchange:	NYSE
Industry:	Home appliances
Company Address:	403 West 4th St. North, Box 39 Newton, IA 50208-0039
Company Phone:	515-787-8344 or 515-787-8339
Transfer Agent:	Harris Trust & Savings Bank
Agent's Address:	P.O. Box A3504 Chicago, IL 60690-3504
Agent's Phone:	888-237-0935
Other than USA:	Yes

Safekeeping:	Yes
Invests:	Every 30 days beginning 1/15
Minimum:	$25
Maximum:	$5,000/month
Min to qualify:	1
Fee on cash inv.:	0!
Fee on div. inv.:	0!
Discount (cash):	0
Discount (div.):	0
Auto invest:	Yes
Auto invest fee:	$0
Selling info:	Sells weekly, by mail, at market, for 15¢/sh.

Company:	**McCormick & Co.**
Symbol:	MKC
Exchange:	NYSE
Industry:	Food mfr., spices, teas, & flavorings
Company Address:	18 Loveton Circle Sparks, MD 21152-6000
Company Phone:	800-424-5855 or 410-771-7301
Transfer Agent:	McCormick & Co., Inc.
Agent's Address:	18 Loveton Circle Sparks, MD 21152-6000
Agent's Phone:	800-424-5855
Other than USA:	Yes

Safekeeping:	Yes
Invests:	Every 30 days beginning 1/10
Minimum:	$50
Maximum:	$50,000/year
Min to qualify:	1
Fee on cash inv.:	0
Fee on div. inv.:	0
Discount (cash):	0
Discount (div.):	0
Auto invest:	No
Auto invest fee:	$0
Selling info:	Sells weekly, by mail or fax, at avg. price, for $15 +12¢/sh.

Company:	**McDermott International Inc.**	Safekeeping:	Yes
		Invests:	Every 7 days beginning varies
Symbol:	MDR	Minimum:	$50
Exchange:	NYSE	Maximum:	$250,000/year
Industry:	Power generation; engineering & marine construction	Min to qualify:	1
		Fee on cash inv.:	$5 + 3¢/sh.
Company Address:	1450 Poydras St. New Orleans, LA 70112-6050	Fee on div. inv.:	5% to $3 + 3¢/sh.
		Discount (cash):	0
Company Phone:	504-587-5682 or 504-587-5400	Discount (div.):	0
Transfer Agent:	FCT (EquiServe)	Auto invest:	Yes
Agent's Address:	P.O. Box 2500 Jersey City, NJ 07303-2500	Auto invest fee:	$2 +3¢/sh.
		Selling info:	Sells daily, by mail or phone, at market, for $15 +12¢/sh.
Agent's Phone:	800-446-2617		
Other than USA:	Yes		

Company:	**McDonald's Corp.**	Safekeeping:	Yes
Symbol:	MCD	Invests:	Every 7 days beginning varies
Exchange:	NYSE	Minimum:	$100
Industry:	Restaurants	Maximum:	$250,000/year
Company Address:	Inv. Relations, Dept. 300, Kroc Dr. Oak Brook, IL 60523	Min to qualify:	25
		Fee on cash inv.:	$5 + 10¢/sh.
Company Phone:	800-228-9623 or 630-623-8430	Fee on div. inv.:	75¢
Transfer Agent:	FCT (EquiServe)	Discount (cash):	0
Agent's Address:	P.O. Box 2591 Jersey City, NJ 07303-2591	Discount (div.):	0
		Auto invest:	Yes
Agent's Phone:	800-621-7825	Auto invest fee:	$1 + 10¢/sh.
Other than USA:	Yes	Selling info:	Sells daily, by mail, phone or fax, at market, for $10 +10¢/sh. w/$5 cap.

Company:	**McGraw-Hill Companies**	Safekeeping:	Yes
Symbol:	MHP	Invests:	Every 7 days beginning varies
Exchange:	NYSE	Minimum:	$100
Industry:	Publishing & information services	Maximum:	$10,000/month
Company Address:	1221 Ave. of the Americas New York, NY 10020-1095	Min to qualify:	1
		Fee on cash inv.:	0!
Company Phone:	212-512-2192 or 212-512-2000	Fee on div. inv.:	0!
Transfer Agent:	ChaseMellon Shareholder Services	Discount (cash):	0
Agent's Address:	P.O. Box 3315 S. Hackensack, NJ 07606	Discount (div.):	0
		Auto invest:	Yes
Agent's Phone:	888-201-5538	Auto invest fee:	$0
Other than USA:	Yes	Selling info:	Sells at least weekly, by mail or phone, at market, for $15 +12¢/sh.

Company:	**McKesson HBOC Inc.**	Safekeeping:	Yes
Symbol:	MCK	Invests:	Every 30 days beginning 1/1
Exchange:	NYSE	Minimum:	$10
Industry:	Drugs, consumer products	Maximum:	$60,000/year
Company Address:	One Post St. San Francisco, CA 94104-5296	Min to qualify:	1
		Fee on cash inv.:	0!
Company Phone:	415-983-8367	Fee on div. inv.:	0!
Transfer Agent:	FCT (EquiServe)	Discount (cash):	0
Agent's Address:	P.O. Box 2500 Jersey City, NJ 07303-2500	Discount (div.):	0
		Auto invest:	Yes
Agent's Phone:	800-414-6280	Auto invest fee:	$1
Other than USA:	No	Selling info:	Sells irregularly, by mail, at market, for $10 +12¢/sh.

Company:	**MCN Energy Group, Inc.**
Symbol:	MCN
Exchange:	NYSE
Industry:	Utility-gas
Company Address:	500 Griswold St.
	Detroit, MI 48226
Company Phone:	800-548-4655
Transfer Agent:	FCT (EquiServe)
Agent's Address:	P.O. Box 2500
	Jersey City, NJ 07303-2500
Agent's Phone:	800-344-9713
Other than USA:	Yes

Safekeeping:	Yes
Invests:	Every 7 days beginning varies
Minimum:	$25
Maximum:	$150,000/year
Min to qualify:	1
Fee on cash inv.:	0!
Fee on div. inv.:	0!
Discount (cash):	0
Discount (div.):	0
Auto invest:	Yes
Auto invest fee:	$1
Selling info:	Sells daily, by phone, mail, or fax, at market, for $10 +12¢/sh.

Company:	**MDS Inc. A**
Symbol:	MHGA
Exchange:	TSE
Industry:	Health care
Company Address:	100 International Blvd.
	Toronto, Ontario M9W 6J6 Canada
Company Phone:	416-675-6777x2691
Transfer Agent:	CIBC Mellon Trust
Agent's Address:	393 University Ave., 5th Floor, P O Box 7010
	Toronto,Ontario M5G 2M7 Canada
Agent's Phone:	800-387-0825
Other than USA:	No U.S. for optional cash

Safekeeping:	No
Invests:	Every 180 days beginning 3/1
Minimum:	$50
Maximum:	$3,000/semiannually Cdn.
Min to qualify:	1
Fee on cash inv.:	0
Fee on div. inv.:	0
Discount (cash):	0
Discount (div.):	5%
Auto invest:	No
Auto invest fee:	$0
Selling info:	Not available

Company:	**MDU Resources Group**
Symbol:	MDU
Exchange:	NYSE
Industry:	Mining, construction material, utility, gas, electric
Company Address:	Box 5650
	Bismarck, ND 58506-5650
Company Phone:	800-437-8000 or 701-222-7900
Transfer Agent:	Norwest Bank Minnesota, N.A.
Agent's Address:	P.O. Box 64854
	St. Paul, MN 55164-0854
Agent's Phone:	800-468-9716
Other than USA:	Yes

Safekeeping:	Yes
Invests:	Every 30 days beginning 1/1
Minimum:	$50
Maximum:	$5,000/month
Min to qualify:	1
Fee on cash inv.:	0!
Fee on div. inv.:	0!
Discount (cash):	0
Discount (div.):	0
Auto invest:	Yes
Auto invest fee:	$0
Selling info:	Sells daily, by phone, mail, or fax, at market, for $3 +15¢/sh.

Company:	**Mead Corp.**
Symbol:	MEA
Exchange:	NYSE
Industry:	Paper, forest prod.
Company Address:	Courthouse Plaza NE
	Dayton, OH 45463
Company Phone:	937-495-6323
Transfer Agent:	Boston Eq. (EquiServe)
Agent's Address:	P.O. Box 8040
	Boston, MA 02266-8040
Agent's Phone:	800-730-4001
Other than USA:	Yes

Safekeeping:	Yes
Invests:	Every 30 days beginning 1/1
Minimum:	$25
Maximum:	$6,000/month
Min to qualify:	1
Fee on cash inv.:	0!
Fee on div. inv.:	0!
Discount (cash):	0
Discount (div.):	0
Auto invest:	No
Auto invest fee:	$0
Selling info:	Sells within 10 bus. days, by phone, at avg. price, for comm.

Company:	**Meadowbrook Insurance Group**	Safekeeping:	Yes
		Invests:	Every 7 days beginning Wed.
Symbol:	MIG	Minimum:	$25
Exchange:	NYSE	Maximum:	$50,000/year
Industry:	Property and casualty insurance	Min to qualify:	1
Company Address:	26600 Telegraph Rd.	Fee on cash inv.:	0!
	Southfield, MI 48075	Fee on div. inv.:	0!
Company Phone:	248-358-1100 or 248-204-8178	Discount (cash):	0
Transfer Agent:	FCT (EquiServe)	Discount (div.):	0
Agent's Address:	P.O. Box 2536	Auto invest:	Yes
	Jersey City, NJ 07303-2536	Auto invest fee:	$0
Agent's Phone:	800-519-3111	Selling info:	Sells daily, by mail or phone, at
Other than USA:	Yes		market, for comm.

Company:	**Medeva PLC**	Safekeeping:	Yes
Symbol:	MDV	Invests:	Every 7 days beginning varies
Exchange:	NYSE	Minimum:	$50
Industry:	Biotechnology & drugs	Maximum:	$250,000/year
Company Address:	c/o BNY,101 Barclay St.,22 West	Min to qualify:	1
	New York, NY 10286	Fee on cash inv.:	$5 + 10¢/sh.
Company Phone:	800-943-9715	Fee on div. inv.:	5% to $5 + 10¢/sh.
Transfer Agent:	Bank of New York	Discount (cash):	0
Agent's Address:	P.O. Box 11258	Discount (div.):	0
	New York, NY 10286	Auto invest:	Yes
Agent's Phone:	888-269-2377	Auto invest fee:	$5 + 10¢/sh.
Other than USA:	Yes	Selling info:	Sells weekly, by mail, at market,
			for $5 +10¢/sh.

Company:	**Medford Bancorp**	Safekeeping:	Yes
Symbol:	MDBK	Invests:	Every 90 days beginning 1/15
Exchange:	OTC	Minimum:	$100
Industry:	Banking	Maximum:	$1,000/quarter
Company Address:	29 High St., Box 151	Min to qualify:	1
	Medford, MA 02155	Fee on cash inv.:	0
Company Phone:	781-395-7700	Fee on div. inv.:	0
Transfer Agent:	Boston Eq. (EquiServe)	Discount (cash):	0
Agent's Address:	P.O. Box 8200	Discount (div.):	0
	Boston, MA 02266-8200	Auto invest:	No
Agent's Phone:	800-426-5523	Auto invest fee:	$0
Other than USA:	Yes	Selling info:	Sells daily, by mail, at market, for
			comm.

Company:	**Media General, Inc. A**	Safekeeping:	Yes
Symbol:	MEGA	Invests:	Every 30 days beginning 1/1
Exchange:	ASE	Minimum:	$25
Industry:	Newspaper, TV	Maximum:	$5,000/month
Company Address:	333 East Franklin St.	Min to qualify:	1
	Richmond, VA 23219	Fee on cash inv.:	0!
Company Phone:	804-649-6000	Fee on div. inv.:	0!
Transfer Agent:	Wachovia (EquiServe)	Discount (cash):	0
Agent's Address:	P.O. Box 8217	Discount (div.):	5%
	Boston, MA 02266-8217	Auto invest:	No
Agent's Phone:	800-633-4236 or 910-770-5000	Auto invest fee:	$0
Other than USA:	Yes	Selling info:	Sells monthly, by mail or fax, at
			avg. price, for comm.

Company:	**Meditrust Companies**	**Safekeeping:**	No
Symbol:	MT	**Invests:**	Every 90 days beginning 2/15
Exchange:	NYSE	**Minimum:**	$100
Industry:	REIT	**Maximum:**	$10,000/quarter
Company Address:	197 First Ave.	**Min to qualify:**	1
	Needham, MA 02194-9127	**Fee on cash inv.:**	0!
Company Phone:	617-433-6000	**Fee on div. inv.:**	0!
Transfer Agent:	Boston Eq. (EquiServe)	**Discount (cash):**	0
Agent's Address:	P.O. Box 8040	**Discount (div.):**	0
	Boston, MA 02266	**Auto invest:**	No
Agent's Phone:	800-730-4001	**Auto invest fee:**	$0
Other than USA:	No	**Selling info:**	Not available

Company:	**Medtronic, Inc.**	**Safekeeping:**	Yes
Symbol:	MDT	**Invests:**	Every 30 days beginning 1/31
Exchange:	NYSE	**Minimum:**	$25
Industry:	Medical	**Maximum:**	$4,000/month
Company Address:	7000 Central Ave. NE	**Min to qualify:**	1
	Minneapolis, MN 55432	**Fee on cash inv.:**	0
Company Phone:	612-514-3035 or 612-514-4000	**Fee on div. inv.:**	0
Transfer Agent:	Norwest Bank Minnesota	**Discount (cash):**	0
Agent's Address:	P.O. Box 64854	**Discount (div.):**	0
	St. Paul, MN 55164-0854	**Auto invest:**	Yes
Agent's Phone:	800-468-9716	**Auto invest fee:**	$0
Other than USA:	Yes	**Selling info:**	Sells daily, by mail or fax, at market, for $3 +15¢/sh.

Company:	**Mellon Bank Corp.**	**Safekeeping:**	Yes
Symbol:	MEL	**Invests:**	Every 7 days beginning varies
Exchange:	NYSE	**Minimum:**	$100
Industry:	Banking	**Maximum:**	$100,000/year
Company Address:	One Mellon Bank Ctr.	**Min to qualify:**	1
	Pittsburgh, PA 15258-0001	**Fee on cash inv.:**	0!
Company Phone:	412-234-5601	**Fee on div. inv.:**	0!
Transfer Agent:	ChaseMellon Shareholder Ser-	**Discount (cash):**	0
	vices	**Discount (div.):**	0
Agent's Address:	P.O. Box 382009	**Auto invest:**	Yes
	Pittsburgh, PA 15250-8009	**Auto invest fee:**	$0
Agent's Phone:	800-205-7699	**Selling info:**	Sells weekly, by mail or phone, at avg. price, for $15 +12¢/sh.
Other than USA:	Yes		

Company:	**Merant plc**	**Safekeeping:**	Yes
Symbol:	MRNT	**Invests:**	Every 7 days beginning varies
Exchange:	OTC	**Minimum:**	$50
Industry:	Technology	**Maximum:**	$250,000/year
Company Address:	c/o BNY,101 Barclay St.,22 West	**Min to qualify:**	1
	New York, NY 10286	**Fee on cash inv.:**	$5 + 10¢/sh.
Company Phone:	800-943-9715	**Fee on div. inv.:**	5% to $5 + 10¢/sh.
Transfer Agent:	Bank of New York	**Discount (cash):**	0
Agent's Address:	P.O. Box 11258	**Discount (div.):**	0
	New York, NY 10286	**Auto invest:**	Yes
Agent's Phone:	888-269-2377	**Auto invest fee:**	$5 + 10¢/sh.
Other than USA:	Yes	**Selling info:**	Sells weekly, by mail, at market, for $5 +10¢/sh.

Company:	**Mercantile Bancorporation, Inc.**	Safekeeping:	Yes
		Invests:	Every 7 days beginning Thursday
Symbol:	MTL	Minimum:	$100
Exchange:	NYSE	Maximum:	$10,000/month
Industry:	Banking	Min to qualify:	1
Company Address:	Box 524	Fee on cash inv.:	$3 + 5¢/sh.
	St. Louis, MO 63166-0524	Fee on div. inv.:	0!
Company Phone:	314-418-2298 or 314-425-8237	Discount (cash):	0
Transfer Agent:	Harris Trust & Savings Bank	Discount (div.):	0
Agent's Address:	P.O. Box A-3504	Auto invest:	Yes
	Chicago, IL 60690-3504	Auto invest fee:	$1.50 + 5¢/sh.
Agent's Phone:	800-720-0417	Selling info:	Sells weekly, by mail, at market,
Other than USA:	Yes		for $10 + 5¢/sh.

Company:	**Mercantile Bankshares Corp.**	Safekeeping:	Yes
		Invests:	Every 90 days beginning 3/31
Symbol:	MRBK	Minimum:	$25
Exchange:	OTC	Maximum:	$5,000/quarter
Industry:	Banking	Min to qualify:	1
Company Address:	Box 1477	Fee on cash inv.:	0!
	Baltimore, MD 21203	Fee on div. inv.:	0!
Company Phone:	410-347-8374 or 410-237-5900	Discount (cash):	0
Transfer Agent:	Bank of New York	Discount (div.):	5%
Agent's Address:	P.O. Box1958	Auto invest:	No
	Newark, NJ 07101-9774	Auto invest fee:	$0
Agent's Phone:	800-524-4458	Selling info:	Not available
Other than USA:	Yes		

Company:	**Merchants Bancorp Inc.**	Safekeeping:	Yes
Symbol:	MBIA	Invests:	Every 90 days beginning 1/31
Exchange:	OTC	Minimum:	$25
Industry:	Bank holding company	Maximum:	$3,000/quarter
Company Address:	1851 West Galena Blvd., Box 289	Min to qualify:	1
	Aurora, IL 60507-0289	Fee on cash inv.:	0
Company Phone:	630-907-9000	Fee on div. inv.:	0
Transfer Agent:	Harris Trust & Savings Bank	Discount (cash):	0
Agent's Address:	P.O. Box A3309	Discount (div.):	0
	Chicago, IL 60690	Auto invest:	No
Agent's Phone:	312-461-6509	Auto invest fee:	$0
Other than USA:	Yes	Selling info:	Sells weekly, by mail, at market,
			for 5% to $3 + comm.

Company:	**Merck & Co., Inc.**	Safekeeping:	Yes
Symbol:	MRK	Invests:	Every 7 days beginning Tues.
Exchange:	NYSE	Minimum:	$50
Industry:	Drugs, specialty chem.	Maximum:	$50,000/year
Company Address:	Box 100, (WS 3AB-40)	Min to qualify:	1
	Whitehouse Station, NJ 08889-0100	Fee on cash inv.:	$5 + 1¢/sh.
Company Phone:	800-613-2104 or 908-423-1000	Fee on div. inv.:	4% to $2 + 1¢/sh.
Transfer Agent:	Norwest Bank Minnesota	Discount (cash):	0
Agent's Address:	P.O. Box 64854	Discount (div.):	0
	St. Paul, MN 55164-0854	Auto invest:	Yes
Agent's Phone:	888-291-3713	Auto invest fee:	$2
Other than USA:	Yes	Selling info:	Sells daily, by phone, mail, or fax,
			at avg. price, for $5 +1¢/sh.

Company:	**Meridian Diagnostics**	**Safekeeping:**	Yes
Symbol:	KITS	**Invests:**	Every 30 days beginning 1/30
Exchange:	OTC	**Minimum:**	$25
Industry:	Mfr. medical diagnostic kits	**Maximum:**	$1,000/month
Company Address:	3471 River Hills Dr.	**Min to qualify:**	1
	Cincinnati, OH 45244	**Fee on cash inv.:**	$3
Company Phone:	800-696-0739 or 513-271-3700	**Fee on div. inv.:**	5% to $3
Transfer Agent:	Fifth Third Bank	**Discount (cash):**	0
Agent's Address:	MD 10AT66, 38 Fountain Sq. Plaza	**Discount (div.):**	0
	Cincinnati, OH 45263	**Auto invest:**	No
Agent's Phone:	800-837-2755	**Auto invest fee:**	$0
Other than USA:	Yes	**Selling info:**	Sells weekly, by mail, at market, for comm.

Company:	**Meritor Automotive, Inc.**	**Safekeeping:**	Yes
Symbol:	MRA	**Invests:**	Every 7 days beginning Friday
Exchange:	NYSE	**Minimum:**	$50
Industry:	Manufacturer of automotive components	**Maximum:**	$100,000/year
		Min to qualify:	1
Company Address:	2135 West Maple Rd.	**Fee on cash inv.:**	$5 + 10¢/sh.
	Troy, MI 48084-7186	**Fee on div. inv.:**	5% to $3 + 10¢/sh.
Company Phone:	248-435-1000	**Discount (cash):**	0
Transfer Agent:	FCT (EquiServe)	**Discount (div.):**	0
Agent's Address:	P.O. Box 2598	**Auto invest:**	Yes
	Jersey City, NJ 07303-2598	**Auto invest fee:**	$2 + 10¢/sh
Agent's Phone:	800-519-3111	**Selling info:**	Sells daily, by mail, fax, or phone, at market, for $10 +12¢/sh.
Other than USA:	Yes		

Company:	**Merrill Lynch**	**Safekeeping:**	No
Symbol:	MER	**Invests:**	Every 30 days beginning 1/18
Exchange:	NYSE	**Minimum:**	$50
Industry:	Finance	**Maximum:**	$unlimited
Company Address:	World Financial Ctr., North Twr.	**Min to qualify:**	1
	New York, NY 10281-1332	**Fee on cash inv.:**	15%
		Fee on div. inv.:	0
Company Phone:	212-602-8459	**Discount (cash):**	0
Transfer Agent:	Merrill Lynch & Co.	**Discount (div.):**	0
Agent's Address:	P.O. Box 20, Church St. Station	**Auto invest:**	No
	New York, NY 10277-1004	**Auto invest fee:**	$0
Agent's Phone:	212-602-8459	**Selling info:**	Sells daily, by phone, at market, for 0
Other than USA:	Yes		

Company:	**Met-Pro Corp.**	**Safekeeping:**	Yes
Symbol:	MPR	**Invests:**	Every 30 days beginning 1/10
Exchange:	NYSE	**Minimum:**	$100
Industry:	Pollution control, fluid handling	**Maximum:**	$5,000/month
Company Address:	Box 144,160 Cassell Rd.	**Min to qualify:**	10
	Harleysville, PA 19438	**Fee on cash inv.:**	0!
Company Phone:	215-723-6751	**Fee on div. inv.:**	0!
Transfer Agent:	American Stock Transfer & Trust	**Discount (cash):**	0
Agent's Address:	40 Wall St., 46th Fl.	**Discount (div.):**	3%
	New York, Ny 10005	**Auto invest:**	Yes
Agent's Phone:	800-278-4353	**Auto invest fee:**	$0
Other than USA:	Yes	**Selling info:**	Sells weekly, by mail or fax, at avg. price, for $15 + comm.

Company:	**MGI Properties**	Safekeeping:	Yes
Symbol:	MGI	Invests:	Every 90 days beginning 1/13
Exchange:	NYSE	Minimum:	$100
Industry:	REIT	Maximum:	$2,500/quarter
Company Address:	One Winthrop Sq.	Min to qualify:	100
	Boston, MA 02110	Fee on cash inv.:	0
Company Phone:	617-422-6000	Fee on div. inv.:	0
Transfer Agent:	BankBoston (EquiServe)	Discount (cash):	3%
Agent's Address:	150 Royall Street	Discount (div.):	3%
	Canton, Ma 02021	Auto invest:	No
Agent's Phone:	800-730-6001	Auto invest fee:	$0
Other than USA:	Yes	Selling info:	Sells irregularly, by mail, at avg. price, for $1 to $15 + comm.

Company:	**Michaels Stores**	Safekeeping:	Yes
Symbol:	MIKE	Invests:	Every 30 days beginning 1/19
Exchange:	OTC	Minimum:	$100
Industry:	Retail,specialty art and home decor	Maximum:	$2,500/month
		Min to qualify:	1
Company Address:	Box 619566	Fee on cash inv.:	0
	Dallas, TX 75261-9566	Fee on div. inv.:	0
Company Phone:	972-409-1300 or 888-515-MIKE	Discount (cash):	0
Transfer Agent:	Harris Trust-Direct Stock Services	Discount (div.):	no
Agent's Address:	P.O. Box A3309	Auto invest:	No
	Chicago, IL 60690-3309	Auto invest fee:	$0
Agent's Phone:	800-577-4676	Selling info:	Sells weekly, by mail, at market, for $10 +12¢/sh.
Other than USA:	No		

Company:	**Michigan Financial Corp.**	Safekeeping:	Yes
Symbol:	MFCB	Invests:	Every 30 days beginning 1/20
Exchange:	OTC	Minimum:	$25
Industry:	Banking	Maximum:	$1,000/quarter
Company Address:	101 West Washington St., Box 10	Min to qualify:	1
	Marquette, MI 49855	Fee on cash inv.:	0
Company Phone:	906-228-6940	Fee on div. inv.:	0
Transfer Agent:	Norwest Bank Minnesota	Discount (cash):	0
Agent's Address:	P.O. Box 64856	Discount (div.):	0
	St. Paul, MN 55164-0856	Auto invest:	No
Agent's Phone:	800-468-9716	Auto invest fee:	$0
Other than USA:	Yes	Selling info:	Sells daily, by mail, at market, for $3 +15¢/sh.

Company:	**Micro Focus Group PLC**	Safekeeping:	Yes
Symbol:	MIFGY	Invests:	Every 7 days beginning varies
Exchange:	OTC	Minimum:	$50
Industry:	International business computing	Maximum:	$250,000/week
Company Address:	c/o BNY,101 Barclay St.,22 West	Min to qualify:	1
	New York, NY 10286	Fee on cash inv.:	$5 + 10¢/sh.
Company Phone:	800-943-9715	Fee on div. inv.:	5% to $5 + 10¢/sh.
Transfer Agent:	Bank of New York	Discount (cash):	0
Agent's Address:	P.O. Box 11258	Discount (div.):	0
	New York, NY 10286	Auto invest:	Yes
Agent's Phone:	888-269-2377	Auto invest fee:	$0
Other than USA:	Yes	Selling info:	Sells weekly, by phone or mail, at market, for $5 +10¢/ADS

Company:	**Mid-America Apt. Comm., Inc.**	Safekeeping:	Yes
		Invests:	Every 90 days beginning 1/31
Symbol:	MAA	Minimum:	$500
Exchange:	NYSE	Maximum:	$10,000/quarter
Industry:	REIT	Min to qualify:	1
Company Address:	6584 Poplar Ave., Ste. 340	Fee on cash inv.:	0
	Memphis, TN 38138	Fee on div. inv.:	0
Company Phone:	901-682-6600	Discount (cash):	3%
Transfer Agent:	First Union Nat'l Bank	Discount (div.):	3%
Agent's Address:	1525 West W.T. Harris Blvd.-3C3	Auto invest:	No
	Charlotte, NC 28288-1153	Auto invest fee:	$0
Agent's Phone:	800-829-8432	Selling info:	Sells weekly, by mail or fax, at avg.
Other than USA:	No		price, for 0

Company:	**Middlesex Water Co.**	Safekeeping:	Yes
Symbol:	MSEX	Invests:	Every 30 days beginning 1/1
Exchange:	OTC	Minimum:	$25
Industry:	Utility-water	Maximum:	$25,000/quarter
Company Address:	1500 Ronson Rd., Box 1500	Min to qualify:	1
	Iselin, NJ 08830	Fee on cash inv.:	0
Company Phone:	732-634-1500	Fee on div. inv.:	0
Transfer Agent:	Registrar & Transfer Co.	Discount (cash):	0
Agent's Address:	10 Commerce Drive	Discount (div.):	0
	Cranford, NJ 07016	Auto invest:	No
Agent's Phone:	800-368-5948	Auto invest fee:	$0
Other than USA:	Yes	Selling info:	Sells monthly, by mail, at market,
			for comm.

Company:	**MidSouth Bancorp, Inc.**	Safekeeping:	Yes
Symbol:	MSL	Invests:	Every 7 days beginning varies
Exchange:	ASE	Minimum:	$100
Industry:	Regional banks	Maximum:	$10,000/quarter
Company Address:	102 Versailles Blvd.,Versailles Ctr.	Min to qualify:	1o
	Lafayette, LA 70501	Fee on cash inv.:	0
Company Phone:	800-213-BANK or 318-237-8343	Fee on div. inv.:	0
Transfer Agent:	ChaseMellon Shareholder Ser-	Discount (cash):	0
	vices	Discount (div.):	0
Agent's Address:	P.O. Box 3338	Auto invest:	Yes
	South Hackensack, NJ 07606-1938	Auto invest fee:	$0
Agent's Phone:	888-216-8113	Selling info:	Sells weekly, by mail or phone, at
Other than USA:	Yes		market, for $15 +12¢/sh.

Company:	**Milacron, Inc.**	Safekeeping:	No
Symbol:	MZ	Invests:	Every 30 days beginning 1/12
Exchange:	NYSE	Minimum:	$25
Industry:	Machinery, factory supplies	Maximum:	$1,000/month
Company Address:	4701 Marburg Ave.	Min to qualify:	1
	Cincinnati, OH 45209-1086	Fee on cash inv.:	0!
Company Phone:	513-841-8100 or 513-841-7499	Fee on div. inv.:	0!
Transfer Agent:	ChaseMellon Shareholder Ser-	Discount (cash):	0
	vices	Discount (div.):	0
Agent's Address:	P.O.Box 3338	Auto invest:	No
	S. Hackensack, NJ 07606-1938	Auto invest fee:	$0
Agent's Phone:	800-426-5754	Selling info:	Sells weekly, by mail or phone, at
Other than USA:	Yes		market, for 12¢/sh.

Company:	**Millipore Corp.**	**Safekeeping:**	Yes
Symbol:	MIL	**Invests:**	Every 90 days beginning 1/28
Exchange:	NYSE	**Minimum:**	$25
Industry:	Mfr. fluid analyzing equipment	**Maximum:**	$3,000/quarter
Company Address:	80 Ashby Rd.	**Min to qualify:**	1
	Bedford, MA 01730-2271	**Fee on cash inv.:**	0
Company Phone:	781-533-6000	**Fee on div. inv.:**	0
Transfer Agent:	Boston Eq. (EquiServe)	**Discount (cash):**	0
Agent's Address:	P.O. Box 8040	**Discount (div.):**	0
	Boston, MA 02266-8040	**Auto invest:**	No
Agent's Phone:	800-730-4001	**Auto invest fee:**	$0
Other than USA:	No	**Selling info:**	Sells within 10 bus. days, by mail, at market, for comm.

Company:	**Mills Corp.**	**Safekeeping:**	Yes
Symbol:	MLS	**Invests:**	Every 30 days beginning 1/20
Exchange:	NYSE	**Minimum:**	$25
Industry:	REIT	**Maximum:**	$100,000/year
Company Address:	1300 Wilson Blvd., Ste.400	**Min to qualify:**	1
	Arlington, VA 22209	**Fee on cash inv.:**	0!
Company Phone:	703-526-5039 or 703-526-5000	**Fee on div. inv.:**	0!
Transfer Agent:	FCT (EquiServe)	**Discount (cash):**	0
Agent's Address:	P.O. Box 2598	**Discount (div.):**	0
	Jersey City, NJ 07303-2598	**Auto invest:**	No
Agent's Phone:	201-324-0498	**Auto invest fee:**	$0
Other than USA:	Yes	**Selling info:**	Sells daily, by mail, at market, for $10 +12¢/sh.

Company:	**Minnesota Mining & Man-ufacturing**	**Safekeeping:**	Yes
		Invests:	Every 30 days beginning 1/12
Symbol:	MMM	**Minimum:**	$10
Exchange:	NYSE	**Maximum:**	$10,000/quarter
Industry:	Diversified mfr.	**Min to qualify:**	1
Company Address:	3M Center 225-1S-15	**Fee on cash inv.:**	0!
	St. Paul, MN 55144-1000	**Fee on div. inv.:**	0!
Company Phone:	651-736-1915 or 651-733-1110	**Discount (cash):**	0
Transfer Agent:	Norwest Bank Minnesota	**Discount (div.):**	0
Agent's Address:	P.O. Box 64854	**Auto invest:**	Yes
	St. Paul, MN 55164-0854	**Auto invest fee:**	$0
Agent's Phone:	800-401-1952	**Selling info:**	Sells daily, by mail or fax, at market, for $3 +15¢/sh.
Other than USA:	Yes		

Company:	**Minnesota Power, Inc.**	**Safekeeping:**	Yes
Symbol:	MPL	**Invests:**	Every 30 days beginning 1/25
Exchange:	NYSE	**Minimum:**	$10
Industry:	Utility-electric	**Maximum:**	$100,000/year
Company Address:	30 West Superior St.	**Min to qualify:**	1
	Duluth, MN 55802-2093	**Fee on cash inv.:**	0
Company Phone:	800-535-3056 or 218-723-3974	**Fee on div. inv.:**	0
Transfer Agent:	Minnesota Power Inc.	**Discount (cash):**	0
Agent's Address:	30 W. Superior St.	**Discount (div.):**	0
	Duluth , MN 55802-2093	**Auto invest:**	Yes
Agent's Phone:	800-535-3056	**Auto invest fee:**	$0
Other than USA:	No	**Selling info:**	Sells daily, by mail or fax, at market, for $5

Company:	**Mobil Corp.**	Safekeeping:	Yes
Symbol:	MOB	Invests:	Every 7 days beginning Wed.
Exchange:	NYSE	Minimum:	$10
Industry:	Petroleum	Maximum:	$7,500/month
Company Address:	3225 Gallows Rd.	Min to qualify:	1
	Fairfax, VA 22037-0001	Fee on cash inv.:	0!
Company Phone:	703-846-3898 or 703-846-3000	Fee on div. inv.:	0!
Transfer Agent:	ChaseMellon Shareholder Services	Discount (cash):	0
Agent's Address:	P.O. Box 3336	Discount (div.):	0
	S. Hackensack, NJ 07606-1936	Auto invest:	No
Agent's Phone:	800-648-9291	Auto invest fee:	$0
Other than USA:	Yes	Selling info:	Sells weekly, by mail or phone, at market, for $5 +10¢/sh.

Company:	**Modern Times Grp.**	Safekeeping:	Yes
Symbol:	MTGNY	Invests:	Every 7 days beginning varies
Exchange:	OTC	Minimum:	$50
Industry:	Media, publishing	Maximum:	$250,000/year
Company Address:	c/o BNY,101 Barclay St.,22 West	Min to qualify:	1
	New York, NY 10286	Fee on cash inv.:	$5 + 10¢/sh.
Company Phone:	800-943-9715	Fee on div. inv.:	5% to $5 + 10¢/sh.
Transfer Agent:	Bank of New York	Discount (cash):	0
Agent's Address:	P.O. Box 11258	Discount (div.):	0
	New York, NY 10286	Auto invest:	Yes
Agent's Phone:	888-269-2377	Auto invest fee:	$5 + 10¢/sh.
Other than USA:	Yes	Selling info:	Sells weekly, by mail, at market, for $5 +10¢/sh.

Company:	**Modine Manufacturing Co.**	Safekeeping:	Yes
		Invests:	Every 30 days beginning 1/5
Symbol:	MODI	Minimum:	$10
Exchange:	OTC	Maximum:	$5,000/month
Industry:	Auto & truck parts	Min to qualify:	1
Company Address:	1500 DeKoven Ave.	Fee on cash inv.:	0!
	Racine, WI 53403-2552	Fee on div. inv.:	0!
Company Phone:	414-636-1200	Discount (cash):	0
Transfer Agent:	Norwest Bank Minnesota	Discount (div.):	0
Agent's Address:	P.O. Box 64854	Auto invest:	Yes
	St. Paul, MN 55164-0854	Auto invest fee:	$0
Agent's Phone:	800-468-9716	Selling info:	Sells within 5 bus. days, by mail or phone, at avg. price, for $10 +15¢/sh.
Other than USA:	Yes		

Company:	**Molson Companies Ltd. A**	Safekeeping:	No
Symbol:	MOLA	Invests:	Every 90 days beginning 1/1
Exchange:	TSE	Minimum:	$100
Industry:	Brewer, food & retailer	Maximum:	$5,000/quarter Cdn.
Company Address:	Scotia Plz.,40 King St.West, Ste.3600	Min to qualify:	1
		Fee on cash inv.:	0!
	Toronto, Ontario M5H 3Z5 Canada	Fee on div. inv.:	0!
		Discount (cash):	0
Company Phone:	416-360-1786	Discount (div.):	0
Transfer Agent:	CIBC Mellon Trust	Auto invest:	No
Agent's Address:	393 University Ave., 5th Fl.	Auto invest fee:	$0
	Toronto, ON M5G 2M7 Canada	Selling info:	Sells irregularly, by mail, at market, for $0
Agent's Phone:	800-387-0825		
Other than USA:	No		

Company:	**Molson Companies Ltd. B**	**Safekeeping:**	No
Symbol:	MOLB	**Invests:**	Every 90 days beginning 1/1
Exchange:	TSE	**Minimum:**	$100
Industry:	Brewer, food & retailer	**Maximum:**	$5,000/quarter Cdn.
Company Address:	Scotia Plz.,40 King St. West,	**Min to qualify:**	1
	Ste.3600	**Fee on cash inv.:**	0!
	Toronto, Ontario M5H 3Z5	**Fee on div. inv.:**	0!
	Canada	**Discount (cash):**	0
Company Phone:	416-360-1786	**Discount (div.):**	0
Transfer Agent:	CIBC Mellon Trust	**Auto invest:**	No
Agent's Address:	393 University Ave., 5th Fl.	**Auto invest fee:**	$0
	Toronto, ON M5G 2M7 Canada	**Selling info:**	Sells irregularly, by mail,
Agent's Phone:	800-387-0825		at market, for $0
Other than USA:	No		

Company:	**Monmouth Capital Corp.**	**Safekeeping:**	No
Symbol:	MONM	**Invests:**	Every 30 days beginning 1/15
Exchange:	OTC	**Minimum:**	$500
Industry:	Real estate	**Maximum:**	$40,000/month
Company Address:	125 Wyckoff Rd.	**Min to qualify:**	1
	Eatontown, NJ 07724	**Fee on cash inv.:**	0!
Company Phone:	732-542-4927	**Fee on div. inv.:**	0!
Transfer Agent:	ChaseMellon Shareholder Services	**Discount (cash):**	5%
Agent's Address:	P.O. Box 750	**Discount (div.):**	5%
	Pittsburgh, PA 15230	**Auto invest:**	No
Agent's Phone:	800-526-0801	**Auto invest fee:**	$0
Other than USA:	Yes	**Selling info:**	Not available

Company:	**Monmouth REIT**	**Safekeeping:**	No
Symbol:	MNRTA	**Invests:**	Every 30 days beginning 1/15
Exchange:	OTC	**Minimum:**	$500
Industry:	REIT	**Maximum:**	$40,000/month
Company Address:	125 Wyckoff Rd., Box 335	**Min to qualify:**	1
	Eatontown, NJ 07724	**Fee on cash inv.:**	0!
Company Phone:	732-542-4927	**Fee on div. inv.:**	0!
Transfer Agent:	ChaseMellon Shareholder Services	**Discount (cash):**	5%
Agent's Address:	P.O. Box 750	**Discount (div.):**	5%
	Pittsburgh, PA 15230	**Auto invest:**	No
Agent's Phone:	800-526-0801	**Auto invest fee:**	$0
Other than USA:	Yes	**Selling info:**	Not available

Company:	**Monsanto Co.**	**Safekeeping:**	Yes
Symbol:	MTC	**Invests:**	Every 30 days beginning 1/12
Exchange:	NYSE	**Minimum:**	$25
Industry:	Agricultural science,	**Maximum:**	$100,000/year
	pharmaceuticals	**Min to qualify:**	1
Company Address:	800 North Lindbergh Blvd.	**Fee on cash inv.:**	2.5% to $4
	St. Louis, MO 63167	**Fee on div. inv.:**	2.5% to $4
Company Phone:	314-694-5432	**Discount (cash):**	0
Transfer Agent:	FCT (EquiServe)	**Discount (div.):**	0
Agent's Address:	P.O. Box 2500	**Auto invest:**	Yes
	Jersey City, NJ 07303-2500	**Auto invest fee:**	$1
Agent's Phone:	888-312-8333	**Selling info:**	Sells daily, by mail or phone, at
Other than USA:	Yes		market, for $10 +12¢/sh.

Company:	**Montana Power (The)**	**Safekeeping:**	Yes
Symbol:	MTP	**Invests:**	Every 15 days beginning 1/13
Exchange:	NYSE	**Minimum:**	$25
Industry:	Utility-electric & gas, telecomm., mining	**Maximum:**	$60,000/year
		Min to qualify:	1
Company Address:	40 East Broadway St. Butte, MT 59701-9394	**Fee on cash inv.:**	3¢/sh.
		Fee on div. inv.:	3¢/sh.
Company Phone:	800-245-6767 or 406-497-2374	**Discount (cash):**	0
Transfer Agent:	Montana Power Co.	**Discount (div.):**	0
Agent's Address:	40 East Broadway Butte, MT 59701-9394	**Auto invest:**	Yes
		Auto invest fee:	$0
Agent's Phone:	800-245-6767	**Selling info:**	Sells biweekly, by mail or fax, at market, for 14¢/sh.
Other than USA:	Yes		

Company:	**Moore Corp. Ltd.**	**Safekeeping:**	No
Symbol:	MCL	**Invests:**	Every 90 days beginning 1/12
Exchange:	NYSE	**Minimum:**	$50
Industry:	Business forms & info. handling prods.	**Maximum:**	$5,000/quarter Cdn.
		Min to qualify:	1
Company Address:	1 First Canadian Pl., Box 78 Toronto, Ont. M5X 1G5 Canada	**Fee on cash inv.:**	0
		Fee on div. inv.:	0
Company Phone:	416-364-2600	**Discount (cash):**	0
Transfer Agent:	CIBC Mellon Trust	**Discount (div.):**	0
Agent's Address:	Box 7010, Adelaide St. Postal Station Toronto, ON Canada M5C 2W9	**Auto invest:**	No
		Auto invest fee:	$0
		Selling info:	Not available
Agent's Phone:	800-387-0825		
Other than USA:	Yes		

Company:	**Morgan (J.P.) & Co.**	**Safekeeping:**	Yes
Symbol:	JPM	**Invests:**	Every 30 days beginning 1/15
Exchange:	NYSE	**Minimum:**	$50
Industry:	Banking	**Maximum:**	$5,000/month
Company Address:	60 Wall St. New York, NY 10260	**Min to qualify:**	1
		Fee on cash inv.:	0
Company Phone:	212-648-9446 or 212-483-2323	**Fee on div. inv.:**	0
Transfer Agent:	FCT (EquiServe)	**Discount (cash):**	0
Agent's Address:	P.O. Box 2500 Jersey City, NJ 07303	**Discount (div.):**	0
		Auto invest:	No
Agent's Phone:	800-519-3111	**Auto invest fee:**	$0
Other than USA:	Yes	**Selling info:**	Sells daily, by mail, at market, for $10 +12¢/sh.

Company:	**Morgan Stanley Asia-Pacific Fund, Inc.**	**Safekeeping:**	No
		Invests:	Every 180 days beginning 1/9
Symbol:	APF	**Minimum:**	$100
Exchange:	NYSE	**Maximum:**	$3,000/year
Industry:	Closed-end fund	**Min to qualify:**	1
Company Address:	c/o Amer. Stk, 40 Wall St., 46th fl. New York, NY 10005	**Fee on cash inv.:**	0
		Fee on div. inv.:	0
Company Phone:	800-221-6726 or 617-557-8844	**Discount (cash):**	0
Transfer Agent:	American Stock Transfer	**Discount (div.):**	0
Agent's Address:	40 Wall St. New York, NY 10005	**Auto invest:**	No
		Auto invest fee:	$0
Agent's Phone:	800-278-4353	**Selling info:**	Sells weekly, by mail, at market, for 4¢/sh.
Other than USA:	Yes		

Company:	**Morgan Stanley Dean Witter & Co.**	Safekeeping:	Yes
		Invests:	Every 15 days beginning 1/1
Symbol:	MWD	Minimum:	$100
Exchange:	NYSE	Maximum:	$40,000/year
Industry:	Financial services	Min to qualify:	1
Company Address:	1585 Broadway	Fee on cash inv.:	0
	New York, NY 10036	Fee on div. inv.:	0
Company Phone:	212-762-8131 or 212-392-2222	Discount (cash):	0
Transfer Agent:	M.S. Dean Witter Trust FSB	Discount (div.):	0
Agent's Address:	Harborside Financial Ctr., Plaza Two	Auto invest:	Yes
		Auto invest fee:	$0
	Jersey City, NJ 07311-3977	Selling info:	Sells irregularly, by mail, at avg.
Agent's Phone:	800-622-2393		price, for $5 + comm.
Other than USA:	No		

Company:	**Motorola, Inc.**	Safekeeping:	Yes
Symbol:	MOT	Invests:	Every 7 days beginning varies
Exchange:	NYSE	Minimum:	$100
Industry:	Electronics	Maximum:	$120,000/year
Company Address:	1303 East Algonquin Rd.	Min to qualify:	1
	Schaumburg, IL 60196	Fee on cash inv.:	$5 + 10¢/sh.
Company Phone:	800-262-8509 or 847-576-4995	Fee on div. inv.:	0!
Transfer Agent:	Harris Trust & Savings Bank	Discount (cash):	0
Agent's Address:	P.O.Box A3309	Discount (div.):	0
	Chicago, IL 60690	Auto invest:	Yes
Agent's Phone:	800-704-4098	Auto invest fee:	$1.50 + 10¢/sh.
Other than USA:	Yes	Selling info:	Sells within 5 bus. days, by mail, at market, for $10 +10¢/sh.

Company:	**Myers Industries, Inc.**	Safekeeping:	Yes
Symbol:	MYE	Invests:	Every 90 days beginning 1/1
Exchange:	ASE	Minimum:	$50
Industry:	Equipment dist. plastic mfg.	Maximum:	$2,500/quarter
Company Address:	1293 South Main St.	Min to qualify:	1
	Akron, OH 44301	Fee on cash inv.:	0!
Company Phone:	330-253-5592	Fee on div. inv.:	0!
Transfer Agent:	FCT (EquiServe)	Discount (cash):	0
Agent's Address:	14 Wall Street	Discount (div.):	0
	New York, NY 10005	Auto invest:	No
Agent's Phone:	201-324-0498	Auto invest fee:	$0
Other than USA:	No	Selling info:	Sells daily, by mail, at avg. price, for $10 +12¢/sh.

Company:	**Mylan Laboratories**	Safekeeping:	Yes
Symbol:	MYL	Invests:	Every 90 days beginning 1/15
Exchange:	NYSE	Minimum:	$50
Industry:	Pharmaceutical products	Maximum:	$5,000/quarter
Company Address:	1030 Century Bldg., 130 Seventh St.	Min to qualify:	25
	Pittsburgh, PA 15222	Fee on cash inv.:	0!
Company Phone:	412-232-0100	Fee on div. inv.:	0!
Transfer Agent:	American Stock Transfer	Discount (cash):	0
Agent's Address:	40 Wall St. - 46th Floor	Discount (div.):	0
	New York, NY 10269-0436	Auto invest:	No
Agent's Phone:	212-936-5100	Auto invest fee:	$0
Other than USA:	No	Selling info:	Sells weekly, by mail, at market, for $7.50 + comm.

Company:	**Nalco Chemical Co.**	Safekeeping:	Yes
Symbol:	NLC	Invests:	Every 90 days beginning 3/10
Exchange:	NYSE	Minimum:	$25
Industry:	Chemicals	Maximum:	$15,000/quarter
Company Address:	One Nalco Ctr.	Min to qualify:	1
	Naperville, IL 60563-1198	Fee on cash inv.:	0
Company Phone:	630-305-1000	Fee on div. inv.:	0
Transfer Agent:	FCT (EquiServe)	Discount (cash):	0
Agent's Address:	P.O. Box 2500	Discount (div.):	0
	Jersey City, NJ 07303	Auto invest:	Yes
Agent's Phone:	800-446-2617	Auto invest fee:	$1
Other than USA:	No	Selling info:	Sells irregularly, by mail, at market, for $10 +12¢/sh.

Company:	**Nash Finch Co.**	Safekeeping:	No
Symbol:	NAFC	Invests:	Every 30 days beginning varies
Exchange:	OTC	Minimum:	$10
Industry:	Wholesale & retail food distribution	Maximum:	$1,000/month
		Min to qualify:	1
Company Address:	7600 France Ave.South, Box 355	Fee on cash inv.:	0!
	Minneapolis, MN 55440-0355	Fee on div. inv.:	0!
Company Phone:	612-832-0534 or 612-844-1155	Discount (cash):	0
Transfer Agent:	Norwest Bank Minnesota	Discount (div.):	0
Agent's Address:	P.O. Box 64854	Auto invest:	No
	St. Paul, MN 55164-0854	Auto invest fee:	$0
Agent's Phone:	800-468-9716	Selling info:	Sells daily, by mail, at market, for $3 +15¢/sh.
Other than USA:	Yes		

Company:	**Nashua Corp.**	Safekeeping:	Yes
Symbol:	NSH	Invests:	Every 45 days beginning 2/15
Exchange:	NYSE	Minimum:	$100
Industry:	Office equip.	Maximum:	$5,000/quarter
Company Address:	Box 2002	Min to qualify:	1
	Nashua, NH 03061-2002	Fee on cash inv.:	0
Company Phone:	603-880-2323 or 603-880-2209	Fee on div. inv.:	0
Transfer Agent:	BankBoston (EquiServe)	Discount (cash):	0
Agent's Address:	Box 8040-MS 45-02-09	Discount (div.):	0
	Boston, MA 02266-8040	Auto invest:	No
Agent's Phone:	781-575-3100	Auto invest fee:	$0
Other than USA:	Yes	Selling info:	Sells within 10 bus. days, by mail, at market, for $0

Company:	**National Australia Bank Ltd.**	Safekeeping:	Yes
		Invests:	Every 7 days beginning varies
Symbol:	NAB	Minimum:	$50
Exchange:	NYSE	Maximum:	$250,000/year
Industry:	Regional banks	Min to qualify:	1
Company Address:	c/o BNY,101 Barclay St.,22 West	Fee on cash inv.:	$5 + 10¢/sh.
	New York, NY 10286	Fee on div. inv.:	5% to $5 + 10¢/sh.
Company Phone:	800-943-9715	Discount (cash):	0
Transfer Agent:	Bank of New York	Discount (div.):	0
Agent's Address:	P.O. Box 11258	Auto invest:	Yes
	New York, NY 10286	Auto invest fee:	$5 + 10¢/sh.
Agent's Phone:	888-269-2377	Selling info:	Sells weekly, by mail, at market, for $5 +10¢/sh.
Other than USA:	Yes		

Company:	**National Bancorp of Alaska**	**Safekeeping:**	Yes
		Invests:	Every 30 days beginning 1/15
Symbol:	NBAK	**Minimum:**	$50
Exchange:	OTC	**Maximum:**	$10,000/quarter
Industry:	Banking	**Min to qualify:**	1
Company Address:	Box 100600	**Fee on cash inv.:**	0
	Anchorage, AK 99510-0600	**Fee on div. inv.:**	0
Company Phone:	888-748-7878 or 907-276-1132	**Discount (cash):**	0
Transfer Agent:	Nat'l Bancorp of AK	**Discount (div.):**	0
Agent's Address:	301 West Northern Lights Blvd.	**Auto invest:**	No
	Anchorage, AK 99503	**Auto invest fee:**	$0
Agent's Phone:	888-748-7878	**Selling info:**	Not available
Other than USA:	No		

Company:	**National City Banc- shares, Inc.**	**Safekeeping:**	Yes
		Invests:	Every 30 days beginning 1/7
Symbol:	NCBE	**Minimum:**	$100
Exchange:	OTC	**Maximum:**	$10,000/month
Industry:	Bank holding co.	**Min to qualify:**	1
Company Address:	227 Main St., Box 868	**Fee on cash inv.:**	0!
	Evansville, IN 47705-0868	**Fee on div. inv.:**	0!
Company Phone:	800-467-1928 or 812-464-9675	**Discount (cash):**	0
Transfer Agent:	Fifth Third Bank	**Discount (div.):**	0
Agent's Address:	38 Fountain Sq. Plaza,	**Auto invest:**	Yes
	MD#1090F5-4129	**Auto invest fee:**	$0
	Cincinnati, OH 45263-8855	**Selling info:**	Sells weekly, by mail, at market,
Agent's Phone:	800-837-2755		for 0!
Other than USA:	No		

Company:	**National City Corp.**	**Safekeeping:**	Yes
Symbol:	NCC	**Invests:**	Every 30 days beginning 1/1
Exchange:	NYSE	**Minimum:**	$50
Industry:	Banking	**Maximum:**	$500/month
Company Address:	Box 5756, Dept. 2101	**Min to qualify:**	1
	Cleveland, OH 44101-0756	**Fee on cash inv.:**	0!
Company Phone:	800-622-4204 or 216-575-2000	**Fee on div. inv.:**	0!
Transfer Agent:	National City Bank	**Discount (cash):**	3%
Agent's Address:	P.O. Box 92301	**Discount (div.):**	3%
	Cleveland, OH 44193-0900	**Auto invest:**	Yes
Agent's Phone:	800-622-6757	**Auto invest fee:**	$0
Other than USA:	Yes	**Selling info:**	Sells weekly, by mail, at market,
			for comm.

Company:	**National Commerce Bancorp.**	**Safekeeping:**	Yes
		Invests:	Every 45 days beginning 1/2
Symbol:	NCBC	**Minimum:**	$100
Exchange:	OTC	**Maximum:**	$3,500/month
Industry:	Banking	**Min to qualify:**	1
Company Address:	One Commerce Sq.	**Fee on cash inv.:**	0!
	Memphis, TN 38150	**Fee on div. inv.:**	0!
Company Phone:	901-523-3434	**Discount (cash):**	0
Transfer Agent:	Bank of New York	**Discount (div.):**	0
Agent's Address:	P.O.Box 1958	**Auto invest:**	No
	Newark, NJ 07101-9774	**Auto invest fee:**	$0
Agent's Phone:	800-524-4458	**Selling info:**	Sells weekly, by mail, at avg. price,
Other than USA:	Yes		for 7¢/sh.

Company:	**National Data Corp.**	Safekeeping:	Yes
Symbol:	NDC	Invests:	Every 30 days beginning 1/30
Exchange:	NYSE	Minimum:	$25
Industry:	Information processing	Maximum:	$1,000/quarter
Company Address:	National Data Plaza	Min to qualify:	1
	Atlanta, GA 30329-2086	Fee on cash inv.:	0!
Company Phone:	404-728-2000 or 404-728-2432	Fee on div. inv.:	0!
Transfer Agent:	SunTrust Bank, Atlanta	Discount (cash):	0
Agent's Address:	P.O. Box 4625	Discount (div.):	0
	Atlanta, GA 30302-4625	Auto invest:	No
Agent's Phone:	800-568-3476	Auto invest fee:	$0
Other than USA:	No	Selling info:	Sells weekly, by mail, at market, for 5¢/sh.

Company:	**National Fuel Gas**	Safekeeping:	Yes
Symbol:	NFG	Invests:	Every 30 days beginning 1/15
Exchange:	NYSE	Minimum:	$25
Industry:	Utility-gas	Maximum:	$5,000/month
Company Address:	10 Lafayette Sq.	Min to qualify:	1
	Buffalo, NY 14203-1899	Fee on cash inv.:	0!
Company Phone:	716-857-6987 or 716-857-7000	Fee on div. inv.:	0!
Transfer Agent:	ChaseMellon Shareholder Services	Discount (cash):	0
Agent's Address:	P.O. Box 3336	Discount (div.):	0
	South Hackensack, NJ 07606-1936	Auto invest:	No
Agent's Phone:	800-648-8166	Auto invest fee:	$0
Other than USA:	Yes	Selling info:	Sells daily, by mail or phone, at market, for $15 + comm.

Company:	**National Health Investors**	Safekeeping:	Yes
Symbol:	NHI	Invests:	Every 30 days beginning varies
Exchange:	NYSE	Minimum:	$100
Industry:	REIT	Maximum:	$5,000/quarter
Company Address:	100 Vine St., Ste. 1402	Min to qualify:	1
	Murfreesboro, TN 37130	Fee on cash inv.:	0
Company Phone:	615-890-9100	Fee on div. inv.:	0
Transfer Agent:	SunTrust Bank, Atlanta	Discount (cash):	0
Agent's Address:	P.O. Box 4625	Discount (div.):	0
	Atlanta, GA 30302-4625	Auto invest:	No
Agent's Phone:	800-568-3476	Auto invest fee:	$0
Other than USA:	Yes	Selling info:	Sells biweekly, by mail, at market, for 8¢/sh.

Company:	**National Service Industries, Inc.**	Safekeeping:	Yes
		Invests:	Every 7 days beginning 1/7
Symbol:	NSI	Minimum:	$25
Exchange:	NYSE	Maximum:	$350,000/year
Industry:	Lighting equip., textile rentals, specialty chemicals, envelopes	Min to qualify:	1
		Fee on cash inv.:	3¢/sh.
Company Address:	1420 Peachtree St., N.E.	Fee on div. inv.:	0!
	Atlanta, GA 30309-3002	Discount (cash):	0
Company Phone:	404-853-1247 or 404-853-1000	Discount (div.):	0
Transfer Agent:	FCT (EquiServe)	Auto invest:	Yes
Agent's Address:	P.O. Box 2598	Auto invest fee:	$0
	Jersey City, NJ 07303-2598	Selling info:	Sells daily, by mail or phone, at market, for $15 +12¢/sh.
Agent's Phone:	888-836-5069		
Other than USA:	Yes		

Company:	**National Westminster Bank plc**	Safekeeping:	Yes
		Invests:	Every 7 days beginning varies
Symbol:	NW	Minimum:	$50
Exchange:	NYSE	Maximum:	$100,000/year
Industry:	Banking	Min to qualify:	1
Company Address:	c/o Morgan Guaranty Trust,	Fee on cash inv.:	$5 + 12¢/sh.
	Box 9073	Fee on div. inv.:	5% up $2.50
	Boston, MA 02205-9948	Discount (cash):	0
Company Phone:	800-428-4237	Discount (div.):	0
Transfer Agent:	Morgan Guaranty Trust Co.	Auto invest:	Yes
Agent's Address:	P.O. Box 9073	Auto invest fee:	$5
	Boston, MA 02205-9948	Selling info:	Sells daily, by phone or mail, at
Agent's Phone:	800-428-4237		avg. price, for $5 +12¢/sh.
Other than USA:	No		

Company:	**National-Standard Co.**	Safekeeping:	Yes
Symbol:	NSD	Invests:	Every 30 days beginning 1/1
Exchange:	NYSE	Minimum:	$10
Industry:	Wire & wire-related prods.	Maximum:	$3,000/month
Company Address:	1618 Terminal Rd.	Min to qualify:	1
	Niles, MI 49120	Fee on cash inv.:	0
Company Phone:	800-777-1618 or 616-683-8100	Fee on div. inv.:	0
Transfer Agent:	Boston Eq. (EquiServe)	Discount (cash):	0
Agent's Address:	P.O. Box 8200	Discount (div.):	0
	Boston, MA 02266-8200	Auto invest:	No
Agent's Phone:	800-426-5523	Auto invest fee:	$0
Other than USA:	No	Selling info:	Sells weekly, by mail, at market,
			for $2.50 +15¢/sh.

Company:	**Nationwide Financial Services A**	Safekeeping:	Yes
		Invests:	Every 7 days beginning varies
Symbol:	NFS	Minimum:	$100
Exchange:	NYSE	Maximum:	$120,000/year
Industry:	Annuity & life insurance products	Min to qualify:	1
Company Address:	One Nationwide Plaza	Fee on cash inv.:	$5 + 3¢/sh.
	Columbus, OH 43215	Fee on div. inv.:	5% to $3 + 3¢/sh.
Company Phone:	614-249-3270 or 614-249-7111	Discount (cash):	0
Transfer Agent:	FCT (EquiServe)	Discount (div.):	0
Agent's Address:	P.O. Box 2598	Auto invest:	Yes
	Jersey City, NJ 07303-2598	Auto invest fee:	$2 + 3¢/sh.
Agent's Phone:	800-446-2617	Selling info:	Sells daily, by mail or phone, at
Other than USA:	Yes		market, for $15 +12¢/sh.

Company:	**NEC Corp.**	Safekeeping:	Yes
Symbol:	NIPNY	Invests:	Every 7 days beginning varies
Exchange:	OTC	Minimum:	$50
Industry:	Audio & video equipment	Maximum:	$250,000/year
Company Address:	c/o BNY,101 Barclay St.,22 West	Min to qualify:	1
	New York, NY 10286	Fee on cash inv.:	$5 + 10¢/sh.
Company Phone:	800-943-9715	Fee on div. inv.:	5% to $5 + 10¢/sh.
Transfer Agent:	Bank of New York	Discount (cash):	0
Agent's Address:	P.O. Box 11258	Discount (div.):	0
	New York, NY 10286	Auto invest:	Yes
Agent's Phone:	888-269-2377	Auto invest fee:	$5 + 10¢/sh.
Other than USA:	Yes	Selling info:	Sells weekly, by mail, at market,
			for $5 +10¢/sh.

Company:	**Neiman Marcus Group**	**Safekeeping:**	Yes	
Symbol:	NMG	**Invests:**	Every 45 days beginning 1/10	
Exchange:	NYSE	**Minimum:**	$25	
Industry:	Retail stores	**Maximum:**	$2,500/45 days	
Company Address:	27 Boylston St., Box 9187	**Min to qualify:**	1	
	Chestnut Hill, MA 02167-9187	**Fee on cash inv.:**	0!	
Company Phone:	617-232-0760	**Fee on div. inv.:**	0!	
Transfer Agent:	Boston Eq. (EquiServe)	**Discount (cash):**	0	
Agent's Address:	P.O. Box 644, MS 45-01-05	**Discount (div.):**	0	
	Boston, MA 02102-0644	**Auto invest:**	No	
Agent's Phone:	800-730-4001	**Auto invest fee:**	$0	
Other than USA:	No	**Selling info:**	Sells within 10 bus. days, by mail, at market, for 0!	

Company:	**Nera A.S. ADS**	**Safekeeping:**	Yes	
Symbol:	NERAY	**Invests:**	Every 7 days beginning varies	
Exchange:	OTC	**Minimum:**	$50	
Industry:	Telecommunications	**Maximum:**	$250,000/week	
Company Address:	c/o BNY,101 Barclay St., 22 West	**Min to qualify:**	1	
	New York, NY 10286	**Fee on cash inv.:**	$5 + 10¢/sh.	
Company Phone:	800-943-9715	**Fee on div. inv.:**	5% to $5 + 10¢/sh.	
Transfer Agent:	Bank of New York	**Discount (cash):**	0	
Agent's Address:	P.O. Box 11258	**Discount (div.):**	0	
	New York, NY 10286	**Auto invest:**	Yes	
Agent's Phone:	888-269-2377	**Auto invest fee:**	$0	
Other than USA:	Yes	**Selling info:**	Sells weekly, by phone or mail, at avg. price, for $5 +10¢/ADS	

Company:	**Nestle SA**	**Safekeeping:**	Yes	
Symbol:	NSRGY	**Invests:**	Every 30 days beginning 1/7	
Exchange:	OTC	**Minimum:**	$20	
Industry:	Food & beverage	**Maximum:**	$60,000/year	
Company Address:	c/o Morgan Guaranty Trust,	**Min to qualify:**	1	
	Box 9073	**Fee on cash inv.:**	5¢/sh.	
	Boston, MA 02205-9948	**Fee on div. inv.:**	5¢/sh.	
Company Phone:	800-428-4237	**Discount (cash):**	0	
Transfer Agent:	Morgan Guaranty Trust Co.	**Discount (div.):**	0	
Agent's Address:	PO Box 9073	**Auto invest:**	No	
	Boston, MA 02205-9948	**Auto invest fee:**	$0	
Agent's Phone:	800-428-4237	**Selling info:**	Sells daily, by mail, at market, for 15¢/sh.	
Other than USA:	Yes			

Company:	**NetCom Systems AB**	**Safekeeping:**	Yes	
Symbol:	NECSY	**Invests:**	Every 7 days beginning varies	
Exchange:	OTC	**Minimum:**	$50	
Industry:	Telecommunications	**Maximum:**	$250,000/year	
Company Address:	c/o BNY,101 Barclay St.,22 West	**Min to qualify:**	1	
	New York, NY 10286	**Fee on cash inv.:**	$5 + 10¢/sh.	
Company Phone:	800-943-9715	**Fee on div. inv.:**	5% to $5 + 10¢/sh.	
Transfer Agent:	Bank of New York	**Discount (cash):**	0	
Agent's Address:	P.O. Box 11258	**Discount (div.):**	0	
	New York, NY 10286	**Auto invest:**	Yes	
Agent's Phone:	888-269-2377	**Auto invest fee:**	$5 + 10¢/sh.	
Other than USA:	Yes	**Selling info:**	Sells weekly, by mail, at market, for $5 +10¢/sh.	

Company:	**New America High Income**	Safekeeping:	No
		Invests:	Every 90 days beginning 3/31
Symbol:	HYB	Minimum:	$100
Exchange:	NYSE	Maximum:	$500/quarter
Industry:	Closed-end fund	Min to qualify:	1
Company Address:	c/o State St. Bk. & Trust, Box 8200	Fee on cash inv.:	75¢ + comm.
	Boston, MA 02266-8200	Fee on div. inv.:	comm.
Company Phone:	800-426-5523 or 617-328-5000	Discount (cash):	0
	x6406	Discount (div.):	0
Transfer Agent:	State Street Bank (EquiServe)	Auto invest:	No
Agent's Address:	P.O. Box 8200	Auto invest fee:	$0
	Boston, MA 02266-8200	Selling info:	Sells irregularly, by mail or phone,
Agent's Phone:	800-426-5523		at market, for $2.50 +15¢/sh.
Other than USA:	Yes		

Company:	**New Century Energies**	Safekeeping:	Yes
Symbol:	NCE	Invests:	Every 30 days beginning 1/15
Exchange:	NYSE	Minimum:	$25
Industry:	Utility-electric, gas	Maximum:	$100,000/year
Company Address:	1225 17th St.	Min to qualify:	1
	Denver, CO 80201-0840	Fee on cash inv.:	comm.
Company Phone:	303-294-2566	Fee on div. inv.:	comm.
Transfer Agent:	Bank of New York	Discount (cash):	0
Agent's Address:	101 Barclay Street	Discount (div.):	0
	New York, NY 10286	Auto invest:	Yes
Agent's Phone:	800-783-4893	Auto invest fee:	$0
Other than USA:	Yes	Selling info:	Sells biweekly, by mail or phone,
			at market, for 10¢/sh.

Company:	**New England Business Service, Inc.**	Safekeeping:	Yes
		Invests:	Every 7 days beginning Wed.
Symbol:	NEB	Minimum:	$50
Exchange:	NYSE	Maximum:	$100,000/year
Industry:	Office supplies	Min to qualify:	1
Company Address:	500 Main St.	Fee on cash inv.:	$5 + 8¢/sh.
	Groton, MA 01471	Fee on div. inv.:	$1.25
Company Phone:	978-449-3425 or 978-448-6111	Discount (cash):	0
Transfer Agent:	BankBoston (EquiServe)	Discount (div.):	0
Agent's Address:	P.O. Box 8040	Auto invest:	Yes
	Boston, MA 02266-8040	Auto invest fee:	$2.50
Agent's Phone:	800-736-3001	Selling info:	Sells weekly, by mail, at market,
Other than USA:	Yes		for $10 +15¢/sh.

Company:	**New England Electric System**	Safekeeping:	Yes
		Invests:	Every 30 days beginning 1/25
Symbol:	NES	Minimum:	$25
Exchange:	NYSE	Maximum:	$5,000/month
Industry:	Utility-electric	Min to qualify:	1
Company Address:	25 Research Dr., Box 770	Fee on cash inv.:	0!
	Westborough, MA 01581	Fee on div. inv.:	0!
Company Phone:	508-389-2000	Discount (cash):	0
Transfer Agent:	Bank of New York	Discount (div.):	0
Agent's Address:	P.O. Box 11258, Church St.	Auto invest:	Yes
	Station-11E	Auto invest fee:	$0
	New York, NY 10286	Selling info:	Sells biweekly, by mail or fax, at
Agent's Phone:	800-466-7215		market, for 5¢/sh.
Other than USA:	Yes		

Company:	**New Germany Fund (The)**	Safekeeping:	Yes
Symbol:	GF	Invests:	Every 30 days beginning 1/15
Exchange:	NYSE	Minimum:	$100
Industry:	Closed-end fund	Maximum:	$36,000/year
Company Address:	c/o Deutsche Bk., 31 West 52nd St.	Min to qualify:	1
	New York, NY 10019	Fee on cash inv.:	comm.
Company Phone:	800-334-1898 or 212-469-7052	Fee on div. inv.:	0!
Transfer Agent:	Investors Bank & Trust Co.-Share-	Discount (cash):	0
	holder Svcs.	Discount (div.):	0
Agent's Address:	P.O. Box 1537	Auto invest:	No
	Boston, MA 02205-1537	Auto invest fee:	$0
Agent's Phone:	800-356-2754	Selling info:	Not available
Other than USA:	Yes		

Company:	**New Holland N.V.**	Safekeeping:	Yes
Symbol:	NH	Invests:	Every 7 days beginning varies
Exchange:	NYSE	Minimum:	$50
Industry:	Agricultural equipment	Maximum:	$100,000/year
Company Address:	c/o Morgan Guaranty Trust,	Min to qualify:	1
	Box 9073	Fee on cash inv.:	$5 + 12¢/sh.
	Boston, MA 02205-9948	Fee on div. inv.:	5% to $2.50
Company Phone:	800-428-4237	Discount (cash):	0
Transfer Agent:	Morgan Guaranty Trust Co.	Discount (div.):	0
Agent's Address:	P.O. Box 9073	Auto invest:	Yes
	Boston, MA 02205-9948	Auto invest fee:	$5
Agent's Phone:	800-428-4237	Selling info:	Sells daily, by mail or phone, at
Other than USA:	No		avg. price, for $5 +12¢/sh.

Company:	**New Jersey Resources Corp.**	Safekeeping:	Yes
		Invests:	Every 15 days beginning 1/1
Symbol:	NJR	Minimum:	$25
Exchange:	NYSE	Maximum:	$60,000/year
Industry:	Utility-gas	Min to qualify:	1
Company Address:	1415 Wyckoff Rd., Box 1468	Fee on cash inv.:	0
	Wall, NJ 07719	Fee on div. inv.:	0
Company Phone:	732-938-1480 or 732-938-1229	Discount (cash):	0
Transfer Agent:	Boston Eq. (EquiServe)	Discount (div.):	0
Agent's Address:	P.O. Box 644, MS 45-02-64	Auto invest:	Yes
	Boston, MA 02102-0644	Auto invest fee:	$0
Agent's Phone:	800-817-3955	Selling info:	Sells daily, by mail or phone, at
Other than USA:	Yes		market, for 10¢ to 15¢/sh.

Company:	**New Plan Excel Realty Trust**	Safekeeping:	Yes
		Invests:	Every 90 days beginning 1/1
Symbol:	NXL	Minimum:	$100
Exchange:	NYSE	Maximum:	$20,000/quarter
Industry:	REIT	Min to qualify:	1
Company Address:	16955 Via Del Campo	Fee on cash inv.:	0
	San Diego, CA 92127	Fee on div. inv.:	0
Company Phone:	619-485-9400x138 or 212-869-3000	Discount (cash):	0
Transfer Agent:	BankBoston (EquiServe)	Discount (div.):	5%
Agent's Address:	P.O. Box 8040	Auto invest:	No
	Boston, MA 02266	Auto invest fee:	$0
Agent's Phone:	800-730-6001	Selling info:	Sells within 10 bus. days, by mail
Other than USA:	Yes		or fax, at market, for 15¢/sh.

Company:	**New York Broker Deutschland**	Safekeeping:	Yes
		Invests:	Every 7 days beginning varies
Symbol:	NYBDY	Minimum:	$50
Exchange:	OTC	Maximum:	$250,000/week
Industry:	Global securities markets	Min to qualify:	1
Company Address:	c/o BNY,101 Barclay St.,22 West	Fee on cash inv.:	$5 + 10¢/sh.
	New York, NY 10286	Fee on div. inv.:	0
Company Phone:	800-943-9715	Discount (cash):	0
Transfer Agent:	Bank of New York	Discount (div.):	0
Agent's Address:	P.O. Box 11258	Auto invest:	Yes
	New York, NY 10286	Auto invest fee:	$0
Agent's Phone:	888-269-2377	Selling info:	Sells weekly, by phone or mail, at
Other than USA:	Yes		market, for $5 +10¢/ADS

Company:	**New York Times Co. A**	Safekeeping:	Yes
Symbol:	NYT	Invests:	Every 90 days beginning 1/20
Exchange:	NYSE	Minimum:	$10
Industry:	Media	Maximum:	$3,000/quarter
Company Address:	229 West 43rd St.	Min to qualify:	1
	New York, NY 10036-3959	Fee on cash inv.:	0
Company Phone:	212-556-1981 or 212-556-4317	Fee on div. inv.:	0
Transfer Agent:	FCT (EquiServe)	Discount (cash):	0
Agent's Address:	P.O. Box 2598	Discount (div.):	0
	Jersey City, NJ 07303-2598	Auto invest:	No
Agent's Phone:	800-414-6280	Auto invest fee:	$0
Other than USA:	No	Selling info:	Sells weekly, by mail or fax, at
			market, for $10 +12¢/sh.

Company:	**Newell Rubbermaid Inc.**	Safekeeping:	Yes
Symbol:	NWL	Invests:	Every 30 days beginning 1/7
Exchange:	NYSE	Minimum:	$10
Industry:	Mfr. consumer & indust. prod.	Maximum:	$30,000/year
Company Address:	6833 Stalter Dr.	Min to qualify:	1
	Rockford, IL 61108	Fee on cash inv.:	0
Company Phone:	800-424-1941 or 815-381-8150	Fee on div. inv.:	0
Transfer Agent:	FCT (EquiServe)	Discount (cash):	0
Agent's Address:	P.O. Box 2500	Discount (div.):	0
	Jersey City, NJ 07303-2500	Auto invest:	Yes
Agent's Phone:	800-317-4445	Auto invest fee:	$1
Other than USA:	No	Selling info:	Sells daily, by phone, mail, or fax,
			at market, for $10 +12¢/sh.

Company:	**Newport Corp.**	Safekeeping:	Yes
Symbol:	NEWP	Invests:	Every 7 days beginning varies
Exchange:	OTC	Minimum:	$50
Industry:	Scientific & technical	Maximum:	$10,000/investment
	instruments	Min to qualify:	1
Company Address:	1791 Deere Ave.	Fee on cash inv.:	$7.50 + 10¢/sh.
	Irvine, CA 92606	Fee on div. inv.:	0
Company Phone:	949-863-3144	Discount (cash):	0
Transfer Agent:	American Stock Transfer	Discount (div.):	0
Agent's Address:	40 Wall Street	Auto invest:	Yes
	New York, NY 10005	Auto invest fee:	$0
Agent's Phone:	888-200-3169	Selling info:	Sells weekly, by mail, at market,
Other than USA:	Yes		for $7.50 +10¢/sh.

Company:	**Newport News Shipbuilding**	Safekeeping:	Yes
		Invests:	Every 5 days beginning varies
Symbol:	NNS	Minimum:	$50
Exchange:	NYSE	Maximum:	$250,000/year
Industry:	Shipbuilding, defense	Min to qualify:	1
Company Address:	4101 Washington Ave.	Fee on cash inv.:	$5 + 10¢/sh.
	Newport News, VA 23607-2770	Fee on div. inv.:	5% to $3 + 10¢/sh.
Company Phone:	800-753-8790 or 757-688-6400	Discount (cash):	0
Transfer Agent:	FCT (EquiServe)	Discount (div.):	0
Agent's Address:	P.O. Box 2500	Auto invest:	Yes
	Jersey City, NJ 07303-2598	Auto invest fee:	$2 + 10¢/sh.
Agent's Phone:	800-519-3111	Selling info:	Sells monthly, by mail or phone,
Other than USA:	Yes		at market, for $15 +12¢/sh.

Company:	**NFC plc**	Safekeeping:	Yes
Symbol:	NFC	Invests:	Every 30 days beginning 1/10
Exchange:	ASE	Minimum:	$25
Industry:	Transportation, railroad, real	Maximum:	$unlimited
	estate in UK	Min to qualify:	1
Company Address:	c/o BNY,101 Barclay St., 22 West	Fee on cash inv.:	7¢/sh.
	New York, NY 10286	Fee on div. inv.:	0
Company Phone:	212-815-2175	Discount (cash):	0
Transfer Agent:	Bank of New York	Discount (div.):	0
Agent's Address:	P.O. Box 11258	Auto invest:	No
	New York, NY 10286	Auto invest fee:	$0
Agent's Phone:	888-269-2377	Selling info:	Sells n/a, by mail, at n/a, for $5
Other than USA:	Yes		+7¢/sh.

Company:	**Niagara Mohawk Holdings Inc.**	Safekeeping:	No
		Invests:	Every 30 days beginning 1/30
Symbol:	NMK	Minimum:	$25
Exchange:	NYSE	Maximum:	$50,000/year
Industry:	Utility-electric, gas	Min to qualify:	1
Company Address:	Box 7058	Fee on cash inv.:	0!
	Syracuse, NY 13261	Fee on div. inv.:	0!
Company Phone:	800-448-5450 or 315-428-6570	Discount (cash):	0
Transfer Agent:	Niagara Mohawk Dividend	Discount (div.):	0
	Reinvestment Dept.	Auto invest:	No
Agent's Address:	P.O. Box 7058	Auto invest fee:	$0
	Syracuse, NY 13261	Selling info:	Sells weekly, by mail or fax, at avg.
Agent's Phone:	800-448-5450		price, for 4¢/sh.
Other than USA:	Yes		

Company:	**Nice Systems Ltd.**	Safekeeping:	Yes
Symbol:	NICEY	Invests:	Every 7 days beginning varies
Exchange:	OTC	Minimum:	$50
Industry:	Computer	Maximum:	$250,000/week
Company Address:	c/o BNY,101 Barclay St., 22 West	Min to qualify:	1
	New York, NY 10286	Fee on cash inv.:	$5 + 10¢/sh.
Company Phone:	800-943-9715	Fee on div. inv.:	0
Transfer Agent:	Bank of New York	Discount (cash):	0
Agent's Address:	P.O. Box 11258	Discount (div.):	0
	New York, NY 10286	Auto invest:	Yes
Agent's Phone:	888-269-2377	Auto invest fee:	$0
Other than USA:	Yes	Selling info:	Sells weekly, by phone or mail, at
			avg. price, for $5 +10¢/ADS

Company:	**Nicor Inc.**	Safekeeping:	Yes
Symbol:	GAS	Invests:	Every 30 days beginning 1/1
Exchange:	NYSE	Minimum:	$50
Industry:	Utility-gas	Maximum:	$5,000/month
Company Address:	1844 Ferry Rd., Box 3014	Min to qualify:	1
	Naperville, IL 60566-7014	Fee on cash inv.:	0!
Company Phone:	630-305-9500	Fee on div. inv.:	0!
Transfer Agent:	Nicor Inc.	Discount (cash):	0
Agent's Address:	1844 Ferry Road	Discount (div.):	0
	Naperville, IL 60566-7014	Auto invest:	No
Agent's Phone:	630-305-9500 x2749	Auto invest fee:	$0
Other than USA:	Yes	Selling info:	Not available

Company:	**Nippon Telephone & Telegraph Corp.**	Safekeeping:	Yes
		Invests:	Every 7 days beginning varies
Symbol:	NTT	Minimum:	$50
Exchange:	NYSE	Maximum:	$100,000/year
Industry:	Communications	Min to qualify:	1
Company Address:	c/o Morgan Guaranty Trust, Box 9073	Fee on cash inv.:	$5 + 12¢/sh.
		Fee on div. inv.:	5% to $2.50
	Boston, MA 02205-9948	Discount (cash):	0
Company Phone:	800-428-4237	Discount (div.):	0
Transfer Agent:	Morgan Guaranty Trust Co.	Auto invest:	Yes
Agent's Address:	P.O. Box 9073	Auto invest fee:	$5
	Boston, MA 02205-9948	Selling info:	Sells daily, by phone or mail, at
Agent's Phone:	800-428-4237		avg. price, for $5 +12¢/sh.
Other than USA:	No		

Company:	**NiSource Inc.**	Safekeeping:	Yes
Symbol:	NI	Invests:	Every 30 days beginning 1/20
Exchange:	NYSE	Minimum:	$25
Industry:	Utility-gas & electric & water	Maximum:	$5,000/quarter
Company Address:	5265 Hohman Ave.	Min to qualify:	1
	Hammond, IN 46320	Fee on cash inv.:	0!
Company Phone:	800-348-6466 or 219-853-5700	Fee on div. inv.:	0!
Transfer Agent:	Harris Trust & Savings Bank	Discount (cash):	0
Agent's Address:	P.O. Box A-3309	Discount (div.):	0
	Chicago, IL 60690-3309	Auto invest:	No
Agent's Phone:	800-554-3406	Auto invest fee:	$0
Other than USA:	Yes	Selling info:	Sells biweekly, by mail or fax, at market, for $5 +7¢/sh.

Company:	**Nokia Corp.**	Safekeeping:	Yes
Symbol:	NOK	Invests:	Every 7 days beginning varies
Exchange:	NYSE	Minimum:	$50
Industry:	Telecommunication systems & equip.	Maximum:	$100,000/year
		Min to qualify:	1
Company Address:	c/o Citibank, NA,111 Wall St., 5th Fl.	Fee on cash inv.:	$2.50 + 8¢/sh.
	New York, NY 10043	Fee on div. inv.:	8¢/sh.
Company Phone:	800-422-2066 or 212-657-1698	Discount (cash):	0
Transfer Agent:	FCT (Citibank)	Discount (div.):	0
Agent's Address:	111 Wall Street, 5th Flr.,Sort 3196	Auto invest:	Yes
	New York, NY 10043	Auto invest fee:	$2.50 + comm.
Agent's Phone:	800-422-2066	Selling info:	Sells weekly, by mail, at market,
Other than USA:	No		for $10 +8¢/sh.

Company:	**Nooney Realty Trust, Inc.**	Safekeeping:	No
Symbol:	NRTI	Invests:	Every 90 days beginning 3/30
Exchange:	OTC	Minimum:	$50
Industry:	REIT	Maximum:	$unlimited
Company Address:	500 N. Broadway	Min to qualify:	1
	St. Louis, MO 63102	Fee on cash inv.:	5% to $2.50 + comm.
Company Phone:	314-206-4600	Fee on div. inv.:	0
Transfer Agent:	ChaseMellon Shareholder Services	Discount (cash):	0
Agent's Address:	P.O. Box 3316	Discount (div.):	0
	South Hackensack, NJ 07606-1916	Auto invest:	No
Agent's Phone:	888-213-0965	Auto invest fee:	$0
Other than USA:	No	Selling info:	Sells weekly, by mail or phone, at market, for comm.

Company:	**Nordson Corp.**	Safekeeping:	Yes
Symbol:	NDSN	Invests:	Every 30 days beginning 1/15
Exchange:	OTC	Minimum:	$10
Industry:	Industrial	Maximum:	$4,000/quarter
Company Address:	28601 Clemens Rd.	Min to qualify:	1
	Westlake, OH 44145-1148	Fee on cash inv.:	0
Company Phone:	440-414-5344	Fee on div. inv.:	0
Transfer Agent:	National City Bank	Discount (cash):	0
Agent's Address:	P.O.Box 92301	Discount (div.):	0
	Cleveland, OH 44193-0900	Auto invest:	No
Agent's Phone:	800-622-6757	Auto invest fee:	$0
Other than USA:	Yes	Selling info:	Sells monthly, by phone, mail, or fax, at market, for 8¢ to 20¢/sh.

Company:	**Norfolk Southern Corp.**	Safekeeping:	No
Symbol:	NSC	Invests:	Every 90 days beginning 3/10
Exchange:	NYSE	Minimum:	$10
Industry:	Railroads	Maximum:	$3,000/quarter
Company Address:	Three Commercial Pl.	Min to qualify:	1
	Norfolk, VA 23510-2191	Fee on cash inv.:	5% to $2.50
Company Phone:	757-629-2600	Fee on div. inv.:	5% to $2.50
Transfer Agent:	Bank of New York	Discount (cash):	0
Agent's Address:	P.O. Box 1958	Discount (div.):	0
	Newark, NJ 07101-9774	Auto invest:	No
Agent's Phone:	800-432-0140	Auto invest fee:	$0
Other than USA:	Yes	Selling info:	Not available

Company:	**Norsk Hydro A.S.**	Safekeeping:	Yes
Symbol:	NHY	Invests:	Every 7 days beginning varies
Exchange:	NYSE	Minimum:	$50
Industry:	Fertilizers, oil, gas, metals	Maximum:	$100,000/year
Company Address:	c/o Morgan Guaranty Trust,	Min to qualify:	1
	Box 9073	Fee on cash inv.:	$5 + 12¢/sh.
	Boston, MA 02205-9948	Fee on div. inv.:	5% to $2.50
Company Phone:	212-688-6606	Discount (cash):	0
Transfer Agent:	Morgan Guaranty Trust Co.	Discount (div.):	0
Agent's Address:	P.O. Box 9073	Auto invest:	Yes
	Boston, MA 02205-9948	Auto invest fee:	$5
Agent's Phone:	800-428-4237	Selling info:	Sells daily, by phone or mail, at avg. price, for $5 +12¢/sh.
Other than USA:	No		

Company:	**Nortel Inversora SA**	Safekeeping:	Yes
Symbol:	NRT	Invests:	Every 7 days beginning varies
Exchange:	NYSE	Minimum:	$50
Industry:	Telecommunications	Maximum:	$100,000/year
Company Address:	c/o Morgan Guaranty Trust,	Min to qualify:	1
	Box 9073	Fee on cash inv.:	$5 + 12¢/sh.
	Boston, MA 02205-9948	Fee on div. inv.:	5% to $2.50
Company Phone:	800-428-4237	Discount (cash):	0
Transfer Agent:	Morgan Guaranty Trust	Discount (div.):	0
Agent's Address:	P.O. Box 9073	Auto invest:	Yes
	Boston,MA 02205-9948	Auto invest fee:	$5 + 12¢/sh.
Agent's Phone:	800-428-4237	Selling info:	Sells daily, by mail or phone, at
Other than USA:	No		avg. price, for $5 +12¢/sh.

Company:	**Nortel Networks**	Safekeeping:	No
Symbol:	NT	Invests:	Every 90 days beginning 3/31
Exchange:	NYSE	Minimum:	$40
Industry:	Communications	Maximum:	$5,000/quarter
Company Address:	8200 Dixie Rd., Ste.100	Min to qualify:	1
	Brampton, Ont. L6T 5P6 Canada	Fee on cash inv.:	0!
Company Phone:	905-863-6044 or 905-863-0000	Fee on div. inv.:	0!
Transfer Agent:	Montreal Trust Company	Discount (cash):	0
Agent's Address:	151 Front Street West-8th floor	Discount (div.):	0
	Toronto, Ont. M5J 2N1 Canada	Auto invest:	No
Agent's Phone:	800-663-9097	Auto invest fee:	$0
Other than USA:	Yes	Selling info:	Sells weekly, by mail, at avg. price,
			for 30¢/sh.

Company:	**North Carolina Natural Gas**	Safekeeping:	Yes
		Invests:	Every 30 days beginning 1/15
Symbol:	NCG	Minimum:	$100
Exchange:	NYSE	Maximum:	$3,000/month
Industry:	Natural gas	Min to qualify:	1
Company Address:	150 Rowan St., Box 909	Fee on cash inv.:	!
	Fayetteville, NC 28302-0909	Fee on div. inv.:	0
Company Phone:	910-323-6204 or 910-483-0315	Discount (cash):	0
Transfer Agent:	Wachovia (EquiServe)	Discount (div.):	5%
Agent's Address:	P.O. Box 8217	Auto invest:	No
	Boston, MA 02266-8217	Auto invest fee:	$0
Agent's Phone:	800-633-4236 or 910-770-5821	Selling info:	Sells weekly, by mail or fax, at
Other than USA:	Yes		market, for comm.

Company:	**North Fork Bancorp**	Safekeeping:	Yes
Symbol:	NFB	Invests:	Every 30 days beginning 1/15
Exchange:	NYSE	Minimum:	$200
Industry:	Banking	Maximum:	$15,000/month
Company Address:	275 Broadhollow Rd.	Min to qualify:	1
	Melville, NY 11747	Fee on cash inv.:	0!
Company Phone:	516-298-5000 or 516-844-1000	Fee on div. inv.:	0!
Transfer Agent:	FCT (EquiServe)	Discount (cash):	0
Agent's Address:	P.O. Box 2598	Discount (div.):	0
	Jersey City, NJ 07303-2598	Auto invest:	No
Agent's Phone:	800-317-4445	Auto invest fee:	$0
Other than USA:	Yes	Selling info:	Sells daily, by phone, mail, or fax,
			at market, for $10 +10¢/sh.

Company:	**Northeast Utilities**	
Symbol:	NU	
Exchange:	NYSE	
Industry:	Utility-electric	
Company Address:	Box 270	
	Hartford, CT 06141-0270	
Company Phone:	800-286-5000 or 860-665-5445	
Transfer Agent:	Northeast Utilities Service	
	Company Shareholder Services	
Agent's Address:	P.O. Box 5006	
	Hartford, CT 06102-5006	
Agent's Phone:	800-999-7269	
Other than USA:	Yes	

Safekeeping:	Yes
Invests:	Every 30 days beginning 1/2
Minimum:	$100
Maximum:	$25,000/month
Min to qualify:	1
Fee on cash inv.:	5¢/sh.
Fee on div. inv.:	0
Discount (cash):	0
Discount (div.):	0
Auto invest:	No
Auto invest fee:	$0
Selling info:	Sells weekly, by mail, at market, for 5¢/sh.

Company:	**Northern States Power**
Symbol:	NSP
Exchange:	NYSE
Industry:	Utility-electric & gas
Company Address:	414 Nicollet Mall
	Minneapolis, MN 55401
Company Phone:	800-527-4677 or 612-330-5560
Transfer Agent:	State Street Bank (EquiServe)
Agent's Address:	414 Nicollet Mall
	Minneapolis, MN 55401-9989
Agent's Phone:	800-527-4677
Other than USA:	Yes

Safekeeping:	Yes
Invests:	Every 30 days beginning 1/10
Minimum:	$25
Maximum:	$10,000/quarter
Min to qualify:	1
Fee on cash inv.:	0!
Fee on div. inv.:	0!
Discount (cash):	0
Discount (div.):	0
Auto invest:	No
Auto invest fee:	$0
Selling info:	Sells weekly, by mail, at market, for $0

Company:	**Northrop Grumman Corp.**
Symbol:	NOC
Exchange:	NYSE
Industry:	Aerospace, defense
Company Address:	1840 Century Park East
	Los Angeles, CA 90067-2199
Company Phone:	310-201-3286 or 310-553-6262
Transfer Agent:	ChaseMellon Shareholder Services
Agent's Address:	P.O. Box 3338
	South Hackensack, Nj 07606-1938
Agent's Phone:	800-279-1242
Other than USA:	Yes

Safekeeping:	No
Invests:	Every 30 days beginning 1/15
Minimum:	$100
Maximum:	$1,000/month
Min to qualify:	1
Fee on cash inv.:	0!
Fee on div. inv.:	0!
Discount (cash):	0
Discount (div.):	0
Auto invest:	No
Auto invest fee:	$0
Selling info:	Not available

Company:	**Northwest Bancorp, Inc.**
Symbol:	NWSB
Exchange:	OTC
Industry:	Savings bank
Company Address:	Liberty St. at Second Ave.
	Warren, PA 16365
Company Phone:	814-726-2140
Transfer Agent:	American Stock Transfer
Agent's Address:	40 Wall St., 46th Fl.
	New York, NY 10005
Agent's Phone:	800-278-4353
Other than USA:	Yes

Safekeeping:	Yes
Invests:	Every 30 days beginning 1/1
Minimum:	$25
Maximum:	$5,000/month
Min to qualify:	5
Fee on cash inv.:	0
Fee on div. inv.:	0
Discount (cash):	0
Discount (div.):	0
Auto invest:	No
Auto invest fee:	$0
Selling info:	Sells within 5 bus. days, by mail, at market, for $10 + comm.

Company:	**Northwest Natural Gas**	Safekeeping:	Yes
Symbol:	NWNG	Invests:	Every 30 days beginning 1/15
Exchange:	OTC	Minimum:	$0
Industry:	Utility-gas	Maximum:	$50,000/year
Company Address:	220 N.W. 2nd Ave.	Min to qualify:	1
	Portland, OR 97209 -3991	Fee on cash inv.:	0!
Company Phone:	800-422-4012x3402 or 503-226-4211	Fee on div. inv.:	0!
Transfer Agent:	Northwest Natural Gas- Share-	Discount (cash):	0
	holder Services	Discount (div.):	0
Agent's Address:	220 N.W. 2nd Ave	Auto invest:	No
	Portland, OR 97209	Auto invest fee:	$0
Agent's Phone:	503-220-2590	Selling info:	Sells weekly, by mail or fax, at
Other than USA:	Yes		market, for $5

Company:	**NorthWestern Corp.**	Safekeeping:	Yes
Symbol:	NOR	Invests:	Every 30 days beginning 1/1
Exchange:	NYSE	Minimum:	$10
Industry:	Utility-electric & gas	Maximum:	$10,000/month
Company Address:	125 S. Dakota Ave., Ste.1100	Min to qualify:	1
	Sioux Falls, SD 57104-6403	Fee on cash inv.:	0!
Company Phone:	800-677-6716 or 605-978-2904	Fee on div. inv.:	0!
Transfer Agent:	NorthWestern Corporation-	Discount (cash):	0
	Shareholder Svcs.	Discount (div.):	0
Agent's Address:	33 Third St. S.E.	Auto invest:	Yes
	Huron, SD 57350-1605	Auto invest fee:	$0
Agent's Phone:	800-677-6716 or 605-352-8411	Selling info:	Sells weekly, by mail, at market,
Other than USA:	Yes		for 6¢/sh.

Company:	**Novo Nordisk A/S B**	Safekeeping:	Yes
Symbol:	NVO	Invests:	Every 7 days beginning varies
Exchange:	NYSE	Minimum:	$50
Industry:	Diabetes care, womens health	Maximum:	$100,000/year
	care	Min to qualify:	1
Company Address:	c/o MGT, ADR Dept., Box 8205	Fee on cash inv.:	$5 + 12¢/sh.
	Boston, MA 02266-8205	Fee on div. inv.:	5% to $2.50
Company Phone:	781-575-4328	Discount (cash):	0
Transfer Agent:	Morgan Guaranty Trust Co.-ADR	Discount (div.):	0
	Dept.	Auto invest:	Yes
Agent's Address:	P.O. Box 8205	Auto invest fee:	$0
	Boston, MA 02266-8205	Selling info:	Sells daily, by phone or mail, at
Agent's Phone:	781-575-4328		avg. price, for $5 +12¢/sh.
Other than USA:	Yes		

Company:	**Nucor Corp.**	Safekeeping:	Yes
Symbol:	NUE	Invests:	Every 30 days beginning 1/11
Exchange:	NYSE	Minimum:	$10
Industry:	Metals, parts	Maximum:	$1,000/month
Company Address:	2100 Rexford Rd.	Min to qualify:	1
	Charlotte, NC 28211	Fee on cash inv.:	0!
Company Phone:	704-366-7000	Fee on div. inv.:	0!
Transfer Agent:	American Stock Transfer	Discount (cash):	0
Agent's Address:	40 Wall Street	Discount (div.):	0
	New York, NY 10005	Auto invest:	No
Agent's Phone:	800-937-5449	Auto invest fee:	$0
Other than USA:	Yes	Selling info:	Sells weekly, by mail, at market,
			for $10 + 4¢/sh.

Company:	**NUI Corp.**
Symbol:	NUI
Exchange:	NYSE
Industry:	Utility-gas
Company Address:	550 Route 202-206, Box 760
	Bedminster, NJ 07921-0760
Company Phone:	908-719-4222 or 908-781-0500
Transfer Agent:	FCT (EquiServe)
Agent's Address:	P.O. Box 2598
	Jersey City, NJ 07303-2598
Agent's Phone:	800-374-5775
Other than USA:	No

Safekeeping:	Yes
Invests:	Every 7 days beginning Wed.
Minimum:	$25
Maximum:	$60,000/year
Min to qualify:	1
Fee on cash inv.:	0!
Fee on div. inv.:	0!
Discount (cash):	0
Discount (div.):	0
Auto invest:	Yes
Auto invest fee:	$0
Selling info:	Sells daily, by mail, at market, for $10 +12¢/sh.

Company:	**OAO Rostelecom**
Symbol:	ROS
Exchange:	NYSE
Industry:	Telecommunications
Company Address:	c/o BNY,101 Barclay St.,22 West
	New York, NY 10286
Company Phone:	800-943-9715
Transfer Agent:	Bank of New York
Agent's Address:	P.O. Box 11258
	New York, NY 10286
Agent's Phone:	888-269-2377
Other than USA:	Yes

Safekeeping:	Yes
Invests:	Every 7 days beginning varies
Minimum:	$50
Maximum:	$250,000/year
Min to qualify:	1
Fee on cash inv.:	$5 + 10¢/sh.
Fee on div. inv.:	0
Discount (cash):	0
Discount (div.):	0
Auto invest:	Yes
Auto invest fee:	$5 + 10¢/sh.
Selling info:	Sells weekly, by mail, at market, for $5 +10¢/sh.

Company:	**OAO Tatneft**
Symbol:	TNT
Exchange:	NYSE
Industry:	Oil & gas operations
Company Address:	c/o BNY,101 Barclay St.,22 West
	New York, NY 10286
Company Phone:	800-943-9715
Transfer Agent:	Bank of New York
Agent's Address:	P.O. Box 11258
	New York, NY 10286
Agent's Phone:	888-269-2377
Other than USA:	Yes

Safekeeping:	Yes
Invests:	Every 7 days beginning varies
Minimum:	$50
Maximum:	$250,000/year
Min to qualify:	1
Fee on cash inv.:	$5 + 10¢/sh.
Fee on div. inv.:	5% to $5 + 10¢/sh.
Discount (cash):	0
Discount (div.):	0
Auto invest:	Yes
Auto invest fee:	$5 + 10¢/sh.
Selling info:	Sells weekly, by mail, at market, for $5 +10¢/sh.

Company:	**Occidental Petroleum Corp.**
Symbol:	OXY
Exchange:	NYSE
Industry:	Oil & gas
Company Address:	10889 Wilshire Blvd.
	Los Angeles, CA 90024-4201
Company Phone:	310-443-6459
Transfer Agent:	ChaseMellon Shareholder Services
Agent's Address:	85 Challenger Road,
	Overpeck Centre
	Ridgefield, New Jersey 07660
Agent's Phone:	800-622-9231
Other than USA:	No

Safekeeping:	Yes
Invests:	Every 30 days beginning 1/15
Minimum:	$50
Maximum:	$1,000/month
Min to qualify:	25
Fee on cash inv.:	0!
Fee on div. inv.:	0!
Discount (cash):	0
Discount (div.):	0
Auto invest:	No
Auto invest fee:	$0
Selling info:	Sells monthly, by mail or phone, at market, for $15 + 3¢ to 12¢/sh.

Company:	**Oce-van der Grinten N.V.**		**Safekeeping:**	Yes
Symbol:	OCENY		**Invests:**	Every 7 days beginning varies
Exchange:	OTC		**Minimum:**	$50
Industry:	Office Equipment		**Maximum:**	$100,000/year
Company Address:	c/o Morgan Guaranty Trust,		**Min to qualify:**	1
	Box 9073		**Fee on cash inv.:**	$5 + 12¢/sh.
	Boston, MA 02205-9948		**Fee on div. inv.:**	5% to $2.50
Company Phone:	800-877-6232		**Discount (cash):**	0
Transfer Agent:	Morgan Guaranty Trust Co.		**Discount (div.):**	0
Agent's Address:	P.O. Box 9073		**Auto invest:**	Yes
	Boston, MA 02205-9948		**Auto invest fee:**	$5 + 12¢/sh.
Agent's Phone:	800-428-4237		**Selling info:**	Sells daily, by mail or phone, at
Other than USA:	No			avg. price, for $5 +12¢/sh.

Company:	**OGE Energy Corp.**		**Safekeeping:**	Yes
Symbol:	OGE		**Invests:**	Every 7 days beginning varies
Exchange:	NYSE		**Minimum:**	$25
Industry:	Utility-electric & gas		**Maximum:**	$100,000/year
Company Address:	Box 321		**Min to qualify:**	1
	Oklahoma City, OK 73101-0321		**Fee on cash inv.:**	0
Company Phone:	405-553-3211 or 405-553-3000		**Fee on div. inv.:**	0
Transfer Agent:	ChaseMellon Shareholder Services		**Discount (cash):**	0
Agent's Address:	P.O. Box 3337		**Discount (div.):**	0
	South Hackensack, NJ 07606		**Auto invest:**	Yes
Agent's Phone:	888-216-8114		**Auto invest fee:**	$0
Other than USA:	Yes		**Selling info:**	Sells weekly, by mail or phone, at
				market, for $10 +12¢/sh.

Company:	**Ohio Casualty Corp.**		**Safekeeping:**	Yes
Symbol:	OCAS		**Invests:**	Every 30 days beginning 1/1
Exchange:	OTC		**Minimum:**	$10
Industry:	Insurance		**Maximum:**	$60,000/year
Company Address:	136 North Third St.		**Min to qualify:**	1
	Hamilton, OH 45025-0001		**Fee on cash inv.:**	5% to $3
Company Phone:	513-867-3462 or 513-867-3000		**Fee on div. inv.:**	5% to $3
Transfer Agent:	FCT (EquiServe)		**Discount (cash):**	0
Agent's Address:	P.O. Box 2500		**Discount (div.):**	0
	Jersey City, NJ 07303-2500		**Auto invest:**	Yes
Agent's Phone:	800-317-4445		**Auto invest fee:**	$1
Other than USA:	Yes		**Selling info:**	Sells daily, by phone or mail, at
				market, for $5 +12¢/sh.

Company:	**Old Guard Group, Inc.**		**Safekeeping:**	Yes
Symbol:	OGGI		**Invests:**	Every 30 days beginning 1/25
Exchange:	OTC		**Minimum:**	$25
Industry:	Insurance		**Maximum:**	$2,000/month
Company Address:	2929 Lititz Pike, Box 3010		**Min to qualify:**	25
	Lancaster, PA 17604		**Fee on cash inv.:**	0
Company Phone:	717-581-6839 or 717-569-5361		**Fee on div. inv.:**	0
Transfer Agent:	American Stock Transfer & Trust		**Discount (cash):**	0
	Co.		**Discount (div.):**	0
Agent's Address:	40 Wall St., 46th Floor		**Auto invest:**	No
	New York, NY 10005		**Auto invest fee:**	$0
Agent's Phone:	800-937-5449		**Selling info:**	Sells weekly, by mail, at market,
Other than USA:	Yes			for $10 + 4¢/sh.

Company:	**Old Kent Financial Corp.**	**Safekeeping:**	No
Symbol:	OK	**Invests:**	Every 30 days beginning 1/15
Exchange:	NYSE	**Minimum:**	$25
Industry:	Banking	**Maximum:**	$5,000/quarter
Company Address:	4420 44th St. SE, Ste. A	**Min to qualify:**	1
	Kentwood, MI 49512	**Fee on cash inv.:**	0!
		Fee on div. inv.:	0!
Company Phone:	616-771-5482	**Discount (cash):**	0
Transfer Agent:	Old Kent Bank	**Discount (div.):**	0
Agent's Address:	4420-44th St. SE, Suite A	**Auto invest:**	No
	Grand Rapids, MI 49512-4011	**Auto invest fee:**	$0
Agent's Phone:	800-652-2657 x771-1034	**Selling info:**	Not available
Other than USA:	No		

Company:	**Old National Bancorp**	**Safekeeping:**	Yes
Symbol:	OLDB	**Invests:**	Every 30 days beginning 1/3
Exchange:	OTC	**Minimum:**	$50
Industry:	Banking	**Maximum:**	$50,000/year
Company Address:	Box 718	**Min to qualify:**	1
	Evansville, IN 47705-0718	**Fee on cash inv.:**	0
		Fee on div. inv.:	0
Company Phone:	812-464-1296	**Discount (cash):**	0
Transfer Agent:	Old National Bancorp	**Discount (div.):**	3%
Agent's Address:	P.O. Box 718	**Auto invest:**	Yes
	Evansville, IN 47705-0718	**Auto invest fee:**	$0
Agent's Phone:	800-677-1749	**Selling info:**	Sells bimonthly, by mail,
Other than USA:	No		at market, for $10

Company:	**Old Republic International Corp.**	**Safekeeping:**	Yes
		Invests:	Every 90 days beginning 3/1
Symbol:	ORI	**Minimum:**	$100
Exchange:	NYSE	**Maximum:**	$5,000/quarter
Industry:	Insurance	**Min to qualify:**	1
Company Address:	307 North Michigan Ave.	**Fee on cash inv.:**	0
	Chicago, IL 60601	**Fee on div. inv.:**	0
Company Phone:	312-346-8100 x279	**Discount (cash):**	0
Transfer Agent:	FCT (EquiServe)	**Discount (div.):**	0
Agent's Address:	P.O. Box 2500	**Auto invest:**	No
	Jersey City, NJ 07303	**Auto invest fee:**	$0
Agent's Phone:	201-324-0313	**Selling info:**	Sells daily, by phone, mail, fax, at
Other than USA:	No		market, for 12¢/sh.

Company:	**Olin Corp.**	**Safekeeping:**	Yes
Symbol:	OLN	**Invests:**	Every 30 days beginning 1/10
Exchange:	NYSE	**Minimum:**	$50
Industry:	Chemicals	**Maximum:**	$5,000/month
Company Address:	501 Merritt 7, Box 4500	**Min to qualify:**	1
	Norwalk, CT 06856-4500	**Fee on cash inv.:**	5% to $2.50 + $5
Company Phone:	203-750-3000 or 203-750-3254	**Fee on div. inv.:**	5% to $2.50
Transfer Agent:	ChaseMellon Shareholder Services	**Discount (cash):**	0
		Discount (div.):	0
Agent's Address:	P.O. Box 3336	**Auto invest:**	No
	South Hackensack, NJ 07606	**Auto invest fee:**	$0
Agent's Phone:	800-306-8594 or 212-613-7147	**Selling info:**	Sells monthly, by mail or phone,
Other than USA:	Yes		at market, for $15 + comm.

Company:	**OLS Asia Holdings Limited**	Safekeeping:	Yes
		Invests:	Every 7 days beginning varies
Symbol:	OLSAY	Minimum:	$50
Exchange:	OTC	Maximum:	$250,000/year
Industry:	Construction	Min to qualify:	1
Company Address:	c/o BNY,101 Barclay St.,22 West	Fee on cash inv.:	$5 + 10¢/sh.
	New York, NY 10286	Fee on div. inv.:	5% to $5 + 10¢/sh.
Company Phone:	800-943-9715	Discount (cash):	0
Transfer Agent:	Bank of New York	Discount (div.):	0
Agent's Address:	P.O. Box 11258	Auto invest:	Yes
	New York, NY 10286	Auto invest fee:	$5 + 10¢/sh.
Agent's Phone:	888-269-2377	Selling info:	Sells weekly, by mail, at market,
Other than USA:	Yes		for $5 +10¢/sh.

Company:	**OM Group**	Safekeeping:	Yes
Symbol:	OMP	Invests:	Every 30 days beginning 1/31
Exchange:	NYSE	Minimum:	$10
Industry:	Specialty chemicals	Maximum:	$5,000/month
Company Address:	50 Public Sq., 3500 Terminal Twr.	Min to qualify:	1
	Cleveland, OH 44113-2204	Fee on cash inv.:	0
Company Phone:	216-781-0083	Fee on div. inv.:	0
Transfer Agent:	National City Bank	Discount (cash):	0
Agent's Address:	P.O. Box 92301	Discount (div.):	0
	Cleveland, OH 44135-0900	Auto invest:	No
Agent's Phone:	800-622-6757 x 8574 or 216-476-8574	Auto invest fee:	$0
Other than USA:	Yes	Selling info:	Sells monthly, by phone or mail, at market, for comm.

Company:	**Omega Healthcare Investor**	Safekeeping:	Yes
		Invests:	Every 30 days beginning 1/15
Symbol:	OHI	Minimum:	$1000
Exchange:	NYSE	Maximum:	$20,000/year
Industry:	REIT	Min to qualify:	1
Company Address:	900 Victors Way, Ste.350	Fee on cash inv.:	0!
	Ann Arbor, MI 48108	Fee on div. inv.:	0!
Company Phone:	734-887-0200	Discount (cash):	0
Transfer Agent:	FCT (EquiServe)	Discount (div.):	5%
Agent's Address:	P O Box 2598	Auto invest:	Yes
	Jersey City, NJ 07303-2598	Auto invest fee:	$0
Agent's Phone:	800-519-3111	Selling info:	Not available
Other than USA:	Yes		

Company:	**Omnicare, Inc.**	Safekeeping:	No
Symbol:	OCR	Invests:	Every 30 days beginning 1/18
Exchange:	NYSE	Minimum:	$10
Industry:	Health care	Maximum:	$1,000/month
Company Address:	100 East River Ctr. Blvd.	Min to qualify:	1
	Covington, KY 41011	Fee on cash inv.:	0!
Company Phone:	606-392-3331 or 606-392-3300	Fee on div. inv.:	0!
Transfer Agent:	FCT (EquiServe)	Discount (cash):	0
Agent's Address:	P.O. Box 2500	Discount (div.):	0
	Jersey City, NJ 07303-2500	Auto invest:	No
Agent's Phone:	800-317-4445	Auto invest fee:	$0
Other than USA:	Yes	Selling info:	Sells daily, by mail or phone, at market, for $10 +12¢/sh.

Company:	**One Valley Bancorp, Inc.**	Safekeeping:	Yes
Symbol:	OV	Invests:	Every 90 days beginning 1/15
Exchange:	NYSE	Minimum:	$25
Industry:	Bank holding company	Maximum:	$3,000/quarter
Company Address:	Box 1793	Min to qualify:	1
	Charleston, WV 25326	Fee on cash inv.:	0!
Company Phone:	304-348-7023 or 304-348-7000	Fee on div. inv.:	0!
Transfer Agent:	Harris Trust & Savings Bank	Discount (cash):	0
Agent's Address:	P.O. Box A-3309	Discount (div.):	0
	Chicago, IL 60690	Auto invest:	No
Agent's Phone:	312-461-2302	Auto invest fee:	$0
Other than USA:	Yes	Selling info:	Sells weekly, by mail or fax, at market, for $0

Company:	**ONEOK, Inc.**	Safekeeping:	Yes
Symbol:	OKE	Invests:	Every 5 days beginning varies
Exchange:	NYSE	Minimum:	$25
Industry:	Integrated energy company	Maximum:	$100,000/year
Company Address:	100 West Fifth St., Box 871	Min to qualify:	1
	Tulsa, OK 74102-0871	Fee on cash inv.:	0!
Company Phone:	918-588-7158 or 918-588-7941	Fee on div. inv.:	0!
Transfer Agent:	FCT (EquiServe)	Discount (cash):	0
Agent's Address:	P.O. Box 2598	Discount (div.):	0
	Jersey City, NJ 07303-2598	Auto invest:	Yes
Agent's Phone:	888-764-5595	Auto invest fee:	$0
Other than USA:	Yes	Selling info:	Sells daily, by mail or phone, at market, for $10 +10¢/sh.

Company:	**Orbital Engine Corp. Ltd.**	Safekeeping:	Yes
Symbol:	OE	Invests:	Every 7 days beginning varies
Exchange:	NYSE	Minimum:	$50
Industry:	Auto & truck parts	Maximum:	$250,000/year
Company Address:	c/o BNY,101 Barclay St.,22 West	Min to qualify:	1
	New York, NY 10286	Fee on cash inv.:	$5 + 10¢/sh.
Company Phone:	800-943-9715	Fee on div. inv.:	0
Transfer Agent:	Bank of New York	Discount (cash):	0
Agent's Address:	P.O. Box 11258	Discount (div.):	0
	New York, NY 10286	Auto invest:	Yes
Agent's Phone:	888-269-2377	Auto invest fee:	$5 + 10¢/sh.
Other than USA:	Yes	Selling info:	Sells weekly, by mail, at market, for $5 +10¢/sh.

Company:	**Otter Tail Power Co.**	Safekeeping:	Yes
Symbol:	OTTR	Invests:	Every 30 days beginning 1/1
Exchange:	OTC	Minimum:	$10
Industry:	Utility-electric	Maximum:	$5,000/month
Company Address:	215 South Cascade St., Box 496	Min to qualify:	1
	Fergus Falls, MN 56538-0496	Fee on cash inv.:	0!
Company Phone:	800-664-1259 or 218-739-8479	Fee on div. inv.:	0!
Transfer Agent:	Otter Tail Power Company	Discount (cash):	0
Agent's Address:	215 S. Cascade St., Box 496	Discount (div.):	0
	Fergus Falls, MN 56538-0496	Auto invest:	No
Agent's Phone:	800-664-1259	Auto invest fee:	$0
Other than USA:	Yes	Selling info:	Sells monthly, by mail, at avg. price, for $0

Company:	**Owens & Minor, Inc.**	Safekeeping:	No
Symbol:	OMI	Invests:	Every 30 days beginning 1/25
Exchange:	NYSE	Minimum:	$25
Industry:	Medical supplies	Maximum:	$25,000/year
Company Address:	Box 27626	Min to qualify:	1
	Richmond, VA 23261-7626	Fee on cash inv.:	0!
Company Phone:	804-747-9794	Fee on div. inv.:	0!
Transfer Agent:	Bank of New York	Discount (cash):	0
Agent's Address:	P.O.Box 1958	Discount (div.):	0
	Newark, NJ 07101-9774	Auto invest:	No
Agent's Phone:	800-524-4458	Auto invest fee:	$0
Other than USA:	No	Selling info:	Sells weekly, by mail, at market, for $5 +10¢/sh.

Company:	**Owens Corning**	Safekeeping:	Yes
Symbol:	OWC	Invests:	Every 7 days beginning varies
Exchange:	NYSE	Minimum:	$100
Industry:	Glass composites & bldg. materials systems	Maximum:	$120,000/year
		Min to qualify:	1
Company Address:	One Owens Corning Pkwy.	Fee on cash inv.:	0
	Toledo, OH 43659	Fee on div. inv.:	0
Company Phone:	419-248-8803 or 419-248-8000	Discount (cash):	0
Transfer Agent:	ChaseMellon Shareholder Services	Discount (div.):	0
Agent's Address:	85 Challenger Road,	Auto invest:	Yes
	Overpeck Centre	Auto invest fee:	$0
	Ridgefield Park, NJ 07660	Selling info:	Sells weekly, by mail or phone, at
Agent's Phone:	800-953-2596		market, for $15 +12¢/sh.
Other than USA:	Yes		

Company:	**P.T. IndoSat**	Safekeeping:	Yes
Symbol:	IIT	Invests:	Every 7 days beginning varies
Exchange:	NYSE	Minimum:	$50
Industry:	Telecommunications	Maximum:	$250,000/year
Company Address:	c/o BNY,101 Barclay St.,22 West	Min to qualify:	1
	New York, NY 10286	Fee on cash inv.:	$5 + 10¢/sh.
Company Phone:	800-943-9715	Fee on div. inv.:	5% to $5 + 10¢/sh.
Transfer Agent:	Bank of New York	Discount (cash):	0
Agent's Address:	P.O. Box 11258	Discount (div.):	0
	New York, NY 10286	Auto invest:	Yes
Agent's Phone:	888-269-2377	Auto invest fee:	$5 + 10¢/sh.
Other than USA:	Yes	Selling info:	Sells weekly, by mail, at market, for $5 +10¢/sh.

Company:	**P.T. Pasifik Satelit Nusantara**	Safekeeping:	Yes
		Invests:	Every 7 days beginning varies
Symbol:	PSNRY	Minimum:	$50
Exchange:	OTC	Maximum:	$250,000/week
Industry:	Satellite telecommunications	Min to qualify:	1
Company Address:	c/o BNY,101 Barclay St.,22 West	Fee on cash inv.:	$5 + 10¢/sh.
	New York, NY 10286	Fee on div. inv.:	5% to $5 + 10¢/sh.
Company Phone:	800-943-9715	Discount (cash):	0
Transfer Agent:	Bank of New York	Discount (div.):	0
Agent's Address:	P.O. Box 11258	Auto invest:	Yes
	New York, NY 10286	Auto invest fee:	$0
Agent's Phone:	888-269-2377	Selling info:	Sells weekly, by phone or mail, at
Other than USA:	Yes		market, for $5 +10¢/ADS

Company:	**P.T. Telkom**	Safekeeping:	Yes
Symbol:	TLK	Invests:	Every 7 days beginning varies
Exchange:	NYSE	Minimum:	$50
Industry:	Telecommunications	Maximum:	$250,000/year
Company Address:	c/o BNY,101 Barclay St.,22 West	Min to qualify:	1
	New York, NY 10286	Fee on cash inv.:	$5 + 10¢/sh.
Company Phone:	800-943-9715	Fee on div. inv.:	5% to $5 + 10¢/sh.
Transfer Agent:	Bank of New York	Discount (cash):	0
Agent's Address:	P.O. Box 11258	Discount (div.):	0
	New York, NY 10286	Auto invest:	Yes
Agent's Phone:	888-269-2377	Auto invest fee:	$5 + 10¢/sh.
Other than USA:	Yes	Selling info:	Sells weekly, by mail, at market, for $5 +10¢/sh.

Company:	**P.T. Tri Polyta**	Safekeeping:	Yes
Symbol:	TPI	Invests:	Every 7 days beginning varies
Exchange:	NYSE	Minimum:	$50
Industry:	Chemicals	Maximum:	$250,000/year
Company Address:	c/o BNY,101 Barclay St.,22 West	Min to qualify:	1
	New York, NY 10286	Fee on cash inv.:	$5 + 10¢/sh.
Company Phone:	800-943-9715	Fee on div. inv.:	5% to $5 + 10¢/sh.
Transfer Agent:	Bank of New York	Discount (cash):	0
Agent's Address:	P.O. Box 11258	Discount (div.):	0
	New York, NY 10286	Auto invest:	Yes
Agent's Phone:	888-269-2377	Auto invest fee:	$5 + 10¢/sh.
Other than USA:	Yes	Selling info:	Sells weekly, by mail, at market, for $5 +10¢/sh.

Company:	**PAB Bankshares, Inc.**	Safekeeping:	Yes
Symbol:	PAB	Invests:	Every 90 days beginning
Exchange:	AMEX	Minimum:	$50
Industry:	Bank holding company	Maximum:	$5,000/year
Company Address:	Box 3469	Min to qualify:	1
	Valdosta, GA 31604	Fee on cash inv.:	0!
Company Phone:	912-241-2775 or 912-241-8051	Fee on div. inv.:	0!
Transfer Agent:	Registrar & Transfer Co.	Discount (cash):	0
Agent's Address:	10 Commerce Drive	Discount (div.):	0
	Cranford, NJ 07016-3572	Auto invest:	No
Agent's Phone:	800-368-5948	Auto invest fee:	$0
Other than USA:	Yes	Selling info:	Sells daily, by mail, at market, for 6¢/sh.

Company:	**Pacific Century Financial Corp.**	Safekeeping:	Yes
		Invests:	Every 30 days beginning 1/10
Symbol:	BOH	Minimum:	$25
Exchange:	NYSE	Maximum:	$5,000/quarter
Industry:	Banking	Min to qualify:	1
Company Address:	Box 2900	Fee on cash inv.:	0!
	Honolulu, HI 96846	Fee on div. inv.:	0!
Company Phone:	808-537-8239 or 808-537-8037	Discount (cash):	0
Transfer Agent:	Continental Stock Transfer & Trust	Discount (div.):	0
		Auto invest:	Yes
Agent's Address:	2 Broadway, 19th Fl.	Auto invest fee:	$0
	New York, NY 10004	Selling info:	Sells weekly, by mail, at market, for $2 + comm.
Agent's Phone:	800-509-5586		
Other than USA:	Yes		

Company:	**Pacific Dunlop Ltd.**	Safekeeping:	Yes
Symbol:	PDLPY	Invests:	Every 7 days beginning varies
Exchange:	OTC	Minimum:	$50
Industry:	Manufacturing & marketing	Maximum:	$100,000/year
Company Address:	6121 Lakeside Dr., Ste.200	Min to qualify:	1
	Reno, NV 89511	Fee on cash inv.:	$5 + 12¢/sh.
Company Phone:	702-824-4600	Fee on div. inv.:	5% to $2.50
Transfer Agent:	Morgan Guaranty Trust Co.	Discount (cash):	0
Agent's Address:	P.O. Box 9073	Discount (div.):	0
	Boston, MA 02205-9948	Auto invest:	Yes
Agent's Phone:	800-428-4237	Auto invest fee:	$0
Other than USA:	No	Selling info:	Sells daily, by phone or mail, at avg. price, for $5 +12¢/sh.

Company:	**Pacific Gulf Properties Inc.**	Safekeeping:	Yes
		Invests:	Every 90 days beginning 1/3
Symbol:	PAG	Minimum:	$100
Exchange:	NYSE	Maximum:	$5,000/quarter
Industry:	REIT	Min to qualify:	1
Company Address:	4220 Von Karman, 2nd Fl.	Fee on cash inv.:	0!
	Newport Beach, CA 92660	Fee on div. inv.:	0!
Company Phone:	949-223-5000	Discount (cash):	0
Transfer Agent:	Harris Trust & Savings Bank	Discount (div.):	0
Agent's Address:	P.O Bo A3309	Auto invest:	No
	Chicago, IL 60690-3309	Auto invest fee:	$0
Agent's Phone:	800-554-3406	Selling info:	Sells weekly, by mail, at market, for comm.
Other than USA:	Yes		

Company:	**Pacificorp**	Safekeeping:	Yes
Symbol:	PPW	Invests:	Every 15 days beginning 1/1
Exchange:	NYSE	Minimum:	$25
Industry:	Utility-electric	Maximum:	$100,000/year
Company Address:	825 N.E. Multnomah St., Ste.1800	Min to qualify:	1
	Portland, OR 97232	Fee on cash inv.:	0
Company Phone:	503-731-2075 or 503-731-2000	Fee on div. inv.:	25¢
Transfer Agent:	Pacificorp Shareholders Services	Discount (cash):	0
Agent's Address:	P.O. Box 14740	Discount (div.):	0
	Portland, OR 97243-0740	Auto invest:	Yes
Agent's Phone:	800-233-5453	Auto invest fee:	$0
Other than USA:	Yes	Selling info:	Sells monthly, by mail, at market, for $2.50 + 5¢/sh.

Company:	**PaineWebber Group**	Safekeeping:	Yes
Symbol:	PWJ	Invests:	Every 90 days beginning 1/1
Exchange:	NYSE	Minimum:	$10
Industry:	Securities broker	Maximum:	$3,000/quarter
Company Address:	1285 Ave. of the Americas	Min to qualify:	1
	New York, NY 10019-6028	Fee on cash inv.:	0!
Company Phone:	212-713-3224 or 212-713-2000	Fee on div. inv.:	0!
Transfer Agent:	ChaseMellon Shareholder Services	Discount (cash):	0
Agent's Address:	85 Challenger Road	Discount (div.):	0
	Overpeck Centre	Auto invest:	No
	Ridgefield Park, NJ 07660	Auto invest fee:	$0
Agent's Phone:	800-851-9677	Selling info:	Sells weekly, by mail or phone, at market, for comm.
Other than USA:	No		

Company:	**Pall Corp.**	Safekeeping:	Yes
Symbol:	PLL	Invests:	Every 30 days beginning 1/10
Exchange:	NYSE	Minimum:	$100
Industry:	Filters	Maximum:	$5,000/month
Company Address:	25 Harbor Park Dr.	Min to qualify:	50
	Port Washington, NY 11050-4630	Fee on cash inv.:	0!
Company Phone:	516-484-3600	Fee on div. inv.:	0!
Transfer Agent:	Wachovia (EquiServe)	Discount (cash):	0
Agent's Address:	P.O. Box 8217	Discount (div.):	0
	Boston, MA 02266-8217	Auto invest:	No
Agent's Phone:	800-633-4236	Auto invest fee:	$0
Other than USA:	Yes	Selling info:	Sells weekly, by mail or fax, at avg. price, for 8¢/sh.

Company:	**Pan Pacific Retail Prop., Inc.**	Safekeeping:	Yes
		Invests:	Every 90 days beginning 1/15
Symbol:	PNP	Minimum:	$100
Exchange:	NYSE	Maximum:	$25,000/quarter
Industry:	REIT	Min to qualify:	1
Company Address:	1631 South Melrose Dr.-Ste. B	Fee on cash inv.:	0!
	Vista, CA 92083	Fee on div. inv.:	0!
Company Phone:	760-727-1002	Discount (cash):	2%
Transfer Agent:	Bank of New York	Discount (div.):	2%
Agent's Address:	P.O. Box 1958	Auto invest:	Yes
	Newark, NJ 07101-9717	Auto invest fee:	$0
Agent's Phone:	800-524-4458	Selling info:	Sells daily, by mail or phone, at avg. price, for $5 + comm.
Other than USA:	Yes		

Company:	**Parker-Hannifin Corp.**	Safekeeping:	Yes
Symbol:	PH	Invests:	Every 30 days beginning 1/1
Exchange:	NYSE	Minimum:	$10
Industry:	Motion control components	Maximum:	$5,000/month
Company Address:	6035 Parkland Blvd.	Min to qualify:	1
	Cleveland, OH 44124-4141	Fee on cash inv.:	0!
Company Phone:	216-896-3000 or 216-896-2584	Fee on div. inv.:	0!
Transfer Agent:	Wachovia (EquiServe)	Discount (cash):	0
Agent's Address:	P.O. Box 8217	Discount (div.):	0
	Boston, MA 02266-8217	Auto invest:	No
Agent's Phone:	800-633-4236	Auto invest fee:	$0
Other than USA:	Yes	Selling info:	Sells weekly, by mail, at market, for 5¢/sh.

Company:	**Paychex, Inc.**	Safekeeping:	Yes
Symbol:	PAYX	Invests:	Every 15 days beginning 1/10-1/25
Exchange:	OTC	Minimum:	$100
Industry:	Accounting service	Maximum:	$10,000/quarter
Company Address:	911 Panorama Trail South,	Min to qualify:	1
	Box 25397	Fee on cash inv.:	0
	Rochester, NY 14625-0397	Fee on div. inv.:	0
Company Phone:	716-383-3406 or 716-385-6666	Discount (cash):	0
Transfer Agent:	American Stock Transfer	Discount (div.):	0
Agent's Address:	40 Wall Street, 46th Floor	Auto invest:	No
	New York, NY 10005	Auto invest fee:	$0
Agent's Phone:	800-937-5449 or 718-921-8200	Selling info:	Sells weekly, by mail or fax, at market, for $0!
Other than USA:	Yes		

Company:	**PECO Energy**	**Safekeeping:**	Yes
Symbol:	PE	**Invests:**	Every 30 days beginning 1/1
Exchange:	NYSE	**Minimum:**	$0
Industry:	Utility-electric	**Maximum:**	$50,000/year
Company Address:	2301 Market St., Box 8699	**Min to qualify:**	1
	Philadelphia, PA 19101	**Fee on cash inv.:**	0!
Company Phone:	215-841-5728 or 215-841-4000	**Fee on div. inv.:**	0!
Transfer Agent:	FCT (EquiServe)	**Discount (cash):**	0
Agent's Address:	P.O. Box 2598	**Discount (div.):**	0
	Jersey City, NJ 07303-2598	**Auto invest:**	No
Agent's Phone:	800-626-8729	**Auto invest fee:**	$0
Other than USA:	Yes	**Selling info:**	Sells daily, by mail or fax, at market, for $2 +12¢/sh.

Company:	**Penney (J.C.)**	**Safekeeping:**	Yes
Symbol:	JCP	**Invests:**	Every 7 days beginning 1/7
Exchange:	NYSE	**Minimum:**	$25
Industry:	Retail department stores	**Maximum:**	$10,000/month
Company Address:	Box 10001	**Min to qualify:**	1
	Dallas, TX 75301	**Fee on cash inv.:**	$1.50 + 6¢/sh.
Company Phone:	800-953-9421	**Fee on div. inv.:**	0
Transfer Agent:	ChaseMellon Shareholder Services	**Discount (cash):**	0
Agent's Address:	P.O. Box 3315	**Discount (div.):**	0
	South Hackensack, NJ 07606	**Auto invest:**	Yes
Agent's Phone:	800-642-9844	**Auto invest fee:**	$0
Other than USA:	Yes	**Selling info:**	Sells daily, by mail or phone, at market, for $15 + 6¢/sh.

Company:	**Pennichuck Corp.**	**Safekeeping:**	Yes
Symbol:	PNNW	**Invests:**	Every 90 days beginning 2/15
Exchange:	OTC	**Minimum:**	$100
Industry:	Holding company	**Maximum:**	$3,000/quarter
Company Address:	Four Water St., Box 448	**Min to qualify:**	1
	Nashua, NH 03061	**Fee on cash inv.:**	0
Company Phone:	603-882-5191 x5309	**Fee on div. inv.:**	0
Transfer Agent:	Boston Eq. (EquiServe)	**Discount (cash):**	0
Agent's Address:	P.O. Box 8040	**Discount (div.):**	5%
	Boston, MA 02266-8040	**Auto invest:**	No
Agent's Phone:	800-730-4001	**Auto invest fee:**	$0
Other than USA:	Yes	**Selling info:**	Not available

Company:	**PennzEnergy Co.**	**Safekeeping:**	Yes
Symbol:	PZE	**Invests:**	Every 30 days beginning 1/15
Exchange:	NYSE	**Minimum:**	$50
Industry:	Oil & gas	**Maximum:**	$60,000/year
Company Address:	Box 4616	**Min to qualify:**	1
	Houston, TX 77210-4616	**Fee on cash inv.:**	0
Company Phone:	888-795-7852 or 713-546-8914	**Fee on div. inv.:**	0
Transfer Agent:	PennzEnergy Company	**Discount (cash):**	0
Agent's Address:	P.O. Box 4351	**Discount (div.):**	0
	Houston, TX 77210-4351	**Auto invest:**	Yes
Agent's Phone:	888-795-7862	**Auto invest fee:**	$0
Other than USA:	Yes	**Selling info:**	Sells weekly, by mail, at market, for $15 +7¢/sh.

Company:	**Pennzoil-Quaker State Co.**	Safekeeping:	Yes
		Invests:	Every 30 days beginning 1/15
Symbol:	PZL	Minimum:	$50
Exchange:	NYSE	Maximum:	$60,000/year
Industry:	Automotive consumer products	Min to qualify:	1
Company Address:	Box 2967	Fee on cash inv.:	0!
	Houston, TX 77252-2967	Fee on div. inv.:	0!
Company Phone:	888-795-7862 or 713-546-8914	Discount (cash):	0
Transfer Agent:	PZ Shareowner Services	Discount (div.):	0
Agent's Address:	P.O. Box 4351	Auto invest:	Yes
	Houston, TX 77210-4351	Auto invest fee:	$0
Agent's Phone:	888-795-7862	Selling info:	Sells weekly, by mail, at avg. price,
Other than USA:	Yes		for $15 +7¢/sh.

Company:	**Pentair, Inc.**	Safekeeping:	Yes
Symbol:	PNR	Invests:	Every 30 days beginning 1/12
Exchange:	NYSE	Minimum:	$10
Industry:	Manufacturing	Maximum:	$3,000/quarter
Company Address:	1500 County Rd., B2 West	Min to qualify:	1
	St. Paul, MN 55113-3105	Fee on cash inv.:	0!
Company Phone:	651-639-5291	Fee on div. inv.:	0!
Transfer Agent:	Norwest Bank Minnesota, N.A.	Discount (cash):	0
Agent's Address:	P.O. Box 64854	Discount (div.):	0
	St. Paul, MN 55164-0854	Auto invest:	No
Agent's Phone:	800-468-9716	Auto invest fee:	$0
Other than USA:	Yes	Selling info:	Sells daily, by mail, at market, for
			$3 +15¢/sh.

Company:	**People's Bank**	Safekeeping:	No
Symbol:	PBCT	Invests:	Every 30 days beginning 1/15
Exchange:	OTC	Minimum:	$100
Industry:	Savings bank	Maximum:	$10,000/month
Company Address:	850 Main St.	Min to qualify:	1
	Bridgeport, CT 06604	Fee on cash inv.:	0!
Company Phone:	203-338-7228 or	Fee on div. inv.:	0!
203-998-7171		Discount (cash):	0
Transfer Agent:	ChaseMellon Shareholders Services	Discount (div.):	0
Agent's Address:	P.O. Box 3316	Auto invest:	No
	South Hackensack, NJ 07606	Auto invest fee:	$0
Agent's Phone:	800-953-2592	Selling info:	Sells daily, by mail or phone, at
Other than USA:	Yes		avg. price, for $15

Company:	**Peoples BancTrust Co., Inc.**	Safekeeping:	Yes
		Invests:	Every 90 days beginning 3/15
Symbol:	PBTC	Minimum:	$100
Exchange:	OTC	Maximum:	$2,000/quarter
Industry:	Bank holding co.	Min to qualify:	25
Company Address:	310 BROAD ST., Box 799	Fee on cash inv.:	0
	Selma, AL 36702-0799	Fee on div. inv.:	0
Company Phone:	334-875-1000	Discount (cash):	0
Transfer Agent:	Peoples BancTrust Co. Attn. Trust	Discount (div.):	0
	Dept.	Auto invest:	No
Agent's Address:	P.O. Box 799	Auto invest fee:	$0
	Selma, AL 36702-0799	Selling info:	Not available
Agent's Phone:	334-875-1000		
Other than USA:	Yes		

Company:	**Peoples Energy Corp.**	**Safekeeping:**	Yes
Symbol:	PGL	**Invests:**	Every 15 days beginning 1/1
Exchange:	NYSE	**Minimum:**	$25
Industry:	Utility-gas	**Maximum:**	$100,000/year
Company Address:	130 East Randolph Dr., Box 2000	**Min to qualify:**	1
	Chicago, IL 60690-0755	**Fee on cash inv.:**	0!
Company Phone:	800-228-6888 or 312-240-4288	**Fee on div. inv.:**	0!
Transfer Agent:	Peoples Energy Corp.	**Discount (cash):**	0
Agent's Address:	P.O. Box 2000	**Discount (div.):**	0
	Chicago, IL 60690-2000	**Auto invest:**	Yes
Agent's Phone:	800-901-8878	**Auto invest fee:**	$0
Other than USA:	No	**Selling info:**	Sells weekly, by mail, at market, for 8¢/sh.

Company:	**Pep Boys**	**Safekeeping:**	Yes
Symbol:	PBY	**Invests:**	Every 90 days beginning 1/20
Exchange:	NYSE	**Minimum:**	$100
Industry:	Auto parts retailer	**Maximum:**	$10,000/quarter
Company Address:	3111 West Allegheny Ave.	**Min to qualify:**	1
	Philadelphia, PA 19132	**Fee on cash inv.:**	0
Company Phone:	215-229-9000	**Fee on div. inv.:**	0
Transfer Agent:	American Stock Transfer	**Discount (cash):**	0
Agent's Address:	40 Wall Street, 46th Fl	**Discount (div.):**	0
	New York, NY 10005	**Auto invest:**	No
Agent's Phone:	800-937-5449 or 718-921-8200	**Auto invest fee:**	$0
Other than USA:	Yes	**Selling info:**	Sells weekly, by mail or fax, at market, for 4¢/sh.

Company:	**Pepsi-Gemex, SA de C.V.**	**Safekeeping:**	Yes
Symbol:	GEM	**Invests:**	Every 7 days beginning varies
Exchange:	NYSE	**Minimum:**	$50
Industry:	Beverages	**Maximum:**	$250,000/year
Company Address:	c/o BNY,101 Barclay St.,22 West	**Min to qualify:**	1
	New York, NY 10286	**Fee on cash inv.:**	$5 + 10¢/sh.
Company Phone:	800-943-9715	**Fee on div. inv.:**	5% to $5 + 10¢/sh.
Transfer Agent:	Bank of New York	**Discount (cash):**	0
Agent's Address:	P.O. Box 11258	**Discount (div.):**	0
	New York, NY 10286	**Auto invest:**	Yes
Agent's Phone:	888-269-2377	**Auto invest fee:**	$5 + 10¢/sh.
Other than USA:	Yes	**Selling info:**	Sells weekly, by mail, at market, for $5 +10¢/sh.

Company:	**PepsiCo Inc.**	**Safekeeping:**	Yes
Symbol:	PEP	**Invests:**	Every 15 days beginning 15 & 30
Exchange:	NYSE	**Minimum:**	$25
Industry:	Beverages and snack foods	**Maximum:**	$5,000/month
Company Address:	Anderson Hill Rd.	**Min to qualify:**	5
	Purchase, NY 10577	**Fee on cash inv.:**	0!
Company Phone:	914-253-3055 or 914-253-3035	**Fee on div. inv.:**	0!
Transfer Agent:	Bank of New York	**Discount (cash):**	0
Agent's Address:	P.O. Box 1958	**Discount (div.):**	0
	NewarK, NJ 07101-9774	**Auto invest:**	No
Agent's Phone:	800-226-0083	**Auto invest fee:**	$0
Other than USA:	Yes	**Selling info:**	Sells weekly, by mail, at market, for $5 +10¢/sh.

Company:	**Petroleum & Resources Corp.**	Safekeeping:	Yes
		Invests:	Every 7 days beginning 1/7
Symbol:	PEO	Minimum:	$50
Exchange:	NYSE	Maximum:	$25,000/investment
Industry:	Investment company	Min to qualify:	1
Company Address:	Seven St. Paul St., #1140	Fee on cash inv.:	$2.50 + 5¢/sh.
	Baltimore, MD 21202	Fee on div. inv.:	10% to $2.50 + 5¢/sh.
Company Phone:	800-638-2479 or 410-752-5900	Discount (cash):	0
Transfer Agent:	Bank of New York	Discount (div.):	0
Agent's Address:	P.O. Box 11258, Church St. Station	Auto invest:	Yes
	New York, NY 10277	Auto invest fee:	$0
Agent's Phone:	800-432-8224	Selling info:	Sells weekly, by mail, at avg. price, for $10 + 5¢/sh.
Other than USA:	Yes		

Company:	**Pfeiffer Vacuum Technology AG**	Safekeeping:	Yes
		Invests:	Every 7 days beginning varies
Symbol:	PV	Minimum:	$50
Exchange:	NYSE	Maximum:	$250,000/year
Industry:	Vacuum pumps & systems	Min to qualify:	1
Company Address:	c/o BNY,101 Barclay St.,22 West	Fee on cash inv.:	$5 + 10¢/sh.
	New York, NY 10286	Fee on div. inv.:	0
Company Phone:	800-943-9715	Discount (cash):	0
Transfer Agent:	Bank of New York	Discount (div.):	0
Agent's Address:	P.O. Box 11258	Auto invest:	Yes
	New York, NY 10286	Auto invest fee:	$5 + 10¢/sh.
Agent's Phone:	888-269-2377	Selling info:	Sells weekly, by mail, at market, for $5 +10¢/sh.
Other than USA:	Yes		

Company:	**Pfizer Inc.**	Safekeeping:	Yes
Symbol:	PFE	Invests:	Every 7 days beginning Thurs.
Exchange:	NYSE	Minimum:	$50
Industry:	Drugs, consumer products	Maximum:	$unlimited
Company Address:	235 East 42nd St.	Min to qualify:	1
	New York, NY 10017-5755	Fee on cash inv.:	0!
Company Phone:	800-PFE-9393 or 212-733-4749	Fee on div. inv.:	0!
Transfer Agent:	FCT (EquiServe)	Discount (cash):	0
Agent's Address:	P.O. Box 2500	Discount (div.):	0
	Jersey City, NJ 07303-2500	Auto invest:	Yes
Agent's Phone:	800-733-9393	Auto invest fee:	$0
Other than USA:	Yes	Selling info:	Sells daily, by mail, at avg. price, for $15 + comm.

Company:	**Pharmacia & Upjohn**	Safekeeping:	Yes
Symbol:	PNU	Invests:	Every 7 days beginning varies
Exchange:	NYSE	Minimum:	$50
Industry:	Drugs	Maximum:	$100,000/year
Company Address:	95 Corporate Dr.	Min to qualify:	1
	Bridgewater, NJ 08807-1265	Fee on cash inv.:	$3 + 8¢/sh.
Company Phone:	888-768-5501	Fee on div. inv.:	5% to $2.50
Transfer Agent:	Harris Trust & Savings Bank	Discount (cash):	0
Agent's Address:	P.O.Box 755	Discount (div.):	0
	Chicago, IL 60690	Auto invest:	Yes
Agent's Phone:	800-323-1849	Auto invest fee:	$1.50 + 8¢/ sh.
Other than USA:	Yes	Selling info:	Sells weekly, by mail, at market, for $10 + 8¢/sh.

Company:	**Phelps Dodge**	Safekeeping:	Yes
Symbol:	PD	Invests:	Every 7 days beginning varies
Exchange:	NYSE	Minimum:	$100
Industry:	Metals	Maximum:	$10,000/month
Company Address:	2600 North Central Ave.	Min to qualify:	10
	Phoeniz, AZ 85004-3014	Fee on cash inv.:	12¢/sh.
Company Phone:	800-528-1182 x8199 or 602-234-8100	Fee on div. inv.:	0!
Transfer Agent:	ChaseMellon Shareholder Services	Discount (cash):	0
Agent's Address:	P.O. Box 3338	Discount (div.):	0
	South Hackensack, NJ 07606-1938	Auto invest:	Yes
Agent's Phone:	800-279-1240	Auto invest fee:	$0
Other than USA:	Yes	Selling info:	Sells monthly, by mail or phone, at avg. price, for $15 +12¢/sh.

Company:	**Philadelphia Suburban Corp.**	Safekeeping:	Yes
		Invests:	Every 90 days beginning 3/1
Symbol:	PSC	Minimum:	$50
Exchange:	NYSE	Maximum:	$30,000/year
Industry:	Utility-water	Min to qualify:	1
Company Address:	762 W. Lancaster Ave.	Fee on cash inv.:	0!
	Bryn Mawr, PA 19010-3489	Fee on div. inv.:	0!
Company Phone:	610-525-1400	Discount (cash):	0
Transfer Agent:	BankBoston (EquiServe)	Discount (div.):	5%
Agent's Address:	P.O. Box 8040	Auto invest:	Yes
	Boston, MA 02266-8040	Auto invest fee:	$0
Agent's Phone:	800-205-8314	Selling info:	Sells biweekly, by mail or phone, at market, for $15 +12¢/sh.
Other than USA:	No		

Company:	**Philip Morris**	Safekeeping:	Yes
Symbol:	MO	Invests:	Every 30 days beginning 1/10
Exchange:	NYSE	Minimum:	$10
Industry:	Tobacco, food, & brewing	Maximum:	$60,000/year
Company Address:	120 Park Ave.	Min to qualify:	1
	New York, NY 10017-5592	Fee on cash inv.:	0!
Company Phone:	212-880-5000	Fee on div. inv.:	0!
Transfer Agent:	FCT (EquiServe)	Discount (cash):	0
Agent's Address:	P.O. Box 2584	Discount (div.):	0
	Jersey City, NJ 07303-2584	Auto invest:	Yes
Agent's Phone:	800-442-0077	Auto invest fee:	$0
Other than USA:	Yes	Selling info:	Sells daily, by phone, mail, or fax, at market, for $10 +12¢/sh.

Company:	**Phillips Petroleum Co.**	Safekeeping:	Yes
Symbol:	P	Invests:	Every 7 days beginning Fri.
Exchange:	NYSE	Minimum:	$50
Industry:	Oil refining, chemicals	Maximum:	$10,000/month
Company Address:	17 Phillips Bldg.	Min to qualify:	1
	Bartlesville, OK 74004	Fee on cash inv.:	0!
Company Phone:	918-661-4689 or 918-661-3700	Fee on div. inv.:	0!
Transfer Agent:	ChaseMellon Shareholder Services	Discount (cash):	0
Agent's Address:	P.O. Box 3336	Discount (div.):	0
	S. Hackensack, NJ 07606	Auto invest:	Yes
Agent's Phone:	800-356-0066	Auto invest fee:	$0
Other than USA:	Yes	Selling info:	Sells weekly, by mail or phone, at market, for $15 + 5¢/sh.

Company:	**Piccadilly Cafeterias Inc.**
Symbol:	PIC
Exchange:	NYSE
Industry:	Restaurants
Company Address:	3232 Sherwood Forest Blvd., Box 2467 Baton Rouge, LA 70821-2467
Company Phone:	504-293-9440
Transfer Agent:	Wachovia (EquiServe)
Agent's Address:	P.O. Box 8217 Boston, MA 02266-8217
Agent's Phone:	800-633-4236
Other than USA:	No
Safekeeping:	Yes
Invests:	Every 90 days beginning 1/1
Minimum:	$100
Maximum:	$5,000/quarter
Min to qualify:	1
Fee on cash inv.:	0!
Fee on div. inv.:	0!
Discount (cash):	0
Discount (div.):	5%
Auto invest:	No
Auto invest fee:	$0
Selling info:	Sells daily, by mail, at market, for 5¢/sh.

Company:	**Piedmont Natural Gas**
Symbol:	PNY
Exchange:	NYSE
Industry:	Utility-gas
Company Address:	1915 Rexford Rd., Box 33068 Charlotte, NC 28233
Company Phone:	800-693-9917 or 704-364-3120
Transfer Agent:	Wachovia (EquiServe)
Agent's Address:	P.O. Box 8217 Boston, MA 02266-8217
Agent's Phone:	800-633-4236
Other than USA:	Yes
Safekeeping:	Yes
Invests:	Every 30 days beginning 1/15
Minimum:	$25
Maximum:	$3,000/month
Min to qualify:	1
Fee on cash inv.:	0!
Fee on div. inv.:	0!
Discount (cash):	0
Discount (div.):	5%
Auto invest:	Yes
Auto invest fee:	$0
Selling info:	Sells daily, by mail or fax, at market, for 5¢/sh.

Company:	**Pier 1 Imports Inc.**
Symbol:	PIR
Exchange:	NYSE
Industry:	Retailing
Company Address:	301 Commerce St., Ste.600 Fort Worth, TX 76102
Company Phone:	817-878-8000
Transfer Agent:	ChaseMellon Shareholder Services
Agent's Address:	P.O. Box 3338 South Hackensack, NJ 07606-1938
Agent's Phone:	888-884-8086
Other than USA:	Yes
Safekeeping:	Yes
Invests:	Every 7 days beginning varies
Minimum:	$50
Maximum:	$5,000/month
Min to qualify:	1
Fee on cash inv.:	0
Fee on div. inv.:	0
Discount (cash):	0
Discount (div.):	0
Auto invest:	Yes
Auto invest fee:	$0
Selling info:	Sells weekly, by mail , at avg. price, for $15 +12¢/sh.

Company:	**Pinnacle West Capital Corp.**
Symbol:	PNW
Exchange:	NYSE
Industry:	Utility-electric
Company Address:	Box 52132 Phoenix, AZ 85072-2132
Company Phone:	800-457-2983 or 602-379-2568
Transfer Agent:	Pinnacle West Capital Corp.
Agent's Address:	P.O. Box 52133 Phoenix, AZ 85072-2133
Agent's Phone:	800-457-2983
Other than USA:	Yes
Safekeeping:	Yes
Invests:	Every 30 days beginning 1/1
Minimum:	$0
Maximum:	$60,000/year
Min to qualify:	1
Fee on cash inv.:	3¢/sh.
Fee on div. inv.:	3¢/sh.
Discount (cash):	0
Discount (div.):	0
Auto invest:	Yes
Auto invest fee:	$0
Selling info:	Sells weekly, by phone, mail, or fax, at avg. price, for 3¢/sh.

Company:	**Pioneer Electronic Corp.**	Safekeeping:	Yes
Symbol:	PIO	Invests:	Every 5 days beginning varies
Exchange:	NYSE	Minimum:	$50
Industry:	Electronics	Maximum:	$100,000/year
Company Address:	c/o Citibank Data Dist., Box 7070	Min to qualify:	1
	Paramus, NJ 07653	Fee on cash inv.:	$5 + 10¢/sh.
Company Phone:	201-236-4142	Fee on div. inv.:	10¢/sh.
Transfer Agent:	Citicorp Data Distribution, Inc.	Discount (cash):	0
Agent's Address:	P.O.Box 7070	Discount (div.):	0
	Paramus, NJ 07653	Auto invest:	Yes
Agent's Phone:	800-422-2066	Auto invest fee:	$5 + 10¢/sh.
Other than USA:	Yes	Selling info:	Sells weekly, by mail, at market, for $10 +10¢/sh.

Company:	**Pioneer Hi-Bred International, Inc.**	Safekeeping:	No
		Invests:	Every 30 days beginning 1/1
Symbol:	PHB	Minimum:	$25
Exchange:	NYSE	Maximum:	$5,000/month
Industry:	Food, seeds	Min to qualify:	1
Company Address:	400 Locust St., Box 14456	Fee on cash inv.:	0!
	Des Moines, IA 50306-3456	Fee on div. inv.:	0!
Company Phone:	515-248-4800	Discount (cash):	0
Transfer Agent:	Boston Eq. (EquiServe)	Discount (div.):	0
Agent's Address:	P.O. Box 8040	Auto invest:	No
	Boston, MA 02266-8040	Auto invest fee:	$0
Agent's Phone:	800-730-4001	Selling info:	Sells daily, by mail, at market, for $5 + 5¢/sh.
Other than USA:	Yes		

Company:	**Pioneer Standard Electronics**	Safekeeping:	Yes
		Invests:	Every 30 days beginning 1/1
Symbol:	PIOS	Minimum:	$25
Exchange:	OTC	Maximum:	$5,000/month
Industry:	Dist. of indus. & end user elec. prods.	Min to qualify:	1
		Fee on cash inv.:	0!
Company Address:	4800 East 131st St.	Fee on div. inv.:	0!
	Cleveland, OH 44105	Discount (cash):	0
Company Phone:	216-587-3600	Discount (div.):	0
Transfer Agent:	National City Bank	Auto invest:	No
Agent's Address:	P.O.Box 92301	Auto invest fee:	$0
	Cleveland, OH 44139-0900	Selling info:	Sells weekly, by mail, at market, for $5 + 8¢ to 20¢/sh.
Agent's Phone:	800-622-6757		
Other than USA:	Yes		

Company:	**Pitney Bowes**	Safekeeping:	Yes
Symbol:	PBI	Invests:	Every 30 days beginning 1/15
Exchange:	NYSE	Minimum:	$100
Industry:	Business equipment	Maximum:	$3,000/quarter
Company Address:	1 Elmcroft Rd., MSC 6140	Min to qualify:	1
	Stamford, CT 06926-0700	Fee on cash inv.:	0!
Company Phone:	203-351-7200 or 203-351-6088	Fee on div. inv.:	0!
Transfer Agent:	FCT (EquiServe)	Discount (cash):	0
Agent's Address:	P.O. Box 2500	Discount (div.):	0
	Jersey City, NJ 07303+2500	Auto invest:	No
Agent's Phone:	800-648-8170	Auto invest fee:	$0
Other than USA:	Yes	Selling info:	Sells daily, by mail or phone, at market, for $15 + comm.

Company:	**PMC Capital, Inc.**	**Safekeeping:**	No
Symbol:	PMC	**Invests:**	Every 30 days beginning 1/5
Exchange:	ASE	**Minimum:**	$50
Industry:	Financial	**Maximum:**	$5,000/month
Company Address:	18111 Preston Rd., Ste. 600	**Min to qualify:**	15
	Dallas, TX 75252	**Fee on cash inv.:**	$3
Company Phone:	972-349-3256 or 972-349-3200	**Fee on div. inv.:**	0!
Transfer Agent:	American Stock Transfer	**Discount (cash):**	0
Agent's Address:	40 Wall Street	**Discount (div.):**	0
	New York, NY 10005	**Auto invest:**	No
Agent's Phone:	212-936-5100	**Auto invest fee:**	$0
Other than USA:	Yes	**Selling info:**	Sells weekly, by mail, at market, for 4¢/sh.

Company:	**PNC Bank Corp.**	**Safekeeping:**	Yes
Symbol:	PNC	**Invests:**	Every 30 days beginning 1/1
Exchange:	NYSE	**Minimum:**	$50
Industry:	Banking	**Maximum:**	$5,000/month
Company Address:	One PNC Plaza, 249 Fifth Ave.	**Min to qualify:**	1
	Pittsburgh, PA 15222-2707	**Fee on cash inv.:**	0!
Company Phone:	800-843-2206 or 412-762-8221	**Fee on div. inv.:**	0!
Transfer Agent:	ChaseMellon Shareholder Services	**Discount (cash):**	0
Agent's Address:	P.O. Box 3316	**Discount (div.):**	0
	South Hackensack, NJ 07606	**Auto invest:**	Yes
Agent's Phone:	800-982-7652	**Auto invest fee:**	$0
Other than USA:	Yes	**Selling info:**	Sells weekly, by mail or phone, at market, for $15 +10¢/sh.

Company:	**Pohang Iron & Steel Co. Ltd.**	**Safekeeping:**	Yes
		Invests:	Every 7 days beginning varies
Symbol:	PKX	**Minimum:**	$50
Exchange:	NYSE	**Maximum:**	$250,000/year
Industry:	Iron & steel	**Min to qualify:**	1
Company Address:	c/o BNY,101 Barclay St.,22 West	**Fee on cash inv.:**	$5 + 10¢/sh.
	New York, NY 10286	**Fee on div. inv.:**	5% to $5 + 10¢/sh.
Company Phone:	800-943-9715	**Discount (cash):**	0
Transfer Agent:	Bank of New York	**Discount (div.):**	0
Agent's Address:	P.O. Box 11258	**Auto invest:**	Yes
	New York, NY 10286	**Auto invest fee:**	$5 + 10¢/sh.
Agent's Phone:	888-269-2377	**Selling info:**	Sells weekly, by mail, at market, for $5 +10¢/sh.
Other than USA:	Yes		

Company:	**Polaroid Corp.**	**Safekeeping:**	Yes
Symbol:	PRD	**Invests:**	Every 90 days beginning 3/30
Exchange:	NYSE	**Minimum:**	$10
Industry:	Photographic equip. & film	**Maximum:**	$3,000/quarter
Company Address:	784 Memorial Dr.	**Min to qualify:**	1
	Cambridge, MA 02139	**Fee on cash inv.:**	5% to $2.50
Company Phone:	718-386-6589 or 718-386-2000	**Fee on div. inv.:**	5% to $2.50
Transfer Agent:	BankBoston (EquiServe)	**Discount (cash):**	0
Agent's Address:	P.O. Box 644, MS:45-02-09	**Discount (div.):**	0
	Boston, MA 02102-0644	**Auto invest:**	No
Agent's Phone:	800-730-4001	**Auto invest fee:**	$0
Other than USA:	No	**Selling info:**	Sells within 10 bus. days, by mail, at market, for 5% to $5 + comm.

Company:	**Popular, Inc.**	Safekeeping:	No
Symbol:	BPOP	Invests:	Every 30 days beginning 1/15
Exchange:	OTC	Minimum:	$25
Industry:	Banking	Maximum:	$10,000/month
Company Address:	Box 362708	Min to qualify:	1
	San Juan, PR 00936-2708	Fee on cash inv.:	0
Company Phone:	787-765-9800 x5637 or 787-764-3908	Fee on div. inv.:	0
Transfer Agent:	Popular,Inc.. Attn: DRP Dept.	Discount (cash):	0
Agent's Address:	Box 362708	Discount (div.):	5%
	San Juan, PR 00936-2708	Auto invest:	No
Agent's Phone:	787-764-1893	Auto invest fee:	$0
Other than USA:	No	Selling info:	Sells within 10 bus. days, by mail, at market, for comm.

Company:	**Portugal Fund**	Safekeeping:	Yes
Symbol:	PGF	Invests:	Every 180 days beginning 2/15
Exchange:	NYSE	Minimum:	$100
Industry:	Closed-end fund	Maximum:	$3,000/semiannually
Company Address:	c/o Credit Suisse, 153 East 53rd St., 58th Fl. New York, NY 10022	Min to qualify:	1
		Fee on cash inv.:	comm.
		Fee on div. inv.:	0
Company Phone:	800-293-1232	Discount (cash):	0
Transfer Agent:	Boston Eq. (EquiServe)	Discount (div.):	0
Agent's Address:	P.O. Box 644, Mail Stop 45-02-09 Boston, MA 02102-0644	Auto invest:	No
		Auto invest fee:	$0
Agent's Phone:	800-730-6001	Selling info:	Not available
Other than USA:	Yes		

Company:	**Portugal Telecom**	Safekeeping:	Yes
Symbol:	PT	Invests:	Every 7 days beginning varies
Exchange:	NYSE	Minimum:	$50
Industry:	Communications services	Maximum:	$250,000/year
Company Address:	c/o BNY,101 Barclay St.,22 West New York, NY 10286	Min to qualify:	1
		Fee on cash inv.:	$5 + 10¢/sh.
Company Phone:	800-943-9715	Fee on div. inv.:	5% to $5 + 10¢/sh.
Transfer Agent:	Bank of New York	Discount (cash):	0
Agent's Address:	P.O. Box 11258 New York, NY 10286	Discount (div.):	0
		Auto invest:	Yes
Agent's Phone:	888-269-2377	Auto invest fee:	$5 + 10¢/sh.
Other than USA:	Yes	Selling info:	Sells weekly, by mail, at market, for $5 +10¢/sh.

Company:	**Post Properties, Inc.**	Safekeeping:	Yes
Symbol:	PPS	Invests:	Every 30 days beginning 1/1
Exchange:	NYSE	Minimum:	$100
Industry:	REIT	Maximum:	$10,000/month
Company Address:	4401 Northside Pkwy., Ste.800 Atlanta, GA 30327-3057	Min to qualify:	1
		Fee on cash inv.:	0!
Company Phone:	404-846-5000	Fee on div. inv.:	0!
Transfer Agent:	Wachovia (EquiServe)	Discount (cash):	0
Agent's Address:	P.O. Box 8217 Boston, MA 02266-8217	Discount (div.):	5%
		Auto invest:	No
Agent's Phone:	781-575-2000	Auto invest fee:	$0
Other than USA:	Yes	Selling info:	Sells weekly, by mail, at market, for 5¢/sh.

Company:	**Potlatch Corp.**
Symbol:	PCH
Exchange:	NYSE
Industry:	Paper & lumber products
Company Address:	601 W. Riverside Ave., Ste.1100
	Spokane, WA 99201
Company Phone:	509-835-1500
Transfer Agent:	Harris Trust & Savings Bank
Agent's Address:	P.O. Box A-3309
	Chicago, IL 60690
Agent's Phone:	312-461-2302
Other than USA:	Yes

Safekeeping:	No
Invests:	Every 30 days beginning 1/3
Minimum:	$25
Maximum:	$1,000/month
Min to qualify:	1
Fee on cash inv.:	0!
Fee on div. inv.:	0!
Discount (cash):	0
Discount (div.):	0
Auto invest:	No
Auto invest fee:	$0
Selling info:	Sells daily, by mail, at market, for 7¢ to 10¢/sh.

Company:	**Potomac Electric Power**
Symbol:	POM
Exchange:	NYSE
Industry:	Utility-electric
Company Address:	Box 97256
	Washington, DC 20090-7256
Company Phone:	800-527-3726 or 202-872-2797
Transfer Agent:	Potomac Elec. Power Company
Agent's Address:	P.O. Box 97256
	Washington, DC 20090-7256
Agent's Phone:	800-527-3726
Other than USA:	Yes

Safekeeping:	Yes
Invests:	Every 30 days beginning 1/30
Minimum:	$25
Maximum:	$5,000/month
Min to qualify:	1
Fee on cash inv.:	0!
Fee on div. inv.:	0!
Discount (cash):	0
Discount (div.):	0
Auto invest:	No
Auto invest fee:	$0
Selling info:	Sells weekly, by mail or fax, at market, for $5 + 4¢/sh.

Company:	**PP&L Resources Inc.**
Symbol:	PPL
Exchange:	NYSE
Industry:	Utility-electric
Company Address:	2 North Ninth St.
	Allentown, PA 18101
Company Phone:	800-345-3085 or 610-774-5151
Transfer Agent:	PP&L Resources, Inc.
Agent's Address:	2 North Ninth Street-GENTW14
	Allentown, PA 18101
Agent's Phone:	800-345-3085
Other than USA:	Yes

Safekeeping:	Yes
Invests:	Every 30 days beginning 1/1
Minimum:	$0
Maximum:	$80,000/year
Min to qualify:	1
Fee on cash inv.:	0!
Fee on div. inv.:	0!
Discount (cash):	0
Discount (div.):	0
Auto invest:	No
Auto invest fee:	$0
Selling info:	Sells weekly, by mail or fax, at avg. price, for 10¢/sh.

Company:	**PPG Industries**
Symbol:	PPG
Exchange:	NYSE
Industry:	Coatings, glass & chemicals, fiberglass
Company Address:	One PPG Pl., #40E
	Pittsburgh, PA 15272
Company Phone:	412-434-3312 or 412-434-3131
Transfer Agent:	ChaseMellon Shareholder Services
Agent's Address:	85 Challenger Road,
	Overpeck Centre
	Ridgefield Park, NJ 07660
Agent's Phone:	800-648-8160
Other than USA:	Yes

Safekeeping:	No
Invests:	Every 30 days beginning 1/12
Minimum:	$10
Maximum:	$3,000/quarter
Min to qualify:	1
Fee on cash inv.:	0
Fee on div. inv.:	0
Discount (cash):	0
Discount (div.):	0
Auto invest:	No
Auto invest fee:	$0
Selling info:	Sells daily, by mail or phone, at market, for $1 + comm.

Company:	**Praxair, Inc.**	Safekeeping:	Yes
Symbol:	PX	Invests:	Every 30 days beginning 1/30
Exchange:	NYSE	Minimum:	$50
Industry:	Industrial gas	Maximum:	$24,000/year
Company Address:	39 Old Ridgebury Rd.	Min to qualify:	1
	Danbury, CT 06810-5113	Fee on cash inv.:	0!
Company Phone:	800-PRAXAIR	Fee on div. inv.:	0!
Transfer Agent:	Bank of New York	Discount (cash):	0
Agent's Address:	P.O. Box 11258, Church St. Station	Discount (div.):	0
	New York, NY 10286	Auto invest:	No
Agent's Phone:	800-432-0140	Auto invest fee:	$0
Other than USA:	Yes	Selling info:	Sells within 10 bus. days, by mail, at market, for $5

Company:	**Presidential Realty B**	Safekeeping:	Yes
Symbol:	PDLB	Invests:	Every 30 days beginning 1/1
Exchange:	ASE	Minimum:	$100
Industry:	REIT	Maximum:	$10,000/quarter
Company Address:	180 South Broadway	Min to qualify:	1
	White Plains, NY 10605	Fee on cash inv.:	0!
Company Phone:	914-948-1300	Fee on div. inv.:	0!
Transfer Agent:	American Stock Transfer	Discount (cash):	0
Agent's Address:	40 Wall Street	Discount (div.):	5%
	New York, NY 10005	Auto invest:	No
Agent's Phone:	800-937-5449 or 718-921-8200	Auto invest fee:	$0
Other than USA:	Yes	Selling info:	Sells weekly, by mail, at market, for 4¢/sh.

Company:	**Prime Bancorp**	Safekeeping:	Yes
Symbol:	PBNK	Invests:	Every 90 days beginning 2/1
Exchange:	OTC	Minimum:	$50
Industry:	Commercial banking	Maximum:	$5,000/quarter
Company Address:	7111 Valley Green Rd.	Min to qualify:	1
	Fort Washington, PA 19034	Fee on cash inv.:	0
Company Phone:	215-836-2400	Fee on div. inv.:	0
Transfer Agent:	American Stock Transfer	Discount (cash):	0
Agent's Address:	40 Wall Street	Discount (div.):	0
	New York, NY	Auto invest:	No
Agent's Phone:	800-937-5449 or 718-921-8200	Auto invest fee:	$0
Other than USA:	No	Selling info:	Sells weekly, by mail, at market, for comm.

Company:	**Prison Realty Trust Inc.**	Safekeeping:	Yes
Symbol:	PZN	Invests:	Every 30 days beginning 1/10
Exchange:	NYSE	Minimum:	$50
Industry:	REIT	Maximum:	$5,000/month
Company Address:	10 Burton Hills Blvd., Ste. 100	Min to qualify:	1
	Nashville, TN 37215	Fee on cash inv.:	0
Company Phone:	615-263-0200 or	Fee on div. inv.:	0
615-263-3000		Discount (cash):	0%-5%
Transfer Agent:	BankBoston (EquiServe)	Discount (div.):	0
Agent's Address:	P.O. Box 8040	Auto invest:	Yes
	Boston, MA 02266-8040	Auto invest fee:	$0
Agent's Phone:	800-793-8940	Selling info:	Sells daily, by , at market, for $15 + 12¢/sh.
Other than USA:	Yes		

Company:	**Procter & Gamble**
Symbol:	PG
Exchange:	NYSE
Industry:	Household goods, personal care, food & beverages
Company Address:	PBox 5572 Cincinnati, OH 45201-5572
Company Phone:	800-742-6253
Transfer Agent:	Procter & Gamble Co.
Agent's Address:	P.O. Box 5572 Cincinnati, OH 45201-5572
Agent's Phone:	800-764-7483
Other than USA:	Yes

Safekeeping:	Yes
Invests:	Every 7 days beginning 1/5
Minimum:	$100
Maximum:	$120,000/year
Min to qualify:	1
Fee on cash inv.:	$2.50 + 3¢/sh.
Fee on div. inv.:	5% to $1 + 3¢/sh.
Discount (cash):	0
Discount (div.):	0
Auto invest:	Yes
Auto invest fee:	$1
Selling info:	Sells daily, by mail, at avg. price, for $2.50 + 3¢/sh.

Company:	**ProLogis Trust**
Symbol:	PLD
Exchange:	NYSE
Industry:	REIT
Company Address:	14100 East 35th Pl. Aurora, CO 80011
Company Phone:	800-566-2706 or 303-375-9292
Transfer Agent:	Boston Eq. (EquiServe)
Agent's Address:	P.O.Box 644 Boston, MA 02102-0644
Agent's Phone:	800-956-3378
Other than USA:	Yes

Safekeeping:	Yes
Invests:	Every 30 days beginning varies
Minimum:	$200
Maximum:	$5,000/month
Min to qualify:	1
Fee on cash inv.:	0!
Fee on div. inv.:	0!
Discount (cash):	2%
Discount (div.):	2%
Auto invest:	Yes
Auto invest fee:	$0
Selling info:	Sells within 13 bus. days, by mail, at market, for 5% to $10 + 5¢/sh.

Company:	**Protective Life Corp.**
Symbol:	PL
Exchange:	NYSE
Industry:	Insurance
Company Address:	Box 2606 Birmingham, AL 35202
Company Phone:	205-868-3515 or 205-879-9230
Transfer Agent:	Bank of New York
Agent's Address:	P.O. Box 1958 Newark, NJ 07101-9774
Agent's Phone:	800-524-4458
Other than USA:	Yes

Safekeeping:	Yes
Invests:	Every 90 days beginning 3/1
Minimum:	$25
Maximum:	$6,000/quarter
Min to qualify:	1
Fee on cash inv.:	0!
Fee on div. inv.:	0!
Discount (cash):	0
Discount (div.):	0
Auto invest:	No
Auto invest fee:	$0
Selling info:	Sells weekly, by mail, at market, for 20¢/sh.

Company:	**Providence Energy Corp.**
Symbol:	PVY
Exchange:	NYSE
Industry:	Utility-gas
Company Address:	100 Weybosset St. Providence, RI 02903
Company Phone:	401-272-9191
Transfer Agent:	Bank of New York
Agent's Address:	P.O. Box 11258-Church St. Station New York, NY 10286
Agent's Phone:	888-269-8845
Other than USA:	Yes

Safekeeping:	Yes
Invests:	Every 30 days beginning 1/15
Minimum:	$25
Maximum:	$5,000/quarter
Min to qualify:	1
Fee on cash inv.:	0!
Fee on div. inv.:	0!
Discount (cash):	0
Discount (div.):	0
Auto invest:	No
Auto invest fee:	$0
Selling info:	Sells weekly, by mail, at market, for $5 +10¢/sh.

Company:	**Provident Bankshares Corp.**	Safekeeping:	No
		Invests:	Every 30 days beginning 1/30
Symbol:	PBKS	Minimum:	$100
Exchange:	OTC	Maximum:	$10,000/quarter
Industry:	Bank holding co.	Min to qualify:	1
Company Address:	114 East Lexington St.	Fee on cash inv.:	0!
	Baltimore, MD 21202	Fee on div. inv.:	0!
Company Phone:	410-277-7000 or 410-277-7343	Discount (cash):	0
Transfer Agent:	BankBoston (EquiServe)	Discount (div.):	0
Agent's Address:	P.O. Box 8040	Auto invest:	No
	Boston, Ma 02266-8040	Auto invest fee:	$0
Agent's Phone:	800-730-4001	Selling info:	Not available
Other than USA:	Yes		

Company:	**Provident Companies, Inc.**	Safekeeping:	No
Symbol:	PVT	Invests:	Every 30 days beginning 1/10
Exchange:	NYSE	Minimum:	$10
Industry:	Life & health insurance	Maximum:	$60,000/year
Company Address:	1 Fountain Sq.	Min to qualify:	1
	Chattanooga, TN 37402	Fee on cash inv.:	3¢/sh.
Company Phone:	423-755-1661 or 423-755-1011	Fee on div. inv.:	3¢/sh.
Transfer Agent:	FCT (EquiServe)	Discount (cash):	0
Agent's Address:	P.O.Box 2598	Discount (div.):	0
	Jersey City, NJ 07303-2598	Auto invest:	No
Agent's Phone:	800-446-2617	Auto invest fee:	$0
Other than USA:	Yes	Selling info:	Sells daily, by phone or mail, at market, for $10 +12¢/sh.

Company:	**Providian Financial**	Safekeeping:	Yes
Symbol:	PVN	Invests:	Every 30 days beginning 1/15
Exchange:	NYSE	Minimum:	$50
Industry:	Financial services, consumer loans	Maximum:	$250,000/year
		Min to qualify:	1
Company Address:	201 Mission St.	Fee on cash inv.:	$5 + 3¢/sh.
	San Francisco, CA 94105	Fee on div. inv.:	5% to $3 + 3¢/sh.
Company Phone:	415-278-4483 or 415-278-6170	Discount (cash):	0
Transfer Agent:	FCT (EquiServe)	Discount (div.):	0
Agent's Address:	P.O. Box 2598	Auto invest:	Yes
	Jersey City, NJ 07303-2598	Auto invest fee:	$2 + comm.
Agent's Phone:	800-317-4445	Selling info:	Sells daily, by phone, mail,fax, or email., at market, for $15 +12¢/sh.
Other than USA:	Yes		

Company:	**Public Service Co. of NC, Inc.**	Safekeeping:	Yes
		Invests:	Every 30 days beginning 1/1
Symbol:	PGS	Minimum:	$25
Exchange:	NYSE	Maximum:	$15,000/quarter
Industry:	Utility-gas	Min to qualify:	1
Company Address:	400 Cox Rd., Box 1398	Fee on cash inv.:	0
	Gastonia, NC 28053-1398	Fee on div. inv.:	0
Company Phone:	800-784-6443 or 704-864-6731	Discount (cash):	0
Transfer Agent:	First Union National Bank of NC	Discount (div.):	5%
Agent's Address:	1525 West W.T. Harris Blvd.-3C3	Auto invest:	Yes
	Charlotte, NC 28288-1153	Auto invest fee:	$0
Agent's Phone:	800-829-8432	Selling info:	Sells weekly, by mail or fax, at market, for 5¢ to 6¢/sh.
Other than USA:	Yes		

Company:	**Public Service Co. of NM**	Safekeeping:	Yes
Symbol:	PNM	Invests:	Every 30 days beginning 1/1
Exchange:	NYSE	Minimum:	$50
Industry:	Utility-electric, gas	Maximum:	$5,000/month
Company Address:	Alvarado Sq., Box 1047	Min to qualify:	1
	Albuquerque, NM 87103-9924	Fee on cash inv.:	comm.
Company Phone:	800-545-4425 or 505-241-2054	Fee on div. inv.:	comm.
Transfer Agent:	PNM Shareholder Records Dept.	Discount (cash):	0
Agent's Address:	Alvarado Square-1104	Discount (div.):	0
	Albuquerque, NM 87158	Auto invest:	Yes
Agent's Phone:	800-545-4425	Auto invest fee:	$0
Other than USA:	Yes	Selling info:	Sells weekly, by mail or fax, at market, for 2.5¢/sh.

Company:	**Public Service Enterprise Grp.**	Safekeeping:	Yes
		Invests:	Every 15 days beginning 1/15
Symbol:	PEG	Minimum:	$50
Exchange:	NYSE	Maximum:	$125,000/year
Industry:	Utility-electric, gas	Min to qualify:	1
Company Address:	80 Park Plaza, T6B	Fee on cash inv.:	0!
	Newark, NJ 07102	Fee on div. inv.:	0!
Company Phone:	800-242-0813 or 973-430-6564	Discount (cash):	0
Transfer Agent:	Public Service Enterprise Group	Discount (div.):	0
	/Stockholder Services	Auto invest:	Yes
Agent's Address:	P.O. Box 1171	Auto invest fee:	$0
	Newark, NJ 07101-1171	Selling info:	Sells biweekly, by mail or fax, at market, for $10 + 2¢/sh.
Agent's Phone:	800-242-0813		
Other than USA:	Yes		

Company:	**Puget Sound Energy**	Safekeeping:	Yes
Symbol:	PSD	Invests:	Every 7 days beginning varies
Exchange:	NYSE	Minimum:	$25
Industry:	Utility-electric, gas	Maximum:	$100,000/year
Company Address:	Box 97034	Min to qualify:	1
	Bellevue, WA 98009-9734	Fee on cash inv.:	comm.
Company Phone:	425-462-3898 or 425-454-6363	Fee on div. inv.:	comm.
Transfer Agent:	ChaseMellon Shareholder Services	Discount (cash):	0
Agent's Address:	85 Challenger Road	Discount (div.):	0
	Ridgefield Park, NJ 07660	Auto invest:	No
Agent's Phone:	800-997-8438	Auto invest fee:	$0
Other than USA:	Yes	Selling info:	Sells weekly, by mail or phone, at market, for comm.

Company:	**Quaker Chemical Corp.**	Safekeeping:	Yes
Symbol:	KWR	Invests:	Every 15 days beginning 1/15
Exchange:	NYSE	Minimum:	$300
Industry:	Specialty chemicals	Maximum:	$24,000/year
Company Address:	Elm & Lee Sts.	Min to qualify:	1
	Conshohocken, PA 19428	Fee on cash inv.:	0
Company Phone:	610-832-4119 or 610-832-4000	Fee on div. inv.:	0
Transfer Agent:	American Stock Transfer & Trust	Discount (cash):	0
Agent's Address:	40 Wall Street	Discount (div.):	0
	New York, NY 10005	Auto invest:	Yes
Agent's Phone:	800-278-4353	Auto invest fee:	$0
Other than USA:	Yes	Selling info:	Sells within 3 bus. days, by mail, at market, for $7.50 + 4¢/sh.

Company:	**Quaker Oats**	Safekeeping:	Yes
Symbol:	OAT	Invests:	Every 7 days beginning varies
Exchange:	NYSE	Minimum:	$50
Industry:	Food & beverages	Maximum:	$120,000/year
Company Address:	Box 049001, Ste.27-7	Min to qualify:	1
	Chicago, IL 60604-9001	Fee on cash inv.:	$5 + 10¢/sh.
Company Phone:	312-222-7818	Fee on div. inv.:	75¢
Transfer Agent:	Harris Trust & Savings Bank	Discount (cash):	0
Agent's Address:	P.O. Box A3504, 311 W. Monroe	Discount (div.):	0
	Chicago, IL 60690-3504	Auto invest:	Yes
Agent's Phone:	800-344-1198	Auto invest fee:	$1.50 + 10¢/sh.
Other than USA:	Yes	Selling info:	Sells weekly, by mail, at market, for $10 +10¢/sh.

Company:	**Quanex Corp.**	Safekeeping:	Yes
Symbol:	NX	Invests:	Every 30 days beginning 1/1
Exchange:	NYSE	Minimum:	$50
Industry:	Mfr. steel, bar aluminum	Maximum:	$10,000/quarter
Company Address:	1900 W. Loop South, Ste.1500	Min to qualify:	1
	Houston, TX 77027	Fee on cash inv.:	0!
Company Phone:	800-231-8176 or 713-961-4600	Fee on div. inv.:	0!
Transfer Agent:	American Stock Transfer	Discount (cash):	0
Agent's Address:	40 Wall Street, 46th Fl.	Discount (div.):	0
	New York, NY 10005	Auto invest:	Yes
Agent's Phone:	800-937-5449 or 800-278-4353	Auto invest fee:	$0
Other than USA:	Yes	Selling info:	Sells weekly, by mail or fax, at market, for $10 + 4¢/sh.

Company:	**Questar Corp.**	Safekeeping:	Yes
Symbol:	STR	Invests:	Every 30 days beginning 1/31
Exchange:	NYSE	Minimum:	$50
Industry:	Integrated nat. gas holding co.,	Maximum:	$100,000/year
	includes oil & gas exploration	Min to qualify:	1
Company Address:	Box 45433	Fee on cash inv.:	0!
	Salt Lake City, UT 84145-0433	Fee on div. inv.:	0!
Company Phone:	801-324-5885 or 801-324-5026	Discount (cash):	0
Transfer Agent:	Questar Corp.,Shareholders	Discount (div.):	0
	Services	Auto invest:	No
Agent's Address:	P.O. Box 45433	Auto invest fee:	$0
	Salt Lake City, UT 84145-0433	Selling info:	Sells biweekly, by mail or fax, at
Agent's Phone:	801-324-5885		market, for 5¢/sh.
Other than USA:	Yes		

Company:	**Ralston Purina Co.**	Safekeeping:	Yes
Symbol:	RAL	Invests:	Every 30 days beginning 1/1
Exchange:	NYSE	Minimum:	$10
Industry:	Dry and semimoist pet food,	Maximum:	$25,000/year
	batteries	Min to qualify:	1
Company Address:	Checkerboard Sq.	Fee on cash inv.:	0!
	St. Louis, MO 63164-0001	Fee on div. inv.:	0!
Company Phone:	800-445-7776 or 314-982-3000	Discount (cash):	0
Transfer Agent:	Ralston Purina	Discount (div.):	0
Agent's Address:	Checkerboard Square	Auto invest:	No
	St. Louis, MO 63164	Auto invest fee:	$0
Agent's Phone:	800-445-7776	Selling info:	Sells weekly, by mail or fax, at
Other than USA:	Yes		market, for 5¢/sh.

Company:	**Rangold & Exploration Co.**	Safekeeping:	Yes
		Invests:	Every 7 days beginning varies
Symbol:	RANGY	Minimum:	$50
Exchange:	OTC	Maximum:	$250,000/year
Industry:	Mining	Min to qualify:	1
Company Address:	c/o BNY,101 Barclay St.,22 West	Fee on cash inv.:	$5 + 10¢/sh.
	New York, NY 10286	Fee on div. inv.:	5% to $5 + 10¢/sh.
Company Phone:	800-943-9715	Discount (cash):	0
Transfer Agent:	Bank of New York	Discount (div.):	0
Agent's Address:	P.O. Box 11258	Auto invest:	Yes
	New York, NY 10286	Auto invest fee:	$5 + 10¢/sh.
Agent's Phone:	888-269-2377	Selling info:	Sells weekly, by mail, at market,
Other than USA:	Yes		for $5 +10¢/sh.

Company:	**Rank Group plc (The)**	Safekeeping:	Yes
Symbol:	RANKY	Invests:	Every 7 days beginning varies
Exchange:	OTC	Minimum:	$50
Industry:	TV, film production, hotels	Maximum:	$100,000/year
Company Address:	c/o Morgan Guaranty Trust,	Min to qualify:	1
	Box 9073	Fee on cash inv.:	$5 + 12¢/sh.
	Boston, MA 02205-9948	Fee on div. inv.:	5% to $2.50
Company Phone:	800-428-4237	Discount (cash):	0
Transfer Agent:	Morgan Guaranty Trust Co.	Discount (div.):	0
Agent's Address:	P.O. Box 9073	Auto invest:	Yes
	Boston, MA 02205-9948	Auto invest fee:	$0
Agent's Phone:	800-428-4237	Selling info:	Sells daily, by phone or mail, at
Other than USA:	No		avg. price, for $5 +12¢/sh.

Company:	**Rauma Oy**	Safekeeping:	Yes
Symbol:	RMA	Invests:	Every 7 days beginning varies
Exchange:	NYSE	Minimum:	$50
Industry:	Constr. & agric. machinery	Maximum:	$250,000/year
Company Address:	c/o BNY,101 Barclay St.,22 West	Min to qualify:	1
	New York, NY 10286	Fee on cash inv.:	$5 + 10¢/sh.
Company Phone:	800-943-9715	Fee on div. inv.:	5% to $5 + 10¢/sh.
Transfer Agent:	Bank of New York	Discount (cash):	0
Agent's Address:	P.O. Box 11258	Discount (div.):	0
	New York, NY 10286	Auto invest:	Yes
Agent's Phone:	888-269-2377	Auto invest fee:	$5 + 10¢/sh.
Other than USA:	Yes	Selling info:	Sells weekly, by mail, at market,
			for $5 +10¢/sh.

Company:	**Rayonier Inc.**	Safekeeping:	Yes
Symbol:	RYN	Invests:	Every 5 days beginning 1/6
Exchange:	NYSE	Minimum:	$50
Industry:	Wood manufacturing	Maximum:	$5,000/quarter
Company Address:	1177 Summer St.	Min to qualify:	1
	Stamford, CT 06905-5529	Fee on cash inv.:	$1.50
Company Phone:	203-348-7000	Fee on div. inv.:	0
Transfer Agent:	Bank of New York	Discount (cash):	0
Agent's Address:	Church St. Station, P.O Box 11258	Discount (div.):	0
	New York, NY 10286-1258	Auto invest:	No
Agent's Phone:	800-432-0140	Auto invest fee:	$0
Other than USA:	Yes	Selling info:	Sells weekly, by mail, at avg. price,
			for $3 + 7¢/sh.

Company:	**Raytheon Co. A**	Safekeeping:	Yes
Symbol:	RTNA	Invests:	Every 30 days beginning 1/25
Exchange:	NYSE	Minimum:	$10
Industry:	Aerospace, defense, elec. & appliances	Maximum:	$25,000/quarter
		Min to qualify:	1
Company Address:	141 Spring St.	Fee on cash inv.:	0
	Lexington, MA 02173	Fee on div. inv.:	0
Company Phone:	781-862-6600 or 781-860-2303	Discount (cash):	0
Transfer Agent:	Boston Eq. (EquiServe)	Discount (div.):	0
Agent's Address:	P.O. Box 8038	Auto invest:	No
	Boston, MA 02266-8038	Auto invest fee:	$0
Agent's Phone:	800-360-4519	Selling info:	Sells within 10 bus. days, by phone or mail, at market, for $10 +15¢/sh.
Other than USA:	Yes		

Company:	**Raytheon Co. B**	Safekeeping:	Yes
Symbol:	RTNB	Invests:	Every 30 days beginning 1/25
Exchange:	NYSE	Minimum:	$10
Industry:	Aerospace, defense, elec. & appliances	Maximum:	$25,000/quarter
		Min to qualify:	1
Company Address:	141 Spring St.	Fee on cash inv.:	0
	Lexington, MA 02173	Fee on div. inv.:	0
Company Phone:	781-862-6600 or 781-860-2303	Discount (cash):	0
Transfer Agent:	Boston Eq. (EquiServe)	Discount (div.):	0
Agent's Address:	P.O. Box 8038	Auto invest:	Yes
	Boston, MA 02266-8038	Auto invest fee:	$0
Agent's Phone:	800-360-4519	Selling info:	Sells weekly, by phone or mail, at market, for $10 +15¢/sh.
Other than USA:	Yes		

Company:	**Reader's Digest Assn., Inc. A**	Safekeeping:	Yes
		Invests:	Every 7 days beginning varies
Symbol:	RDA	Minimum:	$100
Exchange:	NYSE	Maximum:	$10,000/month
Industry:	Magazine, book publishing	Min to qualify:	1
Company Address:	Reader's Digest Rd.	Fee on cash inv.:	$5 + 12¢/sh.
	Pleasantville, NY 10570-7000	Fee on div. inv.:	0
Company Phone:	914-244-7683 or 914-238-1000	Discount (cash):	0
Transfer Agent:	ChaseMellon Shareholder Services	Discount (div.):	0
Agent's Address:	P.O. Box 3338	Auto invest:	Yes
	South Hackensack, NJ 07606-1938	Auto invest fee:	$0
Agent's Phone:	800-230-2771	Selling info:	Sells weekly, by mail or phone, at market, for $15 +12¢/sh.
Other than USA:	Yes		

Company:	**Reader's Digest Assn., Inc. B**	Safekeeping:	Yes
		Invests:	Every 7 days beginning varies
Symbol:	RDB	Minimum:	$100
Exchange:	NYSE	Maximum:	$10,000/month
Industry:	Magazine, book publishing	Min to qualify:	1
Company Address:	Reader's Digest Rd.	Fee on cash inv.:	$5 + 12¢/sh.
	Pleasantville, NY 10570-7000	Fee on div. inv.:	0
Company Phone:	914-244-7683 or 914-238-1000	Discount (cash):	0
Transfer Agent:	ChaseMellon Shareholder Services	Discount (div.):	0
Agent's Address:	P.O. Box 3338	Auto invest:	Yes
	South Hackensack, Nj 07606-1938	Auto invest fee:	$0
Agent's Phone:	800-230-2771	Selling info:	Sells weekly, by mail or phone, at market, for $15
Other than USA:	Yes		

Company:	**Redwood Empire Bancorp**	**Safekeeping:**	Yes
Symbol:	REBC	**Invests:**	Every 30 days beginning 1/15
Exchange:	OTC	**Minimum:**	$100
Industry:	Bank holding company	**Maximum:**	$5,000/month
Company Address:	111 Santa Rosa Ave., Box 402	**Min to qualify:**	1
	Santa Rosa, CA 95402-0402	**Fee on cash inv.:**	0!
Company Phone:	707-573-4800	**Fee on div. inv.:**	0!
Transfer Agent:	ChaseMellon Shareholder Services	**Discount (cash):**	0
Agent's Address:	85 Challenger Road,	**Discount (div.):**	0
	Overpeck Centre	**Auto invest:**	Yes
	Ridgefield, NJ 07660	**Auto invest fee:**	$0
Agent's Phone:	800-522-6645	**Selling info:**	Sells daily, by mail, at avg. price,
Other than USA:	Yes		for $2.50

Company:	**Redwood Trust, Inc.**	**Safekeeping:**	Yes
Symbol:	RWT	**Invests:**	Every 30 days beginning 1/21
Exchange:	OTC	**Minimum:**	$500
Industry:	REIT	**Maximum:**	$5,000/month
Company Address:	591 Redwood Hwy., #3100	**Min to qualify:**	1
	Mill Valley, CA 94941	**Fee on cash inv.:**	0
Company Phone:	415-389-7373	**Fee on div. inv.:**	0
Transfer Agent:	ChaseMellon Shareholder Ser-	**Discount (cash):**	0-2%
	vices	**Discount (div.):**	2%
Agent's Address:	P. O. Box 750	**Auto invest:**	No
	Pittsburgh, PA 15230	**Auto invest fee:**	$0
Agent's Phone:	888-877-2882	**Selling info:**	Sells monthly, by mail, at market,
Other than USA:	No		for $15 +12¢/sh.

Company:	**Regions Financial Corp.**	**Safekeeping:**	Yes
Symbol:	RGBK	**Invests:**	Every 7 days beginning Wed.
Exchange:	OTC	**Minimum:**	$25
Industry:	Banking	**Maximum:**	$120,000/year
Company Address:	417 North 20th St., Box 10247	**Min to qualify:**	1
	Birmingham, AL 35202-0247	**Fee on cash inv.:**	0!
Company Phone:	205-326-7090 or 205-326-7100	**Fee on div. inv.:**	0!
Transfer Agent:	FCT(EquiServe)	**Discount (cash):**	0
Agent's Address:	P.O. Box 2500	**Discount (div.):**	0
	Jersey City, NJ 07303-2500	**Auto invest:**	Yes
Agent's Phone:	800-524-2879	**Auto invest fee:**	$1
Other than USA:	Yes	**Selling info:**	Sells daily, by phone or mail, at
			market, for $15 +12¢/sh.

Company:	**Reliant Energy**	**Safekeeping:**	Yes
Symbol:	REI	**Invests:**	Every 7 days beginning varies
Exchange:	NYSE	**Minimum:**	$50
Industry:	Utility-electric, gas	**Maximum:**	$120,000/year
Company Address:	Box 4657	**Min to qualify:**	1
	Houston, TX 77210	**Fee on cash inv.:**	5¢ to 10¢/sh.
Company Phone:	800-231-6406 or 713-207-3115 or	**Fee on div. inv.:**	5¢ to 10¢/sh.
	713-207-3000	**Discount (cash):**	0
Transfer Agent:	Reliant Energy Shareholder Services	**Discount (div.):**	0
Agent's Address:	P.O. Box 4567	**Auto invest:**	Yes
	Houston, TX 77210	**Auto invest fee:**	$0
Agent's Phone:	800-231-6406	**Selling info:**	Sells weekly, by mail, phone, or
Other than USA:	Yes		fax, at avg. price, for 5¢/sh.

Company:	**ReliaStar Financial Corp.**	Safekeeping:	Yes
Symbol:	RLR	Invests:	Every 30 days beginning 1/13
Exchange:	NYSE	Minimum:	$50
Industry:	Insurance	Maximum:	$5,000/month
Company Address:	20 Washington Ave. South	Min to qualify:	50
	Minneapolis, MN 55401	Fee on cash inv.:	0!
Company Phone:	612-372-5618 or 612-372-5432	Fee on div. inv.:	0!
Transfer Agent:	Norwest Bank Minnesota	Discount (cash):	1%
Agent's Address:	P.O. Box 64854	Discount (div.):	4%
	St. Paul, MN 55164-0854	Auto invest:	No
Agent's Phone:	800-468-9716	Auto invest fee:	$0
Other than USA:	Yes	Selling info:	Sells daily, by mail or fax, at market, for comm.

Company:	**Reliv International, Inc.**	Safekeeping:	Yes
Symbol:	RELV	Invests:	Every 7 days beginning varies
Exchange:	OTC	Minimum:	$50
Industry:	Food processing	Maximum:	$10,000/transaction
Company Address:	136 Chesterfield Industrial,	Min to qualify:	1
	Box 405	Fee on cash inv.:	$7.50 + 10¢/sh.
	Chesterfield, MO 63006	Fee on div. inv.:	0
Company Phone:	888-333-0203	Discount (cash):	0
Transfer Agent:	American Stock Transfer	Discount (div.):	0
Agent's Address:	40 Wall Street	Auto invest:	Yes
	New York, NY 10005	Auto invest fee:	$7.50 + 10¢/sh.
Agent's Phone:	888-333-0203	Selling info:	Sells weekly, by mail, at market, for $7.50 +10¢/sh.
Other than USA:	Yes		

Company:	**Repsol S.A. ADS**	Safekeeping:	Yes
Symbol:	REP	Invests:	Every 7 days beginning varies
Exchange:	NYSE	Minimum:	$50
Industry:	Oil & gas	Maximum:	$250,000/week
Company Address:	c/o BNY,101 Barclay St., 22 West	Min to qualify:	1
	New York, NY 10286	Fee on cash inv.:	$5 + 10¢/sh.
Company Phone:	800-943-9715	Fee on div. inv.:	5% to $5 + 10¢/sh.
Transfer Agent:	Bank of New York	Discount (cash):	0
Agent's Address:	P.O. Box 11258	Discount (div.):	0
	New York, NY 10286	Auto invest:	Yes
Agent's Phone:	888-269-2377	Auto invest fee:	$0
Other than USA:	Yes	Selling info:	Sells weekly, by phone or mail, at avg. price, for $5 +10¢/ADS

Company:	**Republic Bancorp Inc.**	Safekeeping:	Yes
Symbol:	RBNC	Invests:	Every 45 days beginning 1/3
Exchange:	OTC	Minimum:	$10
Industry:	Banking	Maximum:	$5,000/quarter
Company Address:	1070 East Main St., Box 70	Min to qualify:	1
	Owosso, MI 48867	Fee on cash inv.:	0!
Company Phone:	517-725-7004 or 517-725-7337	Fee on div. inv.:	0!
Transfer Agent:	State Street Bank (EquiServe)	Discount (cash):	0
Agent's Address:	P.O. Box 8200	Discount (div.):	0
	Boston, MA 02266-8200	Auto invest:	No
Agent's Phone:	800-257-1770	Auto invest fee:	$0
Other than USA:	No	Selling info:	Sells daily, by phone, mail, or fax, at market, for comm.

Company:	**Republic Group**	
Symbol:	RGC	
Exchange:	NYSE	
Industry:	Paper & paper products	
Company Address:	811 East 30th Ave., Box 1307	
	Hutchinson, KS 67504-1307	
Company Phone:	316-727-2700	
Transfer Agent:	UMB Bank, N.A.	
Agent's Address:	P.O. Box 410064	
	Kansas City, MO 64141-0064	
Agent's Phone:	816-860-7787	
Other than USA:	Yes	

Safekeeping:	Yes
Invests:	Every 30 days beginning 1/15
Minimum:	$50
Maximum:	$10,000/quarter
Min to qualify:	1
Fee on cash inv.:	0
Fee on div. inv.:	0
Discount (cash):	0
Discount (div.):	0
Auto invest:	Yes
Auto invest fee:	$0
Selling info:	Sells weekly, by mail, at market, for $5 + comm.

Company:	**Republic New York Corp.**
Symbol:	RNB
Exchange:	NYSE
Industry:	Commercial banking
Company Address:	452 5th Ave.
	New York, NY 10018
Company Phone:	212-525-6100
Transfer Agent:	American Stock Transfer
Agent's Address:	40 Wall Street, 46th Floor
	New York, NY 10005
Agent's Phone:	800-278-4353
Other than USA:	Yes

Safekeeping:	Yes
Invests:	Every 90 days beginning 1/1
Minimum:	$50
Maximum:	$10,000/quarter
Min to qualify:	1
Fee on cash inv.:	0
Fee on div. inv.:	0
Discount (cash):	0
Discount (div.):	0
Auto invest:	No
Auto invest fee:	$0
Selling info:	Sells weekly, by mail, at market, for $5 + 4¢/sh.

Company:	**Republic Security Financial Corp.**
Symbol:	RSFC
Exchange:	OTC
Industry:	Bank holding company
Company Address:	4400 Congress Ave.
	West Palm Beach, FL 33407-3288
Company Phone:	561-840-1200
Transfer Agent:	American Stock Transfer
Agent's Address:	40 Wall St., 46th Fl.
	New York, NY 10005
Agent's Phone:	718-921-8283
Other than USA:	Yes

Safekeeping:	Yes
Invests:	Every 90 days beginning 3/4
Minimum:	$100
Maximum:	$10,000/quarter
Min to qualify:	1
Fee on cash inv.:	0!
Fee on div. inv.:	0!
Discount (cash):	0
Discount (div.):	0
Auto invest:	No
Auto invest fee:	$0
Selling info:	Sells irregularly, by mail, at market, for comm.

Company:	**Resource Bancshares Mtge. Grp.**
Symbol:	RBMG
Exchange:	OTC
Industry:	Mortgage banking
Company Address:	7909 Parklane Rd.
	Suite 150
	Columbia, SC 29223
Company Phone:	800-933-2890 or 803-741-3000
Transfer Agent:	FCT (EquiServe)
Agent's Address:	P.O. Box 2500
	Jersey City, NJ 07303-2500
Agent's Phone:	800-446-2617
Other than USA:	Yes

Safekeeping:	No
Invests:	Every 90 days beginning 3/31
Minimum:	$100
Maximum:	$15,000/quarter
Min to qualify:	1
Fee on cash inv.:	0
Fee on div. inv.:	0
Discount (cash):	5%
Discount (div.):	5%
Auto invest:	No
Auto invest fee:	$0
Selling info:	Not available

Company:	**Reuters Group plc**	Safekeeping:	Yes
Symbol:	RTRYD	Invests:	Every 7 days beginning Thurs.
Exchange:	OTC	Minimum:	$50
Industry:	Int'l news agency	Maximum:	$100,000/year
Company Address:	1700 Broadway	Min to qualify:	1
	New York, NY 10019	Fee on cash inv.:	$5 + 12¢/sh.
Company Phone:	212-603-3000	Fee on div. inv.:	5% to $2.50
Transfer Agent:	Morgan Guaranty Trust Co.	Discount (cash):	0
Agent's Address:	P.O. Box 9073	Discount (div.):	0
	Boston, MA 02205-9948	Auto invest:	Yes
Agent's Phone:	800-428-4237	Auto invest fee:	$0
Other than USA:	No	Selling info:	Sells daily, by phone or mail, at avg. price, for $5 +12¢/sh.

Company:	**Reynolds & Reynolds Co.**	Safekeeping:	Yes
Symbol:	REY	Invests:	Every 90 days beginning 1/13
Exchange:	NYSE	Minimum:	$100
Industry:	Provider integrated info. mgmt.	Maximum:	$5,000/quarter
	sys. to auto, health care & general	Min to qualify:	1
	business markets	Fee on cash inv.:	0!
Company Address:	Box 2608	Fee on div. inv.:	0!
	Dayton, OH 45401	Discount (cash):	0
Company Phone:	937-485-2000 or 937-485-4460	Discount (div.):	0
Transfer Agent:	Norwest Bank Minnesota	Auto invest:	No
Agent's Address:	P.O. Box 64854	Auto invest fee:	$0
	St. Paul, MN 55164-0854	Selling info:	Sells daily, by mail or fax, at market, for $5 +15¢/sh.
Agent's Phone:	800-468-9716		
Other than USA:	Yes		

Company:	**Reynolds Metals**	Safekeeping:	Yes
Symbol:	RLM	Invests:	Every 30 days beginning 1/1
Exchange:	NYSE	Minimum:	$25
Industry:	Metals	Maximum:	$3,000/quarter
Company Address:	Box 27003	Min to qualify:	1
	Richmond, VA 23261	Fee on cash inv.:	0!
Company Phone:	804-281-2812 or 804-281-2000	Fee on div. inv.:	0!
Transfer Agent:	ChaseMellon Shareholder Services	Discount (cash):	0
Agent's Address:	P.O. Box 3338	Discount (div.):	0
	S. Hackensack, NJ 07606-1938	Auto invest:	No
Agent's Phone:	800-526-0801	Auto invest fee:	$0
Other than USA:	Yes	Selling info:	Sells within 13 bus. days, by mail or phone, at market, for $5 + 6¢/sh.

Company:	**Rhone-Poulenc S.A.**	Safekeeping:	Yes
Symbol:	RP	Invests:	Every 30 days beginning varies
Exchange:	NYSE	Minimum:	$50
Industry:	Chemicals, drugs	Maximum:	$100,000/year
Company Address:	c/o Citibank, NA, 111 Wall St.,	Min to qualify:	1
	5th Fl.	Fee on cash inv.:	$2.50 + comm.
	New York, NY 10043	Fee on div. inv.:	comm.
Company Phone:	800-422-2066 or 212-657-1698	Discount (cash):	0
Transfer Agent:	FCT (Citibank)	Discount (div.):	0
Agent's Address:	111 Wall Street, 5th Floor	Auto invest:	No
	New York, NY 10043	Auto invest fee:	$0
Agent's Phone:	800-422-2066	Selling info:	Sells irregularly, by mail, at market, for $3 + comm.
Other than USA:	No		

Company:	**Rio Tinto plc**	Safekeeping:	Yes
Symbol:	RTP	Invests:	Every 7 days beginning varies
Exchange:	NYSE	Minimum:	$50
Industry:	Mining	Maximum:	$250,000/year
Company Address:	c/o BNY,101 Barclay St.,22 West	Min to qualify:	1
	New York, NY 10286	Fee on cash inv.:	$5 + 10¢/sh.
Company Phone:	800-943-9715	Fee on div. inv.:	5% to $5 + 10¢/sh.
Transfer Agent:	Bank of New York	Discount (cash):	0
Agent's Address:	P.O. Box 11258	Discount (div.):	0
	New York, NY 10286	Auto invest:	Yes
Agent's Phone:	888-269-2377	Auto invest fee:	$5 + 10¢/sh.
Other than USA:	Yes	Selling info:	Sells weekly, by mail, at market, for $5 +10¢/sh.

Company:	**Rite Aid Corp.**	Safekeeping:	Yes
Symbol:	RAD	Invests:	Every 30 days beginning 1/30
Exchange:	NYSE	Minimum:	$25
Industry:	Pharmaceuticals,drug stores	Maximum:	$25,000/year
Company Address:	Box 3165	Min to qualify:	1
	Harrisburg, PA 17105-3165	Fee on cash inv.:	0
Company Phone:	717-761-2633	Fee on div. inv.:	0
Transfer Agent:	Harris Trust & Savings Bank	Discount (cash):	0
Agent's Address:	P.O. Box A3309	Discount (div.):	0
	Chicago, IL 60690-3309	Auto invest:	No
Agent's Phone:	800-554-3406 or 312-461-5698	Auto invest fee:	$0
Other than USA:	Yes	Selling info:	Sells weekly, by mail or fax, at market, for 10¢/sh.

Company:	**RJR Nabisco Holdings Corp.**	Safekeeping:	Yes
		Invests:	Every 7 days beginning Wed.
Symbol:	RN	Minimum:	$100
Exchange:	NYSE	Maximum:	$50,000/year
Industry:	International consumer products	Min to qualify:	1
Company Address:	1301 Ave. of the Americas	Fee on cash inv.:	$5 + comm.
	New York, NY 10019	Fee on div. inv.:	0
Company Phone:	212-258-5706 or 212-258-5600	Discount (cash):	0
Transfer Agent:	FCT (EquiServe)	Discount (div.):	0
Agent's Address:	P.O. Box 2500	Auto invest:	Yes
	Jersey City, NJ 07303-2500	Auto invest fee:	$6 + comm.
Agent's Phone:	800-519-3111	Selling info:	Sells daily, by phone, mail, fax,or e-mail, at market, for 10¢ to 12¢/sh.
Other than USA:	Yes		

Company:	**RLI Corp.**	Safekeeping:	Yes
Symbol:	RLI	Invests:	Every 30 days beginning 1/15
Exchange:	NYSE	Minimum:	$25
Industry:	Insurance	Maximum:	$2,000/month
Company Address:	9025 North Lindbergh Dr.	Min to qualify:	1
	Peoria, IL 61615-1431	Fee on cash inv.:	0!
Company Phone:	800-331-4929 or 309-692-1000	Fee on div. inv.:	0!
Transfer Agent:	Norwest Bank Minnesota	Discount (cash):	0
Agent's Address:	P.O. Box 64854	Discount (div.):	0
	St. Paul, MN 55164-0854	Auto invest:	No
Agent's Phone:	800-468-9716	Auto invest fee:	$0
Other than USA:	No	Selling info:	Sells daily, by mail, at market, for $5 +15¢/sh.

Company:	**Roadway Express, Inc.**	**Safekeeping:**	Yes
Symbol:	ROAD	**Invests:**	Every 7 days beginning varies
Exchange:	OTC	**Minimum:**	$50
Industry:	Trucking	**Maximum:**	$100,000/year
Company Address:	1077 Gorge Blvd., Box 471	**Min to qualify:**	1
	Akron, OH 44309-0471	**Fee on cash inv.:**	$5 + 10¢/sh.
Company Phone:	800-257-2837 or 330-384-1717	**Fee on div. inv.:**	0!
Transfer Agent:	Harris Trust & Savings Bank	**Discount (cash):**	0
Agent's Address:	311 W. Monroe St., 11th Floor	**Discount (div.):**	0
	Chicago, IL 60606	**Auto invest:**	Yes
Agent's Phone:	800-991-8947	**Auto invest fee:**	$1.50 + 10¢/sh.
Other than USA:	Yes	**Selling info:**	Sells within 5 bus. days, by mail, at market, for $10 +10¢/sh.

Company:	**Roanoke Gas Co.**	**Safekeeping:**	Yes
Symbol:	RGCO	**Invests:**	Every 30 days beginning 1/1
Exchange:	OTC	**Minimum:**	$25
Industry:	Utility	**Maximum:**	$20,000/year
Company Address:	519 Kimball Ave. NE , Box 13007	**Min to qualify:**	1
	Roanoke, VA 24030	**Fee on cash inv.:**	0
Company Phone:	540-777-4427	**Fee on div. inv.:**	0
Transfer Agent:	First Union National Bank	**Discount (cash):**	0
Agent's Address:	P.O.Box 1154-Div. Reinvestment	**Discount (div.):**	0
	Dept.	**Auto invest:**	Yes
	Charlotte, NC 28288-1154	**Auto invest fee:**	$0
Agent's Phone:	800-829-8432	**Selling info:**	Not available
Other than USA:	Yes		

Company:	**Robbins & Myers, Inc.**	**Safekeeping:**	Yes
Symbol:	RBN	**Invests:**	Every 30 days beginning 1/30
Exchange:	NYSE	**Minimum:**	$50
Industry:	Pumps, valves, mixers & reactor	**Maximum:**	$5,000/quarter
	systems	**Min to qualify:**	1
Company Address:	1400 Kettering Tower	**Fee on cash inv.:**	0!
	Dayton, OH 45423	**Fee on div. inv.:**	0!
Company Phone:	937-222-2610	**Discount (cash):**	0
Transfer Agent:	National City Bank	**Discount (div.):**	0
Agent's Address:	P.O. Box 94946	**Auto invest:**	No
	Cleveland, OH 44101-4946	**Auto invest fee:**	$0
Agent's Phone:	800-622-6757	**Selling info:**	Sells weekly, by mail, at market, for 5% to $5
Other than USA:	Yes		

Company:	**Rochester G&E**	**Safekeeping:**	Yes
Symbol:	RGS	**Invests:**	Every 30 days beginning 1/25
Exchange:	NYSE	**Minimum:**	$50
Industry:	Utility-electric, gas	**Maximum:**	$5,000/month
Company Address:	89 East Ave.	**Min to qualify:**	10
	Rochester, NY 14649-0001	**Fee on cash inv.:**	0
Company Phone:	716-546-2700	**Fee on div. inv.:**	0
Transfer Agent:	Boston Eq. (EquiServe)	**Discount (cash):**	0
Agent's Address:	P.O. Box 8040	**Discount (div.):**	0
	Boston, MA 02266-8040	**Auto invest:**	No
Agent's Phone:	800-736-3001	**Auto invest fee:**	$0
Other than USA:	Yes	**Selling info:**	Sells daily, by mail, at market, for 5% to $5 +7¢/sh.

Company:	**Rockwell International**	**Safekeeping:**	Yes
Symbol:	ROK	**Invests:**	Every 7 days beginning varies
Exchange:	NYSE	**Minimum:**	$100
Industry:	Global electronic controls & comm.	**Maximum:**	$100,000/year
Company Address:	600 Anton Blvd., Ste.700, Box 5090	**Min to qualify:**	1
	Costa Mesa, CA 92628-5090	**Fee on cash inv.:**	$5 + 10¢/sh.
Company Phone:	714-424-4200 or 714-424-4550	**Fee on div. inv.:**	0
Transfer Agent:	ChaseMellon Shareholder Services	**Discount (cash):**	0
Agent's Address:	P.O. Box 3338	**Discount (div.):**	0
	South Hackensack, NJ 07606-1938	**Auto invest:**	Yes
Agent's Phone:	800-204-7800	**Auto invest fee:**	$0
Other than USA:	Yes	**Selling info:**	Sells weekly, by mail or phone, at market, for $15 +12¢/sh.

Company:	**Rollins Truck Leasing**	**Safekeeping:**	No
Symbol:	RLC	**Invests:**	Every 30 days beginning 1/25
Exchange:	NYSE	**Minimum:**	$25
Industry:	Transportation leasing	**Maximum:**	$2,500/month
Company Address:	One Rollins Plaza, Box 1791	**Min to qualify:**	1
	Wilmington, DE 19899	**Fee on cash inv.:**	5% to $5
Company Phone:	302-426-2700	**Fee on div. inv.:**	0!
Transfer Agent:	Registrar & Transfer Co.	**Discount (cash):**	0
Agent's Address:	10 Commerce Drive	**Discount (div.):**	0
	Cranford, NJ 07016	**Auto invest:**	No
Agent's Phone:	800-368-5948	**Auto invest fee:**	$0
Other than USA:	Yes	**Selling info:**	Sells weekly, by mail, at market, for 5% to $5

Company:	**Roslyn Bancorp, Inc.**	**Safekeeping:**	Yes
Symbol:	RSLN	**Invests:**	Every 30 days beginning 1/15
Exchange:	OTC	**Minimum:**	$100
Industry:	Savings banks	**Maximum:**	$5,000/quarter
Company Address:	1400 Old Northern Blvd.	**Min to qualify:**	25
	Roslyn, NY 11576	**Fee on cash inv.:**	$2.50
Company Phone:	516-621-6000	**Fee on div. inv.:**	0!
Transfer Agent:	Registrar & Transfer Company	**Discount (cash):**	0
Agent's Address:	10 Commerce Drive	**Discount (div.):**	0
	Cranford, NJ 07016	**Auto invest:**	No
Agent's Phone:	800-368-5948	**Auto invest fee:**	$0
Other than USA:	No	**Selling info:**	Sells within 10 bus. days, by mail, at avg. price, for $10 + comm.

Company:	**Rouse Co.**	**Safekeeping:**	Yes
Symbol:	RSE	**Invests:**	Every 90 days beginning 3/30
Exchange:	NYSE	**Minimum:**	$50
Industry:	Real estate developers	**Maximum:**	$unlimited
Company Address:	10275 Little Patuxent Pkwy.	**Min to qualify:**	1
	Columbia, MD 21044-3456	**Fee on cash inv.:**	0!
Company Phone:	410-992-6000 or 410-992-6346.	**Fee on div. inv.:**	0!
Transfer Agent:	Bank of New York	**Discount (cash):**	0
Agent's Address:	P.O. Box 1958	**Discount (div.):**	0
	Newark, NJ 07101-1958	**Auto invest:**	No
Agent's Phone:	800-524-4458	**Auto invest fee:**	$0
Other than USA:	No	**Selling info:**	Sells weekly, by mail, at market, for comm.

Company:	**Rowe Companies (The)**	Safekeeping:	Yes
Symbol:	ROW	Invests:	Every 30 days beginning 1/15
Exchange:	NYSE	Minimum:	$25
Industry:	Furniture	Maximum:	$5,000/month
Company Address:	239 Rowan St.	Min to qualify:	1
	Salem, VA 24153	Fee on cash inv.:	0!
Company Phone:	540-389-8671	Fee on div. inv.:	0!
Transfer Agent:	Wachovia (EquiServe)	Discount (cash):	0
Agent's Address:	P.O. Box 8217	Discount (div.):	0
	Boston, MA 02266-8217	Auto invest:	No
Agent's Phone:	800-633-4236	Auto invest fee:	$0
Other than USA:	Yes	Selling info:	Sells daily, by mail, at avg. price, for 5¢/sh.

Company:	**Royal Ahold**	Safekeeping:	Yes
Symbol:	AHO	Invests:	Every 7 days beginning varies
Exchange:	NYSE	Minimum:	$50
Industry:	Supermarkets	Maximum:	$100,000/year
Company Address:	c/o BNY,101 Barclay St., 22 West	Min to qualify:	1
	New York, NY 10286	Fee on cash inv.:	$5 + 12¢/sh.
Company Phone:	212-815-3874	Fee on div. inv.:	5% to $2.50
Transfer Agent:	Bank of New York	Discount (cash):	0
Agent's Address:	P.O. Box 11258	Discount (div.):	0
	New York, NY 10286	Auto invest:	Yes
Agent's Phone:	888-269-2377	Auto invest fee:	$5
Other than USA:	No	Selling info:	Sells daily, by phone or mail, at avg. price, for $5 +12¢/sh.

Company:	**Royal Dutch Petroleum Co.**	Safekeeping:	Yes
Symbol:	RD	Invests:	Every 7 days beginning 1/2
Exchange:	NYSE	Minimum:	$50
Industry:	Oil & gas	Maximum:	$100,000/year
Company Address:	c/o Morgan Guaranty Trust,	Min to qualify:	1
	Box 9073	Fee on cash inv.:	$5 + 12¢/sh.
	Boston, MA 02205-9948	Fee on div. inv.:	5% to $2.50
Company Phone:	800-428-4237	Discount (cash):	0
Transfer Agent:	Morgan Guaranty Trust Co.	Discount (div.):	0
Agent's Address:	P.O. Box 9073	Auto invest:	Yes
	Boston, MA 02205-9948	Auto invest fee:	$5
Agent's Phone:	800-428-4237	Selling info:	Sells daily, by phone or mail, at avg. price, for $5 +12¢/sh.
Other than USA:	No		

Company:	**Royce Focus Trust, Inc.**	Safekeeping:	Yes
Symbol:	FUND	Invests:	Every 30 days beginning 1/15
Exchange:	OTC	Minimum:	$100
Industry:	Closed end fund	Maximum:	$unlimited
Company Address:	1414 Ave. of the Americas	Min to qualify:	1
	New York, NY 10019	Fee on cash inv.:	75¢ + comm.
Company Phone:	800-221-4268 or 212-508-4572	Fee on div. inv.:	0
Transfer Agent:	State Street Bank (EquiServe)	Discount (cash):	0
Agent's Address:	P.O. Box 8200	Discount (div.):	0
	Boston, MA 02110	Auto invest:	No
Agent's Phone:	800-426-5523	Auto invest fee:	$0
Other than USA:	Yes	Selling info:	Sells within 3 bus. days, by mail, at avg. price, for $2.50 + 15¢/sh.

Company:	**Royce Micro-Cap Trust, Inc.**	**Safekeeping:**	Yes
		Invests:	Every 30 days beginning 1/15
Symbol:	OTCM	**Minimum:**	$100
Exchange:	OTC	**Maximum:**	$unlimited
Industry:	Closed end fund	**Min to qualify:**	1
Company Address:	1414 Ave. of the Americas	**Fee on cash inv.:**	75¢ + comm.
	New York, NY 10019	**Fee on div. inv.:**	0
Company Phone:	800-221-4268 or 212-508-4572	**Discount (cash):**	0
Transfer Agent:	State Street Bank (EquiServe)	**Discount (div.):**	0
Agent's Address:	P.O. Box 8200	**Auto invest:**	No
	Boston, MA 02110	**Auto invest fee:**	$0
Agent's Phone:	800-426-5523	**Selling info:**	Sells within 3 bus. days, by mail,
Other than USA:	Yes		at avg. price, for $2.50 + 15¢/sh.

Company:	**Royce Value Trust, Inc.**	**Safekeeping:**	Yes
Symbol:	RVT	**Invests:**	Every 30 days beginning 1/15
Exchange:	NYSE	**Minimum:**	$100
Industry:	Closed end fund	**Maximum:**	$unlimited
Company Address:	1414 Ave. of the Americas	**Min to qualify:**	1
	New York, NY 10019	**Fee on cash inv.:**	75¢ + comm.
		Fee on div. inv.:	0
Company Phone:	800-221-4268 or 212-508-4572	**Discount (cash):**	0
Transfer Agent:	State Street Bank (EquiServe)	**Discount (div.):**	0
Agent's Address:	P.O. Box 8200	**Auto invest:**	No
	Boston, MA 02110	**Auto invest fee:**	$0
Agent's Phone:	800-426-5523	**Selling info:**	Sells within 3 bus. days, by mail,
Other than USA:	Yes		at avg. price, for $2.50 + 15¢/sh.

Company:	**RPM, Inc.**	**Safekeeping:**	Yes
Symbol:	RPM	**Invests:**	Every 15 days beginning 1/10
Exchange:	NYSE	**Minimum:**	$25
Industry:	Speciality chemicals & paints	**Maximum:**	$5,000/month
Company Address:	2628 Pearl Rd., Box 777	**Min to qualify:**	1
	Medina, OH 44258	**Fee on cash inv.:**	0!
		Fee on div. inv.:	0!
Company Phone:	800-776-4488 or 330-273-5090	**Discount (cash):**	0
Transfer Agent:	Harris Trust & Savings Bank	**Discount (div.):**	0
Agent's Address:	P.O. Box A-3309	**Auto invest:**	Yes
	Chicago, IL 60690-9939	**Auto invest fee:**	$0
Agent's Phone:	800-988-5238	**Selling info:**	Sells daily, by mail, at avg. price,
Other than USA:	Yes		for $0!

Company:	**Ruddick Corp**	**Safekeeping:**	Yes
Symbol:	RDK	**Invests:**	Every 30 days beginning varies
Exchange:	NYSE	**Minimum:**	$20
Industry:	Food supermarkets, thread	**Maximum:**	$3,000/month
Company Address:	1800 Two First Union Ctr.	**Min to qualify:**	1
	Charlotte, NC 28282	**Fee on cash inv.:**	0!
		Fee on div. inv.:	0!
Company Phone:	704-372-5404	**Discount (cash):**	0
Transfer Agent:	Wachovia (EquiServe)	**Discount (div.):**	0
Agent's Address:	P.O. Box 8217	**Auto invest:**	No
	Boston, MA 02266-8217	**Auto invest fee:**	$0
Agent's Phone:	800-633-4236	**Selling info:**	Sells within 3 bus. days, by mail,
Other than USA:	Yes		at market, for comm.

Company:	**Russell Corp.**	**Safekeeping:**	Yes
Symbol:	RML	**Invests:**	Every 30 days beginning 1/20
Exchange:	NYSE	**Minimum:**	$50
Industry:	Textiles & apparel	**Maximum:**	$2,000/month
Company Address:	755 Lee St., Box 272	**Min to qualify:**	50
	Alexander City, AL 35011-0272	**Fee on cash inv.:**	0
Company Phone:	256-500-4000	**Fee on div. inv.:**	0
Transfer Agent:	SunTrust Bank, Atlanta	**Discount (cash):**	0
Agent's Address:	P.O. Box 4625	**Discount (div.):**	0
	Atlanta, GA 30302	**Auto invest:**	No
Agent's Phone:	800-568-3476	**Auto invest fee:**	$0
Other than USA:	Yes	**Selling info:**	Sells 7-10 bus. days , by mail, at market, for comm.

Company:	**Ryanair**	**Safekeeping:**	Yes
Symbol:	RYAAY	**Invests:**	Every 7 days beginning varies
Exchange:	OTC	**Minimum:**	$50
Industry:	Airline transportation	**Maximum:**	$250,000/year
Company Address:	c/o BNY,101 Barclay St.,22 West	**Min to qualify:**	1
	New York, NY 10286	**Fee on cash inv.:**	$5 + 10¢/sh.
Company Phone:	800-943-9715	**Fee on div. inv.:**	5% to $5 + 10¢/sh.
Transfer Agent:	Bank of New York	**Discount (cash):**	0
Agent's Address:	P.O. Box 11258	**Discount (div.):**	0
	New York, NY 10286	**Auto invest:**	Yes
Agent's Phone:	888-269-2377	**Auto invest fee:**	$5 + 10¢/sh.
Other than USA:	Yes	**Selling info:**	Sells weekly, by mail, at market, for $5 +10¢/sh.

Company:	**Ryder System, Inc.**	**Safekeeping:**	Yes
Symbol:	R	**Invests:**	Every 30 days beginning 1/20
Exchange:	NYSE	**Minimum:**	$25
Industry:	Transportation	**Maximum:**	$60,000/year
Company Address:	3600 NW 82nd Ave.	**Min to qualify:**	1
	Miami, FL 33166	**Fee on cash inv.:**	0!
Company Phone:	305-500-3726 or 305-500-4053	**Fee on div. inv.:**	0!
Transfer Agent:	BankBoston (EquiServe)	**Discount (cash):**	0
Agent's Address:	P.O. Box 8040	**Discount (div.):**	0
	Boston, Mass. 02266-8040	**Auto invest:**	No
Agent's Phone:	781-575-3170	**Auto invest fee:**	$0
Other than USA:	No	**Selling info:**	Sells within 7-10 bus. day, by phone or mail, at market, for $1 to $10 + comm.

Company:	**Ryerson Tull Inc.**	**Safekeeping:**	No
Symbol:	RT	**Invests:**	Every 30 days beginning 1/24
Exchange:	NYSE	**Minimum:**	$25
Industry:	Steel distribution	**Maximum:**	$10,000/month
Company Address:	2621 West 15th Pl.	**Min to qualify:**	1
	Chicago, IL 60608	**Fee on cash inv.:**	0
Company Phone:	773-762-2121 or 773-762-2153	**Fee on div. inv.:**	0
	x3206	**Discount (cash):**	0
Transfer Agent:	Harris Trust & Savings Bank	**Discount (div.):**	0
Agent's Address:	P.O. Box A3309	**Auto invest:**	No
	Chicago, IL 60690	**Auto invest fee:**	$0
Agent's Phone:	312-461-4075	**Selling info:**	Sells weekly, by mail, at market, for 7¢/sh.
Other than USA:	Yes		

Company:	**S&T Bancorp, Inc.**	Safekeeping:	Yes
Symbol:	STBA	Invests:	Every 30 days beginning 1/15
Exchange:	OTC	Minimum:	$25
Industry:	Bank holding company	Maximum:	$5,000/quarterly
Company Address:	43 S. Ninth St., Box 190	Min to qualify:	1
	Indiana, PA 15701-0190	Fee on cash inv.:	0
Company Phone:	800-325-2265 or 724-465-1466	Fee on div. inv.:	0
Transfer Agent:	American Stock Transfer & Trust	Discount (cash):	0
Agent's Address:	40 Wall Street	Discount (div.):	0
	New York, NY 10005	Auto invest:	No
Agent's Phone:	800-937-5449	Auto invest fee:	$0
Other than USA:	Yes	Selling info:	Sells weekly, by mail, at market, for comm.

Company:	**S.Y. Bancorp, Inc.**	Safekeeping:	No
Symbol:	SYI	Invests:	Every 90 days beginning 1/2
Exchange:	ASE	Minimum:	$50
Industry:	Banking	Maximum:	$5,000/quarter
Company Address:	1040 East Main St., Box 32890	Min to qualify:	1
	Louisville, KY 40232-2890	Fee on cash inv.:	0
Company Phone:	502-625-9176	Fee on div. inv.:	0
Transfer Agent:	Registrar & Transfer Co.	Discount (cash):	0
Agent's Address:	10 Commerce Drive	Discount (div.):	0
	Cranford, NJ 07016	Auto invest:	No
Agent's Phone:	800-368-5948	Auto invest fee:	$0
Other than USA:	No	Selling info:	Not available

Company:	**Salomon Bros. Fund**	Safekeeping:	Yes
Symbol:	SBF	Invests:	Every 7 days beginning varies
Exchange:	NYSE	Minimum:	$25
Industry:	Capital appreciation fund	Maximum:	$unlimited
Company Address:	7 World Trade Ctr., 38th Fl.	Min to qualify:	1
	New York, NY 10048	Fee on cash inv.:	comm.
Company Phone:	800-446-1013	Fee on div. inv.:	comm.
Transfer Agent:	Bank of New York	Discount (cash):	0
Agent's Address:	Inv. Relations Dept.,Box 11258	Discount (div.):	0
	New York, NY 10286-1258	Auto invest:	Yes
Agent's Phone:	800-432-8224	Auto invest fee:	$0
Other than USA:	No	Selling info:	Sells weekly, by mail or fax, at market, for comm.

Company:	**Sanderson Farms, Inc.**	Safekeeping:	Yes
Symbol:	SAFM	Invests:	Every 7 days beginning varies
Exchange:	OTC	Minimum:	$50
Industry:	Food processing	Maximum:	$10,000/month
Company Address:	225 North 13th Ave., Box 988	Min to qualify:	1
	Laurel, MS 39441-0988	Fee on cash inv.:	$5 + 12¢/sh.
Company Phone:	601-649-4030	Fee on div. inv.:	5% to $10 + 12¢/sh.
Transfer Agent:	ChaseMellon Shareholder Services	Discount (cash):	0
Agent's Address:	P.O. Box 3338	Discount (div.):	0
	South Hackensack, NJ 07606-1938	Auto invest:	Yes
Agent's Phone:	888-810-7452	Auto invest fee:	$5 + 12¢/sh.
Other than USA:	Yes	Selling info:	Sells weekly, by mail, at market, for $15 +12¢/sh.

Company:	**Santos Ltd.**	**Safekeeping:**	Yes
Symbol:	STOSY	**Invests:**	Every 7 days beginning 1/1
Exchange:	OTC	**Minimum:**	$50
Industry:	Oil & Gas	**Maximum:**	$100,000/year
Company Address:	c/o Morgan Guaranty Trust,	**Min to qualify:**	1
	Box 9073	**Fee on cash inv.:**	$5 + 12¢/sh.
	Boston, MA 02205-9948	**Fee on div. inv.:**	5% to $2.50
Company Phone:	800-428-4237	**Discount (cash):**	0
Transfer Agent:	Morgan Guaranty Trust Co.	**Discount (div.):**	0
Agent's Address:	P.O. Box 9073	**Auto invest:**	Yes
	Boston, MA 02205-9948	**Auto invest fee:**	$5
Agent's Phone:	800-428-4237	**Selling info:**	Sells daily, by phone or mail, at
Other than USA:	No		avg. price, for $5 +12¢/sh.

Company:	**Sara Lee Corp.**	**Safekeeping:**	Yes
Symbol:	SLE	**Invests:**	Every 45 days beginning 1/1
Exchange:	NYSE	**Minimum:**	$10
Industry:	Food & consumer products	**Maximum:**	$5,000/quarter
Company Address:	3 First National Plaza	**Min to qualify:**	1
	Chicago, IL 60602-4260	**Fee on cash inv.:**	0
Company Phone:	312-558-8662 or 312-558-4966	**Fee on div. inv.:**	0
Transfer Agent:	Harris Trust & Savings Bank	**Discount (cash):**	0
Agent's Address:	P.O. Box A-3309	**Discount (div.):**	0
	Chicago, IL 60690	**Auto invest:**	No
Agent's Phone:	800-554-3406	**Auto invest fee:**	$0
Other than USA:	Yes	**Selling info:**	Sells weekly, by mail, at market,
			for 5% to $10 +10¢/sh.

Company:	**Savia SA de C.V.**	**Safekeeping:**	Yes
Symbol:	VAI	**Invests:**	Every 7 days beginning varies
Exchange:	NYSE	**Minimum:**	$50
Industry:	Cigarettes, agrobiotechnology, &	**Maximum:**	$250,000/week
	packaging	**Min to qualify:**	1
Company Address:	c/o BNY,101 Barclay St.,22 West	**Fee on cash inv.:**	$5 + 10¢/sh.
	New York, NY 10286	**Fee on div. inv.:**	0
Company Phone:	800-943-9715	**Discount (cash):**	0
Transfer Agent:	Bank of New York	**Discount (div.):**	0
Agent's Address:	P.O. Box 11258	**Auto invest:**	Yes
	New York, NY 10286	**Auto invest fee:**	$0
Agent's Phone:	888-269-2377	**Selling info:**	Sells weekly, by phone or mail, at
Other than USA:	Yes		market, for $5 +10¢/ADS

Company:	**Saville Systems plc**	**Safekeeping:**	Yes
Symbol:	SAVLY	**Invests:**	Every 7 days beginning varies
Exchange:	NASDAQ	**Minimum:**	$50
Industry:	Billing systems	**Maximum:**	$250,000/week
Company Address:	c/o BNY,101 Barclay St.,22 West	**Min to qualify:**	1
	New York, NY 10286	**Fee on cash inv.:**	$5 + 10¢/sh.
Company Phone:	800-943-9715	**Fee on div. inv.:**	5% to $5 + 10¢/sh.
Transfer Agent:	Bank of New York	**Discount (cash):**	0
Agent's Address:	P.O. Box 11258	**Discount (div.):**	0
	New York, NY 10286	**Auto invest:**	Yes
Agent's Phone:	888-269-2377	**Auto invest fee:**	$0
Other than USA:	Yes	**Selling info:**	Sells weekly, by phone or mail, at
			market, for $5 +10¢/ADS

Company:	**Sawako Corp.**
Symbol:	SWKOY
Exchange:	OTC
Industry:	Construction
Company Address:	c/o BNY,101 Barclay St.,22 West
	New York, NY 10286
Company Phone:	800-943-9715
Transfer Agent:	Bank of New York
Agent's Address:	P.O. Box 11258
	New York, NY 10286
Agent's Phone:	888-269-2377
Other than USA:	Yes

Safekeeping:	Yes
Invests:	Every 7 days beginning varies
Minimum:	$50
Maximum:	$250,000/year
Min to qualify:	1
Fee on cash inv.:	$5 + 10¢/sh.
Fee on div. inv.:	5% to $5 + 10¢/sh.
Discount (cash):	0
Discount (div.):	0
Auto invest:	Yes
Auto invest fee:	$5 + 10¢/sh.
Selling info:	Sells weekly, by mail, at market, for $5 +10¢/sh.

Company:	**SBC Communications**
Symbol:	SBC
Exchange:	NYSE
Industry:	Telecommunications
Company Address:	175 East Houston, Box 2933
	San Antonio, TX 78299-2933
Company Phone:	210-821-4105 or 210-351-2044
Transfer Agent:	FCT (EquiServe)
Agent's Address:	P.O. Box 2508
	Jersey City, NJ 07303-2508
Agent's Phone:	800-351-7221
Other than USA:	Yes

Safekeeping:	Yes
Invests:	Every 7 days beginning varies
Minimum:	$50
Maximum:	$120,000/year
Min to qualify:	1
Fee on cash inv.:	0
Fee on div. inv.:	5% to $1
Discount (cash):	0
Discount (div.):	0
Auto invest:	Yes
Auto invest fee:	$0
Selling info:	Sells daily, by phone or mail, at avg. price, for $10 + 5¢/sh.

Company:	**SCANA Corp.**
Symbol:	SCG
Exchange:	NYSE
Industry:	Utility-electric, gas
Company Address:	1426 Main St.
	Columbia, SC 29201-2845
Company Phone:	803-217-9240 or 803-217-9000
Transfer Agent:	SCANA Corp.
Agent's Address:	Shareholder Services (054)
	Columbia, SC 29218-0001
Agent's Phone:	800-763-5891
Other than USA:	No

Safekeeping:	Yes
Invests:	Every 15 days beginning 1/1
Minimum:	$25
Maximum:	$100,000/year
Min to qualify:	1
Fee on cash inv.:	6¢/sh.
Fee on div. inv.:	6¢/sh.
Discount (cash):	0
Discount (div.):	0
Auto invest:	Yes
Auto invest fee:	$0
Selling info:	Sells weekly, by mail or fax, at market, for 18¢/sh.

Company:	**Schawk, Inc.**
Symbol:	SGK
Exchange:	NYSE
Industry:	Prepress graphic arts design
Company Address:	1695 River Rd.
	Des Plaines, IL 60018-3013
Company Phone:	800-621-1909 or 847-827-9494
	x238
Transfer Agent:	FCT (EquiServe)
Agent's Address:	P.O. Box 2598
	Jersey City, NJ 07303-2598
Agent's Phone:	800-446-2617
Other than USA:	Yes

Safekeeping:	Yes
Invests:	Every 7 days beginning varies
Minimum:	$50
Maximum:	$100,000/year
Min to qualify:	1
Fee on cash inv.:	0!
Fee on div. inv.:	0!
Discount (cash):	0
Discount (div.):	0
Auto invest:	Yes
Auto invest fee:	$0
Selling info:	Sells daily, by mail, phone, or fax, at market, for $15 +12¢/sh.

Company:	**Schering-Plough Corp.**
Symbol:	SGP
Exchange:	NYSE
Industry:	Drugs, consumer products
Company Address:	One Giralda Farms
	Madison, NJ 07940-1010
Company Phone:	973-822-7000 or 973-822-7366
Transfer Agent:	Bank of New York
Agent's Address:	P.O. Box 11258, Church St. Station
	New York, NY 10286-1258
Agent's Phone:	800-432-0140
Other than USA:	No

Safekeeping:	Yes
Invests:	Every 15 days beginning 1/10
Minimum:	$25
Maximum:	$36,000/year
Min to qualify:	1
Fee on cash inv.:	0!
Fee on div. inv.:	0!
Discount (cash):	0
Discount (div.):	0
Auto invest:	No
Auto invest fee:	$0
Selling info:	Sells weekly, by mail, at market, for $2.50 + comm.

Company:	**Schnitzer Steel Industries, Inc.**
Symbol:	SCHN
Exchange:	otc
Industry:	Steel & iron
Company Address:	3200 Northwest Yeon Ave.,
	Box 10047
	Portland, OR 97296-0047
Company Phone:	503-224-9900
Transfer Agent:	Bank of New York
Agent's Address:	P.O. Box 1958
	Newark, NJ 07101-9774
Agent's Phone:	800-524-4458
Other than USA:	Yes

Safekeeping:	Yes
Invests:	Every 7 days beginning varies
Minimum:	$50
Maximum:	$10,000/investment
Min to qualify:	1
Fee on cash inv.:	0!
Fee on div. inv.:	0!
Discount (cash):	0
Discount (div.):	0
Auto invest:	Yes
Auto invest fee:	$0
Selling info:	Sells weekly, by mail, at avg. price, for $5 +10¢/sh.

Company:	**Schwab (Charles) Corp.**
Symbol:	SCH
Exchange:	NYSE
Industry:	Financial
Company Address:	101 Montgomery St.
	San Francisco, CA 94104
Company Phone:	415-627-7000 or 415-636-9869
Transfer Agent:	Norwest Bank Minnesota
Agent's Address:	P.O. Box 64854
	St. Paul, MN 55164-0854
Agent's Phone:	800-468-9716 or 612-450-4064
Other than USA:	Yes

Safekeeping:	Yes
Invests:	Every 30 days beginning 1/15
Minimum:	$10
Maximum:	$5,000/month
Min to qualify:	1
Fee on cash inv.:	0!
Fee on div. inv.:	0!
Discount (cash):	0
Discount (div.):	0
Auto invest:	Yes
Auto invest fee:	$0
Selling info:	Sells daily, by mail, at market, for comm.

Company:	**Scientific-Atlanta**
Symbol:	SFA
Exchange:	NYSE
Industry:	Communications equipment
Company Address:	1 Technology Pkwy., South
	Norcross, GA 30092-2967
Company Phone:	800-841-9248 or 770-903-4494
Transfer Agent:	Bank of New York
Agent's Address:	P.O. Box 1958
	Newark, NJ 07101-9774
Agent's Phone:	800-524-4458
Other than USA:	No

Safekeeping:	Yes
Invests:	Every 30 days beginning 1/15
Minimum:	$25
Maximum:	$40,000/year
Min to qualify:	1
Fee on cash inv.:	0!
Fee on div. inv.:	0!
Discount (cash):	0
Discount (div.):	0
Auto invest:	No
Auto invest fee:	$0
Selling info:	Sells weekly, by mail, at market, for $5

Company:	**Scoot.com plc**	Safekeeping:	Yes
Symbol:	SCOP	Invests:	Every 7 days beginning varies
Exchange:	OTC	Minimum:	$50
Industry:	Computer classified info. via internet and telephone	Maximum:	$250,000/week
		Min to qualify:	1
Company Address:	c/o BNY,101 Barclay St.,22 West New York, NY 10286	Fee on cash inv.:	$5 + 0¢/sh.
		Fee on div. inv.:	0
Company Phone:	800-943-9715	Discount (cash):	0
Transfer Agent:	Bank of New York	Discount (div.):	0
Agent's Address:	P.O. Box 11258 New York, NY 10286	Auto invest:	Yes
		Auto invest fee:	$0
Agent's Phone:	888-269-2377	Selling info:	Sells weekly, by phone or mail, at market, for $5 +10¢/ADS
Other than USA:	Yes		

Company:	**SCOR**	Safekeeping:	Yes
Symbol:	SCO	Invests:	Every 7 days beginning varies
Exchange:	NYSE	Minimum:	$50
Industry:	Insurance	Maximum:	$250,000/year
Company Address:	c/o BNY,101 Barclay St.,22 West New York, NY 10286	Min to qualify:	1
		Fee on cash inv.:	$5 + 10¢/sh.
Company Phone:	800-943-9715	Fee on div. inv.:	5% to $5 + 10¢/sh.
Transfer Agent:	Bank of New York	Discount (cash):	0
Agent's Address:	P.O. Box 11258 New York, NY 10286	Discount (div.):	0
		Auto invest:	Yes
Agent's Phone:	888-269-2377	Auto invest fee:	$5 + 10¢/sh.
Other than USA:	Yes	Selling info:	Sells weekly, by mail, at market, for $5 +10¢/sh.

Company:	**Scotiabank**	Safekeeping:	No
Symbol:	BNS	Invests:	Every 30 days beginning varies
Exchange:	TSE	Minimum:	$100
Industry:	Banking	Maximum:	$20,000/year Cdn.
Company Address:	44 King St. West Toronto, Ont. M5H 1H1 Canada	Min to qualify:	1
		Fee on cash inv.:	0
Company Phone:	416-866-5982 or 416-866-4790	Fee on div. inv.:	0
Transfer Agent:	Montreal Trust Company	Discount (cash):	0
Agent's Address:	151 Front Street, 8th Fl. Toronto, Ont. M5J 2N1 Canada	Discount (div.):	0
		Auto invest:	No
Agent's Phone:	800-663-9097 or 416-981-9633	Auto invest fee:	$0
Other than USA:	No U.S.	Selling info:	Sells monthly, by mail, at avg. price, for comm.

Company:	**Scott Technologies, Inc. A**	Safekeeping:	Yes
Symbol:	SCTT	Invests:	Every 30 days beginning 1/15
Exchange:	OTC	Minimum:	$10
Industry:	Indust. manufacturer	Maximum:	$5,000/quarter
Company Address:	5875 Landerbrook Dr., Ste.250 Mayfield Heights, OH 44124	Min to qualify:	1
		Fee on cash inv.:	0
Company Phone:	440-446-1333 or 440-684-3414	Fee on div. inv.:	0
Transfer Agent:	National City Bank	Discount (cash):	0
Agent's Address:	P.O.Box 92301 Cleveland, OH 92301	Discount (div.):	0
		Auto invest:	No
Agent's Phone:	800-622-6757	Auto invest fee:	$0
Other than USA:	Yes	Selling info:	Sells within 10 bus. days, by mail, at market, for 5% to $5

Company:	**Scottish Power PLC**	Safekeeping:	Yes
Symbol:	SPI	Invests:	Every 7 days beginning varies
Exchange:	NYSE	Minimum:	$50
Industry:	Utilities	Maximum:	$250,000/year
Company Address:	c/o BNY,101 Barclay St.,22 West	Min to qualify:	1
	New York, NY 10286	Fee on cash inv.:	$5 + 10¢/sh.
Company Phone:	800-943-9715	Fee on div. inv.:	5% to $5 + 10¢/sh.
Transfer Agent:	Bank of New York	Discount (cash):	0
Agent's Address:	P.O. Box 11258	Discount (div.):	0
	New York, NY 10286	Auto invest:	Yes
Agent's Phone:	888-269-2377	Auto invest fee:	$5 + 10¢/sh.
Other than USA:	Yes	Selling info:	Sells weekly, by mail, at market, for $5 +10¢/sh.

Company:	**Scudder New Asia**	Safekeeping:	No
Symbol:	SAF	Invests:	Every 180 days beginning 2/15
Exchange:	NYSE	Minimum:	$100
Industry:	Closed-end fund	Maximum:	$3,000/semiannually
Company Address:	345 Park Ave.	Min to qualify:	1
	New York, NY 10154-0004	Fee on cash inv.:	75¢ + comm.
Company Phone:	800-349-4281	Fee on div. inv.:	0!
Transfer Agent:	State Street Bank (EquiServe)	Discount (cash):	0
Agent's Address:	P.O.Box 8200	Discount (div.):	5%
	Boston, Mass 02266-8200	Auto invest:	No
Agent's Phone:	800-426-5523 or 617-328-5000	Auto invest fee:	$0
	x6406	Selling info:	Sells daily, by mail, at market, for $2.50 +15¢/sh.
Other than USA:	Yes		

Company:	**Scudder New Europe**	Safekeeping:	No
Symbol:	NEF	Invests:	Every 180 days beginning 2/15
Exchange:	NYSE	Minimum:	$100
Industry:	Closed-end fund	Maximum:	$3,000/semiannually
Company Address:	345 Park Ave.	Min to qualify:	1
	New York, NY 10154-0004	Fee on cash inv.:	$1 + comm.
Company Phone:	800-349-4281	Fee on div. inv.:	0
Transfer Agent:	Boston Eq. (EquiServe)	Discount (cash):	0
Agent's Address:	P.O. Box 8209	Discount (div.):	5%
	Boston, MA 02266-8209	Auto invest:	No
Agent's Phone:	800-426-5523	Auto invest fee:	$0
Other than USA:	Yes	Selling info:	Sells weekly, by mail, at market, for $3.50 +15¢/sh.

Company:	**Sea Containers Ltd. A**	Safekeeping:	Yes
Symbol:	SCRA	Invests:	Every 90 days beginning 2/21
Exchange:	NYSE	Minimum:	$100
Industry:	Marine cargo containers, hotels, restaurants	Maximum:	$5,000/month
		Min to qualify:	50
Company Address:	1155 Ave. of the Americas	Fee on cash inv.:	0
	New York, NY 10036	Fee on div. inv.:	0
Company Phone:	212-302-5066	Discount (cash):	0
Transfer Agent:	Boston Eq. (EquiServe)	Discount (div.):	3%
Agent's Address:	P.O. Box 8040	Auto invest:	No
	Boston, MA 02266-8040	Auto invest fee:	$0
Agent's Phone:	800-730-4001 or 781-575-3170	Selling info:	Sells daily, by mail, at market, for 5% to $15 + comm.
Other than USA:	Yes		

Company:	**Sears, Roebuck and Co.**	Safekeeping:	Yes
Symbol:	S	Invests:	Every 7 days beginning 1/5
Exchange:	NYSE	Minimum:	$50
Industry:	Retail	Maximum:	$150,000/year
Company Address:	3333 Beverly Rd., B5-161A	Min to qualify:	5
	Hoffman Estates, IL 60179	Fee on cash inv.:	5% to $7.50 + 3¢/sh.
Company Phone:	800-732-7780 or 847-286-7385	Fee on div. inv.:	5% to $3 + 3¢/sh.
Transfer Agent:	FCT (EquiServe)	Discount (cash):	0
Agent's Address:	P.O.Box 2552	Discount (div.):	0
	Jersey City, NJ 07303-2552	Auto invest:	Yes
Agent's Phone:	800-732-7780	Auto invest fee:	$1 + 5% to $7.50 + 3¢/sh.
Other than USA:	Yes	Selling info:	Sells daily, by phone or mail, at avg. price, for $15 +12¢/sh.

Company:	**Second Bancorp, Inc.**	Safekeeping:	No
Symbol:	SECD	Invests:	Every 30 days beginning 1/30
Exchange:	OTC	Minimum:	$50
Industry:	General banking	Maximum:	$5,000/quarter
Company Address:	108 Main St. S.W.	Min to qualify:	1
	Warren, OH 44481	Fee on cash inv.:	0
		Fee on div. inv.:	0
Company Phone:	330-841-0234	Discount (cash):	5%
Transfer Agent:	American Stock Transfer	Discount (div.):	5%
Agent's Address:	40 Wall Street, 46th Floor	Auto invest:	No
	New York, NY 10005	Auto invest fee:	$0
Agent's Phone:	800-278-4353	Selling info:	Sells weekly, by mail, at market,
Other than USA:	Yes		for $5 + comm.

Company:	**Sedgwick Group**	Safekeeping:	Yes
Symbol:	SED	Invests:	Every 7 days beginning varies
Exchange:	NYSE	Minimum:	$50
Industry:	Insurance, accident & health	Maximum:	$250,000/year
Company Address:	c/o BNY,101 Barclay St.,22 West	Min to qualify:	1
	New York, NY 10286	Fee on cash inv.:	$5 + 10¢/sh.
Company Phone:	800-943-9715	Fee on div. inv.:	5% to $5 + 10¢/sh.
Transfer Agent:	Bank of New York	Discount (cash):	0
Agent's Address:	P.O. Box 11258	Discount (div.):	0
	New York, NY 10286	Auto invest:	Yes
Agent's Phone:	888-269-2377	Auto invest fee:	$5 + 10¢/sh.
Other than USA:	Yes	Selling info:	Sells weekly, by mail, at market, for $5 +10¢/sh.

Company:	**Select Appointments, PLC.**	Safekeeping:	Yes
		Invests:	Every 7 days beginning varies
Symbol:	SELAY	Minimum:	$50
Exchange:	OTC	Maximum:	$250,000/week
Industry:	Staffing services	Min to qualify:	1
Company Address:	c/o BNY,101 Barclay St.,22 West	Fee on cash inv.:	$5 + 10¢/sh.
	New York, NY 10286	Fee on div. inv.:	5% to $5 + 10¢/sh.
Company Phone:	800-943-9715	Discount (cash):	0
Transfer Agent:	Bank of New York	Discount (div.):	0
Agent's Address:	P.O. Box 11258	Auto invest:	Yes
	New York, NY 10286	Auto invest fee:	$0
Agent's Phone:	888-269-2377	Selling info:	Sells weekly, by phone or mail, at
Other than USA:	Yes		market, for $5 +10¢/ADS

Company:	**Select Software Tools plc**	Safekeeping:	Yes
Symbol:	SLCTY	Invests:	Every 7 days beginning varies
Exchange:	OTC	Minimum:	$50
Industry:	Mfg.of modeling tools for software app.	Maximum:	$250,000/week
		Min to qualify:	1
Company Address:	c/o BNY,101 Barclay St.,22 West New York, NY 10286	Fee on cash inv.:	$5 + 10¢/sh.
		Fee on div. inv.:	5% to $5 + 10¢/sh.
Company Phone:	800-943-9715	Discount (cash):	0
Transfer Agent:	Bank of New York	Discount (div.):	0
Agent's Address:	P.O. Box 11258 New York, NY 10286	Auto invest:	Yes
		Auto invest fee:	$0
Agent's Phone:	888-269-2377	Selling info:	Sells weekly, by phone or mail, at market, for $5 +10¢/ADS
Other than USA:	Yes		

Company:	**Selective Insurance Grp.**	Safekeeping:	No
Symbol:	SIGI	Invests:	Every 90 days beginning 3/1
Exchange:	OTC	Minimum:	$100
Industry:	Insurance	Maximum:	$1,000/quarter
Company Address:	40 Wantage Ave. Branchville, NJ 07890-1000	Min to qualify:	1
		Fee on cash inv.:	0!
Company Phone:	973-948-1762 or 973-948-3000	Fee on div. inv.:	0!
Transfer Agent:	FCT (EquiServe)	Discount (cash):	0
Agent's Address:	P.O. Box 2500 Jersey City, NJ 07303-2500	Discount (div.):	0
		Auto invest:	No
Agent's Phone:	800-446-2617	Auto invest fee:	$0
Other than USA:	Yes	Selling info:	Sells daily, by mail or fax, at market, for $10 +12¢/sh.

Company:	**SEMCO Energy Inc.**	Safekeeping:	Yes
Symbol:	SMGS	Invests:	Every 30 days beginning 1/15
Exchange:	OTC	Minimum:	$25
Industry:	Utility-gas	Maximum:	$100,000/year
Company Address:	405 Water St., Box 5026 Port Huron, MI 48061-5026	Min to qualify:	1
		Fee on cash inv.:	0
Company Phone:	800-255-7647 or 810-989-4104	Fee on div. inv.:	0
Transfer Agent:	SEMCO Energy	Discount (cash):	0
Agent's Address:	405 Water St.,Box 5026 Port Huron, MI 48061-5026	Discount (div.):	0
		Auto invest:	Yes
Agent's Phone:	800-255-7647 or 810-987-2200 x4163	Auto invest fee:	$0
		Selling info:	Sells weekly, by mail or fax, at market, for $5 + 5¢/sh.
Other than USA:	Yes		

Company:	**Sempra Energy**	Safekeeping:	Yes
Symbol:	SRE	Invests:	Every 7 days beginning Tuesday
Exchange:	NYSE	Minimum:	$25
Industry:	Utility-electric, gas	Maximum:	$150,000/year
Company Address:	101 Ash St., Box 129400 San Diego, CA 92112-9400	Min to qualify:	1
		Fee on cash inv.:	0!
Company Phone:	877-736-7727 or 619-696-2901	Fee on div. inv.:	0!
Transfer Agent:	FCT (EquiServe)	Discount (cash):	0
Agent's Address:	P.O. Box 2598 Jersey City, NJ 07303-2598	Discount (div.):	0
		Auto invest:	Yes
Agent's Phone:	877-773-6772	Auto invest fee:	50¢
Other than USA:	Yes	Selling info:	Sells daily, by phone or mail, at market, for $10 + 3¢/sh.

	Senetek plc ADS	
Company:	**Senetek plc ADS**	
Symbol:	SNTKY	
Exchange:	OTC	
Industry:	Health care	
Company Address:	c/o BNY,101 Barclay St., 22 West New York, NY 10286	
Company Phone:	800-943-9715	
Transfer Agent:	Bank of New York	
Agent's Address:	P.O. Box 11258 New York, NY 10286	
Agent's Phone:	888-269-2377	
Other than USA:	No	

Safekeeping:	Yes
Invests:	Every 7 days beginning varies
Minimum:	$50
Maximum:	$250,000/week
Min to qualify:	1
Fee on cash inv.:	$5 + 10¢/sh.
Fee on div. inv.:	5% to $5 + 10¢/sh.
Discount (cash):	0
Discount (div.):	0
Auto invest:	Yes
Auto invest fee:	$0
Selling info:	Sells daily, by phone or mail, at avg. price, for $5 +10¢/ADS

	ServiceMaster Co.
Company:	**ServiceMaster Co.**
Symbol:	SVM
Exchange:	NYSE
Industry:	Consumer and other services
Company Address:	One ServiceMaster Way Downers Grove, IL 60515-1700
Company Phone:	800-288-1065 or 630-271-1300
Transfer Agent:	Harris Trust & Savings Bank
Agent's Address:	P.O. Box A-3309 Chicago, IL 60690
Agent's Phone:	800-858-0840
Other than USA:	Yes

Safekeeping:	Yes
Invests:	Every 30 days beginning 1/25
Minimum:	$25
Maximum:	$25,000/year
Min to qualify:	1
Fee on cash inv.:	0
Fee on div. inv.:	0
Discount (cash):	0
Discount (div.):	0
Auto invest:	No
Auto invest fee:	$0
Selling info:	Sells weekly, by mail, at market, for 7¢/sh.

	Shandong Huaneng Power
Company:	**Shandong Huaneng Power**
Symbol:	SH
Exchange:	NYSE
Industry:	Utilities
Company Address:	c/o BNY,101 Barclay St.,22 West New York, NY 10286
Company Phone:	800-943-9715
Transfer Agent:	Bank of New York
Agent's Address:	P.O. Box 11258 New York, NY 10286
Agent's Phone:	888-269-2377
Other than USA:	Yes

Safekeeping:	Yes
Invests:	Every 7 days beginning varies
Minimum:	$50
Maximum:	$250,000/year
Min to qualify:	1
Fee on cash inv.:	$5 + 10¢/sh.
Fee on div. inv.:	0
Discount (cash):	0
Discount (div.):	0
Auto invest:	Yes
Auto invest fee:	$5 + 10¢/sh.
Selling info:	Sells weekly, by mail, at market, for $5 +10¢/sh.

	Shanghai Petrochemical
Company:	**Shanghai Petrochemical**
Symbol:	SHI
Exchange:	NYSE
Industry:	Oil & gas operations
Company Address:	c/o BNY,101 Barclay St.,22 West New York, NY 10286
Company Phone:	800-943-9715
Transfer Agent:	Bank of New York
Agent's Address:	P.O. Box 11258 New York, NY 10286
Agent's Phone:	888-269-2377
Other than USA:	Yes

Safekeeping:	Yes
Invests:	Every 7 days beginning varies
Minimum:	$50
Maximum:	$250,000/year
Min to qualify:	1
Fee on cash inv.:	$5 + 10¢/sh.
Fee on div. inv.:	5% to $5 + 10¢/sh.
Discount (cash):	0
Discount (div.):	0
Auto invest:	Yes
Auto invest fee:	$5 + 10¢/sh.
Selling info:	Sells weekly, by mail, at market, for $5 +10¢/sh.

Company:	**Shaw Industries**	Safekeeping:	Yes
Symbol:	SHX	Invests:	Every 30 days beginning 12/31
Exchange:	NYSE	Minimum:	$100
Industry:	Carpet mfr.	Maximum:	$2,500/month
Company Address:	Drawer 2128	Min to qualify:	1
	Dalton, GA 30722-2128	Fee on cash inv.:	0!
Company Phone:	706-278-3812	Fee on div. inv.:	0!
Transfer Agent:	Wachovia (EquiServe)	Discount (cash):	0
Agent's Address:	P.O. Box 8217	Discount (div.):	0
	Boston, MA 02266-8217	Auto invest:	No
Agent's Phone:	800-633-4236	Auto invest fee:	$0
Other than USA:	Yes	Selling info:	Sells weekly, by mail, at market, for 5¢/sh.

Company:	**Shell Trans. & Trading Co. plc ADR**	Safekeeping:	Yes
Symbol:	SC	Invests:	Every 30 days beginning 1/10
Exchange:	NYSE	Minimum:	$25
Industry:	Energy petroleum holding co. of Shell Oil in UK	Maximum:	$unlimited
		Min to qualify:	1
		Fee on cash inv.:	$2.50 + 7¢/sh.
Company Address:	c/o BNY,101 Barclay St., 22 West New York, NY 10286	Fee on div. inv.:	$2.50 + 7¢/sh.
		Discount (cash):	0
Company Phone:	212-815-2175	Discount (div.):	0
Transfer Agent:	Bank of New York	Auto invest:	No
Agent's Address:	P.O. Box 11258	Auto invest fee:	$0
	New York, NY 10286	Selling info:	Sells weekly, by mail, at market, for $5 +7¢/sh.
Agent's Phone:	888-269-2377		
Other than USA:	Yes Cdn. only		

Company:	**Sherwin Williams Co.**	Safekeeping:	Yes
Symbol:	SHW	Invests:	Every 30 days beginning 1/15
Exchange:	NYSE	Minimum:	$10
Industry:	Manufacturer & retailer of paint	Maximum:	$2,000/month
Company Address:	101 Prospect Ave., NW	Min to qualify:	1
	Cleveland, OH 44115	Fee on cash inv.:	0!
Company Phone:	216-566-2140 or 216-566-2000	Fee on div. inv.:	0!
Transfer Agent:	Bank of New York	Discount (cash):	0
Agent's Address:	P.O. Box 11258,Church St. Station	Discount (div.):	0
	New York, NY 10286-1258	Auto invest:	No
Agent's Phone:	800-432-0140	Auto invest fee:	$0
Other than USA:	Yes	Selling info:	Sells monthly, by mail, at market, for $0!

Company:	**Shire Pharmaceuticals plc**	Safekeeping:	Yes
Symbol:	SHPGY	Invests:	Every 7 days beginning varies
Exchange:	OTC	Minimum:	$50
Industry:	Pharmaceutical, biotechnology	Maximum:	$100,000/year
Company Address:	c/o Morgan Guaranty Trust,	Min to qualify:	1
	Box 9073	Fee on cash inv.:	$5 + 12¢/sh.
	Boston, MA 02205-9948	Fee on div. inv.:	5% to $2.50
Company Phone:	800-428-4237	Discount (cash):	0
Transfer Agent:	Morgan Guaranty Trust Co.	Discount (div.):	0
Agent's Address:	P.O. Box 9073	Auto invest:	Yes
	Boston, MA 02205-9948	Auto invest fee:	$5
Agent's Phone:	800-428-4237	Selling info:	Sells daily, by phone or mail, at market, for $5 +12¢/sh.
Other than USA:	No		

	Shoreline Financial Corp.	Safekeeping:	Yes
Company:		Invests:	Every 30 days beginning 1/15
Symbol:	SLFC	Minimum:	$50
Exchange:	OTC	Maximum:	$1,000/quarter
Industry:	Bank holding company	Min to qualify:	1
Company Address:	823 Riverview Dr.	Fee on cash inv.:	0!
	Benton Harbor, MI 49022	Fee on div. inv.:	0!
Company Phone:	616-927-2251	Discount (cash):	0
Transfer Agent:	Norwest Bank Minnesota	Discount (div.):	5%
Agent's Address:	P.O. Box 64854	Auto invest:	No
	St. Paul, MN 55164-0854	Auto invest fee:	$0
Agent's Phone:	800-468-9716 or 651-450-4064	Selling info:	Sells daily, by mail, at market, for
Other than USA:	Yes		$5 +15¢/sh.

	SIFCO Industries, Inc.	Safekeeping:	Yes
Company:		Invests:	Every 30 days beginning 1/3
Symbol:	SIF	Minimum:	$20
Exchange:	ASE	Maximum:	$3,000/quarter
Industry:	Precision forging, turbine eng.	Min to qualify:	1
	component repair, mach'd parts	Fee on cash inv.:	0!
Company Address:	970 East 64th St.	Fee on div. inv.:	0!
	Cleveland, OH 44103	Discount (cash):	0
Company Phone:	216-881-8600	Discount (div.):	0
Transfer Agent:	National City Bank	Auto invest:	No
Agent's Address:	P.O. Box 92301	Auto invest fee:	$0
	Cleveland, OH 44135-0900	Selling info:	Sells weekly, by mail, at market,
Agent's Phone:	800-622-6757 x8573 or 216-476-8573		for 20¢/sh.
Other than USA:	Yes		

	SIGCORP	Safekeeping:	Yes
Company:		Invests:	Every 30 days beginning 1/15
Symbol:	SIG	Minimum:	$25
Exchange:	NYSE	Maximum:	$5,000/month
Industry:	Utility-electric, gas	Min to qualify:	1
Company Address:	20 N.W. Fourth St., Box 3606	Fee on cash inv.:	0!
	Evansville, IN 47735-3606	Fee on div. inv.:	0!
Company Phone:	800-227-8625 or 812-464-4599	Discount (cash):	0
Transfer Agent:	SIGCORP	Discount (div.):	0
Agent's Address:	P.O.Box 3606	Auto invest:	No
	Evansville, IN 47735	Auto invest fee:	$0
Agent's Phone:	800-227-8625	Selling info:	Sells weekly, by mail or fax, at avg.
Other than USA:	Yes		price, for comm.

	Signet Group PLC	Safekeeping:	Yes
Company:		Invests:	Every 7 days beginning varies
Symbol:	SIGYY	Minimum:	$50
Exchange:	OTC	Maximum:	$250,000/year
Industry:	Merchandising	Min to qualify:	1
Company Address:	c/o BNY,101 Barclay St.,22 West	Fee on cash inv.:	$5 + 10¢/sh.
	New York, NY 10286	Fee on div. inv.:	5% to $5 + 10¢/sh.
Company Phone:	800-943-9715	Discount (cash):	0
Transfer Agent:	Bank of New York	Discount (div.):	0
Agent's Address:	P.O. Box 11258	Auto invest:	Yes
	New York, NY 10286	Auto invest fee:	$5 + 10¢/sh.
Agent's Phone:	888-269-2377	Selling info:	Sells weekly, by mail, at market,
Other than USA:	Yes		for $5 +10¢/sh.

Company:	**Simpson Industries Inc.**	**Safekeeping:**	Yes
Symbol:	SMPS	**Invests:**	Every 30 days beginning 1/1
Exchange:	OTC	**Minimum:**	$10
Industry:	Automotive	**Maximum:**	$1,000/month
Company Address:	47603 Halyard Dr.	**Min to qualify:**	1
	Plymouth, MI 48170-2429	**Fee on cash inv.:**	0
Company Phone:	734-207-6200	**Fee on div. inv.:**	0
Transfer Agent:	Harris Trust & Savings Bank	**Discount (cash):**	0
Agent's Address:	P.O. Box A3504	**Discount (div.):**	0
	Chicago, IL 60690-3504	**Auto invest:**	No
Agent's Phone:	800-969-6714	**Auto invest fee:**	$0
Other than USA:	Yes	**Selling info:**	Sells weekly, by mail, at market, for $0

Company:	**Sizeler Property Investors Inc.**	**Safekeeping:**	Yes
		Invests:	Every 30 days beginning 1/1
Symbol:	SIZ	**Minimum:**	$10
Exchange:	NYSE	**Maximum:**	$20,000/quarter
Industry:	REIT	**Min to qualify:**	1
Company Address:	2542 Williams Blvd.	**Fee on cash inv.:**	5% to $3
	Kenner, LA 70062	**Fee on div. inv.:**	5% to $3
Company Phone:	504-471-6200 or 504-471-6247	**Discount (cash):**	0
Transfer Agent:	Bank of New York	**Discount (div.):**	0
Agent's Address:	P.O. Box 11258, Church St. Station	**Auto invest:**	No
	New York, NY 10286	**Auto invest fee:**	$0
Agent's Phone:	800-524-4458 or 212-815-2315	**Selling info:**	Sells weekly, by mail, at market, for $5
Other than USA:	No		

Company:	**Sky Financial Group**	**Safekeeping:**	Yes
Symbol:	SKYF	**Invests:**	Every 7 days beginning varies
Exchange:	OTC	**Minimum:**	$50
Industry:	Banking	**Maximum:**	$10,000/month
Company Address:	10 East Main St.	**Min to qualify:**	1
	Salineville, OH 43945	**Fee on cash inv.:**	$2 + 5¢/sh.
Company Phone:	800-576-5007 or 419-327-6300	**Fee on div. inv.:**	0!
Transfer Agent:	Bank of New York	**Discount (cash):**	0
Agent's Address:	P.O. Box 11258, Church St. Station	**Discount (div.):**	0
	New York, NY 10286	**Auto invest:**	Yes
Agent's Phone:	888-683-4901	**Auto invest fee:**	$1 + 5¢/sh.
Other than USA:	Yes	**Selling info:**	Sells daily, by phone or mail, at market, for $10 + 5¢/sh.

Company:	**Slade's Ferry Bancorp**	**Safekeeping:**	Yes
Symbol:	SFBC	**Invests:**	Every 30 days beginning 1/15
Exchange:	OTC	**Minimum:**	$100
Industry:	Banking	**Maximum:**	$5,000/year
Company Address:	100 Slade's Ferry Ave., Box 390	**Min to qualify:**	1
	Somerset, MA 02726	**Fee on cash inv.:**	0
Company Phone:	508-675-2121	**Fee on div. inv.:**	0
Transfer Agent:	Slade's Ferry Bancorp	**Discount (cash):**	0
Agent's Address:	100 Slade's Ferry Ave., Box 390	**Discount (div.):**	0
	Somerset, MA 02726	**Auto invest:**	Yes
Agent's Phone:	508-675-2121	**Auto invest fee:**	$0
Other than USA:	No	**Selling info:**	Not available

Company:	**Smallworld PLC**	Safekeeping:	Yes
Symbol:	SWLDY	Invests:	Every 7 days beginning varies
Exchange:	OTC	Minimum:	$50
Industry:	Computer networks	Maximum:	$250,000/year
Company Address:	5600 Greenwood Plaza Blvd.	Min to qualify:	1
	Englewood, CO 80111	Fee on cash inv.:	$5 + 10¢/sh.
Company Phone:	303-779-6980	Fee on div. inv.:	0
Transfer Agent:	Bank of New York	Discount (cash):	0
Agent's Address:	P.O. Box 11258	Discount (div.):	0
	New York, NY 10286	Auto invest:	Yes
Agent's Phone:	888-269-2377	Auto invest fee:	$5 + 10¢/sh.
Other than USA:	Yes	Selling info:	Sells weekly, by mail, at market, for $5 +10¢/sh.

Company:	**Smith (A.O.) Corp. A**	Safekeeping:	No
Symbol:	SMCA	Invests:	Every 90 days beginning 2/15
Exchange:	ASE	Minimum:	$0
Industry:	Mfg. of electric motors, heating	Maximum:	$5,000/quarter
Company Address:	11270 West Park Pl.	Min to qualify:	1
	Milwaukee, WI 53224-3690	Fee on cash inv.:	0
Company Phone:	414-359-4000	Fee on div. inv.:	0
Transfer Agent:	Firstar Bank Milwaukee, NA	Discount (cash):	0
Agent's Address:	615 E. Michigan St., 4th Floor	Discount (div.):	0
	Milwaukee, WI 53202	Auto invest:	No
Agent's Phone:	800-637-7549	Auto invest fee:	$0
Other than USA:	Yes	Selling info:	Sells Tuesday & Friday, by mail, fax, at market, for comm.

Company:	**Smith (A.O.) Corp. B**	Safekeeping:	No
Symbol:	AOS	Invests:	Every 90 days beginning 2/15
Exchange:	NYSE	Minimum:	$0
Industry:	Mfg. of electric motors, heating	Maximum:	$5,000/quarter
Company Address:	11270 West Park Pl., Box 23972	Min to qualify:	1
	Milwaukee, WI 53223-0972	Fee on cash inv.:	0
Company Phone:	414-359-4009 or 414-359-4000	Fee on div. inv.:	0
Transfer Agent:	Firstar Bank Milwaukee, NA	Discount (cash):	0
Agent's Address:	1555 N.RiverCenter Dr., Ste.	Discount (div.):	0
	301,Box 2077	Auto invest:	No
	Milwaukee, WI 53212	Auto invest fee:	$0
Agent's Phone:	800-637-7549	Selling info:	Sells biweekly, by mail, fax, at market, for comm.
Other than USA:	Yes		

Company:	**SmithKline Beecham plc**	Safekeeping:	Yes
Symbol:	SBH	Invests:	Every 7 days beginning 1/1
Exchange:	NYSE	Minimum:	$50
Industry:	Ethical drugs, health care prods.	Maximum:	$250,000/transaction
Company Address:	c/o BNY,101 Barclay St., 22 West	Min to qualify:	1
	New York, NY 10286	Fee on cash inv.:	$5 + 5¢/sh.
Company Phone:	212-815-2175	Fee on div. inv.:	5% to $5 + 5¢/sh.
Transfer Agent:	Bank of New York	Discount (cash):	0
Agent's Address:	P.O. Box 11258	Discount (div.):	0
	New York, NY 10286	Auto invest:	Yes
Agent's Phone:	800-345-1612	Auto invest fee:	comm.
Other than USA:	No	Selling info:	Sells daily, by mail or phone, at market, for $5 + 5¢/sh.

Company:	**Smucker (J.M.) A**	**Safekeeping:**	Yes
Symbol:	SJMA	**Invests:**	Every 30 days beginning 1/1
Exchange:	NYSE	**Minimum:**	$20
Industry:	Food products	**Maximum:**	$1,500/month
Company Address:	Strawberry Lane	**Min to qualify:**	1
	Orrville, OH 44667	**Fee on cash inv.:**	0!
Company Phone:	330-682-3000	**Fee on div. inv.:**	0!
Transfer Agent:	Harris Trust & Savings Bank	**Discount (cash):**	0
Agent's Address:	311 West Monroe Street,	**Discount (div.):**	0
	Box A3309	**Auto invest:**	No
	Chicago, IL 60690-3309	**Auto invest fee:**	$0
Agent's Phone:	800-942-5909	**Selling info:**	Sells weekly, by mail, at market,
Other than USA:	Yes		for 0!

Company:	**Smucker (J.M.) B**	**Safekeeping:**	Yes
Symbol:	SJMB	**Invests:**	Every 30 days beginning 1/1
Exchange:	NYSE	**Minimum:**	$20
Industry:	Food products	**Maximum:**	$1,500/month
Company Address:	Strawberry Lane	**Min to qualify:**	1
	Orrville, OH 44667	**Fee on cash inv.:**	0!
Company Phone:	330-682-3000	**Fee on div. inv.:**	0!
Transfer Agent:	Harris Trust & Savings Bank	**Discount (cash):**	0
Agent's Address:	311 West Monroe Street,	**Discount (div.):**	0
	Box A3309	**Auto invest:**	No
	Chicago, IL 60690-3309	**Auto invest fee:**	$0
Agent's Phone:	800-554-3406	**Selling info:**	Sells weekly, by mail or fax, at
Other than USA:	Yes		market, for 0!

Company:	**Snap-on Incorporated**	**Safekeeping:**	Yes
Symbol:	SNA	**Invests:**	Every 7 days beginning Friday
Exchange:	NYSE	**Minimum:**	$100
Industry:	Manufacturing of tools	**Maximum:**	$150,000/year
Company Address:	2801 80th St., Box 1430	**Min to qualify:**	1
	Kenosha, WI 53141	**Fee on cash inv.:**	0!
Company Phone:	414-656-5200	**Fee on div. inv.:**	0!
Transfer Agent:	FCT (EquiServe)	**Discount (cash):**	0
Agent's Address:	P.O. Box 2598	**Discount (div.):**	0
	Jersey City, NJ 07303-2598	**Auto invest:**	Yes
Agent's Phone:	800-446-2617	**Auto invest fee:**	$2
Other than USA:	No	**Selling info:**	Sells daily, by mail or fax,
			at market, for $15 +12¢/sh.

Company:	**Sociedad Quimica y Minera**	**Safekeeping:**	Yes
		Invests:	Every 7 days beginning varies
Symbol:	SQM	**Minimum:**	$50
Exchange:	NYSE	**Maximum:**	$250,000/year
Industry:	Chemical manufacturing	**Min to qualify:**	1
Company Address:	c/o BNY,101 Barclay St.,22 West	**Fee on cash inv.:**	$5 + 10¢/sh.
	New York, NY 10286	**Fee on div. inv.:**	5% to $5 + 10¢/sh.
Company Phone:	800-943-9715	**Discount (cash):**	0
Transfer Agent:	Bank of New York	**Discount (div.):**	0
Agent's Address:	P.O. Box 11258	**Auto invest:**	Yes
	New York, NY 10286	**Auto invest fee:**	$5 + 10¢/sh.
Agent's Phone:	888-269-2377	**Selling info:**	Sells weekly, by mail, at market,
Other than USA:	Yes		for $5 +10¢/sh.

Company:	**Solutia Inc.**	Safekeeping:	Yes
Symbol:	SOI	Invests:	Every 30 days beginning 1/12
Exchange:	NYSE	Minimum:	$25
Industry:	Mfg. of chemical based materials	Maximum:	$100,000/year
Company Address:	10300 Olive Blvd., Box 66760	Min to qualify:	1
	St. Louis, MO 63166-6760	Fee on cash inv.:	2.5% to $4
Company Phone:	314-674-1000	Fee on div. inv.:	2.5% to $4
Transfer Agent:	FCT (EquiServe)	Discount (cash):	0
Agent's Address:	P.O. Box 2500	Discount (div.):	0
	Jersey City, NJ 07303-2500	Auto invest:	Yes
Agent's Phone:	888-987-6588	Auto invest fee:	$1
Other than USA:	Yes	Selling info:	Sells daily, by mail, fax, or phone, at market, for $10 +12¢/sh.

Company:	**Sonat, Inc.**	Safekeeping:	No
Symbol:	SNT	Invests:	Every 30 days beginning 1/15
Exchange:	NYSE	Minimum:	$50
Industry:	Oil & gas, gas distrib.	Maximum:	$6,000/quarter
Company Address:	Box 2563	Min to qualify:	1
	Birmingham, AL 35202-2563	Fee on cash inv.:	0!
Company Phone:	800-633-8570 or 205-325-3898	Fee on div. inv.:	0!
Transfer Agent:	ChaseMellon Shareholder Services	Discount (cash):	0
Agent's Address:	P.O. Box 3339	Discount (div.):	0
	South Hackensack, NJ 07606-1939	Auto invest:	No
Agent's Phone:	800-234-0738	Auto invest fee:	$0
Other than USA:	Yes	Selling info:	Sells weekly, by mail or phone, at market, for $15 + comm.

Company:	**Sonoco Products Co.**	Safekeeping:	Yes
Symbol:	SON	Invests:	Every 5 days beginning 1/5
Exchange:	NYSE	Minimum:	$10
Industry:	Industrial & consumer packaging products	Maximum:	$100,000/year
		Min to qualify:	1
Company Address:	North Second St., A46	Fee on cash inv.:	10¢/sh.
	Hartsville, SC 29550	Fee on div. inv.:	0!
Company Phone:	803-383-7277 or 843-383-7635	Discount (cash):	0
Transfer Agent:	BankBoston (EquiServe)	Discount (div.):	0
Agent's Address:	P.O. Box 8218	Auto invest:	Yes
	Boston, MA 02266-8218	Auto invest fee:	10¢/sh.
Agent's Phone:	800-633-4236	Selling info:	Sells weekly, by mail or phone, at market, for 10¢/sh.
Other than USA:	Yes		

Company:	**Sonoma Valley Bank**	Safekeeping:	Yes
Symbol:	SOVY	Invests:	Every 7 days beginning varies
Exchange:	OTC	Minimum:	$50
Industry:	Banking	Maximum:	$10,000/month
Company Address:	202 West Napa St., Box 1228	Min to qualify:	1
	Sonoma, CA 95476	Fee on cash inv.:	$7.50 + 10¢/sh.
Company Phone:	707-935-3200 or 707-935-3290 x220	Fee on div. inv.:	0!
		Discount (cash):	0
Transfer Agent:	American Stock Transfer	Discount (div.):	0
Agent's Address:	40 Wall St., 46th Fl.	Auto invest:	Yes
	New York, NY 10005	Auto invest fee:	$0
Agent's Phone:	800-937-5449	Selling info:	Sells weekly, by mail, fax, at market, for $7.50 +10¢/sh.
Other than USA:	Yes		

Company:	**Sony Corp.**
Symbol:	SNE
Exchange:	NYSE
Industry:	Electronics & entertainment
Company Address:	550 Madison Ave., 33rd Fl.
	New York, NY 10022
Company Phone:	212-833-6800
Transfer Agent:	Morgan Guaranty Trust Co.
Agent's Address:	P.O. Box 9073
	Boston, MA 02205-9948
Agent's Phone:	800-428-4237
Other than USA:	Yes

Safekeeping:	Yes
Invests:	Every 7 days beginning varies
Minimum:	$50
Maximum:	$100,000/year
Min to qualify:	1
Fee on cash inv.:	$5 + 12¢/sh.
Fee on div. inv.:	5% to $2.50
Discount (cash):	0
Discount (div.):	0
Auto invest:	Yes
Auto invest fee:	$0
Selling info:	Sells daily, by phone or mail, at avg. price, for $5 +12¢/sh.

Company:	**Sotheby's Holdings, Inc.**
Symbol:	BID
Exchange:	NYSE
Industry:	Auctioneer
Company Address:	1334 York Ave.
	New York, NY 10021
Company Phone:	800-700-6321
Transfer Agent:	ChaseMellon Shareholder Services
Agent's Address:	85 Challenger Road,
	Overpeck Center
	Ridgefield Park, NJ 07660
Agent's Phone:	800-851-9677 or 201-329-8660
Other than USA:	Yes

Safekeeping:	No
Invests:	Every 30 days beginning 1/15
Minimum:	$100
Maximum:	$5,000/month
Min to qualify:	1
Fee on cash inv.:	0
Fee on div. inv.:	0
Discount (cash):	0
Discount (div.):	0
Auto invest:	No
Auto invest fee:	$0
Selling info:	Sells weekly, by mail or phone, at market, for $10 + comm.

Company:	**South Jersey Ind., Inc.**
Symbol:	SJI
Exchange:	NYSE
Industry:	Utility-gas
Company Address:	1 South Jersey Plaza
	Folsom, NJ 08037-9917
Company Phone:	609-561-9000 ext.4260
Transfer Agent:	SJI Dividend Reinvestment Plan
Agent's Address:	1 South Jersey Plaza
	Folsom, NJ 08037-9917
Agent's Phone:	609-561-9000 x4238
Other than USA:	Yes

Safekeeping:	No
Invests:	Every 90 days beginning 1/2
Minimum:	$25
Maximum:	$100,000/year
Min to qualify:	1
Fee on cash inv.:	0!
Fee on div. inv.:	0!
Discount (cash):	0
Discount (div.):	0
Auto invest:	No
Auto invest fee:	$0
Selling info:	Sells weekly, by mail, at market, for $2.50 + 5¢/sh.

Company:	**Southern Co.**
Symbol:	SO
Exchange:	NYSE
Industry:	Utility-electric
Company Address:	Box 54250
	Atlanta, GA 30308-0250
Company Phone:	800-554-7626 or 404-506-5000
Transfer Agent:	SCS Stockholder Services
Agent's Address:	P.O. Box 54250
	Atlanta, GA 30308-0250
Agent's Phone:	800-554-7626
Other than USA:	Yes

Safekeeping:	Yes
Invests:	Every 15 days beginning 1/10-1/25
Minimum:	$25
Maximum:	$150,000/year
Min to qualify:	1
Fee on cash inv.:	0!
Fee on div. inv.:	0!
Discount (cash):	0
Discount (div.):	0
Auto invest:	Yes
Auto invest fee:	$0
Selling info:	Sells within 5 bus. days, by mail, at avg. price, for 6¢/sh.

Company:	**Southern Financial Bancorp, Inc.**	Safekeeping:	Yes
		Invests:	Every 90 days beginning 2/20
Symbol:	SFFB	Minimum:	$100
Exchange:	OTC	Maximum:	$1,000/quarter
Industry:	Banking	Min to qualify:	1
Company Address:	37 East Main St.	Fee on cash inv.:	0
	Warrenton, VA 20186	Fee on div. inv.:	0
Company Phone:	540-349-3900 or 540-349-3910	Discount (cash):	0
Transfer Agent:	ChaseMellon Shareholder Services	Discount (div.):	0
Agent's Address:	P.O. Box 3338	Auto invest:	No
	South Hackensack, NjJ 07606-1938	Auto invest fee:	$0
Agent's Phone:	800-526-0801	Selling info:	Not available
Other than USA:	Yes		

Company:	**Southern Peru Copper Corp.**	Safekeeping:	Yes
		Invests:	Every 30 days beginning 1/1
Symbol:	PCU	Minimum:	$25
Exchange:	NYSE	Maximum:	$1,000/month
Industry:	Copper mining	Min to qualify:	1
Company Address:	180 Maiden Lane	Fee on cash inv.:	0!
	New York, NY 10038	Fee on div. inv.:	0!
Company Phone:	212-510-2000	Discount (cash):	0
Transfer Agent:	Bank of New York	Discount (div.):	0
Agent's Address:	P.O. Box 11258, Church St. Station	Auto invest:	No
	New York, NY 10286-1258	Auto invest fee:	$0
Agent's Phone:	800-524-4458	Selling info:	Sells weekly, by mail, at avg. price, for $5!
Other than USA:	Yes		

Company:	**Southern Union Co.**	Safekeeping:	Yes
Symbol:	SUG	Invests:	Every 15 days beginning 1/5
Exchange:	NYSE	Minimum:	$50
Industry:	Natural gas distributor	Maximum:	$100,000/year
Company Address:	504 Lavaca St., 8th Fl.	Min to qualify:	1
	Austin, TX 78701	Fee on cash inv.:	$2.50 + 15¢/sh.
Company Phone:	800-773-8938 or 512-477-5852	Fee on div. inv.:	0
Transfer Agent:	Boston Eq. (EquiServe)	Discount (cash):	0
Agent's Address:	P.O. Box 644	Discount (div.):	0
	Boston, MA 02102	Auto invest:	Yes
Agent's Phone:	800-736-3001	Auto invest fee:	$0
Other than USA:	Yes	Selling info:	Sells weekly, by mail, at market, for $10 +15¢/sh.

Company:	**Southtrust Corp.**	Safekeeping:	Yes
Symbol:	SOTR	Invests:	Every 30 days beginning 1/1
Exchange:	OTC	Minimum:	$25
Industry:	Banking	Maximum:	$10,000/month
Company Address:	Box 2554	Min to qualify:	1
	Birmingham, AL 35290	Fee on cash inv.:	0
Company Phone:	800-239-2300 x6868 or 205-254-6868	Fee on div. inv.:	0
	or 205-254-6615	Discount (cash):	0
Transfer Agent:	ChaseMellon Shareholder Services	Discount (div.):	0
Agent's Address:	85 Challenger Road	Auto invest:	No
	Ridgefield Park, NJ 07660	Auto invest fee:	$0
Agent's Phone:	800-205-8317	Selling info:	Sells weekly, by mail or phone, at market, for $5 + comm.
Other than USA:	No		

Company:	**Southwest Gas Corp.**	**Safekeeping:**	Yes
Symbol:	SWX	**Invests:**	Every 15 days beginning 1/1
Exchange:	NYSE	**Minimum:**	$100
Industry:	Utility-gas, & gas distrib.	**Maximum:**	$50,000/year
Company Address:	Box 98510	**Min to qualify:**	1
	Las Vegas, NV 89193-8510	**Fee on cash inv.:**	0!
Company Phone:	800-331-1119 or 702-876-7237	**Fee on div. inv.:**	0!
Transfer Agent:	Southwest Gas Corp.	**Discount (cash):**	0
Agent's Address:	P.O. Box 98511	**Discount (div.):**	0
	Las Vegas, NV 89193-8511	**Auto invest:**	Yes
Agent's Phone:	702-876-7280	**Auto invest fee:**	$0
Other than USA:	Yes	**Selling info:**	Sells weekly, by mail, at market, for 3¢ to 5¢/sh.

Company:	**Southwest Georgia Fin'l Corp.**	**Safekeeping:**	Yes
		Invests:	Every 30 days beginning varies
Symbol:	SGB	**Minimum:**	$5
Exchange:	ASE	**Maximum:**	$5,000/month
Industry:	Banking services	**Min to qualify:**	1
Company Address:	201 First St. S.E.	**Fee on cash inv.:**	0
	Moultrie, GA 31768	**Fee on div. inv.:**	0
Company Phone:	912-985-1120	**Discount (cash):**	0
Transfer Agent:	American Stock Transfer & Trust Co.	**Discount (div.):**	0
		Auto invest:	Yes
Agent's Address:	40 Wall Street	**Auto invest fee:**	$0
	New York, NY 10005	**Selling info:**	Sells weekly, by mail, at market, for 4¢/sh.
Agent's Phone:	800-278-4353		
Other than USA:	Yes		

Company:	**Southwest Water Co.**	**Safekeeping:**	Yes
Symbol:	SWWC	**Invests:**	Every 90 days beginning 1/20
Exchange:	OTC	**Minimum:**	$25
Industry:	Utility-water	**Maximum:**	$3,000/quarter
Company Address:	225 North Barranca Ave., Ste.200	**Min to qualify:**	1
	West Covina, CA 91791-1605	**Fee on cash inv.:**	0
Company Phone:	626-915-1551	**Fee on div. inv.:**	0
Transfer Agent:	ChaseMellon Shareholder Services	**Discount (cash):**	0
Agent's Address:	85 Challenger Road	**Discount (div.):**	5%
	Ridgefield Park, NJ 07660	**Auto invest:**	No
Agent's Phone:	800-356-2017	**Auto invest fee:**	$0
Other than USA:	Yes	**Selling info:**	Sells n/o, by mail or phone, at n/o, for n/o

Company:	**Southwestern Energy Co.**	**Safekeeping:**	Yes
Symbol:	SWN	**Invests:**	Every 30 days beginning 1/5
Exchange:	NYSE	**Minimum:**	$25
Industry:	Diversified-gas	**Maximum:**	$1,000/month
Company Address:	1083 Sain St., Box 1408	**Min to qualify:**	1
	Fayetteville, AR 72602-1408	**Fee on cash inv.:**	$3
Company Phone:	501-521-1141	**Fee on div. inv.:**	5% to $3
Transfer Agent:	FCT (EquiServe)	**Discount (cash):**	0
Agent's Address:	P.O. Box 2598	**Discount (div.):**	0
	Jersey City, NJ 07303-2598	**Auto invest:**	No
Agent's Phone:	800-446-2617	**Auto invest fee:**	$0
Other than USA:	Yes	**Selling info:**	Sells daily, by phone, mail, or fax, at market, for $10 +12¢/sh.

Company:	**Sovereign Bancorp Inc.**	Safekeeping:	Yes
Symbol:	SVRN	Invests:	Every 90 days beginning 2/15
Exchange:	OTC	Minimum:	$50
Industry:	Banking	Maximum:	$5,000/quarter
Company Address:	Box 12646	Min to qualify:	1
	Reading, PA 19612	Fee on cash inv.:	0!
Company Phone:	610-320-8498 or 610-320-8400	Fee on div. inv.:	0!
Transfer Agent:	ChaseMellon Shareholder Services	Discount (cash):	0
Agent's Address:	P.O. Box 3340	Discount (div.):	5%
	South Hackensack, NJ 07606-1940	Auto invest:	No
Agent's Phone:	800-685-4524	Auto invest fee:	$0
Other than USA:	No	Selling info:	Sells daily, by mail, at market, for $15 + 6¢/sh.

Company:	**Sovran Self Storage, Inc.**	Safekeeping:	Yes
Symbol:	SSS	Invests:	Every 30 days beginning 1/22
Exchange:	NYSE	Minimum:	$100
Industry:	REIT	Maximum:	$10,000/month
Company Address:	5166 Main St.	Min to qualify:	1
	Williamsville, NY 14221	Fee on cash inv.:	0!
Company Phone:	716-633-1850	Fee on div. inv.:	0!
Transfer Agent:	American Stock Transfer & Trust	Discount (cash):	2%
Agent's Address:	40 Wall St.	Discount (div.):	2%
	New York, NY 10005	Auto invest:	No
Agent's Phone:	800-278-4353	Auto invest fee:	
Other than USA:	Yes	Selling info:	Sells within 10 bus. days, by mail, at market, for $10 + 4¢/sh.

Company:	**Spain Fund (The)**	Safekeeping:	No
Symbol:	SNF	Invests:	Every 180 days beginning 1/15
Exchange:	NYSE	Minimum:	$100
Industry:	Closed-end fund	Maximum:	$unlimited
Company Address:	c/o All. Capital,1345 Ave. of the	Min to qualify:	1
	Amer.	Fee on cash inv.:	75¢
	New York, NY 10105-0302	Fee on div. inv.:	0
Company Phone:	800-247-4154	Discount (cash):	0
Transfer Agent:	State Street Bank (EquiServe)	Discount (div.):	5%
Agent's Address:	PO Box 8200	Auto invest:	No
	Boston, MA 02266-8200	Auto invest fee:	$0
Agent's Phone:	800-219-4218	Selling info:	Sells within 10 bus. days, by mail or phone, at market, for $2.50 + comm.
Other than USA:	Yes		

Company:	**Spieker Properties**	Safekeeping:	Yes
Symbol:	SPK	Invests:	Every 90 days beginning 1/17
Exchange:	NYSE	Minimum:	$10
Industry:	REIT	Maximum:	$20,000/quarter
Company Address:	2180 Sand Hill Rd., Ste.200	Min to qualify:	1
	Menlo Park, CA 94025	Fee on cash inv.:	5% to $3
Company Phone:	650-854-5600	Fee on div. inv.:	5% to $3
Transfer Agent:	Bank of New York	Discount (cash):	0
Agent's Address:	P.O. Box1958	Discount (div.):	0
	Newark, N.J. 07101-9774	Auto invest:	No
Agent's Phone:	800-524-4458	Auto invest fee:	$0
Other than USA:	Yes	Selling info:	Sells weekly, by mail or fax, at market, for $15 + comm.

Company:	**Sprint Corp. (FON Group)**	**Safekeeping:**	Yes
		Invests:	Every 30 days beginning 1/30
Symbol:	FON	**Minimum:**	$25
Exchange:	NYSE	**Maximum:**	$5,000/quarter
Industry:	Telecommunications	**Min to qualify:**	1
Company Address:	Box 11315	**Fee on cash inv.:**	0
	Kansas City, MO 64112	**Fee on div. inv.:**	0
Company Phone:	800-259-3755 or 913-624-2541	**Discount (cash):**	0
Transfer Agent:	UMB Bank, N.A.	**Discount (div.):**	0
Agent's Address:	P.O. Box 410064	**Auto invest:**	No
	Kansas City, MO 64141-0064	**Auto invest fee:**	$0
Agent's Phone:	816-860-7786	**Selling info:**	Sells weekly, by mail or fax, at
Other than USA:	Yes		market, for $2 + comm.

Company:	**St. Joseph Light & Power**	**Safekeeping:**	Yes
Symbol:	SAJ	**Invests:**	Every 30 days beginning 1/18
Exchange:	NYSE	**Minimum:**	$50
Industry:	Utility-electric, gas	**Maximum:**	$10,000/month
Company Address:	520 Francis St., Box 998	**Min to qualify:**	1
	St. Joseph, MO 64502-0998	**Fee on cash inv.:**	0!
Company Phone:	800-367-4562 or 816-387-6434	**Fee on div. inv.:**	0!
Transfer Agent:	Harris Trust & Savings Bank	**Discount (cash):**	0
Agent's Address:	P.O. Box A-3309	**Discount (div.):**	0
	Chicago, IL 60690	**Auto invest:**	Yes
Agent's Phone:	800-643-8517	**Auto invest fee:**	$0
Other than USA:	Yes	**Selling info:**	Sells daily, by mail, at market, for
			$3 +10¢/sh.

Company:	**St. Paul Bancorp Inc.**	**Safekeeping:**	Yes
Symbol:	SPBC	**Invests:**	Every 30 days beginning 1/15
Exchange:	OTC	**Minimum:**	$50
Industry:	Banking	**Maximum:**	$2,000/month
Company Address:	6700 West North Ave.	**Min to qualify:**	10
	Chicago, IL 60707	**Fee on cash inv.:**	$3.50
Company Phone:	773-804-2284 or 773-622-5000	**Fee on div. inv.:**	0
Transfer Agent:	BankBoston (EquiServe)	**Discount (cash):**	0
Agent's Address:	P.O. Box 8040	**Discount (div.):**	0
	Boston, MA 02266-8040	**Auto invest:**	No
Agent's Phone:	800-730-4001	**Auto invest fee:**	$0
Other than USA:	No	**Selling info:**	Sells daily, by mail, at market, for
			5% to $10 + comm.

Company:	**St. Paul Companies (The)**	**Safekeeping:**	Yes
Symbol:	SPC	**Invests:**	Every 30 days beginning 1/17
Exchange:	NYSE	**Minimum:**	$10
Industry:	Insurance	**Maximum:**	$60,000/year
Company Address:	385 Washington St.	**Min to qualify:**	1
	St. Paul, MN 55102	**Fee on cash inv.:**	0!
Company Phone:	651-310-7911	**Fee on div. inv.:**	0!
Transfer Agent:	Norwest Bank Minnesota, NA	**Discount (cash):**	0
Agent's Address:	P.O. Box 64854	**Discount (div.):**	0
	St. Paul, MN 55164-0854	**Auto invest:**	No
Agent's Phone:	888-326-5102	**Auto invest fee:**	$0
Other than USA:	Yes	**Selling info:**	Sells daily, by phone, at market,
			for $10 +12¢/sh.

Company:	**Standard Commercial Corp.**	Safekeeping:	Yes
		Invests:	Every 30 days beginning 1/15
Symbol:	STW	Minimum:	$25
Exchange:	NYSE	Maximum:	$3,000/quarter
Industry:	Tobacco	Min to qualify:	1
Company Address:	2201 Miller Rd., Box 450	Fee on cash inv.:	0!
	Wilson, NC 27894-0450	Fee on div. inv.:	0!
Company Phone:	252-291-5507	Discount (cash):	0
Transfer Agent:	First Union National Bank of NC	Discount (div.):	0
Agent's Address:	1525 W.T. Harris Blvd., 3C3	Auto invest:	No
	Charlotte, NC 27288-1153	Auto invest fee:	$0
Agent's Phone:	800-829-8432	Selling info:	Sells bimonthly, by mail or fax, at
Other than USA:	Yes		market, for 5¢/sh.

Company:	**Standard Products Co.**	Safekeeping:	Yes
Symbol:	SPD	Invests:	Every 30 days beginning 1/30
Exchange:	NYSE	Minimum:	$20
Industry:	Rubber, plastic & transport equip.	Maximum:	$5,000/month
Company Address:	2401 South Gulley Rd.	Min to qualify:	1
	Dearborn, MI 48124	Fee on cash inv.:	5% to $3
Company Phone:	888-332-4109 or 313-561-1100	Fee on div. inv.:	5% to $3
Transfer Agent:	National City Bank	Discount (cash):	0
Agent's Address:	4100 West 150TH Street	Discount (div.):	0
	Cleveland, OH 44135-1385	Auto invest:	No
Agent's Phone:	800-622-6757 x4289	Auto invest fee:	$0
Other than USA:	Yes	Selling info:	Sells Fridays, by mail or fax, at
			market, for 0

Company:	**Standard Register**	Safekeeping:	Yes
Symbol:	SR	Invests:	Every 30 days beginning 1/5
Exchange:	NYSE	Minimum:	$25
Industry:	Business forms & handling	Maximum:	$60,000/year
Company Address:	Box 1167	Min to qualify:	1
	Dayton, OH 45401	Fee on cash inv.:	0!
Company Phone:	800-755-6405 or 937-221-1540	Fee on div. inv.:	0!
Transfer Agent:	Wachovia (EquiServe)	Discount (cash):	0
Agent's Address:	P.O. Box 8217	Discount (div.):	0
	Boston, MA 02266-8217	Auto invest:	Yes
Agent's Phone:	800-633-4236	Auto invest fee:	$0
Other than USA:	Yes	Selling info:	Sells daily, by mail or fax,
			at market, for 5¢/sh.

Company:	**Stanley Works**	Safekeeping:	Yes
Symbol:	SWK	Invests:	Every 30 days beginning 1/1
Exchange:	NYSE	Minimum:	$25
Industry:	Machinery, tools, hardware,	Maximum:	$5,000/month
	consumer products	Min to qualify:	20
Company Address:	1000 Stanley Dr.	Fee on cash inv.:	0
	New Britain, CT 06053	Fee on div. inv.:	$2
Company Phone:	860-225-5111	Discount (cash):	0
Transfer Agent:	State Street Bank (EquiServe)	Discount (div.):	0
Agent's Address:	P.O. Box 8200	Auto invest:	No
	Boston, MA 0266-8200	Auto invest fee:	$0
Agent's Phone:	800-543-6757	Selling info:	Sells daily, by phone, mail, or fax,
Other than USA:	Yes		at market, for $10 +15¢/sh.

Company:	**State Auto Financial Corp.**	Safekeeping:	Yes
		Invests:	Every 90 days beginning 1/1
Symbol:	STFC	Minimum:	$10
Exchange:	OTC	Maximum:	$3,000/quarter
Industry:	Insurance	Min to qualify:	1
Company Address:	518 East Broad St.	Fee on cash inv.:	0!
	Columbus, OH 43215	Fee on div. inv.:	0!
Company Phone:	614-464-5373 or 614-464-5000	Discount (cash):	0
Transfer Agent:	National City Bank	Discount (div.):	0
Agent's Address:	P.O. Box 92301	Auto invest:	No
	Cleveland, OH 44193-0900	Auto invest fee:	$0
Agent's Phone:	800-622-6757	Selling info:	Sells weekly, by mail, at market,
Other than USA:	Yes		for $2.50

Company:	**State Street Corp.**	Safekeeping:	Yes
Symbol:	STT	Invests:	Every 30 days beginning 1/15
Exchange:	NYSE	Minimum:	$100
Industry:	Financial services	Maximum:	$25,000/month
Company Address:	225 Franklin St.	Min to qualify:	10
	Boston, MA 02110	Fee on cash inv.:	$3.50
Company Phone:	617-786-3000 or 617-664-3477	Fee on div. inv.:	5% to $3
Transfer Agent:	State Street Bank (EquiServe)	Discount (cash):	0
Agent's Address:	P.O. Box 8200	Discount (div.):	0
	Boston, MA 02666-8200	Auto invest:	Yes
Agent's Phone:	800-426-5523	Auto invest fee:	$2.50
Other than USA:	No	Selling info:	Sells daily, by mail or phone, at
			market, for $10 + comm.

Company:	**Sterling Bancorp**	Safekeeping:	Yes
Symbol:	STL	Invests:	Every 30 days beginning varies
Exchange:	NYSE	Minimum:	$150
Industry:	Regional banks	Maximum:	$4,500/month
Company Address:	430 Park Ave., 4th Fl.	Min to qualify:	5
	New York, NY 10022-3505	Fee on cash inv.:	0!
Company Phone:	212-826-8045 or 212-826-8000	Fee on div. inv.:	0!
Transfer Agent:	ChaseMellon Shareholder Services	Discount (cash):	0
Agent's Address:	P.O. Box 3340	Discount (div.):	0
	Hackensack, NJ 07606-1940	Auto invest:	No
Agent's Phone:	800-851-9677	Auto invest fee:	$0
Other than USA:	Yes	Selling info:	Sells weekly, by mail, at market,
			for comm.

Company:	**STET Hellas Telecomm. SA**	Safekeeping:	Yes
		Invests:	Every 7 days beginning varies
Symbol:	STHLY	Minimum:	$50
Exchange:	NYSE	Maximum:	$100,000/year
Industry:	Telecommunications	Min to qualify:	1
Company Address:	c/o Morgan Guaranty Trust,	Fee on cash inv.:	$5 + 12¢/sh.
	Box 9073	Fee on div. inv.:	5% to $2.50
	Boston, MA 02205-9948	Discount (cash):	0
Company Phone:	800-428-4237	Discount (div.):	0
Transfer Agent:	Morgan Guaranty Trust Co.	Auto invest:	Yes
Agent's Address:	P.O. Box 9073	Auto invest fee:	$5
	Boston, MA 02205-9948	Selling info:	Sells daily, by phone or mail, at
Agent's Phone:	800-428-4237		market, for $5 +12¢/sh.
Other than USA:	No		

Company:	**Stifel Financial Corp.**	Safekeeping:	Yes
Symbol:	SF	Invests:	Every 90 days beginning 2/24
Exchange:	NYSE	Minimum:	$25
Industry:	Financial	Maximum:	$5,000/month
Company Address:	501 North Broadway	Min to qualify:	1
	St. Louis, MO 63102	Fee on cash inv.:	0!
Company Phone:	314-342-2000	Fee on div. inv.:	0!
Transfer Agent:	UMB Bank, N.A.	Discount (cash):	0
Agent's Address:	P.O. Box 410064	Discount (div.):	0
	Kansas City, MO 64141	Auto invest:	No
Agent's Phone:	816-860-7787	Auto invest fee:	$0
Other than USA:	Yes	Selling info:	Sells weekly, by mail, at market, for 10¢ to 12¢/sh.

Company:	**STMicroelectronics NV**	Safekeeping:	Yes
Symbol:	STM	Invests:	Every 7 days beginning varies
Exchange:	NYSE	Minimum:	$50
Industry:	Semiconductors	Maximum:	$250,000/year
Company Address:	c/o BNY,101 Barclay St.,22 West	Min to qualify:	1
	New York, NY 10286	Fee on cash inv.:	$5 + 10¢/sh.
Company Phone:	800-943-9715	Fee on div. inv.:	5% to $5 + 10¢/sh.
Transfer Agent:	Bank of New York	Discount (cash):	0
Agent's Address:	P.O. Box 11258	Discount (div.):	0
	New York, NY 10286	Auto invest:	Yes
Agent's Phone:	888-269-2377	Auto invest fee:	$5 + 10¢/sh.
Other than USA:	Yes	Selling info:	Sells weekly, by mail, at market, for $5 +10¢/sh.

Company:	**Stone & Webster, Inc.**	Safekeeping:	Yes
Symbol:	SW	Invests:	Every 30 days beginning 1/15
Exchange:	NYSE	Minimum:	$50
Industry:	Construction & engineering services	Maximum:	$1,500/month
		Min to qualify:	1
Company Address:	245 Summer St.	Fee on cash inv.:	0
	Boston, MA 02210	Fee on div. inv.:	0
Company Phone:	617-589-5111 or 617-589-7473	Discount (cash):	0
Transfer Agent:	ChaseMellon Shareholder Services	Discount (div.):	0
Agent's Address:	P.O. Box 3338	Auto invest:	No
	So. Hackensack, NJ 07606	Auto invest fee:	$0
Agent's Phone:	800-851-9677	Selling info:	Sells within 13 bus. days, by mail or phone, at market, for $15 +12¢/sh.
Other than USA:	Yes		

Company:	**Storage USA, Inc.**	Safekeeping:	Yes
Symbol:	SUS	Invests:	Every 90 days beginning 3/31
Exchange:	NYSE	Minimum:	$50
Industry:	REIT	Maximum:	$25,000/quarter
Company Address:	165 Madison Ave., Ste.1300	Min to qualify:	1
	Memphis, TN 38103	Fee on cash inv.:	0
Company Phone:	901-252-2000	Fee on div. inv.:	0
Transfer Agent:	First Union National Bank of NC	Discount (cash):	0
Agent's Address:	1525 West W.T. Harris Blvd.	Discount (div.):	0
	Charlotte, NC 28288	Auto invest:	No
Agent's Phone:	800-829-8432	Auto invest fee:	$0
Other than USA:	Yes	Selling info:	Sells bimonthly, by mail or fax, at market, for $5 + comm.

Company:	**Stride Rite Corp. (The)**	Safekeeping:	Yes
Symbol:	SRR	Invests:	Every 45 days beginning 2/1
Exchange:	NYSE	Minimum:	$10
Industry:	Apparel, retail & mfr. of shoes	Maximum:	$1,000/month
Company Address:	Box 9191	Min to qualify:	1
	Lexington, MA 02420-9191	Fee on cash inv.:	5% to $2.50
Company Phone:	617-824-6300	Fee on div. inv.:	5% to $2.50
Transfer Agent:	Boston Eq. (EquiServe)	Discount (cash):	0
Agent's Address:	P.O. Box 8040	Discount (div.):	0
	Boston, MA 02266-8040	Auto invest:	No
Agent's Phone:	781-575-3170	Auto invest fee:	$0
Other than USA:	Yes	Selling info:	Not available

Company:	**Suffolk Bancorp**	Safekeeping:	Yes
Symbol:	SUBK	Invests:	Every 90 days beginning 1/1
Exchange:	OTC	Minimum:	$300
Industry:	Banking	Maximum:	$5,000/quarter
Company Address:	6 West 2nd St., Box 9000	Min to qualify:	1
	Riverhead, NY 11901	Fee on cash inv.:	0
Company Phone:	516-727-3800	Fee on div. inv.:	0
Transfer Agent:	American Stock Transfer	Discount (cash):	3%
Agent's Address:	40 Wall Street	Discount (div.):	3%
	New York, NY 10005	Auto invest:	No
Agent's Phone:	800-937-5449 or 718-921-8200	Auto invest fee:	$0
Other than USA:	Yes	Selling info:	Sells weekly, by mail or fax, at market, for $15 + comm.

Company:	**Summit Bancorp**	Safekeeping:	Yes
Symbol:	SUB	Invests:	Every 30 days beginning 1/1
Exchange:	NYSE	Minimum:	$10
Industry:	Banking	Maximum:	$25,000/quarter
Company Address:	301 Carnegie Ctr., Box 2066	Min to qualify:	1
	Princeton, NJ 08543-2066	Fee on cash inv.:	3¢/sh.
Company Phone:	609-987-3452 or 609-987-3200	Fee on div. inv.:	0!
Transfer Agent:	FCT (EquiServe)	Discount (cash):	0
Agent's Address:	P.O. Box 2500	Discount (div.):	0
	Jersey City, NJ 07303-2500	Auto invest:	Yes
Agent's Phone:	201-324-0498	Auto invest fee:	$1
Other than USA:	Yes except Canadians	Selling info:	Sells daily, by mail, at market, for $10 +10¢ to12¢/sh.

Company:	**Summit Properties**	Safekeeping:	Yes
Symbol:	SMT	Invests:	Every 30 days beginning 1/1
Exchange:	NYSE	Minimum:	$100
Industry:	Property management	Maximum:	$10,000/month
Company Address:	212 South Tryon St., Ste.500	Min to qualify:	1
	Charlotte, NC 28281	Fee on cash inv.:	0
Company Phone:	704-334-9905	Fee on div. inv.:	0
Transfer Agent:	First Union National Bank of NC	Discount (cash):	3%
Agent's Address:	230 S. Tryon St., 11th Floor	Discount (div.):	3%
	Charlotte, NC 28288-1154	Auto invest:	No
Agent's Phone:	800-829-8432	Auto invest fee:	$0
Other than USA:	Yes	Selling info:	Sells monthly, by phone, mail, or fax, at market, for 2¢/sh.

Company:	**Sun Bancorp, Inc.**	Safekeeping:	Yes
Symbol:	SUBI	Invests:	Every 90 days beginning 2/17
Exchange:	OTC	Minimum:	$50
Industry:	Banking	Maximum:	$10,000/quarter
Company Address:	2-16 South Market St., Box 57	Min to qualify:	1
	Selinsgrove, PA 17870	Fee on cash inv.:	0
Company Phone:	717-374-1131	Fee on div. inv.:	0
Transfer Agent:	SunBank	Discount (cash):	0
Agent's Address:	2-16 South Market St.,Box 57,	Discount (div.):	0
	Attn: Karen Gaugler	Auto invest:	Yes
	Selinsgrove, PA 17870	Auto invest fee:	$0
Agent's Phone:	717-374-1131	Selling info:	Sells daily, by mail or in person, at
Other than USA:	Yes		market, for $0

Company:	**Suncor Energy Inc.**	Safekeeping:	Yes
Symbol:	SU	Invests:	Every 90 days beginning 3/30
Exchange:	NYSE	Minimum:	$100
Industry:	Oil & gas company	Maximum:	$5,000/quarter Cdn.
Company Address:	112 4th Ave. 5 W., Box 38	Min to qualify:	1
	Calgary, Alta.T2P 2VS Canada	Fee on cash inv.:	0!
Company Phone:	403-269-8757 or 403-269-8100	Fee on div. inv.:	0!
Transfer Agent:	Montreal Trust Company	Discount (cash):	0
Agent's Address:	151 Front St. West-8th Fl.	Discount (div.):	0
	Toronto, Ont., Canada M5J 2N1	Auto invest:	No
Agent's Phone:	416-981-9500	Auto invest fee:	$0
Other than USA:	Yes	Selling info:	Not available

Company:	**Sundstrand Corp.**	Safekeeping:	No
Symbol:	SNS	Invests:	Every 30 days beginning 1/20
Exchange:	NYSE	Minimum:	$25
Industry:	Aerospace, industrial equipment	Maximum:	$3,000/month
Company Address:	4949 Harrison Ave., Box 7003	Min to qualify:	1
	Rockford, IL 61125-7003	Fee on cash inv.:	0!
Company Phone:	815-226-2136	Fee on div. inv.:	0!
Transfer Agent:	Harris Trust & Savings Bank	Discount (cash):	0
Agent's Address:	P.O. Box A3504	Discount (div.):	0
	Chicago, IL 60690-4607	Auto invest:	No
Agent's Phone:	800-293-8207	Auto invest fee:	$0
Other than USA:	Yes	Selling info:	Sells weekly, by mail, at market,
			for $10 + comm.

Company:	**Sunoco Inc.**	Safekeeping:	Yes
Symbol:	SUN	Invests:	Every 30 days beginning 1/29
Exchange:	NYSE	Minimum:	$1
Industry:	Oil & energy	Maximum:	$10,000/quarter
Company Address:	10 Penn Ctr., 1801 Market St.,	Min to qualify:	1
	17th fl.	Fee on cash inv.:	0
	Philadelphia, PA 19103-1699	Fee on div. inv.:	0
Company Phone:	215-977-6082 or 217-977-6106	Discount (cash):	0
Transfer Agent:	FCT (EquiServe)	Discount (div.):	0
Agent's Address:	P.O. Box 2500	Auto invest:	No
	Jersey City, NJ 07303-2500	Auto invest fee:	$0
Agent's Phone:	800-888-8494	Selling info:	Sells daily, by phone or mail, at
Other than USA:	Yes		market, for $10 +12¢/sh.

Company:	**SunSource, Inc.**	Safekeeping:	Yes
Symbol:	SDP	Invests:	Every 90 days beginning 1/10
Exchange:	NYSE	Minimum:	$100
Industry:	Industrial products & services	Maximum:	$2,500/quarter
Company Address:	3000 One Logan Sq.	Min to qualify:	25
	Philadelphia, PA 19103	Fee on cash inv.:	0!
Company Phone:	215-282-1290 x16	Fee on div. inv.:	0!
Transfer Agent:	Registrar & Transfer Company	Discount (cash):	0
Agent's Address:	10 Commerce Drive	Discount (div.):	0
	Cranford, NJ 07016	Auto invest:	No
Agent's Phone:	800-368-5948	Auto invest fee:	$0
Other than USA:	Yes	Selling info:	Sells within 10 bus. days, by mail, at avg. price, for $10 + comm.

Company:	**Sunstone Hotel Investors**	Safekeeping:	Yes
Symbol:	SSI	Invests:	Every 30 days beginning 1/15
Exchange:	NYSE	Minimum:	$100
Industry:	REIT	Maximum:	$3,000/month
Company Address:	903 Calle Amanecer, 3rd Fl.	Min to qualify:	1
	San Clemente, CA 92673	Fee on cash inv.:	$5!
Company Phone:	949-361-3900	Fee on div. inv.:	0
Transfer Agent:	ChaseMellon Shareholder Services	Discount (cash):	0-5%
Agent's Address:	400 S. Hope St., 4th Floor	Discount (div.):	0 -5%
	Los Angeles, CA 90071	Auto invest:	No
Agent's Phone:	888-261-6776	Auto invest fee:	$0
Other than USA:	Yes	Selling info:	Sells weekly, by mail or phone, at market, for $15 +12¢/sh.

Company:	**SunTrust Banks Inc.**	Safekeeping:	Yes
Symbol:	STI	Invests:	Every 30 days beginning 1/15
Exchange:	NYSE	Minimum:	$10
Industry:	Banking	Maximum:	$60,000/year
Company Address:	Box 4418	Min to qualify:	1
	Atlanta, GA 30302-4418	Fee on cash inv.:	0!
Company Phone:	800-568-3476 or 404-588-7822	Fee on div. inv.:	0!
Transfer Agent:	SunTrust Bank, Atlanta	Discount (cash):	0
Agent's Address:	P.O. Box 4625	Discount (div.):	0
	Atlanta, GA 30302-4625	Auto invest:	Yes
Agent's Phone:	800-568-3476	Auto invest fee:	$0
Other than USA:	Yes	Selling info:	Sells biweekly, by mail, at market, for comm.

Company:	**Super-Sol Ltd.**	Safekeeping:	Yes
Symbol:	SAE	Invests:	Every 7 days beginning varies
Exchange:	NYSE	Minimum:	$50
Industry:	Retail, Grocery	Maximum:	$100,000/year
Company Address:	c/o Morgan Guaranty Trust,	Min to qualify:	1
	Box 9073	Fee on cash inv.:	$5 + 12¢/sh.
	Boston, MA 02205-9948	Fee on div. inv.:	0
Company Phone:	212-889-4350	Discount (cash):	0
Transfer Agent:	Morgan Guaranty Trust Co.	Discount (div.):	0
Agent's Address:	P.O. Box 9073	Auto invest:	Yes
	Boston, MA 02205-9948	Auto invest fee:	$5 + 12¢/sh.
Agent's Phone:	800-428-4237	Selling info:	Sells daily, by mail or phone, at avg. price, for $5 +12¢/sh.
Other than USA:	No		

Company:	**Supermercados Unimarc S.A.**	Safekeeping:	Yes
		Invests:	Every 7 days beginning varies
Symbol:	UNR	Minimum:	$50
Exchange:	NYSE	Maximum:	$250,000/year
Industry:	Supermarkets	Min to qualify:	1
Company Address:	c/o BNY,101 Barclay St.,22 West	Fee on cash inv.:	$5 + 10¢/sh.
	New York, NY 10286	Fee on div. inv.:	5% to $5 + 10¢/sh.
Company Phone:	800-943-9715	Discount (cash):	0
Transfer Agent:	Bank of New York	Discount (div.):	0
Agent's Address:	P.O. Box 11258	Auto invest:	Yes
	New York, NY 10286	Auto invest fee:	$5 + 10¢/sh.
Agent's Phone:	888-269-2377	Selling info:	Sells weekly, by mail, at market,
Other than USA:	Yes		for $5 +10¢/sh.

Company:	**Supervalu, Inc.**	Safekeeping:	Yes
Symbol:	SVU	Invests:	Every 30 days beginning 1/15
Exchange:	NYSE	Minimum:	$10
Industry:	Food wholesaler and retailer	Maximum:	$3,000/quarter
Company Address:	Box 990	Min to qualify:	1
	Minneapolis, MN 55440	Fee on cash inv.:	0!
Company Phone:	612-828-4599 or 612-828-4000	Fee on div. inv.:	0!
Transfer Agent:	Norwest Bank Minnesota	Discount (cash):	0
Agent's Address:	P.O. Box 64854	Discount (div.):	0
	St. Paul, MN 55164-0854	Auto invest:	No
Agent's Phone:	800-468-9716	Auto invest fee:	$0
Other than USA:	No	Selling info:	Sells daily, by mail, at market, for
			$3 +15¢/sh.

Company:	**Susquehanna Bancshares**	Safekeeping:	Yes
Symbol:	SUSQ	Invests:	Every 7 days beginning varies
Exchange:	OTC	Minimum:	$50
Industry:	Banking	Maximum:	$25,000/year
Company Address:	26 North Cedar St., Box 1000	Min to qualify:	1
	Lititz, PA 17543-7000	Fee on cash inv.:	$5 + 10¢/sh.
Company Phone:	717-626-4721 x305	Fee on div. inv.:	0!
Transfer Agent:	Bank of New York	Discount (cash):	0
Agent's Address:	P.O. Box 11258,Church St. Station	Discount (div.):	0
	New York, NY 10286-1258	Auto invest:	Yes
Agent's Phone:	800-524-4458	Auto invest fee:	$5 + 10¢/sh.
Other than USA:	Yes	Selling info:	Sells weekly, by mail, at market,
			for $10 +10¢/sh.

Company:	**Synovus Financial Corp.**	Safekeeping:	Yes
Symbol:	SNV	Invests:	Every 7 days beginning varies
Exchange:	NYSE	Minimum:	$50
Industry:	Banking	Maximum:	$250,000/year
Company Address:	Box 120	Min to qualify:	10
	Columbus, GA 31902-0120	Fee on cash inv.:	$2.50 + 8¢/sh.
Company Phone:	706-649-5220	Fee on div. inv.:	0!
Transfer Agent:	State Street Bank (EquiServe)	Discount (cash):	0
Agent's Address:	P.O. Box 8209	Discount (div.):	0
	Boston, Mass. 02266-8209	Auto invest:	Yes
Agent's Phone:	800-503-8903	Auto invest fee:	$0
Other than USA:	Yes	Selling info:	Sells weekly, by mail, at market,
			for $10 +15¢/sh.

Company:	**Sysco Corp.**	Safekeeping:	Yes
Symbol:	SYY	Invests:	Every 30 days beginning 1/23
Exchange:	NYSE	Minimum:	$100
Industry:	Food distribution	Maximum:	$10,000/month
Company Address:	1390 Enclave Pkwy.	Min to qualify:	1
	Houston, TX 77077-2099	Fee on cash inv.:	$5 + 5¢/sh.
Company Phone:	281-584-1458 or 281-584-1390	Fee on div. inv.:	0!
Transfer Agent:	Boston Eq. (EquiServe)	Discount (cash):	0
Agent's Address:	P.O. Box 8040	Discount (div.):	0
	Boston, MA 02266-8040	Auto invest:	Yes
Agent's Phone:	800-730-4001	Auto invest fee:	$5 + 5¢/sh.
Other than USA:	Yes	Selling info:	Sells weekly, by mail, at avg. price, for $10 +15¢/sh.

Company:	**TAG Heuer International SA**	Safekeeping:	Yes
		Invests:	Every 7 days beginning Thurs.
Symbol:	THW	Minimum:	$50
Exchange:	NYSE	Maximum:	$100,000/year
Industry:	Watch mfr.	Min to qualify:	1
Company Address:	c/o Morgan Guaranty Trust,	Fee on cash inv.:	$5 + 12¢/sh.
	Box 9073	Fee on div. inv.:	5% to $2.50
	Boston, MA 02205-9948	Discount (cash):	0
Company Phone:	800-428-4237	Discount (div.):	0
Transfer Agent:	Morgan Guaranty Trust Co.	Auto invest:	Yes
Agent's Address:	P.O. Box 9073	Auto invest fee:	$5
	Boston, MA 02205-9948	Selling info:	Sells daily, by phone or mail, at avg. price, for $5 +12¢/sh.
Agent's Phone:	800-428-4237		
Other than USA:	Yes		

Company:	**Taiwan Fund (The)**	Safekeeping:	No
Symbol:	TWN	Invests:	Every 180 days beginning 2/15
Exchange:	NYSE	Minimum:	$100
Industry:	Closed-end fund	Maximum:	$3,000/semiannually
Company Address:	The Taiwan Fund, 225 Franklin St.	Min to qualify:	1
	Boston, MA 02266-8200	Fee on cash inv.:	75¢ + comm.
Company Phone:	800-636-3242	Fee on div. inv.:	0!
Transfer Agent:	State Street Bank (EquiServe)	Discount (cash):	0
Agent's Address:	P.O. Box 8200	Discount (div.):	5%
	Boston, MA 02266	Auto invest:	No
Agent's Phone:	800-426-5523	Auto invest fee:	$0
Other than USA:	Yes	Selling info:	Sells daily, by mail, at market, for $2.50 +15¢/sh.

Company:	**Tandy Corp.**	Safekeeping:	Yes
Symbol:	TAN	Invests:	Every 15 days beginning 1/10
Exchange:	NYSE	Minimum:	$50
Industry:	Retails consumer electr. & computers	Maximum:	$150,000/year
		Min to qualify:	1
Company Address:	100 Throckmorton St., Ste.1800,	Fee on cash inv.:	$5 + 4¢/sh.
	Box 17180	Fee on div. inv.:	0
	Fort Worth, TX 76102	Discount (cash):	0
Company Phone:	817-415-3022 or 817-390-3700	Discount (div.):	0
Transfer Agent:	BankBoston (EquiServe)	Auto invest:	Yes
Agent's Address:	P.O. Box 8040	Auto invest fee:	$2.50 + 4¢/sh.
	Boston, MA 02266-8040	Selling info:	Sells daily, by mail, at market, for $15 +10¢/sh.
Agent's Phone:	888-218-4374		
Other than USA:	Yes		

Company:	**Tanger Factory Outlet Centers, Inc.**	
Symbol:	SKT	
Exchange:	NYSE	
Industry:	Outlet centers	
Company Address:	1400 W. Northwood St., Box 29168 Greensboro, NC 27429	
Company Phone:	336-274-1666	
Transfer Agent:	Boston Eq. (EquiServe)	
Agent's Address:	P.O. Box 644, MS 45-02-64 Boston, MA 02102	
Agent's Phone:	781-575-3170	
Other than USA:	No	

Safekeeping:	No
Invests:	Every 30 days beginning 1/15
Minimum:	$100
Maximum:	$25,000/quarter
Min to qualify:	1
Fee on cash inv.:	0!
Fee on div. inv.:	0!
Discount (cash):	0
Discount (div.):	0
Auto invest:	No
Auto invest fee:	$0
Selling info:	Sells within 6 bus. days, by mail, at market, for $5 + comm.

Company:	**Taubman Centers, Inc.**
Symbol:	TCO
Exchange:	NYSE
Industry:	Operates & develops shopping centers
Company Address:	200 East Long Lake Rd., Ste.300 Bloomfield Hills, MI 48303
Company Phone:	248-258-6800
Transfer Agent:	ChaseMellon Shareholder Services
Agent's Address:	P.O. Box 750 Pittsburgh, PA 15230
Agent's Phone:	888-877-2889
Other than USA:	Yes

Safekeeping:	Yes
Invests:	Every 7 days beginning varies
Minimum:	$25
Maximum:	$25,000/month
Min to qualify:	1
Fee on cash inv.:	$5 + 12¢/sh.
Fee on div. inv.:	0!
Discount (cash):	0
Discount (div.):	0
Auto invest:	Yes
Auto invest fee:	$5 + 12¢/sh.
Selling info:	Sells daily, by mail, at market, for $15 +12¢/sh.

Company:	**TCF Financial Corp.**
Symbol:	TCB
Exchange:	NYSE
Industry:	Banking
Company Address:	801 Marquette Ave., MC 140-02-C Minneapolis, MN 55402-9002
Company Phone:	612-745-2760 or 612-745-2758
Transfer Agent:	BankBoston (EquiServe)
Agent's Address:	P.O. Box 8040, DRP Unit Boston, MA 02266-8040
Agent's Phone:	800-730-4001
Other than USA:	Yes

Safekeeping:	Yes
Invests:	Every 30 days beginning 1/31
Minimum:	$25
Maximum:	$5,000/quarter
Min to qualify:	1
Fee on cash inv.:	$1
Fee on div. inv.:	0!
Discount (cash):	0
Discount (div.):	0
Auto invest:	No
Auto invest fee:	$0
Selling info:	Sells within 10 days, by mail, at market, for $15

Company:	**TDK Corp.**
Symbol:	TDK
Exchange:	NYSE
Industry:	Ferrite, ceramic, & magnetic tapes
Company Address:	12 Harbor Park Dr. Port Washington, NY 11050
Company Phone:	516-625-0100
Transfer Agent:	Morgan Guaranty Trust Co.
Agent's Address:	P.O. Box 9073 Boston, MA 02205-9948
Agent's Phone:	800-428-4237
Other than USA:	No

Safekeeping:	Yes
Invests:	Every 7 days beginning varies
Minimum:	$50
Maximum:	$100,000/year
Min to qualify:	1
Fee on cash inv.:	$5 + 12¢/sh.
Fee on div. inv.:	5% to $2.50
Discount (cash):	0
Discount (div.):	0
Auto invest:	Yes
Auto invest fee:	$0
Selling info:	Sells daily, by phone or mail, at avg. price, for $5 +12¢/sh.

Company:	**Technitrol Inc.**	Safekeeping:	Yes
Symbol:	TNL	Invests:	Every 90 days beginning 2/2
Exchange:	NYSE	Minimum:	$50
Industry:	Electronic, mechanical products	Maximum:	$5,000/quarter
Company Address:	1210 Northbrook Dr., Ste.385	Min to qualify:	10
	Trevose, PA 19053	Fee on cash inv.:	0
Company Phone:	215-355-2900	Fee on div. inv.:	0
Transfer Agent:	Registrar & Transfer Co.	Discount (cash):	0
Agent's Address:	10 Commerce Drive	Discount (div.):	0
	Cranford, NJ 07016	Auto invest:	No
Agent's Phone:	800-368-5948	Auto invest fee:	$0
Other than USA:	Yes	Selling info:	Not available

Company:	**TECO Energy**	Safekeeping:	Yes
Symbol:	TE	Invests:	Every 30 days beginning 1/15
Exchange:	NYSE	Minimum:	$25
Industry:	Utility-electric, metals & mining	Maximum:	$100,000/year
Company Address:	702 N. Franklin St., Box 111	Min to qualify:	1
	Tampa, FL 33601-0111	Fee on cash inv.:	0!
Company Phone:	800-810-2032 or 813-228-4111	Fee on div. inv.:	0!
Transfer Agent:	Boston Eq. (EquiServe)	Discount (cash):	0
Agent's Address:	P.O. Box 8040	Discount (div.):	0
	Boston, MA 02266-8040	Auto invest:	No
Agent's Phone:	800-650-9222	Auto invest fee:	$0
Other than USA:	Yes	Selling info:	Sells within 10 bus. days, by mail, at market, for comm.

Company:	**Tektronix**	Safekeeping:	Yes
Symbol:	TEK	Invests:	Every 7 days beginning varies
Exchange:	NYSE	Minimum:	$100
Industry:	Electronic instruments & controls	Maximum:	$10,000/month
Company Address:	26600 S.W. Pkwy., Box 1000	Min to qualify:	20
	Wilsonville, OR 97070-1000	Fee on cash inv.:	$5 + 10¢/sh.
Company Phone:	503-682-3411 or 503-685-4113	Fee on div. inv.:	5% to $10 + 12¢/sh.
Transfer Agent:	ChaseMellon Shareholder Services	Discount (cash):	0
Agent's Address:	P.O. Box 3338	Discount (div.):	0
	South Hackensack, NJ 07606-1938	Auto invest:	Yes
Agent's Phone:	800-411-7025	Auto invest fee:	$5 +12/sh.
Other than USA:	Yes	Selling info:	Sells daily, by mail, at market, for $15 +12¢/sh.

Company:	**Tele Celular Sul Participacoes SA**	Safekeeping:	Yes
		Invests:	Every 7 days beginning varies
Symbol:	TSU	Minimum:	$50
Exchange:	NYSE	Maximum:	$250,000/year
Industry:	Telecommunications	Min to qualify:	1
Company Address:	c/o BNY,101 Barclay St.,22 West	Fee on cash inv.:	$5 + 10¢/sh.
	New York, NY 10286	Fee on div. inv.:	5% to $5 + 10¢/sh.
Company Phone:	800-943-9715	Discount (cash):	0
Transfer Agent:	Bank of New York	Discount (div.):	0
Agent's Address:	P.O. Box 11258	Auto invest:	Yes
	New York, NY 10286	Auto invest fee:	$5 + 10¢/sh.
Agent's Phone:	888-269-2377	Selling info:	Sells weekly, by mail, at market, for $5 +10¢/sh.
Other than USA:	Yes		

Company:	**Tele Centro Oeste Celular Participacoes SA**	Safekeeping:	Yes
		Invests:	Every 7 days beginning varies
Symbol:	TRO	Minimum:	$50
Exchange:	NYSE	Maximum:	$250,000/year
Industry:	Telecommunications	Min to qualify:	1
Company Address:	c/o BNY,101 Barclay St.,22 West	Fee on cash inv.:	$5 + 10¢/sh.
	New York, NY 10286	Fee on div. inv.:	5% to $5 + 10¢/sh.
Company Phone:	800-943-9715	Discount (cash):	0
Transfer Agent:	Bank of New York	Discount (div.):	0
Agent's Address:	P.O. Box 11258	Auto invest:	Yes
	New York, NY 10286	Auto invest fee:	$5 + 10¢/sh.
Agent's Phone:	888-269-2377	Selling info:	Sells weekly, by mail, at market,
Other than USA:	Yes		for $5 +10¢/sh.

Company:	**Tele Leste Celular Participacoes SA**	Safekeeping:	Yes
		Invests:	Every 7 days beginning varies
Symbol:	TBE	Minimum:	$50
Exchange:	NYSE	Maximum:	$250,000/year
Industry:	Telecommunications	Min to qualify:	1
Company Address:	c/o BNY,101 Barclay St.,22 West	Fee on cash inv.:	$5 + 10¢/sh.
	New York, NY 10286	Fee on div. inv.:	5% to $5 + 10¢/sh.
Company Phone:	800-943-9715	Discount (cash):	0
Transfer Agent:	Bank of New York	Discount (div.):	0
Agent's Address:	P.O. Box 11258	Auto invest:	Yes
	New York, NY 10286	Auto invest fee:	$5 + 10¢/sh.
Agent's Phone:	888-269-2377	Selling info:	Sells weekly, by mail, at market,
Other than USA:	Yes		for $5 +10¢/sh.

Company:	**Tele Nordesto Celular Participacoes SA**	Safekeeping:	Yes
		Invests:	Every 7 days beginning varies
Symbol:	TND	Minimum:	$50
Exchange:	NYSE	Maximum:	$250,000/year
Industry:	Telecommunications	Min to qualify:	1
Company Address:	c/o BNY,101 Barclay St.,22 West	Fee on cash inv.:	$5 + 10¢/sh.
	New York, NY 10286	Fee on div. inv.:	5% to $5 + 10¢/sh.
Company Phone:	800-943-9715	Discount (cash):	0
Transfer Agent:	Bank of New York	Discount (div.):	0
Agent's Address:	P.O. Box 11258	Auto invest:	Yes
	New York, NY 10286	Auto invest fee:	$5 + 10¢/sh.
Agent's Phone:	888-269-2377	Selling info:	Sells weekly, by mail, at market,
Other than USA:	Yes		for $5 +10¢/sh.

Company:	**Tele Norte Celular Participacoes SA**	Safekeeping:	Yes
		Invests:	Every 7 days beginning varies
Symbol:	TCN	Minimum:	$50
Exchange:	NYSE	Maximum:	$250,000/year
Industry:	Telecommunications	Min to qualify:	1
Company Address:	c/o BNY,101 Barclay St.,22 West	Fee on cash inv.:	$5 + 10¢/sh.
	New York, NY 10286	Fee on div. inv.:	5% to $5 + 10¢/sh.
Company Phone:	800-943-9715	Discount (cash):	0
Transfer Agent:	Bank of New York	Discount (div.):	0
Agent's Address:	P.O. Box 11258	Auto invest:	Yes
	New York, NY 10286	Auto invest fee:	$5 + 10¢/sh.
Agent's Phone:	888-269-2377	Selling info:	Sells weekly, by mail, at market,
Other than USA:	Yes		for $5 +10¢/sh.

Company:	**Tele Norte Leste Participacoes SA**	Safekeeping:	Yes
		Invests:	Every 7 days beginning varies
Symbol:	TNE	Minimum:	$50
Exchange:	NYSE	Maximum:	$250,000/year
Industry:	Telecommunications	Min to qualify:	1
Company Address:	c/o BNY,101 Barclay St.,22 West New York, NY 10286	Fee on cash inv.:	$5 + 10¢/sh.
		Fee on div. inv.:	5% to $5 + 10¢/sh.
Company Phone:	800-943-9715	Discount (cash):	0
Transfer Agent:	Bank of New York	Discount (div.):	0
Agent's Address:	P.O. Box 11258 New York, NY 10286	Auto invest:	Yes
		Auto invest fee:	$5 + 10¢/sh.
Agent's Phone:	888-269-2377	Selling info:	Sells weekly, by mail, at market, for $5 +10¢/sh.
Other than USA:	Yes		

Company:	**Tele Sudeste Celular Participacoes SA**	Safekeeping:	Yes
		Invests:	Every 7 days beginning varies
Symbol:	TSD	Minimum:	$50
Exchange:	NYSE	Maximum:	$250,000/year
Industry:	Telecommunications	Min to qualify:	1
Company Address:	c/o BNY,101 Barclay St.,22 West New York, NY 10286	Fee on cash inv.:	$5 + 10¢/sh.
		Fee on div. inv.:	5% to $5 + 10¢/sh.
Company Phone:	800-943-9715	Discount (cash):	0
Transfer Agent:	Bank of New York	Discount (div.):	0
Agent's Address:	P.O. Box 11258 New York, NY 10286	Auto invest:	Yes
		Auto invest fee:	$5 + 10¢/sh.
Agent's Phone:	888-269-2377	Selling info:	Sells weekly, by mail, at market, for $5 +10¢/sh.
Other than USA:	Yes		

Company:	**Telebras**	Safekeeping:	Yes
Symbol:	TBR	Invests:	Every 7 days beginning varies
Exchange:	NYSE	Minimum:	$50
Industry:	Communications services	Maximum:	$250,000/year
Company Address:	c/o BNY,101 Barclay St.,22 West New York, NY 10286	Min to qualify:	1
		Fee on cash inv.:	$5 + 10¢/sh.
Company Phone:	800-943-9715	Fee on div. inv.:	0
Transfer Agent:	Bank of New York	Discount (cash):	0
Agent's Address:	P.O. Box 11258 New York, NY 10286	Discount (div.):	0
		Auto invest:	Yes
Agent's Phone:	888-269-2377	Auto invest fee:	$5 + 10¢/sh.
Other than USA:	Yes	Selling info:	Sells weekly, by mail, at market, for $5 +10¢/sh.

Company:	**Telebras HOLDRS**	Safekeeping:	Yes
Symbol:	TBH	Invests:	Every 7 days beginning varies
Exchange:	NYSE	Minimum:	$50
Industry:	Telecommunications	Maximum:	$250,000/year
Company Address:	c/o BNY,101 Barclay St.,22 West New York, NY 10286	Min to qualify:	1
		Fee on cash inv.:	$5 + 10¢/sh.
Company Phone:	800-943-9715	Fee on div. inv.:	5% to $5 + 10¢/sh.
Transfer Agent:	Bank of New York	Discount (cash):	0
Agent's Address:	P.O. Box 11258 New York, NY 10286	Discount (div.):	0
		Auto invest:	Yes
Agent's Phone:	888-269-2377	Auto invest fee:	$5 + 10¢/sh.
Other than USA:	Yes	Selling info:	Sells weekly, by mail, at market, for $5 +10¢/sh.

Company:	**Telecom Argentina Stet-France Telecom SA**	**Safekeeping:**	Yes
		Invests:	Every 7 days beginning varies
Symbol:	TEO	**Minimum:**	$50
Exchange:	NYSE	**Maximum:**	$100,000/year
Industry:	Telecommunications	**Min to qualify:**	1
Company Address:	c/o Morgan Guaranty Trust, Box 9073	**Fee on cash inv.:**	$5 + 12¢/sh.
		Fee on div. inv.:	5% to $2.50
	Boston, MA 02205-9948	**Discount (cash):**	0
Company Phone:	800-428-4237	**Discount (div.):**	0
Transfer Agent:	Morgan Guaranty Trust Co.	**Auto invest:**	Yes
Agent's Address:	P.O. Box 9073	**Auto invest fee:**	$5
	Boston, MA 02205-9948	**Selling info:**	Sells daily, by phone or mail, at avg. price, for $5 +12¢/sh.
Agent's Phone:	800-428-4237		
Other than USA:	No		

Company:	**Telecom Corp. of New Zealand Ltd.**	**Safekeeping:**	Yes
		Invests:	Every 7 days beginning varies
Symbol:	NZT	**Minimum:**	$50
Exchange:	NYSE	**Maximum:**	$250,000/year
Industry:	Communications services	**Min to qualify:**	1
Company Address:	c/o BNY,101 Barclay St.,22 West	**Fee on cash inv.:**	$5 + 10¢/sh.
	New York, NY 10286	**Fee on div. inv.:**	5% to $5 + 10¢/sh.
Company Phone:	800-943-9715	**Discount (cash):**	0
Transfer Agent:	Bank of New York	**Discount (div.):**	0
Agent's Address:	P.O. Box 11258	**Auto invest:**	Yes
	New York, NY 10286	**Auto invest fee:**	$5 + 10¢/sh.
Agent's Phone:	888-269-2377	**Selling info:**	Sells weekly, by mail, at market, for $5 +10¢/sh.
Other than USA:	Yes		

Company:	**Telecom Italia SpA**	**Safekeeping:**	Yes
Symbol:	TI	**Invests:**	Every 7 days beginning varies
Exchange:	NYSE	**Minimum:**	$50
Industry:	Communications services	**Maximum:**	$100,000/year
Company Address:	c/o Morgan Guaranty Trust,Box 9073	**Min to qualify:**	1
		Fee on cash inv.:	$5 + 12¢/sh.
	Boston, MA 02205-9948	**Fee on div. inv.:**	5% to $2.50
Company Phone:	800-428-4237	**Discount (cash):**	0
Transfer Agent:	Morgan Guaranty Trust Co.	**Discount (div.):**	0
Agent's Address:	P.O. Box 9073	**Auto invest:**	Yes
	Boston, MA 02205-9948	**Auto invest fee:**	$5 + 12¢/sh.
Agent's Phone:	800-428-4237	**Selling info:**	Sells daily, by mail or phone, at avg. price, for $5 +12¢/sh.
Other than USA:	No		

Company:	**Teleflex Incorporated**	**Safekeeping:**	Yes
Symbol:	TFX	**Invests:**	Every 30 days beginning 1/15
Exchange:	NYSE	**Minimum:**	$50
Industry:	Electronic instruments & controls	**Maximum:**	$2,500/month
Company Address:	630 West Germantown Pike, Ste.450	**Min to qualify:**	10
		Fee on cash inv.:	0!
	Plymouth Meeting, PA 19462	**Fee on div. inv.:**	0!
Company Phone:	610-834-6301	**Discount (cash):**	0
Transfer Agent:	American Stock Transfer & Trust	**Discount (div.):**	0
Agent's Address:	40 Wall St., 46th Floor	**Auto invest:**	No
	New York, NY 10005	**Auto invest fee:**	$0
Agent's Phone:	800-278-4353 or 718-921-8283	**Selling info:**	Sells within 7 bus. days, by mail, at market, for $15 + comm.
Other than USA:	Yes		

Company:	**Telefonica del Peru SA**	Safekeeping:	Yes
Symbol:	TDP	Invests:	Every 7 days beginning varies
Exchange:	NYSE	Minimum:	$50
Industry:	Telecommunications	Maximum:	$100,000/year
Company Address:	c/o Morgan Guaranty Trust,	Min to qualify:	1
	Box 9073	Fee on cash inv.:	$5 + 12¢/sh.
	Boston, MA 02205-9948	Fee on div. inv.:	5% to $2.50
Company Phone:	800-428-4237	Discount (cash):	0
Transfer Agent:	Morgan Guaranty Trust Co.	Discount (div.):	0
Agent's Address:	P.O. Box 9073	Auto invest:	Yes
	Boston, MA 02205-9948	Auto invest fee:	$5
Agent's Phone:	800-428-4237	Selling info:	Sells daily, by phone or mail, at
Other than USA:	No		avg. price, for $5 +12¢/sh.

Company:	**Telefonos de Mexico, SA de C.V.**	Safekeeping:	Yes
		Invests:	Every 7 days beginning varies
Symbol:	TMX	Minimum:	$50
Exchange:	NYSE	Maximum:	$100,000/year
Industry:	Telecommunications	Min to qualify:	1
Company Address:	c/o Morgan Guaranty Trust,	Fee on cash inv.:	$5 + 12¢/sh.
	Box 9073	Fee on div. inv.:	5% to $2.50
	Boston, MA 02205-9948	Discount (cash):	0
Company Phone:	800-428-4237	Discount (div.):	0
Transfer Agent:	Morgan Guaranty Trust Co.	Auto invest:	Yes
Agent's Address:	P.O. Box 9073	Auto invest fee:	$0
	Boston, MA 02205-9948	Selling info:	Sells daily, by phone or mail, at
Agent's Phone:	800-428-4237		avg. price, for $5 +12¢/sh.
Other than USA:	No		

Company:	**Telemig Celular Participacoes SA**	Safekeeping:	Yes
		Invests:	Every 7 days beginning varies
Symbol:	TMB	Minimum:	$50
Exchange:	NYSE	Maximum:	$250,000/year
Industry:	Telecommunications	Min to qualify:	1
Company Address:	c/o BNY,101 Barclay St.,22 West	Fee on cash inv.:	$5 + 10¢/sh.
	New York, NY 10286	Fee on div. inv.:	5% to $5 + 10¢/sh.
Company Phone:	800-943-9715	Discount (cash):	0
Transfer Agent:	Bank of New York	Discount (div.):	0
Agent's Address:	P.O. Box 11258	Auto invest:	Yes
	New York, NY 10286	Auto invest fee:	$5 + 10¢/sh.
Agent's Phone:	888-269-2377	Selling info:	Sells weekly, by mail, at market,
Other than USA:	Yes		for $5 +10¢/sh.

Company:	**Telephone & Data Systems**	Safekeeping:	Yes
		Invests:	Every 30 days beginning 1/1
Symbol:	TDS	Minimum:	$10
Exchange:	ASE	Maximum:	$5,000/quarter
Industry:	Telecommunications	Min to qualify:	10
Company Address:	30 North LaSalle St., Ste. 4000	Fee on cash inv.:	0!
	Chicago, IL 60602-2507	Fee on div. inv.:	0!
Company Phone:	312-630-1900	Discount (cash):	0
Transfer Agent:	Harris Trust & Savings Bank	Discount (div.):	5%
Agent's Address:	P.O. Box A3309	Auto invest:	No
	Chicago, IL 60690	Auto invest fee:	$0
Agent's Phone:	312-360-5337	Selling info:	Not available
Other than USA:	Yes		

Company:	**Telesp Celular Participacoes SA**	Safekeeping:	Yes
Symbol:	TCP	Invests:	Every 7 days beginning varies
Exchange:	NYSE	Minimum:	$50
Industry:	Telecommunications	Maximum:	$250,000/year
Company Address:	c/o BNY,101 Barclay St.,22 West New York, NY 10286	Min to qualify:	1
		Fee on cash inv.:	$5 + 10¢/sh.
Company Phone:	800-943-9715	Fee on div. inv.:	5% to $5 + 10¢/sh.
Transfer Agent:	Bank of New York	Discount (cash):	0
Agent's Address:	P.O. Box 11258 New York, NY 10286	Discount (div.):	0
		Auto invest:	Yes
Agent's Phone:	888-269-2377	Auto invest fee:	$5 + 10¢/sh.
Other than USA:	Yes	Selling info:	Sells weekly, by mail, at market, for $5 +10¢/sh.

Company:	**Telesp Participacoes SA**	Safekeeping:	Yes
Symbol:	TSP	Invests:	Every 7 days beginning varies
Exchange:	NYSE	Minimum:	$50
Industry:	Telecommunications	Maximum:	$250,000/year
Company Address:	c/o BNY,101 Barclay St.,22 West New York, NY 10286	Min to qualify:	1
		Fee on cash inv.:	$5 + 10¢/sh.
Company Phone:	800-943-9715	Fee on div. inv.:	5% to $5 + 10¢/sh.
Transfer Agent:	Bank of New York	Discount (cash):	0
Agent's Address:	P.O. Box 11258 New York, NY 10286	Discount (div.):	0
		Auto invest:	Yes
Agent's Phone:	888-269-2377	Auto invest fee:	$5 + 10¢/sh.
Other than USA:	Yes	Selling info:	Sells weekly, by mail, at market, for $5 +10¢/sh.

Company:	**Telstra Corp. Ltd.**	Safekeeping:	Yes
Symbol:	TLS	Invests:	Every 7 days beginning varies
Exchange:	NYSE	Minimum:	$50
Industry:	Communications services	Maximum:	$250,000/year
Company Address:	c/o BNY,101 Barclay St.,22 West New York, NY 10286	Min to qualify:	1
		Fee on cash inv.:	$5 + 10¢/sh.
Company Phone:	800-943-9715	Fee on div. inv.:	0
Transfer Agent:	Bank of New York	Discount (cash):	0
Agent's Address:	P.O. Box 11258 New York, NY 10286	Discount (div.):	0
		Auto invest:	Yes
Agent's Phone:	888-269-2377	Auto invest fee:	$5 + 10¢/sh.
Other than USA:	Yes	Selling info:	Sells weekly, by mail, at market, for $5 +10¢/sh.

Company:	**TELUS Corp.**	Safekeeping:	Yes
Symbol:	TTO	Invests:	Every 30 days beginning 1/16
Exchange:	TSE	Minimum:	$100
Industry:	Telecommunications	Maximum:	$20,000/year Cdn.
Company Address:	10020-100th St., 30th Fl. Edmonton, Alberta T5J 0N5 Canada	Min to qualify:	1
		Fee on cash inv.:	0
		Fee on div. inv.:	0
Company Phone:	800-667-4871	Discount (cash):	0
Transfer Agent:	Montreal Trust Co.	Discount (div.):	0
Agent's Address:	600, 530 8 Ave. SW Calgary, Alta T2P 3S8 Canada	Auto invest:	No
		Auto invest fee:	$0
Agent's Phone:	800-558-0046	Selling info:	Sells irregularly, by mail or fax, at market, for $7.50 + 4¢/sh.
Other than USA:	Yes		

Company:	**Temple-Inland**
Symbol:	TIN
Exchange:	NYSE
Industry:	Containers, paper, fin'l svcs.
Company Address:	Drawer N
	Diboll, TX 75941
Company Phone:	409-829-1313
Transfer Agent:	FCT (EquiServe)
Agent's Address:	P.O. Box 13531
	Newark, NJ 07188-0001
Agent's Phone:	800-446-2617 or 201-324-1225
Other than USA:	No

Safekeeping:	Yes
Invests:	Every 90 days beginning 3/15
Minimum:	$25
Maximum:	$1,000/quarter
Min to qualify:	1
Fee on cash inv.:	0!
Fee on div. inv.:	0!
Discount (cash):	0
Discount (div.):	0
Auto invest:	No
Auto invest fee:	$0
Selling info:	Sells daily, by phone, mail, or fax, at market, for $10 +10¢/sh.

Company:	**Tennant Co.**
Symbol:	TANT
Exchange:	OTC
Industry:	Floor maintenance equipment
Company Address:	701 N. Lilac Dr.
	Minneapolis, MN 55440
Company Phone:	612-540-1341 or 612-540-1200
Transfer Agent:	Norwest Bank Minnesota
Agent's Address:	P.O. Box 64854
	St. Paul, MN 55164-0854
Agent's Phone:	800-468-9716
Other than USA:	Yes

Safekeeping:	Yes
Invests:	Every 90 days beginning 3/15
Minimum:	$50
Maximum:	$5,000/quarter
Min to qualify:	1
Fee on cash inv.:	0
Fee on div. inv.:	0
Discount (cash):	0
Discount (div.):	0
Auto invest:	No
Auto invest fee:	$0
Selling info:	Sells daily, by phone or mail, at market, for $5 +15¢/sh.

Company:	**Tenneco Inc.**
Symbol:	TEN
Exchange:	NYSE
Industry:	Packaging & automotive parts
Company Address:	1275 King St.
	Greenwich, CT 06831-2946
Company Phone:	203-863-1175 or 203-863-1000
Transfer Agent:	FCT (EquiServe)
Agent's Address:	P.O. Box 2598
	Jersey City, NJ 07303-2598
Agent's Phone:	800-649-9891 or 800-519-3111
Other than USA:	Yes

Safekeeping:	Yes
Invests:	Every 7 days beginning Thurs.
Minimum:	$50
Maximum:	$250,000/year
Min to qualify:	1
Fee on cash inv.:	$5 + 10¢/sh.
Fee on div. inv.:	$1 to $3 + 10¢/sh.
Discount (cash):	0
Discount (div.):	0
Auto invest:	Yes
Auto invest fee:	$2 + 10¢/sh.
Selling info:	Sells daily, by mail, phone, fax, at market, for $15 +12¢/sh.

Company:	**Texaco Inc.**
Symbol:	TX
Exchange:	NYSE
Industry:	Fully integrated oil company
Company Address:	2000 Westchester Ave.
	White Plains, NY 10650-0001
Company Phone:	800-283-9785
Transfer Agent:	Texaco Inc.
Agent's Address:	2000 Westchester Ave., Investor Services
	White Plains, NY 10650-0001
Agent's Phone:	800-283-9785
Other than USA:	Yes

Safekeeping:	Yes
Invests:	Every 3x/month days beginning varies
Minimum:	$50
Maximum:	$120,000/year
Min to qualify:	1
Fee on cash inv.:	4¢/sh.
Fee on div. inv.:	4¢/sh
Discount (cash):	0
Discount (div.):	0
Auto invest:	Yes
Auto invest fee:	$0
Selling info:	Sells biweekly, by mail or fax, at market, for 4¢/sh.

Company:	**Textron, Inc.**	Safekeeping:	Yes
Symbol:	TXT	Invests:	Every 30 days beginning 1/1
Exchange:	NYSE	Minimum:	$25
Industry:	Aerospace, diversified	Maximum:	$120,000/year
	manufacturer	Min to qualify:	1
Company Address:	40 Westminster St.	Fee on cash inv.:	0!
	Providence, RI 02903	Fee on div. inv.:	0!
Company Phone:	401-421-2800 or 401-457-2353	Discount (cash):	0
Transfer Agent:	FCT (EquiServe)	Discount (div.):	0
Agent's Address:	P.O. Box 2500	Auto invest:	Yes
	Jersey City, NJ 07303-2500	Auto invest fee:	$1
Agent's Phone:	800-519-3111	Selling info:	Sells daily, by phone or mail, at
Other than USA:	Yes		market, for $10 +12¢/sh.

Company:	**Thai Fund**	Safekeeping:	No
Symbol:	TTF	Invests:	Every 180 days beginning 2/15
Exchange:	NYSE	Minimum:	$100
Industry:	Closed-end fund	Maximum:	$3,000/semiannually
Company Address:	c/o Boston EquiServe, Box 1681	Min to qualify:	1
	Boston, MA 02105-1681	Fee on cash inv.:	comm.
Company Phone:	800-730-6001	Fee on div. inv.:	comm.
Transfer Agent:	Boston Eq. (EquiServe)	Discount (cash):	0
Agent's Address:	P.O. Box 8040	Discount (div.):	0
	Boston, MA 02266	Auto invest:	No
Agent's Phone:	800-730-6001	Auto invest fee:	$0
Other than USA:	No	Selling info:	Sells bimonthly, by mail,
			at market, for $0

Company:	**Thistle Group Holdings, Co.**	Safekeeping:	Yes
		Invests:	Every 90 days beginning 1/13
Symbol:	THTL	Minimum:	$100
Exchange:	OTC	Maximum:	$1,000/quarter
Industry:	Unitary thrift holding company	Min to qualify:	100
Company Address:	6060 Ridge Ave.	Fee on cash inv.:	0
	Philadelphia, PA 19128	Fee on div. inv.:	0
Company Phone:	215-483-2800x212	Discount (cash):	0
Transfer Agent:	Registrar & Transfer	Discount (div.):	0
Agent's Address:	10 Commerce Drive	Auto invest:	No
	Cranford, NJ 07016	Auto invest fee:	$0
Agent's Phone:	800-368-5948	Selling info:	Not available
Other than USA:	Yes		

Company:	**Thomas & Betts Corp.**	Safekeeping:	Yes
Symbol:	TNB	Invests:	Every 30 days beginning 1/1
Exchange:	NYSE	Minimum:	$10
Industry:	Electrical electronics	Maximum:	$24,000/year
Company Address:	8155 T&B Blvd.	Min to qualify:	1
	Memphis, TN 38125	Fee on cash inv.:	0!
Company Phone:	901-252-8943 or 901-252-8000	Fee on div. inv.:	0!
Transfer Agent:	FCT (EquiServe)	Discount (cash):	0
Agent's Address:	P.O. Box 2598	Discount (div.):	0
	Jersey City, NJ 07303-2598	Auto invest:	No
Agent's Phone:	800-446-2617	Auto invest fee:	$0
Other than USA:	Yes	Selling info:	Sells daily, by phone, mail, or fax,
			at market, for $5 +12¢/sh.

Company:	**Thomas Industries**	
Symbol:	TII	
Exchange:	NYSE	
Industry:	Mfr. compressors & vacuum pumps	
Company Address:	Box 35120, 4360 Brownsboro Rd., #300 Louisville, KY 40232-5120	
Company Phone:	502-893-4600	
Transfer Agent:	Fifth Third Bank	
Agent's Address:	38 Fountain Sq. Plaza, MD 1090FS Cincinnatii, OH 45263	
Agent's Phone:	800-837-2755	
Other than USA:	Yes	

Safekeeping:	Yes
Invests:	Every 30 days beginning 1/1
Minimum:	$25
Maximum:	$3,000/month
Min to qualify:	1
Fee on cash inv.:	0!
Fee on div. inv.:	0!
Discount (cash):	0
Discount (div.):	0
Auto invest:	No
Auto invest fee:	$0
Selling info:	Sells daily, by mail, at market, for comm.

Company:	**Thorn plc**
Symbol:	THRNY
Exchange:	NYSE
Industry:	Media & publishing
Company Address:	c/o Morgan Guaranty Trust, Box 9073 Boston, MA 02205-9948
Company Phone:	800-428-4237
Transfer Agent:	Morgan Guaranty Trust Co.
Agent's Address:	P.O. Box 9073 Boston, MA 02205-9948
Agent's Phone:	800-428-4237
Other than USA:	No

Safekeeping:	Yes
Invests:	Every 7 days beginning varies
Minimum:	$50
Maximum:	$100,000/year
Min to qualify:	1
Fee on cash inv.:	$5 + 12¢/sh.
Fee on div. inv.:	5% to $2.50
Discount (cash):	0
Discount (div.):	0
Auto invest:	Yes
Auto invest fee:	$5
Selling info:	Sells daily, by phone or mail, at avg. price, for $5 +12¢/sh.

Company:	**Thornburg Mortgage Asset**
Symbol:	TMA
Exchange:	NYSE
Industry:	REIT
Company Address:	119 East Marcy St. Santa Fe, NM 87501
Company Phone:	505-989-1900
Transfer Agent:	Continental Stock Transfer & Trust
Agent's Address:	2 Broadway, 19th Fl. New York, NY 10004
Agent's Phone:	800-509-5586 x525
Other than USA:	Yes

Safekeeping:	Yes
Invests:	Every 30 days beginning 1/15
Minimum:	$100
Maximum:	$5,000/month
Min to qualify:	1
Fee on cash inv.:	0!
Fee on div. inv.:	0!
Discount (cash):	0-5%
Discount (div.):	0-5%
Auto invest:	No
Auto invest fee:	$0
Selling info:	Not available

Company:	**Tidewater Inc.**
Symbol:	TDW
Exchange:	NYSE
Industry:	Offshore oil & gas services
Company Address:	601 Poydras St., Ste. 1900 New Orleans, LA 70130
Company Phone:	504-568-1010
Transfer Agent:	Boston Eq. (EquiServe)
Agent's Address:	P.O. Box 8040 Boston, MA 02266
Agent's Phone:	781-575-3170
Other than USA:	Yes

Safekeeping:	Yes
Invests:	Every 45 days beginning 2/3
Minimum:	$25
Maximum:	$5,000/quarter
Min to qualify:	1
Fee on cash inv.:	5% to $2.50 + comm.
Fee on div. inv.:	5% to $2.50 + comm.
Discount (cash):	0
Discount (div.):	0
Auto invest:	No
Auto invest fee:	$0
Selling info:	Sells daily, by mail, at market, for 5% to $5 +15¢/sh.

Timber Co. (The)

Company:	Timber Co. (The)
Symbol:	TGP
Exchange:	NYSE
Industry:	Timber, wood fiber
Company Address:	133 Peachtree St. N.E., Box 105605 Atlanta, GA 30348
Company Phone:	404-586-0275
Transfer Agent:	FCT (EquiServe)
Agent's Address:	P.O. Box 2500 Jersey City, NJ 07303
Agent's Phone:	800-519-3111
Other than USA:	Yes
Safekeeping:	Yes
Invests:	Every 30 days beginning 1/10
Minimum:	$25
Maximum:	$5,000/month
Min to qualify:	1
Fee on cash inv.:	5% to $3
Fee on div. inv.:	5% to $3
Discount (cash):	0
Discount (div.):	0
Auto invest:	Yes
Auto invest fee:	5% to $3 + $2
Selling info:	Sells daily, by phone, mail, or fax, at avg. price, for $10 +12¢/sh.

Time Warner Inc.

Company:	Time Warner Inc.
Symbol:	TWX
Exchange:	NYSE
Industry:	Communications
Company Address:	75 Rockefeller Plaza New York, NY 10019
Company Phone:	212-484-6971
Transfer Agent:	ChaseMellon Shareholder Services
Agent's Address:	P.O. Box 3338 South Hackensack, Nj 07606-1938
Agent's Phone:	800-279-1238
Other than USA:	No
Safekeeping:	Yes
Invests:	Every 30 days beginning 1/10
Minimum:	$25
Maximum:	$10,000/quarter
Min to qualify:	1
Fee on cash inv.:	0
Fee on div. inv.:	0
Discount (cash):	0
Discount (div.):	5%
Auto invest:	No
Auto invest fee:	$0
Selling info:	Sells weekly, by mail or phone, at market, for $5 + comm.

Times Mirror Co. (The)

Company:	Times Mirror Co. (The)
Symbol:	TMC
Exchange:	NYSE
Industry:	Communications
Company Address:	Times Mirror Sq. Los Angeles, CA 90053
Company Phone:	213-237-3700 or 213-237-3955
Transfer Agent:	Harris Trust & Savings Bank
Agent's Address:	P.O. Box A3309 Chicago, IL 60890
Agent's Phone:	800-929-6781
Other than USA:	No
Safekeeping:	Yes
Invests:	Every 90 days beginning 3/9
Minimum:	$100
Maximum:	$10,000/quarter
Min to qualify:	1
Fee on cash inv.:	0!
Fee on div. inv.:	0!
Discount (cash):	0
Discount (div.):	0
Auto invest:	No
Auto invest fee:	$0
Selling info:	Not available

Timken Co.

Company:	Timken Co.
Symbol:	TKR
Exchange:	NYSE
Industry:	Industrial products, bearings, alloy steels
Company Address:	Box 6928, GNE-04 Canton, OH 44706-0928
Company Phone:	330-471-3832 or 330-417-3378
Transfer Agent:	FCT (EquiServe)
Agent's Address:	P.O. Box 2598 Jersey City, NJ 07303-2598
Agent's Phone:	800-555-9898
Other than USA:	Yes
Safekeeping:	Yes
Invests:	Every 7 days beginning varies
Minimum:	$100
Maximum:	$250,000/year
Min to qualify:	1
Fee on cash inv.:	$3 + 10¢/sh.
Fee on div. inv.:	0!
Discount (cash):	0
Discount (div.):	0
Auto invest:	Yes
Auto invest fee:	$1
Selling info:	Sells weekly, by mail or phone, at market, for $15 +12¢/sh.

Company:	**TNP Enterprises**	Safekeeping:	Yes
Symbol:	TNP	Invests:	Every 30 days beginning 1/15
Exchange:	NYSE	Minimum:	$25
Industry:	Utility-electric	Maximum:	$100,000/year
Company Address:	4100 International Plaza	Min to qualify:	1
	Ft. Worth, TX 76109	Fee on cash inv.:	0
Company Phone:	800-435-2822 or 817-737-1316	Fee on div. inv.:	0
Transfer Agent:	Bank of New York	Discount (cash):	0
Agent's Address:	P.O. Box 1958	Discount (div.):	0
	Newark, NJ 07101	Auto invest:	No
Agent's Phone:	800-524-4458	Auto invest fee:	$0
Other than USA:	Yes	Selling info:	Sells weekly, by phone or mail, at avg. price, for $5 + 25¢/sh.

Company:	**Tomkins PLC**	Safekeeping:	Yes
Symbol:	TKS	Invests:	Every 7 days beginning varies
Exchange:	NYSE	Minimum:	$50
Industry:	Conglomerates	Maximum:	$250,000/year
Company Address:	c/o BNY,101 Barclay St.,22 West	Min to qualify:	1
	New York, NY 10286	Fee on cash inv.:	$5 + 10¢/sh.
Company Phone:	800-943-9715	Fee on div. inv.:	5% to $5 + 10¢/sh.
Transfer Agent:	Bank of New York	Discount (cash):	0
Agent's Address:	P.O. Box 11258	Discount (div.):	0
	New York, NY 10286	Auto invest:	Yes
Agent's Phone:	888-269-2377	Auto invest fee:	$5 + 10¢/sh.
Other than USA:	Yes	Selling info:	Sells weekly, by mail, at market, for $5 +10¢/sh.

Company:	**Torchmark Corp.**	Safekeeping:	Yes
Symbol:	TMK	Invests:	Every 45 days beginning 2/1
Exchange:	NYSE	Minimum:	$100
Industry:	Insurance & financial	Maximum:	$3,000/45 days
Company Address:	2001 Third Ave. South	Min to qualify:	1
	Birmingham, AL 35233-2186	Fee on cash inv.:	5% to $2.50 + 3¢/sh.
Company Phone:	205-325-2051 or 205-325-4200	Fee on div. inv.:	5% to $2.50 + 3¢/sh.
Transfer Agent:	FCT (EquiServe)	Discount (cash):	0
Agent's Address:	P.O. Box 2500	Discount (div.):	0
	Jersey City, NJ 07303	Auto invest:	No
Agent's Phone:	800-446-2617	Auto invest fee:	$0
Other than USA:	Yes	Selling info:	Sells daily, by mail, phone, or fax, at market, for $10 +12¢/sh.

Company:	**Toro Co. (The)**	Safekeeping:	Yes
Symbol:	TTC	Invests:	Every 30 days beginning 1/12
Exchange:	NYSE	Minimum:	$10
Industry:	Machinery	Maximum:	$1,000/month
Company Address:	8111 Lyndale Ave. South	Min to qualify:	1
	Bloomington, MN 55420-1196	Fee on cash inv.:	0
Company Phone:	612-888-8801 or 612-887-7141	Fee on div. inv.:	0
Transfer Agent:	Norwest Bank Minnesota, NA	Discount (cash):	0
Agent's Address:	P.O. Box 64854	Discount (div.):	0
	St. Paul, MN 55164-0854	Auto invest:	No
Agent's Phone:	800-468-9716	Auto invest fee:	$0
Other than USA:	Yes	Selling info:	Sells daily, by mail or fax, at market, for $3 +15¢/sh.

Company:	**TOTAL S.A.**	Safekeeping:	Yes
Symbol:	TOT	Invests:	Every 7 days beginning varies
Exchange:	NYSE	Minimum:	$50
Industry:	Oil & gas	Maximum:	$250,000/year
Company Address:	c/o BNY,101 Barclay St.,22 West	Min to qualify:	1
	New York, NY 10286	Fee on cash inv.:	$5 + 10¢/sh.
Company Phone:	800-943-9715	Fee on div. inv.:	5% to $5 + 10¢/sh.
Transfer Agent:	Bank of New York	Discount (cash):	0
Agent's Address:	P.O. Box 11258	Discount (div.):	0
	New York, NY 10286	Auto invest:	Yes
Agent's Phone:	888-269-2377	Auto invest fee:	$5 + 10¢/sh.
Other than USA:	Yes	Selling info:	Sells weekly, by mail, at market, for $5 +10¢/sh.

Company:	**Total System Services, Inc.**	Safekeeping:	Yes
		Invests:	Every 30 days beginning 1/31
Symbol:	TSS	Minimum:	$50
Exchange:	NYSE	Maximum:	$250,000/year
Industry:	Credit card data processing serv. for financial institutions	Min to qualify:	10
		Fee on cash inv.:	$2.50 + 8¢/sh.
Company Address:	Box 120	Fee on div. inv.:	0
	Columbus, GA 31902-0120	Discount (cash):	0
Company Phone:	706-649-5220	Discount (div.):	0
Transfer Agent:	State Street Bank (EquiServe)	Auto invest:	Yes
Agent's Address:	P.O. Box 8209	Auto invest fee:	$0
	Boston, MA 02266-8209	Selling info:	Sells weekly, by mail, at market, for $10 +15¢/sh.
Agent's Phone:	800-503-8903		
Other than USA:	Yes		

Company:	**Tran Rail Holdings Ltd.**	Safekeeping:	Yes
Symbol:	TNZRY	Invests:	Every 7 days beginning varies
Exchange:	OTC	Minimum:	$50
Industry:	Holding co.	Maximum:	$250,000/year
Company Address:	c/o BNY,101 Barclay St.,22 West	Min to qualify:	1
	New York, NY 10286	Fee on cash inv.:	$5 + 10¢/sh.
Company Phone:	800-943-9715	Fee on div. inv.:	5% to $5 + 10¢/sh.
Transfer Agent:	Bank of New York	Discount (cash):	0
Agent's Address:	P.O. Box 11258	Discount (div.):	0
	New York, NY 10286	Auto invest:	Yes
Agent's Phone:	888-269-2377	Auto invest fee:	$5 + 10¢/sh.
Other than USA:	Yes	Selling info:	Sells weekly, by mail, at market, for $5 +10¢/sh.

Company:	**Transalta Corp.**	Safekeeping:	No
Symbol:	TA	Invests:	Every 90 days beginning 1/1
Exchange:	TSE	Minimum:	$0
Industry:	Utility-electric	Maximum:	$5,000/quarter Cdn.
Company Address:	411 8th Ave. SW	Min to qualify:	1
	Calgary, Alta. T2K 4M3 Canada	Fee on cash inv.:	0
Company Phone:	800-387-0825 or 416-813-4600	Fee on div. inv.:	0
Transfer Agent:	CIBC Mellon Trust	Discount (cash):	0
Agent's Address:	393 University Ave., 5th Fl.	Discount (div.):	0
	Toronto, Ont. M5G 2M7 Canada	Auto invest:	No
Agent's Phone:	800-387-0825	Auto invest fee:	$0
Other than USA:	Yes	Selling info:	Not available

Company:	**Transamerica Corp.**	Safekeeping:	Yes
Symbol:	TA	Invests:	Every 30 days beginning 1/30
Exchange:	NYSE	Minimum:	$10
Industry:	Insurance & financial	Maximum:	$60,000/year
Company Address:	600 Montgomery St.	Min to qualify:	1
	San Francisco, CA 94111	Fee on cash inv.:	0!
Company Phone:	415-983-4000	Fee on div. inv.:	0!
Transfer Agent:	FCT (EquiServe)	Discount (cash):	0
Agent's Address:	P.O. Box 2598	Discount (div.):	0
	Jersey City, NJ 07303	Auto invest:	Yes
Agent's Phone:	800-756-8200	Auto invest fee:	$1
Other than USA:	Yes	Selling info:	Sells daily, by mail or phone, at market, for $10 +12¢/sh.

Company:	**TransCanada Pipelines Ltd.**	Safekeeping:	No
		Invests:	Every 90 days beginning 1/31
Symbol:	TRP	Minimum:	$35
Exchange:	NYSE	Maximum:	$7,000/quarter
Industry:	Natural gas pipeline	Min to qualify:	1
Company Address:	Box 1000, Station M	Fee on cash inv.:	0
	Calgary, Alta. T2P 4K5 Canada	Fee on div. inv.:	0
Company Phone:	800-361-6522	Discount (cash):	0
Transfer Agent:	Montreal Trust Company	Discount (div.):	5%
Agent's Address:	#600-530 8th Ave. SW	Auto invest:	No
	Calgary, Alberta Canada T2P 3S8	Auto invest fee:	$0
Agent's Phone:	800-558-0046 or 403-267-6555	Selling info:	Not available
Other than USA:	Yes		

Company:	**Transocean Offshore, Inc.**	Safekeeping:	Yes
Symbol:	RIG	Invests:	Every 7 days beginning varies
Exchange:	NYSE	Minimum:	$25
Industry:	Offshore oil & gas drilling services	Maximum:	$5,000/month
Company Address:	4 Greenway Plaza	Min to qualify:	1
	Houston, TX 77046	Fee on cash inv.:	0!
Company Phone:	713-871-7500	Fee on div. inv.:	0!
Transfer Agent:	Bank of New York	Discount (cash):	0
Agent's Address:	P.O. Box 1958	Discount (div.):	0
	Newark, NJ 07101-9774	Auto invest:	Yes
Agent's Phone:	800-524-4458 or 800-727-7033	Auto invest fee:	$0
Other than USA:	Yes	Selling info:	Sells weekly, by mail or phone, at avg. price, for $10 +10¢/sh.

Company:	**Tredegar Industries, Inc.**	Safekeeping:	Yes
Symbol:	TG	Invests:	Every 30 days beginning 1/1
Exchange:	NYSE	Minimum:	$25
Industry:	Diversified mfr. plastic & metal prods.	Maximum:	$4,000/month
		Min to qualify:	1
Company Address:	1100 Boulders Pkwy.	Fee on cash inv.:	0!
	Richmond, VA 23225	Fee on div. inv.:	0!
Company Phone:	804-330-1044 or 804-330-1000	Discount (cash):	0
Transfer Agent:	American Stock Transfer	Discount (div.):	0
Agent's Address:	40 Wall Street, 46th Fl.	Auto invest:	No
	New York, NY 10005	Auto invest fee:	$0
Agent's Phone:	800-937-5449 or 718-921-8200	Selling info:	Sells weekly, by mail, at market, for 4¢/sh.
Other than USA:	Yes		

Company:	**Tribune Co.**	**Safekeeping:**	Yes
Symbol:	TRB	**Invests:**	Every 5 days beginning Thurs.
Exchange:	NYSE	**Minimum:**	$50
Industry:	Publishing, broadcasting,	**Maximum:**	$120,000/year
	education	**Min to qualify:**	1
Company Address:	435 North Michigan Ave.	**Fee on cash inv.:**	$5 + 10¢/sh.
	Chicago, IL 60611-4041	**Fee on div. inv.:**	5% to $3 + 10¢/sh.
Company Phone:	312-222-9100 or 312-222-3787	**Discount (cash):**	0
Transfer Agent:	FCT (EquiServe)	**Discount (div.):**	0
Agent's Address:	P.O. Box 2598	**Auto invest:**	Yes
	Jersey City, NJ 07303-2598	**Auto invest fee:**	$2 + 10¢/sh.
Agent's Phone:	800-446-2617	**Selling info:**	Sells within 5 bus. days, by phone
Other than USA:	No		or mail, at market, for $10
			+12¢/sh.

Company:	**Tricom, S.A.**	**Safekeeping:**	Yes
Symbol:	TDR	**Invests:**	Every 7 days beginning varies
Exchange:	NYSE	**Minimum:**	$50
Industry:	Telecommunications	**Maximum:**	$250,000/year
Company Address:	c/o BNY,101 Barclay St.,22 West	**Min to qualify:**	1
	New York, NY 10286	**Fee on cash inv.:**	$5 + 10¢/sh.
Company Phone:	800-943-9715	**Fee on div. inv.:**	5% to $5 + 10¢/sh.
Transfer Agent:	Bank of New York	**Discount (cash):**	0
Agent's Address:	P.O. Box 11258	**Discount (div.):**	0
	New York, NY 10286	**Auto invest:**	Yes
Agent's Phone:	888-269-2377	**Auto invest fee:**	$5 + 10¢/sh.
Other than USA:	Yes	**Selling info:**	Sells weekly, by mail, at market,
			for $5 +10¢/sh.

Company:	**Tricon Global Restau-**	**Safekeeping:**	Yes
	rants, Inc.	**Invests:**	Every 30 days beginning 1/30
Symbol:	YUM	**Minimum:**	$20
Exchange:	NYSE	**Maximum:**	$5,000/month
Industry:	Operates quick service	**Min to qualify:**	1
	restaurants	**Fee on cash inv.:**	0!
Company Address:	1441 Gardiner Lane	**Fee on div. inv.:**	0!
	Louisville, KY 40213	**Discount (cash):**	0
Company Phone:	888-2YUMYUM or 502-874-8300	**Discount (div.):**	0
Transfer Agent:	Boston Eq. (EquiServe)	**Auto invest:**	No
Agent's Address:	P.O. Box 8038	**Auto invest fee:**	$0
	Boston, MA 02266-8038	**Selling info:**	Sells weekly, by mail or phone, at
Agent's Phone:	888-439-4986		market, for $5 + 5¢/sh.
Other than USA:	Yes		

Company:	**True North**	**Safekeeping:**	Yes
	Communications	**Invests:**	Every 30 days beginning 1/1
Symbol:	TNO	**Minimum:**	$25
Exchange:	NYSE	**Maximum:**	$1,000/month
Industry:	Advertising	**Min to qualify:**	1
Company Address:	101 East Erie St.	**Fee on cash inv.:**	0!
	Chicago, IL 60611-2897	**Fee on div. inv.:**	0!
Company Phone:	312-425-6570	**Discount (cash):**	0
Transfer Agent:	FCT (EquiServe)	**Discount (div.):**	0
Agent's Address:	P.O. Box 2500	**Auto invest:**	No
	Jersey City, NJ 07303	**Auto invest fee:**	$0
Agent's Phone:	800-446-2617	**Selling info:**	Sells monthly, by mail or phone,
Other than USA:	No		at market, for $10 +12¢/sh.

Company:	**TrustCo Bank Corp NY**	Safekeeping:	Yes
Symbol:	TRST	Invests:	Every 7 days beginning varies
Exchange:	OTC	Minimum:	$25
Industry:	Banking	Maximum:	$unlimited
Company Address:	320 State St.	Min to qualify:	1
	Schenectady, NY 12305	Fee on cash inv.:	0!
Company Phone:	518-381-3601 or 518-377-3311	Fee on div. inv.:	0!
Transfer Agent:	TrustCo Bank	Discount (cash):	0
Agent's Address:	P.O. Box 1082	Discount (div.):	0
	Schenectady, NY 12301-1082	Auto invest:	No
Agent's Phone:	518-381-3601	Auto invest fee:	$0
Other than USA:	Yes	Selling info:	Sells within 10 bus. days, by mail, at market, for $0

Company:	**TRW Inc.**	Safekeeping:	Yes
Symbol:	TRW	Invests:	Every 45 days beginning 1/30
Exchange:	NYSE	Minimum:	$10
Industry:	Air bags, defense, automotive	Maximum:	$1,000/45 days
Company Address:	1900 Richmond Rd.	Min to qualify:	1
	Cleveland, OH 44124-3760	Fee on cash inv.:	0!
Company Phone:	216-291-7506	Fee on div. inv.:	0!
Transfer Agent:	TRW Inc. Shareholder Services	Discount (cash):	0
Agent's Address:	1900 Richmond Road	Discount (div.):	0
	Cleveland, OH 44124	Auto invest:	No
Agent's Phone:	216-291-7654	Auto invest fee:	$0
Other than USA:	Yes	Selling info:	Sells every 45 days, by mail or fax, at market, for 8¢/sh.

Company:	**Tubos de Acero de Mexico SA**	Safekeeping:	Yes
		Invests:	Every 7 days beginning varies
Symbol:	TAM	Minimum:	$50
Exchange:	ASE	Maximum:	$100,000/year
Industry:	Mfr. steel pipe & tubing	Min to qualify:	1
Company Address:	c/o Morgan Guaranty Trust,	Fee on cash inv.:	$5 + 12¢/sh.
	Box 9073	Fee on div. inv.:	5% to $2.50
	Boston, MA 02205-9948	Discount (cash):	0
Company Phone:	800-428-4237	Discount (div.):	0
Transfer Agent:	Morgan Guaranty Trust Co.	Auto invest:	Yes
Agent's Address:	P.O. Box 9073	Auto invest fee:	$5
	Boston, MA 02205-9948	Selling info:	Sells daily, by phone or mail, at avg. price, for $5 +12¢/sh.
Agent's Phone:	800-428-4237		
Other than USA:	No		

Company:	**TV Azteca**	Safekeeping:	Yes
Symbol:	TZA	Invests:	Every 7 days beginning varies
Exchange:	NYSE	Minimum:	$50
Industry:	Broadcasting & cable TV	Maximum:	$250,000/year
Company Address:	c/o BNY,101 Barclay St.,22 West	Min to qualify:	1
	New York, NY 10286	Fee on cash inv.:	$5 + 10¢/sh.
Company Phone:	800-943-9715	Fee on div. inv.:	0
Transfer Agent:	Bank of New York	Discount (cash):	0
Agent's Address:	P.O. Box 11258	Discount (div.):	0
	New York, NY 10286	Auto invest:	Yes
Agent's Phone:	888-269-2377	Auto invest fee:	$5 + 10¢/sh.
Other than USA:	Yes	Selling info:	Sells weekly, by mail, at market, for $5 +10¢/sh.

Twin Disc, Inc.

Company:	Twin Disc, Inc.
Symbol:	TDI
Exchange:	NYSE
Industry:	Mfr. ind. equip.
Company Address:	1328 Racine St.
	Racine, WI 53403-1758
Company Phone:	414-638-4100
Transfer Agent:	Firstar Bank Milwaukee, NA
Agent's Address:	P.O. Box 2054
	Milwaukee, WI 53202
Agent's Phone:	800-637-7549
Other than USA:	Yes
Safekeeping:	No
Invests:	Every 90 days beginning 3/1
Minimum:	$10
Maximum:	$2,000/month
Min to qualify:	1
Fee on cash inv.:	0
Fee on div. inv.:	0
Discount (cash):	0
Discount (div.):	0
Auto invest:	No
Auto invest fee:	$0
Selling info:	Sells biweekly, by mail or fax, at market, for $0

TXU Electric & Gas Co.

Company:	TXU Electric & Gas Co.
Symbol:	TXU
Exchange:	NYSE
Industry:	Utility-electric
Company Address:	1601 Bryan St., Ste. EP33068
	Dallas, TX 75201
Company Phone:	800-828-0812 or 214-812-2478
Transfer Agent:	Texas Utilities Shareholder Services
Agent's Address:	P.O. Box 225249
	Dallas, TX 75222-5249
Agent's Phone:	800-828-0812
Other than USA:	No
Safekeeping:	Yes
Invests:	Every 7 days beginning varies
Minimum:	$25
Maximum:	$100,000/year
Min to qualify:	10
Fee on cash inv.:	0!
Fee on div. inv.:	0!
Discount (cash):	0
Discount (div.):	0
Auto invest:	Yes
Auto invest fee:	$0
Selling info:	Sells weekly, by mail or fax, at market, for $10 +7¢/sh.

Tyco International Ltd.

Company:	Tyco International Ltd.
Symbol:	TYC
Exchange:	NYSE
Industry:	Fire prot., elec.comp., health care prod.
Company Address:	Gibbons Bldg., 10 Queen St., Ste.301
	Hamilton, HM11 Bermuda
Company Phone:	603-778-9700 or 441-292-8674
Transfer Agent:	ChaseMellon Shareholder Services
Agent's Address:	85 Challenger Road,
	Overpeck Centre
	Ridgefield Park, NJ 07660
Agent's Phone:	800-685-4509
Other than USA:	Yes
Safekeeping:	Yes
Invests:	
Minimum:	
Maximum:	$no drp plan
Min to qualify:	1
Fee on cash inv.:	0
Fee on div. inv.:	0
Discount (cash):	0
Discount (div.):	0
Auto invest:	No
Auto invest fee:	$0
Selling info:	Sells weekly, by mail or phone, at market, for $2.50 + comm.

Tyson Foods - A

Company:	Tyson Foods - A
Symbol:	TSN
Exchange:	NYSE
Industry:	Integrated poultry business
Company Address:	2210 West Oaklawn, Box 2020
	Springdale, AR 72765-2020
Company Phone:	501-290-4826 or 501-290-4000
Transfer Agent:	FCT (EquiServe)
Agent's Address:	P.O. Box 2598
	Jersey City, NJ 07303-2598
Agent's Phone:	800-317-4445
Other than USA:	Yes
Safekeeping:	Yes
Invests:	Every 7 days beginning Thurs.
Minimum:	$50
Maximum:	$unlimited
Min to qualify:	1
Fee on cash inv.:	0!
Fee on div. inv.:	0!
Discount (cash):	0
Discount (div.):	0
Auto invest:	Yes
Auto invest fee:	$1
Selling info:	Sells daily, by phone or mail, at market, for $15 +10¢/sh.

Company:	**U S West, Inc.**
Symbol:	USW
Exchange:	NYSE
Industry:	Telecommunications
Company Address:	1801 California St., Ste. 4320
	Denver, CO 80202
Company Phone:	800-879-4357 or 303-896-1277
Transfer Agent:	Boston Eq. (EquiServe)
Agent's Address:	P.O. Box 8936
	Boston, MA 02266-8936
Agent's Phone:	800-537-0222
Other than USA:	Yes

Safekeeping:	Yes
Invests:	Every 7 days beginning varies
Minimum:	$100
Maximum:	$100,000/year
Min to qualify:	10
Fee on cash inv.:	0
Fee on div. inv.:	$1
Discount (cash):	0
Discount (div.):	0
Auto invest:	Yes
Auto invest fee:	$0
Selling info:	Sells daily, by phone, at market, for $10 + 6¢/sh.

Company:	**U.S. Bancorp**
Symbol:	USB
Exchange:	NYSE
Industry:	Banking
Company Address:	601 Second Ave. South
	Minneapolis, MN 55402-4302
Company Phone:	800-947-9820 or 612-973-2264
Transfer Agent:	FCT (EquiServe)
Agent's Address:	P.O. Box 2598
	Jersey City, NJ 07303-2598
Agent's Phone:	800-446-2617
Other than USA:	Yes

Safekeeping:	Yes
Invests:	Every 30 days beginning 1/1
Minimum:	$25
Maximum:	$60,000/year
Min to qualify:	1
Fee on cash inv.:	0!
Fee on div. inv.:	0!
Discount (cash):	0
Discount (div.):	0
Auto invest:	Yes
Auto invest fee:	$1
Selling info:	Sells biweekly, by mail or phone, at market, for $10 +12¢/sh.

Company:	**U.S. Trust Corp.**
Symbol:	UTC
Exchange:	NYSE
Industry:	Financial services & banking
Company Address:	114 West 47th St.
	New York, NY 10036
Company Phone:	800-548-6565 or 212-852-1332
Transfer Agent:	U.S. Trust Corp.
Agent's Address:	770 Broadway, 13th floor
	New York, NY 10003
Agent's Phone:	800-548-6565 or 212-420-6671
Other than USA:	Yes

Safekeeping:	Yes
Invests:	Every 30 days beginning 1/25
Minimum:	$30
Maximum:	$1,000/month
Min to qualify:	1
Fee on cash inv.:	0
Fee on div. inv.:	0
Discount (cash):	0
Discount (div.):	0
Auto invest:	No
Auto invest fee:	$0
Selling info:	Sells weekly, by mail, at market, for comm.

Company:	**UGI Corp.**
Symbol:	UGI
Exchange:	NYSE
Industry:	Utility-gas & electric, propane
Company Address:	Box 858
	Valley Forge, PA 19482
Company Phone:	610-337-1000
Transfer Agent:	ChaseMellon Shareholder Services
Agent's Address:	P.O. Box 3338
	South Hackensack, NJ 07606-1938
Agent's Phone:	800-756-3353
Other than USA:	Yes

Safekeeping:	Yes
Invests:	Every 30 days beginning 1/1
Minimum:	$25
Maximum:	$3,000/quarter
Min to qualify:	1
Fee on cash inv.:	0!
Fee on div. inv.:	0!
Discount (cash):	0
Discount (div.):	0
Auto invest:	No
Auto invest fee:	$0
Selling info:	Sells within 10 bus. days, by mail or phone, at market, for $2.50 +10¢ to12¢/sh.

Company:	**Ultramar Diamond Shamrock**	Safekeeping:	Yes
		Invests:	Every 90 days beginning 3/14
Symbol:	UDS	Minimum:	$100
Exchange:	NYSE	Maximum:	$25,000/year
Industry:	Refining oil, retail marketing	Min to qualify:	1
Company Address:	Box 696000	Fee on cash inv.:	0!
	San Antonio, TX 78269-6000	Fee on div. inv.:	0!
Company Phone:	210-592-2000 or 210-592-2009x3	Discount (cash):	0
Transfer Agent:	Registrar & Transfer Co.	Discount (div.):	0
Agent's Address:	10 Commerce Drive	Auto invest:	No
	Cranford, NJ 07016	Auto invest fee:	$0
Agent's Phone:	800-368-5948	Selling info:	Sells weekly, by mail, at market,
Other than USA:	No		for 0!

Company:	**UMB Financial Corp.**	Safekeeping:	Yes
Symbol:	UMBF	Invests:	Every 30 days beginning 1/3
Exchange:	OTC	Minimum:	$50
Industry:	Financial	Maximum:	$3,000/quarter
Company Address:	1010 Grand Blvd., Box 419226	Min to qualify:	1
	Kansas City, MO 64141-6226	Fee on cash inv.:	0!
Company Phone:	800-821-2171 or 816-860-7000 or	Fee on div. inv.:	0!
	816-860-7888	Discount (cash):	0
Transfer Agent:	UMB Bank, N.A.	Discount (div.):	0
Agent's Address:	P.O. Box 410064	Auto invest:	No
	Kansas City, MO 64141-0064	Auto invest fee:	$0
Agent's Phone:	816-860-7891	Selling info:	Sells weekly, by mail, at market,
Other than USA:	Yes		for $3 + comm.

Company:	**Unicom Corp.**	Safekeeping:	Yes
Symbol:	UCM	Invests:	Every 30 days beginning 1/1
Exchange:	NYSE	Minimum:	$25
Industry:	Utility-electric	Maximum:	$60,000/year
Company Address:	One First National Plz.,	Min to qualify:	1
	Box A-3005	Fee on cash inv.:	10¢/sh.
	Chicago, IL 60690-3005	Fee on div. inv.:	0!
Company Phone:	800-950-2377	Discount (cash):	0
Transfer Agent:	FCT (EquiServe)	Discount (div.):	0
Agent's Address:	P.O. Box 2500	Auto invest:	Yes
	Jersey City, NJ 07303	Auto invest fee:	$0
Agent's Phone:	800-950-2377	Selling info:	Sells daily, by phone, mail, or fax,
Other than USA:	Yes		at market, for 10¢/sh.

Company:	**Unilever N.V.**	Safekeeping:	Yes
Symbol:	UN	Invests:	Every 7 days beginning varies
Exchange:	NYSE	Minimum:	$50
Industry:	Int'l consumer products	Maximum:	$100,000/year
Company Address:	390 Park Ave.	Min to qualify:	1
	New York, NY 10022	Fee on cash inv.:	$5 + 12¢/sh.
Company Phone:	212-906-3398	Fee on div. inv.:	5% to $2.50
Transfer Agent:	Morgan Guaranty Trust Co.	Discount (cash):	0
Agent's Address:	P.O. Box 9073	Discount (div.):	0
	Boston, MA 02205-9948	Auto invest:	Yes
Agent's Phone:	800-428-4237	Auto invest fee:	$5
Other than USA:	No	Selling info:	Sells daily, by phone or mail, at
			avg. price, for $5 +12¢/sh.

Company:	**Unilever plc**
Symbol:	UL
Exchange:	NYSE
Industry:	Int'l consumer products
Company Address:	c/o Morgan Guaranty Trust,
	Box 9073
	Boston, MA 02205-9948
Company Phone:	800-428-4237
Transfer Agent:	Morgan Guaranty Trust Co.
Agent's Address:	P.O. Box 9073
	Boston, MA 02205-9948
Agent's Phone:	800-428-4237
Other than USA:	No

Safekeeping:	Yes
Invests:	Every 7 days beginning varies
Minimum:	$50
Maximum:	$100,000/year
Min to qualify:	1
Fee on cash inv.:	$5 + 12¢/sh.
Fee on div. inv.:	5% to $2.50
Discount (cash):	0
Discount (div.):	0
Auto invest:	Yes
Auto invest fee:	$5
Selling info:	Sells daily, by phone or mail, at avg. price, for $5 +12¢/sh.

Company:	**Union Carbide Corp.**
Symbol:	UK
Exchange:	NYSE
Industry:	Chemicals & plastics
Company Address:	39 Old Ridgebury Rd.
	Danbury, CT 06817-0001
Company Phone:	203-794-3093 or 203-794-3647
Transfer Agent:	Union Carbide Corp.
Agent's Address:	Shareholder Svcs.G1328, 39 Old
	Ridgebury Road
	Danbury, CT 06817-0001
Agent's Phone:	800-934-3350
Other than USA:	Yes

Safekeeping:	Yes
Invests:	Every 30 days beginning 1/30
Minimum:	$25
Maximum:	$1,000/month
Min to qualify:	1
Fee on cash inv.:	0!
Fee on div. inv.:	0!
Discount (cash):	0
Discount (div.):	0
Auto invest:	No
Auto invest fee:	$0
Selling info:	Sells within 10 bus. days , by mail or fax, at market, for 6¢/sh.

Company:	**Union Pacific Corp.**
Symbol:	UNP
Exchange:	NYSE
Industry:	Transportation, railroad
Company Address:	1717 Main St., Ste.5900
	Dallas, TX 75201-4605
Company Phone:	214-743-5600 or 214-743-5676
Transfer Agent:	Harris Trust & Savings Bank
Agent's Address:	P.O. Box A3504, Shareholder Svcs.
	311/11
	Chicago, IL 60690-3504
Agent's Phone:	800-317-2512
Other than USA:	Yes

Safekeeping:	Yes
Invests:	Every 30 days beginning 1/1
Minimum:	$10
Maximum:	$60,000/year
Min to qualify:	1
Fee on cash inv.:	0
Fee on div. inv.:	0
Discount (cash):	0
Discount (div.):	0
Auto invest:	No
Auto invest fee:	$0
Selling info:	Sells weekly, by mail, at market, for $0!

Company:	**Union Planters**
Symbol:	UPC
Exchange:	NYSE
Industry:	Banking
Company Address:	7130 Goodlett Farms Pkwy.
	Memphis, TN 38018
Company Phone:	800-900-4548 or 901-580-6000
Transfer Agent:	Union Planters Bank, N.A.
Agent's Address:	Box 523, 1 South Church St.,
	Ste. 500
	Belleville, IL 62220
Agent's Phone:	800-900-4548
Other than USA:	Yes

Safekeeping:	Yes
Invests:	Every 90 days beginning 3/1
Minimum:	$100
Maximum:	$2,000/quarter
Min to qualify:	1
Fee on cash inv.:	0!
Fee on div. inv.:	0!
Discount (cash):	0
Discount (div.):	0
Auto invest:	No
Auto invest fee:	$0
Selling info:	Not available

Company:	**Unionamerica Holdings plc**	Safekeeping:	Yes
		Invests:	Every 7 days beginning varies
Symbol:	UA	Minimum:	$50
Exchange:	NYSE	Maximum:	$100,000/year
Industry:	Medical & health ins.	Min to qualify:	1
Company Address:	c/o BNY,101 Barclay St., 22 West	Fee on cash inv.:	$5 + 12¢/sh.
	New York, NY 10286	Fee on div. inv.:	5% to $2.50
Company Phone:	212-815-3874	Discount (cash):	0
Transfer Agent:	Bank of New York	Discount (div.):	0
Agent's Address:	P.O. Box 11258	Auto invest:	Yes
	New York, NY 10286	Auto invest fee:	$5
Agent's Phone:	888-269-2377	Selling info:	Sells daily, by phone or mail, at
Other than USA:	No		avg. price, for $5 +12¢/sh.

Company:	**UnionBanCal Corp.**	Safekeeping:	Yes
Symbol:	UNBC	Invests:	Every 90 days beginning 1/10
Exchange:	OTC	Minimum:	$25
Industry:	Banking	Maximum:	$3,000/quarter
Company Address:	400 California St., 13th Fl.	Min to qualify:	1
	San Francisco, CA 94104	Fee on cash inv.:	0
Company Phone:	415-765-2969	Fee on div. inv.:	0
Transfer Agent:	Harris Trust Co. of CA	Discount (cash):	0
Agent's Address:	601 S. Figueroa St.-Suite 4900	Discount (div.):	5%
	Los Angeles, CA 90017	Auto invest:	No
Agent's Phone:	800-554-3406	Auto invest fee:	$0
Other than USA:	yes	Selling info:	Not available

Company:	**UniSource Energy Corp.**	Safekeeping:	Yes
Symbol:	UNS	Invests:	Every 15 days beginning varies
Exchange:	NYSE	Minimum:	$50
Industry:	Electric utilities	Maximum:	$unlimited
Company Address:	Box 711	Min to qualify:	1
	Tucson, AZ 85702	Fee on cash inv.:	0
Company Phone:	520-884-3661 or 520-571-4000	Fee on div. inv.:	0
Transfer Agent:	Bank of New York	Discount (cash):	0
Agent's Address:	P.O. Box 11258, Church St. Station	Discount (div.):	0
	New York, NY 10286	Auto invest:	Yes
Agent's Phone:	888-269-8845	Auto invest fee:	$0
Other than USA:	Yes	Selling info:	Sells weekly, by mail, at market,
			for $5 +10¢/sh.

Company:	**Unisource Worldwide, Inc.**	Safekeeping:	Yes
Symbol:	UWW	Invests:	Every 30 days beginning 1/10
Exchange:	NYSE	Minimum:	$25
Industry:	Dist. paper prods. & supply	Maximum:	$5,000/month
	systems	Min to qualify:	1
Company Address:	1100 Cassatt Ave., Box 3000	Fee on cash inv.:	0!
	Berwyn, PA 19312-0935	Fee on div. inv.:	0!
Company Phone:	610-722-3593 or 610-722-3513	Discount (cash):	0
Transfer Agent:	National City Bank	Discount (div.):	0
Agent's Address:	P.O. Box 92301-N	Auto invest:	No
	Cleveland, OH 44193-0900	Auto invest fee:	$0
Agent's Phone:	800-622-6757	Selling info:	Sells weekly, by mail, at market,
Other than USA:	Yes		for $3 + 9¢ to 20¢/sh.

Company:	**United Bancorp Inc.**	Safekeeping:	Yes
Symbol:	UBCP	Invests:	Every 90 days beginning 3/20
Exchange:	OTC	Minimum:	$100
Industry:	Banking	Maximum:	$5,000/quarter
Company Address:	4th at Hickory St., Box 10	Min to qualify:	1
	Martins Ferry, OH 43935	Fee on cash inv.:	0
Company Phone:	888-275-5566 x120	Fee on div. inv.:	0
Transfer Agent:	American Stock Transfer	Discount (cash):	0
Agent's Address:	40 Wall Street 46th Floor	Discount (div.):	0
	New York, NY 10005	Auto invest:	No
Agent's Phone:	800-278-4353 or 718-921-8283	Auto invest fee:	$0
Other than USA:	Yes	Selling info:	Sells weekly, by mail, at market, for 0

Company:	**United Bankshares, Inc.**	Safekeeping:	No
Symbol:	UBSI	Invests:	Every 90 days beginning varies
Exchange:	OTC	Minimum:	$25
Industry:	Banking	Maximum:	$10,000/quarter
Company Address:	514 Market St., Box 1508	Min to qualify:	1
	Parkersburg, WV 26101	Fee on cash inv.:	0!
Company Phone:	304-424-8764 or 304-424-8800	Fee on div. inv.:	0!
Transfer Agent:	ChaseMellon Shareholder Services	Discount (cash):	0
Agent's Address:	85 Challenger Road	Discount (div.):	0
	Ridgefield Park, NJ 07660	Auto invest:	No
Agent's Phone:	800-756-3353	Auto invest fee:	$0
Other than USA:	Yes	Selling info:	Not available

Company:	**United Dominion Realty Trust**	Safekeeping:	Yes
		Invests:	Every 90 days beginning 1/30
Symbol:	UDR	Minimum:	$50
Exchange:	NYSE	Maximum:	$25,000/quarter
Industry:	REIT	Min to qualify:	1
Company Address:	10 South Sixth St.	Fee on cash inv.:	0!
	Richmond, VA 23219-3802	Fee on div. inv.:	0!
Company Phone:	804-780-2691	Discount (cash):	0
Transfer Agent:	ChaseMellon Shareholder Services	Discount (div.):	5%
Agent's Address:	P.O. Box 3338	Auto invest:	No
	South Hackensack, NJ 07606-1938	Auto invest fee:	$0
Agent's Phone:	800-526-0801	Selling info:	Sells within 13 bus. days, by mail, at market, for $5 + comm.
Other than USA:	Yes		

Company:	**United Illuminating Co.**	Safekeeping:	Yes
Symbol:	UIL	Invests:	Every 30 days beginning 1/1
Exchange:	NYSE	Minimum:	$10
Industry:	Utility-electric	Maximum:	$4,000/month
Company Address:	157 Church St., Box 1564	Min to qualify:	1
	New Haven, CT 06506-0901	Fee on cash inv.:	4¢/sh.
Company Phone:	203-499-2591 or 203-499-2409	Fee on div. inv.:	4¢/sh.
Transfer Agent:	American Stock Transfer & Trust Co.	Discount (cash):	0
		Discount (div.):	0
Agent's Address:	40 Wall St., 46th Fl.	Auto invest:	No
	New York, NY 10005	Auto invest fee:	$0
Agent's Phone:	800-937-5449 or 800-278-4353	Selling info:	Sells biweekly, by mail, at market, for 4¢/sh.
Other than USA:	Yes		

Company:	**United Industrial Corp.**
Symbol:	UIC
Exchange:	NYSE
Industry:	Equipment
Company Address:	570 Lexington Ave.
	New York, NY 10022
Company Phone:	212-752-8787
Transfer Agent:	American Stock Transfer & Trust
Agent's Address:	40 Wall Street-46th Floor
	New York, NY 10005
Agent's Phone:	800-278-4353 or 800-937-5449
Other than USA:	No

Safekeeping:	Yes
Invests:	Every 30 days beginning 1/10
Minimum:	$100
Maximum:	$5,000/month
Min to qualify:	1
Fee on cash inv.:	0!
Fee on div. inv.:	0!
Discount (cash):	0
Discount (div.):	0
Auto invest:	No
Auto invest fee:	$0
Selling info:	Sells within 5 bus. days, by mail, at avg. price, for $10 + comm.

Company:	**United National Bancorp**
Symbol:	UNBJ
Exchange:	OTC
Industry:	Banking
Company Address:	1130 Route 22 East
	Bridgewater, NJ 08807-0010
Company Phone:	908-429-2405 or 908-429-2200
Transfer Agent:	Bank of New York
Agent's Address:	101 Barclay Street
	New York, NY 10286
Agent's Phone:	800-524-4458
Other than USA:	Yes

Safekeeping:	Yes
Invests:	Every 7 days beginning varies
Minimum:	$50
Maximum:	$100,000/year
Min to qualify:	1
Fee on cash inv.:	0!
Fee on div. inv.:	0!
Discount (cash):	0
Discount (div.):	0
Auto invest:	Yes
Auto invest fee:	$0
Selling info:	Sells weekly, by mail, fax, phone,email, at market, for 10¢/sh.

Company:	**United Technologies**
Symbol:	UTX
Exchange:	NYSE
Industry:	Aerospace, climate control systems
Company Address:	One Financial Plaza
	Hartford, CT 06101
Company Phone:	860-728-7000
Transfer Agent:	FCT (EquiServe)
Agent's Address:	P.O. Box 2598
	Jersey City, NJ 07303-2598
Agent's Phone:	800-519-3111
Other than USA:	Yes

Safekeeping:	Yes
Invests:	Every 30 days beginning 1/10
Minimum:	$100
Maximum:	$120,000/year
Min to qualify:	10
Fee on cash inv.:	0!
Fee on div. inv.:	0!
Discount (cash):	0
Discount (div.):	0
Auto invest:	No
Auto invest fee:	0
Selling info:	Sells weekly, by mail or phone, at market, for $10 +12¢/sh.

Company:	**United Water Resources Inc.**
Symbol:	UWR
Exchange:	NYSE
Industry:	Utility-water
Company Address:	200 Old Hook Rd.
	Harrington Park, NJ 07640-1799
Company Phone:	201-767-2811 or 201-784-9434
Transfer Agent:	ChaseMellon Shareholder Services
Agent's Address:	P.O. Box 3336
	South Hackensack, NJ 07606-1936
Agent's Phone:	800-230-2685
Other than USA:	Yes

Safekeeping:	No
Invests:	Every 30 days beginning 1/1
Minimum:	$25
Maximum:	$3,000/quarter
Min to qualify:	1
Fee on cash inv.:	0!
Fee on div. inv.:	0!
Discount (cash):	0-10%
Discount (div.):	0-10%
Auto invest:	No
Auto invest fee:	$0
Selling info:	Not available

Company:	**United Wisconsin Services**	**Safekeeping:**	Yes
Symbol:	UWZ	**Invests:**	Every 30 days beginning 1/1
Exchange:	NYSE	**Minimum:**	$100
Industry:	Group health insurance services	**Maximum:**	$100,000/year
Company Address:	401 West Michigan St.	**Min to qualify:**	1
	Milwaukee, WI 53203-2896	**Fee on cash inv.:**	0!
Company Phone:	414-226-5756 or 414-226-6833	**Fee on div. inv.:**	0!
Transfer Agent:	Firstar Bank Milwaukee, NA	**Discount (cash):**	0
Agent's Address:	615 E. Michigan Street, 4th Flr.	**Discount (div.):**	0
	Milwaukee, WI 53202	**Auto invest:**	No
Agent's Phone:	800-637-7549	**Auto invest fee:**	$0
Other than USA:	Yes	**Selling info:**	Sells irregularly, by mail, at market, for comm.

Company:	**Unitil Corp.**	**Safekeeping:**	Yes
Symbol:	UTL	**Invests:**	Every 90 days beginning 2/14
Exchange:	ASE	**Minimum:**	$25
Industry:	Public utility holding company	**Maximum:**	$5,000/quarter
Company Address:	6 Libery Lane West	**Min to qualify:**	1
	Hampton, NH 03842-1720	**Fee on cash inv.:**	0!
Company Phone:	800-999-6501 or 603-772-0775	**Fee on div. inv.:**	0!
Transfer Agent:	Boston Eq. (EquiServe)	**Discount (cash):**	0
Agent's Address:	P.O. Box 8040, Mail Stop 45-02-62	**Discount (div.):**	5%
	Boston, MA 02266-8040	**Auto invest:**	No
Agent's Phone:	800-736-3001	**Auto invest fee:**	$0
Other than USA:	No	**Selling info:**	Sells within 10 days, by mail, at market, for 2¢ to 15¢/sh.

Company:	**Unitrin, Inc.**	**Safekeeping:**	Yes
Symbol:	UNIT	**Invests:**	Every 7 days beginning varies
Exchange:	OTC	**Minimum:**	$50
Industry:	Insurance	**Maximum:**	$100,000/year
Company Address:	One East Wacker Dr.	**Min to qualify:**	1
	Chicago, IL 60601	**Fee on cash inv.:**	$5 + 3¢/sh.
Company Phone:	312-661-4520 or 312-661-4600	**Fee on div. inv.:**	3% to $3 + 3¢/sh.
Transfer Agent:	FCT (EquiServe)	**Discount (cash):**	0
Agent's Address:	P.O. Box 2598	**Discount (div.):**	0
	Jersey City, NJ 07303-2598	**Auto invest:**	Yes
Agent's Phone:	800-446-2617	**Auto invest fee:**	$2 + 3¢/sh.
Other than USA:	Yes	**Selling info:**	Sells weekly, by mail or phone, at market, for $10 +12¢/sh.

Company:	**Universal Corp.**	**Safekeeping:**	No
Symbol:	UVV	**Invests:**	Every 30 days beginning 1/1
Exchange:	NYSE	**Minimum:**	$10
Industry:	Leaf tobacco, bldg prod., agri-products	**Maximum:**	$1,000/month
		Min to qualify:	1
Company Address:	1501 N. Hamilton St., Box 25099	**Fee on cash inv.:**	0!
	Richmond, VA 23260	**Fee on div. inv.:**	0!
Company Phone:	804-254-1303 or 804-254-8689	**Discount (cash):**	0
Transfer Agent:	Norwest Bank Minnesota, NA	**Discount (div.):**	0
Agent's Address:	P.O. Box 64854	**Auto invest:**	Yes
	St. Paul, MN 55164-0854	**Auto invest fee:**	$0
Agent's Phone:	800-468-9716	**Selling info:**	Sells weekly, by mail, at market, for 5¢/sh.
Other than USA:	No		

Company:	**Universal Foods Corp.**	**Safekeeping:**	Yes
Symbol:	UFC	**Invests:**	Every 30 days beginning 1/30
Exchange:	NYSE	**Minimum:**	$25
Industry:	Flavors, colors, food ingredients	**Maximum:**	$1,500/month
Company Address:	433 East Michigan St., Box 737	**Min to qualify:**	1
	Milwaukee, WI 53201	**Fee on cash inv.:**	0!
Company Phone:	800-558-9892 or 414-347-3779	**Fee on div. inv.:**	0!
Transfer Agent:	Firstar Bank Milwaukee, NA	**Discount (cash):**	0
Agent's Address:	P.O. Box 2077	**Discount (div.):**	0
	Milwaukee, WI 53201	**Auto invest:**	No
Agent's Phone:	800-637-7549	**Auto invest fee:**	$0
Other than USA:	Yes	**Selling info:**	Sells biweekly, by mail, fax, at market, for comm. + 3¢ to 5¢/sh.

Company:	**Universal Health Rlty. Income Trust**	**Safekeeping:**	Yes
		Invests:	Every 30 days beginning 1/30
Symbol:	UHT	**Minimum:**	$25
Exchange:	NYSE	**Maximum:**	$5,000/month
Industry:	REIT	**Min to qualify:**	1
Company Address:	367 South Gulph Rd., Box 61558	**Fee on cash inv.:**	5% to $3
	King of Prussia, PA 19406-0958	**Fee on div. inv.:**	5% to $3
Company Phone:	610-265-0688	**Discount (cash):**	0
Transfer Agent:	Boston Eq. (EquiServe)	**Discount (div.):**	0
Agent's Address:	P.O. Box 8040, Mail Stop 45-02-64	**Auto invest:**	No
	Boston, MA 02266-8040	**Auto invest fee:**	$0
Agent's Phone:	800-730-6001	**Selling info:**	Sells daily, by mail, at market, for 5% to $10
Other than USA:	No		

Company:	**Unocal Corp.**	**Safekeeping:**	Yes
Symbol:	UCL	**Invests:**	Every 30 days beginning 1/10
Exchange:	NYSE	**Minimum:**	$50
Industry:	Oil exploration and production	**Maximum:**	$10,000/month
Company Address:	2141 Rosecrans Ave., Ste. 4000	**Min to qualify:**	25
	El Segundo, CA 90245	**Fee on cash inv.:**	5% to $3 + 5¢/sh.
Company Phone:	800-252-2233 or 310-726-7665	**Fee on div. inv.:**	5¢/sh.
Transfer Agent:	ChaseMellon Shareholder Services	**Discount (cash):**	0
Agent's Address:	85 Challenger Road	**Discount (div.):**	0
	Ridgefield Park, NJ 07660	**Auto invest:**	No
Agent's Phone:	800-279-1249	**Auto invest fee:**	$0
Other than USA:	No	**Selling info:**	Sells daily, by mail or phone, at market, for $15 + comm.

Company:	**UNUM Corp.**	**Safekeeping:**	Yes
Symbol:	UNM	**Invests:**	Every 30 days beginning 1/15
Exchange:	NYSE	**Minimum:**	$100
Industry:	Life & health insurance	**Maximum:**	$60,000/year
Company Address:	2211 Congress St.	**Min to qualify:**	1
	Portland, ME 04122	**Fee on cash inv.:**	0!
Company Phone:	207-770-4330 or 207-770-2211	**Fee on div. inv.:**	0!
Transfer Agent:	FCT (EquiServe)	**Discount (cash):**	0
Agent's Address:	P.O. Box 2500	**Discount (div.):**	0
	Jersey City, NJ 07303-2500	**Auto invest:**	No
Agent's Phone:	800-519-3111 or 201-324-1225	**Auto invest fee:**	$0
Other than USA:	Yes	**Selling info:**	Sells within 2 bus. days, by phone or mail, at market, for $10 +12¢/sh.

Company:	**Urban Shopping Centers**	**Safekeeping:**	Yes
Symbol:	URB	**Invests:**	Every 7 days beginning Thursday
Exchange:	NYSE	**Minimum:**	$50
Industry:	REIT	**Maximum:**	$60,000/year
Company Address:	900 N. Michigan Ave., Ste. 1500	**Min to qualify:**	1
	Chicago, IL 60611	**Fee on cash inv.:**	$5 + 12¢/sh.
Company Phone:	312-915-2000	**Fee on div. inv.:**	0!
Transfer Agent:	FCT (Equiserve)	**Discount (cash):**	0
Agent's Address:	P.O. Box 2598	**Discount (div.):**	0
	Jersey City, NJ 07303-2598	**Auto invest:**	Yes
Agent's Phone:	800-446-2617	**Auto invest fee:**	5% to $3 +12¢/sh.
Other than USA:	Yes	**Selling info:**	Sells daily, by phone or mail, at market, for $10 +12¢/sh.

Company:	**USBancorp, Inc.**	**Safekeeping:**	Yes
Symbol:	UBAN	**Invests:**	Every 30 days beginning 1/3
Exchange:	OTC	**Minimum:**	$10
Industry:	Banking	**Maximum:**	$2,000/month
Company Address:	Main & Franklin, Box 430	**Min to qualify:**	1
	Johnstown, PA 15907-0430	**Fee on cash inv.:**	0!
Company Phone:	814-533-5202	**Fee on div. inv.:**	0!
Transfer Agent:	Boston Eq. (EquiServe)	**Discount (cash):**	0
Agent's Address:	P.O. Box 8040	**Discount (div.):**	0
	Boston, MA 02266-8040	**Auto invest:**	No
Agent's Phone:	800-730-4001	**Auto invest fee:**	$0
Other than USA:	Yes	**Selling info:**	Sells daily, by mail, at market, for $10 + comm.

Company:	**USP Real Estate Inv. Trust**	**Safekeeping:**	Yes
		Invests:	Every 30 days beginning 1/15
Symbol:	USPTS	**Minimum:**	$0
Exchange:	OTC	**Maximum:**	$unlimited
Industry:	REIT	**Min to qualify:**	1
Company Address:	4333 Edgewood Rd. NE	**Fee on cash inv.:**	comm.
	Cedar Rapids, IA 52499-5441	**Fee on div. inv.:**	0!
Company Phone:	319-398-8895	**Discount (cash):**	0
Transfer Agent:	Boston Eq. (EquiServe)	**Discount (div.):**	0
Agent's Address:	P.O. Box 8200	**Auto invest:**	No
	Boston, MA 02266-8200	**Auto invest fee:**	$0
Agent's Phone:	800-426-5523	**Selling info:**	Not available
Other than USA:	Yes		

Company:	**UST Corp.**	**Safekeeping:**	Yes
Symbol:	USTB	**Invests:**	Every 90 days beginning 1/24
Exchange:	OTC	**Minimum:**	$100
Industry:	Banking	**Maximum:**	$3,000/quarter
Company Address:	40 Court St.	**Min to qualify:**	1
	Boston, MA 02108	**Fee on cash inv.:**	0!
Company Phone:	617-726-7000	**Fee on div. inv.:**	0!
Transfer Agent:	UST Corp. DRP Plan-Asset	**Discount (cash):**	0
	Management Dept.	**Discount (div.):**	0
Agent's Address:	40 Court Street	**Auto invest:**	No
	Boston, MA 02108	**Auto invest fee:**	$0
Agent's Phone:	617-726-7262	**Selling info:**	Not available
Other than USA:	No		

Company:	**UST Inc.**	Safekeeping:	Yes
Symbol:	UST	Invests:	Every 15 days beginning 1/15
Exchange:	NYSE	Minimum:	$10
Industry:	Tobacco, liquor	Maximum:	$10,000/month
Company Address:	100 West Putnam Ave.	Min to qualify:	1
	Greenwich, CT 06830	Fee on cash inv.:	0!
Company Phone:	203-661-1100	Fee on div. inv.:	0!
Transfer Agent:	Boston Eq. (EquiServe)	Discount (cash):	0
Agent's Address:	P.O. Box 8040	Discount (div.):	0
	Boston, MA 02266-8040	Auto invest:	No
Agent's Phone:	800-730-4001	Auto invest fee:	$0
Other than USA:	Yes	Selling info:	Sells within 5 days , by mail, at market, for 5% to $5 + comm.

Company:	**USX-Marathon Group**	Safekeeping:	Yes
Symbol:	MRO	Invests:	Every 30 days beginning 1/10
Exchange:	NYSE	Minimum:	$50
Industry:	Oil & gas	Maximum:	$5,000/month
Company Address:	600 Grant St., Rm. 611	Min to qualify:	1
	Pittsburgh, PA 15219-4776	Fee on cash inv.:	0
Company Phone:	412-433-4801 or 412-433-6870	Fee on div. inv.:	0
Transfer Agent:	USX Corp.	Discount (cash):	0-3%
Agent's Address:	600 Grant Street, Rm. 611	Discount (div.):	0-3%
	Pittsburgh, PA 15219-4776	Auto invest:	No
Agent's Phone:	412-433-4801	Auto invest fee:	$0
Other than USA:	Yes	Selling info:	Sells weekly, by mail, at market, for 5¢/sh.

Company:	**USX-U.S. Steel Group**	Safekeeping:	Yes
Symbol:	X	Invests:	Every 30 days beginning 1/11
Exchange:	NYSE	Minimum:	$50
Industry:	Steel products manufacturer	Maximum:	$5,000/month
Company Address:	600 Grant St., Rm. 611	Min to qualify:	1
	Pittsburgh, PA 15219-4776	Fee on cash inv.:	0!
Company Phone:	412-433-4801 or 412-433-1121	Fee on div. inv.:	0!
Transfer Agent:	USX Corp.	Discount (cash):	0-3%
Agent's Address:	600 Grant Street, Rm. 611	Discount (div.):	0-3%
	Pittsburgh, PA 15219-4776	Auto invest:	No
Agent's Phone:	412-433-4801	Auto invest fee:	$0
Other than USA:	Yes	Selling info:	Sells weekly, by mail or fax, at market, for 5¢/sh.

Company:	**UtiliCorp United**	Safekeeping:	Yes
Symbol:	UCU	Invests:	Every 30 days beginning 1/12
Exchange:	NYSE	Minimum:	$50
Industry:	Utility-electric, gas	Maximum:	$10,000/month
Company Address:	Box 13287	Min to qualify:	1
	Kansas City, MO 64199-3287	Fee on cash inv.:	0!
Company Phone:	800-487-6661 or 816-421-6600	Fee on div. inv.:	0!
Transfer Agent:	FCT (EquiServe)	Discount (cash):	0
Agent's Address:	P.O. Box 2506	Discount (div.):	5%
	Jersey City, NJ 07303-2506	Auto invest:	Yes
Agent's Phone:	800-884-5426	Auto invest fee:	$0
Other than USA:	Yes	Selling info:	Sells daily, by phone, mail, or fax, at market, for $15 +12¢/sh.

Company:	**Valley National Bancorp**	Safekeeping:	Yes
Symbol:	VLY	Invests:	Every 30 days beginning 1/1
Exchange:	NYSE	Minimum:	$50
Industry:	Banking	Maximum:	$5,000/month
Company Address:	1455 Valley Rd.	Min to qualify:	1
	Wayne, NJ 07470	Fee on cash inv.:	0!
Company Phone:	800-522-4100 or 973-305-3380	Fee on div. inv.:	0!
Transfer Agent:	American Stock Transfer	Discount (cash):	0
Agent's Address:	40 Wall Street	Discount (div.):	0
	New York, NY 10005	Auto invest:	Yes
Agent's Phone:	800-278-4353	Auto invest fee:	$0
Other than USA:	No	Selling info:	Sells weekly, by mail, at market, for 4¢/sh.

Company:	**Valley Resources, Inc.**	Safekeeping:	Yes
Symbol:	VR	Invests:	Every 7 days beginning varies
Exchange:	ASE	Minimum:	$25
Industry:	Utility-gas	Maximum:	$75,000/year
Company Address:	1595 Mendon Rd., Box 7900	Min to qualify:	1
	Cumberland, RI 02864-0700	Fee on cash inv.:	0!
Company Phone:	401-334-1188 x 2302	Fee on div. inv.:	0!
Transfer Agent:	Bank of New York	Discount (cash):	0
Agent's Address:	P.O. Box 11258, Church St. Station	Discount (div.):	5%
	New York, NY 10286	Auto invest:	Yes
Agent's Phone:	800-524-4458	Auto invest fee:	$0
Other than USA:	Yes	Selling info:	Sells weekly, by mail, at market, for $5 + comm.

Company:	**Valmet Corp.**	Safekeeping:	Yes
Symbol:	VA	Invests:	Every 7 days beginning varies
Exchange:	NYSE	Minimum:	$50
Industry:	Intl. paper manufacturer	Maximum:	$250,000/week
Company Address:	c/o BNY,101 Barclay St.,22 West	Min to qualify:	1
	New York, NY 10286	Fee on cash inv.:	$5 + 10¢/sh.
Company Phone:	800-943-9715	Fee on div. inv.:	5% to $5 + 10¢/sh.
Transfer Agent:	Bank of New York	Discount (cash):	0
Agent's Address:	P.O. Box 11258	Discount (div.):	0
	New York, NY 10286	Auto invest:	Yes
Agent's Phone:	888-269-2377	Auto invest fee:	$0
Other than USA:	Yes	Selling info:	Sells weekly, by phone or mail, at market, for $5 +10¢/sh.

Company:	**Valspar Corp**	Safekeeping:	Yes
Symbol:	VAL	Invests:	Every 7 days beginning varies
Exchange:	NYSE	Minimum:	$100
Industry:	Mfr. chemicals, paints & coatings	Maximum:	$10,000/month
Company Address:	1101 Third St. South	Min to qualify:	1
	Minneapolis, MN 55415	Fee on cash inv.:	$5 + 12¢/sh.
Company Phone:	612-332-7371	Fee on div. inv.:	0
Transfer Agent:	ChaseMellon Shareholder Services	Discount (cash):	0
Agent's Address:	P.O. Box 3338	Discount (div.):	0
	South Hackensack, NJ 07606-1938	Auto invest:	Yes
Agent's Phone:	800-842-7629	Auto invest fee:	$3 + 12¢/sh.
Other than USA:	Yes	Selling info:	Sells weekly, by mail or phone, at market, for $15 +12¢/sh.

Company:	**Varian Medical Systems, Inc.**	Safekeeping:	Yes
		Invests:	Every 30 days beginning 1/1
Symbol:	VAR	Minimum:	$50
Exchange:	NYSE	Maximum:	$40,000/year
Industry:	Electronic devices	Min to qualify:	1
Company Address:	3050 Hansen Way	Fee on cash inv.:	5% to $5 + comm.
	Palo Alto, CA 94304-1000	Fee on div. inv.:	5% to $5
Company Phone:	650-424-5369 or 650-493-4000	Discount (cash):	0
Transfer Agent:	FCT (EquiServe)	Discount (div.):	0
Agent's Address:	P.O. Box 2598	Auto invest:	Yes
	Jersey City, NJ 07303-2598	Auto invest fee:	$1
Agent's Phone:	800-756-8200	Selling info:	Sells daily, by phone, mail, or fax,
Other than USA:	No		at market, for 5% to $5 +12¢/sh.

Company:	**VEBA Aktiengesellschaft**	Safekeeping:	Yes
Symbol:	VEB	Invests:	Every 7 days beginning varies
Exchange:	NYSE	Minimum:	$50
Industry:	Oil & Gas	Maximum:	$100,000/year
Company Address:	c/o Morgan Guaranty Trust,	Min to qualify:	1
	Box 9073	Fee on cash inv.:	$5 + 12¢/sh.
	Boston, MA 02205-9948	Fee on div. inv.:	5% to $2.50
Company Phone:	800-428-4237	Discount (cash):	0
Transfer Agent:	Morgan Guaranty Trust Co.	Discount (div.):	0
Agent's Address:	P.O. Box 9073	Auto invest:	Yes
	Boston, MA 02205-9948	Auto invest fee:	$5 + 12¢/sh.
Agent's Phone:	800-428-4237	Selling info:	Sells daily, by mail or phone, at
Other than USA:	No		avg. price, for $5 +12¢/sh.

Company:	**Venator Group**	Safekeeping:	Yes
Symbol:	Z	Invests:	Every 30 days beginning 1/1
Exchange:	NYSE	Minimum:	$20
Industry:	Retail stores	Maximum:	$60,000/year
Company Address:	233 Broadway	Min to qualify:	1
	New York, NY 10279-0003	Fee on cash inv.:	0!
Company Phone:	212-553-2391 or 212-553-2600	Fee on div. inv.:	0!
Transfer Agent:	FCT (EquiServe)	Discount (cash):	0
Agent's Address:	P.O. Box 2500	Discount (div.):	0
	Jersey City, NJ 07303-2500	Auto invest:	No
Agent's Phone:	800-519-3111	Auto invest fee:	$0
Other than USA:	No	Selling info:	Sells daily, by phone, mail, or fax,
			at market, for $10 +12¢/sh.

Company:	**VF Corp.**	Safekeeping:	No
Symbol:	VFC	Invests:	Every 90 days beginning 3/20
Exchange:	NYSE	Minimum:	$10
Industry:	Apparel, casual	Maximum:	$3,000/quarter
Company Address:	Box 21488	Min to qualify:	1
	Greensboro, NC 27420	Fee on cash inv.:	5% to $2.50
Company Phone:	336-547-6000	Fee on div. inv.:	5% to $2.50
Transfer Agent:	FCT (EquiServe)	Discount (cash):	0
Agent's Address:	P.O. Box 2500-Suite 4694	Discount (div.):	0
	Jersey City, NJ 07303-2500	Auto invest:	No
Agent's Phone:	201-324-1225	Auto invest fee:	$0
Other than USA:	Yes	Selling info:	Sells daily, by mail, at market, for
			$10 +12¢/sh.

Company:	**VimpelCom**	Safekeeping:	Yes
Symbol:	VIP	Invests:	Every 7 days beginning varies
Exchange:	NYSE	Minimum:	$50
Industry:	Cellular telecommunications	Maximum:	$250,000/week
Company Address:	c/o BNY,101 Barclay St.,22 West	Min to qualify:	1
	New York, NY 10286	Fee on cash inv.:	$5 + 10¢/sh.
Company Phone:	800-943-9715	Fee on div. inv.:	0
Transfer Agent:	Bank of New York	Discount (cash):	0
Agent's Address:	P.O. Box 11258	Discount (div.):	0
	New York, NY 10286	Auto invest:	Yes
Agent's Phone:	888-269-2377	Auto invest fee:	$0
Other than USA:	Yes	Selling info:	Sells weekly, by phone or mail, at market, for $5 +10¢/sh.

Company:	**Vina Concha y Toro, S.A.**	Safekeeping:	Yes
Symbol:	VCO	Invests:	Every 7 days beginning varies
Exchange:	NYSE	Minimum:	$50
Industry:	Winery	Maximum:	$250,000/year
Company Address:	c/o BNY,101 Barclay St.,22 West	Min to qualify:	1
	New York, NY 10286	Fee on cash inv.:	$5 + 10¢/sh.
Company Phone:	800-943-9715	Fee on div. inv.:	5% to $5 + 10¢/sh.
Transfer Agent:	Bank of New York	Discount (cash):	0
Agent's Address:	P.O. Box 11258	Discount (div.):	0
	New York, NY 10286	Auto invest:	Yes
Agent's Phone:	888-269-2377	Auto invest fee:	$5 + 10¢/sh.
Other than USA:	Yes	Selling info:	Sells weekly, by mail, at market, for $5 +10¢/sh.

Company:	**Vista Bancorp, Inc.**	Safekeeping:	Yes
Symbol:	VBNJ	Invests:	Every 90 days beginning 3/10
Exchange:	OTC	Minimum:	$25
Industry:	Banking	Maximum:	$100 sh./quarter
Company Address:	305 Roseberry St., Box 5360	Min to qualify:	1
	Phillipsburg, NJ 08865	Fee on cash inv.:	0
Company Phone:	908-859-9500	Fee on div. inv.:	0
Transfer Agent:	Vista Bancorp, Inc.	Discount (cash):	0
Agent's Address:	305 Roseberry St., Box 5360	Discount (div.):	0
	Phillipsburg, NJ 08865	Auto invest:	No
Agent's Phone:	908-859-9500	Auto invest fee:	$0
Other than USA:	No	Selling info:	Not available

Company:	**Vodafone AirTouch plc**	Safekeeping:	Yes
Symbol:	VOD	Invests:	Every 7 days beginning varies
Exchange:	NYSE	Minimum:	$50
Industry:	Intl. mobile telecommunications	Maximum:	$250,000/week
Company Address:	c/o BNY,101 Barclay St.,22 West	Min to qualify:	1
	New York, NY 10286	Fee on cash inv.:	$5 + 10¢/sh.
Company Phone:	800-943-9715	Fee on div. inv.:	5% to $5 + 10¢/sh.
Transfer Agent:	Bank of New York	Discount (cash):	0
Agent's Address:	P.O. Box 11258	Discount (div.):	0
	New York, NY 10286	Auto invest:	Yes
Agent's Phone:	888-269-2377	Auto invest fee:	$0
Other than USA:	Yes	Selling info:	Sells weekly, by phone or mail, at market, for $5 +10¢/ADS

Company:	**Volvo B**	**Safekeeping:**	Yes
Symbol:	VOLVY	**Invests:**	Every 30 days beginning 1/15
Exchange:	OTC	**Minimum:**	$25
Industry:	Swedish auto mfr.	**Maximum:**	$5,000/month
Company Address:	570 Lexington Ave., 20th Fl.	**Min to qualify:**	1
	New York, NY 10022	**Fee on cash inv.:**	0
Company Phone:	212-418-7400 or 212-418-7431	**Fee on div. inv.:**	0
Transfer Agent:	Norwest Bank Minnesota	**Discount (cash):**	0
Agent's Address:	P.O. Box 64854	**Discount (div.):**	0
	St. Paul, MN 55164-0854	**Auto invest:**	No
Agent's Phone:	800-468-9716	**Auto invest fee:**	$0
Other than USA:	Yes	**Selling info:**	Not available

Company:	**Vulcan Materials Co.**	**Safekeeping:**	Yes
Symbol:	VMC	**Invests:**	Every 30 days beginning 1/10
Exchange:	NYSE	**Minimum:**	$10
Industry:	Construction, industrial	**Maximum:**	$60,000/year
	chemicals	**Min to qualify:**	1
Company Address:	Box 385014	**Fee on cash inv.:**	5% to $2.50 + 3¢/sh.
	Birmingham, AL 35238-5014	**Fee on div. inv.:**	5% to $2.50 + 3¢/sh.
Company Phone:	205-298-3000 or 205-298-3202	**Discount (cash):**	0
Transfer Agent:	FCT (EquiServe)	**Discount (div.):**	0
Agent's Address:	P.O. Box 2598	**Auto invest:**	No
	Jersey City, NJ 07303-2598	**Auto invest fee:**	$0
Agent's Phone:	800-519-3111	**Selling info:**	Sells daily, by phone or mail, at
Other than USA:	Yes		market, for $10 +12¢/sh.

Company:	**Wachovia Corp.**	**Safekeeping:**	Yes
Symbol:	WB	**Invests:**	Every 30 days beginning 1/1
Exchange:	NYSE	**Minimum:**	$20
Industry:	Banking	**Maximum:**	$15,000/month
Company Address:	100 North Main St., Box 3099	**Min to qualify:**	1
	Winston-Salem, NC 27150	**Fee on cash inv.:**	0!
Company Phone:	336-732-5787 or 336-770-5000	**Fee on div. inv.:**	0!
Transfer Agent:	Wachovia (EquiServe)	**Discount (cash):**	0
Agent's Address:	P.O. Box 8218	**Discount (div.):**	0
	Boston, MA 02266-8218	**Auto invest:**	Yes
Agent's Phone:	800-633-4236	**Auto invest fee:**	$0
Other than USA:	Yes	**Selling info:**	Sells within 10 bus. days, by mail
			or fax, at avg. price, for comm.

Company:	**Wacoal Corp.**	**Safekeeping:**	Yes
Symbol:	WACLY	**Invests:**	Every 7 days beginning varies
Exchange:	OTC	**Minimum:**	$50
Industry:	Apparel, accessories	**Maximum:**	$250,000/year
Company Address:	c/o BNY,101 Barclay St.,22 West	**Min to qualify:**	1
	New York, NY 10286	**Fee on cash inv.:**	$5 + 10¢/sh.
Company Phone:	800-943-9715	**Fee on div. inv.:**	0
Transfer Agent:	Bank of New York	**Discount (cash):**	0
Agent's Address:	P.O. Box 11258	**Discount (div.):**	0
	New York, NY 10286	**Auto invest:**	Yes
Agent's Phone:	888-269-2377	**Auto invest fee:**	$5 + 10¢/sh.
Other than USA:	Yes	**Selling info:**	Sells weekly, by mail, at market,
			for $5 +10¢/sh.

Company:	**Wal-Mart Stores**	Safekeeping:	Yes
Symbol:	WMT	Invests:	Every daily days beginning 1/1
Exchange:	NYSE	Minimum:	$50
Industry:	Operates discount stores	Maximum:	$150,000/year
Company Address:	702 S.W. 8th St.	Min to qualify:	1
	Bentonville, AR 72716-8001	Fee on cash inv.:	$5 + 10¢/sh.
Company Phone:	501-273-6463 or 501-273-4000	Fee on div. inv.:	0!
Transfer Agent:	FCT (EquiServe)	Discount (cash):	0
Agent's Address:	P.O. Box 2540	Discount (div.):	0
	Jersey City, NJ 07303-2540	Auto invest:	Yes
Agent's Phone:	800-438-6278	Auto invest fee:	$1 + 10¢/sh.
Other than USA:	Yes	Selling info:	Sells daily, by phone or mail, at market, for $20 +10¢/sh.

Company:	**Walgreen Co.**	Safekeeping:	Yes
Symbol:	WAG	Invests:	Every 7 days beginning varies
Exchange:	NYSE	Minimum:	$50
Industry:	Retail stores	Maximum:	$60,000/year
Company Address:	200 Wilmont Rd., MS 2261	Min to qualify:	1
	Deerfield, IL 60015	Fee on cash inv.:	$5 + 10¢/sh.
Company Phone:	847-914-2972 or 847-940-2500	Fee on div. inv.:	0!
Transfer Agent:	Harris Trust & Savings Bank	Discount (cash):	0
Agent's Address:	P.O. Box A-3309	Discount (div.):	0
	Chicago, IL 60690	Auto invest:	Yes
Agent's Phone:	888-368-7346	Auto invest fee:	$1.50 + 10¢/sh.
Other than USA:	Yes	Selling info:	Sells weekly, by mail or fax, at market, for $10 +10¢/sh.

Company:	**Walt Disney Co.**	Safekeeping:	Yes
Symbol:	DIS	Invests:	Every 7 days beginning varies
Exchange:	NYSE	Minimum:	$100
Industry:	Recreation, film	Maximum:	$250,000/year
Company Address:	500 South Buena Vista St.	Min to qualify:	10
	Burbank, CA 91521-9722	Fee on cash inv.:	$5 + 3¢/sh.
Company Phone:	818-560-1000 or 818-553-7200	Fee on div. inv.:	0
Transfer Agent:	Walt Disney Co. Investment Plan,	Discount (cash):	0
	General Post Office	Discount (div.):	0
Agent's Address:	P.O. Box 7773	Auto invest:	Yes
	Burbank, CA 91510-7773	Auto invest fee:	$1
Agent's Phone:	818-553-7200	Selling info:	Sells irregularly, by mail,
Other than USA:	Yes		at market, for $10 + 3¢/sh.

Company:	**Warner Chilcott PLC**	Safekeeping:	Yes
Symbol:	WCRXY	Invests:	Every 7 days beginning varies
Exchange:	OTC	Minimum:	$50
Industry:	Biotechnology & drugs	Maximum:	$250,000/year
Company Address:	c/o BNY,101 Barclay St.,22 West	Min to qualify:	1
	New York, NY 10286	Fee on cash inv.:	$5 + 10¢/sh.
Company Phone:	800-943-9715	Fee on div. inv.:	0
Transfer Agent:	Bank of New York	Discount (cash):	0
Agent's Address:	P.O. Box 11258	Discount (div.):	0
	New York, NY 10286	Auto invest:	Yes
Agent's Phone:	888-269-2377	Auto invest fee:	$5 + 10¢/sh.
Other than USA:	Yes	Selling info:	Sells weekly, by mail, at market, for $5 +10¢/sh.

Company:	**Warner-Lambert Co.**	**Safekeeping:**	Yes
Symbol:	WLA	**Invests:**	Every 5 days beginning Thursday
Exchange:	NYSE	**Minimum:**	$50
Industry:	Drugs, consumer products	**Maximum:**	$unlimited
Company Address:	201 Tabor Rd.	**Min to qualify:**	1
	Morris Plains, NJ 07950-2693	**Fee on cash inv.:**	$5 + 3¢/sh.
Company Phone:	973-540-4874 or 973-540-2000	**Fee on div. inv.:**	5% to $3 + 3¢/sh.
Transfer Agent:	FCT (EquiServe)	**Discount (cash):**	0
Agent's Address:	P.O. Box 2500	**Discount (div.):**	0
	Jersey City, NJ 07303-2500	**Auto invest:**	Yes
Agent's Phone:	800-446-2617	**Auto invest fee:**	$2 + 3¢/sh.
Other than USA:	Yes	**Selling info:**	Sells daily, by phone or mail, at avg. price, for $15 +12¢/sh.

Company:	**Washington Gas Light Co.**	**Safekeeping:**	Yes
Symbol:	WGL	**Invests:**	Every 30 days beginning 1/1
Exchange:	NYSE	**Minimum:**	$25
Industry:	Utility-gas	**Maximum:**	$20,000/quarter
Company Address:	1100 H St. NW	**Min to qualify:**	1
	Washington, DC 20080	**Fee on cash inv.:**	5¢/sh.
Company Phone:	800-221-9427 or 703-750-5636	**Fee on div. inv.:**	5¢/sh.
Transfer Agent:	Bank of New York	**Discount (cash):**	0
Agent's Address:	101 Barclay St., Investor Relations	**Discount (div.):**	0
	New York, NY 10286	**Auto invest:**	No
Agent's Phone:	888-269-8845	**Auto invest fee:**	$0
Other than USA:	Yes	**Selling info:**	Sells weekly, by mail or fax, at market, for 3¢ to 5¢/sh.

Company:	**Washington Mutual, Inc.**	**Safekeeping:**	Yes
Symbol:	WM	**Invests:**	Every 30 days beginning 1/15
Exchange:	NYSE	**Minimum:**	$50
Industry:	Banking	**Maximum:**	$10,000/quarter
Company Address:	1201 3rd Ave., WMT 0735	**Min to qualify:**	1
	Seattle, WA 98101	**Fee on cash inv.:**	0
Company Phone:	206-461-4744 or 206-461-8856	**Fee on div. inv.:**	0
Transfer Agent:	ChaseMellon Shareholder Services	**Discount (cash):**	0
Agent's Address:	P.O. Box 3315	**Discount (div.):**	0
	S. Hackensack, NJ 07606-1915	**Auto invest:**	Yes
Agent's Phone:	800-234-5835	**Auto invest fee:**	$0
Other than USA:	Yes	**Selling info:**	Sells bimonthly, by mail or phone, at market, for $5 + comm.

Company:	**Washington REIT**	**Safekeeping:**	Yes
Symbol:	WRE	**Invests:**	Every 30 days beginning 1/30
Exchange:	NYSE	**Minimum:**	$100
Industry:	REIT	**Maximum:**	$25,000/quarter
Company Address:	6110 Executive Blvd., Ste.800	**Min to qualify:**	1
	Rockville, MD 20852	**Fee on cash inv.:**	0!
Company Phone:	800-565-9748 or 301-984-9400	**Fee on div. inv.:**	0!
Transfer Agent:	American Stock Transfer	**Discount (cash):**	0
Agent's Address:	40 Wall Street, 46th Floor	**Discount (div.):**	0
	New York, NY 10005	**Auto invest:**	Yes
Agent's Phone:	800-937-5449 or 800-278-4353 or	**Auto invest fee:**	$0
	718-921-8200	**Selling info:**	Sells monthly, by mail or fax, at market, for $10 + 4¢/sh.
Other than USA:	Yes		

Company:	**Washington Trust Bancorp, Inc.**	Safekeeping:	Yes
		Invests:	Every 90 days beginning 1/15
Symbol:	WASH	Minimum:	$25
Exchange:	OTC	Maximum:	$10,000/quarter
Industry:	Banking	Min to qualify:	1
Company Address:	23 Broad St., Box 512	Fee on cash inv.:	0!
	Westerly, RI 02891-0512	Fee on div. inv.:	0!
Company Phone:	401-348-1309 or 401-348-1200	Discount (cash):	0
Transfer Agent:	Washington Trust Company	Discount (div.):	0
Agent's Address:	P.O. Box 512	Auto invest:	Yes
	Westerly, RI 02891-0512	Auto invest fee:	$0
Agent's Phone:	401-348-1200	Selling info:	Not available
Other than USA:	No		

Company:	**Waste Management, Inc.**	Safekeeping:	Yes
Symbol:	WMI	Invests:	Every 7 days beginning 1/7
Exchange:	NYSE	Minimum:	$50
Industry:	Waste management, energy, &	Maximum:	$100,000/year
	environmental	Min to qualify:	1
Company Address:	1001 Fannin, Ste.4000	Fee on cash inv.:	$5 + 10¢/sh.
	Houston, TX 77002	Fee on div. inv.:	0!
Company Phone:	713-512-6548 or 713-512-6200	Discount (cash):	0
Transfer Agent:	Harris Trust & Savings Bank	Discount (div.):	0
Agent's Address:	P.O. Box A-3309	Auto invest:	Yes
	Chicago, IL 60690	Auto invest fee:	$1.50 + 10¢/sh.
Agent's Phone:	800-245-7630	Selling info:	Sells weekly, by mail, at market,
Other than USA:	Yes		for $10 +10¢/sh.

Company:	**Waterford Wedgewood plc**	Safekeeping:	Yes
Symbol:	WATFZ	Invests:	Every 7 days beginning varies
Exchange:	OTC	Minimum:	$50
Industry:	Mfr. china & crystal	Maximum:	$100,000/year
Company Address:	c/o BNY,101 Barclay St., 22 West	Min to qualify:	1
	New York, NY 10286	Fee on cash inv.:	$5 + 12¢/sh.
Company Phone:	212-815-2175	Fee on div. inv.:	5% to $2.50
Transfer Agent:	Bank of New York	Discount (cash):	0
Agent's Address:	P.O. Box 11258	Discount (div.):	0
	New York, NY 10286	Auto invest:	Yes
Agent's Phone:	888-269-2377	Auto invest fee:	$5
Other than USA:	No	Selling info:	Sells daily, by phone or mail, at
			avg. price, for $5 +12¢/sh.

Company:	**Wausau-Mosinee Paper Corp.**	Safekeeping:	Yes
		Invests:	Every 90 days beginning 2/15
Symbol:	WMO	Minimum:	$25
Exchange:	NYSE	Maximum:	$5,000/quarter
Industry:	Paper & lumber	Min to qualify:	1
Company Address:	1244 Kronenwetter Dr.	Fee on cash inv.:	0!
	Mosinee, WI 54455-9099	Fee on div. inv.:	0!
Company Phone:	715-693-4470	Discount (cash):	0
Transfer Agent:	Harris Trust & Savings Bank	Discount (div.):	0
Agent's Address:	P.O. Box A3309	Auto invest:	No
	Chicago, IL 60690	Auto invest fee:	$0
Agent's Phone:	877-424-1980	Selling info:	Sells weekly, by mail, at market,
Other than USA:	No		for 7¢ to 10¢/sh.

Company:	**WebsterFinancial Corp.**	**Safekeeping:**	Yes
Symbol:	WBST	**Invests:**	Every 90 days beginning 2/12
Exchange:	OTC	**Minimum:**	$100
Industry:	Banking	**Maximum:**	$10,000/month
Company Address:	Webster Plaza	**Min to qualify:**	1
	Waterbury, CT 06702	**Fee on cash inv.:**	0
Company Phone:	203-753-2921	**Fee on div. inv.:**	0
Transfer Agent:	American Stock & Transfer	**Discount (cash):**	0
Agent's Address:	40 Wall St., 46th Floor	**Discount (div.):**	0
	New York, NY 10005	**Auto invest:**	No
Agent's Phone:	800-278-4353 or 718-921-8283	**Auto invest fee:**	$0
Other than USA:	Yes	**Selling info:**	Sells weekly, by mail, at market, for 0

Company:	**Weeks Corp.**	**Safekeeping:**	Yes
Symbol:	WKS	**Invests:**	Every 30 days beginning 1/1
Exchange:	NYSE	**Minimum:**	$100
Industry:	REIT	**Maximum:**	$7,500/month
Company Address:	4497 Park Dr.	**Min to qualify:**	1
	Norcross, GA 30093	**Fee on cash inv.:**	0
Company Phone:	770-923-4076	**Fee on div. inv.:**	0
Transfer Agent:	Wachovia (EquiServe)	**Discount (cash):**	0
Agent's Address:	P.O. Box 8217	**Discount (div.):**	3%
	Boston, MA 02266-8217	**Auto invest:**	No
Agent's Phone:	800-633-4236	**Auto invest fee:**	$0
Other than USA:	Yes	**Selling info:**	Sells weekly, by mail, at market, for 5¢/sh.

Company:	**Weingarten Realty Investors**	**Safekeeping:**	Yes
		Invests:	Every 30 days beginning 1/15
Symbol:	WRI	**Minimum:**	$100
Exchange:	NYSE	**Maximum:**	$25,000/month
Industry:	REIT	**Min to qualify:**	1
Company Address:	2600 Citadel Plaza Dr., Box 924133	**Fee on cash inv.:**	0
	Houston, TX 77292-4133	**Fee on div. inv.:**	0
Company Phone:	713-866-6000 or 219-965-2236	**Discount (cash):**	0
Transfer Agent:	ChaseMellon Shareholder Services	**Discount (div.):**	0
Agent's Address:	85 Challenger Road	**Auto invest:**	Yes
	Ridgefield Park, NJ 07660	**Auto invest fee:**	$0
Agent's Phone:	800-550-4689	**Selling info:**	Sells weekly, by mail or phone, at market, for $15 +12¢/sh.
Other than USA:	Yes		

Company:	**Weis Markets, Inc.**	**Safekeeping:**	Yes
Symbol:	WMK	**Invests:**	Every 90 days beginning 2/26
Exchange:	NYSE	**Minimum:**	$10
Industry:	Retail stores	**Maximum:**	$3,000/quarter
Company Address:	1000 S. Second St., Box 471	**Min to qualify:**	50
	Sunbury, PA 17801-0471	**Fee on cash inv.:**	0
Company Phone:	717-286-4571	**Fee on div. inv.:**	0
Transfer Agent:	American Stock Transfer	**Discount (cash):**	0
Agent's Address:	40 Wall Street-46th Floor	**Discount (div.):**	0
	New York, NY 10005	**Auto invest:**	No
Agent's Phone:	800-937-5449 or 718-921-8210	**Auto invest fee:**	$0
Other than USA:	No	**Selling info:**	Sells weekly, by mail, at market, for comm.

Company:	**Wells Fargo & Co.**	**Safekeeping:**	Yes
Symbol:	WFC	**Invests:**	Every 7 days beginning Thurs.
Exchange:	NYSE	**Minimum:**	$25
Industry:	Banking	**Maximum:**	$10,000/month
Company Address:	Sixth & Marquette Ave.	**Min to qualify:**	1
	Minneapolis, MN 55479-1016	**Fee on cash inv.:**	$3 + 3¢/sh.
Company Phone:	888-662-7865 or 612-667-7919	**Fee on div. inv.:**	4% to $4 + 3¢/sh.
Transfer Agent:	Norwest Bank Minnesota	**Discount (cash):**	0
Agent's Address:	P.O. Box 64854	**Discount (div.):**	0
	St. Paul, MN 55164-0854	**Auto invest:**	Yes
Agent's Phone:	800-468-9716	**Auto invest fee:**	$1
Other than USA:	Yes	**Selling info:**	Sells daily, by phone or mail, at avg. price, for $10 + 3¢/sh.

Company:	**Wendy's International, Inc.**	**Safekeeping:**	Yes
		Invests:	Every 30 days beginning 1/10
Symbol:	WEN	**Minimum:**	$20
Exchange:	NYSE	**Maximum:**	$20,000/year
Industry:	Restaurant	**Min to qualify:**	1
Company Address:	4288 W. Dublin Granville Rd.,	**Fee on cash inv.:**	0!
	Box 256	**Fee on div. inv.:**	0!
	Dublin, OH 43017-0256	**Discount (cash):**	0
Company Phone:	614-764-3019 or 614-764-3044	**Discount (div.):**	0
Transfer Agent:	American Stock Transfer	**Auto invest:**	Yes
Agent's Address:	40 Wall Street, 46th Fl.	**Auto invest fee:**	$0
	New York, NY 10005	**Selling info:**	Sells weekly, by mail or fax, at market, for $2 + 4¢/sh.
Agent's Phone:	800-278-4353		
Other than USA:	Yes		

Company:	**WesBanco, Inc.**	**Safekeeping:**	Yes
Symbol:	WSBC	**Invests:**	Every 90 days beginning 1/2
Exchange:	OTC	**Minimum:**	$10
Industry:	Banking	**Maximum:**	$5,000/quarter
Company Address:	1 Bank Plaza	**Min to qualify:**	1
	Wheeling, WV 26003	**Fee on cash inv.:**	0
Company Phone:	304-234-9000 or 304-234-9208	**Fee on div. inv.:**	0
Transfer Agent:	American Stock Transfer	**Discount (cash):**	0
Agent's Address:	40 Wall Street, 46th Floor	**Discount (div.):**	0
	New York, NY 10005	**Auto invest:**	Yes
Agent's Phone:	800-278-4353	**Auto invest fee:**	$0
Other than USA:	No	**Selling info:**	Sells weekly, by mail, at market, for comm.

Company:	**West Pharmaceutical Services Inc.**	**Safekeeping:**	Yes
		Invests:	Every 30 days beginning 1/1
Symbol:	WST	**Minimum:**	$50
Exchange:	NYSE	**Maximum:**	$5,000/month
Industry:	Packaging components,	**Min to qualify:**	1
	pharmaceutical svcs.	**Fee on cash inv.:**	0!
Company Address:	101 Gordon Dr.	**Fee on div. inv.:**	0!
	Lionville, PA 19341	**Discount (cash):**	0
Company Phone:	610-594-2900 or 610-594-3346	**Discount (div.):**	0
Transfer Agent:	American Stock Transfer	**Auto invest:**	No
Agent's Address:	40 Wall Street	**Auto invest fee:**	$0
	New York, N.Y. 10005	**Selling info:**	Sells weekly, by mail, at market, for 4¢/sh.
Agent's Phone:	800-937-5449 or 718-921-8200		
Other than USA:	No		

Company:	**Westamerica Bancorp**	Safekeeping:	No
Symbol:	WABC	Invests:	Every 30 days beginning 1/15
Exchange:	OTC	Minimum:	$100
Industry:	Banking	Maximum:	$3,000/month
Company Address:	Box 1250, Inv. Relations, A-2B	Min to qualify:	1
	Suisun City, CA 94585-1250	Fee on cash inv.:	0!
Company Phone:	707-863-6992 or 800-848-1088	Fee on div. inv.:	0!
Transfer Agent:	ChaseMellon Shareholder Services	Discount (cash):	0
Agent's Address:	P.O. Box 3338	Discount (div.):	0
	South Hackensack, NJ 07606-1938	Auto invest:	No
Agent's Phone:	800-953-2490	Auto invest fee:	$0
Other than USA:	Yes	Selling info:	Sells monthly, by mail or phone, at avg. price, for $15 +10¢/sh.

Company:	**Westcoast Energy Inc.**	Safekeeping:	Yes
Symbol:	WE	Invests:	Every 90 days beginning 3/31
Exchange:	NYSE	Minimum:	$50
Industry:	Gas pipeline operations	Maximum:	$5,000/quarter Cdn.
Company Address:	1333 West Georgia St.	Min to qualify:	1
	Vancouver, BC Canada V6E 3K9	Fee on cash inv.:	0!
Company Phone:	604-488-8021 or 604-488-8000	Fee on div. inv.:	0!
Transfer Agent:	Montreal Trust Company	Discount (cash):	0
Agent's Address:	510 Burrard Street	Discount (div.):	5%
	Vancouver, BC V6C 3B9 Canada	Auto invest:	No
Agent's Phone:	888-661-5566	Auto invest fee:	$0
Other than USA:	Yes	Selling info:	Not available

Company:	**WesterFed Financial Corp.**	Safekeeping:	Yes
		Invests:	Every 90 days beginning 2/21
Symbol:	WSTR	Minimum:	$100
Exchange:	OTC	Maximum:	$2,500/quarter
Industry:	Savings and loan	Min to qualify:	1
Company Address:	110 East Broadway	Fee on cash inv.:	0!
	Missoula, MT 59802	Fee on div. inv.:	0!
Company Phone:	406-721-5254	Discount (cash):	0
Transfer Agent:	TrustCorp	Discount (div.):	0
Agent's Address:	8 Third Street, Suite 301	Auto invest:	No
	P.O. Box 2309	Auto invest fee:	$0
	Great Falls, MT 59403-5526	Selling info:	Sells irregularly, by mail,
Agent's Phone:	800-634-5526		at market, for comm.
Other than USA:	Yes		

Company:	**Western Investment RE Trust**	Safekeeping:	No
		Invests:	Every 90 days beginning 3/15
Symbol:	WIR	Minimum:	$500
Exchange:	ASE	Maximum:	$5,000/quarter
Industry:	REIT	Min to qualify:	1
Company Address:	2200 Powell St., Ste. 600	Fee on cash inv.:	0
	Emeryville, CA 94608	Fee on div. inv.:	0
Company Phone:	888-831-5770 or 510-597-0160	Discount (cash):	0
Transfer Agent:	ChaseMellon Shareholder Services	Discount (div.):	0
Agent's Address:	P.O. Box 3315	Auto invest:	No
	South Hackensack, NJ 07606	Auto invest fee:	$0
Agent's Phone:	800-982-7649	Selling info:	Not available
Other than USA:	Yes		

Company:	**Western Resources, Inc.**	Safekeeping:	Yes
Symbol:	WR	Invests:	Every 15 days beginning 1/1
Exchange:	NYSE	Minimum:	$50
Industry:	Utility-electric, gas	Maximum:	$10,000/month
Company Address:	818 S. Kansas Ave., Box 750320	Min to qualify:	1
	Topeka, KS 66675-0320	Fee on cash inv.:	0!
Company Phone:	800-527-2495 or 785-575-6394	Fee on div. inv.:	0!
Transfer Agent:	Western Resources	Discount (cash):	2%
Agent's Address:	P.O. Box 750320	Discount (div.):	2%
	Topeka, KS 66675-0320	Auto invest:	Yes
Agent's Phone:	800-527-2495	Auto invest fee:	$0
Other than USA:	Yes	Selling info:	Sells weekly, by mail or fax, at avg price, for 7¢/sh.

Company:	**Westernbank Puerto Rico**	Safekeeping:	Yes
Symbol:	WBPR	Invests:	Every 7 days beginning varies
Exchange:	OTC	Minimum:	$50
Industry:	Banking	Maximum:	$5,000/investment
Company Address:	19 West Mckinley St.	Min to qualify:	1
	Mayaguez, PR 00680	Fee on cash inv.:	$2 + 7¢/sh.
Company Phone:	809-934-8000	Fee on div. inv.:	$1.50 + 7¢/sh.
Transfer Agent:	Bank of New York	Discount (cash):	0
Agent's Address:	P.O. Box 11258	Discount (div.):	0
	New York, NY 10286	Auto invest:	Yes
Agent's Phone:	888-269-2377	Auto invest fee:	$2 + 7¢/sh.
Other than USA:	Yes	Selling info:	Sells daily, by mail or phone, at market, for $5 +7¢/sh.

Company:	**Westpac Banking Corp.**	Safekeeping:	Yes
Symbol:	WBK	Invests:	Every 7 days beginning varies
Exchange:	NYSE	Minimum:	$50
Industry:	Commercial banking-Australia	Maximum:	$100,000/year
Company Address:	c/o Morgan Guaranty Trust,	Min to qualify:	1
	Box 9073	Fee on cash inv.:	$5 + 12¢/sh.
	Boston, MA 02205-9948	Fee on div. inv.:	5% to $2.50
Company Phone:	800-428-4237	Discount (cash):	0
Transfer Agent:	Morgan Guaranty Trust Co.	Discount (div.):	0
Agent's Address:	P.O. Box 9073	Auto invest:	Yes
	Boston, MA 02205-9948	Auto invest fee:	$5
Agent's Phone:	800-428-4237	Selling info:	Sells daily, by phone or mail, at avg. price, for $5 +12¢/sh.
Other than USA:	No		

Company:	**Westvaco Corp.**	Safekeeping:	Yes
Symbol:	W	Invests:	Every 7 days beginning varies
Exchange:	NYSE	Minimum:	$25
Industry:	Paper, chemicals	Maximum:	$5,000/quarter
Company Address:	299 Park Ave.	Min to qualify:	1
	New York, NY 10171	Fee on cash inv.:	0!
Company Phone:	800-432-9874 or 212-688-5000	Fee on div. inv.:	0!
Transfer Agent:	Bank of New York	Discount (cash):	0
Agent's Address:	P.O. Box 11258, Church St. Station	Discount (div.):	0
	New York, NY 10286-1258	Auto invest:	Yes
Agent's Phone:	800-432-0140	Auto invest fee:	$0
Other than USA:	Yes	Selling info:	Sells weekly, by mail, at market, for 5¢/sh.

Company:	**Weyerhaeuser Co.**	Safekeeping:	Yes
Symbol:	WY	Invests:	Every 30 days beginning 1/1
Exchange:	NYSE	Minimum:	$100
Industry:	Forestry & wood products	Maximum:	$25,000/quarter
Company Address:	Box 2999	Min to qualify:	1
	Tacoma, WA 98477-2999	Fee on cash inv.:	$5 + comm.
Company Phone:	253-924-2345	Fee on div. inv.:	4% to $1.50
Transfer Agent:	ChaseMellon Shareholder Services	Discount (cash):	0
Agent's Address:	P.O. Box 3315	Discount (div.):	0
	S. Hackensack, NJ 07606	Auto invest:	No
Agent's Phone:	800-561-4405	Auto invest fee:	$0
Other than USA:	Yes	Selling info:	Sells weekly, by mail or phone, at market, for $15 + comm.

Company:	**Whirlpool Corp.**	Safekeeping:	Yes
Symbol:	WHR	Invests:	Every 7 days beginning varies
Exchange:	NYSE	Minimum:	$100
Industry:	Household appliances	Maximum:	$250,000/year
Company Address:	2000 N. M-63 #3001	Min to qualify:	1
	Benton Harbor, MI 49022-2692	Fee on cash inv.:	$5 + 3¢/sh.
Company Phone:	616-926-3189 or 616-923-5000	Fee on div. inv.:	5% to $3 + 3¢/sh.
Transfer Agent:	FCT (EquiServe)	Discount (cash):	0
Agent's Address:	P.O. Box 2500	Discount (div.):	0
	Jersey City, NJ 07303-2500	Auto invest:	Yes
Agent's Phone:	800-446-2617	Auto invest fee:	$2 + 3¢/sh.
Other than USA:	Yes	Selling info:	Sells daily, by phone or mail, at market, for $15 +12¢/sh.

Company:	**Whitman Corp.**	Safekeeping:	Yes
Symbol:	WH	Invests:	Every 7 days beginning varies
Exchange:	NYSE	Minimum:	$50
Industry:	Beverages	Maximum:	$120,000/year
Company Address:	3501 Algonquin Rd.	Min to qualify:	1
	Rolling Meadows, IL 60008	Fee on cash inv.:	5% to $5 + 3¢/sh.
Company Phone:	847-818-5000	Fee on div. inv.:	5% to $3 + 3¢/sh.
Transfer Agent:	FCT (EquiServe)	Discount (cash):	0
Agent's Address:	P.O. Box 2598	Discount (div.):	0
	Jersey City, NJ 07303-2598	Auto invest:	Yes
Agent's Phone:	800-446-2617	Auto invest fee:	$2 + comm
Other than USA:	Yes	Selling info:	Sells daily, by phone, mail, or fax, at market, for $15 +12¢/sh.

Company:	**Whitney Holding Co.**	Safekeeping:	Yes
Symbol:	WTNY	Invests:	Every 90 days beginning 1/3
Exchange:	OTC	Minimum:	$50
Industry:	Bank holding co.	Maximum:	$5,000/quarter
Company Address:	Box 61260	Min to qualify:	1
	New Orleans, LA 70161-1260	Fee on cash inv.:	0
Company Phone:	504-586-7272 or 504-586-3627	Fee on div. inv.:	0
Transfer Agent:	Bank of New York	Discount (cash):	0
Agent's Address:	Box 11258,Church St. Station,11E	Discount (div.):	0
	New York, NY 10286-1402	Auto invest:	No
Agent's Phone:	800-432-0140	Auto invest fee:	$0
Other than USA:	Yes	Selling info:	Not available

Company:	**WICOR, Inc.**
Symbol:	WIC
Exchange:	NYSE
Industry:	Utility-gas
Company Address:	626 East Wisconsin Ave.
	Milwaukee, WI 53202
Company Phone:	800-236-3453 or 414-291-6561
Transfer Agent:	ChaseMellon Shareholder Services
Agent's Address:	85 Challenger Road
	Ridgefield Park, NJ 07660
Agent's Phone:	800-621-9609
Other than USA:	Yes

Safekeeping:	Yes
Invests:	Every 7 days beginning varies
Minimum:	$100
Maximum:	$10,000/month
Min to qualify:	1
Fee on cash inv.:	0!
Fee on div. inv.:	0!
Discount (cash):	0
Discount (div.):	0
Auto invest:	Yes
Auto invest fee:	$0
Selling info:	Sells weekly, by mail or phone, at avg. price, for $15 +12¢/sh.

Company:	**Wilmington Trust Co.**
Symbol:	WL
Exchange:	NYSE
Industry:	Banking
Company Address:	1100 N. Market St., Rodney Sq.
	North
	Wilmington, DE 19890-0001
Company Phone:	800-441-7120 or 302-651-1000
Transfer Agent:	Norwest Bank Minnesota
Agent's Address:	P.O. Box 64854
	St. Paul, MN 55164-0854
Agent's Phone:	800-999-9867
Other than USA:	No

Safekeeping:	Yes
Invests:	Every 30 days beginning 1/15
Minimum:	$10
Maximum:	$5,000/quarter
Min to qualify:	1
Fee on cash inv.:	0!
Fee on div. inv.:	0!
Discount (cash):	0
Discount (div.):	0
Auto invest:	Yes
Auto invest fee:	$0
Selling info:	Sells daily, by mail or fax, at market, for 0!

Company:	**Winn-Dixie Stores, Inc.**
Symbol:	WIN
Exchange:	NYSE
Industry:	Retail stores
Company Address:	5050 Edgewood Ct., Box B
	Jacksonville, FL 32203-0297
Company Phone:	904-783-5000
Transfer Agent:	FCT (EquiServe)
Agent's Address:	P.O. Box 2500
	Jersey Dity, NJ 07303-2500
Agent's Phone:	888-822-5593
Other than USA:	No

Safekeeping:	Yes
Invests:	Every 30 days beginning 1/2
Minimum:	$10
Maximum:	$10,000/month
Min to qualify:	10
Fee on cash inv.:	0!
Fee on div. inv.:	0!
Discount (cash):	0
Discount (div.):	0
Auto invest:	Yes
Auto invest fee:	$1
Selling info:	Sells daily, by phone, mail, or fax, at market, for $10 +12¢/sh.

Company:	**Wisconsin Energy Corp.**
Symbol:	WEC
Exchange:	NYSE
Industry:	Utility-electric, gas
Company Address:	231 West Michigan St., Box #2949
	Milwaukee, WI 53201
Company Phone:	800-881-5882 or 414-221-2118
Transfer Agent:	Boston Eq. (EquiServe)
Agent's Address:	P.O. Box 9156
	Boston MA 02205-9156
Agent's Phone:	800-558-9663
Other than USA:	No

Safekeeping:	Yes
Invests:	Every 15 days beginning 1/1
Minimum:	$25
Maximum:	$50,000/quarter
Min to qualify:	1
Fee on cash inv.:	0!
Fee on div. inv.:	0!
Discount (cash):	0
Discount (div.):	0
Auto invest:	Yes
Auto invest fee:	$0
Selling info:	Sells daily, by phone or mail, at market, for 5¢/sh.

Company:	**Witco Corp.**	Safekeeping:	No
Symbol:	WIT	Invests:	Every 30 days beginning 1/1
Exchange:	NYSE	Minimum:	$10
Industry:	Chemicals	Maximum:	$20,000/year
Company Address:	One American Lane	Min to qualify:	1
	Greenwich, CT 06831-2559	Fee on cash inv.:	0
Company Phone:	800-884-4440 or 203-552-2282	Fee on div. inv.:	0
Transfer Agent:	FCT (EquiServe)	Discount (cash):	0
Agent's Address:	P.O. Box 2500	Discount (div.):	0
	Jersey City, NJ 07303	Auto invest:	No
Agent's Phone:	201-324-0313	Auto invest fee:	$0
Other than USA:	Yes	Selling info:	Sells daily, by phone, mail, or fax, at market, for $10 +12¢/sh.

Company:	**WLR Foods, Inc.**	Safekeeping:	Yes
Symbol:	WLRF	Invests:	Every 30 days beginning Friday
Exchange:	OTC	Minimum:	$100
Industry:	Food	Maximum:	$20,000/year
Company Address:	Box 7000	Min to qualify:	1
	Broadway, VA 22815-7000	Fee on cash inv.:	0!
Company Phone:	540-896-0418 or 540-896-0425	Fee on div. inv.:	0!
Transfer Agent:	WLR Foods	Discount (cash):	0
Agent's Address:	P.O. Box 7000	Discount (div.):	0
	Broadway, VA 22815	Auto invest:	No
Agent's Phone:	540-896-0425	Auto invest fee:	$0
Other than USA:	Yes	Selling info:	Not available

Company:	**Woodward Governor Co.**	Safekeeping:	Yes
Symbol:	WGOV	Invests:	Every 90 days beginning 3/1
Exchange:	OTC	Minimum:	$25
Industry:	Electronic inst. & controls	Maximum:	$1,000/quarter
Company Address:	5001 North Second St.	Min to qualify:	1
	Rockford, IL 61125	Fee on cash inv.:	4% to $2.50
Company Phone:	815-877-7441	Fee on div. inv.:	0!
Transfer Agent:	Wachovia (EquiServe)	Discount (cash):	0
Agent's Address:	P.O. Box 8217	Discount (div.):	0
	Boston, MA 02266-8217	Auto invest:	No
Agent's Phone:	800-633-4236	Auto invest fee:	$0
Other than USA:	Yes	Selling info:	Sells within 10 bus. days, by mail, at market, for comm.

Company:	**Worthington Foods, Inc.**	Safekeeping:	Yes
Symbol:	WFDS	Invests:	Every 30 days beginning 1/1
Exchange:	OTC	Minimum:	$25
Industry:	Food processing	Maximum:	$1,000/month
Company Address:	900 Proprietors Rd.	Min to qualify:	1
	Worthington, OH 43085	Fee on cash inv.:	0!
Company Phone:	614-885-9511	Fee on div. inv.:	0!
Transfer Agent:	National City Bank	Discount (cash):	0
Agent's Address:	P.O. Box 92301	Discount (div.):	0
	Cleveland, OH 44193-0900	Auto invest:	No
Agent's Phone:	800-622-6757	Auto invest fee:	$0
Other than USA:	Yes	Selling info:	Sells weekly, by mail, at market, for 0!

Company:	**Worthington Industries**	Safekeeping:	Yes
Symbol:	WTHG	Invests:	Every 30 days beginning 1/31
Exchange:	OTC	Minimum:	$50
Industry:	Metals	Maximum:	$5,000/month
Company Address:	1205 Dearborn Dr.	Min to qualify:	1
	Columbus, OH 43085	Fee on cash inv.:	0!
Company Phone:	614-438-3210	Fee on div. inv.:	0!
Transfer Agent:	BankBoston (EquiServe)	Discount (cash):	0
Agent's Address:	P.O. Box 840, MS 45-02-64	Discount (div.):	0
	Boston, MA 02266-8040	Auto invest:	Yes
Agent's Phone:	800-730-4001	Auto invest fee:	$0
Other than USA:	Yes	Selling info:	Sells within 10 bus. days, by mail only, at market, for $0

Company:	**WPS Resources Corp.**	Safekeeping:	Yes
Symbol:	WPS	Invests:	Every 30 days beginning 1/20
Exchange:	NYSE	Minimum:	$25
Industry:	Utility-electric, gas	Maximum:	$100,000/year
Company Address:	Box 19001	Min to qualify:	1
	Green Bay, WI 54307-9001	Fee on cash inv.:	0
Company Phone:	800-236-1551 or 920-433-1050	Fee on div. inv.:	0
Transfer Agent:	WPS Resources Corp.	Discount (cash):	0
Agent's Address:	P.O. Box 19001	Discount (div.):	0
	Green Bay, WI 54307-9001	Auto invest:	No
Agent's Phone:	800-236-1551	Auto invest fee:	$0
Other than USA:	Yes	Selling info:	Sells within 10 days, by mail, at market, for 25¢/sh.

Company:	**Wrigley (Wm. Jr.) Co.**	Safekeeping:	Yes
Symbol:	WWY	Invests:	Every 30 days beginning 1/1
Exchange:	NYSE	Minimum:	$50
Industry:	Chewing gum prod.	Maximum:	$5,000/month
Company Address:	410 North Michigan Ave.	Min to qualify:	1
	Chicago, IL 60611-4287	Fee on cash inv.:	0!
Company Phone:	800-824-9681 or 312-645-4197	Fee on div. inv.:	0!
Transfer Agent:	FCT (EquiServe)	Discount (cash):	0
Agent's Address:	P.O. Box 2500	Discount (div.):	0
	Jersey City, NJ 07303-2500	Auto invest:	No
Agent's Phone:	800-446-2617	Auto invest fee:	$0
Other than USA:	Yes	Selling info:	Sells monthly, by mail, at avg. price, for $0!

Company:	**Xeikon, N.V.**	Safekeeping:	Yes
Symbol:	XEIKY	Invests:	Every 7 days beginning varies
Exchange:	OTC	Minimum:	$50
Industry:	Digital color printing systems	Maximum:	$250,000/week
Company Address:	c/o BNY,101 Barclay St.,22 West	Min to qualify:	1
	New York, NY 10286	Fee on cash inv.:	$5 + 10¢/sh.
Company Phone:	800-943-9715	Fee on div. inv.:	5% to $5 + 10¢/sh.
Transfer Agent:	Bank of New York	Discount (cash):	0
Agent's Address:	P.O. Box 11258	Discount (div.):	0
	New York, NY 10286	Auto invest:	Yes
Agent's Phone:	888-269-2377	Auto invest fee:	$0
Other than USA:	Yes	Selling info:	Sells weekly, by phone or mail, at market, for $5 +10¢/ADS

Company:	**Xenova Grp. plc**
Symbol:	XNVAY
Exchange:	OTC
Industry:	Health care
Company Address:	c/o BNY, 101 Barclay St., 22 West
	New York, NY 10286
Company Phone:	800-943-9715
Transfer Agent:	Bank of New York
Agent's Address:	P.O. Box 11258
	New York, NY 10286
Agent's Phone:	888-269-2377
Other than USA:	Yes

Safekeeping:	Yes
Invests:	Every 7 days beginning varies
Minimum:	$50
Maximum:	$250,000/week
Min to qualify:	1
Fee on cash inv.:	$5 + 10¢/sh.
Fee on div. inv.:	0
Discount (cash):	0
Discount (div.):	0
Auto invest:	Yes
Auto invest fee:	$0
Selling info:	Sells weekly, by phone or mail, at avg. price, for $5 +10¢/ADS

Company:	**Xerox Corp.**
Symbol:	XRX
Exchange:	NYSE
Industry:	Business equipment
Company Address:	800 Long Ridge Rd., Box 1600
	Stamford, CT 06904
Company Phone:	203-968-3000
Transfer Agent:	Boston Eq. (EquiServe)
Agent's Address:	P.O. Box 8038
	Boston, MA 02206-8038
Agent's Phone:	800-828-6396
Other than USA:	Yes

Safekeeping:	Yes
Invests:	Every 30 days beginning 1/1
Minimum:	$10
Maximum:	$5,000/month
Min to qualify:	1
Fee on cash inv.:	0
Fee on div. inv.:	0
Discount (cash):	0
Discount (div.):	0
Auto invest:	No
Auto invest fee:	$0
Selling info:	Sells weekly, by mail, at market, for $10 +15¢/sh.

Company:	**Yankee Energy System**
Symbol:	YES
Exchange:	NYSE
Industry:	Utility-natural gas
Company Address:	599 Research Pkwy.
	Meriden, CT 06450-1030
Company Phone:	203-639-4643 or 203-639-4000
Transfer Agent:	ChaseMellon Shareholder Services
Agent's Address:	P.O. Box 3315
	South Hackensack, NJ 07606-1915
Agent's Phone:	888-451-0192
Other than USA:	No

Safekeeping:	Yes
Invests:	Every 30 days beginning 1/15
Minimum:	$100
Maximum:	$10,000/month
Min to qualify:	1
Fee on cash inv.:	$1.50
Fee on div. inv.:	0!
Discount (cash):	0
Discount (div.):	0
Auto invest:	No
Auto invest fee:	$0
Selling info:	Sells weekly, by mail or phone, at avg. price, for $5 + 6¢/sh.

Company:	**York Financial Corp.**
Symbol:	YFED
Exchange:	OTC
Industry:	Banking, savings and loan
Company Address:	101 South George St., Box 15068
	York, PA 17401
Company Phone:	717-846-8777
Transfer Agent:	American Stock Transfer
Agent's Address:	40 Wall St., 46th Fl.
	New York, NY 10005
Agent's Phone:	800-278-4353
Other than USA:	No

Safekeeping:	Yes
Invests:	Every 90 days beginning 2/15
Minimum:	$25
Maximum:	$2,500/quarter
Min to qualify:	1
Fee on cash inv.:	0!
Fee on div. inv.:	0!
Discount (cash):	0
Discount (div.):	10%
Auto invest:	Yes
Auto invest fee:	$0
Selling info:	Sells weekly, by mail, at market, for comm.

Company:	**York International Corp.**	Safekeeping:	Yes
Symbol:	YRK	Invests:	Every 7 days beginning varies
Exchange:	NYSE	Minimum:	$100
Industry:	Mfr. climate control systems, HVAC	Maximum:	$10,000/month
Company Address:	631 South Richland Ave.	Min to qualify:	1
	York, PA 17403	Fee on cash inv.:	$5
Company Phone:	717-771-7451 or 717-771-7890	Fee on div. inv.:	0
Transfer Agent:	ChaseMellon Shareholder Services	Discount (cash):	0
Agent's Address:	P.O. Box 3338	Discount (div.):	0
	South Hackensack, NJ 07606-1938	Auto invest:	Yes
Agent's Phone:	800-437-6726	Auto invest fee:	$0
Other than USA:	Yes	Selling info:	Sells weekly, by mail or phone, at market, for $15 +12¢/sh.

Company:	**YPF Sociedad Anonima**	Safekeeping:	Yes
Symbol:	YPF	Invests:	Every 7 days beginning varies
Exchange:	NYSE	Minimum:	$50
Industry:	Argentinian oil & gas producer	Maximum:	$250,000/week
Company Address:	c/o BNY,101 Barclay St.,22 West	Min to qualify:	1
	New York, NY 10286	Fee on cash inv.:	$5 + 10¢/sh.
Company Phone:	800-943-9715	Fee on div. inv.:	5% to $5 + 10¢/sh.
Transfer Agent:	Bank of New York	Discount (cash):	0
Agent's Address:	P.O. Box 11258	Discount (div.):	0
	New York, NY 10286	Auto invest:	Yes
Agent's Phone:	888-269-2377	Auto invest fee:	$0
Other than USA:	Yes	Selling info:	Sells weekly, by phone or mail, at market, for $5 +10¢/ADS

Company:	**Zeneca Group plc**	Safekeeping:	Yes
Symbol:	ZEN	Invests:	Every 7 days beginning varies
Exchange:	NYSE	Minimum:	$50
Industry:	Pharmaceutical R & D	Maximum:	$100,000/year
Company Address:	c/o Morgan Guaranty Trust,	Min to qualify:	1
	Box 9073	Fee on cash inv.:	$5 + 12¢/sh.
	Boston, MA 02205-9948	Fee on div. inv.:	5% to $2.50
Company Phone:	800-428-4237	Discount (cash):	0
Transfer Agent:	Morgan Guaranty Trust Co.	Discount (div.):	0
Agent's Address:	P.O. Box 9073	Auto invest:	Yes
	Boston, MA 02205-9948	Auto invest fee:	$5
Agent's Phone:	800-428-4237	Selling info:	Sells daily, by phone or mail, at avg. price, for $5 +12¢/sh.
Other than USA:	No		

Company:	**Zindart Ltd.**	Safekeeping:	Yes
Symbol:	ZNDTY	Invests:	Every 7 days beginning varies
Exchange:	OTC	Minimum:	$50
Industry:	Recreational products	Maximum:	$250,000/year
Company Address:	c/o BNY,101 Barclay St.,22 West	Min to qualify:	1
	New York, NY 10286	Fee on cash inv.:	$5 + 10¢/sh.
Company Phone:	800-943-9715	Fee on div. inv.:	0
Transfer Agent:	Bank of New York	Discount (cash):	0
Agent's Address:	P.O. Box 11258	Discount (div.):	0
	New York, NY 10286	Auto invest:	Yes
Agent's Phone:	888-269-2377	Auto invest fee:	$5 + 10¢/sh.
Other than USA:	Yes	Selling info:	Sells weekly, by mail, at market, for $5 +10¢/sh.

Company:	**Zions Bancorp.**	Safekeeping:	No
Symbol:	ZION	Invests:	Every 90 days beginning 1/20
Exchange:	OTC	Minimum:	$10
Industry:	Banking	Maximum:	$5,000/quarter
Company Address:	One South Main, Ste.1380	Min to qualify:	1
	Salt Lake City, UT 84111	Fee on cash inv.:	0
Company Phone:	801-524-4787	Fee on div. inv.:	0
Transfer Agent:	Zions First National Bank	Discount (cash):	0
Agent's Address:	One South Main St.	Discount (div.):	0
	Salt Lake City, UT 84111	Auto invest:	No
Agent's Phone:	801-524-4624	Auto invest fee:	$0
Other than USA:	No	Selling info:	Not available

Company:	**Zweig Fund (The)**	Safekeeping:	Yes
Symbol:	ZF	Invests:	Every 30 days beginning 1/15
Exchange:	NYSE	Minimum:	$100
Industry:	Capital appreciation fund	Maximum:	$$3,000/month
Company Address:	900 3rd Ave., c/o Zweig Advisors	Min to qualify:	1
	New York, NY 10022	Fee on cash inv.:	comm.
Company Phone:	212-755-9860	Fee on div. inv.:	comm.
Transfer Agent:	State Street Bank (EquiServe)	Discount (cash):	0
Agent's Address:	P.O. Box 370042	Discount (div.):	0
	Boston, MA 02241-0742	Auto invest:	Yes
Agent's Phone:	800-272-2700	Auto invest fee:	$0
Other than USA:	No	Selling info:	Sells daily, by mail, at market, for 5¢/sh.

INDEX

Page numbers in bold refer to Direct Investment Plan profiles for particular companies. Page numbers followed by *f* and *t* refer to figures and tables respectively.

OTHER NEW OFFERINGS FROM THE MOTLEY FOOL

IN BOOKSTORES NOW

To find out about other Motley Fool products, visit us online at www.FoolMart.com (AOL keyword: FoolMart) or call 1-888-665-FOOL for more information

or

send in the order form below to receive your free Motley Fool Catalog.

Yes... send me my free copy of The FoolMart Catalog

Name _____

Address _____

_____

_____

E-mail Address _____
(optional)

DP-1

Send to:
FoolMart
123 N. Pitt Street
Alexandria, VA 22314

FOOLISH INVESTING ADVICE
DELIVERED TO YOU EVERY MONTH

Now you can have The Motley Fool delivered to your door every month. We've taken the best of what we do on our website and incorporated it into *The Motley Fool Monthly*, the first financial magazine that's truly fun, informative, and easy to understand. *The Motley Fool Monthly* is great for folks who don't have time to visit Fool.com every day, and is also ideal for new investors who are just getting started.

Every 32-page issue includes:

- The latest news and analysis on the market
- Personal finance advice on topics ranging from taxes to buying a home
- Topics from our Fool's School to help you become a smarter investor
- Our latest and greatest stock ideas
- Articles from The Motley Fool's co-founders, David and Tom Gardner

SUBSCRIBE NOW!

❑ Yes... start my subscription to *The Motley Fool Monthly* at the rate of $39.00 for one year (12 monthly issues).

Name _____

Address _____

_____

_____

E-mail (optional) _____

Payment Method: ❑ Check or Money Order ❑ VISA ❑ MC ❑ AE ❑ Discover

Credit Card Number _____

Expiration Date _____

Name as it appears on card _____

Signature _____

Send to:

FoolMart
123 N. Pitt Street
Alexandria, VA 22314

1-888-665-FOOL
www.foolmart.com

100% Satisfaction Guarantee

We're so sure that you're going to love *The Motley Fool Monthly* that if it fails to meet your expectations at any time, we'll gladly refund the remainder of your subscription.

DP-1